Brad E. Davis and David Nichols

Plants IN DESIGN

A GUIDE TO DESIGNING
WITH SOUTHERN
LANDSCAPE PLANTS

University of Georgia Press   Athens

To my parents and grandparents, the Davises, Bowers, and Lineberrys; your toils on the farms and soils of southern Appalachia has borne fruits perhaps you never imagined. I am forever grateful and indebted to you.

To my wife, Amanda, your patience, support, and bearing with me allowed this book to come to existence. I am forever thankful for you. To our children, Isabelle, Callie, Lilia, and Josiah: You are the trees of tomorrow, and the future full of hope and joy in you.

BRAD

A Wormsloe
FOUNDATION
nature book

© 2021 by the University of Georgia Press

Athens, Georgia 30602

www.ugapress.org

All rights reserved

Designed by Mindy Basinger Hill

Set in Adobe Calson Pro and Copihue

Printed and bound by TOPPAN Leefung Printing, Ltd.
www.kingstimeprinting.com

The paper in this book meets the guidelines for permanence and durability of the Committee on Production Guidelines for Book Longevity of the Council on Library Resources.

Most University of Georgia Press titles are available from popular e-book vendors.

Printed in China

25 24 23 22 21 C 5 4 3 2 1

Library of Congress Cataloging-in-Publication Data

Names: Davis, Brad E., author. | Nichols, David, Associate Professor, 1956– author.

Title: Plants in design : a guide to designing with southern landscape plants / Brad E. Davis, David Nichols.

Description: Athens, Georgia : The University of Georgia Press, [2021] | Includes bibliographical references and index.

Identifiers: LCCN 2020045083 | ISBN 9780820341736 (hardback)

Subjects: LCSH: Landscape plants—Southern States. | Planting design—Southern States.

Classification: LCC SB407 .D37 2021 | DDC 635.90975—dc23

LC record available at https://lccn.loc.gov/2020045083

Contents

- vii — Ackowledgments
- 1 — Introduction: A Design Resource
- 5 — Seeing Plants as Elements of Design
- 19 — Plants as Architecture: Forming Outdoor Space Using the Principles of Design
- 37 — Plant Lists for Difficult Situations
- 43 — Terminology Used in This Book

SPECIES ACCOUNTS

- 53 — Large Deciduous Trees
- 95 — Medium Deciduous Trees
- 121 — Small Deciduous Trees
- 165 — Evergreen Trees
- 197 — Large Evergreen Shrubs
- 243 — Large Deciduous Shrubs
- 273 — Medium Evergreen Shrubs
- 299 — Medium Deciduous Shrubs
- 321 — Small Shrubs
- 351 — Ornamental Grasses
- 375 — Perennials, Bulbs, and Ground Covers
- 469 — Turfgrasses
- 479 — Annuals
- 493 — Ferns
- 509 — Vines and Climbers
- 531 — Interior Plants
- 543 — Invasive Exotic Plants

- 563 — References
- 569 — Image Credits
- 571 — Index of Common Names
- 577 — Index of Scientific Names

Acknowledgments

I want to thank the students, friends, family, and colleagues who generously gave of their time and expertise and made this book possible. You all soldiered on with us, encouraging us and making the work better.

I especially thank our colleagues at UGA and around the Southeast for their input and editing: Maureen O'Brien, Neal Weatherly, Shelley Cannady, Dan Nadenicek, Dr. Matthew Chappell, Dr. John Ruter, Dr. Susan Hamilton, and many more.

I also thank our dear students at UGA. So many wonderful graduate students assisted over the years in everything: scouting photos, information gathering, and organization. Thank you to Stephen Bell, Joanna Stephens, Andrew Bailey, and Thomas Baker. Thank you to all of the students who joined us on trips around the United States and abroad to see great gardens and designed places and waited on us while we snapped just one more photo.

Brad E. Davis

First, I'd like to convey my appreciation to some of the retired faculty of the College of Environment and Design who helped mentor me as an entry-level faculty member: Scott Weinberg, Gregg Coyle, Allen Stovall, and Bruce Ferguson. Special thanks to Bill Mann for going on all those trips with me and to Neal Weatherly for prodding me for so many years. And to Dan Nadenicek for his support and patience while we were working on this book.

I'd also like to thank Maureen O'Brien for her help in seeing that the Founders Memorial Garden was taken care of so well while I was distracted by this effort. And thanks to Jon Davies of the UGA Press for his patience in helping two guys who really didn't know how a book went together.

Although they are no longer here, I must acknowledge the love of plants that was instilled in me by my parents and by my Aunts Gladys and Juanita. I grew up surrounded by trees and native wildflowers. We all went on frequent trips to dig up many of those plants, so after all these years, my apologies to all the state parks and natural areas that we visited.

David Nichols

PLANTS IN DESIGN

Introduction A DESIGN RESOURCE

The idea for this book came out of our love for plants and well-designed landscapes and our general frustration with the lack of concise information for gardeners and designers creating planting plans. There is a great need for books that focus on plants at a regional scale. A book that covers plants for the entire country can be quite misleading. We hope that this book serves as a "go-to" palette for those creating planting designs in temperate zones 6–9.

Many great books have been written on the subject of planting design and plants, and we are indebted to the wealth of knowledge that has been accumulated by gardeners, horticulturalists, landscape designers, and landscape architects around the globe. Overlap exists between all these allied fields, and on large complex projects all may be involved in some phase of the work, but each has its area of specialty. A landscape designer is primarily focused on planting design, with limited attention to hardscape features such as patios, decks, pergolas, and the like. A landscape architect is typically commissioned to create a planting plan, but this is but one element in a large suite of services, including a site-grading and drainage plan; vehicular and pedestrian circulation; plans for stormwater management; construction details for significant site features in concrete, wood, and stone; and management plans for long-term care of the landscape over time, just to list a few aspects of typical practice. Landscape architects are charged to protect the health, safety, and welfare of the public as licensed professionals governed by state-level licensure boards for architects, engineers, and landscape architects. Landscape design is not a licensed field and is typically tied to installation and landscape maintenance.

In this book, we have striven to strike a balance between listing plants that should be used more often and omitting dozens of cultivars that may be difficult to locate or that do not perform well in most landscape settings. We encourage a fresh look at plants as important elements of art in the landscape.

WHY ANOTHER PLANTS AND PLANTING DESIGN BOOK?

While working on this book we occasionally were asked the question: Why write yet another plants book—hasn't this subject been exhausted? To this we politely respond, No! In fact, the need for a concise yet comprehensive resource has probably never been greater. This is due in part to recent revisions to the USDA hardiness zones map, which has denoted most of the eastern United States as much as an entire zone warmer than in previous years. An equally compelling reason for a new book is found in the increasing number of new cultivar releases each year, which can be maddening when searching for plants that have been proven to be hardy and reliable for design use, only to find that many new and "improved" cultivars have replaced the old ones. This would not be a problem if all new releases could be trusted to perform well; however, many hot new cultivars have proven to be less than impressive in many landscape settings. One example is the latest craze over multiple colors of *Echinacea*. Although the marketing engines of the nursery industry are no doubt profiting greatly over this proliferation of new forms of *Echinacea*, careful observation of the vast majority of these plants reveals that they suffer from reduced vigor and minimal flowering when installed in the landscape. What good is a giant flower in a new color if the overall plant looks like hell? A more effective system of evaluation and release to the public is needed. Evaluations of plants can be found in various forms, such as the list of winners, based on performance, issued each year by the American Perennial Plant Association; other plant associations provide similar resources. Visits to botanical gardens and trial gardens around the world also reveal the truth of landscape performance over time. Similarly, the writings of trusted authors and researchers such as Michael Dirr (woody plants), Allan Armitage (herbaceous perennials), and Rick Darke (ornamental grasses) can be extremely helpful. However, the encyclopedic books by Dirr and Armitage both acknowledge the problem of cultivarism gone out of control, with too many new forms each year and not enough information on whether these new plants really offer anything new and improved or simply reiterate essentially the same plants or, much worse, introductions that do not perform well. We have been extremely cautious and selective in our mention of cultivars in order to provide the reader with a trustworthy list of plants that can both be found in the nursery industry and perform well. This may be frustrating for the plant enthusiast wanting to experiment with the latest and greatest, but we hope this book will be extremely helpful to those creating planting designs and looking for a sure bet when landscape performance really matters.

The designer or landscape architect generally cannot use a client's landscape as a trial garden. Too many failed installations quickly lead to a failed business and a poor reputation. This gleaning of plant lists comes out of our combined seventy-plus years of gardening, visiting gardens, and designing gardens around the Southeast.

ORGANIZATION AND SCOPE OF THE BOOK

Anyone familiar with books on plants will note a significant departure from the typical alphabetical organization of plants using the botanical names. The problem with this type of organization is that it requires planners to know what they are looking for before turning the pages. A list of botanical names may be perfectly acceptable for scientific reference and fact finding; however, someone interested in choosing plants for a specific design may become lost. A planting designer, much like a painter who spreads his or her color options around the edges of a palette, needs a palette of plant options. Each design calls for a unique mix of plants based on many criteria, such as site suitability and aesthetic and cultural considerations. To achieve this palette, this book covers many genres of plants, from turfgrasses and herbaceous perennials to woody shrubs and trees. A designer must consider all these genres when composing a landscape.

Among the many criteria that must be considered when designing with plants, two must be considered first. The first criterion is the scale of the plant, meaning how big it will eventually become. The second is whether a location needs an evergreen or a deciduous plant. These broad categorical decisions set the stage in a design for the overall character and feel of a space. After these choices have been made, one may move on to more finite decisions, such as flowering, fruit, seasonal change, texture, and color. This order of process is taught in planting design courses around the world and should result in a well-planned landscape that requires less maintenance and has the capacity to grow and evolve over time. We hope that this book will serve those living and designing with plants by providing an easy-to-use palette of options for any design situation.

PLANTS COVERED AND NOT COVERED: A DELICATE BALANCE

Writing a book on such a diversity of plant categories, from trees down to bulbs and ground covers, is a massive undertaking. However, any designer or landscape architect will agree that in designing a landscape one must consider all of these options. Too many American landscapes dominated by vast expanses of lawn fail to offer the diversity of life found in nature. Our goal is to strike a delicate balance between great plants and plants that should be used more, as well as plants that can be reasonably sourced within the nursery industry. We filtered out all plants that are too obscure to be sourced easily. While the plant collector may thoroughly enjoy the pursuit of rare and hard-to-find species and cultivars, the planting designer must be able to locate a plant within some reasonable time frame and distance. A planting designer must also be confident that the plants specified for a design will perform well and please the client. Selected growers' catalogs and websites are referenced in the selection of plant lists and related cultivars for inclusion in this book. Have we left out some great plants? No doubt we have, and we hope readers will write to us about their experiences with other great plants for inclusion in future editions. The world of plants is constantly changing, and great new species and cultivars do emerge and prove themselves design worthy over time.

ON NATIVE PLANTS

The reader may note a bias toward native plants. This is not accidental. Increasingly, research indicates the far-reaching harmful impacts of the overuse of nonnative plant material. These impacts go beyond the most obvious problem plants,

PLANTS IN DESIGN

such as privet and kudzu, which have become infamous for their invasive tendencies in the Southeast. Recent publications such as Douglas Tallamy's book *Bringing Nature Home* point to the inability of our indigenous pollinators to feed on the foliage and other plant parts of introduced species. This has far-reaching implications for our local ecosystems, insect and animal populations that feed on insects, and even our ability to produce food crops. While our stance is not a policy of natives only, we do advocate for a more careful process of evaluation and introduction of nonnative plants. There are many exotic plants that perform well in temperate regions yet for various reasons do not reproduce at high rates and thus do not outpace native species. Many nonnative plants do support the adult life stages of indigenous pollinators, so the issue is a complex one. More careful evaluation is needed to understand the ecological fit of each plant for each place.

WHO SHOULD BE DOING PLANTING DESIGN?

As landscape architects who happen to love plants, we freely admit that too often planting designs by landscape architects fail to capture the imagination and offer the beauty and mystery of great gardens and the natural world. Piet Oudolf and Noel Kingsbury write in their book *Designing with Plants* that "some gardens, particularly those created by landscape architects, are like monuments: frozen" (1999, 94). In a similar vein, the authority on woody plants, Michael Dirr, writes in his account of Otto Luyken laurel, "'Tis a favorite of the landscape architecture clan and appears on their plans with the regularity of erasure marks" (2011, 632). These critiques of planting designs by landscape architects point to an overreliance in American landscapes on stiff, plastic-looking evergreens and lawn, with little seasonal change or adaptation over time. While this has too often been the case, there are many notable exceptions, and many of these are featured in this book. For example, the inspiring landscapes of Wolfgang Oehme and James van Sweden of the firm Oehme, van Sweden (OvS) are rich in detailed plantings and elegant in their accommodation of human function. However, too many gardens by horticulturalists and landscape designers are rich in plant diversity but lacking in structure, planning, and arrangement of space, and they need a stronger sense of visual order. So what is the answer? Working together! We have relied on the expertise and trial landscapes of many great horticulturalists in compiling this book, and we are indebted to them. We are also indebted to many great landscape architects who have shared their work and ability to create memorable and beautiful places. Landscape architects bring a holistic set of skills to the design table, creating landscapes that are strong in structure and function for human use and rich in plantings. Landscape architects have long understood and championed the need for public access to great green spaces, landscapes, and gardens. In the spirit of great gardens and landscapes, we hope that this book will inspire even greater planting design by offering a rich and robust palette in a concise resource.

Our goal is to show plants used appropriately in all designed settings. Whenever possible we have a representative design photo for each species in the landscape. People need to see plants not only for identification as a horticultural specimen but also, more importantly, used appropriately in design. This more holistic view of plants requires a deep understanding of using plants as structures to carve out and define outdoor space, as well as using plants as filler, focal points, and visual interest that invite human use and enjoyment. Planting designers must consider a large palette, from trees and shrubs down to grasses and perennials and creeping herbs to fill nooks and crannies. Great landscapes work at both the masterplan and fine detail levels. We hope that this book will encourage and facilitate use of a diverse range of plants and will embolden the planting designer to create landscapes that are rich, diverse, complex, beautiful, and life sustaining.

FIGURE 1 *Hamamelis virginiana* in early November flower, Founders Memorial Garden, UGA.

Seeing Plants as Elements of Design

One of the goals of this book is to help the reader learn to see plants in a new way. We hope to make planting design more accessible to the professional and the public by organizing plants into a palette of choices. Planting designers must consider many aesthetic and ecological factors in order to choose the right plants. When designers learn to examine the inherent design qualities of each individual plant, then their planting design can come together just as skillfully as an effective interior design in which all the fabrics and other materials have been painstakingly chosen to complement, contrast, and augment one another, forming a visually appealing composition. A successful interior design must also function in a way that supports the use of the room over time. Will the flooring endure? Is the room a wet or humid space? Does the space support getting work done, or is it for leisure and relaxation? These kinds of functional questions are quite similar, whether asked for an interior or a landscape design, and they serve as a helpful metaphor for thinking about function and aesthetics in planting design. This section offers a brief discussion of aesthetic and functional considerations in choosing plants. Later chapters of the book present individual plant descriptions and offer species-level functional and ecological information. Learning to see a plant and connect with its inherent qualities requires careful observation and repeated encounters with the plant over time and in different stages of growth and different seasons. Slowly, over time, a designer acquires a deeper knowledge of the plant and its full personality and can then make more thoughtful decisions about its place in the landscape.

A DEEPER AWARENESS

In his book *A Philosophy for Planting Design*, Wayne Womack discusses the importance of having empathy with plants. By examining the inherent personality of a plant, the designer is able to better connect a plant to place and to the other elements of the design. Womack writes that "to have a favorite plant suggests a deeper connection" (2006, 11). The kind of pause and reflection necessary to truly understand an individual plant and imagine all of its possibilities is captured in his description of our native witch hazel (figs. 1 and 2):

I spoke of empathy, that intellectual or emotional identification with another person whereby we seem to have an understanding of their motives and moods. I believe that an understanding can be extended to include plants as well. By becoming more aware of the nature of a plant we allow it to reveal its character to us. Let me give an example. I have always been drawn to the witch hazel family. Every species I have come across has fascinated me, and I am always on the search for new ones to get to know. Here I will focus on the native species which I encounter most frequently in Louisiana, *Hamamelis virginiana*. The native witch hazel is a challenge. It is a solitary plant seldom crowded by other plants since it is not prone to colonize. Its every detail is visually quite distinct from other plants with which it associates in the wild. In the spring as its leaves unfold there are tints of copper and pink which give an arresting blush to the light green foliage with its aqua highlights. The leaf edges have a distinctly smooth and broadly curving undulation. There is a velvety texture to the new leaves which changes to a rougher, resistant touch as they mature. The arching stems develop a zigzag pattern adding a sense of movement to the overall appearance of the plant. All of these details are displayed on a relatively transparent, multi-trunked structural habit which, while visually strong, blends with the surroundings. The most striking seasonal moment in the plant's development is the translucent yellow fall color, which makes it a standout in October and November. The trunks, with their smooth grey bark, serve to highlight the event. The abundant but unobtrusive flowers, with their strap-like petals in cream to yellow, are remarkable in that they occur in late fall when few native plants are in flower. They have a delicate, spicy fragrance which adds complexity to the aromas of autumn.

From these observations it becomes apparent that we are dealing with a plant of much subtle detail and intimacy. Its details are so refined and elusive that they become vague in my memory and I must return again and again to renew my acquaintance with the plant. The witch hazel is not a plant that will make as bold an effect as a crape myrtle or a redbud. It is not a showy plant but reserved, even modest in appearance. There is, however, always the suggestion of change and becoming with the continuing variety of its seasonal effects. It is an intriguing plant in its way of locating and exhibiting its subtleties to maximum effect. Let's place this information within a design attitude. Here is a plant with a strong but subtle presence. It is not a plant that becomes more effective in quantity, in that there is enough to discover in one of them as it grows and matures and assumes its place in a planting. It is a plant which should be situated for close viewing and ease of access so as to make it possible to regularly renew one's familiarity with it through the seasons. It can occupy an unobtrusive place and yet provide a highly individual character. With skill a designer can help it become as expressive in a garden as in its own woodland haunts. (Womack 2006, 15–17)

Other great garden writers write in a similarly personal way about their deep knowledge of plants as acquired over time. Michael Dirr, professor of horticulture and author of over twenty books on plants, enjoys an almost cultlike following. We would argue that this following is equally the result of his frank and candid commentary on the appearance and personality of plants, as well as his astute botanical descriptions. To read Dirr is to take a journey with him through the landscape. In *Manual of Woody Landscape Plants*, he writes of his uncertainty and dislike of the commercially popular plant *Chamaecyparis pisifera* 'Filifera Aurea': "The most common forms in cultivation are 'Filifera,' (green) and 'Filifera Aurea,' a rather ghastly golden yellow form that can grow 15 to 20' high. In my worst dreams, the large specimen by the waterfall at Longwood Gardens always surfaces" (Dirr 2009, 252). The reader cannot hold back a smile and a chuckle of agreement upon reading such comments.

As there will likely be a fair number of landscape architects and designers reading this book (we hope), let us return to the candid remark about *Prunus laurocerasus* by Dirr in Dirr's *Trees and Shrubs for Warm Climates*: "'Tis a favorite of the landscape architecture clan, appearing on their plans with the regularity of erasure marks.... Shot hole—a disease complex that produces buckshot-like holes in leaves which enlarge, rendering the plant 'mad dog' ugly—can be troublesome" (2011, 632–633). Dirr's critique of the overuse of laurels and the general lack of plant diversity in the plans is a fair one

FIGURE 2 Fall foliage of *Hamamelis virginiana* just as leaves drop to reveal the early November flowers in Athens, Ga.

FIGURE 3 Spring ephemerals in late March, Lurie Garden, Chicago, Ill. Gustafson Guthrie Nichol, landscape architects, with Piet Oudolf, horticulturalist.

FIGURE 4 Can you believe this is planted? Native plants creating an urban wild in Brooklyn Bridge Park, Brooklyn, N.Y. Created by Michael Van Valkenburgh Associates, Inc.

and should be taken to heart. This critique lies at the heart of the inspiration for this book—that there is a need for more inspired and diverse planting design. Indeed, some of the more exciting and successful landscape architecture projects in recent years take a fresh approach, embracing great botanical diversity and collaborating with ecologists and horticulturalists to create places of great delight to the visitor, such as the High Line in New York City, Millennium Park and the Lurie Garden in downtown Chicago (fig. 3), and Fourth Ward Park along the beltline in Atlanta, Georgia.

The argument for greater complexity and diversity isn't simply a visual one. In *Bringing Nature Home*, Douglas Tallamy writes of the necessary plant diversity to support lower trophic levels, which support all higher forms of life. He argues that our oversimplified and sterile suburban landscapes of turf dotted with a few evergreens are essentially sterile places that do not support life. These vast expanses of land, if planted and maintained with greater diversity, could serve as a "last refuge" for the biotic diversity on which all life depends (fig. 4).

The following paragraphs offer a discussion of the basic elements of the art and principles of landscape design. Considering the unique aspects of each plant is critical to the completion of a great design.

FIGURE 5 *left* Italian cypresses are used to form walls and the focal point at Villa La Foce, near Montepulciano, Italy.

FIGURE 6 *bottom left* In the gardens at Cornerstone Sonoma, California, several species of *Carex* and grasses are used to form a soft and subtle ground plane against which the iron sculpture contrasts nicely.

FIGURE 7 *right top* Several grassy-looking plants such as *Juncus*, *Carex*, and *Iris* species are used to soften the water's edge here in Brooklyn Bridge Park. Design by Michael Van Valkenburgh Associates, Inc.

FIGURE 8 *right bottom* *Panicum virgatum* remains upright even in winter, providing its wonderful color and textural contrast in Fourth Ward Park, Atlanta. Designed by HDR.

LINE

Seeing line as it is expressed by an individual plant or by a group of plants is an important step in developing a sharp visual awareness and a design vocabulary related to the use of plants as elements of design.

Line Expression by Individual Plants The line quality of individual plants can be a useful tool in identification as one learns to see the character and personality of plants. The concept of line relates to many aspects of a plant, from its leaf edges and vein pattern to its branch structure and tree architecture and its overall outline and form. On a detail level, the leaf edges of many plants can be unique and memorable. For example, the characteristic wavy leaf margin of our native witch hazel is distinctive: it's a bit like a ruffled potato chip (fig. 2). Larger characteristics such as branch habit and structure can also be very species specific and help with both identification and selection for specific design purposes. For example, trees such as flowering dogwood, *Cornus florida*, and live oak, *Quercus virginiana*, have spreading forms with strong horizontal branches. These types of trees often appear to almost float in the landscape and lend a graceful and relaxed feel to it. This can be a wonderful quality in creating a very human-scale place. However, this habit and form can be a problem for streets and busy pedestrian sidewalks where low-hanging horizontal branches would be in the way. In contrast, plants with strong vertical lines possess great visual energy and draw the eye up toward the sky, buildings, and other landscape elements. These plants can have a powerful effect in framing views or creating focal points. The Italian cypress, *Cupressus sempervirens*, shown in figure 5, always draws attention with its commanding vertical lines. Grasses or grasslike plants such as those in figures 6, 7, and 8 have varying degrees of vertical lines, some stiff and upright, others softly arching. The effect is often striking when contrasted with other materials.

Lines Seen in the Larger Landscape The inherent line quality of plants assists the planting designer in relating individual plant choices to the overall scheme of a garden or larger landscape. Equally important are the implied or perceived lines in the greater landscape. The outline of a tree canopy or of mountaintops or buildings in a distant view forms a perceived line that may be used as the backdrop in the design of a closer space. Line types possess inherent qualities when drawn over the landscape, and these qualities elicit predictable responses from the observer. For example, straight lines move the eye quickly and draw attention to the endpoint, as in figure 9. Horizontal lines are understood in the landscape as restful or at peace. Vertical lines interject energy and draw the eye up. Diagonal lines are also energetic and create movement through the landscape. Curving lines create soft relaxed movement. In figure 10, the soft curves of the path contrast and offer a restful counterpoint to the erratic outline of the treetops in the distance. In figure 11, the grove of silhouetted tree trunks creates a beautiful frame through which to view the amphitheater beyond. The soft curving lines of the trunks provide a vertical visual break to the horizontally curving lines of the amphitheater. In figure 12, the zigzagging lines of the boardwalk provide visual energy and movement through the space, and they contrast with the soft surrounding landscape. Many plants express strong horizontal or vertical line qualities, and this may be a key factor in choosing the right plant for a design based on larger spatial and contextual considerations.

Lines and Landscape Function A designer must be conscious of the power of lines to guide the human eye and body through the landscape. Lines become visible in the landscape as both real and perceived. Real lines may be expressed where two or more materials meet, such as a pathway next to plantings. Lines may be hard, as in figures 9–12. Notice the contrast between the grass and the mulch path in figure 10. The sweeping path becomes a line in the landscape, first leading the eye and then beckoning the user to move through the landscape. Bed edges or bed lines and hardscape edges function in a similar way, not only defining and separating planting from other areas in the design in a functional way but also drawing the eye through the space. One must always consider the visual power of these lines, first drawn in plan but ultimately defining the visual and functional experience for the user in the built space.

COLOR

Color is a powerful and complex element of art that must be considered in planting design. While the form and scale of a plant are probably the foremost of all factors to be considered in making plant choices, color wields great visual power, and the human eye and psyche are greatly affected by it. Plants express color in many ways, from their flowers and

FIGURE 9 *top left* The hard and straight lines of this sidewalk near Hilton Head, S.C., draw the user into the depths of the tunnel of contrasting contorted lines of the live oak branches.

FIGURE 10 *top right* A soft curving mulch path at the Bloedel Reserve, Bainbridge Island, Wash., offers a more subtle contrast to the adjacent meadow, yet it beckons one to explore the landscape beyond, perhaps at a slower pace.

FIGURE 11 *bottom left* The trunks of *Prunus cerasifera* act as a window frame between the public sidewalk and the park.

FIGURE 12 *bottom right* The zigzag boardwalk through marshy areas at the Bloedel Reserve offers just the right visual energy and contrast to the soft mishmash of wetland plants.

fruit to their foliage and bark. Their color expression can also change drastically with the seasons. Because of this and so many other factors bearing on planting design, it is helpful to use what landscape architects call the "overlay method." This approach involves using individual sheets of transparent paper: the designer draws and solves one or two plant layout challenges on each sheet and then stacks sheets on top of each other. It is a very helpful way to visualize overlapping criteria and find solutions. This method is also quite useful for mapping what plants will do each season in terms of color by using one layer of paper per season. These layered analyses allow the designer to examine whether plants will bloom in the same season, whether the color combinations will be pleasing and effective, if conflicts or gaps in seasonal interest exist, if there is a good balance of evergreen versus deciduous plants, and so on. In figures 13, 14, and 15, overlays are used to check for seasonal change in the planting design for the Lurie Garden in Millennium Park, Chicago.

Without launching into a lengthy section on color, we will lay out the basic principles and major schemes to consider. Starting with a scheme or strategy for color is a step in the right direction. The color wheel in figure 16 provides a helpful visual to aid in understanding color relationships described in the following paragraphs.

Primary Colors, Shades, and Tints The primary colors—red, yellow, and blue—can be naturally derived and are the colors from which all others are mixed. In their pure form, they are extremely bright, stimulating, and reminiscent of plastic children's play equipment or the flower plantings at the drive-through line of a fast-food restaurant (yellow marigolds, red salvia, maybe some blue ageratum, topped off with some lava or white marble chip mulch). A primary color scheme is greatly improved by altering the pure color into shades (adding black) and tints (adding white). Think of a French baroque interior, with shades of deep red, deep blue, and gold. On the tint side, consider pale blue, pale pink, and pale yellow.

Analogous Schemes Using multiple shades and tints of the same color in a planting scheme can create very rich and complex combinations that are pleasing to the eye. Figure 17 depicts analogous colors, meaning those next to each other on the color wheel. Analogous colors (e.g., orange and yellow or green and blue) are visually harmonious with each other.

Seasonal overlays of the Lurie Garden by Gustafson Guthrie Nichol. These seasonal drawings ensure there is something interesting happening every month of the year for public enjoyment and education. FIGURE 13 *top* Spring. FIGURE 14 *middle* Summer through fall. FIGURE 15 *bottom* Winter.

FIGURE 16 Color wheel graphic.

FIGURE 17 Various shades and tints of red and orange make a pleasing combination of summer annuals in this analogous color bed at Queen Elizabeth Park, Vancouver, B.C.

Monochromatic Schemes The use of only one color (including green) creates a monochromatic scheme. This is a very low risk approach and can be visually stunning when multiple shades and tints of only one color are used together. Wonderful examples of this color strategy can be seen each year at Chanticleer Garden in Wayne, Pennsylvania (fig. 18) and were used to great effect in the purple border at Sissinghurst Castle by the famous British perennial garden designer Vita Sackville-West and her contemporary Gertrude Jekyll.

Complementary Schemes A complementary scheme combines colors opposite each other on the color wheel. Complements augment and balance each other. Using one complement as the dominant color with a smaller amount of the opposite color as an accent creates a more harmonious and unified scheme, as in figures 19 and 20.

Individual colors tend to affect the feeling and mood of a design because of their inherent visual energy. Warm colors such as red and yellow are stimulating, whereas cool colors such as green and blue have a calming effect. Consider the use of each space and the contextual influences in making the decision on the right color scheme.

TEXTURE

Plants offer an incredible study in texture, one of the basic elements of art. In order to create gardens and landscapes that are memorable and beautiful throughout all seasons, the planting designer must consider plant textures and how they appear when placed next to each other in a planting composition.

The casual observer or beginning planting designer may not notice plant textures immediately but will focus first on form and color. However, careful consideration of texture, in addition to the other elements of art, creates a landscape of greater visual complexity and richness.

Texture is defined on a sliding scale, from fine on one end to coarse on the other. Consider *Muhlenbergia capillaris*, Muhly grass. It offers an extremely fine visual effect, with its thin wiry foliage and extremely fine flower and seed panicles, which appear to float in the landscape like a soft purple fog. On the other end of the spectrum is *Musa basjoo*, the cold-hardy Japanese banana. Its enormous leaves stand out in the landscape, calling attention to themselves and acting as a focal point. Since coarse textures tend to steal the human eye, a planting designer must be mindful of their powerful visual impact and use them carefully in planting compositions. This is even more evident in temperate gardens such as those in the southeastern United States, where tropical and coarse-textured plants may be used as perennials (which disappear for the winter). They stand out as extremely coarse against the temperate summer landscape, whereas in tropical

top to bottom

FIGURE 18 With mostly shades of green and just a touch of yellow, this monochromatic scheme at Chanticleer Garden in Wayne, Pa., allows the eye to enjoy contrasts in texture and form.

FIGURE 19 The complements purple and yellow and their shades and tints are used to augment one another in this combination of annual petunias, marigolds, *Santolina*, and *Agave*, in Stanley Park, Vancouver, B.C.

FIGURE 20 The orange of native butterfly weed, *Asclepias tuberosa*, is combined with purples from lavender and oregano in the scree garden at Chanticleer Garden in Wayne, Pa. It's an ingenious combination, as these plants share a love of hot dry sunny sites, the colors augment one another in a secondary triad, and the assemblage of forms, scales, and textures works together to create a successful tapestry.

FIGURE 21 Careful attention to textural variety (and color and form) creates a feast for the eyes in this perennial garden combination. This photo was taken in the Tennis Court garden at Chanticleer Garden in June 2012. The coarse-textured perennial is clary sage, *Salvia sclarea* var. *turkestanica*.

locales they blend in with other native plants, which often include many coarse textures. A plant with a medium texture might appear quite coarse next to *Muhlenbergia capillaris* but finer next to *Musa basjoo*.

Should a garden be designed to blend with its surroundings or to stand out? Some planting designers consider the use of coarse textures to be too visually jarring and in bad taste, while others purposefully place plants of textural extremes next to each other to create drama and focal points in the landscape. Consider the visual drama created by the many color and textural contrasts in figure 21. The choice of an approach must be based on a garden's context, the client's wishes, and other factors that contribute to the totality of the landscape.

In addition to its visual aspect, plant texture is tactile, and some plants invite touch, such as *Stachys byzantina*, lamb's ear. The tactile textural qualities of plants are most effective upon close inspection or in very detailed and human-scale planting designs such as a courtyard, a container, an intricately planted perennial border, or a garden for the visually impaired, where plants with both great tactile qualities and fragrances are used.

Consider the exquisite texture garden at Swarthmore College (fig. 22). In this garden, the extremes of fine and coarse textures have been carefully arranged to provide the visitor with a rich visual and tactile experience. Texture is the obvious dominant element of art being expressed in this garden; however, the other elements of art, as well as cultural requirements, have also been considered, resulting in a successful garden.

Texture also has an impact on the spatial qualities and "feel" of a landscape. It is generally understood that coarse textures advance in the landscape, or appear to be closer to the observer, while fine textures recede or appear farther away. This aspect of texture can be useful to the planting designer in manipulating a space to feel either larger or smaller.

FORM: FITTING THE PLACE

Plants naturally take on distinct forms as they stretch for the light or respond to other environmental factors and fill their unique niche in a plant community. An awareness of natural form and a plant's structure or architecture is important when selecting a plant that best fits the space and functional requirements of a design. Form can be defined

FIGURE 22 Extremes of texture from coarse to very fine are massed to frame a distinct lawn and bench space in the texture garden at Swarthmore College. In this garden, color has been restrained so that form and texture take center stage.

as the three-dimensional volume that a plant occupies at maturity. Forms are easily described by geometric terms such as "oval," "rounded," and "conical." It is helpful to visualize common plant forms as somewhat simplified geometric shapes in order to envision how to use them successfully. (See the form diagrams in the terminology section, p. 45, fig. 60.) An easy example of fitting plant form to space and function is seen in the use of vase-shaped or upright arching trees as street trees. A tree such as American elm, *Ulmus americana* 'Liberty', naturally extends its branches at an upward angle, thus reducing conflicts with pedestrians and vehicles on a city street. Maintenance is greatly reduced in nearly any design context by selecting a form that works for the space.

Another very culturally relevant example lies in the common need for low plantings in front of buildings. Too often, very little thought goes into the plant selection for foundation landscapes, and shrubs that naturally will grow to great heights get stuffed along the foundation of the building. In these situations, the plantings must be sheared multiple times per year to keep the plant from blocking windows and damaging the building facade. By carefully selecting plants with low-growing, mounding, or spreading forms, the maintenance and long-term aesthetic value of the landscape are much improved. Arguably, the worst offender of foundation

FIGURE 23 The play of light on plants and space is especially dramatic at Great Dixter, Northiam, England, where hard topiary forms are juxtaposed with soft perennials and grasses. Light and shadow play beautifully and reveal the geometry of the faceted topiaries while causing the translucent foliage, seed heads, and flowers to glow in the same light. The dance between the two is hypnotic and exquisite.

planting selection is the ubiquitous *Loropetalum chinense rubrum*, redleaf Chinese witch hazel. The nondwarf forms of *Loropetalum* will grow to be 25' tall and can be limbed up as small trees (and there are wonderful examples in downtown Savannah). Why force them into 3' boxed hedges?

FORM, HUMAN PSYCHOLOGY, AND THE PRINCIPLES OF DESIGN

Plant forms can elicit a predictable response from the viewer. Tight and upright columnar forms draw the eye up toward the sky and can appear very formal and stiff, acting like a focal point, especially when used singly. Conversely, weeping

FIGURE 24 *top* The regular spacing and parallel placement of red maples as street trees on the UGA campus provide a sense of rhythm, movement, and formality, especially dramatic in full fall color. The simple and bold act of a line of trees, even when they are part of a streetscape and not a formal allée, can create considerable order and drama in the landscape.

FIGURE 25 *middle* The repetition of plants with chartreuse foliage in the Tennis Court Garden at Chanticleer provides a sense of unity and visual cohesiveness, even in the midst of such botanical diversity. The eye is drawn into the garden, and the visitor must explore.

FIGURE 26 *bottom* The sharp form, color, and textural contrasts between the agaves and Mexican feather grass create a mesmerizing visual treat. The repetition of only the two plants, bisected by the curving path, creates a strong sense of visual order and pattern. Design by OvS.

FIGURE 30 Thornless honeylocust trees are often perfect for urban streets, where their light canopy provides shade and softness without being too dark and heavy.

FIGURE 27 *top* Clipped topiaries in containers reinforce the axial view and dramatic visual relationship between the entry doors of the house and the reflecting pool and fountain.

FIGURE 28 *middle* Plants and hard materials can be used to create pattern and movement. At the Los Angeles Natural History Museum, the vertical and changing angle of the stone slabs is energetic and keeps the eye and the user moving down the stone pathway. Design by Studio-MLA.

FIGURE 29 *bottom* Even on a bright sunny day, the heaviness and dark presence of *Magnolia grandiflora* is evident. This can be a visual asset, as in this spot on the UGA campus, where the magnolias bookend the building, frame the view, and add power to the building's presence.

forms draw the eye down to the ground or water's surface and appear relaxed and peaceful. Spreading and ground cover forms are visually at rest and help connect other, more upright forms back to the ground plane when used in combination. Rounded forms are fairly balanced and are visually stable, while irregular forms and contrived forms such as topiaries have more visual energy and attract more attention. Contrast can be a great tool in planting design to direct the eye to a point in the composition by juxtaposing opposite forms, textures, color complements, or multiple attributes all at once. Planting designers may prefer to contrast only one attribute at a time, while others may layer several contrasts at once for more visual impact.

PUTTING THE PRINCIPLES OF DESIGN TOGETHER: REPETITION, BALANCE, CONTRAST, UNITY, EMPHASIS, MOVEMENT, PATTERN, RHYTHM

The repetition of form can alter the visual impact of a landscape. Repetition of columnar forms, such as a line of Italian cypresses, termed an "allée," draws the eye horizontally, and the familiar double row has a hypnotic, tunnel-like effect as it draws one deeper into the landscape. Repetition of form, color, texture, and other design attributes helps create unity and a visually cohesive composition. Repetition of plant forms, in conjunction with a response to other contextual elements such as architecture, can create a sort of "conversation" between plantings and built elements to create patterns and a sense of rhythm between all landscape elements. See figures 25 through 29 for some examples of these principles of design in completed projects. For the reader wanting more on the topic of planting design, there are many great books that address the use of plants to express the principles of design in more detail. For a wonderful historical context and a good read on the evolution of the history of planting and garden styles, read Nancy Leszczynski's book *Planting the Landscape: A Professional Approach to Garden Design.* To explore through diagrams and sketches the way that plants can be used as objects of design, see *Residential Landscape Architecture*, by Norman Booth and James Hiss, or, equally as good, *The Planting Design Handbook*, by Nick Robinson. All three of these are excellent texts for a course in planting design.

LIGHT AND SHADOW, VALUE

Subtler and more ephemeral, light and shadow effects create changing moods and lend a somewhat spiritual dimension to the landscape, compelling one to return to experience the landscape again and again. Light effects correlate with landscape comfort (shade during the hot summer months) and also safety (using transparent plants to avoid too much enclosure and hiding places). In a more romantic way, consider the light effects of sunlight through grasses or of dappled sunlight through the light and open canopy of serviceberry, *Amelanchier × grandiflora.* Compare these effects to the dark and heavy presence of *Magnolia grandiflora*, southern magnolia. Each design's context aids in considering the light conditions and desired impact of the selected plant material. Note the different light effects created by magnolia and honeylocust in figures 29 and 30.

Light also affects the perception of other elements such as color and texture. Warm colors are even more vibrant in bright sun but may be dull in shade, whereas cool colors come to life in shade but can be washed out in bright sunlight. Light colors help to brighten a dark space, and dark colors can lend weight and substance to a space that is too open and bright.

In this section we have examined the many ways that plants may be considered based on their artistic and aesthetic attributes. In the next section we will discuss how plants can be selected and combined to successfully address the scale or size of a space.

Plants as Architecture FORMING OUTDOOR SPACE

USING THE PRINCIPLES OF DESIGN

SPACE, SCALE, AND DEGREES OF ENCLOSURE

Careful attention must be given to the spatial qualities of a design in relation to the site and to the desired function of the site (often termed the "design program" by landscape architects). Three-dimensional space, its size, and its visual permeability in relation to the human user have a profound impact on the feel, comfort level, and functionality of the place. The psychology of space has long been studied by environmental psychologists and urban designers, and much is known about the human response to various landscape typologies. For example, large open spaces like a soccer or football field may be intimidating to a single user, and people will often skirt the edges of such a space rather than walk straight across them. In the public realm, small spaces that are too enclosed or isolated communicate a sense of danger. Plantings for small spaces in the public realm should be carefully chosen to provide partial privacy and filtering of views without completely blocking views, creating an unsafe space. In the private realm, a secluded and private space with heavy plantings may be acceptable and quite desirable because it offers the user a private haven that serves as a retreat and place of respite from daily stress.

In addition to these landscape typologies, we assert that planting design can create a variety of spatial experiences within any one design, be it public or private, as in figure 31. A residential garden could offer a range of experiences, from a quiet and private spot for one person, to a gathering place that accommodates a table for six to ten people (see figure 32), to a larger, more open space for recreation, walking, or larger group activities. This spectrum of spaces in a design invites varied uses over time and increases a landscape's functional and aesthetic value. Consider the many scales in which one may experience the landscape in figure 33A–F. Public parks and greenways can be greatly improved by the addition of smaller, more intimate spots where people can rest and observe the activities in larger adjacent spaces. Think of these as the small eddies that form along the main current of a creek or river. Public parks often provide large open expanses of lawn and trees with little definition of smaller spaces and supporting planting that invite a slow stroll or a shady and more private place to sit and relax. While an expanse of lawn may be perfect for recreation and sports, the smaller adjacent nooks (think back to the stream eddy idea) support other uses and invite a greater overall diversity of users to the public realm. Smaller-scale spaces and plantings encourage curiosity and provide the opportunity to examine plants up close, witness and enjoy the activity of pollinators, and observe the way plants change with the seasons.

The reader will notice that the foremost organizing factor for the plants covered in this book is that of scale. Landscape architects and landscape designers know that the correct scale or size of plant material for a given location is of utmost importance. In fact, most planting design courses in landscape architecture programs emphasize a phased process of design in which plants are first placed in the appropriate scale. After this important decision has been made, one may progress to increasingly finite attributes such as foliage, flowering, and seasonal change.

Selecting an appropriate scale of plant material is directly related to the development of an understanding of the size and scale of the site to be designed. Planting design is done by landscape architects across an enormous scale, from an intimate residential courtyard at the small end, to city streets, parks, and many miles of transit and utility corridors at the larger end. In general, the opportunity for detailed planting design and plant selection lies at the small end of the scale. City parks, streets, and campuses require consideration of a much larger land area and may emphasize planning for future shade and screening that is affected by incompatible land uses. Planting design at this level is more about tree

FIGURE 31 *above* A smaller and more intimate bench space is tucked at the edge of a larger lawn area in this Columbus, Ga., garden by Bill Smith and Associates. This spatial arrangement provides a spot where visitors can have a conversation while still being able to view activities beyond.

FIGURE 32 *right* Almost hidden from public view, this side garden in Charleston provides an intimate getaway.

FIG. 33 SCALE PHOTOS A–F

Planting design must address the interrelationship between small and large scale, private and public. Successful planting design helps craft a variety of outdoor usable space for people to choose how they wish to engage with the natural world.

A *Intimate Nooks and Crannies*

In highly detailed gardens no opportunity to create interest should be overlooked. In this garden container richness of detail is provided through the combination of carefully selected plants with complimentary colors and textures. Attention to material selection and using plants in containers, cracks in walls, pockets between steps and walks, and other tiny spaces create fine detail, an invitation to pause and linger in the landscape, and provide a clear message of great care to the observer.

B *Private Spaces*

This small courtyard is the tropical garden at Chanticleer estate in Wayne, Pennsylvania. Plants are used to create privacy and an intimate feeling, just off to the side of a much larger and more open terrace. This contrast in public versus private is important in creating spaces for different activities and moods.

C *Neighborhood Yards and Parks*

In this very formal backyard in Atlanta, Georgia, plants are used architecturally to direct the viewer toward the distant infinity edge of the pool and the feeling of endless property beyond, even though the backyard itself is relatively small. Design by LandPlus Associates.

At this Wayne, Pennsylvania, residence the owner has reclaimed the front yard as semiprivate space using plants as a semipermeable visual barrier to the street. The yard is simultaneously welcoming and secluded enough for uses that might typically be relegated to a back or side yard.

Post Office Park provides a peaceful respite in the heart of Boston. Trees, shrubs, and perennials provide shade, a visual shield, noise reduction, and spaces varying in size and scale for individuals and groups. Design by Halvorsen Design Partnership.

Mature London Plane Trees (*Plantanus × acerifolia*) create a green haven and a much-loved meeting place in Bryant Park, New York City. The trees create a cathedral-like shaded edge where the user can choose between open lawn and sunshine or shady nook.

FIG. 33 SCALE PHOTOS A–F *(continued)*

D *Corridors and Trails*

E–F *Expansive Views and Large Open Spaces*

The linear arrangement of maple trees on the left, and arborvitae hedge on the right keeps the pedestrian moving down the corridor at Nike headquarters outside Portland, Oregon. Planting design along pedestrian and bicycle trails can speed up or slow down the experience based on the level of detail and degree of repetition. Slower spaces for pause and rest can be planted in a more detailed way, peeling off to the side as a collecting point like eddies along a stream.

A hilltop residence in Knoxville, Tennessee, affords a breathtaking view of the Tennessee River. The garden offers detailed spaces up close (small scale spots for benches and small gatherings) while keeping the grand vista open. Design by SWH landscape architects.

Large-scale design for places like Naumkeag, a sprawling private estate designed by Nathan Barrett and later Fletcher Steele, requires thinking in terms of forests and meadows, views and vistas, acres and miles. Planting at this scale is about painting with a very broad brush and thinking about large-scale management and maintenance. It is even more important at this scale to embrace the character of the land—its natural systems and processes—as the guiding concepts for the design.

selection and massing of only a few plants for large areas; however, these kinds of projects often include smaller pedestrian-oriented spaces or pockets that are more like a residential garden or small pocket park. These are small projects within a project and should be given their own special consideration at a more detailed scale. Why does this matter? Good planting design should craft a memorable human experience of the place. It should inspire wonder at the marvels of nature and the plant kingdom. In a small space where one can sit and is invited to linger, whether residential garden or urban pocket park, one can better appreciate a high level of detail. At this intimate scale, there is an opportunity to layer many plants within a small space and create a rich and changing sensory experience—much like peering into a jewel box. In contrast, a larger project such as a street or transit corridor may only be viewed at high speeds while traveling. Observers cannot appreciate details while moving at a high speed. Large-scale projects can involve sweeping masses of trees and large shrubs or meadows of grasses and forbs, but fine-scaled perennials, bulbs, and ground covers would be largely missed and unappreciated, as well as difficult to maintain.

MASSING AND VISUAL COMPLEXITY

In large spaces, grouping or massing of plants is necessary for visual cohesiveness and a sense of order. Massing of plants creates a legible pattern for the viewer. Even natural plant communities can have visually legible patterns that lend a sense of order and stability. In small-scale spaces, it is possible that large simple masses of plants can be a bit boring and not offer enough visual complexity, interest, or mystery. In a large space, the lack of any massing or patterning may appear disordered, chaotic, and unintentional. The planting designer must be aware of the relationship between human scale and the degree of plant massing and pattern necessary for a sense of visual order.

The following sections offer a discussion of some of the considerations one must make in planting design when working at different scales. We hope these examples from current landscape architects and garden designers serve as an inspiration and a jumping-off point. They are by no means exhaustive or applicable to all places, as there are too many factors in every project that must be considered. However, they do serve as examples of planting design done with careful attention to scale, and they may help connect you to the right sections of the book for assistance in thinking about plant selection and in preparing your own planting designs.

NOOKS AND CRANNIES

The tiniest of spaces can host an amazing diversity of plant life. A walk down nearly any sidewalk in the Southeast shows this to be true, with everything from crabgrass to princess tree seedlings coming up between the cracks in the concrete. Cracks and nooks and crannies can be an opportunity to embellish a place with great detail and care. The English tradition of planted steps is a great historic example, where stone steps between garden levels were sometimes designed with open pockets in the stone work specifically for plants. This level of detail is a sign of great care and invites visitors to slow down and enjoy the intricacy of the place. Note the level of detailed plantings in figure 34 and the contrasting masses and large scale of plantings in figure 35.

Figure 36 is taken from a garden in Columbus, Georgia, designed by landscape architect Bill Smith. Strawberry begonia, *Saxifraga stolonifera*, is planted to creep between tread and riser and in the corners of the steps. The small round leaves with silver venation repeat the gray and silver tones of the stone while softening the hard edges. Southern shield fern, *Thelypteris kunthii*, provides the next layer and offers a color shift to a more yellow green. The result is a visual reward for all who pass and a pleasant moment as one takes the steps.

ALLEYWAYS

Alleyways and tight spaces between buildings and walls can be very human-scale places where every square inch provides an opportunity for detail design. In these often

FIGURE 34 *left* Vine-covered walls, planted steps, and grade changes create intimacy and interest, even at this threshold and gateway, in Great Dixter, Christopher Lloyd's masterpiece garden.

FIGURE 35. *right* Large swaths of wave-shaped hedges and ribbon-like block plantings of grasses and perennials provide visual interest in the sunken space and keep the eye and the passerby moving. Thames Barrier Park, London.

FIGURE 36 Moss and strawberry begonia, *Saxifraga stolonifera*, soften the stone step edges and create much detailed interest in this Columbus, Ga., garden, designed by Atlanta landscape architect Bill Smith.

linear spaces, visitors can be invited to sit along the way or move more slowly and enjoy detailed planting. In the alley shown in figure 37, the Atlanta-based landscape architecture firm Land Plus Associates used small ground covers, vines, and perennials to create a feast for the eyes, whether viewing the alley from windows or walking down the stepping-stone path of the alley space. These tighter spaces might only be large enough for one person sitting in a chair surrounded by plants or walking down a pathway through lush plantings. The user is large in relation to usable space in this example.

COURTYARDS AND SMALL GARDEN ROOMS

A courtyard offers a high level of structure and is in many cases the first transition space between architecture and the open landscape or garden, as in figure 37, with a plan view in figure 38. The highly controlled nature of a courtyard, whether formed entirely by walls or by hedged plant material, tends to feel comfortable and safe and can be likened to the living room of a house. A courtyard might be 12' square or even 40', but the nature of the space invites visitors to linger there and perhaps enjoy a meal at a table or conversation while sitting on outdoor furniture. In a courtyard or small garden room, there is an opportunity to use both hardscape and planting at a very detailed level, allowing a sitting observer to examine and enjoy material choices, as in figures 39 and 40.

FIGURE 37 A tight alley is turned into a desirable space by use of plants to climb walls, creep between stones, and provide focal points along the way and from indoor views from windows. Land Plus Associates, Atlanta, Ga.

YARDS AND SMALL PARKS

In a somewhat larger landscape space such as a suburban yard or public park, the landscape extends beyond the immediate view of the observer. This is an excellent opportunity to invite the user to wander and explore, as in figure 41. Pathways and plants can lead one through the landscape and offer the possibility of discovery around the corner. The human is small in this context, and a designer may decide to focus detailed plantings at points of interest or important nodes. In the connections, the planting may be simpler and focus more on massing trees and large shrubs to form space. A designer can consider the value of natural areas to reduce maintenance and provide habitat.

FIGURE 38 *above* Plan image, Land Plus Associates, Atlanta.

FIGURE 39 *left* A small courtyard designed by SWH Associates in Knoxville, Tenn., serves as a private haven for the owners.

FIGURE 40 *below left* This lush rear courtyard by Land Plus Associates in Atlanta, Ga., is carefully planted to soften hard edges, provide a rich tapestry of plant textures, and frame views of the koi pond from the adjacent screened-in porch.

FIGURE 41 *below right* A series of spaces is evident from this pathway view, with a bench as the focal point in the distance. One is invited to walk and explore. Private residence by SWH Associates in Knoxville, Tenn.

FIGURE 42 *top* Fourth Ward Park, Atlanta, Ga., by HDR. The excellent planting design features wetland native species adapted to thrive in both drought and flood conditions. Plants were also selected based on their ornamental attributes. The resulting park is an exquisite blend of ecological function, aesthetic beauty, and public interaction.

FIGURE 43 *bottom* The master plan for Fourth Ward Park, Phase 1 by HDR, Phase 2 by Wood and Partners.

LARGE PARKS AND PUBLIC OPEN SPACES

Large parks and connected open spaces provide the opportunity for recreation and for walking and bicycle trails. The scale of these spaces is much greater than the human scale, and any detailed planting must be focused at key nodes and places of rest or where the site use changes to a smaller-scale space and program. The planting approach for such vast landscapes should shift to habitat creation and greater plant diversity through native tree planting, as in figure 42, with a plan view of the design in figure 43. A designer can utilize seed mixes of perennial grasses and forbs for seasonal interest and wildlife value without the need for constant mowing and intense horticulture.

EXTENSIVE GREEN INFRASTRUCTURE

As cities plan for extensive pedestrian and bicycle greenway trails and transit corridors, there is a new opportunity to reconnect humans with nature. These landscapes may extend many miles; therefore, the planting design approach must focus on tree planting and minimal maintenance. An exciting area of research lies at this critical intersection of the public desire for beauty and sense of control over the landscape and the reality of minimal public funding for maintenance. Designed seed mixes or seeds with plugs and small container plants featuring forbs offer a low-cost installation possible across many acres and may only require an annual mowing or bush hog (use of a large mowing deck pulled by a large farm tractor) or burn where possible. Success in establishing a seeded meadow requires careful site preparation (often with herbicides) to eradicate overly aggressive and competitive plants such as rhizomatous grasses like Bermuda and Johnson grass. Often, poor soils are desirable to control growth—at first a baffling concept in light of traditional gardening approaches involving soil amendments to increase fertility. The seed mix must include species that grow well and layer together to create multiple flowering events throughout the growing season. The exact approach to establishment of and recipe for the seed mix varies greatly based on the ecoregion and the conditions of the site, the client's expectations, and the management regimen. Examples of success and novel approaches to establishment can be seen in the work of James Hitchmough and his projects in Europe and China. Recently completed Tongva Park in Santa Monica, California, features a beautiful and regionally inspired meadow-like design by John Greenlee. In the eastern United States, Larry Weaner is well known for his successful meadows.

The growing public appreciation and desire for these flowering meadows offer a glimmer of hope to end the overdependence on lawns and maintenance-intensive turf that dominate public lands. The Beltline project in Atlanta is one such example (figs. 44 and 45). Miles and hundreds of acres of land are being planted with trees and seeded with native grasses and forbs to offer city dwellers new modes of mobility and greater access to (designed) natural places. Interestingly, these designed meadows can be applied across a vast scale, yet the species diversity afforded by the seed mix results in great complexity per square foot, offering the close observer a feast for the eyes. This approach is valuable for restoration and more ecosystem-supportive care of roadsides and utility corridors.

There exists a subtle tension between the worlds of landscape architecture and horticulture, where the idea of massing and pattern (typical for landscape architects) versus a very plantcentric approach to planting design (typical for horticulturalists) can lead to a mutual skepticism. This skepticism can be seen in books, websites, and publications from all sides. Consider the source! Tony Avent, famous plantsman and owner of Plant Delights Nursery near Raleigh, North Carolina, often alludes to these different approaches with humor and sarcasm in lectures and on his website with the slogan "drifts of one." Tony, a world-class collector of plants and an advocate for diversity in planting design, makes fun of the boring plans of landscape architects who sometimes overemphasize plant massing and use an overly simplified plant palette. On the flip side, many landscape architects raise an eyebrow at the one-of-everything approach that sometimes comes out of the horticulture camps. The solution for better work is to work together. Arguably, some of the finest recent projects demonstrate the value of

FIGURE 44 Atlanta residents enjoy a crisp fall ride down the Beltline. *Andropogon virginicus* leans into the photo with its rich amber fall color, while oaks and maples provide color in the distance.

FIGURE 45 Large-scale planning for the Beltline trail system around Atlanta involves a nature experience for city dwellers. Tree planting and grassy meadow establishment are major components of the planting strategy. Perkins&Will, Atlanta, Ga.

collaboration, such as the internationally famous High Line in Manhattan, a collaboration between landscape architect James Corner and horticulturalist Piet Oudolf.

BAD PLANTING DESIGN

We are surrounded every day by poor choices of plant material. In the residential realm, it's the shrubs planted 2' from the house foundation. If left unpruned, these shrubs grow taller than the house, blocking windows and generally creating a messy, unkempt appearance. Why does this happen? The reasons are many. Too often, the design itself is poorly done by someone with only a cursory knowledge of plants and their actual growth habits. More often than this, plants are installed by a building contractor without any professional advice. Many times the landscape architect or designer is to blame for lack of knowledge about plants. Sometimes the nursery industry is to blame by printing plant tags that do not indicate the realistic size of the plant after a few years. We always tell our students to be wary of any claims of "dwarf" plant material. "Dwarf" is a highly relative term and may mean the shrub only grows 15' tall rather than 25! Sometimes a plant released for sale to the public as the latest and greatest dwarf form has only been observed in a test plot for a few years, so nobody knows how big it will be in twenty years. To add to the problem, the public's taste in landscape design is now cemented in the "mulch aesthetic," where plants cannot be allowed to touch each other (see figs. 47 and 48). Thomas Rainer is a landscape architect and author of the excellent book *Planting in a Post-wild World: Designing Plant Communities for Resilient Landscapes*. He writes humorously of our "addiction to mulch" and advocates for the use of layered plantings as living green mulch, mimicking natural plant assemblages.

Mistakes are also made in larger public projects. Too many plazas, parking lots, and streets in temperate zones serve as hot examples of places where more and bigger trees are needed. This is not simply a problem of tree selection but a larger problem of undervaluing the contributions that trees and green space make to our cities and the public realm and the lack of allocating the necessary space for successful growth and longevity. Without planning for adequate root and canopy space, large shade-providing trees cannot be planted or expected to perform well over the long term. The problem is a deeper one of not adequately valuing the landscape and its role in supporting all of life on the earth.

top to bottom

FIGURE 46 A typical scene in suburban America, where it is apparently a rule that plants may not touch and shrubs must be balled regularly. Are the plants plastic?

FIGURE 47 What is the concept here? Must the azaleas be flat topped? How much more lovely the spring bloom and overall scene would be with naturally formed plants!

FIGURE 48. A familiar unpleasant scene in strip mall land, where plants must not touch, and no trees provide shade over the hot asphalt.

On a brighter note, it is exciting to be living in a time when there seems to be an increasing interest and public investment in public green open space and access to nature. The public is increasingly more knowledgeable of the health benefits of easy access to green space and a more active lifestyle that promotes walking and deemphasizes the automobile. Edward O. Wilson's biophilia hypothesis suggests that at a genetic level humans are wired to love and be in community with the natural world. Social ecologist Stephen Kellert took this idea further and wrote that our genetic connection to the natural world and our ability to appreciate and value it atrophy over time when we are separated from nature. This is an alarming idea, as so many people around the globe live in increasingly dense cities with no access to nature. Stephen and Rachel Kaplan, environmental psychologists, have coined the term "attention restoration theory," the idea that urban environments create a unique kind of mental fatigue ("directed attention fatigue," or a decrease in one's ability to focus on tasks) and that nature is uniquely capable of restoring the ability to concentrate and focus. These links between health and well-being and access to nature increasingly point to the need for quality green spaces in our cities. Projects around the world serve as examples of these essential connections to nature, such as the ambitious and visionary Beltline project in Atlanta. This project will eventually provide both a form of public mass transit and an associated emerald necklace of parks and greenway trails for Atlanta. In Chattanooga, recent downtown projects have reconnected the city with its waterfront along the Tennessee River. In both cities, these green infrastructure projects are driving new development because people want to live within walking distance to green space and nature. With these new projects come new opportunities to reconnect humanity to the natural world, so the need for inspired planting design has never been greater. Run-of-the-mill landscaping will not suffice. The planting design of these urban wilds must be diverse and complex, leaving viewers unaware that they are looking at a designed space, as depicted beautifully in figure 49.

FIGURE 49 This wonderful park/playground/habitat refuge is in Vancouver, B.C., designed by PWL Partnership. Many species, such as *Carex*, *Juncus*, and *Calamagrostis*, are woven into a naturalistic tapestry for beauty and ecological function.

DESIGN MATRICES

We have used the preceding pages to discuss the many ways of seeing plants as instruments of design. Throughout this book, plants are presented with their particular design qualities and uses, along with identification features and their cultural requirements and natural associations. With so many things to consider at once in preparing a planting plan, we have found charts to be very helpful so that many criteria—aesthetic and ecological—can be considered at once. We hope readers will find the design matrices in each section of this book to be quite useful. Apart from these tables, this book is first organized by scale, followed by whether a plant is evergreen or deciduous. This is a significant departure from many alphabetically organized horticultural texts and is inspired by the decision-making process of preparing a planting plan. Landscape architects and garden designers throughout history have understood the importance of often considering these two factors first in the process of planting design.

The evergreen or deciduous character of plant material is quite important, as it relates to the visual permeability, seasonality, and even energy efficiency of nearby sites and structures. Many landscape architects use a rule of thumb when planning a landscape in which they strive for around 40 percent evergreen and 60 percent deciduous plant material. The rationale for this is that too much evergreen material can appear heavy and tends to offer less in terms of year-round seasonal interest and change. Too little evergreen material can create a landscape that feels too empty, particularly in the winter. This is a loose rule of thumb and can be argued against depending on other factors such as region, immediate context, and client preference. Interestingly, in recent decades, as grasses and perennials have become more available and more appreciated, it appears that in at least some landscapes there is a decreasing use of evergreens because of the use of structural herbaceous plants such as grasses that remain upright during the winter and create a compelling winter scene.

CONSIDERING THE SITE

The temperate regions of North America boast some of the richest floras in the world. This richness has evolved out of conditions such as fertile soils, a long, warm growing season, and generally abundant rainfall. The southern Appalachian region is considered a temperate rainforest, with many areas of high elevation receiving well over 60" of rain per year. The large number of plants covered in this text are only a small sampling of the number of species that occur naturally or that can be grown in temperate regions. This richness makes planting design quite fun, but it is also a rather daunting task with many possibilities. One important way of narrowing the possibilities is to look very carefully at regional patterns and how those are expressed on an individual site. Every site has its own story to tell through its physical and geographic qualities. These must be analyzed, understood, and used as a way to narrow the planting palette and make plant choices that will prosper because they fit the site conditions. This process of reading a site, or site analysis, is the proper beginning of any landscape design and development activity.

It is helpful to first understand the land patterns and geographic characteristics of a region and how they influence plant communities. Plant communities evolve over time because of many factors, including geography, soils, slopes, hydrological patterns, climate, elevation, and disturbance. Knowledge of characteristic plant communities common to your region or the region of a design project forms an excellent baseline of plants that are more likely to succeed in a new installation. Native plant communities and their associated site conditions serve as excellent models for use on other sites sharing similar attributes. The state of Georgia and its physiographic regions and subsequent plant communities are profiled in *The Natural Communities of Georgia*, edited by Jonathan Ambrose, L. Katherine Kirkman, and Leslie Edwards. As shown in figure 50, the major plant communities of the state follow roughly the same patterns across the state as geography, elevation, soil, and hydrology. These plant communities are well documented and serve as an initial palette of options for planting design. We have not organized this book by community because we wanted to include some nonnative plants. However, we highly recommend *The Living Landscape* by Rick Darke and Doug Tallamy, a rich resource on planting design by natural community. On your own site, consider the many functional and ecological factors that will influence plant performance over the long term.

FIGURE 50 *opposite page*
Plant communities of Georgia.

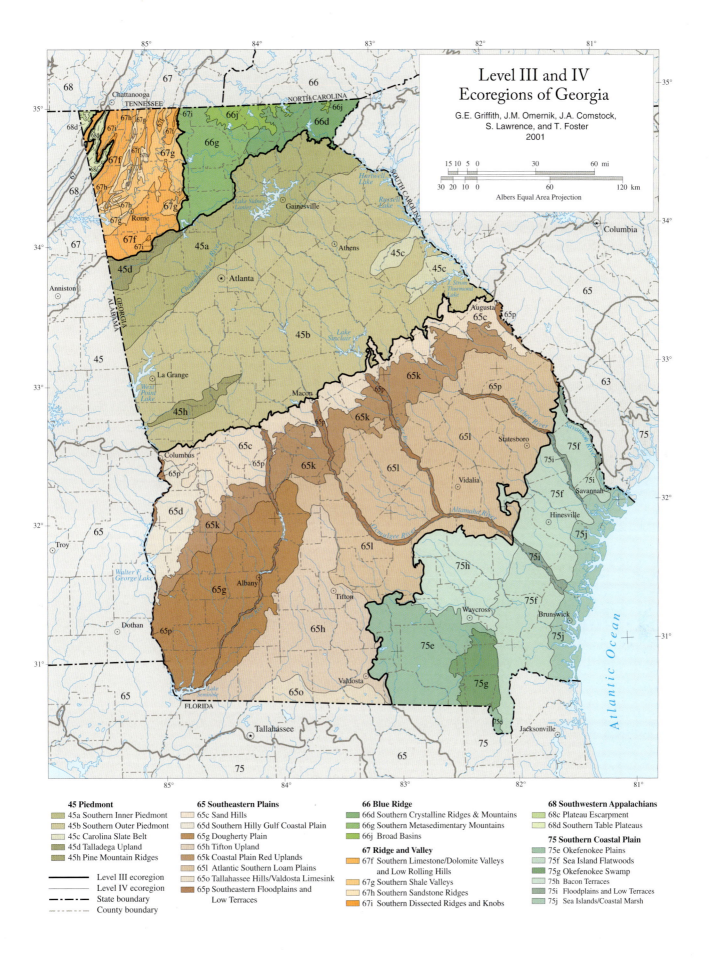

SOIL TYPES, MOISTURE, AND COMPACTION

What is the soil composition in terms of clay, silt, and sand? An ideal soil is typically defined as close to equal portions of these three particles, with 50 percent pore space for water movement and oxygen. However, most native plant communities have evolved to thrive in less than ideal conditions, and these native assemblages can serve as excellent choices for most sites, with careful attention to soils and other site attributes. Soil compaction can be an extremely limiting factor and should be addressed by aeration and addition of organic material. What is the moisture-holding capacity of the soil? Does it stay wet? Is it dry most of the time? How fast does it dry out after rain?

Throughout this book in each plant description, we describe the preferred soil moisture levels or tolerance range for each plant species. In ecological terms, we describe soil moisture on a gradient from dry to wet. An accurate understanding of soil moisture is essential for optimum plant performance over time.

Dry	Mostly dry	Moist and well drained	Mostly moist	Wet
Xeric	Subxeric	Submesic	Mesic	Hydric

FIGURE 51 Sun/shade patterns from morning to afternoon.

EXISTING VEGETATION AND SUN AND SHADE PATTERNS

The planting designer must evaluate existing vegetation onsite and work to enhance and preserve existing trees and plant communities. In many cases, these assets have accrued over time and will not be matched by new plantings for perhaps decades. Working with the sun and shade patterns that are created by both existing vegetation and architectural structures provides opportunities for greater species diversity, greater visual interest, and a planting that will perform and mature far better over time. Pockets of afternoon shade are particularly important for hot climates, as they can provide the necessary relief from heat stress for plants such as *Hydrangea macrophylla* and *Cornus florida*, allowing their use in a design that may otherwise be too hot and exposed for such plants. Conversely, a warm, south-facing wall may provide a spot just warm enough in winter to sneak in a plant from one or two zones southward. Many gardeners in zone 7 have used this strategy to include much-coveted camellias and gardenias. Note the sun and shade patterns from morning to afternoon in figure 51.

TOPOGRAPHY AND SLOPE ASPECT

The lay of the land will influence the types of plant communities that grow there. In the Southeast, north-facing steep slopes are cooler and wetter than south- or west-facing slopes, which are hotter and drier. The slope aspect greatly impacts the human comfort and usability of both the architecture and the landscape. In the best designs, the building is designed to respond to site conditions, with room and window and door placement responding to slope aspect, existing vegetation, and all site conditions (see fig. 52). However, even in less ideal situations, where the building has more or less been plopped from a catalog onto the site, new plantings can be used strategically to create shade and greater comfort over time. Research has shown that in the Southeast the afternoon shade from mature trees results in as much as a 30 percent savings on summer energy bills. Conversely, deciduous trees that allow the winter sun to penetrate and warm south-facing rooms can increase winter comfort and reduce heating bills.

HYDROLOGY

The movement patterns and speed of water across a site must be carefully dealt with in site design. From a planting perspective, it is critical to understand water patterns and site conditions and the soil moisture gradient throughout the year. While excessive moisture too close to the building envelope cannot be tolerated, wet conditions in other places on the site can be a visual and functional asset. Rain gardens and planted stormwater systems recharge local groundwater and improve water quality. They are an exciting area of progress toward better environmental quality. These wet areas can be visually interesting when planted with wet soil–loving plants. They are increasingly being utilized in home landscapes and city streets. Many of the photos of moist to wet soil–loving plants throughout this book depict designed rain gardens, green streets, and planted stormwater systems.

WIND PATTERNS

Dominant wind patterns can be effectively addressed and utilized through planting design. In the Southeast, most summer winds are out of the south and west, as shown in figure 53. To encourage a cooling effect, the planting design

FIGURE 52 The slope aspect, or directional exposure, of a site greatly influences sunlight and moisture levels, impacts from wind, and energy consumption.

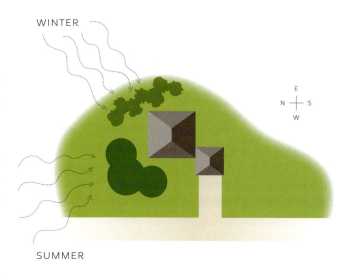

FIGURE 53 Prevailing wind directions in summer and winter need consideration for proper placement of plantings.

should avoid blocking these breezes by placement of large dense evergreens, although these same evergreens can be used as a windbreak to reduce the force of cold northern winds in the winter. Newly planted trees and large shrubs typically need staking for stability and root development during the first year, especially in site locations exposed to high winds. Plants with large broad leaves can be easily damaged by high winds and need to be planted in more protected locations.

WILDLIFE CORRIDORS

The overwhelmingly prevalent philosophy behind many gardens and planted landscapes is one of resistance to wildlife and insect damage and pressure. The frustration of having one's hostas mowed to the ground by deer, rabbits, or slugs is certainly understandable. However, the need to utilize our everyday gardens as habitat has been made clear by the writings and research of Doug Tallamy and others and by movements such as the pollinator network, which aims to promote monarch butterfly–friendly landscapes and habitats. One of the great ironies of American society can be found in the American suburbs, where vast lawns are maintained primarily for traditional and ceremonial reasons. Few suburban dwellers utilize much of their own turf-dominated miniestates, nor do they want to spend the time and money maintaining this space. A more valuable and compelling use of so much land can be found in interconnected wildlife

FIGURE 54 We must view each parcel of property as an important piece in the bigger puzzle.

interconnecting wildlife corridors and walking / bike trails.

corridors. Neighborhoods and cities can be designed around such corridors, as illustrated in figure 54, and they can also serve as recreation corridors for people. To change a landscape from wildlife proof to wildlife attracting invites a new layer of interest and engagement with the natural world.

The United States Department of Agriculture Hardiness Zone Map (fig. 55) indicates the average minimum winter temperatures and maps these across the country. These zones illustrate the approximate areas in which plants can tolerate the winter lows. A very useful interactive map is available online and allows the user to zoom down to the county level. This map was updated in 2012 based on a larger data set of temperature over time and to reflect warming trends. Many zip codes moved at least a half zone warmer in this change.

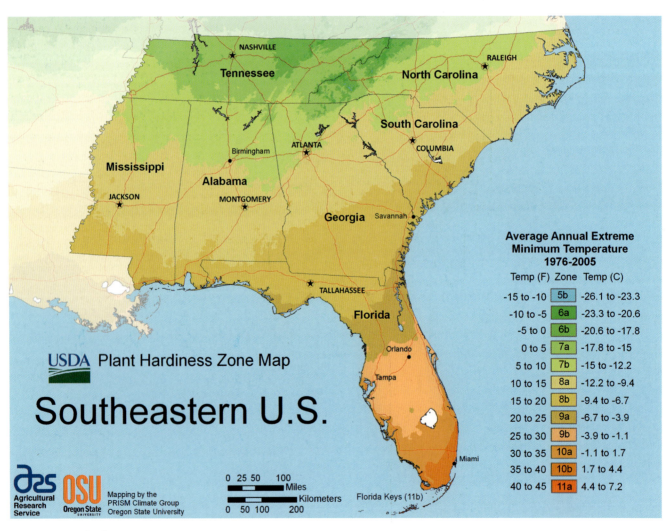

FIGURE 55 USDA hardiness zones.

CHANGE OVER TIME

Perhaps one of the most difficult aspects of planting design is to understand and anticipate growth and change over time. The element of time sets the science and art of planting design apart from most other forms of creative enterprise. Good planting design embodies the idea of stewardship and of partnering with nature to create a better world for the generations to come.

The planting designer must reject the idea that a landscape is static. The client must be informed that as plants grow and change, the landscape will need editing and human intervention to mediate change. A frequently encountered example of this is in shrub layer plantings installed in combination with young trees. Shrub layer planting refers to a large area that is planted with mostly shrubs and trees (perhaps grasses and perennials too) and is often mulched in anticipation of shrub and tree growth and plants touching each other to form solid masses, thus reducing sun to soil contact, weed germination, and maintenance. As trees mature, the ground plane becomes shady, and many of the initial sun-loving plants decline and disappear. At this point the lower layers must be reworked and replanted. To some degree a total redesign may be avoided by the use of plants with a naturally wide light tolerance range (e.g., our native oak leaf hydrangea tolerates full sun and moderate shade quite well). However, inevitably some layers will decline as trees mature, and new layers will need to be installed.

Anticipating and embracing change as trees and other plantings mature is a step toward environmental stewardship and the preservation of healthy plant communities and the living systems they support. The careful editing of plantings based on change works to increase biodiversity and species richness. The philosophy here is one of careful shaping and maintenance.

This idea of stewardship opposes mainstream landscaping in contemporary society, which too often is simply un-

FIGURE 56 The growth of trees easily transcends the lifespan of humans. To plan for growth and change is to plan for the well-being of future generations.

FIGURE 57 A careful design process leads to wise plant choices.

change over time

SITE INVENTORY AND ANALYSIS +	DESIGN	PLANT SELECTION
climate?	function?	plant matrices
hydrology?	spacial separation?	species accounts
soils?	scale?	
topography?	aesthetics?	
sun and shade?	spirit of place?	
views?	mood?	
local plant communities?	form / color / texture?	
wildlife?	seasonal interest?	

derstood to be and applied as decoration. In this view, the landscape is cheap, easily discarded, and easily replaced. The role and value of plantings in human life is increasingly well understood and documented. For enduring places and a healthier world, society must learn to value and understand landscape quality and the layered richness that builds over time (fig. 1). Planting designers and landscape architects can help by creating a landscape management plan and vision for each landscape to be used by future managers of the landscape. Designers should create design programs that answer these questions: What is the ultimate purpose of the design? What are the ways that natural and heavily planted land can increase while decreasing turf, mulch, and other low diversity, overly managed, and environmentally poor landscapes?

USING THIS BOOK

This section has provided a discussion of the many functional and aesthetic factors that must be considered in mak-ing wise plant choices (fig. 57). When preparing a planting design, one must consider these factors in order to fully utilize the plant descriptions and design matrices contained in this book. We have endeavored to organize the book in such a way that through the design process, including site inventory and analysis, as well as design development, the designer will be able to define the key criteria that lead to the best plant choices. Need a large tree for a wet site? Go to the sections on large and medium trees and compare the many possibilities listed, along with other attributes for consideration such as flowering, fruit, fall color, texture, and more. Need a low shrub or perennial for hot dry sun? Search through the sections on shrubs and herbaceous perennials and compare options as you work to synthesize many criteria. Most importantly, design plantings and select plants with passion. The end user will reap the benefits for many years, and the world will be a little bit better because of your thoughtful and caring approach.

Plant Lists for Difficult Situations

Life would be so much easier for designers if every site had deep, rich soils and was located in full sun with a little light shade in a few places. A plant palette for that type of site would be virtually limitless. While those situations are ideal, in reality, landscape architects often struggle with finding suitable plants that can survive and thrive in less than ideal situations in the landscape. These situations occur frequently, even in small portions of a site where most of the habitat may be ideal. Although all landscape architects should know where to put each plant in the composition into a spot where it can successfully compete with its neighbors and display its full potential, the following situations test even the most knowledgeable and resourceful designer.

These lists are merely intended to be starting points for these types of unique sites. For example, if there is only about 4" of clay soil before you hit solid bedrock in a sunny dry location, you cannot expect to transplant larger shrubs or trees to that location. Certainly, those shrubs or trees will not survive those soil conditions. If a site includes a perched water table or hardpan, where a layer of impervious rock or dense clay prevents the movement of water and air through the soil, then choice of plants that could thrive would be greatly limited. In addition, none of these lists for site conditions recognizes the potential presence of deer in the neighborhood.

Asterisks next to the name indicate a plant that is native to the southeastern United States.

DRY SHADE *(e.g., under a mature tree on the north side of a building)*

Ground covers	*Acanthus mollis*
	Aspidistra elatior
	*Carex pennsylvanica**
	Cyrtomium falcatum
	*Dryopteris marginalis**
	Helleborus orientalis
	Ophiopogon japonicus
	*Polystichum acrostichoides**
	Rohdea japonica
	Trachelospermum asiaticum
	Vinca minor
Shrubs	*Fatsia japonica*
	Ficus carica
	Podocarpus macrophyllus
	Prunus laurocerasus
	(all cultivars)
	Ruscus aculeatus
	*Rhaphidophyllum hystrix**

Climbing vines	*Ficus pumila*
	*Parthenocissus quinquefolia**
	*Smilax smallii**
Small trees	*Carpinus caroliniana**
	*Ostrya virginiana**

SUNNY DRY LOCATIONS WITH LIMITED SOIL DEPTH *(locations in full sun with less than 8" of rocky or sandy soil to bedrock or hardpan)*

Ground covers and herbaceous perennials	*Dianthus* spp.
	*Echinacea purpurea**
	*Glandularia canadensis**
	Iberis sempervirens
	Perovskia atriplicifolia
	*Phlox subulata**
	Salvia spp.
	Sedum acre
	Hylotelephium 'Autumn Joy'
	Tradescantia pallida

Ornamental grasses	*Leymus arenarius* 'Blue Dune'		*Berberis thunbergii*
	Nassella tenuissima		*Buddleja davidii*
	Pennisetum alopecuriodes		*Callicarpa americana**
	*Sorghastrum nutans**		*Callistemon citrinus*
	*Sporobolus heterolepis**		(zone 8b southward)
Shrubs	*Agave americana**		*Cycas revoluta* (zone 8b southward)
	Juniperus conferta		*Eriobotrya japonica*
	Juniperus horizontalis		*Feijoa selloana*
	Rosmarinus officinalis		*Hibiscus syriacus*
	*Yucca aloifolia**		*Ilex vomitoria* (all cultivars)*
	*Yucca filamentosa**		*Juniperus* (all species)
	*Yucca gloriosa**		*Kerria japonica*
	*Yucca recurvifolia**		*Lantana camara*

Lonicera fragrantissima

Nerium oleander

SUNNY DRY LOCATIONS WITH MODERATE SOIL DEPTH

(locations with at least 12" of rocky or sandy soil to bedrock or hardpan)

Ground covers and herbaceous perennials	*Achillea* spp.		*Photinia* × *fraseri*
	Baptisia australis		*Punica granatum*
	Dianthus spp.		*Punica granatum nana*
	*Echinacea purpurea**		*Pyracantha* spp.
	*Glandularia canadensis**		*Rhaphidophyllum hystrix**
	Hylotelephium 'Autumn Joy'		*Rhus aromatica**
	Iberis sempervirens		*Rosmarinus officinalis*
	*Packera aurea**		*Spiraea* (all species
	Perovskia atriplicifolia		and their cultivars)
	*Phlox subulata**		*Viburnum* × *pragense*
	Salvia spp.		*Vitex agnus-castus*
	Sedum acre		*Yucca aloifolia**
	Tradescantia pallida		*Yucca filamentosa**
Ornamental grasses	*Andropogon virginicus**		*Yucca gloriosa**
	Calamagrostis × *acutiflora*		*Yucca recurvifolia**
	'Karl Foerster'	Trees	*Aralia spinosa**
	Cortaderia selloana		*Butia capitata*
	Leymus arenarius 'Blue Dune'		*Carya glabra**
	*Muhlenbergia capillaris**		*Carya tomentosa**
	*Nassella tenuissima**		*Cedrus atlantica*
	*Panicum virgatum**		*Cedrus deodara*
	Pennisetum alopecuriodes		*Cercis canadensis**
	*Sorghastrum nutans**		*Cunninghamia lanceolata*
	*Sporobolus heterolepis**		*Cupressus sempervirens*
Shrubs	*Agave americana**		*Ilex opaca**
	Berberis julianae		*Juniperus virginiana**

Lagerstroemia spp.

Maclura pomifera

*Ostrya virginiana**

Parrotia persica

Pinus (all species)
Pistacia chinensis
*Quercus coccinea**
*Quercus falcata**
*Quercus montana**
*Quercus stellata**
*Quercus velutina**
Rhus (all species)*
*Robinia pseudoacacia**
*Sabal palmetto**
Trachycarpus fortunei
*Ulmus alata**

MOIST SUNNY AREAS   *(locations such as drainage swales and stormwater detention basins that stay damp but not inundated for several days after storms during the growing season and for several months in winter)*

Ground covers and herbaceous perennials
Canna × *generalis*
Colocasia esculenta
*Conoclinium coelestinum**
*Equisetum hyemale**
*Eutrochium fistulosum**
*Eutrochium maculatum**
*Eutrochium purpureum**
Hedychium coronarium
Helianthus spp.*
*Hibiscus coccineus**
*Hibiscus moscheutos**
Iris ensata
Iris pseudacorus
Iris sibirica
Iris × *Louisiana**
*Lobelia cardinalis**
Macrothelypteris torresiana
*Monarda didyma**
*Osmunda cinnamomea**
*Osmunda regalis**
Ruellia brittoniana
*Thelypteris kunthii**
*Tradescantia virginiana**

Ornamental grasses
Acorus calamus
Acorus gramineus
*Carex muskingumensis**
*Carex stricta**

*Chasmanthium latifolium**
*Juncus effusus**
*Panicum virgatum**
*Sorghastrum nutans**
*Tripsacum dactyloides**

Shrubs
*Agarista populifolia**
*Cephalanthus occidentalis**
*Clethra alnifolia**
*Ilex glabra**
*Ilex verticillata**
*Ilex vomitoria**
*Illicium floridanum**
*Illicium parviflorum**
*Itea virginica**
*Morella cerifera**
*Osmanthus americanus**
*Sambucus nigra canadensis**

Trees
*Acer negundo**
*Acer rubrum**
*Acer saccharinum**
Acer × *freemanii*
*Betula nigra**
*Carpinus caroliniana**
*Celtis laevigata**
*Chionanthus virginicus**
*Fraxinus pennsylvanica**
*Gleditsia triacanthos inermis**
*Liquidambar styraciflua**
*Liriodendron tulipifera**
*Magnolia grandiflora**
*Magnolia virginiana**
Metasequoia glyptostroboides
*Nyssa sylvatica**
*Ostrya virginiana**
*Persea borbonia**
*Persea palustris**
*Platanus occidentalis**
*Quercus lyrata**
*Quercus michauxii**
*Quercus nigra**
Quercus palustris
*Quercus phellos**
*Quercus texana**
*Sabal palmetto**
Salix babylonica

Salix nigra*
Taxodium distichum*
Ulmus americana*

WET SUNNY AREAS *(locations that remain moist year-round and are often inundated during winter and periodically during the growing season; shrubs and especially field-grown nursery trees need to be acclimated before planting in wet locations)*

Ground covers and herbaceous perennials	*Colocasia esculenta*
	Iris pseudacorus
	Iris × Louisiana*
	Osmunda cinnamomea*
	Osmunda regalis*
Ornamental grasses	*Acorus calamus*
	Carex stricta*
	Juncus (all species)
	Panicum virgatum*
	Typha angustifolia*
Shrubs	*Cephalanthus occidentalis**
	Ilex verticillata*
	Morella cerifera*
Trees	*Quercus texana**
	Salix babylonica
	Salix nigra*
	Taxodium distichum*

MOIST TO WET SHADED AREAS
(locations with limited direct sunlight during the growing season and soils that remain moist year-round and may be inundated periodically during the winter and spring)

Ground covers and herbaceous perennials	*Colocasia esculenta*
	Equisetum hyemale*
	Macrothelypteris torresiana
	Onoclea sensibilis*
	Osmunda cinnamomea*
	Osmunda regalis*
	Tradescantia virginiana*
	Woodwardia areolata*
Ornamental grasses	*Acorus calamus**
	Acorus gramineus
Trees	*Carpinus caroliniana**
	Ostrya virginiana*

BUTTERFLY GARDENS *(plants whose flowers are particularly attractive to insects, including butterflies, but may not be attractive to the larval stages of the insects)*

Ground covers, herbaceous perennials, and annuals	*Asclepias tuberosa**
	Conoclinium coelestinum*
	Echinacea purpurea*
	Eutrochium maculatum*
	Eutrochium purpureum*
	Eutrochium fistulosum*
	Helianthus spp.*
	Hemerocallis spp.
	Hylotelephium 'Autumn Joy'
	Lantana camara
	Lobelia cardinalis*
	Monarda didyma*
	Pentas lanceolata
	Phlox paniculata*
	Rudbeckia fulgida*
	Salvia spp.*
	Solidago spp.*
	Tagetes spp.
	Zinnia spp.
Shrubs	*Abelia × grandiflora* (all cultivars)
	Buddleja davidii
	Cephalanthus occidentalis*
	Clethra alnifolia*
	Fatsia japonica
	Itea virginica*
	Photinia × fraseri
	Prunus laurocerasus (all cultivars)
	Rhaphiolepis umbellata
	Rhododendron canescens*
	Rhododendron catawbiense*
	Rhododendron eriocarpum
	Rhododendron indicum
	Rhododendron minus*
	Rhododendron obtusum
	Rhus aromatica*
	Rosa 'Radrazz'
	Sambucus nigra canadensis*
	Sarcococca confusa
	Spiraea japonica
	Spiraea cantoniensis
	Spiraea prunifolium

	Spiraea vanhouttei
	Vitex agnus-castus
	Weigela florida
Trees	*Amelanchier* × *grandiflora*
	*Aralia spinosa**
	*Catalpa bignonioides**
	*Catalpa speciosa**
	*Cercis canadensis**
	Crataegus spp.*
	Koelreuteria bipinnata
	Koelreuteria paniculata
	Lagerstroemia spp.
	Malus spp.
	*Nyssa sylvatica**
	*Oxydendrum arboreum**
	*Prunus serotina**
	*Rhus copallinum**
	*Rhus glabra**
	*Rhus typhina**
	*Robinia pseudoacacia**

HUMMINGBIRD ATTRACTORS

(plants whose colorful, tubular-shaped flowers are particularly attractive to hummingbirds)

Vines	*Bignonia capreolata**
	*Campsis radicans**
	*Gelsemium sempervirens**
	*Lonicera sempervirens**
Shrubs	*Buddleja davidii*
	Hibiscus syriacus
	*Rhododendron canescens**
	Rhododendron indicum
	Weigela florida
Trees	*Aesculus pavia**
	*Catalpa bignonioides**
	*Catalpa speciosa**
	Malus spp.
	*Robinia pseudoacacia**

Ground covers, herbaceous perennials, and annuals

	*Aquilegia canadensis**
	*Asclepias tuberosa**
	Canna × *generalis*
	Digitalis purpurea
	Hemerocallis spp.

	Hibiscus spp.*
	Hosta spp.
	*Liatris spicata**
	*Lobelia cardinalis**
	*Monarda didyma**
	Penstemon spp.*
	Petunia × *hybrida*
	Salvia spp.*

DEER DESSERT *(while deer will eat or at least nibble at anything if they get hungry enough, these plants are guaranteed to be severely damaged or even vanish if deer are present in your neighborhood)*

Ground covers, herbaceous perennials, and annuals	*Begonia semperflorens*
	Caladium spp.
	Hemerocallis spp.
	Hosta spp.
	Impatiens hawkeri
	Impatiens walleriana
	Petunia × *hybrida*
	*Phlox paniculata**
	*Rudbeckia fulgida**
	Solenostemon scutellarioides
	*Tradescantia virginiana**
	Tulipa × *hybrida*
	Viola wittrockiana
Vines	*Hydrangea anomala petiolaris*
	*Lonicera sempervirens**
Shrubs	*Hydrangea arborescens**
	Hydrangea macrophylla
	Pittosporum tobira
	*Sambucus nigra canadensis**
	*Thuja occidentalis**
Trees	*Chionanthus virginicus**
	*Cornus florida**
	Magnolia stellata
	Malus spp.
	*Nyssa sylvatica**
	Prunus campanulata
	*Prunus caroliniana**
	Prunus × *incam* 'Okame'
	*Prunus serotina**
	Prunus serrulata 'Kanzan'
	Prunus subhirtella

Prunus × *yedoensis*
Styrax japonicus

While deer may not eat them, virtually all small trees are susceptible to bucks rubbing their antlers on them, stripping their bark, and ultimately killing them.

PLANTS TO AVOID WITH YOUNG CHILDREN

Parents and pet owners are always concerned that their children or best friends might be poisoned by browsing on their landscape plants. Unfortunately, if one were to eat enough of any of the plants covered in this book, a series of technicolor yawns and/or a serious tango with the toilet is the likely outcome. There is a reason why none of these plants are classified as vegetables. We don't recommend eating the foliage or fruit of any of the plants in this book unless we have noted in a plant's account that it is edible. The ASPCA and the extension services of North Carolina, Alabama, and California all have web pages that list poisonous plants if you need further proof.

The good news is that those plants that will make a child or pet ill if consumed taste so bad that it would take a concerted effort to consume enough of the foliage to actually become seriously ill. The first time your parents gave you Brussels sprouts or broccoli when you were a child, you likely didn't think, "Wow, these are great. I want more." Therefore, our focus in this list is to point out the plants that possess foliage that could cause physical pain, injury, or skin rash if an individual were to fall into or brush against these plants.

Shrubs	*Agave americana*
	Berberis julianae
	Berberis thunbergii
	Chaenomeles speciosa
	Loropetalum chinense
	Loropetalum chinense rubrum
	Pyracantha spp.
	Rhapidophyllum hystrix
	Rosa spp.
	Yucca aloifolia
	Yucca filamentosa
	Yucca gloriosa
Vines	*Toxicodendron radicans*
Trees	*Aralia spinosa*
	Crataegus spp.
	Maclura pomifera
	Robinia pseudoacacia
Grasses	*Cortaderia selloana*
Perennials	*Acanthus spinosus*

Terminology Used in This Book

For each of the plants covered in this book, we address important points that the designer needs to know when making decisions about which plants to use and where to place them in their compositions. The following is a description of each feature addressed in the book.

PLANT NAMES

We have listed both the botanical name and the most frequently used common name for each plant. The botanical name of a plant includes both the genus and species names in Latin. The first letter of the genus name is capitalized; the species name is lowercased. Botanical names for plants are recognized across the world. However, that same plant's common name varies across the world and even within various regions of the same country. For example, *Liriodendron tulipifera* is known as tulip poplar, tulip tree, yellow poplar, and even yellow wood in different regions of the eastern United States.

Botanical names are used by landscape architects to specify plants in order to assure the plant ordered is what shows up on the project site. A word of warning: the botanical names of several species have changed in the time we have been working on this book. For example, when we started, banana shrub was known as *Michelia figo*. It is now recognized as *Magnolia figo*. If you ever hear us speak badly of botanical taxonomists, it is because they keep changing the botanical names. Come on, folks, get it right the first time! Anyway, we use the U.S. Department of Agriculture Plants Database (https://plants.usda.gov/java/), the Royal Horticultural Society Horticultural Database (http://apps.rhs.org.uk/horticulturaldatabase/), and the Missouri Botanical Garden Plant Finder (http://www.missouribotanicalgarden.org/plantfinder/plantfindersearch.aspx) as our authorities for the correct botanical names in this book.

Several plants in this book have an × between their genus and species names. The × is used to indicate a cross between two plants in the same genus. As an example, *Osmanthus ×* *fortunei* is a cross between tea olive, *Osmanthus fragrans*, and holly leaf osmanthus, *Osmanthus heterophyllus*.

In addition to their species name, some plants also have a variety name. A variety of a species exhibits one or more features that differ from the species itself, and that feature is able to be reproduced in at least some of the variety's offspring. For example, *Prunus persica* is a peach tree that produces fruit with a soft, fuzzy skin. *Prunus persica nucipersica* is a nectarine that has fruit with a smooth skin. If the seeds of nectarines are allowed to germinate, grow, and flower, some of the resulting trees would produce fruit with smooth skins. The variety name of a species is also in Latin and follows the species name in lowercase.

Many of the plants covered in this text also have what are termed "cultivars." A cultivar of a species exhibits some characteristic such as leaf color, flower color, or cold hardiness that is different from that of the species. Maybe a branch of a plant sprouted a stem that exhibited a mutation that enticed someone to attempt to reproduce that stem by vegetative means such as a rooted cutting or by layering the stem. However, unlike a variety of the species, the offspring of a cultivar reverts back to the characteristics of the species. A cultivar must be reproduced by vegetative means. We talk more about cultivars at the end of this section.

HARDINESS ZONES

Hardiness zones for each plant are based upon the 2012 USDA Plant Hardiness Zone Map for the United States (https://planthardiness.ars.usda.gov/PHZMWeb/). The plants covered in this book are primarily suited for zones 7a, 7b, 8a, and 8b, which cover a wide swath of the southeastern United States, from northern Florida to northern Virginia and southern Kentucky and west through Arkansas and eastern Texas. Most of these plants are also suited for coastal portions of the Pacific Northwest, from Vancouver and Victoria, British Columbia, through Seattle and Portland, as well as portions of the East Coast up to New York City and Boston.

PLANT SIZE

For trees and shrubs, we offer the following classification system. It is based upon the size that a typical plant in a reasonably good cultural environment could expect to reach. The expected sizes of herbaceous perennials are covered in the table at the beginning of that section. It is important to remember that most vines will grow as tall as the structure they are given to climb upon.

LARGE TREES	MEDIUM TREES	SMALL TREES
+60' tall	35'–60' tall	15'–35' tall

LARGE SHRUBS	MEDIUM SHRUBS	SMALL SHRUBS
+8' tall	4'–8' tall	<4' tall

GROWTH RATE

The growth rate for each plant is largely dependent upon the plant's ultimate size. For example, for a large tree, a fast growth rate would exceed 3' per year. However, a large shrub that exceeds 1' in size per year would be considered fast growing. The table below illustrates growth rates for different categories of plants. The individual growth rate for all plants is based upon the plant growing under its ideal light and soil conditions. Recognize that most plants start off growing much slower after planting than they do with maturity.

TEXTURE

Texture refers to the patterns of light and shade created by the plant. It may be thought of as the light and dark spaces of plant tissue and void space. The texture is usually dependent upon the size of the foliage, stems, and internodes of the plant. In some cases, the texture may actually vary depending upon the season of the year, particularly for deciduous trees and shrubs.

Texture is important to a designer. A viewer's eye is attracted to coarse texture, while finer-textured plants tend to recede into the background. Coarse-textured plants can make a large space seem smaller or a small space feel much more intimate. On the other hand, fine-textured plants can make small spaces appear a little larger.

The majority of plants have a medium texture. As a result, designers often look for plants that have either a coarse or a fine texture in order to incorporate some contrast into borders and shrub compositions.

FORM

Form refers to the outline of the plant. Think of it as an image in silhouette. Just as most plants have a medium texture, most also tend to assume an oval to broadly oval form. Designers are often interested in plants with forms that provide contrast. Plants with conical or columnar forms tend to attract the eye, as do those with a spreading habit.

Plant Growth Rates

LARGE TREES		MEDIUM TREES		SMALL TREES	
Fast	Up to 3' per year	Fast	18"–24" per year	Fast	12"–18" per year
Medium	18"–24" per year	Medium	12"–18" per year	Medium	8"–12" per year
Slow	<12" per year	Slow	8"–12" per year	Slow	<8' per year

LARGE SHRUBS		MEDIUM SHRUBS		SMALL SHRUBS	
Fast	12"+ per year	Fast	8"–12" per year	Fast	6"–8" per year
Medium	8"–12" per year	Medium	6"–8" per year	Medium	4"–6" per year
Slow	<8" per year	Slow	<6" per year	Slow	<4" per year

PERENNIALS		FERNS		INTERIOR PLANTS	
Fast	12"+ per year	Fast	8"–12" per year	Fast	8"–12" per year
Medium	8"–12" per year	Medium	4"–8" per year	Medium	4"–8" per year
Slow	<8" per year	Slow	<4" per year	Slow	<4" per year

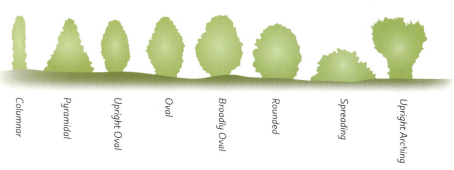

FIGURE 58 *top left* A composition at Stanley Park, Vancouver, B.C.

FIGURE 59 *top right* The Sunken Garden in Butchart Gardens, Victoria, B.C.

FIGURE 60 *right* Plant forms.

Figure 60 provides the terms used to describe a plant's form. These descriptive terms apply to both trees and shrubs.

LEAF TYPES

Leaves are classified as being either simple or compound. For woody plants, the determining factor is where the leaf attaches to the stem of the plant and the adjacent bud. Simple leaves have a blade (which we usually call the leaf) and a short stem or petiole that serves to attach the leaf to the woody stem of the plant.

Compound leaves contain multiple blades called "leaflets," which are connected to the petiole of the leaf by an extension of the petiole, called a "rachis." Compound leaves can be difficult for plant novices to comprehend. It may be easiest to think of what happens to a deciduous plant in the fall. The entire leaf structure of a compound leaf falls away from the woody stem in autumn.

Pinnately compound leaves have leaflets on both sides of the rachis. Depending upon the species, the leaf may consist of either an even or odd number of leaflets.

Palmately compound leaves are similar to pinnately compound leaves, except that the leaflets are arranged like fin-

FIGURE 61 Simple leaf.

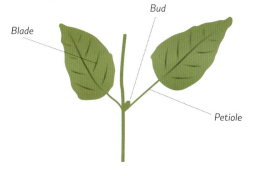

FIGURE 62 Pinnately compound leaf.

FIGURE 63 Palmately compound leaf.

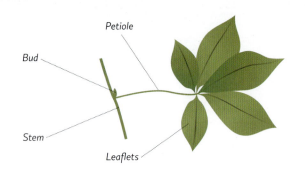

FIGURE 64 Bipinnately compound leaf.

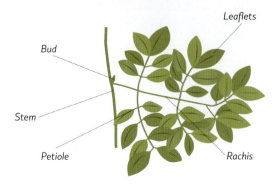

FIGURE 65 Leaf arrangements.

Opposite   Alternate   Whorled

FIGURE 66 Leaf shapes.

Linear   Lanceolate   Oblanceolate   Spatulate   Elliptic   Ovate   Obovate   Oval   Cordate

FIGURE 67 Leaf margins.

Entire   Serrate   Doubly Serrate   Dentate   Crenate   Lobed

FIGURE 68 Leaf tips.

Rounded   Acute   Acuminate   Emarginate

gers. Buckeyes are among the most common species with palmately compound leaves.

Bipinnately compound leaves are twice divided with leaflets. Again, the entire structure will fall away in autumn.

LEAF ARRANGEMENT

Leaf arrangement refers to how the leaves and buds arise from the stem. The foliage of most species is either alternately or oppositely arranged along the stem. Only a few plants are whorled.

Leaf shape also helps in plant identification. Just keep in mind that not every leaf on a plant is consistent in its shape, but the majority of leaves will fit into one of these categories.

Leaf margin refers to the edge of the leaf blade. Again, one of the terms listed in figure 67 will fit the description of the majority of the leaves on the plant.

Finally, the shape of the leaf tip is noted in most of the plant identifying descriptions.

FERN FOLIAGE

The terminology used to describe parts of a fern is different from that used for other types of plants. For example, what one would call a "leaf" on most plants is termed a "frond" on a fern. As with other plant types, the leaf or frond is composed of the blade and the petiole, except that in the case of ferns, the petiole is termed a "stipe." At the point on the frond where the leaflets begin, the stipe becomes the rachis of the frond. Speaking of leaflets, they are known as "pinnae" on a fern. An individual leaflet is a "pinna." If the pinnae are further divided or bipinnate, the final division is termed a "pinnule." Thus, a bipinnate frond has pinnae and pinnules. Young fronds are referred to as fiddleheads as they begin to emerge from the crown of the fern because as they uncurl themselves they resemble the head of a violin or cello.

FLOWERS

While all plants, except ferns, produce flowers, we only go into detail about the flowers if they provide some reason why that plant might be selected for use in a design. Some plants have very small but highly fragrant flowers, like tea olive. In those cases, we talk about the flowers only to point out their fragrance, not their potential to attract the eye of the beholder. There are some plants whose flowers are neither showy nor fragrant enough to provide a reason for their use in a design. They may have other unique features like fall foliage color, form, and texture that stand out, but their flowers do not. For example, oak trees, junipers, and even some herbaceous perennials are used for reasons other than their flowers. In those cases, we point out that the flowers are insignificant for the designer.

Some terms describe a plant's flowers. A "monecious" plant has both male and female flowers on the same plant. Think of a corn plant. Its male flowers compose the tassel at the top of the cornstalk, while the female flowers lower down on the stalk ultimately provide the corn kernels once they've been fertilized or pollinated.

Another example is a pine tree. We've all seen the clouds of yellow pollen that are produced from the small flower structures on the ends of the branches in the spring. Some of that pollen that doesn't end up on our cars or in our noses fertilizes the female flowers, which produce the tiny seeds within the pine cone lower down on the branches. Oak trees are similar.

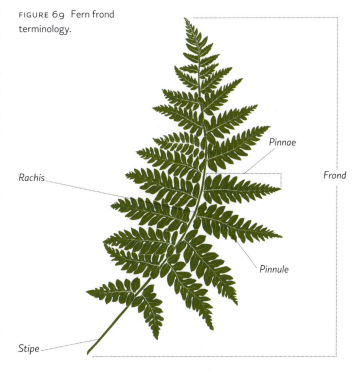

FIGURE 69 Fern frond terminology.

FIGURE 70 *left* Camellia with single-petaled flowers.   FIGURE 71 *middle* Camellia with double-petaled flowers.
FIGURE 72 *right* Camellia with multiple-petaled flowers.

On the other hand, a "dioecious" plant contains flowers of only one sex. A female holly or persimmon tree needs to have a male tree nearby to provide the pollen that will ultimately produce the female tree's fruit.

For those plants that do have significant, attractive flowers, we may mention that a particular flower has single or double petals. For most but not all plants, the petals are what provide the color that catches your eye. Gardenias and camellias are some of the best plants to illustrate the difference between flowers with single or double petals. In fact, some camellia cultivars have even more than two sets of petals. The number of sets of petals doesn't necessarily make a flower more or less attractive. We mention this solely to help identify a particular plant.

The final item we mention when talking about flowers is whether they occur individually along the stem or as part of a flower structure such as a raceme or corymb that contains multiple individual flowers. Think of a camellia, with its individual flowers, versus something like a hydrangea or viburnum, with a large corymb composed of small individual flowers. While this distinction between whether a plant has individual flowers or a flower structure is significant to taxonomists, for design compositions, it is really not critical. As long as the flowers are attractive, the designer doesn't care whether they occur singly or in a structure.

FLOWER FRAGRANCE

Flower fragrance is not something that can be scientifically quantified. Everyone senses fragrance differently. Someone may think of a plant's flowers as being sweet as perfume, while someone else may find the same fragrance unpleasant or even repulsive. Even the distance from the plant that the fragrance can be sensed varies by individual.

For example, some authors speak about the bountiful sweet fragrance of winter daphne, *Daphne odora*, and sweetshrub, *Calycanthus floridus*. Personally, I have to bend over and stick my nose into the flowers of both plants to sense anything. And in the case of sweetshrub, what I sense reminds me of the smell of rotting apples on the ground in late summer.

So if we consider a plant's flowers to be highly fragrant, it means that one can sense the fragrance from a distance of 30' or more away from the plant. Moderately fragrant means that someone would need to be no more than 10' away to sense the fragrance, and lightly fragrant means that an individual would need to be closer than 5'. If a plant has lightly fragrant flowers, you might need to stick your nose in the flower and take a deep breath in order to smell anything.

FRUIT

We don't get into the specifics of a plant's fruit unless the fruit offers some reason to use that plant in a design. Obviously, if the fruit provides an ornamental attribute, we address it. In addition, we mention whether the fruit is an important food source for wildlife, even if the fruit is not important for the composition of a landscape plan.

We don't always identify the type of fruit a plant produces, which may cause consternation among the taxonomists. We could care less whether a fruit is a drupe, pome, or berry as long as it provides some reason to choose that plant for a design. In our defense, we are trying to write a book for designers, not taxonomists.

LIGHT CONDITIONS

The cultural conditions to which a plant is subjected are the most important factors in whether or not that plant ultimately provides the appearance that the designer originally envisioned for the composition. Obviously, all plants require some level of light in order to generate sugars in their foliage for food. Provided they have adequate moisture for their root systems, most plants could grow in full sunlight, meaning at least eight hours of direct sunlight per day during the summer months. There are some plants, however, that perform better under various levels of shading during the summer months. And a few, particularly those that are borderline cold-hardy in a particular region, benefit by being in shaded protected positions in winter. For the purposes of this text, here is what we mean by the various light levels.

FULL SUN At least eight hours of direct sunlight from mid-May to mid-September.
LIGHT SHADE Four to six hours of direct sunlight, with preferably none between noon and 3:00 p.m. in summer.
MODERATE SHADE Two to four hours of direct sunlight, with none between 11:00 a.m. and 4:00 p.m. in summer.
FULL SHADE No direct sunlight between 9:00 a.m. and 5:00 p.m. from mid-May to mid-September.

SOIL CONDITIONS

Soil Basics

Most of our soils have been formed in their current location over thousands of years. A few soils, such as those along the floodplains of streams, have been transported by erosive forces. An upland soil that has not been subjected to erosion over time would typically have four layers or horizons. The top layer is the O horizon. It may be only 1"–2" deep and is composed of decayed and decaying organic material from plant debris. The next layer, the A horizon, ranges from 4" to 12" deep and is typically what is referred to as topsoil. It is a mixture of organic material and mineral particles and is where the overwhelming majority of all plant roots are found. Below the A horizon is the B horizon, which ranges from 6" to about 30" deep and is composed of minerals and particles that have leached downward from the A horizon over time. Below that is the C horizon, which consists of minerals and decomposed parent bedrock particles.

Throughout much of the Southeast, particularly in the Piedmont region, both the O and A horizons are often

FIGURE 73 *below* Mock orange with single flowers.

FIGURE 74 *right* Garden hydrangeas with flowers in corymbs.

absent as a result of farming practices in the nineteenth and early twentieth centuries, which caused these horizons to erode into nearby streams and rivers. Just look at a local stream in the Piedmont after a heavy rainfall event and notice how brown the water is from all the sediment that is still being transported today as a result of past practices. The floodplains of these streams are very rich and productive soils, but most of us don't live on a bottomland.

Even those areas that were not subjected to past farming practices have often been subjected to more recent destructive processes. The ability to move large volumes of soil quickly on construction sites with heavy machinery in urbanizing areas has resulted in the loss of the topsoil and left compacted subsoils in place that greatly affect the ability of plants to thrive.

As a result, we find ourselves often trying to grow plants in subsoil material, which is why we recommend adding organic material to the planting mixture. Organic material improves the ability of the soil to hold moisture and nutrients, as well as improving the environment for important soil microorganisms.

In addition, since we're starting with subsoil material, it is important when we install new plants to ensure that the root ball is slightly higher than the surrounding soil level to provide good surface drainage away from the plant. Otherwise, the surrounding subsoil material can act like a pot and hold so much water that the plant's roots die from lack of oxygen.

Soil pH

Soil pH is a measurement of the reaction of the soil solution and is measured on a scale of 1 to 14, with 7 being considered a neutral reaction. Soil pH measurements under 7 are considered to be acidic, while those above 7 are alkaline in reaction. The pH is largely influenced by the bedrock material from which the soil is derived and from the average level of rainfall, which is naturally acidic in reaction. Areas with greater rainfall, like the southeastern states, usually have acidic soils, while those found in western Texas and Oklahoma, which have much lower rainfall levels, are often neutral to somewhat alkaline in reaction.

Most plants in the Southeast, whether native or exotic, perform best with a somewhat acidic soil pH in the range of 5.5–6.5. A few plants—azaleas, camellias, and pin oak quickly come to mind—prefer the lower end of that ideal range. It is the rare plant that prefers or even tolerates a near-neutral to slightly alkaline soil reaction, which is why we always try to point them out.

Soil Moisture

While plants need to be able to absorb moisture to survive and grow, their roots also need oxygen in order to be able to respire and absorb the moisture. Lacking adequate oxygen in the soil, the roots of many plants begin to drown, and those plants soon die. The appearance of a plant under drought stress is similar to one whose roots are drowning in a soil with excessive moisture.

Most plants prefer a moist but well-drained soil. This means that the soil is able to retain adequate moisture for plant absorption for seven to fourteen days after a moderate summer rainfall event. Excessive soil moisture, particularly during the growing season, can stress many plants. Those plants that can tolerate and even thrive in consistently moist soils are rare. Those that can do so in soils that remain saturated for long periods or even throughout the growing season are even more rare, which is why we note them.

On the other hand, many plants can tolerate a period of several days of dry soil, but far fewer are able to tolerate several weeks without adequate moisture. Those that can survive and thrive for a period of a month or more during a summer with low moisture levels are not only drought resistant but also able to tolerate dry soils, which it is important to note.

For the purposes of this book, here is what we mean by the various soil moisture levels provided for each plant. Remember that these levels deal only with the top 12" of the soil mixture in which the plant is growing. A moderate rainfall event will be considered as a one-year storm with a one-hour storm duration in the Piedmont region of Georgia, which equates to approximately a 1.35" rainfall event.

WET Soil such as that found on the margins of a stream or pond. The soil may be inundated periodically throughout the year, especially during late winter and early spring, and remain damp even in summer.

MOIST The soil holds adequate moisture for plant growth for fourteen to twenty-eight days after a moderate summer rainfall event and remains damp from late autumn to midspring.

MOIST BUT WELL DRAINED The soil is able to hold adequate

moisture for plant growth for seven to ten days after a moderate summer rainfall event.

WELL DRAINED The soil is able to hold adequate moisture for plant growth for four to six days after a moderate summer rainfall event.

DRY The soil is able to hold adequate moisture for plant growth for no more than three days after a moderate summer rainfall event.

INSTALLATION

In this section, we recommend the time of year when a particular plant should be installed. If the time is not addressed, then the plant can be installed anytime during the year. We also recommend the spacing of the plants as they are installed. Under appropriate cultural conditions, a grouping of shrubs could be expected to grow together into a solid mass in approximately five years. In the case of a grouping of trees, the tree canopies could be expected to grow together in approximately twenty years.

We also mention the sizes that are available from the nursery industry for most of the woody plants. The sizes are based upon the *American Standard for Nursery Stock*, published by the American Horticulture Association in conjunction with the American National Standards Institute. The publication is available free online.

Assuming that many readers may not be familiar with nursery stock standard sizes, we offer the following explanation. Most of the herbaceous plants for sale at a local retail nursery or a Lowe's or Home Depot garden center will be in either 1-quart or 1-gallon size. The woody shrubs will likely be in 3- to 5-gallon sizes. Any container-grown trees in these nursery centers will likely be in 7- to 15-gallon sizes maximum. A 15-gallon plant is likely the largest that a healthy person could handle without assistance.

Many wholesale growers grow trees in the ground and then dig them up, wrap the roots in a burlap ball, and ship the trees to the local nursery for sale. Field-grown trees are classified by their height and by the diameter of the trunk measured 6" above the ground for trees up to 4" in diameter or at 12" above the ground for trees greater than 4". Most homeowners would struggle with a shade tree larger than 10'–12' in height with a 1½" diameter. Most landscape installation crews composed of two or three people could

handle a 12'–14' tree with a 2"–2½" diameter without any type of machinery to help lift and place the tree.

PLANT MAINTENANCE

In this section, we briefly try to address each plant's particular issues, such as pruning the plant to control the size or to stimulate additional branching and the need to provide supplemental water during the growing season to reduce stress on the plant or to stimulate new growth. We also touch on fertilization requirements for some plants and the use of organic mulches to conserve soil moisture, moderate soil temperatures, and reduce the establishment of unwanted weeds around the plant.

Pruning

We recommend that any pruning should not change the overall natural form of the plant. For example, glossy abelia (*Abelia × grandiflora*) normally reaches 8'–10' in height, with an arching, fountain-like form. If it becomes too tall for a particular situation, then the proper pruning technique is to remove taller branches back to a lower node (bud location) on the offending stems. This preserves the natural form of the plant. We would never recommend shearing the abelia with hedge shears, although it is frequently pruned that way, since that would destroy its natural form. If you feel the need to shear an abelia, you've probably got the wrong plant for that location in your design. Plus, whenever you shear a larger plant, you just create more work for yourself down the line, because after shearing, that plant is going to grow faster and need to be sheared increasingly often.

The worst example of bad pruning technique is usually exhibited in late winter each year by numerous lawn maintenance workers who decide that your crape myrtle needs to be butchered to stimulate more branches. One theory is that those maintenance companies feel a little guilty at that time of the year because they are charging a monthly fee, but the tree leaves have already been collected, the beds have a fresh layer of pine straw, and the turfgrass doesn't need to be mowed for another month or two. So to make the property owner feel like the maintenance company deserves that monthly payment and to make it look like there is something serious that needs to be done, workers destroy the lovely form and attractive trunks of a crape myrtle. Think about it: they never do this sort of thing to a flowering crabapple, redbud, or cherry tree, only to the poor crape myrtle.

There are some plants on which shearing is acceptable. For example, if you've got a border planting of dwarf yaupon hollies, *Ilex vomitoria* 'Nana', in a formal bed, it's OK to shear them to keep them low. Dwarf yaupons naturally develop a rounded to spreading outline, so shearing them lower will not affect their natural form. Let them grow together to form a mass rather than a group of little round balls.

Deadheading

Deadheading is a type of pruning in which old flower heads are pruned in order to stimulate additional flowering. To be fully effective, deadheading should be supplemented with water and/or fertilization. For certain plants, the use of deadheading is an accepted practice. Many warm-season flowering annuals benefit from deadheading. Certain flowering shrubs such as butterfly bush, chastetree, and even crape myrtle can be stimulated to provide additional flowers through proper deadheading techniques.

PESTS AND DISEASES

Every plant can be attacked at some point by a variety of insects and viral, fungal, or bacterial microorganisms. The key in denying a serious foothold to these agents is to prevent the plant from being stressed. The old saying, "Put the right plant in the right place," should always be at the forefront of any design.

Excessive soil moisture, drought, wounds to the trunk, lack of adequate sunlight, root compaction, and a less than ideal soil pH are among the most common factors that stress a plant. Continuing stresses ultimately weaken plants over time, providing opportunities for these organisms to cause serious problems. Grouping together plants that prefer similar cultural conditions and then providing those conditions are always helpful methods when composing a design.

Assuming that all cultural requirements are being met, there are still some plants that are prone to more problems than others. For example, native elms, cherries, and even the much beloved pecan tree all tend to have something attacking them at any given point in time. The key is that if these trees have not been greatly weakened by continual stresses, then they are usually able to resist serious injury.

For this text, we have listed only the most common in-fectious agents for each species. One should not assume that other agents could not cause issues. If you have a plant that appears to have an insect or disease problem, provide a sample of the infected tissue to a local county extension agent for identification and recommendation for treatment.

As far as possible, we also try to identify those plants that are prone to damage by white-tailed deer. For numerous reasons, the deer populations in rural, suburban, and even urban areas have multiplied in recent decades. Neighborhoods that never had to consider the impact that deer might have upon their plantings must do so now.

Much of the information dealing with the impact of deer upon ornamental plants is available through various state agricultural extension service online publications and serves as our primary reference material. In cases where specific plants are not addressed by any of these extension service publications, we use personal experience and personal observations. However, it is important to always keep in mind that no plant is completely safe from browsing by a really hungry deer.

NOTES AND CULTIVARS

Remember from earlier in this section that a cultivar of a species is selected because of characteristics that differ from the species, but plants that exhibit those characteristics can only be reproduced by vegetative means.

Rather than trying to list every possible cultivar for a particular plant, we've limited the cultivars to those that are widely grown in the nursery industry. We have been frustrated with other publications when we read about a particular cultivar of a plant and then are not able to locate anyone who actually grows it.

Popular cultivars grown by the nursery industry change over time. This is particularly true for many of the annuals and herbaceous plants that can be reproduced, evaluated, and grown much more quickly than can woody plants.

In some cases, we also may point out a related species that may not be as widely recognized. In those cases, we mention some important features or cultural preferences that can help in positive identification.

LARGE DECIDUOUS TREES

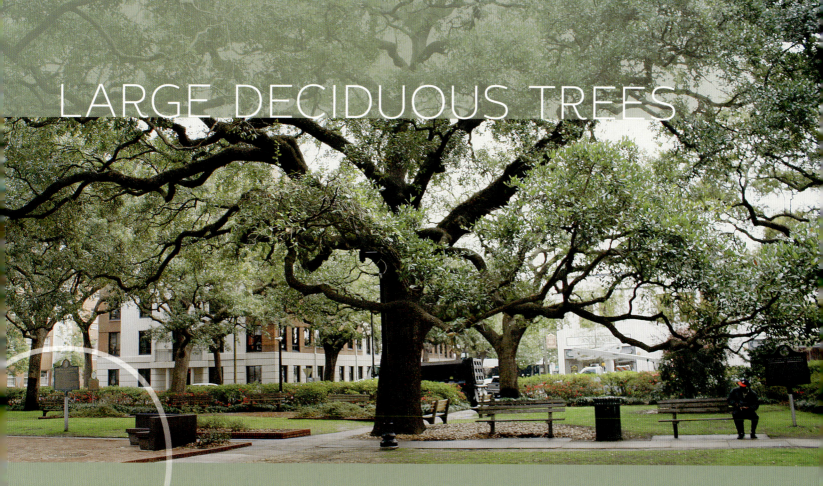

above Live oak in Reynold's Square, Savannah, Ga.

ur long hot sunny and humid summer days in the Southeast can be miserable. In the dog days of summer, shade is a highly valued commodity. The large deciduous trees in this section are the principal contributors to shade for our homes, streets, parks, and urban plazas. Of course, these trees do more than just provide cooling shade. From an ecological standpoint, the overhead canopy they provide is the best instrument to break up the destructive force of raindrops on the soil, and the trees' extensive root systems help to hold soils in place and prevent erosion. In fact, an undisturbed woodland is the best type of land cover: it absorbs stormwater runoff and allows precipitation to infiltrate the soil rather than contributing runoff to our urban drainage systems.

But in addition to providing shade and benefiting the environment, these trees form the canopy that helps to define space in our designed environments. They form the roof, so to speak, over our outdoor environments. By doing so, these large trees can make a designed space much more hospitable than would be the case if the space were barren of trees and allowed to bleed out into the surrounding environment.

While these large trees typically don't add much to the design in the way of showy flowers or ornamental fruit, their fruit is, in fact, a very important source of food for a variety of wildlife. The fruit of virtually all these trees is eaten by some type of native wildlife. As an added design bonus, a number of these tree species are among the best providers of color to the fall landscape. In addition, the mere presence of many of these species tells us a great deal about the soil and moisture conditions of a particular site, as well as how long it has been since the site was disturbed by human activity. Trees also provide the opportunity to use other plants in the middle canopy and ground layers of the design that require some shade during the most intense parts of the day. Just try to grow camellias, rhododendrons, or hydrangeas without a little midday shade.

For the purposes of design, we consider any tree that would be expected to reach at least 60' in height in a design to be included in this large category. Those trees that usually mature at smaller sizes are covered in the next two sections.

Keep in mind that for these trees to reach their maximum size and provide all their benefits, you've got to provide enough space for their roots. If they are restricted to only 8' or 10' squared, they will never approach the size you may have in mind for them. The larger the unrestricted root zone you can provide, the larger these trees will ultimately become and the longer they will live. If you are picturing large majestic trees to provide a framework for your design, make sure to provide adequate space for their roots.

BOTANICAL NAME	SUNLIGHT	SOILS	TEXTURE	NOTABLE ATTRIBUTES	FALL FOLIAGE	NATIVE TO SOUTHEAST
Acer platanoides	Full sun to moderate shade	Moist but well drained	Medium coarse	Milky-white petiole sap	Fair yellow	No, native to Europe
Acer rubrum	Full sun to moderate shade	Wet to moist but well drained	Medium	Red late winter flowers	Great orange red to dark red	Yes
Acer saccharinum	Full sun to light shade	Moist to well drained	Medium coarse	Very fast growth rate	Fair yellow	Yes
Acer saccharum	Full sun to moderate shade	Moist but well drained	Medium coarse	Primary source of maple syrup	Great bright yellow to orange	Yes
Acer × freemanii	Full sun to light shade	Moist to moist but well drained	Medium	Combines silver and red maples	Good orange to deep red	No, but both parents are
Carya glabra	Full sun to moderate shade	Well drained	Medium	Impact-resistant wood	Great bright yellow	Yes
Carya illinoinensis	Full sun to light shade	Moist but well drained	Medium coarse	Attractive form in open areas	Fair yellow	Yes
Carya tomentosa	Full sun to moderate shade	Well drained	Coarse	Messy in refined landscapes	Great bright yellow	Yes
Celtis laevigata	Full sun to moderate shade	Moist to well drained	Medium fine	Salt spray and pH tolerant	Good yellow	Yes
Fagus grandifolia	Full sun to full shade	Moist but well drained	Medium	Smooth silver bark	Fair coppery yellow	Yes
Fraxinus americana	Full sun to light shade	Moist but well drained	Medium	Salt spray and pH tolerant	Fair to good yellow orange	Yes
Fraxinus pennsylvanica	Light to moderate shade	Moist to moist but well drained	Medium	Some salt and pH tolerance	Fair to good yellow	Yes
Ginkgo biloba	Full sun to light shade	Moist but well drained	Medium	Moderate salt spray tolerance	Great bright yellow	No, native to Asia
Juglans nigra	Full sun to light shade	Well drained	Medium coarse	Messy in refined landscapes	Poor yellow	Yes
Liquidambar styraciflua	Full sun to light shade	Moist to well drained	Medium	Drought and salt tolerant	Good yellow to deep purple	Yes
Liriodendron tulipifera	Full sun	Moist but well drained	Medium coarse	Tennessee state tree	Fair yellow	Yes
Metasequoia glyptostroboides	Full sun to light shade	Wet to well drained	Fine	Strong pyramidal form	Poor rusty brown	No, native to Asia
Platanus occidentalis	Full sun to light shade	Moist to moist but well drained	Coarse	White inner bark	Poor yellow	Yes
Quercus acutissima	Full sun to light shade	Moist but well drained	Medium coarse	Moderate salt tolerance	Poor yellow	No, native to Asia
Quercus alba	Full sun to moderate shade	Moist but well drained	Medium coarse	Highly salt spray tolerant	Fair reddish purple	Yes
Quercus coccinea	Full sun to light shade	Well drained	Medium coarse	Drought tolerant	Good scarlet red	Yes
Quercus falcata	Full sun to light shade	Well drained	Medium coarse	Drought and salt tolerant	Poor reddish brown	Yes
Quercus hemisphaerica	Full sun to light shade	Moist but well drained	Medium fine	Moderate salt spray tolerance	None	Yes
Quercus lyrata	Full sun to light shade	Moist to moist but well drained	Medium coarse	Tolerates winter floods	Poor yellow brown	Yes
Quercus michauxii	Full sun to light shade	Moist to moist but well drained	Coarse	Tolerates brief winter flooding	Fair red to crimson	Yes

BOTANICAL NAME	SUNLIGHT	SOILS	TEXTURE	NOTABLE ATTRIBUTES	FALL FOLIAGE	NATIVE TO SOUTHEAST
Quercus montana	Full sun to light shade	Well drained	Medium coarse	Drought tolerant	Fair yellow brown	Yes
Quercus nigra	Full sun to light shade	Moist to well drained	Medium fine	Tolerates moist to wet soils	None	Yes
Quercus palustris	Full sun	Moist to moist but well drained	Medium	Tolerates winter floods	Fair reddish brown	No, native to Ohio River basin
Quercus phellos	Full sun to light shade	Moist to moist but well drained	Medium fine	Highly salt spray tolerant	Good yellow	Yes
Quercus rubra	Full sun to light shade	Moist but well drained	Medium coarse	Moderate salt spray tolerance	Fair yellow to crimson	Yes
Quercus shumardii	Full sun	Moist but well drained	Medium coarse	Moderate salt spray tolerance	Fair yellow to red	Yes
Quercus stellata	Full sun	Well drained	Coarse	Drought tolerant	Fair yellow to orange red	Yes
Quercus texana	Full sun	Wet to moist but well drained	Medium	Tolerates wet soils	Good orange to deep red	Yes but not to Georgia
Quercus velutina	Full sun to light shade	Well drained	Coarse	Drought tolerant	Poor yellow brown	Yes
Quercus virginiana	Full sun to moderate shade	Moist but well drained	Medium	Highly salt spray tolerant	None	Yes
Taxodium distichum	Full sun to light shade	Wet to well drained	Fine	Louisiana state tree, wet soils	Poor bronzy brown	Yes
Ulmus alata	Full sun to light shade	Moist but well drained to dry	Medium fine	Drought and pH tolerant	Poor to fair yellow	Yes
Ulmus americana	Full sun to light shade	Moist to moist but well drained	Medium	Salt spray, pH, and some floods	Poor to fair yellow	Yes

top left Norway maple foliage.

top right Norway maple allée at Longwood Gardens, Kennett Square, Pa.

middle Form.

bottom 'Crimson King' Norway maple.

Acer platanoides NORWAY MAPLE

Norway maple has been a popular and highly planted tree in the mid-Atlantic states, New England, and upper Midwest. Its ease of transplanting, fast growth rate, tolerance of urban conditions, and fall foliage color led to it being one of the most heavily planted street trees after the decline of the American elm. Unfortunately, it proved to be highly invasive in those areas as well and is now on many states' lists of invasive plants. It appears to languish in the southeastern states, growing more slowly and lacking notable fall foliage color. There are far better trees for the Southeast, but at least the Norway maple has not proven invasive here.

ZONES & ORIGIN 3b–8a. Native to Europe and western Asia.

SIZE & GROWTH RATE 50'–70' tall, 30'–50' wide, medium fast growing.

TEXTURE & FORM Medium coarse texture and oval to broadly oval form.

FOLIAGE Simple oppositely arranged dark green leaves have mostly five, occasionally seven, bristle-tipped lobes with U-shaped sinuses and coarsely toothed margins. Fall color is a weak yellow in the South. The petiole produces a milky-white sap.

FLOWERS Insignificant yellow–green early spring flowers.

FRUIT Fruit is a wide-spreading paired samara. Flowering and fruiting may not occur in the Southeast.

LIGHT & SOIL Full sun to moderate shade and moist to moist but well-drained soil.

MAINTENANCE Norway maple prefers consistent summer moisture. It doesn't perform well in hot, dry, windy locations.

INSTALLATION Norway maple is still widely grown in northern nurseries. It is available in containers or field grown, and it transplants well in larger sizes.

PESTS & DISEASES Norway maple isn't well adapted to the heat and humidity of the Southeast. The short summer day lengths of the Southeast compared with this tree's native habitat contribute to a slower growth rate. Deer eat buds and young foliage.

NOTES & CULTIVARS

'Crimson King' reaches 50'–60' tall with a broadly oval form and deep crimson leaves.

'Crimson Sentry' is similar but has an upright oval form.

'Deborah' has red spring foliage and crinkled leaf margins.

'Emerald Queen' has dark green foliage and bright yellow fall foliage.

Acer rubrum RED MAPLE

For fall foliage color, few trees surpass that provided by red maple. Native to the eastern United States, it is found from low moist bottomlands and swamps to drier mountain ridges, making it one of the most widespread trees in the country. Red maples are popular for streets, parks, and yards due to their wide availability, ease of transplanting, fast growth, and dependable fall foliage.

ZONES & ORIGIN   3b–9b. Native across the eastern United States.

SIZE & GROWTH RATE   50'–70' tall, 30'–50' wide, medium fast growing.

TEXTURE & FORM   Medium texture and broadly oval form.

FOLIAGE   Simple opposite leaves 2"–6" long have three to five lobes, V-shaped sinuses, and serrate margins. Fall foliage is an eye-catching orange to red in early to midautumn.

FLOWERS   Tiny red-tinted late winter flowers are visible against clear blue winter skies from late January through February in Athens.

FRUIT   Red samaras in late February and March provide food for many species of wildlife.

LIGHT & SOIL   Full sun to moderate shade and moist to moist but well-drained acidic soils.

MAINTENANCE   Young trees are susceptible to damage by lawn maintenance equipment. They produce a lot of shade and have shallow roots, making it difficult to grow other plants beneath them. Provide mulch beneath the canopy or plant drought-resistant and shade-tolerant ground covers beneath trees.

INSTALLATION   Field-grown trees up to 5" in caliper are readily available and successfully transplanted in the dormant season. Space 40' apart and avoid planting around water, irrigation, or sewer lines, as their roots are notorious for invading these water sources.

PESTS & DISEASES   Life span is about 60 years with no serious problems. Deer rarely cause problems.

NOTES & CULTIVARS
'Autumn Flame' produces an orange-red early fall foliage with a rounded form and small leaves.
'Brandywine' is a hybrid of 'Autumn Flame' and 'October Glory', with dark red midautumn foliage and an oval form.
'October Glory' develops a broadly oval form with burgundy-red late autumn foliage.
'Red Sunset' has good heat tolerance, broadly oval form, and orange-red early to midautumn foliage.

top Foliage.

bottom Native tree on woodland edge.

left 'October Glory' cultivars on the UGA campus.   *right* On Baldwin Street on the UGA campus.

top left Fall color on the UGA campus.
top right Fall color on the UGA Health Sciences campus.
middle Foliage.
bottom Mature bark.

Acer saccharinum SILVER MAPLE

Silver maple is a fast-growing tree found exclusively along streams and bodies of water from north Georgia to Canada. While noted for its tolerance to flooding, it also performs adequately on better-drained sites and has been widely promoted for quick shade. Unfortunately, trees are weak-wooded, are easily damaged by ice and winds, and don't produce outstanding fall foliage. Crosses between silver and red maple combine silver maple's fast growth with the fall foliage of red maple.

ZONES & ORIGIN 3b–9b. Native to bottomlands and streams of the eastern United States.

SIZE & GROWTH RATE 60'–80' tall, 40'–60' wide, fast growing.

TEXTURE & FORM Medium coarse texture and oval to broadly oval form.

FOLIAGE Simple opposite leaves 4"–8" long have 3–5 lobes with coarsely toothed margins and silvery-white undersides. The middle lobe is distinctly longer than the others and narrower at its base than toward the tip. Sinuses between the lobes are mostly V-shaped. A pale yellow fall foliage is rarely good. A scaly gray bark peels in strips.

FLOWERS Insignificant greenish-yellow late winter flowers.

FRUIT Insignificant paired samaras mature in mid- to late spring.

LIGHT & SOIL Full sun to light shade with a wet to moist but well-drained acidic soil.

MAINTENANCE Silver maple is notorious for producing surface roots and sprouts from those roots. Remove any unwanted sprouts and avoid using this tree around storm drains and water or irrigation lines, since the roots find any moisture leaks and multiply rapidly.

INSTALLATION Silver maples are rare in nurseries and, if available, are usually either seedlings or in small containers. Young trees can be successfully used in stream restoration projects or other areas that sustain late winter and spring flooding. Due to their weak brittle limbs, avoid planting silver maples near structures or parking areas.

PESTS & DISEASES Trees are fairly short-lived, 30–50 years in most cases. Weak limbs break in storms and allow the infiltration of insects and fungal diseases, which contribute to the tree's decline. Deer nibble the foliage but don't favor it

NOTES & CULTIVARS
None listed.

Acer saccharum SUGAR MAPLE

For brilliant yellow to orange fall foliage, few trees exceed the sugar maple. It is an outstanding shade tree with a dense canopy that provides generous shade beneath. Although not as heat tolerant or drought resistant as red maple, it is still a dependable tree that is easily transplanted in larger sizes. Rising sap in early spring is the primary source of maple syrup, and the leaf is the symbol on the Canadian flag.

Foliage

ZONES & ORIGIN 3b–8a. Native from north Georgia to Ontario.

SIZE & GROWTH RATE 50'–70' tall, 40'–60' wide, medium growing.

TEXTURE & FORM Medium coarse texture and oval to broadly oval form.

FOLIAGE Simple dark green opposite leaves 4"–6" long have mostly five lobes with U-shaped sinuses between the lobes. Fall foliage is bright yellow to orange red.

FLOWERS Insignificant early spring flowers.

FRUIT Insignificant early summer samaras.

LIGHT & SOIL In the Southeast, light shade with a moist but well-drained slightly acidic soil is ideal. It tolerates moderate shade or full sun with adequate moisture.

MAINTENANCE Provide a consistent moisture during summer for several years until the root system is well established. Thin bark on young trees, like the bark on red maple, should be protected from lawn equipment. Surface roots can cause problems.

INSTALLATION Sugar maple is best used in open areas, and it is not well adapted to urban streetscapes. Large-caliper field-grown trees are widely available. Space 40'–50' apart.

PESTS & DISEASES Few serious disease problems have been reported. Scorched leaf tips are a sign of drought stress on well-drained sites in the Southeast. Deer will nibble.

NOTES & CULTIVARS

'Bailsta' has orange-red fall foliage.

'Green Mountain' has improved heat and drought tolerance and yellow fall foliage.

'Legacy' has good heat and drought tolerance, rounded form, and orange-red fall color.

Southern sugar maple, *Acer barbatum*, reaches 50' with leaves half the size of sugar maple. Never abundant, it occurs as an understory tree on the lower slopes of shaded woods, developing some yellow fall foliage and retaining its tan leaves into early winter.

top left Fall color on the UGA campus.
top right Fall color in downtown Athens, Ga.
bottom Fall color in an Athens neighborhood.

left Form and fall color.
middle Fall color in 2014.
right Same tree in 2017.

Acer × freemanii FREEMAN MAPLE

Freeman maples are the results of crosses between red maple, *Acer rubrum*, and silver maple, *Acer saccharinum*. Selections of these crosses combine the fast growth of silver maple with the fall-foliage color of the red maple. However, they also combine some of the less desirable characteristics of these two species, such as a somewhat brittle wood, a short life expectancy, and a proclivity for surface roots that invade leaking water or sewer lines. Fall color is usually good, nearly equal to that from quality red or sugar maple cultivars. Utilize their upright form and tough nature for street, parking lot, and sidewalk plantings.

Foliage.

ZONES & ORIGIN 3b–9a. A cross between two native species.

SIZE & GROWTH RATE 50'–70' tall, 30'–40' wide, fast growing.

TEXTURE & FORM Medium texture and oval form.

FOLIAGE Simple opposite leaves 3"–6" long have three to five lobes resembling the silver maple, with silvery undersides and an extended middle lobe. Fall color is yellow orange to deep red, depending upon the cultivar, and is superior to that of silver maple.

FLOWERS Insignificant early spring flowers.

FRUIT Insignificant samaras; some cultivars are sterile.

LIGHT & SOIL Full sun to light shade with a moist to moist but well-drained acidic soil is ideal. They tolerate wet to flooded soils for brief periods in winter.

MAINTENANCE Provide water during summer for several years until the root system is well established and avoid planting it near leaking water sources. Like silver maple, it is prone to storm damage to the fast-growing but weak-wooded branches.

INSTALLATION Field-grown trees are readily available in sizes up to 5" in caliper. For continuous canopy, plant 30'–40' apart.

PESTS & DISEASES Serious problems are rare, provided the tree is not stressed. Deer will browse young small trees.

NOTES & CULTIVARS

'Armstrong' reaches 60', with a distinctly upright oval form and early orange-red fall color.

'Autumn Blaze' is the most commonly available cultivar, reaching 60', with an oval form and bright orange-red fall color.

'Autumn Fantasy' reaches 50', with crimson-red fall foliage.

Carya glabra PIGNUT HICKORY

Pignut hickory is an important component of mature upland oak-hickory forests, where it occurs on a variety of sites, from upland ridges to lower slopes. In spite of its outstanding yellow fall foliage, it is rarely used in designs due to difficulty in propagation and successful transplanting. However, mature specimens are certainly worth protecting. Pignut hickory serves as an important food source for many woodland animal species due to the high fat content of its nuts. Its dense, impact-resistant wood is valued for axes, hammers, baseball bats, and fuel.

ZONES & ORIGIN 4a–9b. Native from Florida to southern Michigan.

SIZE & GROWTH RATE 70'–90' tall, 40'–60' wide, medium slow growing.

TEXTURE & FORM Medium texture and upright oval to oval form.

FOLIAGE Pinnately compound alternate leaves have mostly five, rarely seven, sessile leaflets that turn bright yellow in autumn. The leaflets, 3"–6" long, are lustrous above, with finely serrate margins and acuminate tips. Obovate-shaped terminal leaflets are the largest, while lower leaflets are ovate-lanceolate in shape.

FLOWERS Insignificant early spring flowers.

FRUIT Pear-shaped nuts are enclosed in thin green husks that mature in early to midautumn.

LIGHT & SOIL Trees prefer full sun but tolerate moderate shade in the Southeast. They do best on moist but well-drained sites but also occur on dry, thin soils.

MAINTENANCE To preserve existing trees, avoid parking construction equipment or doing any earthwork within the drip line of the tree.

INSTALLATION Container seedlings are rarely available from specialty growers. Make sure the roots are not girdling the stem in the containers.

PESTS & DISEASES Weevils commonly infest the nuts, causing early drop of infected ones before maturity but no permanent damage. Deer will occasionally browse the foliage.

NOTES & CULTIVARS
Shagbark hickory, *Carya ovata*, also has mostly five leaflets and can reach 100' tall. It is mostly found on bottomland soils in the Southeast but can occur on upland sites as well. Easily identified by its gray scaly bark, it develops good yellow fall foliage and rounded edible nuts.

top Foliage and bark.
middle Fall color.
bottom Fall color in Chattanooga.

Form at Chattanooga National Cemetery.

Carya illinoinensis PECAN

While not an important landscape tree, pecan is nevertheless an important species in the Southeast. Early settlers found it growing on rich bottomland sites along the Mississippi River basin. In addition to the value of the tree's nuts as a food source, the tree's light colored wood is highly valued for paneling, furniture, and cabinets. For designers, pecans are not a good choice to plant but are worth protecting on project sites for their shade and attractive vaselike branching structure. However, falling nuts can make a mess on pavements. Pecan is the state tree of Texas, but Texas ranks behind Georgia in commercial nut production.

top left Foliage.
top right Pecan as a focal point.
middle Shade tree at an Athens residence.
bottom Providing shade at the Georgia Center.

ZONES & ORIGIN 5b–9a. Native to bottomland soils from Texas to Indiana.

SIZE & GROWTH RATE 80'–120' tall, 60'–80' wide, medium slow growing.

TEXTURE & FORM Medium coarse texture and broadly oval form.

FOLIAGE Pinnately compound alternate leaves have 11–21 dark green leaflets. The leaflets are up to 7" long, with serrate margins and a sickle-like shape. Leaves emerge mid- to late spring and begin dropping in early autumn, with a slight yellow color.

FLOWERS Insignificant midspring flowers.

FRUIT Narrowly elliptical brown nuts enclosed by a thin husk mature in midautumn. The edible sweet nuts have a high fat content and are valued for cookies, candies, and pies. They are an important food source for many wildlife species.

LIGHT & SOIL Full sun to light shade, with a moist but well-drained soil.

MAINTENANCE Nut production requires a high level of nutrition, frequent spraying for pests, and monitoring for zinc deficiencies.

INSTALLATION Trees up to 10' tall are available from specialty growers for late winter planting. Space 50'–60' apart.

PESTS & DISEASES Numerous pests affect pecan. Aphids are universal, fall webworms form white tents and cause partial defoliation, pecan scab causes early nut abortion and defoliation in severe cases. Orchards spray up to 12 times per season to control pecan scab.

NOTES & CULTIVARS
'Elliot', 'Excel', and 'Gloria Grande' are cultivars recommended for homeowners interested in growing their own pecans in Georgia.

Carya tomentosa MOCKERNUT HICKORY

Mockernut hickory is reportedly the most common hickory in the Southeast. Rarely available commercially due to the difficulty of transplanting, its large nuts are an important wildlife food source, and its bright yellow late fall foliage is among the most attractive of our native trees. It is well worth preserving on construction sites, though it can be somewhat messy in refined landscapes. Mockernuts reportedly live up to 500 years in nature and have long been valued for their light colored, impact-resistant wood.

ZONES & ORIGIN   4b–9a. Native from eastern Texas to Massachusetts.

SIZE & GROWTH RATE   60'–90' tall, 30'–50' wide, slow growing.

TEXTURE & FORM   Coarse texture and oval to broadly oval form.

FOLIAGE   Pinnately compound alternate leaves have mostly seven, rarely five or nine leaflets. Undersides of the leaflets and rachis are covered in coarse yellowish-brown hairs and have a pungent odor when crushed. Fall foliage is bright yellow in late autumn. Bark on mature trees is light gray, with ridges forming a diamond pattern on the trunk.

FLOWERS   Insignificant midspring flowers.

FRUIT   Round brown nuts are enclosed in a thick husk that is slightly larger than a golf ball and mature in midautumn, although many fall prematurely during the summer. The nuts have a high fat content and are edible, though tough to crack, and serve as food for many wildlife species.

LIGHT & SOIL   Mockernut hickory prefers full sun and well-drained soils but tolerates heavy shade when young and is very drought tolerant.

MAINTENANCE   Mockernuts can be messy in refined landscapes. Nuts start falling in midsummer and continue into late autumn, and the large leaves are easily blown about by winds. Avoid parking cars beneath mature trees to avoid loud bangs and dents.

INSTALLATION   Specialty nurseries may have bare-root seedlings or small containers. Make sure the root system is not girdling the stem of the tree.

PESTS & DISEASES   A number of insects chew on the foliage and attack the nuts but rarely cause any serious damage.

NOTES & CULTIVARS
None available.

Fall color in Chattanooga.

top Foliage.
middle Foliage and nuts with thick husks.
bottom Form and fall color in Athens.

top left Hackberry foliage.
top right Sugar hackberry form.
middle Bark.
bottom Sugar hackberry foliage and fruit.

Celtis laevigata   SUGAR HACKBERRY · SUGARBERRY

Sugar hackberry is a native tree that is better appreciated from a distance than up close. Its attractive fall foliage is delightful along woodland edges, where its somewhat unsightly traits can be hidden. Sugar hackberry fruit provides food for many birds but can also cause a mess on pavements. Native to moist bottomlands but also occurring along fencerows and woodland edges on upland sites, it is considered aggressive due to the number of seedlings it produces. Jim Cothran (2003) noted that it was planted in early southern cities but is now rarely found in nurseries.

ZONES & ORIGIN 5b–10a. Native from Florida and Texas to Illinois.

SIZE & GROWTH RATE 60'–80' tall, 40'–60' wide, medium fast growing.

TEXTURE & FORM Medium fine texture with an upright oval form that becomes broadly oval with maturity.

FOLIAGE Simple alternate leaves 2"–4" long are ovate to lanceolate shaped with long tapering tips, have asymmetrical bases, and have either entire margins or a few teeth on the upper half. Yellow fall foliage is fairly good. Trunks and older branches have a smooth gray bark covered with wartlike growths.

FLOWERS Insignificant.

FRUIT Small berry-like drupes mature to dark purple in late summer.

LIGHT & SOIL Hackberry prefers full sun and a moist to a well-drained soil but tolerates moderate shade and near-neutral pH soils. It reportedly tolerates salt spray.

MAINTENANCE Numerous seedlings are produced in ground covers, shrub beds, and unmaintained areas. A surface root system and dense canopy make it difficult to grow other plants beneath it.

INSTALLATION Hackberries are rarely grown in nurseries but transplant well.

PESTS & DISEASES Small leaf nipple galls are common but do not cause serious damage.

NOTES & CULTIVARS

- 'All Seasons' reportedly provides a more consistent canopy and fall foliage color but is difficult to locate.
- Hackberry, *Celtis occidentalis*, is a native of better-drained uplands from zones 3b–9a. It has mostly ovate leaves with coarsely serrate margins, a sandpaper-like upper surface, and acuminate tips. The two species reportedly hybridize where both occur.

Fagus grandifolia AMERICAN BEECH

American beech is a stately, shade-tolerant native across much of the eastern United States. Its smooth silvery-gray bark has served as a historical record by authors who have engraved their tales and initials on this long-lived tree. Beech produces a dense canopy with branches low to the ground for many years. It is best observed from afar to avoid its spiny nuts and prevent compaction to its sensitive roots. In nature, the beech is considered a climax species: it begins as an understory tree under heavy shade for many years before reaching the upper canopy.

ZONES & ORIGIN 4a–9a. Native to lower slopes from Florida to Michigan.

SIZE & GROWTH RATE 60'–80' tall, 50'–70' wide, slow growing.

TEXTURE & FORM Medium texture. A pyramidal form in youth becomes rounded with age.

FOLIAGE Simple alternate leaves 2"–5" long are elliptic shaped with coarsely serrate margins and prominent depressed veins. Dark yellow to bronze fall foliage becomes tan in winter and remains until spring. Bark is smooth light gray, with long narrow brown buds.

FLOWERS Insignificant.

FRUIT Three angular nuts are enclosed in a prickly angular husk. The edible nuts have a high fat content and serve as food for many wildlife species.

LIGHT & SOIL Beech grows in full sun to full shade with a moist but well-drained slightly acidic soil. Summer droughts may cause leaf scorch.

MAINTENANCE The dense canopy and shallow roots make it difficult to grow other plants beneath the beech. Mature trees are sensitive to disturbance.

INSTALLATION This tree is somewhat rare in nurseries, but small field-grown trees transplant successfully during the dormant season. Space trees 50' apart.

PESTS & DISEASES Beech blight bark disease has devastated large populations in the Northeast and the Appalachians, though it is not yet serious in the Southeast. Deer nibble the foliage.

NOTES & CULTIVARS
European beech, *Fagus sylvatica*, is most famous for its numerous dark purple-leafed cultivars, which are often lumped together under the name "copper beech." Hardy from zones 5a–7b, and several weeping cultivars and a narrowly upright oval cultivar, 'Dawyck', are also available.

top left Fall foliage on the UGA campus.
top right Purple European beech at Longwood Gardens.
middle Foliage.
bottom Tan winter foliage in north Georgia.

top left Form in full sun.
top middle Form and fall color in light shade.
top right Fall foliage.
bottom Foliage.

Fraxinus americana WHITE ASH

White ash has been often used as a street tree, particularly in midwestern states, due to its dense canopy, fall foliage, fast growth, and tolerance to a range of soil conditions. However, it is often better appreciated from a distance than up close due to its messy seed, susceptibility to insects and diseases, and somewhat brittle wood. Late summer and early autumn drought in the South can cause foliage to drop early before any significant fall color display. The light color and impact resistance of the wood of both the white and green ash have made them popular for baseball bats.

ZONES & ORIGIN 4a–9a. Native from north Florida to Canada.

SIZE & GROWTH RATE 60'–80' tall, 40'–60' wide, fast growing.

TEXTURE & FORM Medium texture and broadly oval form.

FOLIAGE Odd pinnately compound opposite leaves with usually seven leaflets 3"–5" long. The elliptic to ovate-shaped leaflets have mostly entire or occasionally serrate margins and soft white pubescence beneath. Fall color is a fair yellow orange. Mature bark develops both chunky and diamond-shaped ridges.

FLOWERS Ash are dioecious, with insignificant flowers.

FRUIT Numerous winged samaras are produced on female trees and can be unsightly. Avoid them by specifying male trees.

LIGHT & SOIL Full sun with a moist but well-drained soil is ideal. It tolerates light shade, slightly alkaline soils, somewhat drier sites, and moderate salt spray.

MAINTENANCE White ash doesn't seem to be quite as prone to insects and disease as is the green ash. Nevertheless, careful monitoring and good soil conditions will achieve better results.

INSTALLATION Field-grown trees transplant well in larger sizes. Space 40'–60' apart.

PESTS & DISEASES Numerous insects subsist on white ash foliage, including some butterfly species larvae. The emerald ash borer from Asia has killed many trees in midwestern states and is confirmed in the Southeast, making widespread use of ash highly questionable. Deer should not pose problems.

NOTES & CULTIVARS
'Autumn Applause' and 'Autumn Purple' are male cultivars with deep purple fall foliage.
'Skyline' is a male with a symmetrical oval form.

Fraxinus pennsylvanica GREEN ASH

Green ash shares many attributes with the white ash. It has been widely planted for street and shade trees due to its fast growth, ability to tolerate a wide range of soil conditions, ease of transplanting, and fall foliage color. However, it also shares the potential insect and disease problems of the white ash, making it questionable for heavy use in designs. Using a diversity of species reduces the potential for devastation brought on by either weather or pests.

ZONES & ORIGIN 3a–9a. Native to open bottomlands of the central and eastern United States.

SIZE & GROWTH RATE 60'–80' tall, 40'–60' wide, fast growing.

TEXTURE & FORM Medium texture and oval to broadly oval form.

FOLIAGE Odd pinnately compound opposite leaves have mostly seven dark green ovate leaflets with either serrate or entire margins and flattened leaf scars. While often promoted for its bright yellow fall foliage, late summer droughts and several fungal diseases often cause early leaf drop.

FLOWERS A dioecious species with insignificant flowers.

FRUIT Female trees produce numerous winged samaras that, while unsightly, provide food for some wildlife.

LIGHT & SOIL Full sun to light shade and a moist but well-drained soil are ideal. It tolerates slightly alkaline soils, salt spray, and moist soils with late winter and early spring flooding.

MAINTENANCE Ideal cultural conditions are critical to afford resistance to numerous insects and fungal diseases that thrive on green ash. It appears more susceptible to fungal diseases than white ash.

INSTALLATION Large, field-grown trees are readily available and transplant easily. For massing or street trees, space 40' apart.

PESTS & DISEASES Insects, fungal diseases, and brittle wood make it questionable to depend too much on green ash in designs. Use them to supplement less susceptible shade trees in the canopy.

NOTES & CULTIVARS
The following male cultivars are readily available:

'Cimmzam' has an upright oval form with reddish-purple fall foliage.
'Oconee' has improved heat tolerance.
'Summit' is pyramidal in youth, becoming broadly oval with age.

top Foliage.
middle Mature form.
bottom left Form.
bottom right Fall foliage.

Ginkgo biloba GINKGO · MAIDENHAIR TREE

Ginkgo is an extremely popular tree due to its outstanding bright yellow fall foliage, wide availability, ease of transplanting, dependability over time, and lack of insect and disease problems. It has a somewhat awkward appearance in youth, with an open canopy and only a few strongly horizontal branches, and it is sometimes used as a bonsai or an espalier to take advantage of this habit. With age, its canopy fills in to form a broadly oval outline. Classified as a gymnosperm, it is a longed-lived tree, with specimens over 1,000 years old reported and fossil records dating millions of years.

ZONES & ORIGIN 4b–8b. Native to China.

SIZE & GROWTH RATE 60'–100' tall, 40'–60' wide, medium slow growing.

TEXTURE & FORM Medium coarse texture with an upright oval form in youth, becoming broadly oval with maturity.

FOLIAGE Fan-shaped leaves with parallel veins and wavy margins occur in clusters on short spurs on the stems. Fall foliage is an outstanding bright yellow, with the leaves falling over a short time period.

FLOWERS A dioecious species with insignificant flowers.

FRUIT Female trees produce a plumlike fruit that turns yellow orange in autumn and produces a foul odor when it falls and is crushed by pedestrians or vehicles. Avoid planting female trees.

LIGHT & SOIL Full sun to light shade with a moist but well-drained soil is ideal. Ginkgo tolerates drought, urban pollution, deicing salt, and moderate salt spray.

MAINTENANCE Selectively prune to maintain a desired form and provide supplemental water for the first summer.

INSTALLATION Container and large field-grown trees are readily available and can be transplanted from fall to spring as close as 20' apart for narrow upright cultivars.

PESTS & DISEASES No serious problems. Deer don't like them.

NOTES & CULTIVARS
The following male cultivars are commonly available:

'Fairmount', 'Magyar', and 'Princeton Sentry' have upright oval forms.
'Golden Globe' develops a broadly oval to rounded form.
'Presidential Gold' has an oval to broadly oval form from the tree at the front of the UGA President's House on Prince Avenue in Athens.

top left Fall color at the UGA President's House.
top right Espalier at Swarthmore College.
middle Foliage.
bottom Fall color on the UGA campus.

Juglans nigra BLACK WALNUT

It may be difficult to believe that a native tree with an attractive open canopy is not necessarily something to be valued in refined landscapes, but it is true in the case of the black walnut. Its heavy nuts can dent vehicles, bang building roofs, and cause pedestrians to turn an ankle. The foliage and roots also contain a compound that inhibits the growth of many other plants. However, as long as the walnut is not near a paved surface or roof, it's well worth trying to preserve the tree on a site. Its lumber is highly valued for fine furniture and rifle stocks.

Foliage and fruit.

ZONES & ORIGIN 4b–9a. Native but never very common from Florida to Minnesota.

SIZE & GROWTH RATE 60'–80' tall, 40'–60' wide, medium growing.

TEXTURE & FORM Coarse texture and broadly oval form.

FOLIAGE Odd pinnately compound alternate leaves 2' long have 11–23 leaflets and a terminal leaflet that often falls by midsummer. The narrowly ovate leaflets have serrate margins and acuminate tips. Leaves often drop in early autumn, without fall color. Dark gray bark has deep ridges and furrows.

FLOWERS Insignificant flowers.

FRUIT Fruit is a nut enclosed within a thick rounded yellow-green husk that matures and falls in mid- to late autumn. The edible and tasty kernel serves as a food source for many wildlife species but is difficult to remove due to the hard shell.

LIGHT & SOIL Primarily found on bottomlands, the tree prefers full sun with a moist but well-drained soil and near-neutral pH but tolerates drought and moderate salt spray.

MAINTENANCE Leaves begin falling in late summer. The nuts start falling in mid-autumn and need to be removed quickly in refined landscapes, since they can easily cause someone to fall.

INSTALLATION Trees are rarely available in nurseries due to the difficulty of transplanting.

PESTS & DISEASES Many insects and fungal diseases affect black walnuts but rarely cause serious health issues. Deer don't like them.

NOTES & CULTIVARS Cultivars for commercial nut production are available but not normally carried by ornamental nurseries.

left Form. *middle and right* Early summer foliage on the UGA campus and at the Schmitt residence, Athens, GA.

Liquidambar styraciflua SWEETGUM

Anyone who has owned a sweetgum tree probably finds it hard to develop enthusiasm for another one. An aggressive early successional species that quickly occupies old fields, its fruit is the one character that most people remember. Yet sweetgum provides excellent fall foliage color, grows quickly on a variety of sites, transplants readily, has very few pest issues, and provides a formal conical outline for many years. So talk your neighbor into planting one, or just make sure to place it where people don't have to walk beneath it. The common name comes from Native Americans who chewed the dried hardened sap.

top Foliage.
middle Fall color.
bottom left and right Form.

ZONES & ORIGIN 5b–10a. Native to lower elevations from Florida to Illinois.

SIZE & GROWTH RATE 80'–100' tall, 40'–60' wide, medium fast growing.

TEXTURE & FORM Medium texture with a pyramidal to oval form.

FOLIAGE Simple star-shaped alternate leaves have five lobes and serrate margins. Fall foliage ranges from bright yellow to crimson to deep purple depending upon the individual tree. Young stems often develop corky wings.

FLOWERS Insignificant.

FRUIT A round light green spiny capsule falls from early August to late July.

LIGHT & SOIL Full sun to light shade and moist but well-drained acidic soil are ideal. Sweetgum occurs on moist sites, as well as drier uplands, and tolerates drought, as well as light salt spray.

MAINTENANCE Sweetgums are messy trees, producing many seedlings, gumballs that fall year-round, and leaves that drop for an extended period in autumn. The gumballs are painful for bare feet, don't decay quickly, and are difficult to rake or blow out of lawns. The shallow root system also produces sprouts.

INSTALLATION Sweetgum is readily available and transplants well in larger sizes. Space trees 30'–50' apart.

PESTS & DISEASES No disease problems. Deer avoid it.

NOTES & CULTIVARS
'Hapdell', known as Happi Daze, is fruitless, with dark maroon fall color.
'Moraine' is hardy to zone 4b with red fall foliage.
'Rotundiloba' is a fruitless cultivar with rounded lobes, although some branches can revert to the species and produce fruit.

Liriodendron tulipifera TULIP OR YELLOW POPLAR

Tulip poplar is the state tree of Tennessee and the largest native tree in the eastern United States. Trees in the Appalachian coves reached over 150' tall, with diameters approaching 10', and were heavily timbered in the late nineteenth and early twentieth centuries due to their long straight trunk with few knots. In the landscape industry, it is valued for its fast growth, yellow fall foliage, and somewhat formal upright appearance. While it doesn't provide much shade, consider it for tight spaces or to line walks and drives to take advantage of its upright form.

ZONES & ORIGIN 5a–9a. Native from Florida to southern Michigan.

SIZE & GROWTH RATE 80'–120' tall, 25'–50' wide, fast growing.

TEXTURE & FORM Medium coarse texture and upright oval form.

FOLIAGE Simple tulip-shaped dark green alternate leaves 3"–6" long have four lobes and entire margins. Fall foliage is bright yellow, but many leaves drop early.

FLOWERS Tulip-shaped flowers 2"–3" in diameter with greenish-yellow petals and orange markings are held on the ends of branches in midspring (mid-April to mid-May in Athens) but are seldom appreciated unless you are in a building looking down at the tree.

FRUIT An insignificant cone-shaped cluster of samaras.

LIGHT & SOIL Full sun and moist to moist but well-drained soil are ideal. Prolonged summer droughts cause early leaf drop.

MAINTENANCE The thin bark of young trees is easily damaged by lawn equipment. Limbs are prone to breaking in wind and ice storms.

INSTALLATION Field-grown trees are easily transplanted in fairly large sizes, but due to their fast growth, smaller trees quickly catch up in size after a few years. Plant in late winter to early spring and space trees 30'–50' apart.

PESTS & DISEASES Aphids cause problems with trees under drought stress, and deer nibble on young trees.

NOTES & CULTIVARS
'Arnold' and 'Fastigiatum' reach 60', with narrowly upright oval to columnar forms.
'Little Volunteer' reaches 40', with a pyramidal form and leaves about half the size of the species.

top left and middle Form in a Vancouver, B.C., plaza.
top right Fall foliage at UGA.
bottom Foliage and flowers.

left Fall color.
middle Form.
right 'Ogon' at the Coastal Maine Botanical Gardens in Boothbay.

Metasequoia glyptostroboides DAWN REDWOOD

Few trees catch the eye as easily as dawn redwood. Its highly formal outline stands out in the landscape, making it a candidate for formal plantings, as well as for specimen trees for parks and other large open spaces. Often mistaken for the bald cypress, it can be differentiated by having branches growing upward at a 45-degree angle to the main trunk and drooping at their ends, depressions (armpits) on the trunk where the branches attach, and oppositely arranged branchlets that hold the needles. Its fast growth, wide availability, and ease of transplanting have contributed to its popularity. Tolerating moist to wet soils and drought makes dawn redwood suited for use along stormwater detention basins and swales. Fossil records indicate that it is more than 25 million years of age and that it once grew in North America.

ZONES & ORIGIN 5b–8b. Native to China.

SIZE & GROWTH RATE 80'–120' tall, 40'–60' wide, fast growing.

TEXTURE & FORM Fine texture and conical form.

FOLIAGE Flat bright green needles are held on oppositely arranged branchlets on the stems. The needles turn a reddish-brown color in late autumn and fall along with the branchlets that hold them. The gray bark expands into strips as the tree grows to reveal some reddish-orange inner bark.

FLOWERS Insignificant flowers.

FRUIT A small rounded cone matures in early autumn.

LIGHT & SOIL Best growth occurs with full sun and a moist but well-drained soil. It tolerates moist to wet soils and is quite drought tolerant as well.

MAINTENANCE Fallen needles can be difficult to rake or blow together to collect due to their small surface area.

INSTALLATION Field-grown and container trees are readily available and easily transplanted. For a formal allée, plant approximately 40' on center.

PESTS & DISEASES No serious problems. Deer don't like them.

NOTES & CULTIVARS
Listed cultivars are still quite rare in the nursery industry.

'National' is reportedly more upright in habit than the species.

'Ogon' Gold Rush has bright yellow foliage.

Foliage.

Platanus occidentalis SYCAMORE · PLANETREE

Sycamore is a massive native tree found on rich open bottomlands. An attractive exfoliating bark that resembles a camouflage pattern is mostly obscured by the foliage until winter, when the low sun angle highlights its exfoliating bark and reveals a white inner bark. Although widely used for street tree and urban plantings, sycamore has a number of pest problems that appear under those stressful conditions. For that reason, it may be better suited for parks, golf courses, and other large open spaces that better mimic its natural environment.

ZONES & ORIGIN 4b–9a. Native to the eastern United States.

SIZE & GROWTH RATE 80'–120' tall, 60'–80' wide, fast growing.

TEXTURE & FORM Coarse texture and broadly oval form.

FOLIAGE Simple alternate leaves 4"–9" long have three to five lobes with coarsely toothed margins. The leaves are densely pubescent in spring and develop no significant fall color.

FLOWERS Insignificant flowers.

FRUIT A round green golf ball–sized cluster of fibrous seeds on a long slender stalk turns mustard colored in autumn and causes maintenance problems in refined landscapes.

LIGHT & SOIL Full sun with a moist but well-drained soil is ideal. It tolerates light shade, moist soils, winter flooding, and slightly alkaline soils.

MAINTENANCE Sycamores are messy. Broken limbs are a constant problem due to the tree's fast growth, and leaves and fruit drop from midsummer to winter.

INSTALLATION Large field-grown trees are readily available and transplant easily at 50'–70' on center.

PESTS & DISEASES Sycamore is highly susceptible to powdery mildew and anthracnose, which causes defoliation in spring. It is also susceptible to lace bugs and several borers, which appear to cause more problems on urban trees than on those in natural environments.

NOTES & CULTIVARS
London planetree, *Platanus × acerifolia*, is a cross between American and Oriental sycamores. Hardy to zone 5b and promoted to be more pest resistant than the native sycamore, it now appears to suffer similar problems. Sycamore cultivars are rare, but London planetree cultivars 'Bloodgood' and 'Yarwood' are easily located.

top Foliage.

middle Prominent white bark in Athens.

An allée at Cornell University in Ithaca, N.Y.

Occidental Park in Seattle.

Quercus acutissima SAWTOOTH OAK

Sawtooth oak is one of the fastest-growing oak species. It has been widely promoted for wildlife management areas because of its abundant annual acorn crops, which are produced at an earlier age than those of many native oaks. In the landscape, it becomes a broadly spreading shade tree, often broader than tall, that appears to tolerate a variety of soil conditions. A somewhat coarse texture and large quantity of acorns make it a better choice for large open spaces such as parks and highways than for urban plazas and residential yards.

top Foliage.

bottom Acorns and acorn caps.

ZONES & ORIGIN 5b–9a. Native to Asia.

SIZE & GROWTH RATE 50'–60' tall, 60'–80' wide, medium fast growing.

TEXTURE & FORM Medium coarse texture with a rounded form at maturity.

FOLIAGE Simple lustrous dark green alternate leaves 4"–7" long are narrowly ovate in shape, with bristle-tipped margins and prominent parallel veins. Leafing out in early spring, the tree develops some yellow fall foliage, which eventually turns tan and remains into late winter. Gray bark develops deep ridges and furrows.

FLOWERS Insignificant.

FRUIT Oval-shaped acorns are approximately 1" in size. The unusual-looking acorn cap, with long curving scales, covers about two-thirds of the acorn. Trees produce large acorn crops annually, which are eaten by a number of wildlife species but can be messy in yards or parks.

LIGHT & SOIL Full sun with a moist but well-drained slightly acidic soil is ideal. It tolerates some salt spray and moderate droughts.

MAINTENANCE Due to the tree's dense canopy, turf is difficult to grow beneath mature trees. Seedlings will sprout in ground cover beds, so the best option may be to mulch beneath mature trees. There are reports of sawtooth oaks escaping into woodlands when planted on wildlife management areas. Urban trees currently don't appear to cause problems but should be watched carefully in the future.

INSTALLATION Bare-root, container, and field-grown trees are available and transplant well. For continuous canopy coverage, space 60' apart.

PESTS & DISEASES No serious problems.

NOTES & CULTIVARS
No cultivars are commonly available.

left and right Form on UGA campus.

left and middle Summer appearance at the Nichols residence in Athens, Ga.

right Winter outline in Athens.

Quercus alba WHITE OAK

White oak is an outstanding shade tree valued for its late autumn foliage and acorns, which are favored by many wildlife species, particularly white-tailed deer. One of the stateliest trees in the Southeast, it can reach over 120' tall and live for several hundred years on good sites. White oaks are climax species on many sites due to their ability to grow under shade for many years before reaching the top of the canopy. Their slower growth and reputation for being difficult to transplant favored other species such as maples for quick shade on new projects. However, regular root pruning allows large white oaks to be transplanted successfully. While questionable for urban situations, for long-term shade in parks, golf courses, and estates, few trees surpass white oak.

ZONES & ORIGIN 3b–8b. Native to the eastern United States.

SIZE & GROWTH RATE 60'–100' tall, 50'–80' wide, medium slow growing.

TEXTURE & FORM Medium coarse texture and broadly oval form.

FOLIAGE Simple blue-green alternate leaves 5"–9" long have five to eleven rounded lobes. Leaves turn dark red to purple in late autumn. A light gray scaly bark is typical of the native white oak group.

FLOWERS Insignificant midspring flowers.

FRUIT Oblong acorns ¾" long with a scaly cap covering a third of the nut mature in midautumn. Favored by many wildlife species, heavy acorn crops are produced every two to three years.

LIGHT & SOIL Full sun and a moist but well-drained slightly acidic soil are ideal. It tolerates moderate shade, drought, and salt spray.

MAINTENANCE Leaves drop from midautumn to early winter, requiring extended attention. Provide supplemental water during extended droughts for several years after planting.

INSTALLATION Container trees and root-pruned field-grown trees can be transplanted successfully and are becoming widely available. Space 50'–60' apart.

PESTS & DISEASES Stressed trees are susceptible to several fungal diseases that can be fatal. Earthwork around mature trees or extended droughts weaken the tree and provide entry to these diseases. Deer eat the foliage of small trees.

NOTES & CULTIVARS No cultivars available.

Foliage at the Nichols residence in Athens, Ga.

Quercus coccinea SCARLET OAK

Scarlet oak develops one of the most attractive fall foliage displays of any native oak. Its scarlet-red late fall foliage stands out among other large oak species. Unfortunately, a sensitivity to higher pH soils and a difficulty in successfully transplanting larger trees have caused scarlet oak to be somewhat difficult to locate in nurseries and rarely specified on projects. Although occurring on drier upland sites, it can actually grow faster than many other oaks on locations with better soils.

Fall foliage and buds.

ZONES & ORIGIN 5a–8b. Native to uplands from Alabama to New England.

SIZE & GROWTH RATE 60'–80' tall, 40'–60' wide, medium growing.

TEXTURE & FORM Medium coarse texture and oval to broadly oval form.

FOLIAGE Simple glossy green alternate leaves 4"–7" long have five to nine bristle-tipped lobes with C-shaped sinuses cut nearly to the midrib. Outstanding late autumn foliage becomes scarlet to deep crimson. Reddish-brown terminal buds ⅛" long are shaped like rugby balls. Trunks on mature trees are shallowly ridged and furrowed and become buttressed just above the soil.

FLOWERS Insignificant.

FRUIT Rounded acorns ½"–¾" with concentric rings about the tips and caps appear covered in varnish. Acorns require two years to mature and are eaten by several wildlife species.

LIGHT & SOIL Full sun to moderate shade and moist but well-drained moderately acidic soil are ideal. It tolerates droughts and light salt spray.

MAINTENANCE Provide supplemental water during extended droughts for several years after planting. Avoid earthwork around mature trees.

INSTALLATION Field-grown trees can be somewhat difficult to transplant. Container-grown trees are more successful.

PESTS & DISEASES Trees are susceptible to fatal fungal diseases when weakened from earthwork around their roots or prolonged droughts. Deer rarely bother them.

NOTES & CULTIVARS
No cultivars are generally available. Scarlet oak is grown from seed and produces one of the smallest quantities of viable acorns of any oak. Many nurseries listing scarlet oak actually carry another species such as northern red oak or hybrids between scarlet and pin or Shumard oaks.

left and middle Fall foliage in Athens.   *right* Late autumn native tree at a woodland edge in Athens.

left Form at Chattanooga National Cemetery.

middle Form at a Chattanooga residence.

right Form at Samford University, Birmingham, Ala.

Quercus falcata SOUTHERN RED OAK

Southern red oak is a long-lived native upland tree. While it doesn't offer a lot of ornamental attributes, existing trees have provided welcome shade for many people over the years, and their sturdy branches have supported many backyard swings. For those reasons, existing trees on construction projects should be protected from destruction or site grading. It is probably the easiest native red oak to identify due to leaves that resemble a turkey's foot and develop a droopy, hang-down appearance on mature trees.

ZONES & ORIGIN 6a–9a. Native to uplands of the Southeast.

SIZE & GROWTH RATE 60'–80' tall, 50'–70' wide, slow growing.

TEXTURE & FORM Medium coarse texture and broadly oval form.

FOLIAGE Simple dark glossy green alternate leaves 5"–9" long have three to seven bristle-tipped lobes with pale hairs beneath and tend to droop downward on the twigs. Leaves in full sun have three lobes, with an extended middle lobe resembling a turkey's foot. Poor reddish-brown fall foliage remains into winter. Medium to dark gray bark has broad ridges with narrow furrows.

FLOWERS Insignificant flowers.

FRUIT Rounded acorns ½" long with caps covering about a third of the nut are bitter tasting but eaten by a number of wildlife species.

LIGHT & SOIL Full sun to light shade and a well-drained moderately acidic soil are ideal. It tolerates drought and is reportedly tolerant of moderate salt spray.

MAINTENANCE Trees usually drop some leaves throughout early autumn and for an extended period in late autumn.

INSTALLATION Rarely available even in containers.

PESTS & DISEASES Existing trees are extremely sensitive to earthwork around their roots. Deer rarely touch them.

NOTES & CULTIVARS

Nurseries rarely carry trees due to difficulty in transplanting and slow growth rate.

Cherrybark oak, *Quercus pagoda*, is now recognized as a separate species, but it was long thought of as a variety of southern red oak. It grows on bottomlands from zones 6a–8b. It has more regularly lobed leaves and grows faster and taller than southern red oak. No cultivars of either species are available.

Foliage.

Quercus hemisphaerica LAUREL OAK · DARLINGTON OAK

Laurel oak is a semievergreen tree that is popular for urban streets and plazas. Its pyramidal outline in youth, fairly fast growth, and semievergreen nature convince many communities to use it as a prop for holiday lighting. With the trees' ability to be successfully transplanted in large sizes, they would seem like a no-brainer for urban areas. Their downside is that they are shorter-lived than many oaks, 60–80 years, and they are somewhat brittle-wooded, potentially dropping branches on parked cars, pedestrians, and structures beneath them.

ZONES & ORIGIN 6a–9a. Native to uplands of the southeastern Coastal Plain.

SIZE & GROWTH RATE 50'–70' tall, 40'–60' wide, medium growing.

TEXTURE & FORM Medium fine texture. A pyramidal form in youth becomes broadly oval to rounded with maturity.

FOLIAGE Simple leathery dark green alternate leaves 1"–3" long remain green until late winter and are elliptical to oblanceolate shaped, with mostly acute tips. A smooth gray bark eventually develops shallow ridges and furrows.

FLOWERS Insignificant flowers.

FRUIT Rounded sessile acorns ½" long have caps covering about a third of the nut and are a food source for many smaller animals.

LIGHT & SOIL Full sun to light shade and moist but well-drained slightly acidic soil are ideal. Once established, they tolerate droughts and moderate salt spray.

MAINTENANCE Trees produce an abundance of acorns each year that, although easily crushed by pedestrians, can create messes on pavements, and they drop their leaves in late winter or early spring.

INSTALLATION Field-grown trees are easily transplanted. For urban plantings, space at least 40' apart.

PESTS & DISEASES Brittle limbs can fail under ice or heavy winds. A number of pathogens can enter mature trees through wounds and cause rot of the heartwood.

NOTES & CULTIVARS Laurel oak and swamp laurel oak, *Quercus laurifolia*, are similar in appearance. Swamp laurel oak grows in wet locations of the Coastal Plain and goes deciduous in early winter. Its leaves tend to be slightly broader and somewhat longer than those of laurel oak, with blunt or rounded tips.

Foliage.

below left Street trees in downtown Athens.   *below right top* Mature form at the UGA campus.
below right bottom Younger tree form at the UGA campus.

Quercus lyrata OVERCUP OAK

If you pictured a perfect shade tree in your mind, you would likely imagine something that was broader than tall with a dense canopy and strong horizontal branches suitable for a swing or hammock. Until recent years, few trees other than live oak fit that description. However, in the past 20 years, nurseries have been discovering and growing overcup oak. Similar in form to live oak at maturity, it is long-lived and transplants easily. Its popularity has soared in recent years for shading residential streets, parking lots, yards, and parks, as well as for stream restorations to take advantage of its moist soil tolerance.

ZONES & ORIGIN 6a–9a. Native to bottomlands of the southeastern Coastal Plain and Mississippi River basin.

SIZE & GROWTH RATE 50'–70' tall and wide, medium growing.

TEXTURE & FORM Medium coarse texture, pyramidal form in youth becoming rounded with age.

FOLIAGE Simple alternate leaves 6"–10" long resemble a red oak but lack bristle tips and are pubescent beneath. They are oblong to obovate shaped, with five to nine irregularly shaped lobes and a narrow tapering base. Leaves emerge late and drop early, with a sickly yellow-brown color. A short trunk with light gray scaly bark resembles white oak.

FLOWERS Insignificant flowers.

FRUIT A flattened spherical acorn ¾" long is broader than long, with a scaly cap covering most of the nut. Trees produce abundant acorns each year that drop in early autumn and are popular with many wildlife species.

LIGHT & SOIL Full sun to light shade and moist to moist but well-drained soil are ideal. It is very tolerant of dormant-season flooding.

MAINTENANCE Provide supplemental water for several years after planting during droughts. Autumn acorns present problems for pedestrians on pavements.

INSTALLATION Although they tolerate flooding, nursery-grown trees need to be acclimated to moister soils for several years prior to planting. To anticipate the trees' mature size and spread, plant them at least 50' apart.

PESTS & DISEASES No serious disease problems. Deer eat foliage of small trees.

NOTES & CULTIVARS 'Highbeam' develops upward-angled branches and broadly oval form.

top left Fall foliage.
top right Mature form at UGA.
middle Foliage.
bottom Mature acorn.

Quercus michauxii SWAMP CHESTNUT OAK

One of the most attractive oak trees is also one of the rarer trees in the nursery industry. Many people don't recognize this tree, but it certainly deserves greater attention. Its upright habit and tolerance of a range of soil conditions make it suitable for use in tough urban or residential developments. But it is the attractive deep red late fall foliage that really demands greater use of the swamp chestnut oak. Take advantage of its fall color and form for parks, golf courses, and residential streetscapes.

ZONES & ORIGIN 6a–9a. Native to bottomlands of the Piedmont and Coastal Plain.

SIZE & GROWTH RATE 60'–80' tall, 30'–50' wide, medium slow growing.

TEXTURE & FORM Coarse texture and oval form.

FOLIAGE Simple obovate-shaped alternate leaves 6"–10" long have crenate margins, prominent depressed veins above, and dense white hairs beneath. They turn crimson in mid- to late autumn. A scaly light gray bark resembles that of white oak.

FLOWERS Insignificant.

FRUIT Nearly sessile oval acorns are slightly over 1" long, with scaly caps covering nearly half of the nut. The sweet acorns are edible raw and favored by wildlife, but they are messy in refined landscapes.

LIGHT & SOIL Full sun to light shade and moist to moist but well-drained slightly acidic soil are ideal. Once established, it tolerates drought but not flooding during the growing season.

MAINTENANCE Large acorns can be difficult for impaired individuals when walking, and the large leaves act like sails when they fall and catch the wind.

INSTALLATION For streets and sidewalks, space at least 40' apart. Provide supplemental water for several years during extended summer droughts.

PESTS & DISEASES No serious problems unless stressed by prolonged drought or by continually wet or compacted soil.

NOTES & CULTIVARS
Trees are still fairly rare in the nursery industry, probably due to their somewhat slow growth rate. Most nurseries grow them as container plants, although they appear to transplant well as field-grown trees. The light colored wood is valued for use in baskets.

top Late fall foliage.
middle Swamp chestnut oak's typical white oak bark.
bottom Young tree form.

Mature form.

Quercus montana CHESTNUT OAK

Many urbanites may never see a chestnut oak, since it usually occurs on very dry upland ridges and is rarely available from nurseries. Many authors note it to be somewhat small in size, slow growing, and virtually impossible to transplant. While that may be true for native trees on upland sites, the reality is that field-grown nursery trees grow as quickly as any native oak and can be transplanted successfully in fairly large sizes. Long-lived and with few disease problems, it would be a good choice to provide shade in large open areas.

ZONES & ORIGIN 5a–8b. Native to dry ridges from New England to Alabama.

SIZE & GROWTH RATE 60'–80' tall, 40'–60' wide, medium growing. On sites with thin rocky soils, it grows slowly and may only reach 30'–50' tall.

TEXTURE & FORM Medium coarse texture and oval to broadly oval form.

FOLIAGE Simple broadly elliptical alternate leaves 5"–8" long have crenate margins, prominent depressed veins, and a poor yellow fall color. Unlike that of most members of the white oak group, the gray bark develops deep furrows and broad ridges.

FLOWERS Insignificant flowers.

FRUIT Broadly oval acorns are slightly over 1" long, with caps covering about a third of the nut. The large acorns drop in early autumn and are extremely popular with wildlife.

LIGHT & SOIL Full sun and moist but well-drained moderately acidic soil are ideal. It tolerates moderate shade and severe drought with establishment.

MAINTENANCE Large acorns can turn ankles, especially for elderly pedestrians. The large leaves act like sails in winds.

INSTALLATION Chestnut oak is grown from seed, and although it transplants well, few nurseries grow it. If found, space 50' apart.

PESTS & DISEASES No serious problems. Deer rarely bother them.

NOTES & CULTIVARS
Chestnut oaks are differentiated from swamp chestnut oaks by their broadly elliptical leaves with glabrous undersides, yellow fall foliage, and deeply ridged and furrowed bark. Swamp chestnut oaks have obovate leaves with soft hairy undersides, crimson fall foliage, and light gray scaly bark.

Form at UGA.

top Foliage.
middle Bark.
bottom Mature form in Chattanooga.

Quercus nigra WATER OAK

Water oak is a tardily deciduous native of floodplains and bottomlands in the Southeast but occurs on upland locations as well. Water oaks are best when they are planted in open locations where they can develop an attractive form reminiscent of live oaks and pecans in orchards. On Coastal Plain sites where both water oak and southern live oak occur, the presence of water oak helps differentiate minute differences in elevation and soil drainage, since live oaks cannot tolerate poorly drained soils. Use water oak for shade along streets, walks, and parks and for stormwater detention in parking lot islands.

ZONES & ORIGIN 6b–10a. Native to bottomlands of the Southeast.

SIZE & GROWTH RATE 80'–100' tall, 60'–80' wide, medium growing.

TEXTURE & FORM Medium fine texture in leaf, but medium in winter, with a pyramidal form in youth eventually becoming broadly oval to spreading.

FOLIAGE Simple obovate to spatulate alternate leaves 2"–4" long have three rounded lobes. Leaves on young seedlings often resemble southern red or willow oaks. Fall color is nonexistent, with some leaves remaining green into January. A smooth gray bark in youth eventually develops shallow ridges and furrows.

FLOWERS Insignificant flowers.

FRUIT Round acorns are approximately ½" long, with a cap covering a quarter of the nut.

LIGHT & SOIL Full sun to light shade with a moist to well-drained soil. It tolerates drought and soils that are wet for much of the dormant season.

MAINTENANCE Water oaks are messy, with leaves falling from September into January, large numbers of acorns each year that fall over an extended period of time, and numerous seedlings in ground cover and shrub beds.

INSTALLATION While water oak transplants well, many nurseries carry only container-grown trees. It takes searching to find large field-grown trees. Plant 50'–60' apart.

PESTS & DISEASES Water oaks are somewhat short-lived, typically 60 to 80 years. They are prone to storm damage, which provides entry to numerous insects and fungi. They are a common host for mistletoe.

NOTES & CULTIVARS
No cultivars are available.

Foliage.

top left Form at Reinhardt University, Waleska, Ga.

bottom left Mature form at Reinhardt University.

right Young trees on the UGA campus.

left Lower branches droop, middle remain level, and upper ascend on the UGA campus.
middle In Brooklyn, N.Y.
right In an Athens neighborhood.

Quercus palustris PIN OAK

Pin oak is one of the most heavily planted oaks in the eastern United States. Its ease of transplanting, somewhat formal canopy, tolerance to wet and compacted soils, and good fall color have made it a popular choice for urban and residential streets, as well as urban parks and plazas. It is one of the easier red oaks to identify due to its lower branches angling toward the ground, while the middle branches are held horizontal, and the upper branches ascend upward from the trunk.

ZONES & ORIGIN 5a–8a. Native to bottomlands of the Ohio and mid–Mississippi River basins.

SIZE & GROWTH RATE 60'–80' tall, 30'–50' wide, medium growing.

TEXTURE & FORM Medium fine texture and upright oval to oval form.

FOLIAGE Simple lustrous green alternate leaves 3"–7" long have usually five but occasionally seven bristle-tipped lobes with deep U-shaped sinuses, truncate bases, tapering acuminate tips, and reddish-brown to crimson fall color.

FLOWERS Insignificant flowers.

FRUIT Rounded acorns ½" long with flattened tops have caps covering about a quarter of the nut. The small acorns are valued by wildlife managers for migrating waterfowl.

LIGHT & SOIL Provide full sun with a moist to moist but well-drained moderately acidic soil. Established trees tolerate extended flooding during winter but are extremely sensitive to higher pH soils.

MAINTENANCE Lower branches often need to be removed to allow vehicle and pedestrian movement beneath the tree. On younger trees, dead foliage often remains into winter, and the thin bark is susceptible to damage by lawn equipment.

INSTALLATION Select trees that nurseries have pruned to ensure only one main leader. With their fairly narrow canopy, pin oaks can be planted as close as 30'–40' apart. Newly planted trees should be allowed to acclimate before being subjected to wet soils.

PESTS & DISEASES Pin oak is particularly prone to bacterial leaf scorch, which eventually kills the tree, and develops iron chlorosis on soils with a near-neutral pH. Nuttall oak is a recommended alternative in zones 7–9.

NOTES & CULTIVARS
No cultivars available.

Foliage.

Quercus phellos WILLOW OAK

Willow oak is one of the most versatile of the large deciduous trees. It has one of the most refined appearances of any oak, and its fairly formal conical outline for the first 30 to 40 years provides an opportunity to use it for urban or residential streets, as well as for plazas or other urban environments. As it matures into a looser, less formal appearance with age, its dense canopy provides excellent shade for residences or other large open-space situations. With its ease of transplanting, wide availability, fairly fast growth rate, and adaptability to a variety of sites, willow oak should be on everyone's short list of potential shade trees.

ZONES & ORIGIN 5a–8b. Native to bottomlands from New Jersey to Texas.

SIZE & GROWTH RATE 70'–100' tall, 50'–70' wide, medium growing.

TEXTURE & FORM Medium fine texture, pyramidal form in youth but broadly oval with age.

FOLIAGE Simple alternate leaves 2"–5" long are linear-lanceolate in shape with a fairly good yellow late fall color. Thin, silvery-gray bark develops shallow furrows and flattened ridges.

FLOWERS Insignificant flowers.

FRUIT Rounded acorns ½" long have caps covering about a third of the nut. The small acorns are a valued food source for small rodents and waterfowl.

LIGHT & SOIL Full sun to light shade and moist but well-drained moderately acidic soil are ideal. Unlike other bottomland oaks, willow oak doesn't tolerate flooded soils but becomes drought tolerant with age and is very tolerant of salt spray.

MAINTENANCE Willow oaks produce dense canopies when young and don't clean themselves well, so some pruning may be required to remove dead branches and thin the canopy. The fall foliage drops over a short time period and is easily removed.

INSTALLATION Large, field-grown trees transplant easily. For street and sidewalks, space 40'–50' apart.

PESTS & DISEASES No serious problems.

NOTES & CULTIVARS
Many nurseries grow willow oaks from seed.
'Hightower' is the most available cultivar with a consistent canopy.
'Shiraz' produces crimson fall foliage.

top Foliage.
middle Young tree form in Atlanta.
bottom Young tree form on the UGA campus.
right Mature form and fall color.

Young tree in the Founders Memorial Garden.

Quercus rubra NORTHERN RED OAK

Northern red oak is an excellent choice for a shade tree in large open spaces, yards, and urban areas. One of the faster-growing oaks, it is valued for its dense symmetrical crown, which can provide heavy shade. While the tree is widely promoted for red fall foliage, fall color in the Southeast is only fair at best, since this tree is better adapted to cooler regions than to the heat and droughts of southeastern summers. The lumber is valued for furniture, flooring, and cabinets.

ZONES & ORIGIN 3b–8a. Native to cool moist slopes of eastern North America.

SIZE & GROWTH RATE 70'–100' tall, 50'–70' wide, medium growing.

TEXTURE & FORM Medium coarse texture and broadly oval to rounded form.

FOLIAGE Simple dark dull green obovate leaves 5"–9" long have seven to eleven bristle-tipped lobes, with the upper lobes pointing toward the tip, and sinuses extending less than halfway to the midrib. Reddish-brown sharply pointed buds aid in identification. Fall foliage is a fair yellow orange to reddish brown in the South. A gray bark develops wide flattened ridges with shallow furrows.

FLOWERS Insignificant flowers.

FRUIT Rounded acorns ¾" long have streaks along their length and shallow turban-like caps covering a quarter of the nut. Acorns provide food for many insect and wildlife species.

LIGHT & SOIL Full sun to light shade and a moist but well-drained fairly acidic soil are ideal. It reportedly tolerates salt spray.

MAINTENANCE Northern red oak develops iron chlorosis with pH levels above 6. Trees in full sun near sidewalks or drives may require the removal of some lower branches.

INSTALLATION Trees up to 6" in caliper are available and easily transplanted successfully. Space at least 50' apart.

PESTS & DISEASES Oak wilt is a deadly fungal disease of forest trees but is rare in landscapes. Deer nibble small trees.

NOTES & CULTIVARS Sometimes listed by nurseries as *Quercus borealis* and confused with black oak, but black oak buds are large, angled, hairy, and tan to light gray, while northern red has smaller reddish-brown sharply pointed buds.

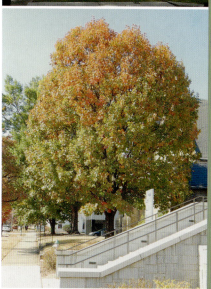

top Foliage.
middle Young tree form.
bottom Same tree with fall color.

top Foliage.
middle Young tree form at the Wray Nicholson House on the UGA campus.
bottom Fall color.

Mature tree form on the UGA Health Sciences campus.

Quercus shumardii SHUMARD OAK

Shumard oak is often considered as the southern equivalent of the pin oak. Both trees grow in bottomland areas, are easily transplanted, and need full sun. Like pin oak, Shumard oak is a fairly fast grower among the oaks, with the potential to provide good fall foliage, although it doesn't always meet expectations. Important differences are Shumard's tolerance of near-neutral soil pH levels and an inability to survive prolonged wet or flooded soils. While not as distinctive in form as pin oak, Shumard is generally a better choice for much of the Southeast due to its tolerance of warmer climates.

ZONES & ORIGIN 5b–9b. Native to well-drained bottomlands from northern Florida to Indiana.

SIZE & GROWTH RATE 60'–80' tall, 40' by 60' wide, medium growing.

TEXTURE & FORM Medium texture and oval to broadly oval form.

FOLIAGE Simple lustrous green alternate leaves 4"–8" long have five to nine lobes with many bristles and sinuses extending over halfway to the midrib. Prominent tan tufts of hairs in the vein axils beneath help in identification. Tan to gray buds are short and sharply pointed. Fall foliage varies greatly with individual genetics from a poor yellow to an outstanding red.

FLOWERS Insignificant flowers.

FRUIT Broadly oval acorns 1" long have shallow turban-like caps covering less than a quarter of the nut.

LIGHT & SOIL Full sun with moist but well-drained slightly acidic soil is ideal. It tolerates near-neutral pH soils, moderate salt spray, and drought with establishment.

MAINTENANCE Like many oaks, the acorns may cause problems on sidewalks or highly maintained lawns.

INSTALLATION Large field-grown trees are fairly available and easily transplanted. For streets and sidewalks, space 50' on center.

PESTS & DISEASES While susceptible to numerous insects and fungal diseases, trees in good cultural conditions have few issues. Deer eat young seedlings.

NOTES & CULTIVARS Many nurseries grow Shumards from seed, so cultivars are rarely available. Select Trees nursery lists 'Panache' and 'Prominence' with consistent canopies and orange to red fall foliage.

Quercus stellata POST OAK

Post oak is a good indicator tree of well-drained soils in the Southeast. Found on dry ridgetops and slopes with western or southern exposure, post oak is usually associated with species such as black and chestnut oaks and mockernut hickory. Mature trees in open sun produce a dense canopy and outstanding shade. Although rarely used in the landscape industry due to their slow growth, post oaks are worthy of maintaining on construction sites by limiting earthwork and soil compaction beneath their canopy. Their decay-resistant wood was used for fenceposts, hence the common name.

Foliage

ZONES & ORIGIN 6a–9a. Native to well-drained uplands from Texas to Pennsylvania.

SIZE & GROWTH RATE 60'–80' tall, 40'–60' wide, slow growing.

TEXTURE & FORM Coarse texture, upright oval form in youth, broadly oval with age.

FOLIAGE Simple leathery dark glossy green alternate leaves 5"–8" long are mostly obovate in shape, with three to five lobes providing a cross-like shape. Undersides of young leaves have a dense, mustard-colored mat of hairs that disappears by late summer. Reddish-brown buds are short and rounded. Fall foliage is only a fair orange yellow on mature trees, though younger trees may show some crimson. A light gray scaly bark is typical of the native white oak group.

FLOWERS Insignificant flowers.

FRUIT Rounded acorns are approximately ¾" long with caps covering about half of the nut. While the acorns are valued by wildlife, post oak rarely produces abundant crops.

LIGHT & SOIL Full sun with a well-drained soil. Trees tolerate some salt spray and are quite drought tolerant.

MAINTENANCE Dead leaves on young trees remain through winter, falling during early spring.

INSTALLATION Post oaks are rarely listed by nurseries. Those that do grow them from seed provide trees that top out at 6'–8' tall in 15-gallon containers. Plant during the dormant season and ensure good surface drainage away from the tree at planting.

PESTS & DISEASES Trees are long-lived with few serious pest problems.

NOTES & CULTIVARS
No cultivars available.

Foliage at the Founders Memorial Garden, at a Chattanooga residence, and at the Martha Berry Estate, Rome, Ga.

top Foliage.
middle Fall color on the UGA campus.
bottom left Young tree form
right Fall color on the UGA Health Sciences Campus.

Quercus texana NUTTALL OAK

The popularity of Nuttall oak has exploded in recent years as more designers and nurseries become familiar with the toughness and ease of transplanting of this formerly somewhat obscure tree. It provides an excellent alternative for many situations in which pin or Shumard oak might have been considered in the past. Its tolerance of southern summer heat, ability to tolerate the slightly higher soil pH levels frequently found in urban situations, and superior fall foliage color compared to Shumard and pin oaks have all contributed to its surge in popularity. Utilize its upright form for urban sidewalks, yards and parks, and any locations that may be wet in winter and dry in summer.

ZONES & ORIGIN 6b–9a. Native to the lower Mississippi River basin.

SIZE & GROWTH RATE 50'–70' tall, 30'–50' wide, medium fast growing.

TEXTURE & FORM Medium texture and oval to broadly oval form.

FOLIAGE Simple dark dull green leaves 4"–8" long have five to nine, usually seven, bristle-tipped lobes, irregular sinuses, and tapering bases. New spring growth has a reddish tint, while fall color ranges from yellow orange to deep red. A smooth gray bark in youth develops shallow furrows and flattened ridges with orange streaks with age.

FLOWERS Insignificant flowers.

FRUIT Egg-shaped acorns are approximately 1" long, with goblet-shaped caps covering about a third of the nut. Heavy crops are produced annually, providing food for rodents, turkeys, wild hogs, and waterfowl.

LIGHT & SOIL Full sun with wet to well-drained soils. They tolerate flooding and drought, as well as near-neutral pH soils, but don't like shade.

MAINTENANCE Like those of many oaks, the acorns can present problems in highly maintained landscapes. However, unlike many other oaks, the tree drops its leaves over a relatively short time period in autumn.

INSTALLATION Field-grown trees are widely available and easily transplanted successfully. For street trees, space 40'–50' apart.

PESTS & DISEASES No serious problems.

NOTES & CULTIVARS
'Arcade' and 'Sangria' have burgundy spring foliage and yellow-orange fall color.
'Highpoint' provides a more consistent canopy with upswept branches.

Quercus velutina BLACK OAK

Black oaks are native upland trees often associated with post, chestnut, and scarlet oaks on upland sites. They are one of the most widespread oaks, behind only white and northern red oaks in their distribution. While valued for its lumber and providing an important wildlife food source, black oak is rarely considered for landscape applications because of its slow growth and the difficulty in successfully transplanting larger trees. The lack of outstanding fall foliage, the tree's coarse nature, and an inconsistent form further limit its value in designs. Designers should consider protecting mature trees on construction sites to provide shade.

ZONES & ORIGIN 4b–8b. Native to well-drained uplands across the eastern United States.

SIZE & GROWTH RATE 60'–80' tall, 40'–60' wide, slow growing. Trees may only reach 50'–60' tall on dry sites.

TEXTURE & FORM Coarse texture and upright oval form in youth, broadly oval with age.

FOLIAGE Simple lustrous dark green alternate leaves 5"–10" long have seven, occasionally five or nine, bristle-tipped lobes with irregular sinuses cut about halfway to the midrib; the lobes are densely pubescent beneath. Fall color is a poor yellow brown. Tan to light gray terminal buds ¼"–½" long with five angled sides are the largest of the red oaks. Dark gray to nearly black bark has chunky ridges and deep furrows.

FLOWERS Insignificant flowers.

FRUIT Rounded acorns ½"–¾" long have coarsely scaled caps covering nearly half the nut and are eaten by small rodents, deer, and turkeys.

LIGHT & SOIL Full sun to moderate shade and moist but well-drained moderately acidic soil are preferred. It tolerates drought and near-neutral pH soils.

MAINTENANCE Like those of many oaks, the acorns and large leaves require additional attention in highly maintained landscapes.

INSTALLATION Some specialty nurseries grow them from seed in containers. Plant during the dormant season in sunny locations.

PESTS & DISEASES Oak wilt is a deadly fungal disease of red oaks stressed by excessive drought or damage to the root system from earthwork. Deer don't bother them.

NOTES & CULTIVARS
No cultivars are available.

top left Foliage.

top middle Mature tree bark.

top right View behind a red maple in Chattanooga.

bottom Tree on a woodland edge in Athens.

left At the Castle, Beaufort, S.C.

top right Oak allée at Belfair Plantation near Hilton Head, S.C.

bottom right Young tree form at the Georgia State Botanical Garden.

Foliage.

Quercus virginiana LIVE OAK

The state tree of Georgia is probably the most widely recognized tree of the Southeast. Its dense canopy and spreading form with massive branches reaching down to the ground draped by Spanish moss have formed one of the most lasting natural images of the South. Live oak is a long-lived species that can withstand the destructive damage of hurricanes while surrounding trees are shattered. It makes an outstanding shade tree in zones 8–10 for yards, campuses, parking lots, and boulevards. Get your hammock and swing ready.

ZONES & ORIGIN 7b–11a. Native to maritime forests from Texas to Virginia.

SIZE & GROWTH RATE 40'–80' tall, 60'–100' wide, medium growing.

TEXTURE & FORM Medium fine texture and rounded form in youth become medium coarse and spreading with age.

FOLIAGE Leathery dark green simple leaves 1½"–4" long are elliptic shaped with mostly entire margins. Leaves on seedlings may have sharply serrate margins resembling hollies. A dark gray to black bark is deeply furrowed and becomes chunky. Often considered evergreen, the trees actually drop their leaves in late winter, with new foliage emerging soon after.

FLOWERS Insignificant flowers.

FRUIT Narrowly oblong acorns ¾"–1" long with caps covering about a third of the nut are held on long stems and provided food for Native Americans and many wildlife species.

LIGHT & SOIL Full sun to light shade with a moist but well-drained acidic soil is ideal. It tolerates heavy salt spray, moderate shade, and drought but not wet soils.

MAINTENANCE Mature trees produce numerous seedlings in shrub and ground cover beds. Leaves fall in late winter and early spring.

INSTALLATION Large field-grown trees are readily available and easily transplanted. For a cathedral-like effect, plant approximately 50' apart.

PESTS & DISEASES Oak wilt disease causes problems in Texas but is rare in other parts of the Southeast.

NOTES & CULTIVARS

'Boardwalk' and 'Park Side' provide consistently broadly oval to spreading forms.

'Cathedral' is broadly pyramidal in youth, maturing to a broadly oval form.

'High Rise' is narrowly pyramidal in youth, maturing to an oval form.

Taxodium distichum BALD CYPRESS

If live oak is the most recognized tree in the Southeast, bald cypress is a close second. This long-lived deciduous conifer, the state tree of Louisiana, frequents wetlands, where it can become massive in size. Its ability to tolerate both wet and dry conditions favors its use for wetland restorations and stormwater basins, while its pyramidal form is attractive for formal designs and allées. Trees were once heavily timbered for their soft decay-resistant heartwood.

ZONES & ORIGIN 5a–10b. Native to wetlands of the Coastal Plain and mid–Mississippi River basin.

SIZE & GROWTH RATE 80'–100' tall, 30'–50' wide, medium growing.

TEXTURE & FORM Fine texture and strongly pyramidal form with horizontal branching.

FOLIAGE Feathery bright green foliage on short spirally arranged lanceolate branchlets approximately 1" long turn reddish brown in autumn. Light gray bark has shallow furrows with flattened exfoliating ridges, revealing cinnamon-colored inner bark.

FLOWERS Insignificant flowers.

FRUIT Small rounded bluish-green cones appear in midsummer before turning brown in autumn.

LIGHT & SOIL Full sun to light shade with moist to well-drained slightly acidic soil is ideal. Established trees tolerate wet soils, drought, and light salt spray.

MAINTENANCE Trees near pavements may require removal of lower branches to allow circulation beneath. Trees develop a buttressed base and in moist to wet soils develop knees 2'–8' tall around the tree.

INSTALLATION Although established trees tolerate several months of inundation, field-grown trees should be acclimated by planting them on mounds slightly above water level. Seedling and container trees can be planted in shallow standing water. For allées, plant on 40' centers.

PESTS & DISEASES No serious diseases. The nutria, a large South American rodent, destroys seedlings in wetlands in zones 9 and 10.

NOTES & CULTIVARS
'Autumn Gold' has a denser, narrower canopy.
'Cascade Falls' reaches 20' with a weeping habit.
'Monarch of Illinois' displays a broadly oval form.
'Shawnee Brave' has a columnar form.
Pond cypress, *Taxodium ascendens*, has scalelike leaves clasping the branchlets. It shares many similar traits but is generally smaller and not as common in nurseries.

top Foliage and cones.

bottom Bald cypress knees in a swamp at Magnolia Plantation and Gardens near Charleston, S.C.

top An allée at Longwood Gardens.

bottom Fall foliage on the UGA campus.

Ulmus alata WINGED ELM

top Foliage.
middle Fall color in Athens.
bottom On Hill Street in Athens.

Winged elm is a native tree found primarily on well-drained uplands but occasionally on better-drained bottomlands. It has the potential to develop an attractive form similar to that of the American elm but often displays an irregular branching habit, with some branching bending downward. It often aggressively occupies abandoned upland sites and has extremely heavy and dense wood that is difficult to split.

ZONES & ORIGIN 6a–9b. Native from Florida and Texas to southern Illinois.

SIZE & GROWTH RATE 50'–80' tall, 30'–50' wide, medium fast growing.

TEXTURE & FORM Medium fine texture and oval form.

FOLIAGE Simple ovate to elliptical alternate leaves 1½"–2½" long have doubly serrate margins and slightly asymmetrical bases and are occasionally scabrous on the upper surface. Fall color is usually a poor yellow, with leaves often falling early before developing color. Corky ridges are common on young, fast-growing stems. A light gray bark has shallow furrows and scaly ridges.

FLOWERS Insignificant.

FRUIT Insignificant early spring samaras.

LIGHT & SOIL Full sun to light shade and well-drained soils are ideal. It tolerates higher pH levels and drought.

MAINTENANCE Mature trees constantly drop twigs and branches.

INSTALLATION Small container or field-grown trees should be spaced 40'–50' apart in late fall and winter.

PESTS & DISEASES Native elms are prone to a number of fungal diseases and a range of leaf-eating and bark-boring insects that cause unsightly foliage, early defoliation, or death. The most devastating diseases are Dutch elm disease, verticillium wilt, and phloem necrosis. While winged elm is more resistant than American elm to Dutch elm disease, careful monitoring of existing trees and disposal of infected trees are essential.

NOTES & CULTIVARS

Trees are extremely rare in nurseries, with no cultivars listed.

Rock elm, *Ulmus thomasii*, is another native elm found on well-drained uplands with limestone bedrock from Tennessee through the Great Lakes states. Hardy to zone 3a and more shade tolerant than winged elm, it can reach 60'–70' in height and also develops corky ridges on stems.

At the T. R. R. Cobb House in Athens.

left Fall foliage on the UGA campus.
middle Form at Longwood Gardens.
right Upright, arching, and branching trees.

Ulmus americana AMERICAN ELM

American elm has long been prized for its outstanding shade, fast growth, tolerance of urban conditions, and ease of transplanting. It was valued for providing a cathedral-like canopy over residential and urban streets. It became the most heavily planted urban tree in the United States until trees were devastated during the mid-1900s, when Dutch elm disease, an exotic fungus carried by bark beetles, left whole communities barren but taught us to diversify urban plantings. Disease-resistant cultivars lend hope that the stately American elm may once again arch over streets and shade our communities.

ZONES & ORIGIN 3a–9b. Native to bottomlands across eastern North America.

SIZE & GROWTH RATE 70'–100' tall, 50'–70' wide, fast growing.

TEXTURE & FORM Medium texture with upright arching branches and vase-shaped form.

FOLIAGE Simple broadly elliptic alternate leaves, 4"–6" long, have doubly serrate margins, acuminate tips, asymmetrical bases, and prominent depressed veins. Yellow fall foliage is usually poor. Mature bark is light gray and ridged and furrowed.

FLOWERS Insignificant late winter flowers.

FRUIT Insignificant early spring samaras.

LIGHT & SOIL Full sun to light shade with moist to well-drained soils. It tolerates salt spray, near-neutral pH, drought, and short periods of winter flooding.

MAINTENANCE American elm's branching structure makes trees prone to storm damage.

INSTALLATION Large field-grown trees are easily transplanted. Space 60' apart.

PESTS & DISEASES Like winged elm, a number of pests attack American elm, with symptoms ranging from early defoliation to death.

NOTES & CULTIVARS
Although Dutch elm disease never appeared as serious in the Southeast as in other regions, the use of disease-resistant cultivars is recommended.

'Jefferson' is a clone of a tree on the National Mall that reaches 60' with good resistance.
'Princeton' is the earliest and still most common cultivar with improved resistance.
'Valley Forge' exhibits the highest level of resistance.

Slippery elm, *Ulmus rubra*, is another native bottomland and lower-slope species from zones 4a–9a. Is it similar in appearance to American elm but has hairs on the undersides of the leaves and young stems and abruptly acuminate leaves.

Foliage

MEDIUM DECIDUOUS TREES

Medium sized deciduous trees are primarily used for augmentation in a design. In the wild, most of the trees in this category would be classified as woodland-edge plants. Since they typically are not tall enough or broad spreading enough to cast adequate shade for buildings, vehicles, or pedestrians, they are utilized to bring the scale of a designed space down to a more comfortable level for human interaction while displaying their own unique attributes.

For example, a number of these trees provide outstanding fall foliage. By grouping them in positions where they receive adequate sunlight and typically no more than light shade, they are able to display their foliage while blending into their surroundings for much of the remainder of the year.

And unlike their larger cousins, several of these trees provide attractive flowers that can be utilized in the design. Due to the trees' smaller height, their flowers tend to be more visible to the human eye and in a few instances even introduce some fragrance into the landscape.

Several of these trees are utilized primarily for their sculptural qualities. Unlike most large trees, which rarely have a unique form, several of these trees maintain striking outlines throughout their lifetimes. These forms may allow them to be used in tight spaces between buildings where larger-canopy trees would never fit. They can also command the attention of the viewer to a specific location in the landscape or in some instances actually be the focal point of the design themselves.

Be aware that these trees typically do not have long lifespans. Unlike many of the large deciduous trees, which may live for well over 100 years, most of these trees rarely exceed 80 years of age, and many begin to decline in vigor after 50–60 years. So utilize their attributes wisely, but be aware that they won't be around forever.

above Honey-locusts in Boston's Norman B. Leventhal Park.

BOTANICAL NAME	SUNLIGHT	SOILS	TEXTURE	NOTABLE ATTRIBUTES	FALL FOLIAGE	NATIVE TO SOUTHEAST
Acer negundo	Full sun	Moist to dry	Medium coarse	Tolerates wet and high pH soils	Poor yellow	Yes
Aesculus hippocastanum	Light to moderate shade	Moist but well drained	Coarse	Tolerates alkaline soils	Poor yellow	No, Europe
Betula nigra	Full sun to light shade	Moist to moist but well drained	Medium fine	Attractive exfoliating bark	Poor yellow	Yes
Carpinus betulus 'Fastigiata'	Full sun to light shade	Moist but well drained	Medium fine	Formal appearance	Good yellow	No, Europe
Catalpa bignonioides	Full sun to light shade	Well drained	Coarse	Showy white spring flowers	Poor yellow	Yes
Cercidiphyllum japonicum	Full sun to light shade	Moist but well drained	Medium fine	Formal appearance	Great yellow to orange	No, Asia
Cladrastis kentukea	Light to moderate shade	Moist but well drained	Medium	Showy white spring flowers	Great bright yellow	Yes
Diospyros virginiana	Full sun to moderate shade	Moist to well drained	Medium	Salt, drought, and pH tolerant	Fair yellow orange to red	Yes
Gleditsia triacanthos inermis	Full sun to light shade	Moist to moist but well drained	Fine	Salt spray and pH tolerant	Poor	Yes
Maclura pomifera	Full sun to light shade	Well drained	Medium coarse	Some salt and pH tolerance	Fair yellow	No, southern plains states
Magnolia macrophylla	Full sun to moderate shade	Moist but well drained	Coarse	Exotic texture, fragrant flowers	Fair bright yellow	Yes
Nyssa sylvatica	Full sun to light shade	Moist to well drained	Medium	Drought and salt tolerant	Outstanding red to crimson	Yes
Ostrya virginiana	Full sun to full shade	Moist to dry	Medium	Drought and pH tolerant	Poor yellow to yellow brown	Yes
Oxydendrum arboreum	Full sun to moderate shade	Well drained	Medium	Attractive early summer flowers	Outstanding orange to red	Yes
Pistacia chinensis	Full sun	Well drained	Medium fine	Drought and pH tolerant	Outstanding orange to red	No, Asia
Prunus serotina	Full sun to light shade	Moist but well drained	Medium	Wildlife food source	Fair yellow to red	Yes
Quercus robur 'Fastigiata'	Full sun	Moist but well drained	Medium	Columnar form, pH, salt tolerant	Poor yellow	No, Europe
Robinia pseudoacacia	Full sun	Well drained	Medium fine	Fragrant flowers, pH, salt tolerant	None	Yes
Salix babylonica	Full sun	Wet to moist but well drained	Fine	Restful, pendulous form	None	No, Europe and Asia
Salix nigra	Full sun	Wet to moist but well drained	Fine	Wetland restoration	None	Yes
Sassafras albidum	Full sun to light shade	Moist but well drained	Medium	Wildlife food source	Outstanding red to orange	Yes
Tilia cordata	Full sun to light shade	Moist but well drained	Medium	Tolerates slightly alkaline	Good yellow	No, native to Europe
Ulmus pumila	Full sun	Well drained	Medium coarse	Salt spray and pH tolerant	None	No, Asia
Zelkova serrata	Full sun to light shade	Moist but well drained	Medium	Drought and pH tolerant	Fair yellow to crimson	No, Native to Asia

Acer negundo BOXELDER

Boxelder is a fast-growing early successional floodplain species. Mature trees are somewhat unsightly in appearance. As a result, it is more often used for streambank stabilizations than as an ornamental in the Southeast. Western states take advantage of its toughness for urban plantings and shelterbelts.

ZONES & ORIGIN 3a–9a. Native to the eastern and midwestern United States.

SIZE & GROWTH RATE 40'–60' tall, 30'–50' wide, and fast growing.

TEXTURE & FORM Medium coarse texture and broadly oval form.

FOLIAGE Opposite pinnately compound leaves have mostly five but occasionally three or seven leaflets. Seedlings are often mistaken for poison ivy. Yellow-green leaflets 2"–4" long are ovate shaped with coarsely serrate margins. Fall color is nonexistent. Light gray bark is shallowly ridged and furrowed.

LIGHT & SOIL Full sun with a moist to dry soil. It tolerates drought and alkaline soils.

MAINTENANCE Boxelder is short-lived, with brittle wood that breaks easily in storms and a surface root system that makes it difficult to grow other plants beneath it. Numerous seedlings invade shrub and ground cover beds and unmaintained alleys and roadsides.

NOTES & CULTIVARS Boxelder is dioecious and lacks showy flowers. Female trees produce many unsightly late spring samaras, which remain into winter.

Foliage.

Early fall foliage in a wooded edge.

left Foliage and fruit.

right Late spring flowers at J. F. Kennedy Park, Cambridge, Mass.

Aesculus hippocastanum HORSECHESTNUT

Horsechestnut is not well adapted to the southeastern summer heat but is valued for its showy flowers, form, and fall color in cooler climates. It produces showy white panicles of late spring flowers and remains low-branched for many years.

ZONES & ORIGIN 4a–8a. Native to southeastern Europe.

SIZE & GROWTH RATE 50'–70' tall, 30'–50' wide, medium slow growing.

TEXTURE & FORM Coarse texture with an oval form.

FOLIAGE Oppositely arranged palmately compound leaves have seven obovate leaflets with prominent depressed veins, doubly serrate margins, and dense hairs on the petiole and midribs. Prominent brown midsummer buds are covered with a sticky syrup-like substance. Yellow fall foliage in cooler climates is lacking in the Southeast.

LIGHT & SOIL Horsechestnut prefers light to moderate shade and moist but well-drained soils, but it tolerates alkaline soils.

MAINTENANCE Rounded golf ball–sized nuts with spiny husks can turn ankles or dent cars.

NOTES & CULTIVARS
'Baumannii' has pinkish-white double flowers. Yellow buckeye, *Aesculus flava*, is a shade-tolerant native of the Appalachian Mountains, where it reaches 80' tall with prominent yellow flowers in moist coves. Ohio buckeye, *Aesculus glabra*, is native to bottomlands from Tennessee to the Great Lakes and reaches 30'–50' tall.

Betula nigra RIVER BIRCH

The attractive exfoliating bark, fine texture, upright form, and multitrunked character of young river birch make them best appreciated up close. A light open canopy allows dappled sunlight to reach the ground. Consider them for courtyards, patios, and walkways with decorative lighting to highlight their assets. Unfortunately, they have a relatively short time span in which their attributes are assets in the landscape. The exfoliating bark occurs on relatively young trunks and branches, but as the trees reach 20 to 30 years old, the bark becomes ridged and furrowed.

top Exfoliating bark on young trees.

middle A residential entry court with Asian jasmine.

bottom River birch allée at Gibbs Gardens near Atlanta.

ZONES & ORIGIN 3b–9a. Native to sandy streambanks of the Southeast.

SIZE & GROWTH RATE 40'–60' tall, 30–50' wide, medium fast growing.

TEXTURE & FORM Medium fine texture with a pyramidal form in youth, becoming broadly oval.

FOLIAGE Medium green simple alternate leaves are 1½"–3" long and triangular-ovate shaped with doubly serrate margins. Yellow fall foliage is poor. Young trunks and limbs have exfoliating bark and pinkish-tan inner bark.

FLOWERS Insignificant early spring flowers.

FRUIT Insignificant nutlet.

LIGHT & SOIL Full sun to light shade and moist to moist but well-drained acidic soils. It tolerates some dormant-season flooding but is not very drought tolerant until well established.

MAINTENANCE Weak wood is easily damaged in storms. Surface roots make it difficult to grow other plants beneath mature trees and may cause pavement buckling. Leaves fall for an extended period in autumn.

INSTALLATION Field-grown trees are easily transplanted in large sizes. For a continuous canopy, plant 30'–40' on center. For stream restorations or stormwater retention areas, trees should be acclimated to moist soils or planted slightly higher than expected water levels.

PESTS & DISEASES Typical lifespan is about 60 years, with numerous pests that can defoliate trees and shorten that time unless the tree is well sited and maintained.

NOTES & CULTIVARS
Native trees are single trunked, but nurseries often plant several trees together to provide multiple trunks.
'Heritage' is the most common cultivar, with dark green foliage, fast growth, and improved drought resistance.
'Dura Heat' has improved heat tolerance and a denser canopy.

Form at Callaway Gardens, Pine Mountain, Ga.

MEDIUM DECIDUOUS TREES

Carpinus betulus
'FASTIGIATA' · UPRIGHT EUROPEAN HORNBEAM

For someone looking for a tree with a formal symmetrical appearance and dependable fall foliage, the upright European hornbeam could be an excellent selection. Although it doesn't provide showy flowers, the upright hornbeam offers a form similar to 'Aristocrat' and 'Cleveland' Callery pears but without their invasive nature. It develops an upright habit, with low branching and a dense canopy, making it a good choice for formal allées, and trees can be planted close together and pruned into tall hedges or for agricultural windbreaks. Tolerant of urban conditions, it is a good choice for tight spaces around buildings or for street tree plantings where overhanging branches of other trees might be damaged by large trucks. Consider it for an accent plant in residential compositions.

Foliage and buds.

ZONES & ORIGIN 5a–8a. Native to southern Europe.

SIZE & GROWTH RATE 30'–50' tall, 10'–25' wide, medium slow growing.

TEXTURE & FORM Medium fine texture with a pyramidal to upright oval form.

FOLIAGE Simple alternately arranged dark green leaves are 2"–3½" long, with an ovate shape and finely doubly serrate margins. Leaves have prominently depressed veins and develop a good yellow color in late autumn; the tree often holds leaves into mid-December. Bark is a smooth gray.

FLOWERS Insignificant.

FRUIT Insignificant nutlets, which may not occur in southeastern states.

LIGHT & SOIL Full sun to moderate shade and a moist but well-drained soil. It tolerates drought, as well as near-neutral to slightly alkaline soils.

MAINTENANCE Leaves fall late in the year after most other trees, but the foliage is easily collected by blowing or raking and decomposes readily.

INSTALLATION Trees up to 14'–16' tall are successfully transplanted in late winter or early spring. Provide supplemental water for the first summer during prolonged droughts. Plant 20' on center for a continuous canopy.

PESTS & DISEASES No serious problems have been reported.

NOTES & CULTIVARS
'Cornerstone' provides an oval to broadly oval form.
'Frans Fontaine' provides a narrower, more upright form.
'Pyramidalis' is another name used for 'Fastigiata'.

left Form in downtown Vancouver, B.C.
middle Form in Portland, Ore.
right Late fall foliage at UGA.

Foliage and flowers.

Catalpa bignonioides SOUTHERN CATALPA

Catalpas are among the most overlooked native trees in the nursery industry. Their bold heart-shaped foliage provides an exotic tropical appearance. Combine that with their showy white spring flowers, and you have a tree that really stands out in the landscape. With a messy character and a tendency to inhibit other plants from growing beneath their canopies, catalpas are best utilized along woodland edges or large open spaces.

ZONES & ORIGIN 5a–9b. Native to lower elevations of the Southeast.

SIZE & GROWTH RATE 30'–50' tall and wide, medium fast growing.

TEXTURE & FORM Coarse texture with a broadly oval form.

FOLIAGE Simple ovate to cordate leaves are 6"–12" long, with entire margins and acuminate tips. The yellow-green leaves have an opposite or whorled arrangement. Fall color is insignificant. Gray bark is shallowly ridged and furrowed.

FLOWERS Lightly fragrant showy white tubular-shaped flowers occur on terminal panicles in mid- to late spring. In Athens, flowering typically occurs for seven to ten days in early to mid-May.

FRUIT Narrow bright green capsules 8"–15" long resembling large bean pods are visible from late spring to autumn, when they mature into an unsightly brown and often remain into winter.

LIGHT & SOIL Full sun to light shade with a moist to moist but well-drained slightly acidic to near-neutral pH soil.

MAINTENANCE Catalpas are messy, dropping spent flowers, foliage, dead twigs, and capsules.

INSTALLATION Young container or bare-root trees are easily transplanted but difficult to find in commercial nurseries.

PESTS & DISEASES Catalpa sphinx moth caterpillar consumes the foliage in late spring. The caterpillar, grown commercially for fish bait, can defoliate the tree, but catalpas can sprout new leaves. Repeated defoliations over several successive years can cause dieback and death.

NOTES & CULTIVARS
Northern catalpa, *Catalpa speciosa*, is also native, growing from zones 4b–9b. Similar in appearance, it is slightly larger (40'–60' in height), with a broadly oval form, moderate salt spray tolerance, and late May flowers. While neither species is widely grown in nurseries, both deserve consideration.

top Foliage and fruit.

middle Late spring flowers in Athens.

bottom Late spring flowers with Siberian iris and switchgrass at Chanticleer.

Cercidiphyllum japonicum KATSURA TREE

Katsura is a graceful tree that offers a number of attributes for consideration. A pyramidal form in youth gradually becomes upright oval in light shade or broadly oval in sun. A very clean neat demeanor with highly attractive fall foliage, medium fine texture, and a low-branching habit make it suitable for intimate designs, as well as for larger spaces. Katsuras tend to perform better in cooler climates but will perform well in the Southeast with proper attention.

left Weeping katsura at the Vince Dooley residence in Athens.

top right Mature form at Longwood Gardens parking lot.

middle Foliage.

bottom Form at the Bloedel Reserve, Bainbridge Island, Wash.

ZONES & ORIGIN 5a–8a. Native to Asia.

SIZE & GROWTH RATE 40'–60' tall, 20'–40' wide, medium growing.

TEXTURE & FORM Medium fine texture. Pyramidal in youth, variable form with maturity.

FOLIAGE Simple opposite cordate-shaped leaves are 2"–4" long with crenate-serrate margins. Young leaves emerge reddish purple in spring before maturing to blue-green with silvery undersides. Fall foliage is an excellent yellow to orange red. A smooth bark in youth develops shallow furrows and peeling ridges with maturity.

FLOWERS Dioecious, with insignificant flowers.

FRUIT Insignificant.

LIGHT & SOIL Full sun to light shade with a consistently moist but well-drained acidic to near-neutral pH soil.

MAINTENANCE Young trees suffer from prolonged summer droughts and may require supplemental water for several years after planting. Surface roots can cause problems with pavements and plantings.

Katsura is available as either a single or multitrunked tree, with a natural tendency to be multitrunked with ascending branches. Care should be taken to make sure that all branches have a strong connection to the trunk to avoid storm damage.

INSTALLATION Container and field-grown trees are successfully transplanted in late winter and early spring. They are perhaps best sited near ponds or streams, where their roots can eventually grow into soils that provide consistent moisture during the summer. Space as close as 30' on center.

PESTS & DISEASES No serious problems.

NOTES & CULTIVARS
'Pendulum' is a weeping form reaching 15'–25' tall with an equal or greater spread and is an excellent choice for locations that can be viewed up close.

Cladrastis kentukea YELLOWWOOD

Yellowwood is a somewhat rare understory tree found in cool moist coves of mature forests from North Carolina to Missouri that deserves much greater use in the landscape. It is a clean neat tree that typically doesn't create a lot of seedlings beneath and is adaptable to a wide range of conditions, except for prolonged summer droughts. Yellowwood consistently provides attractive bright yellow fall foliage, and its pleasantly fragrant and showy late spring flowers are a treat in enclosed spaces. Combine them with plants that prefer similar cultural conditions, such as boxwoods, ferns, and pachysandras.

ZONES & ORIGIN 4b–8b. Native to the Southeast.

SIZE & GROWTH RATE 35'–50' tall and wide, medium growth rate.

TEXTURE & FORM Medium texture and rounded form.

FOLIAGE Pinnately compound alternate leaves have seven (rarely five or nine) oval to obovate leaflets with entire margins. It has a smooth gray bark and bright yellow fall foliage.

FLOWERS Pendulous panicles of showy and lightly fragrant flowers 12"–20" long occur in mid- to late spring (late April and early May in Athens). Heavy flowering occurs about every three years, with only sporadic flowering between.

FRUIT Flattened light green bean pods 2"–4" long appear in late spring and remain into winter.

LIGHT & SOIL Light to moderate shade with a moist but well-drained near-neutral pH soil is ideal. Unlike most legumes, yellowwood does not have the ability to fix nitrogen in the soil.

MAINTENANCE A thin bark makes it susceptible to mechanical damage. Yellowwood benefits from supplemental water during prolonged summer droughts.

INSTALLATION Container and small field-grown trees are successfully planted in late winter and early spring. For a continuous canopy, plant 35'–40' on center.

PESTS & DISEASES Stressed trees are prone to several fungal diseases. Deer eat seedlings and young trees. Ascending branches are susceptible to damage from winter snow and ice loads.

NOTES & CULTIVARS
Yellowwood is somewhat rare in nurseries and often grown in containers or as small field-grown trees.
'Perkins Pink' produces light pink flowers and is the only cultivar commonly found.

top Foliage.

middle In bloom at Swarthmore College.

left and right Fall color in the Founders Memorial Garden.

top Midsummer foliage and fruit.
middle Mature bark on the UGA campus.
bottom Oriental persimmon at the Ram Giberson residence, Athens.

Diospyros virginiana PERSIMMON

Many people have seen a persimmon at one time or another and probably not recognized it, even though it is one of the most widespread trees throughout the Southeast. Persimmon grows on a variety of sites, from dry uplands to moist streambanks and swamp edges. It commonly occurs along fencerows and shaded woodland edges but is rarely utilized in designs. Persimmon provides fair fall foliage, while its fruit provides food for a variety of wildlife.

ZONES & ORIGIN 5a–10a. Native across the southeastern and midwestern states.

SIZE & GROWTH RATE 30'–50' tall, 20'–30' wide, medium slow growing.

TEXTURE & FORM Medium texture with an upright oval to oval form.

FOLIAGE Simple alternately arranged dark green leaves are 2"–6" long and elliptical to ovate shaped with entire margins. The leaves tend to droop during the season and develop a fair but undependable yellow-orange to red fall color. The bark is dark gray, with thick chunky blocks on mature trees that resemble an alligator's hide.

FLOWERS A dioecious species, with non-showy mid- to late spring flowers.

FRUIT Green plumlike berries turn yellow orange in midautumn. The fruit is sweet and edible after a hard frost and an excellent source of wildlife food. Immature fruits are extremely astringent. At some point, everyone should try an unripened persimmon, just for the experience.

LIGHT & SOIL Persimmon tolerates full sun to moderate shade with moist to well-drained soils. It tolerates drought, dormant-season flooding, salt spray, and alkaline soils.

MAINTENANCE Fallen fruit can be messy on pavements.

INSTALLATION Persimmon is extremely difficult to transplant successfully in larger sizes.

PESTS & DISEASES Leaf spot infections and tent caterpillars are common and can be unsightly but not serious.

NOTES & CULTIVARS
Selected cultivars are available for fruit production in containers from specialty native or fruit nurseries.
'Early Golden' and 'Wabash' are the most popular.
Oriental persimmon, *Diospyros kaki*, is hardy to 7b and reaches 15'–20' tall, with sweet apple-sized fruit. A number of cultivars are available, as well as crosses with the native persimmon.

Behind crape myrtles in an Athens office park.

Gleditsia triacanthos inermis THORNLESS HONEYLOCUST

Honeylocust is one of the most popular trees in landscape architecture. Its light airy canopy allows filtered sunlight to reach the ground, providing dappled shading to pavements, while its mature size is perfectly suited to a comfortable pedestrian scale. It is heavily planted in urban plazas and courtyards, as well as streets and sidewalks, to the point that numerous pest problems have emerged, particularly in the Southeast. Combine it judiciously with other trees to take advantage of its characteristics while providing species diversity.

top Foliage.
middle left Street trees in Seattle.
middle right Trees in Boston's Norman B. Leventhal Park.
bottom In Battery Park, New York City.

ZONES & ORIGIN 4a–9a. Native to bottomlands from Louisiana to Pennsylvania and Nebraska.

SIZE & GROWTH RATE 40'–60' tall, 30'–50' wide, medium fast growing.

TEXTURE & FORM Fine texture, broadly oval form.

FOLIAGE Odd pinnately or bipinnately compound leaves are 6"–8" long and alternately arranged. Bright yellow fall foliage is undependable in the Southeast. Gray bark develops long narrow plates at maturity.

FLOWERS Insignificant yellow-green racemes 2"–4" long occur in midspring.

FRUIT Twisted flattened bean pods 10"–18" long mature in autumn and are a favored wildlife food. Cultivars are usually fruitless.

LIGHT & SOIL Full sun with a moist to moist but well-drained soil is ideal. It tolerates salt spray, deicing salts, and alkaline soils but is susceptible to drought stress in urban environments.

MAINTENANCE To reduce the risk of fungal infections, never prune in summer or fall.

INSTALLATION Field-grown trees are easily transplanted in large sizes in the dormant season. Plant 35'–45' apart for a continuous canopy.

PESTS & DISEASES Urban trees stressed by drought are susceptible to a number of pests, including borers, which can introduce fungal cankers.

NOTES & CULTIVARS
Common cultivars are selections of northern trees and best suited for cooler climates.

'Imperial', with a rounded canopy, is susceptible to degradation from high ozone levels but resistant to fungal cankers.

'Shademaster' is broadly oval with ascending branches.

'Skyline' has a pyramidal form with ascending branches.

'Sunburst' produces yellow new foliage that fades to light green but is highly susceptible to fungal infections.

top left Fall foliage at the Wray Nicholson House.

top right Form at Chattanooga National Cemetery.

middle Foliage.

bottom Baseball-size fruit.

Maclura pomifera OSAGE ORANGE · HEDGE APPLE

Native Americans discovered such wide applications for Osage orange that it was soon carried to other regions of the country, even though it is native to only a small area of the southern plains. The hard decay-resistant wood was used for wagon wheels, fenceposts, furniture, fuel, and bows. Before barbed wire was invented, the tree was planted for windbreaks and hedgerows to take advantage of its thorny stems. While rarely used today in the Southeast, Osage orange has been planted for street trees in the midwestern and Great Plains states due to its tolerance of urban conditions, drought, and higher pH soils.

ZONES & ORIGIN 4b–9a. Native to the Red River basin of Texas and Oklahoma.

SIZE & GROWTH RATE 40'–60' tall, 30'–50' wide, fast growing in youth but medium with age.

TEXTURE & FORM Medium coarse texture with an oval to broadly oval form.

FOLIAGE Simple glossy green alternate leaves are 2"–5" long, ovate shaped, with entire margins, acuminate tips, and a milky-white sap. Yellow fall foliage is fair to poor. Young actively growing stems have prominent thorns, which are absent on older branches. A chunky gray bark reveals some orange inner bark.

FLOWERS Osage orange is dioecious, with neither sex showy.

FRUIT Female trees produce a light green grapefruit-sized round fruit resembling a small brain that matures in early autumn.

LIGHT & SOIL Full sun to light shade with a moist but well-drained soil is ideal. It tolerates moist soils, drought, alkaline soils, and some salt spray.

MAINTENANCE The heavy fruit drop over a four-to-six-week period in autumn and can easily dent cars or cause someone to turn an ankle. The shallow root system is often visible on the ground surface and often produces sprouts.

INSTALLATION Although easily transplanted, Osage orange is rare in nurseries. Bareroot or container plants are most likely to be found in midwestern and Great Plains nurseries.

PESTS & DISEASES Virtually disease free, provided the soil is well drained.

NOTES & CULTIVARS
'Wichita' is a thornless male tree but difficult to locate.

Magnolia macrophylla BIGLEAF MAGNOLIA

Bigleaf magnolia is a rare native found on cool moist woodland slopes in deep rich soils. Its bold exotic appearance is a real eye-catcher, with huge leaves that are among the largest of any North American species. It is often used to simulate tropical environments. Combine it with native ferns for woodland gardens along streams or water features.

ZONES & ORIGIN 5b–9a. Native to the southeastern United States.

SIZE & GROWTH RATE 30'–50' tall, 20'–40' wide, slow growing.

TEXTURE & FORM Coarse texture and oval to broadly oval form.

FOLIAGE Simple oblong to obovate leaves 18"–30" long with entire margins, earlike lobes at their base, and a silvery-white pubescence beneath are clustered at the ends of branches. Fall color is a poor yellow, with leaves often dropping early. Mature bark is smooth gray.

FLOWERS Lightly fragrant white flowers up to 12" in diameter open over several weeks in mid- to late spring (late April to mid-May in Athens).

FRUIT Oval cone-like fruit with rosy-red midautumn seeds is eaten by birds.

LIGHT & SOIL Light shade is ideal with a moist but well-drained acidic soil. It tolerates full sun with adequate moisture and moderate shade, but flowering is reduced in shade. Provide supplemental water during droughts.

MAINTENANCE The large leaves are damaged by late summer from falling debris punching holes in them. Fallen leaves and cones are messy in autumn.

INSTALLATION Occasionally found in specialty nurseries. Plant in late winter to early spring and provide supplemental water during droughts.

PESTS & DISEASES In spite of its slow growth, the wood is brittle and easily damaged in severe winds and ice.

NOTES & CULTIVARS
Several cultivars are reported but difficult to locate.
Fraser magnolia, *Magnolia fraseri*, is native to cool streambanks of the Appalachians and grows 30'–50' tall, with obovate leaves 10"–18" long with pronounced lobes at their bases.
Cucumber magnolia, *Magnolia acuminata*, is native to bottomlands of the eastern United States. Hardy to zone 4b, it grows 50'-80' with elliptical leaves 6"–12" long without lobes.

top to bottom

Foliage and late spring flowers.

Midautumn fruit.

In a therapeutic garden at Northeast Georgia Medical Center in Gainesville, Ga.

Form at Berkshire Botanical Garden, Stockbridge, Mass.

left SW 12th Avenue Green Street project, Portland, Ore.

middle Fall foliage in an Athens neighborhood.

right Fall foliage on the UGA campus.

Nyssa sylvatica BLACKGUM

Blackgum is a tough native tree found on a variety of sites, from moist streambanks to dry ridgetops. Rather nondescript for much of the year, except in autumn, when its highly attractive fall foliage stands out. It is one of the earliest trees to provide fall color, usually late September to mid-October in Athens. Its adaptability and toughness have made blackgum popular for yards and parks, street and sidewalk plantings, parking lots where its straight trunk and narrow canopy don't interfere with vehicles, and stormwater retention areas, since it tolerates both moist soils and drought.

Foliage and fruit.

ZONES & ORIGIN 5a–9b. Native from Florida and Texas to Michigan and Maine.

SIZE & GROWTH RATE 40'–60' tall, 20'–40' wide, medium growing.

TEXTURE & FORM Medium texture with an oval form.

FOLIAGE Simple alternate leaves are 2"–6" long, elliptical to obovate in shape, lustrous above, with entire margins and acuminate tips. Fall foliage is an outstanding orange red to scarlet or crimson in early to midautumn. It develops a strongly horizontal branching habit and tan-colored bark with shallow ridges and furrows.

FLOWERS Dioecious, with insignificant flowers valued for honey.

FRUIT Female trees produce small oval bluish-purple drupes that mature in early autumn. Though not showy, they are attractive to birds and other wildlife.

LIGHT & SOIL Full sun to light shade with a moist to well-drained soil. Blackgum tolerates moderate salt spray, drought, and moist soils with acclimation.

MAINTENANCE Fall foliage drops earlier than that of many trees. Birds eating the fruit can create messes on pavements and cars.

INSTALLATION Field-grown trees are widely available in sizes as large as 4"–5" in caliper. Transplanted trees grow slowly for several years. Plant 20'–30' on center for continuous canopies.

PESTS & DISEASES A leaf spot fungus is common and, while unsightly, doesn't cause long-term problems. Young trees are heavily grazed by deer.

NOTES & CULTIVARS
'Red Rage' has improved resistance to leaf spot fungus, dark green leaves, and outstanding red fall foliage.
'Wildfire' provides red new spring foliage.

Ostrya virginiana HOPHORNBEAM

Hophornbeam is a native understory species that occurs primarily on drier upland sites but is occasionally found on bottomland locations. While it doesn't possess any outstanding ornamental attributes, it is a tough tree that tolerates urban environments and is surprisingly long-lived. Its shade tolerance allows it to be used around tall buildings or for naturalizing in understory plantings. It is also sometimes called ironwood for its hard dense wood, which is difficult to cut.

ZONES & ORIGIN 3b–9a. Native from northern Florida to Canada.

SIZE & GROWTH RATE 25'–40' tall, 20'–30' wide, slow growing.

TEXTURE & FORM Medium texture with a pyramidal to broadly oval form.

FOLIAGE Simple alternate leaves are 2"–5" long, ovate shaped, with sharply doubly serrate margins and acuminate tips. Leaves have a rough sandpapery feel to their upper surface and are pubescent beneath. Fall foliage is a poor yellow brown. Grayish brown bark on mature trees peels in long narrow strips.

FLOWERS Insignificant early spring flowers as the leaves emerge.

FRUIT Fruits are flattened nutlets enclosed in inflated hairy sacs on structures 1"–2" long that resemble hops used in brewing operations. The hairs irritate the skin if handled. The fruit matures in early autumn and, while not showy, is interesting up close.

LIGHT & SOIL It grows in full sun to full shade and prefers moist but well-drained acidic soil, but it tolerates consistently moist soils, drought, and alkaline soils.

MAINTENANCE No special attention required.

INSTALLATION Although the tree is rare due to its slow growth and lack of outstanding visual interest, a few nurseries provide small field-grown trees, usually 2" or less in caliper. Transplant in early spring.

PESTS & DISEASES No serious problems. Deer don't like them.

NOTES & CULTIVARS

Hophornbeam is often confused with ironwood, *Carpinus caroliniana*. Both are native understory species that are similar in size with similar foliage. A good way to differentiate the two is their bark: smooth gray with muscular ridges for ironwood versus gray brown and shredding on hophornbeam. They occasionally occur together on lower slopes and floodplains, but hophornbeam also occurs on drier sites.

top Early summer foliage and flowers.
middle and bottom right Autumn foliage and fruit in downtown Athens.
bottom left Mature form at a Birmingham residence.

Oxydendrum arboreum SOURWOOD

Many people only notice sourwood on scenic autumn drives along wooded roadsides, where they observe its brilliant color and maybe stop at a roadside establishment for a jar of clear honey produced from its flowers. Its brilliant reds are among the most vivid of our native trees and cause many to overlook its attractive white early summer flowers. Rarely used in ornamental compositions due to its slow growth and reputation for being difficult to transplant, it would be an excellent addition near a patio or a perennial border, where its flowers attract butterflies and other insects.

top Foliage and late spring flowers.
middle Fall foliage and fruit capsules on the UGA campus.
bottom left Fall in the Founders Memorial Garden.
bottom right Fall color at the State Botanical Garden of Georgia.

ZONES & ORIGIN 5a–8b. Native to well-drained woods from Louisiana to Pennsylvania.

SIZE & GROWTH RATE 30'–50' tall, 20'–30' wide, slow growing.

TEXTURE & FORM Medium texture with an oval to upright oval form.

FOLIAGE Alternate simple leaves are 3"–7" long, elliptical in shape, with very finely serrate margins and a sour taste. The leaves turn an outstanding orange red to crimson in midautumn. Branches and leaves typically have a drooping habit. The bark of mature trees is gray, with chunky deep ridges and furrows.

FLOWERS Attractive and lightly fragrant small white flowers hang from drooping racemes on the ends of branches in late spring and early summer. The flowers are favored by beekeepers to produce a clear honey.

FRUIT Insignificant capsules remain on the racemes into winter and aid in identification.

LIGHT & SOIL Sourwood grows in full sun to moderate shade with a moist but well-drained acidic soil. It tolerates drought and moderate salt spray.

MAINTENANCE A very clean neat tree.

INSTALLATION Sourwood is related to mountain laurel and rhododendron and requires a strongly acidic soil pH. It has a reputation for being difficult to transplant. Best results are from using small container-grown plants from late autumn to early spring.

PESTS & DISEASES No serious problems. Deer occasionally browse young tender shoots.

NOTES & CULTIVARS
Sourwood is difficult to propagate, so only a few nurseries grow them from seed in containers or as small field-grown trees less than 2" in caliper.

Pistacia chinensis CHINESE PISTACHE

After watching the installation and subsequent establishment of Chinese pistache trees in the parking lot islands of an Athens shopping center during one of the hottest and driest summers on record, I am convinced that there is not a tougher tree available. Chinese pistache has long been valued for its outstanding fall color, even in zones 8 and 9. In recent years, it has gone from being rare in nurseries to being widely grown. A clean well-behaved tree with a rounded uniform habit that resembles a golf ball on a tee, it is an outstanding choice for urban environments, as well as for residential applications where it can shade open patios. Its uniform habit lends itself to being used in somewhat formal arrangements to line streets, driveways, or golf course fairways.

ZONES & ORIGIN 6b–10a. Native to China.

SIZE & GROWTH RATE 30'–40' tall and wide, with a medium growth rate.

TEXTURE & FORM Medium fine texture with a rounded form.

FOLIAGE Alternate pinnately compound leaves have 10–16 even-numbered leaflets. Lanceolate leaflets are dark lustrous green, with entire margins and slightly asymmetrical bases. Crushed leaflets smell like radishes. Fall foliage ranges from a good yellow orange to an outstanding scarlet red, depending upon individual genetics. Gray bark has shallow ridges and furrows, occasionally revealing a salmon-colored inner bark.

FLOWERS A dioecious species, with neither sex being showy.

FRUIT Female trees produce small pea-sized drupes on open panicles that are red in summer and mature to a purplish black in midautumn but aren't particularly showy.

LIGHT & SOIL Provide full sun and a well-drained soil. It is extremely tolerant of drought and alkaline soils.

MAINTENANCE Young trees look a little awkward and top-heavy for several years after transplanting and benefit from support until the roots become established.

INSTALLATION Field-grown trees as large as 6" in caliper are available. For a continuous canopy, plant 30'–40' apart on center. Select trees in fall to ensure good foliage color.

PESTS & DISEASES No serious problems.

NOTES & CULTIVARS
'Keith Davey' is a male tree.

top left Mature form in Athens.
top right The same tree in the fall.
middle Foliage and fruit.
bottom Fall color at Stanford University.

Prunus serotina BLACK CHERRY

Black cherry is an important native tree of woodland edges. Somewhat showy white early spring flowers produce dark red to black midsummer fruit that is popular with birds and other wildlife and used in wines, jellies, and liqueurs. The wood is valued for furniture and rifle stocks, while the inner bark is used for cough medicines.

ZONES & ORIGIN 3b–9b. Native from central Florida to southern Ontario.

SIZE & GROWTH RATE 40'–60' tall, 20'–40' wide, fast growing.

TEXTURE & FORM Medium texture with a broadly oval form.

FOLIAGE Alternate simple elliptical leaves are 2"–5" long, with serrate margins and tiny glands on the petiole at the leaf base. Yellow to red fall foliage is often poor due to early defoliation. Young bark is light gray, with prominent horizontal lenticels, but becomes darker and scaly at maturity.

LIGHT & SOIL Full sun to light shade and a moist but well-drained acidic soil.

MAINTENANCE Tent caterpillars, aphids, borers, and fungal diseases are common. Mature trees produce numerous seedlings.

NOTES & CULTIVARS Foliage contains hydrogen cyanide, which is poisonous to humans and livestock in large quantities. Deer browse the foliage with no apparent harm.

top Early spring foliage and flowers. *bottom* Early spring foliage and form.

Quercus robur 'Fastigiata' UPRIGHT ENGLISH OAK

Upright English oak is an eye-catching tree that is valued for its dense narrow canopy and that lends itself to use as an accent tree in compositions or for use in formal allées to line streets and walks. It is better suited to cooler climates such as the Pacific Northwest, where it doesn't encounter the heat and humidity of southeastern summers. It is available in 4"–5" calipers.

ZONES & ORIGIN 5b–8b. Native to Europe and northern Africa.

SIZE & GROWTH RATE 30'–50' tall, 10'–15' wide, medium slow growing.

TEXTURE & FORM Medium texture with a columnar form.

FOLIAGE Simple oblong to obovate bluish-green leaves are alternately arranged, with three to seven pairs of rounded lobes. Fall color is a poor yellow brown. Oblong acorns 1" long mature in late summer.

LIGHT & SOIL Full sun with a moist but well-drained soil; tolerant of salt spray and high pH.

MAINTENANCE Powdery mildew is common in the Southeast.

NOTES & CULTIVARS
'Crimson Spire' is a cross with *Quercus alba* with reddish-brown fall foliage.
'Regal Prince' is a cross with *Quercus bicolor*, with lustrous dark green leaves and good mildew resistance.
'Skyrocket' has improved mildew resistance.

top Foliage. *bottom* Form in downtown Athens.

Robinia pseudoacacia BLACK LOCUST

Black locust is an extremely tough native tree that is often considered a pest, since it often forms thickets in abandoned upland fields, roadsides, and neglected urban sites. Passing it off as a weed overlooks its attractive and fragrant white midspring flowers and light airy canopy, which allows filtered sunlight to reach the ground. With an ability to fix nitrogen in the soil, it can handle the toughest environmental conditions. Due to issues with honeylocust in the Southeast, it might be considered as an alternative to provide filtered sunlight on paved areas or for habitat plantings in zoological gardens.

Foliage and midspring flowers.

ZONES & ORIGIN   4b–9a. Native to the Appalachian and Ozark Mountains.

SIZE & GROWTH RATE   40'–60' tall, 30'–50' wide, fast growing.

TEXTURE & FORM   Medium fine texture with an oval form.

FOLIAGE   Alternate pinnately compound leaves have 11 to 17 blue-green elliptical leaflets with prominent spines at their base. Leaves begin falling in late summer and early autumn without developing any color. Young branches have numerous spines, while mature bark is dark gray and deeply furrowed.

FLOWERS   Sweetly fragrant and somewhat showy white flowers occur on drooping racemes in midspring (mid- to late April in Athens).

FRUIT   Fruit is an unattractive brown bean pod 4" long that remains into winter.

LIGHT & SOIL   Full sun to light shade with moist but well-drained soils. It tolerates drought, salt spray, deicing salts, and alkaline soils.

MAINTENANCE   Brittle tree limbs are easily damaged in storms. Leaves fall early in autumn but are easily handled by mowers or leaf blowers.

INSTALLATION   Trees are fairly rare in nurseries. Some growers provide them in containers or as small field-grown trees. Plant during the dormant season at 40' spacing.

PESTS & DISEASES   Black locust is subject to a number of diseases and pests. Numerous seedlings arise in full sun near mature trees. Deer don't touch them.

NOTES & CULTIVARS
Strong decay-resistant wood was used for railroad ties and fenceposts. These cultivars are more common in nurseries than the species:

'Purple Robe' produces dark pink flowers. 'Frisia' has yellow-green foliage.

left *Robinia pseudoacacia* 'Frisia' at the entrance to the Bloedel Reserve.
middle *Robinia pseudoacacia* 'Frisia' at the Bloedel Reserve.
right Form at Lewis and Clark College, Portland, Ore.

Late summer at Nike World Corporate Campus, Beaverton, Ore.

top Foliage.
middle Early spring at Gibbs Gardens.
bottom Midsummer form at Butchart Gardens.

Salix babylonica WEEPING WILLOW

Few trees are more widely recognized than weeping willow. With its fine texture and restful drooping branches highlighted by thin pendulous stems and foliage that softly flutters in the slightest breeze, it conjures images of lazy, carefree days. When it is located around ponds or lazy streams, it elicits a desire to relax on a hammock and take a summer nap. However, they are messy trees best appreciated from a distance rather than up close.

ZONES & ORIGIN   4a–9b. Native to southern Europe and western Asia.

SIZE & GROWTH RATE   35'–50' height and spread, very fast growing.

TEXTURE & FORM   Fine texture with a broadly oval to rounded form.

FOLIAGE   Simple light green leaves are alternately arranged and 3"–6" long, with finely serrate margins. The narrowly lanceolate leaves are silvery green beneath and held on thin pendulous yellow-green stems. Willows are among the first trees to leaf out in spring, and they hold their leaves into late autumn without developing significant color. Mature trees have dark gray ridged and furrowed bark.

FLOWERS   Insignificant flowers.

FRUIT   Insignificant fruit.

LIGHT & SOIL   Full sun with a moist but well-drained to wet soil.

MAINTENANCE   Weeping willows are messy, with branches easily broken in storms. An extensive surface root system easily invades tiny leaks in irrigation pipes, water lines, septic tank field lines, or sewers.

INSTALLATION   Trees are commonly available in sizes up to 4" in caliper. Because they are so fast growing, consider buying trees that are 6'–8' tall instead. In two to three years, small trees will be 15'–20' tall. For a continuous canopy, space 40'–50' apart.

PESTS & DISEASES   Numerous insects and fungal diseases cause willows to be short-lived. Approximately 30 years is the life expectancy in the Southeast.

NOTES & CULTIVARS
Corkscrew willow, *Salix matsudana* 'Tortuosa' reaches 20–30' tall, with a medium fine texture and broadly oval form. Native to China and best adapted for zones 5a–7a, its twisting contorted stems are most pronounced in the winter landscape. It is widely available and fast growing but short-lived.

Salix nigra BLACK WILLOW

Black willow is a pioneer species of streambanks and wetlands. Extremely fast growing but brittle wooded, with numerous pests, it rarely survives over 25 years before being overtaken by other species. Nevertheless, it is an important tree for wetland and streambank restorations, where cut branches inserted into soil quickly take root to impede soil erosion. Split branches were used for baskets. The inner bark and twigs were chewed for pain and fever relief by Native Americans.

ZONES & ORIGIN 3a–9b. Native to open moist sites from Florida and Texas to Canada.

SIZE & GROWTH RATE 30'–50' in height and spread, very fast growing.

TEXTURE & FORM Fine texture and broadly oval form.

FOLIAGE Simple alternately arranged light green leaves are 3"–5" long and narrowly lanceolate, with finely serrate margins. Insignificant flowers provide early spring food for honeybees, while the fibrous seeds provide nesting material for birds. Mature trees have a dark ridged and scaly bark.

LIGHT & SOIL Full sun with a moist but well-drained to wet soil.

MAINTENANCE Willows are easily broken in storms. Deer and beaver browse heavily.

NOTES & CULTIVARS Coastal plain willow, *Salix caroliniana*, is smaller and hybridizes with black willow.

Foliage.

Mature tree along the New River, Woodlawn, Va.

Sassafras albidum SASSAFRAS

Sassafras is an attractive native tree found in well-drained open fields, woodland edges, and fencerows. It often forms thickets due to its proclivity to sprout from the roots. Sassafras develops a rich fall foliage color, while its fruit provides food for birds and other wildlife, and its foliage is eaten by swallowtail butterfly larvae. Though difficult to transplant, sassafras is certainly worth protecting and utilizing along woodland edges, paths, or open perennial borders.

Foliage types.

ZONES & ORIGIN 5b–9a. Native from Texas to Massachusetts.

SIZE & GROWTH RATE 30'–50' tall, 20'–40' wide, medium growing.

TEXTURE & FORM Medium texture with an irregularly oval form.

FOLIAGE Simple alternate leaves 3"–7" long are elliptic shaped with a lemony odor when crushed. Leaves on mature trees have entire margins and a gray ridged and furrowed bark in a diamond pattern. Young trees and branches have leaves with two (right- and left-hand mittens) or three prominent lobes. Fall foliage is an excellent orange to red.

FLOWERS Insignificant greenish-yellow flowers occur in early spring before the leaves emerge.

FRUIT Tiny deep purple drupes on female trees mature in late summer.

LIGHT & SOIL Sassafras prefers full sun to light shade with a moist but well-drained slightly acidic soil, but it tolerates drought.

MAINTENANCE Watch for sprouts around existing trees.

INSTALLATION Trees are difficult to successfully transplant and rare in nurseries as a result. Transplant container or small field-grown trees in late winter to early spring.

PESTS & DISEASES Laurel wilt, a fungal disease carried by an Asian beetle, is killing sassafras in southeastern coastal areas where bay trees (*Persea*) are common. Deer browse young trees but rarely do serious damage.

NOTES & CULTIVARS
No cultivars available.

People are more likely to be familiar with products derived from sassafras than with the tree itself. Ground dried leaves (filé) are used for seasoning and thickening gumbo. Tea made from the roots was used to treat a number of ailments, as well as to flavor root beer and candies, but it is no longer used due to health concerns.

left Early spring flowers.
middle Fall color in Athens.
right Clump at Lewis and Clark College.

Tilia cordata LITTLELEAF LINDEN

Littleleaf linden is a clean neat tree that has long been popular for streets and parks in the Northeast. With its pyramidal form, dense canopy, and low branching to the ground for many years, it can form tall screens and is sometimes utilized for clipped hedges, particularly in Europe. Fragrant late spring flowers, fairly good fall color, and a formal outline are additional benefits. It is better adapted to locations with cooler summers, so care should be taken with it in zones 7 and 8.

ZONES & ORIGIN 3b–8a. Native to Europe and western Asia.

SIZE & GROWTH RATE 50'–70' tall, 30'–50' wide, medium slow growing.

TEXTURE & FORM Medium texture, pyramidal form when young, becoming oval with age.

FOLIAGE Simple dark green cordate-shaped alternate leaves 1½"–3" long have serrate margins and acuminate tips. Fall foliage is bright yellow but not always dependable. A smooth gray bark when young becomes dark gray brown and ridged and furrowed with maturity.

FLOWERS Creamy-white flowers on pendulous cymes with a pale green leaflike bract occur in late spring (mid-May in Athens). Though not showy and remaining only a short time, they are quite fragrant. Old flower structures and bracts remain into winter.

FRUIT Insignificant small nut.

LIGHT & SOIL Full sun to light shade with a moist but well-drained soil is ideal. While tolerating slightly alkaline soils, it is not particularly drought tolerant and benefits from afternoon shade in the South.

MAINTENANCE Trees near pavements require removal of lower branches to allow circulation beneath. It is very difficult to grow other plants beneath *Tilia* due to its dense canopy and shallow surface roots.

INSTALLATION Field-grown trees are available and easily transplanted during the dormant season. For formal allées, space 30'–40' apart.

PESTS & DISEASES Aphids are fairly common, and Japanese beetles can defoliate trees.

NOTES & CULTIVARS
'Greenspire', with a broadly pyramidal form, is the most popular cultivar.
Basswood, *Tilia americana*, is a fast-growing native of the Midwest. Its highly fragrant late spring flowers are favored by beekeepers for honey.

top left Clipped lindens at Longwood Gardens' Italian Garden.

top right Spring foliage and flower structures at Berkshire Botanical Garden.

middle Spring foliage and flower structures on the UGA campus.

bottom Spring foliage and flower structures at a residence in Athens.

Ulmus pumila SIBERIAN ELM

Siberian elm was often used in the Great Plains states as a substitute for American elm due to its resistance to Dutch elm disease, fast growth, and ability to tolerate drought and adverse soil conditions. It was even promoted as a hedge plant in dust bowl states. In the Southeast it lives an unsightly short life due to its magnetic attraction to leaf-eating insects and diseases, as well as its brittle wood, which causes branches to break without advance warning. With the release of Dutch elm disease–resistant cultivars of American elm, there is little reason to now consider Siberian elm. There are just too many native trees with superior longevity and ornamental attributes to waste time and money on it.

ZONES & ORIGIN 4a–9b. Native to Siberia and China.

SIZE & GROWTH RATE 40'–60' tall, 30'–50' wide, fast growing.

TEXTURE & FORM Medium coarse texture with a broadly oval to rounded form.

FOLIAGE Simple alternate leaves are lustrous dark green with an asymmetrical base and are mostly ovate or occasionally elliptic in shape. The leaves, which are 1½"–3" long, have doubly serrate margins and acute or short acuminate tips. Fall color is nonexistent in the Southeast, but it may get some yellow color in cooler zones. Slender light gray twigs have rounded dark brown buds ⅛" long with fine hairs on the end. A dark gray to black bark is deeply ridged and furrowed.

FLOWERS Insignificant late winter flowers.

FRUIT Insignificant oval-shaped mid-spring samaras.

LIGHT & SOIL Provide full sun and a well-drained soil. It tolerates drought, alkaline soils, and some salt spray.

MAINTENANCE Siberian elm is a messy tree, dropping limbs and branches. Though reportedly invasive in cooler regions, it doesn't cause problems in southeastern states.

INSTALLATION Field-grown trees are widely available from Ohio River Valley and Texas nurseries. Plant from midautumn to spring.

PESTS & DISEASES Numerous pests, including insects and fungal diseases, cause Siberian elm to be unsightly in appearance and generally short-lived in the southeastern states.

NOTES & CULTIVARS A few are listed, but none are commonly available.

top Foliage and buds.
middle Bark.
bottom Form on the UGA campus.

Zelkova serrata ZELKOVA

Zelkova has been promoted as an alternative to the American elm. With upright arching branches, a dense canopy, and a consistent broadly oval form, it provides a branching and shade pattern that is similar to American elm. It has far fewer disease and insect issues than elms and adapts well to urban conditions. Best of all, it's not as aggressive as many elms. As a result, zelkova is an excellent choice for urban plazas and street and sidewalk plantings or even just as a shade tree for homes and yards. Its only drawback is that its lower branches can get in the way of taller trucks when used to shade streets or driveways.

ZONES & ORIGIN 5a–9a. Native to Asia.

SIZE & GROWTH RATE 50'–70' tall, 40'–60' wide, medium fast growing.

TEXTURE & FORM Medium texture with upright arching branches and broadly oval form.

FOLIAGE Simple ovate to elliptical alternate leaves 2"–5" long have serrate margins and rounded to slightly asymmetrical bases. Inconsistent fall color ranges from yellow to rusty brown to crimson. Young branches have prominent lenticels that resemble those of cherry trees, while older trunks develop exfoliating bark with a rusty-orange inner bark. The trunk explodes around 6' tall into numerous ascending branches.

FLOWERS Insignificant early spring flowers.

FRUIT Insignificant drupes.

LIGHT & SOIL Full sun and a moist but well-drained soil are ideal. Zelkova tolerates higher pH levels, drought, and air pollution.

MAINTENANCE Squirrels cut the small twigs in summer as they devour the fruit, leaving a mess of leaves and twigs beneath.

INSTALLATION Easily transplanted year-round in large field-grown sizes up to 6" in caliper. For a continuous canopy, plant 40'–60' apart.

PESTS & DISEASES Susceptible to storm damage due to narrow branch crotch angles. Wounds to the bark provide entrance to deadly canker diseases, particularly during extreme droughts.

NOTES & CULTIVARS
'Green Vase' is a fast grower with a slightly narrower canopy.
'Halka' reaches 40'–50' with a rounded form.
'Murashino' has an upright oval form.
'Village Green' is broader spreading, almost rounded in form.

top left Form at Reinhardt University.
top right Fall foliage on the UGA campus.
middle Foliage.
bottom Mature bark.

SMALL DECIDUOUS TREES

above Crape myrtles on the UGA campus.

Trees in this category generally mature at 30' in height or less. In nature, they would most often be found along the edges of established woods. While they may provide shade for small shrubs or ground cover plants, rarely could these trees be considered important in providing shade for people. Rather, they are more often used to bring the scale of a space down to one that is more comfortable for human interactions. As a result, they are often placed in locations where humans will closely interact with them. They are often used in courtyards and patios and near building entrances to make humans feel more relaxed in their environment by transitioning from towering buildings, immense plazas, or huge shade trees down to a more intimate dimension.

In addition, in many designs, these small trees often function as the stars in a well-designed composition. They tend to captivate us with their attributes and are often highly photogenic with their striking charms. Eye-catching flowers, eye-popping fall foliage, appealing fruit or bark, or even just a handsome trunk or branching habit are among their attractions. Many possess attributes that allow them to be appreciated throughout the year and not simply when they are in flower or exhibiting autumn foliage. Due to their alluring features, we tend to enjoy them more when they are nearby, even though many possess attributes that appeal equally well from a distance.

However you use them, make sure to provide a suitable environment for them to flourish. Pay particular attention to their requirements for sunlight and soil moisture levels. Since these trees are often located where nearby buildings and pavements have interrupted natural processes, appropriate conditions may be difficult to provide.

BOTANICAL NAME	SUNLIGHT	SOILS	TEXTURE	NOTABLE ATTRIBUTES	FALL FOLIAGE	NATIVE TO SOUTHEAST
Acer buergerianum	Full sun to light shade	Well drained	Medium fine	Multitrunks, exfoliating bark	Good yellow to orange to red	No, Asia
Acer griseum	Light shade	Moist but well drained	Medium fine	Attractive exfoliating bark	Outstanding late season red	No, Asia
Acer palmatum	Light shade	Moist but well drained acidic	Fine	Specimen plant	Outstanding yellow to red	No, Asia
Aesculus pavia	Light shade	Moist but well drained acidic	Coarse	Scarlet red early spring flowers	Poor yellow	Yes
Amelanchier × grandiflora	Full sun to light shade	Moist but well drained	Fine	Edible fruit, early spring flowers	Outstanding red to orange	Yes
Aralia spinosa	Full sun to moderate shade	Moist to well drained	Coarse	Flowers and fruit attract wildlife	Fair yellow to purple	Yes
Carpinus caroliniana	Full sun to full shade	Moist to well drained	Medium fine	Muscular ridges on smooth bark	Fair yellow to purple	Yes
Cercis canadensis	Full sun to light shade	Well drained	Medium coarse	Attractive spring flowers	Fair yellow	Yes
Chionanthus retusus	Full sun to light shade	Moist but well drained	Medium	Showy white spring flowers	None	No, Asia
Chionanthus virginicus	Full sun to moderate shade	Moist to well drained	Coarse	Showy white spring flowers	None	Yes
Cornus florida	Full sun to light shade	Moist but well drained	Medium	Attractive spring flowers, fall fruit	Outstanding red to crimson	Yes
Cornus kousa	Full sun to light shade	Moist but well drained acidic	Medium	Attractive spring flowers, fall fruit	Outstanding orange to red	No, Asia
Cotinus coggygria	Full sun to light shade	Well drained	Medium	Billowy pink summer flowers	Outstanding orange to red	No, Europe and Asia
Crataegus spp.	Full sun to light shade	Moist but well drained	Medium fine	Attractive spring flowers, fall fruit	Rarely good due to diseases	Yes
Franklinia altamaha	Light shade	Moist but well drained	Medium	Fragrant, late summer flowers	Good yellow to orange red	Yes
Halesia tetraptera	Light to moderate shade	Moist but well drained acidic	Medium	White spring flowers	Poor yellow	Yes
Koelreuteria bipinnata	Full sun	Well drained	Medium coarse	Yellow late summer flowers	Fair yellow	No, Asia
Koelreuteria paniculata	Full sun	Well drained	Medium	Yellow early summer flowers	Good yellow	No, Asia
Lagerstroemia spp.	Full sun to light shade	Well drained	Medium fine	Summer flowers, attractive bark	Outstanding red to yellow orange	No, Asia
Magnolia stellata	Full sun to light shade	Moist to moist but well drained	Medium	Fragrant white spring flowers	Poor yellow	No, Asia
Magnolia × loebneri	Full sun to light shade	Moist but well drained acidic	Medium	Late winter flowers	Poor yellow	No, man-made cross from Asia
Magnolia × soulangeana	Full sun to light shade	Moist but well drained acidic	Coarse	Late winter purple flowers	Fair yellow	No, man-made cross from Asia
Malus spp.	Full sun to light shade	Moist but well drained acidic	Medium	Spring flowers fall fruit	Poor yellow	No, crosses from Asian species
Parrotia persica	Full sun to light shade	Well drained	Medium	Attractive exfoliating bark	Outstanding red to yellow orange	No, Persia
Prunus campanulata	Full sun to light shade	Moist but well drained acidic	Medium	Late winter rosy-red flowers	Fair bronzy yellow	No, Asia

BOTANICAL NAME	SUNLIGHT	SOILS	TEXTURE	NOTABLE ATTRIBUTES	FALL FOLIAGE	NATIVE TO SOUTHEAST
Prunus cerasifera 'Atropurpurea'	Full sun	Well drained	Medium	Spring flowers, purple foliage	Good purple	No, Persia
Prunus persica	Full sun	Moist but well drained	Medium	Early spring flowers	None	No, Asia
Prunus serrulata 'Kanzan'	Full sun	Moist but well drained	Medium	Double pink spring flowers	Fair yellow orange	No, Asia
Prunus × incam 'Okame'	Full sun to light shade	Moist but well drained	Medium fine	Smoky pink late winter flowers	Fair, dull orange	No, man-made cross from Asia
Prunus subhirtella	Full sun to light shade	Moist but well drained acidic	Medium	Pink to white spring flowers	Good yellow orange	No, Asia
Prunus × yedoensis	Full sun	Moist but well drained	Medium	Early spring white flowers	Good yellow orange	No, cross from Asian species
Rhus copallinum	Full sun	Well drained	Medium coarse	Red fall and winter fruit	Outstanding bright red	Yes
Rhus glabra	Full sun	Well drained	Medium coarse	Red fall and winter fruit	Outstanding dark red	Yes
Rhus typhina	Full sun	Well drained	Medium coarse	Red fall and winter fruit	Outstanding scarlet red	Yes
Styphnolobium japonicum	Full sun	Moist but well drained	Medium fine	White midsummer flowers	Poor yellow	No, Asia
Styrax japonicus	Light shade	Moist but well drained acidic	Medium fine	White midspring flowers	Fair yellow orange	No, Asia

top left Street trees on the UGA campus.
top right Street trees in Gainesville, Ga.
middle Fall foliage.
bottom Bark.

Acer buergerianum TRIDENT MAPLE

Trident maple is an attractive small tree that is likely unfamiliar to many people. Only recently widely available in nurseries, it is a tough tree that tolerates drought and is easily transplanted. Best known for its showy fall foliage and an attractive exfoliating bark, it is available in either single or multiple trunks. Consider combining it with a drought-tolerant ground cover such as candytuft, verbena, or monkey grass in raised planters for patios or courtyards. While it is perfectly suited for small yards, take advantage of its attractive bark for uplighting near building entrances and for bonsai collections.

ZONES & ORIGIN   6a–8b. Native to China.

SIZE & GROWTH RATE   25'–35' tall, 20'–30' wide, medium slow growing.

TEXTURE & FORM   Medium fine texture and broadly oval form.

FOLIAGE   Simple opposite leaves are 1½"–3" long, lustrous dark green in color, with rounded bases and margins that may be entire or irregularly serrate. The duck-foot-shaped leaves have three lobes, V-shaped sinuses, acuminate tips, and three prominent veins. Bright yellow to orange to red fall foliage is usually good, even in the Southeast. An exfoliating tan to light gray bark reveals an orange inner bark. The degree of exfoliation varies with each tree's genetics.

FLOWERS   Insignificant yellow-green flowers in mid-April.

FRUIT   Paired samaras appear in late spring and remain into winter. Fruiting is heavy and can be somewhat unsightly.

LIGHT & SOIL   Provide full sun to light shade and slightly acidic well-drained soils. It tolerates drought, compacted soils, and moderate salt spray.

MAINTENANCE   Leaves drop in late autumn. The samaras often remain into winter. Otherwise, trident maple is fairly clean, with no special maintenance issues.

INSTALLATION   Trees are widely available in sizes up to 6" in caliper in both single and multitrunks. They transplant best in late winter but can be transplanted virtually year-round, even in summer. Space 25' apart for a continuous canopy.

PESTS & DISEASES   No serious problems. Deer browse them but rarely cause severe damage.

NOTES & CULTIVARS
'Aeryn' is vegetatively propagated, so it provides consistency in its form and yellow-red fall color.

Acer griseum PAPERBARK MAPLE

Paperbark maple is equally striking both from a distance and up close. Its rich deep red fall color can be appreciated from a distance, while its attractive exfoliating bark and branching habit are best valued from nearby. It is an excellent choice for courtyards, patios, or building entrances where people will pass nearby. In those situations, consider utilizing some decorative night lighting to highlight its exfoliating character. Combine it with low-growing plants like ferns and hostas that won't hide its bark.

top Late fall foliage.
middle Exfoliating bark.
bottom left Composition with pieris, hydrangeas, and blue Atlas cedars.
bottom right Roof garden at Massachusetts General Hospital, Boston.

ZONES & ORIGIN 5a–8a. Native to China.

SIZE & GROWTH RATE 20'–30' tall and 15'–25' wide with a slow growth rate.

TEXTURE & FORM Medium fine texture with an oval form, becoming broadly oval with age.

FOLIAGE Oppositely arranged dark blue-green trifoliate leaves 2½"–6" long are elliptic to obovate in shape, with shallow lobes and soft dense hair beneath and on the petiole. Deep red fall color develops late, usually November in Athens. A rich reddish-brown exfoliating bark peels into paper-thin sheets, revealing a light brown or tan inner bark.

FLOWERS Insignificant early spring flowers.

FRUIT Sparse and insignificant winged samaras.

LIGHT & SOIL It prefers light shade with a moist but well-drained soil but tolerates full sun to moderate shade and a near-neutral pH.

MAINTENANCE Provide supplemental water during extreme droughts throughout its lifetime.

INSTALLATION Field-grown or container trees are best planted in late winter or early spring. For grouping, they can be planted as close as 15' on center.

PESTS & DISEASES Few disease or pest problems have been reported. Deer will browse, but they rarely cause severe damage.

NOTES & CULTIVARS

Few of the samaras are viable, so paperbark maple is still somewhat rare in nurseries. Hand select trees to ensure the quality of the exfoliating bark. Young trees should exhibit this feature and will not develop it later.

'Cinnamon Flake' and 'Gingerbread' are crosses between paperbark maple and Nikko maple, *Acer maximowiczianum*. They are similar in size and fall foliage color to paperbark maple and grow somewhat faster, but they are rare in nurseries.

top Foliage.

middle left Form in the Founders Memorial Garden.

middle right *Acer palmatum* 'Sango Kaku' branches.

bottom Fall color at Stanford University.

Acer palmatum JAPANESE MAPLE

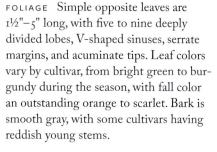

Japanese maple is an extremely diverse species, with numerous cultivars exhibiting variable sizes, leaf shapes, leaf colors, and growth habits. Their delicate fine-textured foliage and graceful branch structure are why so many are trained as bonsai. Those same features make them suitable for use as specimen plants in courtyards and patios or near building entrances; they also do well as accent plants in perennial or shrub borders. Many are available with multiple trunks, and all look good when combined with natural materials such as stone, wood, and ferns. Add some decorative night lighting so they can be appreciated both after dark and during daytime. Both the upright and spreading forms are suitable for use in container plantings. Spreading forms are particularly nice near streams and waterfalls or even just to disguise an odd edge or corner.

ZONES & ORIGIN 5b–9a. Native to Korea and Japan.

SIZE & GROWTH RATE 15'–30' tall and wide, depending upon the cultivar, medium slow growing.

TEXTURE & FORM Fine texture with a broadly oval to spreading form depending on the cultivar.

FOLIAGE Simple opposite leaves are 1½"–5" long, with five to nine deeply divided lobes, V-shaped sinuses, serrate margins, and acuminate tips. Leaf colors vary by cultivar, from bright green to burgundy during the season, with fall color an outstanding orange to scarlet. Bark is smooth gray, with some cultivars having reddish young stems.

FLOWERS Insignificant early spring flowers.

FRUIT Sparse and insignificant winged samaras.

LIGHT & SOIL Light shade and a moist but well-drained acidic soil are ideal. They tolerate full sun to moderate shade, but plants in full sun are prone to scorched leaves.

MAINTENANCE Thin bark is easily damaged by mowers and trimmers.

INSTALLATION Plant during the dormant season to allow root establishment before summer. Provide supplemental water during droughts.

PESTS & DISEASES No serious problems under optimal cultural conditions. Deer browse but rarely cause serious problems.

NOTES & CULTIVARS Hundreds of cultivars are listed in various references and catalogs. Other than camellias and daylilies, few plants inspire as much interest in cross-pollination and propagation. With that in mind, this is an attempt to group commonly available cultivars into varietal groups based upon leaf type and color and should not be construed as taxonomically accurate.

Species cultivars have green foliage and sinuses extending no more than two-thirds the length of the leaf.

'Bihou' grows 12'–18' tall, 8'–12' wide, with yellow fall foliage and bright yellow young twigs.

'Glowing Embers' reaches 20'–30' tall and wide, with yellow, orange, scarlet, and crimson fall colors all on the same branch.

'Ryusen' reaches 10'–15' tall, 6'–8' wide, with an upright oval form, pendulous branches, and orange-red fall foliage.

'Sango Kaku' reaches 20'–30' tall and wide, with bright green foliage, yellow-orange fall color, and coral-colored young stems in winter.

Atropurpureum variety cultivars produce dark red to burgundy new foliage and sinuses that generally extend no more than two-thirds the length of the leaf.

'Bloodgood' is the most common cultivar, reaching 15'–25' tall and wide, with scarlet late autumn foliage.

'Crimson Prince' reaches 15'–25' tall, 10'–20' wide, with scarlet fall foliage.

'Wolff Emperor 1', 'Nigrum', and 'Oshio-Beni' reach 15'–20' tall, 12'–15' wide, with scarlet fall foliage.

'Moonfire' reaches 15'–20' tall, 10'–15' wide, with crimson fall foliage.

left Acer palmatum 'Bloodgood' foliage.

middle Acer palmatum 'Bloodgood' in the Founders Memorial Garden.

right Acer palmatum 'Bloodgood' on the UGA campus.

Cultivars of the *dissectum* variety have sinuses extending nearly the entire length of the leaf, with thin linear lobes.

'Seiryu' has a faster growth rate, reaching 15'–25' tall, and orange to crimson fall foliage.

'Waterfall', with light green foliage, grows 6'–10' tall, with a spreading form and yellow-orange fall color.

'Dissectum Atropurpureum' cultivars have sinuses extending nearly the entire length of the leaf, thin linear lobes, and dark red to burgundy new foliage.

'Dissectum Nigrum' and 'Ever Red' grow 6'–10' tall and wide, with pendulous branches and scarlet fall foliage.

'Inabashidare' and 'Red Select' reach 6'–10' tall, 8'–12' wide, with spreading forms, pendulous branches, and scarlet fall color.

'Red Dragon' grows 6'–8' tall and wide, with a rounded form, bronzy-red summer foliage, and scarlet fall color.

'Tamukeyama' reaches 6'–10' tall, 10'–15' wide, with a mounded form, coppery-red summer foliage, and scarlet fall color.

top Acer palmatum dissectum at Longwood Gardens.

bottom Acer palmatum dissectum with daylilies.

top Foliage.

bottom Form and foliage at the Giberson residence, Athens.

top left Trees in a north Georgia woodland.

top middle Foliage and early spring flowers at a café in New York City.

top right Flowers and foliage in New York City.

bottom Foliage and early spring flowers.

Aesculus pavia RED BUCKEYE

Red buckeyes are small understory trees found on rich bottomland soils of the Southeast. One of the earliest native plants to leaf out in spring, it is valued for its attractive red early spring flowers, which are favored by migratory hummingbirds. Trees begin to flower at a young age and provide a coarse texture that contrasts with surrounding plants. Combine it with a native shrub such as piedmont azalea or fothergilla and an early spring wildflower such as trillium, bloodroot, or foamflower along woodland edges or paths or in shrub borders.

ZONES & ORIGIN 6a–9a. Native from Texas to North Carolina.

SIZE & GROWTH RATE 15'–25' tall, 10'–20' wide, medium slow growing.

TEXTURE & FORM Coarse texture and broadly oval to rounded form.

FOLIAGE Palmately compound opposite leaves with mostly five leaflets emerge reddish purple before turning dark green in summer. The obovate leaflets, 2½"–6½" long, have serrate margins and prominent depressed veins. Leaves drop early without significant color. A smooth gray-brown bark eventually develops a flaky character.

FLOWERS Attractive scarlet-red tubular-shaped flowers on terminal panicles emerge in early to midspring (late March to mid-April in Athens).

FRUIT Light brown rounded capsules 1" in diameter mature in early autumn. While not showy, they are toxic to humans and cattle.

LIGHT & SOIL Light shade and a consistently moist but well-drained acidic soil are ideal. It tolerates full sun to full shade but develops few flowers in full shade.

MAINTENANCE Thin bark is easily damaged by maintenance equipment. Foliage falls early, requiring attention in lawns.

INSTALLATION Red buckeye is difficult to locate and usually only available in containers. Provide a loose, well-drained soil and supplemental water during droughts.

PESTS & DISEASES No serious problems as long as trees receive adequate moisture. Deer don't bother them.

NOTES & CULTIVARS
Red horsechestnut, *Aesculus × carnea*, is a cross between red buckeye and horsechestnut, *Aesculus hippocastanum*. Hardy from zones 5b to 8a, it reaches 30'–40' tall with a coarse texture, dense rounded canopy, and large pinkish-red midspring flowers.

Amelanchier × *grandiflora* SERVICEBERRY

Serviceberry provides year-round interest in designs. Its fine texture and multistem habit offer the opportunity to highlight it as an accent or specimen plant in compositions. Attractive early spring flowers combine well with redbuds or early flowering shrubs in borders. Highly visible flowers and showy fall foliage make it popular for massing along woodland edges, where its early summer fruit provides a feeding frenzy for birds. With its cold-hardiness, serviceberry could even be used as a container plant to enliven smaller spaces.

ZONES & ORIGIN 3b–8b. A cross between two native species.

SIZE & GROWTH RATE 15'–25' tall, 10'–20' wide, medium growing.

TEXTURE & FORM Fine texture and broadly oval form.

FOLIAGE Alternate simple leaves are 1"–3" long, ovate to elliptic in shape, with finely serrate margins. Leaf undersides are softly pubescent when young. Fall color is an outstanding orange to deep red. The smooth light gray bark has vertical stripes.

FLOWERS Showy racemes of white flowers occur in early to midspring (late March to early April in Athens) but only last about a week.

FRUIT Small blueberry-sized pomes turn red and finally purple in early summer. The edible fruits taste like blueberries, but birds often devour them before they fully ripen.

LIGHT & SOIL Light shade with a moist but well-drained slightly acidic soil is ideal. It tolerates full sun and moderate salt spray.

MAINTENANCE A thin bark is easily damaged by maintenance equipment. If planting in a turf area, mulch around the trunk.

INSTALLATION Field-grown trees with multiple trunks in sizes up to 3"–4" in caliper are readily available. Transplant during the dormant season and provide supplemental water during summer droughts.

PESTS & DISEASES Serviceberry is susceptible to aphids, scale, leaf spot disease, rust, and powdery mildew. Selected cultivars provide greater resistance. Deer seldom cause serious problems.

NOTES & CULTIVARS
'Autumn Brilliance' is the most popular cultivar, with improved disease resistance.
'Forest Prince' provides disease-resistant foliage, rounded form, and flowers along the length of the stems.
'Princess Diana' provides dark green foliage with good disease resistance.

top to bottom

Late spring foliage and fruit.

Early spring flowers.

Fall foliage on the UGA campus.

Flowering with redbuds on a north Georgia roadside.

SMALL DECIDUOUS TREES

top left Stems and spines.

bottom left Foliage and late summer flower heads.

right Used as an ornamental tree in Vancouver, B.C.

Aralia spinosa DEVIL'S WALKINGSTICK

A rare but widespread native with an exotic appearance, devil's walkingstick is found on bottomlands, in drainage ravines, and along woodland edges, where it forms thickets from root sprouts. Terminal panicles of creamy-white midsummer flowers and early autumn purple fruits are favorites of insects and birds. Use it in perennial and shrub borders, but keep it away from children.

ZONES & ORIGIN 5a–9b. Native from Florida and Texas to New England.

SIZE & GROWTH RATE 12'–25' tall, 10'–15' wide, and fast growing.

TEXTURE & FORM Coarse texture and an umbrella-like broadly oval form.

FOLIAGE Alternate bipinnately compound leaves 2'–3' long have ovate leaflets 2"–4" long with serrate margins and sharp spines on the rachis and young stems. Foliage is clustered at the ends of scarce branches and drops early, with some yellow to purple color. Gray-brown bark on mature trees has few spines, but fast-growing stems have numerous spines.

LIGHT & SOIL Full sun to moderate shade and a moist to well-drained soil. It tolerates drought and alkaline soils.

NOTES & CULTIVARS
Easily transplanted in containers from specialty growers. Use steel edging to restrain roots and new sprouts.

Carpinus caroliniana IRONWOOD · MUSCLEWOOD

Ironwood is a climax species found on moist lower slopes from Florida to Michigan and is among the longest-lived small trees. Foresters consider it a pest in managed timberlands due to its hard dense wood, which makes cutting difficult. Take advantage of its clean habit and neat appearance for specimen plantings to highlight its muscular trunk or for understory plantings to take advantage of its shade tolerance. It has even been sheared into a formal aerial hedge at Dumbarton Oaks. Its tolerance of moist soils in sun or shade makes it worthy of consideration for stormwater retention areas.

ZONES & ORIGIN 3b–9b. Native to the eastern United States.

SIZE & GROWTH RATE 20'–35' tall, 15'–30' wide, slow growing.

TEXTURE & FORM Medium fine texture and broadly oval to rounded form.

FOLIAGE Alternate simple leaves are 2"–4" long, elliptic to ovate shaped, with serrate or doubly serrate margins, acuminate tips, and prominently depressed veins. Leaves are held on thin zigzagged stems with pendulous tips. Fall color in sun is a fair yellow. Trees in shade develop red to purple late autumn foliage. A smooth gray bark develops muscular ridges with age.

FLOWERS Insignificant male catkins are visible before the leaves emerge in early spring.

FRUIT Insignificant clusters of nutlets on leaflike bracts are an important food source for squirrels, pheasants, and turkeys.

LIGHT & SOIL Light shade with a moist soil is ideal. Ironwood tolerates full sun to full shade, well-drained soils, and some dormant-season flooding.

MAINTENANCE Ironwood is a very clean neat tree that doesn't drop foliage or fruit year-round. Its small leaves are easily collected after dropping. Established trees decline from earth-moving operations within the root zone.

INSTALLATION Field-grown trees in sizes up to 8" in caliper can be transplanted in late winter. For massing, space 20' on center. Multitrunk trees are available. Provide supplemental water for several years during summer droughts.

PESTS & DISEASES No serious problems. Deer browse the twigs but don't prefer them.

NOTES & CULTIVARS
'Palisade' has an upright oval form.

top to bottom

Fall foliage and fruiting structures.

Bark.

Winter form on the UGA campus.

Street trees in Athens.

Cercis canadensis EASTERN REDBUD

Nothing announces the coming of spring like redbud. Airy pink flowers appear before most trees leaf out and last for several weeks. For the rest of the year, redbud is rather ordinary. Take advantage of its early flowering by using it with early blooming shrubs such as bridalwreath spiraea, serviceberry, and forsythia or mass it with dogwoods along woodland edges. A tough tree tolerant of urban conditions, redbud could be used for street, sidewalk, and plaza plantings.

top Cordate-shaped foliage.
middle *Cercis canadensis* 'Forest Pansy' in Seattle's Freeway Park.
bottom left *Cercis canadensis* 'Forest Pansy' in Wayne, Pa.
bottom right Early spring flowers on the UGA campus.

ZONES & ORIGIN 5a–9b. Native to open uplands from Florida to Michigan.

SIZE & GROWTH RATE 20'–35' tall, 15'–25' wide, medium fast growing.

TEXTURE & FORM Medium coarse texture and broadly oval form.

FOLIAGE Simple, cordate, alternate leaves are 2"–5" long, with entire margins and swollen petioles at both ends. Fall foliage is a fair yellow. Young stems are reddish brown, while mature bark is light brown and scaly.

FLOWERS Showy lavender-pink flowers appear for two to three weeks in early spring (mid-March to early April in Athens).

FRUIT Flattened green bean pods, up to 4" long, turn tan in midsummer and remain into winter.

LIGHT & SOIL Full sun to light shade with a well-drained soil. It tolerates drought and slightly alkaline soil.

MAINTENANCE Numerous seedlings germinate in open areas.

INSTALLATION Field-grown redbuds are available in single and multiple trunks up to 5" in caliper. Transplant in early spring. Space 30' for massing.

PESTS & DISEASES Avoid pruning during spring and summer to reduce risk of fungal canker disease. Young trees are susceptible to damage from maintenance equipment. Deer seldom cause problems.

NOTES & CULTIVARS
'Appalachian Red' produces reddish-pink flowers.
'Covey' and 'Lavender Twist' are weeping forms reaching 6'–8' tall and 6'–10' wide.
'Flame' is a sterile cultivar producing double flowers, but it is difficult to find.
'Forest Pansy' provides new purple spring foliage, fading to dark green in summer.
'Royal White' produces white flowers.
Cercis canadensis texensis is a southern plains variety reaching about 20' tall, with smaller rounder lustrous leathery leaves.
'Oklahoma' provides magenta-pink flowers.
'Texas White' has white flowers.

Chionanthus retusus WHITE FRINGETREE

Few small flowering trees are as trouble free as white fringetree. With no serious pest problems and a tolerance for summer droughts, they deserve greater consideration in the landscape. For a week or so in midspring, the tree explodes with a cloud of white flowers that few plants can rival. Female trees produce small fruit in fall that attracts birds into the garden. Consider it for patios and courtyards or for shrub borders to span the interval between spring-blooming azaleas and spiraeas and later-blooming peonies and hydrangeas.

ZONES & ORIGIN 5b–9b. Native to Asia.

SIZE & GROWTH RATE 15'–35' tall, 20'–35' wide, medium slow growing.

TEXTURE & FORM Medium texture and broadly oval to rounded form.

FOLIAGE Simple leathery dark green opposite leaves are 2"–5" long, oval to elliptic in shape, with lustrous upper surfaces. Leaves are held late and develop a fair yellow color that is better farther north. Tan bark on younger branches develops some exfoliating character, while older trunks have gray ridged and furrowed bark.

FLOWERS Lightly fragrant bright white flowers with strap-shaped petals occur in showy terminal panicles for about one week in midspring (mid-April in Athens). The tree is primarily dioecious, with male trees being showier, but some individuals have perfect flowers.

FRUIT Female trees produce an attractive blueberry-sized oval drupe that turns bluish purple in early to midautumn and is popular with birds.

LIGHT & SOIL Provide full sun to light shade and a moist but well-drained soil. Established plants are fairly drought tolerant.

MAINTENANCE Prune after flowering is completed in spring to avoid removing next year's flower buds. It can be maintained as a large shrub for shrub borders. Birds can cause messes on pavements from eating the fruit.

INSTALLATION Plants are difficult to locate. A few nurseries provide container and smaller field-grown plants with single or multiple trunks. Container plants can be planted year-round. Field-grown trees transplant better while dormant.

PESTS & DISEASES No serious pest problems.

NOTES & CULTIVARS
'Tokyo Tower' reaches 15' with a columnar to upright oval form.

top left Flowering at Berry College's Kilpatrick Commons.

top right Flowering along a garden path at the Jane Bath residence, Oconee County, Ga.

middle Foliage and autumn fruit.

bottom Midspring flowers.

left Flowers at Longwood Gardens.
top right Flowers at Swarthmore College.
bottom right Flowers in Athens.

Chionanthus virginicus
FRINGETREE · GRANCY GRAYBEARD

Fringetree is a native understory plant found from moist bottomlands to dry ridge rock outcrops. While widespread but rare, it is often overlooked even where it occurs due to a nondescript character for much of the year. Although it is primarily used as a large shrub because of its natural multitrunked and low-branched habit, with proper pruning it can reach the size of a small tree. Place it in the rear of a shrub border with southern indica azaleas and pittosporum, or use it for understory woodland plantings with leucothoe, native rhododendrons, and mountain laurel.

Foliage and late summer fruit.

ZONES & ORIGIN 5a–9b. Native from Florida and Texas to Massachusetts.

SIZE & GROWTH RATE 15'–20' tall, 10'–20' wide, medium slow growing.

TEXTURE & FORM Coarse texture with a broadly oval form.

FOLIAGE Simple opposite leaves are 2½"–6" long, elliptic to obovate shaped, with entire margins and acuminate tips. Leaves are lustrous green above, while the undersides and young stems have soft fine hairs. Fall color is a poor yellow. Reddish-brown young twigs mature to a light gray shallowly ridged and furrowed bark.

FLOWERS Creamy-white flowers with strap-shaped petals are held in panicles along the branches for seven to ten days in midspring (mid-April in Athens). The flowers appear shortly before those of *Chionanthus retusus*. Fringetree is dioecious, with male trees somewhat showier than females.

FRUIT Female trees produce bluish-black oval drupes in late summer that are somewhat hidden by the foliage but are attractive to birds.

LIGHT & SOIL Light shade and a moist but well-drained slightly acidic soil are ideal. It tolerates full sun to moderate shade, drought, a near-neutral soil pH, and wet winter soils.

MAINTENANCE Provide mulch around the trunks to protect the plants from maintenance equipment.

INSTALLATION Fringetree is somewhat rare in nurseries. Container and field-grown plants are best transplanted in mid- to late autumn. Provide supplemental water for the first few summers during droughts.

PESTS & DISEASES No disease problems. Deer will browse the foliage.

NOTES & CULTIVARS
'Prodigy' has a rounded form and dark green foliage.

Cornus florida DOGWOOD

For many people, spring officially arrives when the dogwoods and azaleas begin their marriage of colors. Dogwood's white bracts combine with any color of azalea. Combining dogwoods with azaleas, viburnums, redbuds, spiraeas, and late-blooming camellias provides an eye-opening splash of spring color. Consider adding them to woodland edges with ferns, hostas, and native wildflowers, and take advantage of their outstanding fall foliage and fruit.

ZONES & ORIGIN 5b–9b. Native from Texas to Massachusetts.

SIZE & GROWTH RATE 20'–30' tall, 15'–25' wide, medium slow growing.

TEXTURE & FORM Medium texture and broadly oval form.

FOLIAGE Simple opposite leaves are 2½"–6" long, elliptic in shape, with entire margins and abruptly acuminate tips. Fall foliage is an outstanding deep orange to red. Mature trees develop a layered effect with horizontal branching. A thin gray bark in youth becomes chunky with age.

FLOWERS Tiny yellow-green flowers occur within four showy white bracts in early to midspring (late March to mid-April in Athens). The obovate bracts, 2" long, have a brown cleft in the center of their rounded tips. The variety *rubra* develops pink bracts.

FRUIT Clusters of attractive bright red midautumn drupes are quickly devoured by birds.

LIGHT & SOIL Light shade with a moist but well-drained slightly acidic soil is ideal. They grow in full sun to moderate shade. Flowering and fall color are reduced with shade.

MAINTENANCE Due to the tree's shallow root systems, provide supplemental water during summer droughts.

INSTALLATION Site trees for early morning sun to help prevent fungal problems. Container plants or field-grown trees as large as 3" in caliper are easily transplanted during the dormant season. Space 25' apart, and mulch trees in lawn areas.

top Foliage and autumn fruit.
bottom Spring bracts and flowers.

A pink-flowered cultivar at UGA.

SMALL DECIDUOUS TREES

Fall foliage in Athens.

top Layered form.

bottom In bloom with 'George L. Tabor' azaleas on the UGA campus.

PESTS & DISEASES Memories of hillsides covered with the snow-like blossoms of blooming native dogwoods are largely a thing of the past due to anthracnose, which destroyed many trees starting in the late 1970s. Breeding efforts have increased disease resistance, and planting in locations that receive morning sun helps alleviate disease problems. Deer heavily browse young trees.

NOTES & CULTIVARS
'Appalachian Blush' has excellent powdery mildew resistance and white bracts with pink edges.
'Appalachian Spring' provides outstanding resistance to anthracnose.
'Cherokee Princess' is a heavy-flowering cultivar with large white bracts and good anthracnose resistance.
'Cloud Nine' flowers at an early age, with overlapping bracts and good mildew resistance.
Cornus florida rubra cultivars perform best in zones 5b–8a.
'Cherokee Brave' produces reddish-pink bracts with white centers and some powdery mildew resistance.
'Cherokee Chief' has deep reddish-pink bracts and red new foliage.
'Cherokee Sunset' has red flower bracts and variegated foliage but is susceptible to powdery mildew.

Cornus kousa KOUSA DOGWOOD · KOREAN DOGWOOD

Kousa dogwood offers many attributes that have made the native dogwood one of the most popular understory trees for years: outstanding fall foliage, attractive autumn fruit, and showy late spring flowers with the added bonus of improved disease resistance. Add an attractive exfoliating bark, and you have a tree that looks great around patios and building entrances, as well as from a distance in shrub beds or along woodland edges. Combine them with late spring perennials such as peonies, daylilies, and irises for color combinations in borders.

ZONES & ORIGIN 5a–9a. Native to Asia.

SIZE & GROWTH RATE 20'–30' tall, 15'–25' wide, medium slow growing.

TEXTURE & FORM Medium texture with a broadly oval to rounded form.

FOLIAGE Simple opposite dark green ovate leaves are 2"–4" long, with entire margins, acuminate tips, and often an asymmetrical base. Fall foliage color is an outstanding orange to crimson. Mature trees develop an exfoliating bark that varies upon the individual genetics of each tree but is often quite attractive.

FLOWERS Tiny yellow-green flower clusters occur in the center of four attractive creamy-white bracts in mid- to late spring (late April to late May in Athens). The ovate bracts, 2" long, with acuminate tips, lack the cleft found on *Cornus florida* bracts.

FRUIT Rounded pendulous drupes turn pinkish red in midautumn but are not very attractive to wildlife.

LIGHT & SOIL Full sun to light shade with a moist but well-drained acidic soil.

MAINTENANCE Provide supplemental water for the first few summers.

INSTALLATION Field-grown trees are readily available from nurseries and easily transplanted during the dormant season. Space 20'–25' apart.

PESTS & DISEASES Kousa dogwood resists dogwood anthracnose and is rarely browsed by deer, but it is somewhat susceptible to powdery mildew.

NOTES & CULTIVARS
'Elizabeth Lustgarten' grows 6'–10' with an oval form and pendulous branches.
'Milky Way' grows 20' tall and wide, with heavy flowering.
'Satomi' has pink flower bracts.
Cornus kousa angustata 'Empress of China' provides creamy-white June flowers with evergreen foliage that acquires a purple tint in late autumn.

top Late spring foliage and flowers.
bottom Fall fruit in Athens.

Stellar Series dogwoods are selections of crosses between *Cornus florida* and *Cornus kousa* from Rutgers University. Flowering in mid-April in Athens, they are sterile trees with deep red fall color and improved resistance to anthracnose, powdery mildew, and dogwood borers.

'Aurora' has large rounded white overlapping bracts.
'Celestial' has white overlapping bracts.
'Constellation' is the most popular cultivar, with white bracts.
'Stellar Pink' produces pink bracts.

top Flowers and form at Signal Mountain, Tenn.
bottom Late spring at Mt. Cuba Gardens, Wilmington, Del.

Cotinus coggygria SMOKETREE

top and middle Late spring foliage and flower structures at Chanticleer.
bottom left With daylilies and hosta.
bottom right Late spring flowering.

Smoketree gets its name from its late spring flowers with hairlike strands that appear like smoky pink clouds on the ends of the branches. Its cultivars are far more common than the species. The cultivars are noted for their colorful spring to autumn foliage. Many people sacrifice the flowers by heavily pruning to promote new branches and foliage and maintain the tree as a large shrub in borders to provide a contrasting backdrop for other plants. Smoketree looks better from a distance than up close and is better adapted to cooler drier climates.

ZONES & ORIGIN 5a–8b. Native to southern Europe and western Asia.

SIZE & GROWTH RATE 12'–18' tall and wide, medium growing.

TEXTURE & FORM Medium texture with a rounded form.

FOLIAGE Simple alternate blue-green leaves are 1"–3" long, oval to obovate shaped, with entire margins, rounded or occasionally emarginate tips, and a spicy odor when crushed. Deep orange to reddish-purple fall foliage is outstanding in full sun.

FLOWERS Insignificant tiny greenish-yellow flowers occur in panicles in mid- to late spring (late April to mid-May in Athens). Long smoky pink hairlike flower strands are very showy for several weeks before turning tan in midsummer.

FRUIT Insignificant drupes.

LIGHT & SOIL Full sun to light shade with a well-drained soil and near-neutral pH. Drought tolerant.

MAINTENANCE Pruning helps maintain a dense canopy and avoid a straggly appearance. Prune before midsummer.

INSTALLATION Popular cultivars are available in large containers or as small field-grown trees. Plant during the dormant season, and space 10'–12' apart for hedges.

PESTS & DISEASES Few problems on well-drained locations. Deer rarely browse it.

NOTES & CULTIVARS

'Royal Purple' and 'Velvet Cloak' are popular cultivars with dark burgundy spring foliage that turns reddish purple in summer in full sun and reddish-pink flower filaments.

Cotinus obovatus is a rare tree with good fall foliage color that grows 30'–40' tall on open sites with limestone outcrops from northern Georgia to southern Missouri and is hardy from zones 6b to 8a.

left and top right Midspring flowers and foliage at Chanticleer Garden. *bottom right* Late fall and winter fruit.

Crataegus spp. HAWTHORN

Hawthorns compose a large genus with a number of species native to various parts of the Southeast. In nature, hawthorns freely hybridize, making positive identification difficult. They are generally large shrubs or small trees with dense twigs and numerous thorns located in open areas with a medium growth rate. In colonial times, hawthorns were often pruned into barrier hedges to take advantage of their thorns. Essentially, they can form a living barbed-wire fence. In designs, they are often massed to take advantage of their spring flowers and fall fruit and occasionally used for specimen plants. Hawthorns produce attractive white midspring flowers and clusters of mostly red autumn fruit. As members of the rose family, they are prone to many serious disease problems, which makes it difficult to recommend their use. Borers, fire blight, rust, aphids, spider mites, and assorted leaf spot diseases make their lifespans short and often unsightly. With that in mind, the following is a quick summary of the two most commercially important hawthorns.

Crataegus phaenopyrum
WASHINGTON HAWTHORN

Washington hawthorn grows 20'– 30' tall and wide with a pyramidal form that becomes rounded with age. Hardy from zones 4b to 8b, it has a medium fine texture and dense twiggy habit. Simple leaves are triangular-ovate shaped, up to 3" long, with serrate margins and three to five lobes. The leaves can turn yellow to orange in fall but often succumb to fungal diseases without developing color. Mature bark is gray and somewhat scaly and often covered in thorns. Attractive clusters of creamy-white flowers occur in midspring (late April to early May in Athens), with the odor of aged road kill on hot summer days. Pea-sized pomes turn a brilliant red in midautumn and remain on the tree into winter. They perform best in full sun and a moist but well-drained soil but tolerate drought and an alkaline soil pH.

Crataegus viridis 'WINTER KING' · WINTER KING HAWTHORN

Winter king hawthorn grows 15'– 25' in height and spread, with a medium fine texture and vase-shaped form that becomes rounded with age. Hardy from zone 5a to 9a and found on bottomland sites from north Florida and Texas to Pennsylvania, it performs best above zone 7b. Attractive clusters 2" long of tiny white flowers with a slightly unpleasant odor occur in midspring (mid-April in Athens). The pea-sized fruit turn orange red in late autumn and remain well into winter. The simple leaves, which are 2" long, are broadly oval or occasionally obovate in shape, with doubly serrate margins and a deep red fall color. A silvery-gray bark develops a scaly exfoliating habit to reveal an orange inner bark. Winter king is widely available in sizes up to 2" in caliper and should be planted in early spring in full sun with a moist but well-drained soil.

top left Foliage and late summer flowers.

right Form at Longwood Gardens.

bottom left Fall foliage.

Franklinia altamaha FRANKLINIA

Anyone who has seen a healthy mature Franklinia has probably vowed to obtain one at some point in their life. The early autumn camellia-like white flowers provide a sweet fragrance and are followed by outstanding fall foliage. Sadly, they cannot be grown in much of the Southeast due to a soil-borne root fungus perhaps introduced by cotton. We recommend them for large containers in courtyards or on patios.

ZONES & ORIGIN 6b–9a. Native to southeastern Georgia.

SIZE & GROWTH RATE 15'–25' tall, 10'–20' wide, medium growing.

TEXTURE & FORM Medium texture and broadly oval form.

FOLIAGE Simple obovate leaves are 3½"–8" long, with acute tips, finely tapered bases, and finely serrate margins, and they are often clustered near the ends of twigs. It provides a good orange to crimson fall foliage.

LIGHT & SOIL Provide light shade with a loose, moist, but well-drained acidic soil. Franklinia doesn't tolerate wet feet, but it doesn't like to dry out either.

MAINTENANCE For massing, plant 20' on center. Provide a loose soil mix and supplemental water during droughts.

NOTES & CULTIVARS
Use artificial soil mixes without pine bark to avoid introducing the fungus into the roots of Franklinia. No cultivars available.

Halesia tetraptera CAROLINA SILVERBELL

Carolina silverbell is an understory tree found on the lower slopes of shaded woodlands and well-drained bottomlands of the upper Piedmont and mountains of the Southeast. It does well in shaded locations, provided it receives consistent moisture. Attractive white flowers attract hummingbirds but last for only a short period in midspring. Consider using it around water features, in the rear of shrub borders, and along woodland edges and paths.

ZONES & ORIGIN 5a–8b. Native from Alabama to West Virginia.

SIZE & GROWTH RATE 20'–35' tall, 15'–25' wide, medium slow growing.

TEXTURE & FORM Medium texture with a broadly oval form.

FOLIAGE Simple alternate leaves 3"–6" long are ovate to elliptic shaped, with soft silvery-white hairs beneath and serrate margins. Fall color is a poor yellow, with the foliage often falling without developing any color, but it is more consistent farther north. Young bark has lighter vertical stripes, while mature bark is shallowly ridged and furrowed and is low-branched for many years.

FLOWERS Pendulous bell-shaped white flowers occur in clusters of four or five below the branches in midspring with the new foliage (early April in Athens). Though not as showy as dogwoods, the trees flower in heavier shade and are popular with hummingbirds and beekeepers for honey.

FRUIT Insignificant light green four-winged drupes mature in late summer and remain into winter.

LIGHT & SOIL Light to moderate shade with a moist but well-drained acidic soil. Silverbell grows in full sun but is not drought tolerant.

MAINTENANCE Provide adequate mulch and supplemental water during summer droughts.

INSTALLATION Field-grown silverbells are available in single and multiple trunks in sizes up to 2" in caliper, but they transplant more successfully from containers. For massing, space 12'–15' apart.

PESTS & DISEASES No serious pest problems. Deer rarely browse them.

NOTES & CULTIVARS
'Arnold's Pink' and 'Rosea', with light pink flowers, are available in small containers from specialty nurseries. *Halesia diptera* is native to the southeastern Coastal Plain and hardy to zone 6b. Its flowers are more open, and its drupes have two wings.

top *Halesia diptera* flowers and foliage.
middle *Halesia diptera* at New York City's High Line.
bottom *Halesia diptera* at Chanticleer Garden.

Spring trees in north Georgia.

left Late summer flowers.

right Late summer street tree in Athens.

top Bipinnately compound leaves.

bottom Early fall fruit.

Koelreuteria bipinnata CHINESE FLAME TREE

Chinese flame tree is a small fast-growing tree that provides a show in late summer and early autumn when few plants are blooming. Its late summer flowers last for several weeks and are followed by salmon-colored seedpods into early October. Due to its fast growth, trees reach mature sizes in only 10–12 years and tolerate tough urban environments. It is attractive from a distance but messy up close, so use it for massing in open areas or for sidewalk and parking lot shade, but think carefully before placing it around patios or courtyards.

ZONES & ORIGIN 7b–10b. Native to China.

SIZE & GROWTH RATE 25'–40' tall and wide, fast growing.

TEXTURE & FORM Medium coarse texture, broadly oval form with age.

FOLIAGE Alternate bipinnately compound leaves are up to 2' long. Ovate leaflets 2"–4" long are lustrous dark green above, with entire margins. Fall color is a fair yellow. Grayish-brown bark is shallowly ridged and furrowed on mature trees.

FLOWERS Showy terminal panicles of small bright yellow flowers occur for several weeks in late summer (mid-August to mid-September in Athens). The panicles are up to 2' long, with hundreds of flowers on each.

FRUIT Three-sided papery capsules turn an attractive salmon color for several weeks in early to midautumn (mid-September to mid-October in Athens) before turning tan and remaining into winter.

LIGHT & SOIL Provide full sun and well-drained soils. It tolerates drought, slightly alkaline soils, and moderate salt spray.

MAINTENANCE Trees are short-lived, approximately 30 years, and easily damaged by heavy winds and ice. Selective pruning is recommended in late winter and early spring to eliminate weak branch crotches. Spent flowers, leaves, and seedpods drop in fall, with broken branches year-round.

INSTALLATION Due to its fast growth, small container plants planted in early to midspring perform best. Young trees have an awkward appearance and benefit from support for the first year but begin flowering by three years of age.

PESTS & DISEASES No serious problems. Deer seldom browse it.

NOTES & CULTIVARS
None listed.

Koelreuteria paniculata GOLDENRAINTREE

Goldenraintree kicks off summer with an explosion of yellow flowers. Lasting several weeks in early summer, the bright yellow flowers cover the tree, then fall to the ground like yellow rain. This is a vigorous tree that doesn't skip a beat when planted in tough urban situations, so take advantage of its fast growth to provide some quick color and shade for parking lots and sidewalks. Use it for massing, and either combine it with a ground cover like lantana or verbena or pair it with garden hydrangeas. It is best viewed from a distance, since it tends to be a little messy, with broken twigs and falling seedpods, so be careful about placing it around patios or in courtyards.

Early summer flowers and foliage.

ZONES & ORIGIN   5b–9b. Native to Asia.

SIZE & GROWTH RATE   20'–35' tall and wide, fast growing.

TEXTURE & FORM   Medium texture with a broadly oval form.

FOLIAGE   Odd pinnately compound leaves 6"–18" long have 9 to 17 leaflets. The dark green leaflets have coarsely serrate margins, are often deeply lobed, and are sometimes trifoliate. Fall color is a good yellow. Light gray bark is shallowly ridged and furrowed.

FLOWERS   Showy terminal panicles of small bright yellow flowers occur for about two weeks in late May to early June in Athens. Hundreds of flowers are on each panicle.

FRUIT   Three-sided light green papery capsules resembling small Chinese lanterns appear after flowering, turning tan in summer and remaining into winter.

LIGHT & SOIL   Provide full sun to light shade and well-drained soil. It tolerates drought, alkaline soils, and moderate salt spray.

MAINTENANCE   Goldenraintree produces numerous seedlings, particularly in ground cover beds, and may be invasive in some areas. Prune branches to eliminate weak crotches in late winter.

INSTALLATION   Usually only container grown due to their fast growth. Plant in early spring, and provide support for the first year.

PESTS & DISEASES   No serious problems. Deer seldom browse it.

NOTES & CULTIVARS
'Fastigiata' reaches 30' with a 4'–6' spread but is rare in nurseries and does not flower heavily.

left and middle Flowering on the UGA campus.   *right* Flowers at Reinhardt University.

Lagerstroemia spp. CRAPE MYRTLE

Crape myrtles are typically small trees that provide interest throughout the year. Though best known for their extended show of summer flowers in a variety of colors, their outstanding fall foliage is equally attractive. Often overlooked are their muscularly ridged trunks and exfoliating bark, which are especially attractive up close. Crape myrtle is one of the few plants that is just as attractive in parking lots or along roadsides as it is in courtyards or on patios. Many cultivars now offered are crosses between *Lagerstroemia indica* and *fauriei* that provide abundant flowers and improved disease resistance. Several smaller cultivars work well as large or small shrubs.

ZONES & ORIGIN 6b–10b. Native to Asia.

SIZE & GROWTH RATE 15'–30' tall, 15'–25' wide, medium fast growing.

TEXTURE & FORM Medium fine texture and broadly oval form.

FOLIAGE Opposite simple leaves are 1"–3" long, elliptic to obovate shaped, with entire margins and orange to red fall color. Usually multitrunked, with older trunks developing attractive tan-colored muscular ridges and exfoliating bark.

FLOWERS Large showy panicles in pink, white, red, or purple occur for several weeks in midsummer, with sporadic flowering into September. Some cultivars begin blooming in June, but most begin in July.

FRUIT Nonshowy capsules through winter.

LIGHT & SOIL Provide full sun to light shade and well-drained soils. They tolerate drought, higher pH levels, and moderate salt spray.

MAINTENANCE Remove suckers from the base and roots. Never prune main stems or trunks unless they are damaged. Severe pruning to increase flowering produces weakened plants over time that are prone to powdery mildew and destroys their natural form.

INSTALLATION Widely available in both large containers and field-grown plants, they can be planted year-round, though the best time is usually early spring. Provide 20'–25' minimum spacing for larger cultivars.

PESTS & DISEASES Aphids, leaf spot, and powdery mildew can be problems, particularly on *L. indica* cultivars.

top left 'Sarah's Favorite'.
top right 'Near East' and 'Carolina Beauty'.
middle 'Red Rocket'.
bottom Fall color on the UGA campus.

Attractive winter habit near Charleston, S.C.

NOTES & CULTIVARS

These cultivars are listed by size, with an attempt to list the best and most available. Flowering dates are for zone 8a. An asterisk indicates a hybrid cultivar.

Small Tree Forms (18'–30')

*'Apalachee'—light lavender early July flowers, reddish-brown fall color, to 20'
*'Arapaho'—bright red early July flowers, red to maroon fall color, to 20'
*'Biloxi'—light pink mid-July flowers, orange-red fall foliage, to 30'
'Carolina Beauty'—pinkish-red mid-July flowers, orange fall foliage, to 20'
*'Choctaw'—bright pink mid-July flowers, orange-red fall foliage, to 25'
'Dynamite'—bright red early July flowers, orange fall color, to 25'
*'Muskogee'—light lavender mid-June flowers, yellow to red fall color, to 30'
*'Natchez'—white early June flowers, cinnamon-brown bark, orange-red fall color, to 30'
'Red Rocket'—cherry-red mid-July flowers, reddish-orange fall color, to 20'
'Sarah's Favorite'—white mid-June flowers, yellow-orange fall color, hardy to zone 6a, to 25'
'Seminole'—pink mid-June flowers, yellow fall color, rounded form, to 20'
*'Tuscarora'—dark pink early July flowers, orange-red fall color, to 25'
*'Tuskegee'—dark pink late June flowers, orange-red fall color, spreading form, to 25'

Large Shrub or Small Tree Forms (10'–18')

*'Catawba'—lavender-purple mid-July flowers, reddish-orange fall color, to 15'
*'Comanche'—dark pink mid-July flowers, orange-red fall color, to 18'
*'Lipan'—lavender-pink mid-July flowers, orange fall foliage, to 18'
'Near East'—light pink mid-July flowers, yellow-orange fall color, spreading form, to 18'
*'Osage'—pink early July flowers, yellow-orange fall color, to 18'
*'Sioux'—pink late June flowers, yellow-red fall color, to 18'
*'Yuma'—medium lavender late July flowers, maroon-red fall color, to 18'

Large Shrub Forms (5'–10')

*'Acoma'—white flowers mid-June, red fall color, rounded form, to 10'
*'Caddo'—vivid pink mid-July flowers, orange-red fall color, spreading form, to 8'
*'Hopi'—pink late June flowers, orange-red fall color, spreading form, to 10'
*'Pecos'—pink mid-July flowers, maroon fall color, rounded form, to 10'
*'Tonto'—dark pinkish-red mid-July flowers, maroon fall color, to 10'
*'Zuni'—lavender-pink late July flowers, orange-red fall color, to 10'

Small to Medium Shrub Forms (3'–5')

'Cherry Dazzle'—bright red flowers in July and August, orange-red fall foliage, mounding form 3' tall by 5' wide
'Dazzle Me Pink'—medium pink flowers in mid-July, mounded form, to 4'
*'Pocomoke'—rose-pink flowers in July and August, to 4' tall by 4' wide
'Ruby Dazzle'—bronzy-red foliage, pink flowers in early August, mounded form, to 3'

Magnolia stellata STAR MAGNOLIA

Star magnolia is often considered as a large shrub rather than a small tree because of its multitrunked habit and slow growth rate. The rewards for using it are lovely lightly fragrant late winter to early spring flowers. Star magnolia is often used as a specimen plant near courtyards, decks, and patios and even performs well in large containers for use in those settings. Consider using it in border plantings with quince, forsythia, daffodils, and tulips, which bloom at the same time.

ZONES & ORIGIN   4b–8b. Native to Japan.

SIZE & GROWTH RATE   10'–15' tall, 10'–12' wide, slow growing.

TEXTURE & FORM   Medium texture and broadly oval to rounded form.

FOLIAGE   Alternate simple leaves are 2"–5" long, elliptic to obovate shaped, with entire margins and acute or occasionally rounded tips. Fall color is a poor yellow. It forms a dense twiggy mass with multiple smooth light gray trunks.

FLOWERS   Lightly fragrant white flowers appear for several weeks in late winter and early spring (mid-February to early March in Athens). The flowers, 2"–4" wide, have 12 to 30 tepals, which are a combination of petals and sepals. Flowers are susceptible to hard frosts as they are opening.

FRUIT   Insignificant cone-like fruit.

LIGHT & SOIL   Light shade and moist but well-drained acidic soils are ideal. It tolerates full sun to moderate shade and slightly moist soils.

MAINTENANCE   Mulch to keep roots cool and moist. Prune in midspring to allow time for next year's flower buds to form.

INSTALLATION   Star magnolia is available in containers and small field-grown plants usually less than 6' tall. Plant in spring and provide supplemental water for the first summer and during severe droughts.

PESTS & DISEASES   Deer, rabbits, and opossums browse the foliage and bark.

NOTES & CULTIVARS
'Centennial' produces large white flowers.
'Pink Stardust' produces large light pink flowers.
'Royal Star' is the predominant cultivar, with pink flower buds that open into large white flowers one to two weeks after the species.

top   Foliage.
bottom   Flower.

left   Form at the Ram Giberson residence.
right   Late winter flowers in Athens.

left Late winter flowers on the UGA campus.

right Form.

Magnolia × loebneri LOEBNER MAGNOLIA

Loebner magnolias are crosses between two Japanese species, *Magnolia kobus* and *Magnolia stellata*. Their attractive early season flowers make a show for several weeks but are susceptible to hard late season frosts, which turn them to brown mush. Trees exposed to early morning sun are at a greater risk of frost damage to the flowers. Their clean character, late winter flowers, and appealing multitrunked habit make them well suited for intimate protected courtyards, which could also help protect the flowers from damaging freezes. Combine them with flowering quince, daffodils, winter daphne, and edgeworthia, which bloom at the same time.

ZONES & ORIGIN 4b–8b. A cross between Japanese species.

SIZE & GROWTH RATE 20'–30' tall and wide, medium growing.

TEXTURE & FORM Medium texture and broadly oval form but pyramidal in youth.

FOLIAGE Alternate simple leaves are 3"–6" long, elliptic to oblong shaped, with entire margins and acute or occasionally rounded or notched tips. Yellow fall foliage is usually poor.

FLOWERS Showy flowers appear for several weeks in late winter to early spring (early February to early March in Athens). The flowers, which are 4"–6" wide, with 9 to 16 tepals, are white to rosy pink, depending upon the cultivar. Flowers are extremely susceptible to freezing temperatures as they are opening.

FRUIT An insignificant cone-like fruit is rarely produced.

LIGHT & SOIL Provide full sun to light shade with a moist to moist but well-drained slightly acidic soil.

MAINTENANCE Provide supplemental water for the first few years until well established. Prune immediately after flowering is completed to avoid removing next year's flower buds.

INSTALLATION Cultivars are widely available as field-grown trees up to 10'–12' in height and are best planted in spring.

PESTS & DISEASES No serious problems. Deer rarely browse them.

NOTES & CULTIVARS

'Ballerina' produces white flowers with a light pink blush at the base of the tepals.

'Leonard Messel' has large flowers that are white on the inside and rosy pink on the outside, with a medium slow growth rate.

'Merrill' produces white flowers with a faster growth rate.

top Foliage.

bottom Flowers.

top left Flowering in Athens.
top right Form on Milledge Avenue in Athens.
middle Foliage.
bottom Flowers.

Magnolia × *soulangeana* SAUCER MAGNOLIA

Saucer magnolia is the best known of the early season flowering magnolias. It is a cross between *Magnolia denudata*, a tall tree with white late winter flowers, and *Magnolia lilliflora*, a large shrub with purple early spring flowers. The selected cultivars possess highly attractive early spring pinkish-purple flowers. They are effective in masses or individually along shrub and perennial borders. Consider underplanting them with daffodils, forsythia, and edgeworthia for complementary colors.

ZONES & ORIGIN 5a–9b. A cross between two Asian species.

SIZE & GROWTH RATE 20'–30' tall and wide, medium growing.

TEXTURE & FORM Coarse texture and broadly oval form.

FOLIAGE Alternate simple leaves are 3"–7" long, broadly elliptic to obovate shaped, with entire margins, acute tips, and pubescence when young. Fall color is a fair yellow. Twigs have large hairy terminal flower buds. Trees are usually low-branched and multitrunked, with a smooth gray bark.

FLOWERS Highly attractive cup-shaped flowers occur in late winter to early spring (late February to mid-March in Athens), with some flowers opening in midautumn as well. The flowers are dark pink to purple outside, white on the inside, and susceptible to late frosts.

FRUIT Rare and insignificant fruit.

LIGHT & SOIL Provide full sun to light shade and moist but well-drained slightly acidic soils.

MAINTENANCE Provide supplemental water for several years during summer droughts. Spent flowers are messy. A thin bark is easily damaged by maintenance equipment.

INSTALLATION Transplant in early spring. Field-grown trees up to 3" in caliper are widely available.

PESTS & DISEASES No problems. Deer rarely browse it.

NOTES & CULTIVARS
'Alexandrina' is hardy to 4b and blooms several weeks later, with deep red-purple flowers.
'Lennei' is a faster grower, with dark red flowers.
'Rustica Rubra' has goblet-shaped reddish-purple flowers.
The U.S. National Arboretum released a series of cultivars that are crosses between *Magnolia stellata* 'Rosea' and *Magnolia lilliflora* 'Nigra'. They grow 8'–12' tall, with rosy-purple early to midspring flowers. The most common cultivars are the late bloomers 'Jane' and 'Judy' and an early bloomer, 'Ann'.

Malus spp. FLOWERING CRABAPPLE

Flowering crabapples are among the most colorful spring flowering trees for the design palette. These versatile trees are available in a range of sizes and forms, as well as flower colors, that fits almost any niche. Highly popular in masses and as individual trees in border plantings, they are sometimes overlooked because they bloom at the same time as dogwoods and redbuds. Disease issues in humid climates require specifying disease-resistant cultivars and thoughtful consideration of their use.

top Flowers.
bottom Fruit.

ZONES & ORIGIN 4a–8a. Cultivars from hybrids of predominantly Asian species.

SIZE & GROWTH RATE 10'–25' tall and wide, medium growing.

TEXTURE & FORM Medium texture with oval to spreading form, depending upon the cultivar.

FOLIAGE Alternate simple leaves are 2"–5" long, ovate to elliptic shaped, with crenate-serrate margins and acuminate tips. A few cultivars have lobed leaves. Fall color is not dependable in the Southeast.

FLOWERS Showy red, pink, or white single or double flowers cover the tree for seven to ten days, with the new foliage in late March to early April in Athens. Some cultivars are lightly fragrant. Flower buds are colorful for a week before opening.

FRUIT Fruit is a tart edible pome ⅜"–1½" in diameter in yellow or red, depending upon the cultivar. It ripens in early autumn and is generally showy, with several cultivars producing fruit that attracts wildlife.

LIGHT & SOIL Full sun with a moist but well-drained acidic soil is ideal. Light shade reduces flowering and increases disease susceptibility.

MAINTENANCE Remove root sprouts and thin the canopy after flowering to improve air circulation.

INSTALLATION Field-grown trees are readily available in sizes up to 3" in caliper. Plant during the dormant season and space 20'–30' apart for massing.

PESTS & DISEASES Apple scab causes early summer defoliation. Cedar apple rust fungus defoliates in early to midsum-

Early spring flowering in Athens.

top left Flowers in bloom at the Wray Nicholson House.

top right Form at the Douglas residence.

bottom Espalier in the Founders Memorial Garden.

mer. Fire blight kills new spring growth. Aphids, scale, Japanese beetles, borers, white-tailed deer, and powdery mildew combine to make life interesting.

NOTES & CULTIVARS

These common cultivars from southeastern nurseries show improved disease resistance.

- 'Adirondack' is a slow grower to 18' with an oval form, red buds with white flowers, and orange-red fruit.
- 'Callaway' provides a rounded form to 25' with pink buds, large white flowers, and large dark red fruit.
- 'Candy Mint Sargent' grows to 12' with a spreading form, pinkish-white flowers, and dark red fruit.
- 'Coralburst' reaches 12' tall with a rounded form, double rosy-pink flowers, and small reddish-orange fruit.
- *floribunda* grows to 25' with a spreading form, dark pink buds, and pinkish-white fragrant flowers.
- 'Harvest Gold' grows to 25' with an oval form, pink buds, white flowers, and small yellow fruit.
- 'Prairiefire' grows to 20' with a rounded form, bright red flowers, small dark red fruit, and red new foliage that turns dark green in summer.
- 'Profusion' grows to 25' with a rounded to broadly oval form, salmon-pink flowers, maroon fruit, and purple new foliage that turns bronzy green.
- 'Red Jade' reaches 12' with a spreading form, pendulous branches, dark pink buds, white flowers, and bright red fruit.
- 'Red Jewel' reaches 15' with an oval form, white flowers, and bright red fruit.
- 'Robinson' is a fast grower to 25' with a rounded form, deep pink flowers, and bright red fruit.
- 'Snowdrift' reaches 20' with a rounded form, pink buds, white flowers, and tiny orange-red fruit.
- 'Spring Snow' reaches 25' with a rounded form, fragrant white flowers, and few fruit.
- 'Sugar Tyme' grows to 20' with an oval form, fragrant white flowers, and small red fruit.
- *Malus* × *zumi* var. *calocarpa* grows to 25' with a spreading form, pinkish-red buds, lightly fragrant white flowers, and small red fruit.

Parrotia persica PARROTIA · PERSIAN IRONWOOD

Parrotia doesn't fit the description of most small trees. Despite flowering in early spring before the leaves, its flowers are not showy. And, unlike most small trees, it lives for over 100 years. It is known primarily for its superb fall foliage, dense low-branching canopy, clean demeanor, tolerance of urban conditions, and attractive exfoliating bark. Its toughness makes it popular for street tree plantings, traffic circles, raised planters, and screens and buffers. Don't overlook using it as a specimen tree for small spaces to take advantage of its branching habit and exfoliating bark.

ZONES & ORIGIN 5a–8b. Native to Iran and Iraq.

SIZE & GROWTH RATE 25'–35' tall, 15'–30' wide, medium slow growing.

TEXTURE & FORM Medium texture with an oval form in youth, rounded with age.

FOLIAGE Alternate simple leaves are 3"–5" long, mostly obovate shaped, with coarse rounded teeth above the middle and uneven bases. New foliage emerges reddish purple, while fall color ranges from an outstanding yellow to orange to scarlet. Parrotia is multitrunked, with very low branches, and a subtle but attractive exfoliating bark reveals splotches of tan, green, and beige inner bark.

FLOWERS Insignificant flowers with red anthers but lacking petals and sepals emerge in early spring before the foliage.

FRUIT Insignificant small brown woody capsules.

LIGHT & SOIL Full sun to light shade and well-drained soil are ideal. It tolerates drought and slightly alkaline soils.

MAINTENANCE With branches virtually to the ground, some limbs may need to be removed to show the exfoliating bark.

INSTALLATION Field-grown trees are somewhat available and easily transplanted in the dormant season. For a continuous mass, plant 25' on center and ensure good surface drainage.

PESTS & DISEASES No serious problems.

NOTES & CULTIVARS

While the species is somewhat available in the Southeast, parrotia cultivars are primarily grown in the Pacific Northwest and Great Lakes areas and are usually smaller in size. 'Vanessa' and 'Ruby Vase' are more upright, with oval forms.

top Foliage.

bottom Fall foliage on the UGA campus.

left Thirty-plus-year-old forms at the State Botanical Garden of Georgia.

right Old specimen at the Bloedel Reserve, Bainbridge, Wash.

Late winter flowers in Oconee County, in the Founders Memorial Garden, and in Savannah.

Prunus campanulata TAIWAN FLOWERING CHERRY

Taiwan flowering cherry is the earliest flowering but least cold-hardy of the flowering cherries. Its rosy-red flowers brighten the late winter landscape when virtually nothing else shows signs of life. It has been highly popular in the lower parts of zone 8 and zone 9, where it often blooms by mid-January. In the northern parts of its range, hard freezes can destroy the flowers after they open. It is a mostly nondescript tree when not in bloom, so consider locating it in the back of shrub borders with *Hamamelis* × *intermedia*.

Flowers

ZONES & ORIGIN 8a–9b. Native to Taiwan and Japan.

SIZE & GROWTH RATE 15'–25' tall, 15'–20' wide, fast growing.

TEXTURE & FORM Medium texture and broadly oval form.

FOLIAGE Alternate simple leaves are 3"–4" long, ovate shaped, with doubly serrate margins and acuminate tips. Fall color is a fair bronzy yellow. Raised lenticels form stripes along its gray bark.

FLOWERS Pendulous bell-shaped pinkish-red flowers occur in clusters of three to five below the stems for several weeks in late winter (late January to late February in Athens) and endure frosts and light freezes without damage.

FRUIT Small rounded drupes maturing to black in late spring are not showy, but they are popular with birds.

LIGHT & SOIL Full sun to light shade with a moist but well-drained slightly acidic soil. It tolerates moderate droughts.

MAINTENANCE Seedlings can cause problems in the lower parts of its range.

INSTALLATION Gulf Coast nurseries carry trees up to 4" in caliper. Due to their fast growth, smaller trees may be a better choice. Plant during the dormant season, and space 25' for massing.

PESTS & DISEASES Borers, Japanese beetles, scale, aphids, and other pests catch up to it within 20 years.

NOTES & CULTIVARS
Prunus × 'First Lady' is a cross between Taiwan and Okame cherries. A fast grower, reaching 25'–30' with an oval form, and hardy to zone 6a, with dark rosy-red flowers closely resembling Taiwan cherry but blooming several weeks later.

Prunus cerasifera 'Atropurpurea' PURPLELEAF PLUM

Purpleleaf plums are trees that you either love or hate. For most folks, a little goes a long way. Its reddish-purple foliage commands attention, whether you are standing still or traveling 60 mph. Wherever it is used, it will stand out. Use it in shrub or perennial borders to complement or contrast adjacent flower and foliage colors, but make sure to avoid placing it in front of red brick walls or buildings.

Early spring flowers.

ZONES & ORIGIN 4b–8b. Native to Persia.

SIZE & GROWTH RATE 15'–25' tall and wide, fast growing.

TEXTURE & FORM Medium texture and broadly oval to rounded form.

FOLIAGE Alternate ovate simple leaves, 1½"–3" long, have serrate margins and acuminate tips and emerge red before turning reddish purple to coppery purple in summer. Shaded leaves turn greenish purple. The gray bark has irregular shallow ridges.

FLOWERS Lightly fragrant dusty light pink flowers emerge with the foliage for seven to ten days in early spring (mid-March in Athens). Flowers, which are 1" wide, have five oval petals but are somewhat camouflaged by the purple foliage.

FRUIT Small reddish-purple drupes maturing in midsummer are devoured by birds but hidden within the purple foliage.

LIGHT & SOIL Provide full sun with a moist but well-drained soil that is slightly acidic to neutral pH. It tolerates drought after establishment.

MAINTENANCE Root suckers are common and should be removed. It can be invasive in drier climates such as the Pacific Northwest.

INSTALLATION Transplant container or field-grown trees during the dormant season. Space trees 25' apart for continuous canopies. Provide supplemental water for the first summer.

PESTS & DISEASES Borers, aphids, scale, and various fungal diseases generally limit purpleleaf plums to a life expectancy of 20–30 years.

NOTES & CULTIVARS
Prunus cerasifera with green leaves and white flowers is rarely grown. 'Newport' is a purple-leafed hybrid of *Prunus cerasifera*, *P. salicina*, and *P. americana* that is hardy to zone 4a, reaches 15' in height and spread, and flowers later than 'Atropurpurea'. 'Thundercloud' is hardy to zone 5a and reaches 15'–20' in height and spread.

left At the Oregon Vietnam Veterans Memorial in Portland.
middle In Vancouver, B.C.
right At Butchart Gardens.

White flowering at Magnolia Plantation and Gardens.

Prunus persica FLOWERING PEACH

Ornamental peach is noted for its showy single and double flowers in colors of red, pink, and white in early spring before the leaves emerge (mid-March in Athens). Some cultivars have burgundy-colored foliage. Peaches need a minimum number of hours of cold temperatures to set flower buds, which limits their range in the Southeast. Due to their disease issues, consider using them in large containers on patios and in courtyards rather than planting them in the landscape.

Pink and red at Magnolia Plantation and Gardens.

ZONES & ORIGIN 5b–8b. Native to China.

SIZE & GROWTH RATE 12'–20' tall, 15'–20' wide, fast growing.

TEXTURE & FORM Medium texture and rounded form.

FOLIAGE Alternate simple lanceolate leaves 2"–5" long have serrate margins and acuminate tips. Foliage diseases often cause early defoliation. A gray bark has horizontal lenticels, while young stems are reddish brown.

LIGHT & SOIL Full sun and a moist but well-drained acidic soil.

MAINTENANCE Peaches are very short-lived, fewer than 15 years. Borers, aphids, scale, caterpillars, and numerous fungal diseases all contribute to their short life. Prune after flowering to avoid small inedible midsummer peaches.

NOTES & CULTIVARS
Corinthian hybrids with upright oval forms are available with white, pinkish-white, and pinkish-red flowers.

Prunus serrulata 'Kanzan'   KANZAN CHERRY

Kanzan cherry is the last of the popular flowering cherries to bloom in spring. Kanzan is the only one that blooms as the leaves are emerging, and it continues in bloom with the leaves nearly fully developed. Yet in spite of this, it still puts on such a show with its rounded bubblegum-pink flowers that people tend to stop and stare when they encounter it. Kanzans are good choices for massing in combination with spiraeas and azaleas in border plantings or for patios and courtyards, where their spreading form can shade the ground plane.

Flowers close up on the UGA campus.

ZONES & ORIGIN   5b–8b. Native to Japan.

SIZE & GROWTH RATE   20'–25' in height and spread, fast growing.

TEXTURE & FORM   Medium texture with rounded to spreading form.

FOLIAGE   Alternate lustrous dark green simple leaves 3"–5½" long are elliptic to oval shaped, with sharply serrate margins and acuminate tips. Leaves emerge coppery red in spring and develop a fair yellow-orange fall color.

FLOWERS   Bubblegum-pink double flowers 2" wide emerge with new foliage over several days in early spring (late March to early April in Athens), with the show lasting 10 to 14 days.

FRUIT   Insignificant.

LIGHT & SOIL   Full sun with moist but well-drained soils. It tolerates short droughts and near-neutral pH soils.

MAINTENANCE   Provide supplemental water during summer droughts, and protect the thin bark from maintenance equipment.

INSTALLATION   Readily available in up to 5" in caliper, but smaller trees may be better due to their fast growth. Plant by early spring, provide supplemental water for the first year, and space 25'–30' on center.

PESTS & DISEASES   Trees begin to decline after 15 to 20 years, with few living beyond 30 years. Borers, aphids, various fungal diseases, and deer are all culprits.

NOTES & CULTIVARS

'Shirotae' and 'Mt. Fuji' reach 18' with spreading forms and lightly fragrant semidouble white flowers with a light pink blush that are 2" wide.

'Snow Goose' is a hybrid between *Prunus incisa* and *P. serrulata speciosa*, growing to 20' with a rounded form and single white flowers.

Flowers on the UGA campus and in Athens.

Flowers close up on the UGA campus and at a Charleston residence.

Prunus × *incam* 'Okame'   OKAME CHERRY

Okame cherry is an eye-catching late winter flowering tree that blooms about the same time as Loebner magnolia. Like Loebner, it is susceptible to late winter freezes while in flower. Selected from a cross between Taiwan cherry, *Prunus campanulata*, and Fuji cherry, *P. incisa*, it is a fast-growing tree whose small size makes it suited for small yards, courtyards, and patios. Use it for massing to take advantage of those spectacular late winter flowers, but avoid placing it in front of a red brick wall without some tall evergreen background.

ZONES & ORIGIN 6a–9a. A cross between two Asian species.

SIZE & GROWTH RATE 20'–25' tall, 15'–20' wide, fast growing.

TEXTURE & FORM Medium fine texture with a vase-shaped form in youth, broadly oval at maturity.

FOLIAGE Alternate simple leaves 1¾"–3" long are elliptic shaped, with serrate margins, acuminate tips, and rounded glands at their base. Fall color is a dull orange, usually not outstanding, and developing late. Reddish-brown bark develops prominent raised lenticels, which form stripes along the trunk.

FLOWERS Showy smoky pink flowers emerge in late winter and last 10 to 14 days (mid- to late February in Athens). The flowers have a red calyx, which appears about a week before the flowers open.

FRUIT Insignificant drupes appear in late spring.

LIGHT & SOIL Provide full sun to light shade with a moist but well-drained acidic soil. Susceptible to droughts, it benefits from supplemental water during summers.

MAINTENANCE Angled branches are susceptible to storm damage, so remove branches with narrow crotches. The thin bark is susceptible to damage from lawn maintenance equipment.

INSTALLATION Trees are widely available and transplant easily as field-grown trees in sizes up to 3" in caliper during the dormant season. With its fast growth rate, a smaller tree may be a better bargain. For masses, space trees 20'–25' apart.

PESTS & DISEASES Trees are short-lived, 15 to 25 years, with borers and Japanese beetles proving the biggest threats. Deer browse young plants.

NOTES & CULTIVARS
None listed.

Prunus subhirtella HIGAN CHERRY

Higan cherries were considered as crosses between two Japanese species. The tree is now considered a separate species, but the old name, *Prunus × subhirtella*, is still frequently encountered. Higan cherry is known for its two varieties: *pendula*, with pendulous branches and weeping form, and *autumnalis*, with ascending branches and broadly oval form. Several cultivars are available within both varieties.

ZONES & ORIGIN 5b–8b. Native to Japan.

SIZE & GROWTH RATE 20'–35' tall, 20'–30' wide, medium growing.

TEXTURE & FORM Medium texture and broadly oval form.

FOLIAGE Alternate lustrous dark green simple leaves 3½"–5" long are narrowly elliptic, with serrate margins, acuminate tips, and prominent depressed veins. Fall color is often a good yellow orange.

FLOWERS Clusters of light pinkish-white flowers occur in early spring (mid- to late March in Athens), with a few flowers in autumn.

FRUIT Insignificant purple-black early summer drupes.

LIGHT & SOIL Full sun to light shade with moist but well-drained slightly acidic soils.

MAINTENANCE Provide supplemental water during extended summer droughts.

INSTALLATION Trees up to 4" in caliper are readily available. Plant during the dormant season on 25'–30' centers.

PESTS & DISEASES Similar issues as other ornamental cherries but longer-lived.

NOTES & CULTIVARS

Prunus subhirtella pendula cultivars are usually grafted about 5' high onto rootstock of mazzard cherry, *P. avium*. Sprouts below the graft must be removed to maintain the intended form. Weeping cherries lend themselves for use as accent or specimen plants rather than for massing. Their pendulous branches are quite graceful, and the light pinkish-white early spring flowers covering the tree only add to that impression.

'Pendula' has pink buds opening to pinkish white.

'Pendula Plena Rosea' produces double light pink flowers.

Prunus subhirtella autumnalis is often multitrunked, developing a broadly oval form to 35' with low ascending branches.

'Autumnalis' has a vase-shaped branching habit, with pinkish-white flowers, and could be a longer-living substitute for Yoshino cherry.

'Autumnalis Rosea' has light pink semi-double flowers.

Accolade cherry (*Prunus × 'Accolade'*) has semidouble pink flowers and grows from zones 4b to 8a.

top left In north Georgia.
top right Flowers close up.
middle At Reinhardt University.
bottom On the UGA campus.

left Form in flower.
right Mid-March at the Georgia Center.

top Flowers.
bottom Foliage.

Prunus × yedoensis YOSHINO CHERRY

Producing a cloud of smoky white early spring flowers, Yoshino cherry is a dependable, fast-growing, but short-lived tree for the Southeast. It is often used in masses, for border plantings, as accents, and even for street and sidewalk plantings to take advantage of its tolerance for urban conditions. Place it against a dark background for best effect. In addition to its flowers, it provides good yellow-orange fall foliage. Japan donated several thousand trees to the United States in 1912. They were planted along the Tidal Basin and other locations in Washington, D.C., and the trees are celebrated in the Macon, Georgia, Cherry Blossom Festival each spring.

ZONES & ORIGIN 5b–8b. A selection of a cross between two Japanese species.

SIZE & GROWTH RATE 25'–35' tall, 20'–30' wide, fast growing.

TEXTURE & FORM Medium texture and broadly oval form.

FOLIAGE Alternate oval to elliptic simple leaves 2½"–5" long have doubly serrate margins, acuminate tips, and prominent glands on the petioles. Fall color is a good yellow orange. Gray bark has prominent lenticels, which form horizontal lines.

FLOWERS Showy smoky white flowers cover trees for 10 days in early spring (mid- to late March in Athens).

FRUIT Tiny insignificant black midsummer drupes.

LIGHT & SOIL Full sun with moist but well-drained soils. It tolerates moderate drought and neutral to slightly alkaline soil.

MAINTENANCE Remove root suckers, and protect the bark from maintenance equipment.

INSTALLATION Trees 5" in caliper are readily available. Smaller trees transplant better and reach mature sizes in just a few years. Space 30' apart during the dormant season.

PESTS & DISEASES Trees begin to decline in vigor after about 20 years, with few living more than 40 years.

NOTES & CULTIVARS
Many older trees around the Tidal Basin are actually 'Akebono', with very lightly pink flowers.
'Shidare Yoshino' has a weeping form to 30' with single white flowers.
Snow Fountain, *Prunus* 'Snofozam', has an oval form to 15' medium slow growth rate, single white flowers, and cascading branches that reach the ground.

Rhus copallinum WINGED SUMAC

Winged sumac is native to abandoned upland fields, woodland edges, and roadsides throughout the eastern states. A pioneer species, it is among the first woody plants to establish following disturbances. Sumacs are best known for their flaming fall foliage, but they have other attributes to contribute. Their coarse texture, umbrella-like canopy, and multiple stems lend an exotic tropical appearance in compositions. Their fruit attracts birds in the fall and winter. Use them in masses or individually mixed into border plantings.

Foliage.

ZONES & ORIGIN 4b–10b. Native across the eastern United States.

SIZE & GROWTH RATE 10'–20' tall and wide, very fast growing.

TEXTURE & FORM Medium coarse texture with a rounded form and umbrella-like canopy.

FOLIAGE Odd pinnately compound leaves have 11–17 lustrous dark green leaflets. Narrowly ovate leaflets are 1½"–3" long, with acute tips and mostly entire margins, and they are softly pubescent beneath. The rachis has leaflike wings. Midautumn foliage is an outstanding reddish orange to crimson. Young stems are pink to tan with red lenticels and covered with a soft dense pubescence. Smooth light gray mature bark has prominent raised lenticels.

FLOWERS Greenish-yellow flower panicles are held above the foliage in early to midsummer.

FRUIT A dioecious plant, female trees produce somewhat showy sticky red drupes in summer that are eaten by birds in winter.

LIGHT & SOIL Full sun and loose well-drained soils. It tolerates drought and acidic to fairly alkaline soils.

MAINTENANCE Sumacs spread by sprouting new plants from the roots. When using them in border plantings, consider some type of edge restraint to contain them.

INSTALLATION A few specialty growers provide them in small containers, usually 5 gallons or smaller. They can be transplanted virtually year-round. For massing, space 15' apart in loose soil.

PESTS & DISEASES Leaf spot fungal diseases can cause early defoliation.

NOTES & CULTIVARS
Chinese sumac, *Rhus chinensis*, with a winged leaf rachis, can be differentiated by its dull green leaflets with serrate margins. Fall color is yellow orange and not nearly as attractive as that of *R. copallinum*.

left Fall foliage   *right* Form on the UGA campus.

Rhus glabra SMOOTH SUMAC

Like winged sumac, smooth sumac is a pioneer species of abandoned fields, roadsides, and woodland edges. The most common sumac, it is native throughout the lower 48 states and parts of southern Canada, and it is well adapted to difficult sites. Recognized for their outstanding early fall foliage and exotic appearance, sumacs are extremely short-lived. In nature, they become shaded out by taller but slower-growing species such as sweetgum, winged elm, and tulip poplar. However, in designed landscapes, this natural succession process can be suspended. Individual trees may only survive for 10 years, but by removing them and allowing root sprouts to form new trees, a grouping of sumacs can be maintained indefinitely.

top Foliage.
middle Foliage and summer fruit.
bottom Fall foliage.

ZONES & ORIGIN 3b–9a. Native to the United States and Canada.

SIZE & GROWTH RATE 10'–20' tall and wide, very fast growing.

TEXTURE & FORM Medium coarse texture with an umbrella-like canopy and rounded form.

FOLIAGE Odd pinnately compound leaves have 15 to 25 lustrous dark green leaflets. Individual leaflets are 2"–5" long, narrowly ovate shaped, with serrate margins, acuminate tips, and a pinkish-red rachis. Fall color is an outstanding orange red to scarlet to crimson in early autumn. Mature bark is brownish gray.

FLOWERS Sumacs are dioecious, with greenish-yellow flowers on 6"–10" terminal panicles in late spring to early summer.

FRUIT Female trees produce somewhat attractive sticky red drupes in late summer that are eaten by birds in winter.

LIGHT & SOIL Full sun and loose well-drained soils. It tolerates drought, very light shade, and acidic to somewhat alkaline soils.

MAINTENANCE For border plantings, consider edge restraints to keep root sprouts contained. Individual trees will need to be removed every 10 to 12 years as they decline to allow root sprouts to develop into tree forms.

INSTALLATION Plant containerized trees on 15' centers in a loose soil mixture to facilitate the spread of the roots.

PESTS & DISEASES Few serious problems, but leaf spot infections can cause early defoliation. While not heavily browsed, smooth sumac is a favored rub for male white-tailed deer.

NOTES & CULTIVARS
None listed.

Rhus typhina STAGHORN SUMAC

Staghorn sumac closely resembles smooth sumac except that the undersides of its leaflets and twigs are covered in soft hairs similar to those on male deer antlers. Like smooth and winged sumacs, staghorn sumac's fall color is outstanding, and its red fruit attracts wildlife. Also like the other sumacs, its coarse texture, umbrella-like canopy, and multiple stems lend an exotic tropical appearance in compositions. Teas made from the leaflets and fruit taste like lemonade and are high in vitamin C. The cultivars 'Lacinata' and 'Tiger Eyes' will provide contrast and catch the viewer's eyes in mixed composition borders.

ZONES & ORIGIN 3b–8a. Native from Georgia to Minnesota.

SIZE & GROWTH RATE 15'–25' tall and wide, fast growing.

TEXTURE & FORM Medium coarse texture and rounded form.

FOLIAGE Pinnately compound leaves have 13 to 25 narrowly ovate leaflets with serrate margins and orange-red to scarlet fall color. The rachis and young stems are densely pubescent.

FLOWERS Greenish-yellow flowers on terminal panicles in late spring to early summer.

FRUIT Female trees produce somewhat attractive sticky red drupes in late summer that are eaten by birds in winter.

LIGHT & SOIL Full sun with well-drained acidic to slightly alkaline soil.

MAINTENANCE Like other sumacs, new plants sprout from the roots. Remove older trees every five to ten years to maintain the tree mass.

INSTALLATION Specialty growers provide trees in small containers. They can be transplanted virtually year-round. For massing, space 15' apart in loose soil.

PESTS & DISEASES Few issues, as long as they get plenty of sun. Like other sumacs, staghorn sumacs are not long-lived, but removing older trees and allowing the younger suckers to mature will keep a planting looking good.

NOTES & CULTIVARS
'Bailtiger' Tiger Eyes only reaches about 6' in height, with bright yellow-green finely lobed leaflets. It is slower growing and reportedly produces fewer root suckers than other sumacs.
'Dissecta' and 'Laciniata' have finely lobed leaflets and a medium fine texture in leaf. 'Laciniata' is a female plant. Both are more common in nurseries than the species.

top left In bloom at the Vince and Barbara Dooley residence, Athens.
top right At a residence in Columbus
middle Flowers and foliage.
bottom Flowers.

Styphnolobium japonicum JAPANESE PAGODA TREE

Japanese pagoda tree tolerates difficult locations, including urban environments. Its creamy-white midsummer flowers offer interest when few other plants are blooming. Light dappled shade produced by the canopy of young trees is also a bonus. Though it is a little too messy for courtyards and patios, use it along streets, entry drives, or parking lots. The tree is a member of the legume family and was listed as *Sophora japonica* for years, but recent research indicates it has a different number of chromosomes than other *Sophora* members and lacks the ability to fix nitrogen in the soil.

Foliage and summer flower structure.

ZONES & ORIGIN 5b–8b. Native to China.

SIZE & GROWTH RATE 25'–35' tall and wide, medium fast growing.

TEXTURE & FORM Medium fine texture in leaf, medium in winter with a broadly oval form.

FOLIAGE Alternate pinnately compound leaves have mostly 17 bright green ovate leaflets with entire margins and acute tips. Yellow fall foliage is fair to poor. Young green twigs have tan lenticels. Mature bark is brownish gray with shallow ridges.

FLOWERS Showy lightly fragrant creamy-white flowers occur in terminal panicles in midsummer (July in Athens).

FRUIT Knobby green bean pods with up to five beans inside mature to yellow in late summer. The pods and beans have a high moisture content and sticky sap. If ingested, they can cause serious digestive system distress.

LIGHT & SOIL Provide full sun with moist but well-drained soil. It tolerates slightly acidic to slightly alkaline soils, urban environments, moderate droughts, and moderate salt spray.

MAINTENANCE Inspect trees regularly for dead branches. Trees can be messy when dropping the fruit in winter.

INSTALLATION Trees are difficult to locate from southeastern nurseries and transplant best during the dormant season or early spring. Ensure good surface drainage and space 30'–35' for massing.

PESTS & DISEASES Trees have weak branch angles and brittle wood that can be damaged in severe winds and under snow and ice.

NOTES & CULTIVARS
A weeping cultivar, 'Pendula', is extremely difficult to locate.
'Regent' is the most common cultivar and is promoted as blooming at a younger age than the species.

left Form at Swarthmore College.
middle Form on the UGA campus.
right Early fall foliage with fruit.

Styrax japonicus JAPANESE SNOWBELL

Japanese snowbell is a refined tree whose attributes are best appreciated up close. Its small size and lightly fragrant white flowers lend themselves to use in patios and courtyards, where its qualities are more visible. Accentuate it with night lighting and combine it with ferns or other moisture-loving plants. Or plant it beneath the light shade of mature pines in shrub or perennial borders and contrast its texture with rhododendrons and hostas. It is somewhat rare in nurseries, but the search effort may pay off in the long run.

ZONES & ORIGIN 5b–8b. Native to Asia.

SIZE & GROWTH RATE 20'–30' tall, 15'–25' wide, medium slow growing.

TEXTURE & FORM Medium fine texture and broadly oval form.

FOLIAGE Alternate simple leaves are 1"–3½" long, dark lustrous green, and elliptic to ovate shaped, with entire or slightly wavy margins and acuminate tips. Some yellow-orange to red fall color is rarely outstanding. Smooth light gray bark when young becomes shallowly fissured with age.

FLOWERS Lightly fragrant white bell-shaped flowers droop below the branches in clusters of three to five in midspring (late April to early May in Athens). While not showy from afar, they are attractive up close.

FRUIT Insignificant fleshy green drupes.

LIGHT & SOIL Light shade with moist but well-drained slightly acidic soils are ideal. It tolerates full sun to moderate shade and light salt spray but not drought.

MAINTENANCE Keep it moist with supplemental water during the summer.

INSTALLATION Container or small field-grown trees transplant best in early spring and survive better than larger trees.

PESTS & DISEASES Deer heavily browse small plants. Otherwise, no serious problems have been reported.

NOTES & CULTIVARS
'Pendula' is a weeping form, reaching 15' tall.
'Pink Chimes' has light pink flowers. Both cultivars are difficult to locate.
American Snowbell, *Styrax americanus*, is a large shrub or small tree native to moist bottomlands and swamp edges in the southeastern United States, with fragrant white flowers in late April and May. Fairly rare, it reaches 12' tall and prefers light shade, but it tolerates full sun to full shade.

top left In bloom at the Vince and Barbara Dooley residence, Athens.
top right At a residence in Columbus.
middle Flowers and foliage.
bottom Flowers.

EVERGREEN TREES

Mature evergreen trees in the landscape lend a feeling of permanence and stability. They serve as markers of place and of territory and were often cited on historic maps and land surveys. They are often seen planted as sentinels, standing guard adjacent to important civic buildings and university halls, dominating town squares, and flanking historic residences. A familiar scene is easily painted in the eastern United States of pastureland punctuated by old eastern red cedars, standing lonely and strong. The sculptural beauty of old evergreens such as these causes one to be reflective and consider the fleeting nature of human life and the ability of trees to transcend many generations.

Indeed, the use of evergreen trees in designed landscapes should take inspiration from their seemingly timeless qualities. They should be placed with age and maturity in mind, set to endure and become ever richer in character and sculptural form.

While not all of the evergreen trees listed in this section are long-lived, many of them are, and many are transformed by old age into sculptural forms that look significantly different from their youthful appearance. A classic example is the deodar cedar, which has a fully branched to the ground conical form in youth, a looser overall oval form as a middle-aged tree, and finally a flat-topped bonsai-like form in old age, with no bottom limbs remaining. This process may take seventy-five years, so planting the tree in a location that allows space for the transformation is important.

In this section, as in other sections, we have been broad in our selection. Many texts would separate out palms, for example, but we have included them here as simply evergreen trees. Let the designer decide whether a needle or broad-leaved evergreen tree is right functionally and aesthetically for the design and whether the tropical appear-

above Eastern red cedars frame and punctuate the pastoral view at Hedgerow Farm in Bishop, Ga.

ance of a palm is warranted or a frosty needle evergreen is needed.

Evergreen trees may exhibit a wide range of foliage types. First, broad evergreens such as southern magnolia and cherry laurel have large, usually thick, and somewhat waxy and glossy foliage. Second, needle evergreens such as pines have long thin waxy foliage arranged in bundles (called fascicles), with numbers of needles per bundle varying with the species. The third type is the junipers, with often scaly foliage whose leaves are tightly wrapped "scales" around thin branches, the appearance being somewhat like a coral or sponge from the ocean. The fourth and less common type is the awl-leaved evergreens (also junipers), whose leaves are shaped like an awl. Just what is an awl, you ask? It is a somewhat rounded-triangular-pointed tool used to punch or pierce leather and other materials.

For a more in-depth accounting of evergreen trees, we highly recommend the book *Landscaping with Conifers and Gingko for the Southeast*, by Tom Cox and John Ruter. Also see detailed accounts in Michael Dirr's *Manual of Woody Landscape Plants*. We are indebted to these and many other experts who for decades have been growing and evaluating evergreen trees for use in gardens and landscapes. Their work has opened the door to many possibilities in today's designed landscapes. Every year the availability of great native and introduced plants seems to only get better.

BOTANICAL NAME	SUNLIGHT	SOILS	TEXTURE	NOTABLE ATTRIBUTES	SALT TOLERANCE	NATIVE TO SOUTHEAST
UNDER 30' TALL						
Butia capitata	Full sun to moderate shade	Moist but well drained	Coarse	Showy flowers edible fruit	Moderate	No, native to South America
Ilex × attenuata 'Fosteri'	Full sun to moderate shade	Well drained	Medium fine	Showy red winter fruit	Slight to moderate	Cross between native species
Ilex latifolia	Light to moderate shade	Well drained	Coarse	Showy red winter fruit	None	No, native to Asia
Magnolia grandiflora 'Little Gem'	Full sun to moderate shade	Moist to moist but well drained	Coarse	Showy fragrant summer flowers	Slight to moderate	Yes
Magnolia grandiflora 'Mgtig'	Full sun to moderate shade	Moist to moist but well drained	Coarse	Showy fragrant summer flowers	Slight to moderate	Yes
Magnolia grandiflora 'Alta'	Full sun to moderate shade	Moist to moist but well drained	Coarse	Showy fragrant summer flowers	Slight to moderate	Yes
Persea palustris	Full sun to moderate shade	Moist to moist but well drained	Medium coarse	Wildlife food source	Slight to moderate	Yes
Pinus bungeana	Full sun to light shade	Moist but well drained to dry	Fine	Attractive exfoliating bark	None	No, native to Asia
Pinus thunbergii	Full sun	Moist but well drained to dry	Medium	Windswept form	Moderate	No, native to Asia
Prunus caroliniana	Full sun to light shade	Moist but well drained to dry	Medium	Spring flowers, wildlife food	Moderate	Yes
Trachycarpus fortunei	Full sun to moderate shade	Well drained	Coarse	Tropical effect	Moderate	Yes
OVER 30' TALL						
Cedrus atlantica	Full sun	Moist but well drained to dry	Fine	Stately habit with maturity	Moderate	No, native to Africa
Cedrus deodara	Full sun	Moist but well drained to dry	Fine	Stately habit with maturity	Moderate	No, native to Asia
Cryptomeria japonica	Full sun to light shade	Moist but well drained to dry	Medium	Formal outline	Slight	No, native to Asia
Cunninghamia lanceolata	Full sun to moderate shade	Moist but well drained to dry	Coarse	Multitrunked tree	Highly	No, native to Asia
× Cuprocyparis leylandii	Full sun to light shade	Moist but well drained to dry	Fine	Formal outline	Slight to moderate	No, nonnative cross

BOTANICAL NAME	SUNLIGHT	SOILS	TEXTURE	NOTABLE ATTRIBUTES	SALT TOLERANCE	NATIVE TO SOUTHEAST
Cupressus sempervirens	Full sun	Moist but well drained to dry	Fine	Highly formal appearance	Moderate	No, Europe to Persia
Ilex opaca	Full sun to moderate shade	Moist but well drained, acidic	Medium	Showy red winter fruit	Moderate	Yes
Ilex × attenuata 'East Palatka'	Full sun to moderate shade	Moist but well drained, acidic	Medium	Showy red winter fruit	Moderate	Cross between native species
Ilex × attenuata 'Savannah'	Full sun to moderate shade	Moist but well drained, acidic	Medium	Showy red winter fruit	Moderate	Cross between native species
Ilex × 'Nellie R. Stevens'	Full sun to moderate shade	Well drained	Medium	Red winter fruit, dark green foliage		No, cross of nonnative species
Juniperus virginiana	Full sun to moderate shade	Well drained	Fine	Windswept form with age	Highly	Yes
Magnolia grandiflora	Full sun to moderate shade	Moist to moist but well drained	Coarse	Fragrant showy summer flowers	Moderate	Yes
Magnolia grandiflora 'Claudia Wannamaker'	Full sun to moderate shade	Moist to moist but well drained	Coarse	Fragrant showy summer flowers	Moderate	Yes
Magnolia grandiflora 'Bracken's Brown Beauty'	Full sun to moderate shade	Moist to moist but well drained	Coarse	Fragrant showy summer flowers	Moderate	Yes
Magnolia grandiflora 'D. D. Blanchard'	Full sun to moderate shade	Moist to moist but well drained	Coarse	Fragrant showy summer flowers	Moderate	Yes
Magnolia virginiana	Full sun to light shade	Moist to moist but well drained	Medium coarse	Fragrant late spring flowers	Moderate	Yes
Pinus echinata	Full sun to light shade	Moist but well drained to dry	Medium fine	Wildlife food	None	Yes
Pinus elliottii	Full sun	Moist to well drained	Medium coarse	Fast growth for screening	Slight	Yes
Pinus palustris	Full sun to light shade	Moist but well drained to dry	Coarse	Wildlife food and habitat	Moderate to highly	Yes
Pinus strobus	Full sun to light shade	Moist but well drained	Fine	Most shade-tolerant pine	None	Yes
Pinus taeda	Full sun	Moist to well drained	Medium coarse	Wildlife food and habitat source	Slight	Yes
Pinus virginiana	Full sun to light shade	Well drained	Medium	Tolerates difficult sites	None	Yes
Sabal palmetto	Full sun to moderate shade	Moist but well drained to dry	Coarse	Fruit are wildlife food source	Highly	Yes
Tsuga canadensis	Light to full shade	Moist but well drained	Fine	Wildlife food and habitat	None	Yes

top Pindo palms in Los Angeles.
middle and bottom In Savannah.
bottom right On Hilton Head Island.

Butia capitata PINDO PALM · JELLY PALM

A real eye-catcher, the pindo palm provides an immediate tropical visual effect in the landscape with its explosion of long silvery-green leaves. The color of the foliage, the tree's habit, its cold-hardiness, and its overall mature height, which is lower than that of many palms, make it a good choice for many landscapes. It can be used effectively as a specimen accent at the corner of a building or standing alone or in groupings. You may want to stagger the heights of palms at installation for more interest. The delicious fruits of this palm mature to an orangey-yellow color and can be used for making jams and jellies, giving it the common name jelly palm.

ZONES & ORIGIN 8a–10b. Native from Argentina to central Brazil.

SIZE & GROWTH RATE 15'–20' tall, 10'–15' wide, slow growing.

TEXTURE & FORM Coarse texture and rounded form.

FOLIAGE Considered a "feather-leaved" palm. Silvery-blue-green pinnately compound fronds 4'–6' even 10' long stiffly arch and curl on long spiny petioles. Old leaves persist for years unless removed.

FLOWERS Creamy-yellow to reddish flowers occur on an inflorescence that is 3'–4' long. Bloom times are difficult to predict, sometimes spring or early summer, or sometimes into early autumn.

FRUIT Yellow to orange 1" rounded fruit mature in summer and are edible, with a taste somewhat like pineapple.

LIGHT & SOIL Full sun and well-drained soil are ideal. It tolerates light shade, slightly acidic to slightly alkaline soil pH, and drought and is highly tolerant of salt spray.

MAINTENANCE Old spent leaves remain for several years and can be unattractive. Remove old fronds at the base on the trunk of the palm.

INSTALLATION Plants are available in containers or as ball-and-burlap. It is attractive as a specimen, or space trees 12' apart in groupings of staggered heights or planted with taller palm species above it.

PESTS & DISEASES No major issues. Plants may experience some freeze damage to foliage in zone 8 and may even be killed by severe freezes in the single digits. Deer don't bother them.

NOTES & CULTIVARS
No cultivars commonly available.

Planting at Nike World Corporate Campus, Beaverton, Ore.

Cedrus atlantica ATLAS CEDAR

The majesty and grandeur of a mature Atlas cedar inspire awe. This tree is living sculpture throughout its life; it is stiff and very open as a juvenile and somewhat oval to rounded in middle age, becoming flat topped and almost windswept in old age. The blue-green foliage is a welcome color shift in the southeastern plant palette. This tree must be planted where it will have space to achieve its full mature grandeur, either as a specimen in a lawn or meadow or carefully grouped with thought to its eventual size and visual presence.

ZONES & ORIGIN 6a–9a. Native to the Atlas Mountains of northwestern Africa.

SIZE & GROWTH RATE 40'–60' tall, 30'–40' wide, slow growing.

TEXTURE & FORM Medium texture with a pyramidal form through adolescence, becoming broadly oval with maturity.

FOLIAGE Foliage varies in color from blue green to grayish green to almost silvery. Needles ½"–1½" long occur in radial tufts along stems. The trunk often becomes unique and twisted in shape, with gray, lightly ridged, and furrowed bark more reminiscent of a hardwood tree than a needle evergreen.

FLOWERS Ovoid or egg-shaped female cones 4" long are held upright on the branches and have an attractive contrasting purplish hue. Male cones occur in early fall, producing abundant yellow pollen.

FRUIT Insignificant cones.

LIGHT & SOIL Requires full sun and, ideally, moist but well-drained soils. It tolerates moderate salt spray and is very drought tolerant with establishment. A better choice than *Cedrus deodara* for hot dry sites.

MAINTENANCE A fairly clean tree that will self-mulch with falling needles.

INSTALLATION Container and field-grown trees are available. Space 30' minimum from other trees to achieve eventual specimen status.

PESTS & DISEASES No serious issues, but good drainage is essential. Woodpeckers often make holes in the trunk.

NOTES & CULTIVARS
Cedrus atlantica 'Glauca Pendula' is a weeping form that can be trained to create interesting cascading forms, providing the effect of curtains against a wall.
Cedrus libani is the most cold-hardy of the cedars to zone 5b.

top to bottom 'Pendula' in Athens, Ga., at the University of Washington, and in Volunteer Park, Seattle, Wash.

Cedrus deodara DEODAR CEDAR

A mature deodar cedar is like a work of fine art. After you see one hovering gracefully in the landscape, you will be forever changed, haunted by its beauty. Deodars possess a handsome set of attributes, including sculptural form, graceful branches with somewhat pendulous tips, and fine-textured needles of a blue to silvery-green color. Like so many evergreen trees, deodars morph in form, from pyramidal to conical in youth, to somewhat more oval in middle age, and finally to flat topped and sculptural in old age. Each phase has a beauty of its own. This tree is best planted where it can achieve specimen status in a lawn or meadow or at least have adequate space from other large trees and shrubs. Mature specimens around the South speak to this tree's usefulness in southern landscapes.

Blue-tinged new growth.

ZONES & ORIGIN 7a–9a. Native to the western Himalayas.

SIZE & GROWTH RATE 40'–70' tall, 20'–40' wide, medium slow growing.

TEXTURE & FORM Medium fine texture, with a conical to pyramidal form in youth, more irregular and even flat topped in maturity.

FOLIAGE Small needle-like leaves about 1" long in clusters range from blue green to silvery blue green. Bark on mature trees is grayish brown, with a fissured pattern more like that of a hardwood tree than other southern conifers.

FLOWERS Conspicuous blue-green female cones 4" tall occur upright on upper branches in early autumn. Male cones with yellow pollen are smaller and clustered together.

FRUIT Cones are not ornamental but provide visual interest.

LIGHT & SOIL Full sun with a well-drained near-neutral pH soil. It tolerates moderate salt spray.

MAINTENANCE Older needles shed in spring and fall.

INSTALLATION Container and field-grown trees are available. Provide good drainage and ample space from buildings or other trees.

PESTS & DISEASES Canopy dieback from cankers, weevils, or cold injury. Deer don't bother them.

NOTES & CULTIVARS
'Feelin Blue' is a shrub form.
'Mystic Ice' is stiffer in form, with silvery-blue foliage.
'Shalimar' is reportedly more cold-hardy, with blue-green foliage.
'Wyndemere' is pendulous in form, with blue-green foliage.

top left A mature specimen at Lewis and Clark College, Portland, Ore.

bottom left A residential planting in Athens, Ga.

right A middle-aged specimen in Philadelphia, Pa.

Cryptomeria japonica
JAPANESE CEDAR · JAPANESE CRYPTOMERIA

Japanese cryptomeria is a fast-growing yet enduring and attractive tall evergreen tree. Its rich dark green color, conical form, and unique foliage texture make it a great screening plant. It can also be used as a specimen or in drifts, if the property is large enough. Minor aesthetic problems include the tendency to hold on to dead foliage for long time periods and to discolor somewhat to a bronze purple in winter; however, newer cultivars appear to be less prone to both issues. Dwarf shrub-like cultivars are also available.

ZONES & ORIGIN 6a–8b. Native to Japan and China.

SIZE & GROWTH RATE 50'–60' tall, 25'–40' wide, medium slow growing.

TEXTURE & FORM Medium texture with a pyramidal to conical form.

FOLIAGE Dark green needles 1" long are arranged spirally on stems to form small somewhat drooping branchlets. Inner branches often turn brown and remain on the plant for several years. Foliage may turn a bronze purple in winter. Peeling bark is noticeable on older trees.

FLOWERS Insignificant flowers.

FRUIT Small female cones ½"–1" long are spherical to globular in shape.

LIGHT & SOIL Provide full sun to light shade and moist but well-drained soils. It tolerates drought once established and is reportedly slightly salt tolerant.

MAINTENANCE If needed, heavy pruning should occur in spring before new growth. Avoid pruning during summer. Inner dead branches should be removed periodically to maintain a clean appearance.

INSTALLATION Large container and field-grown trees up to 12' tall are readily available. Plant at least 25' apart for full branching to base over the long term. Avoid planting where exposed to high winds.

PESTS & DISEASES None serious. Poor air circulation can cause fungal problems such as needle blight and dieback. Root rot can occur in poorly drained sites. Deer don't bother them.

NOTES & CULTIVARS
Pay attention to cultivars that may keep their green color during winter, such as 'Ben Franklin' and 'Yoshino'. Other notable cultivars: 'Black Dragon', 'Elegans' (10'–15' with a dense, bushy habit), 'Elegans Aurea', 'Gracillis', 'Lobii', 'Sekkan-sugi', and 'Yellow Twig'.

top left An evergreen backdrop at Chanticleer Garden.
top right Screening in a residential setting.
middle Beautiful conical form.
bottom Curious spirally arranged foliage.

Cunninghamia lanceolata COMMON CHINA FIR

There is at least one China Fir lurking and waiting to pounce in just about every old neighborhood in the South. While its appearance in older landscapes makes us nostalgic, it looks a little bit awkward and clumsy. In slightly more technical terms, this is due to its somewhat drooping and coarse-textured branches, which have very stiff plastic-looking glossy green foliage, and its tendency to hold on to old brown clumps of dead foliage for long periods of time. On a more positive note, there's hardly a tougher tree around, and China fir becomes an impressive evergreen specimen when given enough space. The blue-foliaged form, 'Glauca', is somewhat more attractive but hard to find.

Stiff shiny foliage.

ZONES & ORIGIN 6a–9a. Native to China.

SIZE & GROWTH RATE 30'–75' tall, 10'–30' wide, medium growing.

TEXTURE & FORM Coarse texture with a pyramidal form when young, becoming upright oval with age.

FOLIAGE Medium green lanceolate needles 1"–2½" long and 1/16"–1/8" wide are spirally arranged and curve backward toward the stem. Tips of the needles are quite sharp, with a plastic-like feel. Dead foliage remains on the tree for several years and can be unsightly in appearance.

FLOWERS Insignificant flowers.

FRUIT Ovoid cones 1½"–2½" remain on the tree for several years.

LIGHT & SOIL Provide full sun to light shade with a moist but well-drained to well-drained acidic soil. It is very drought and salt tolerant.

MAINTENANCE Most people find its tendency to hold old foliage unattractive. Dead branches can be pruned out with much pain on younger trees, but this becomes very difficult on mature specimens.

INSTALLATION Container plants are somewhat available. Site the tree as a specimen.

PESTS & DISEASES No serious issues. Deer don't even glance at them.

NOTES & CULTIVARS
Economically important crop to China. Wood is durable, light, easily worked, and easily produced because of the tree's growth rate and ability to resprout from roots and stump. 'Glauca' has a bluish cast to the foliage.

left A 100+-year-old specimen at Hills and Dales in Lagrange, Ga.

middle This older specimen shows the tendency to hold on to old brown clumps of foliage.

right An old multitrunk specimen in Athens, Ga.

× *Cuprocyparis leylandii* LEYLAND CYPRESS

The Leyland cypress has become the go-to screen plant and is used to the point of complete boredom. To be sure, it grows fast and creates a quick visual barrier, but it is not without problems. Bagworms or an ice storm can turn it into matchsticks in a hurry. The price for such fast growth is often weak branches and even a weak root system that is susceptible to being blown over in high winds. More enduring evergreens exist and should be chosen in small-scale landscapes, but for some applications the growth speed of Leyland cypress may still make it the best choice. It grows taller and wider than most people realize, and when the trees are planted too close together the bottom branches thin and shed, negating the trees' original intended use as a screen.

ZONES & ORIGIN 6a–10b. An intergeneric cross between Monterrey cypress, *Cupressus macrocarpa*, and Alaska cedar, *Chamaecyparis nootkatensis*.

SIZE & GROWTH RATE 60'–80' tall, 15'–20' wide, fast growing.

TEXTURE & FORM Fine texture with a pyramidal to columnar form.

FOLIAGE Dark green to bluish-green feathery foliage, depending on the cultivar, with scaly needles on flattened sprays. It holds its color well in winter.

FLOWERS Insignificant.

FRUIT Insignificant small rounded cones.

LIGHT & SOIL Full sun to light shade, requires good drainage, and tolerates drought and salt spray.

MAINTENANCE Responds well to hard pruning and hedging.

INSTALLATION For screening, space 15'–20' on center. Container plants transplant better than ball-and-burlap due to their fibrous/stringy root system.

PESTS & DISEASES Because of overuse, many disease problems have surfaced over the years. Bagworm, fungus, canker, and root rot are all notable problems. Air circulation and good soil drainage are key to successful plantings. Deer may eat buds and new foliage but rarely cause severe damage.

NOTES & CULTIVARS
Leyland cypresses have become popular Christmas trees in the South due to their fast growth rate (up to 3' a year) and tolerance of shearing. Blue- and gold-foliaged cultivars, as well as more columnar cultivars, exist for the collector.

top Scaly foliage held in flat handlike sprays.
middle left It always gets larger than one anticipates.
middle right An effective screen.
bottom March 1, 2009, 6" of snow in Watkinsville, Ga.

A creative parking screen in Savannah, Ga.

top to bottom

Juveniles with lavender in Cortona, Italy.

Container accents at the State Botanical Garden of Georgia.

Lending an Italian feel to an estate in Columbus, Ga.

An old grove at Villa La Foce, Montepulciano, Italy.

Cupressus sempervirens ITALIAN CYPRESS

It can be difficult for a designer to avoid an all-out love affair with the Italian cypress. Who among us hasn't pined over images of Italian villas with long allées of Italian cypresses? For drama in the landscape there is almost no better evergreen. Its tight narrow columnar form demands attention and becomes hypnotic when used in groupings or allées, drawing the eye upward when used singularly or horizontally when used in a line or allée. Its strong form should also create pause, as it can be too visually dominant for small-scale spaces. Use with discretion. Culturally, it prefers a hot dry climate, and too much humidity and poorly drained soils can lead to disease problems if the tree is not sited carefully.

ZONES & ORIGIN 7b–10b. Native to the Mediterranean region and Persia.

SIZE & GROWTH RATE 30'–50' tall, 4'–6' wide, medium growing.

TEXTURE & FORM Fine texture and narrow upright columnar form.

FOLIAGE Dense bright dark green scalelike foliage whorled around the stem, forming branchlets.

FLOWERS Insignificant.

FRUIT Insignificant small oval to rounded cones are whitish green in summer, brown in fall.

LIGHT & SOIL Provide full sun with well-drained to dry soils. It tolerates drought, salt spray, and alkaline soil pH.

MAINTENANCE Structural pruning required to ensure strong central leader.

INSTALLATION Container plants are available in a variety of sizes. Space 8'–10' apart for groupings or allées. Remember that they do not tolerate shade or poorly drained soils, so avoid planting on the north or east side of a structure.

PESTS & DISEASES Most problems are caused by poor soil drainage and air circulation. Bagworms and spider mites are the primary insect pests, while a variety of fungal diseases can disfigure or kill plants. It is questionable how much one should count on their performance in the humidity of the southeastern states.

NOTES & CULTIVARS

Use with caution; overuse can have a negative impact on your design.

'Glauca' has blue-green foliage.

'Stricta' is very common, with a dull green foliage color.

'Swane's Golden' has yellow-green foliage.

Ilex latifolia

LUSTERLEAF HOLLY, MAGNOLIALEAF HOLLY

Of all the large tree-form hollies, lusterleaf is the most tropical in appearance with its large glossy leaves. People often initially confuse it with magnolia, hence the common name magnolialeaf holly. Lusterleaf holly is great for creating visual screens in partially shaded conditions, as it prefers lower light and seems to tolerate competition from nearby trees well. Its shade tolerance allows it to maintain foliage lower to the ground better than hollies that prefer more sun. Its foliage may have some damage in winter when it is located in a sunny location exposed to wind.

ZONES & ORIGIN 7a–9b. Native to China and Japan.

SIZE & GROWTH RATE 20'–25' tall, 10'–15' wide, slow growing.

TEXTURE & FORM Coarse texture and densely pyramidal form.

FOLIAGE Simple alternate leaves are oval to oblong shaped, medium green in color, up to 8" long and 3" wide, with a leathery appearance, coarsely spiny margins, and acute tips.

FLOWERS A dioecious species, with neither sex providing significant flowers.

FRUIT Dull orange-red berries occur in dense clusters along the stems. The fruit color up in mid- to late autumn and remain into midspring.

LIGHT & SOIL Provide light to moderate shade and moist but well-drained soils. Plants become drought tolerant after establishment.

MAINTENANCE Some selective pruning may be needed to maintain a full dense shape.

INSTALLATION Field-grown and container trees are available. Space 8'–12' on center for screens or groupings.

PESTS & DISEASES No serious issues, and deer don't touch them.

NOTES & CULTIVARS
Emily Bruner holly, *Ilex* × 'Emily Bruner', is a cross between lusterleaf and Chinese holly. It reaches 20' with a dense pyramidal form and similar-looking but smaller foliage than lusterleaf.
Mary Nell holly, *Ilex* × 'Mary Nell', is a cross between lusterleaf and the result of a cross between Burford holly and *Ilex pernyi* 'Red Delight'. It develops a pyramidal form to 25' in height and is a heavy-fruiting holly with dark lustrous green leaves that are smaller and have spinier margins than lusterleaf.

top Large shiny leaves and showy clusters of fruit in winter.

middle Often mistaken for magnolia at a distance.

bottom At Hills and Dales, with abelia in the foreground.

At Hills and Dales, Lagrange, Ga.

Ilex opaca AMERICAN HOLLY

The fruit is not always this abundant.

A most regal and enduring holly, our American holly and its cultivars offer an impressive and long-lived evergreen tree that should be used more in planted landscapes. It will grow in a wide range of soil and light conditions, and cultivar development has yielded some truly beautiful forms, some of which grow faster than the notoriously slow species. In addition to describing the stunning visual appearance of this tree, entomologist Douglas Tallamy (2012) writes of the importance of our native hollies (and other native plants) to local pollinators and the entire food web. They are best used as a specimen or grouping but may not be the best choice for hedging/screening, as the lower limbs eventually drop.

ZONES & ORIGIN 5b–9b. Native from east Texas to Massachusetts.

SIZE & GROWTH RATE 30'–50' tall, 15'–30' wide, slow growing.

TEXTURE & FORM Medium texture with a pyramidal form.

FOLIAGE Slightly lustrous light green simple leaves are 2"–3" long, elliptic shaped, and alternately arranged, with variable spines. Smooth light gray bark.

FLOWERS Dioecious species, with neither sex showy.

FRUIT Female trees provide attractive red berries that remain through winter. Cedar waxwings go crazy over the berries in late winter. Bird watchers report drunken birds from the partially fermented berries.

LIGHT & SOIL Full sun to light shade with a moist but well-drained acidic soil is best, but it tolerates moderate to full shade, drought, and moderate salt spray.

MAINTENANCE Minimal structural pruning may be required. Old specimens will lose lower limbs.

INSTALLATION Space 12'–15' on center for groupings. Field-grown trees do not transplant as well as container-grown trees.

PESTS & DISEASES Few serious problems. Leaf miners and scale can occur. Deer don't bother them.

NOTES & CULTIVARS
'Canary' produces yellow fruit.
'Carolina #2' and 'Dan Fenton' provide dark green foliage and heavy fruiting.
'Greenleaf' grows quicker, with a bright cheerful green foliage and beautiful bright red berries, a welcome sight on cold gray winter days.
'Jersey Princess' is a vigorous grower, with dark green foliage, heavy fruiting, and better cold-hardiness.

left At Gibbs Gardens near Atlanta, Ga.
top right At the University of the South in Sewanee, Tenn.
bottom right At Swarthmore College.

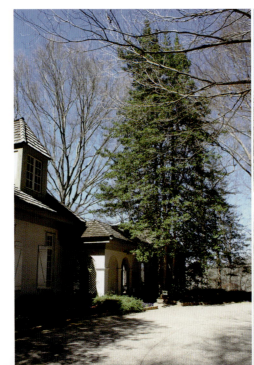

Ilex × attenuata 'East Palatka' EAST PALATKA HOLLY

Ilex × attenuata cultivars are crosses between *Ilex opaca* and *I. cassine*, both natives of the Southeast. The selections of these crosses make fine evergreen trees for landscape use with somewhat formal outlines. Numerous cultivars of the crosses have been selected and are readily available in the landscape industry. 'East Palatka' is reported to be a naturally occurring hybrid first discovered near East Palatka, Florida, in 1927. It forms a large conical to nearly oval form, with almost spineless medium green leaves and heavy red fruit production. Beautiful specimens exist all over the South, and it is worthy of use.

ZONES & ORIGIN 7a–9b, a hybrid between native hollies *Ilex cassine* and *I. opaca*.

SIZE & GROWTH RATE 30'–50' tall, 15'–30' wide, medium growing.

TEXTURE & FORM Medium texture with an upright oval to narrowly pyramidal form.

FOLIAGE Alternate simple leaves are lustrous medium green, elliptic to obovate in shape, with an entire margin and single spine on the tip.

FLOWERS Inconspicuous midspring female flowers.

FRUIT Berries 3/16"–1/4" diameter turn bright red in autumn and often remain into spring. While attractive, the smaller-sized fruit is not as showy as the fruit on some of the American holly cultivars nor as plentiful as that on Savannah hollies.

LIGHT & SOIL Full sun to light shade with a moist but well-drained somewhat acidic soil is ideal. They tolerate moderate salt spray and become somewhat drought tolerant with establishment but are sensitive to poorly drained soils.

MAINTENANCE They can be sheared to maintain a compact form in landscapes. East Palatka holly's natural form is graceful if not sheared, with a slightly airy pyramidal form and drooping branches.

INSTALLATION Container plants transplant best. Space 10'–15' apart for large screens, but they also make excellent specimen trees.

PESTS & DISEASES Leaf miners, scale, and spittlebugs can be issues some years. Sphaeropsis fungal disease causes witches'-broom and is a serious problem in central Florida.

NOTES & CULTIVARS
East Palatka holly is the least cold-hardy of the three *Ilex × attenuata*.

top Light green obovate leaves and small but abundant fruit are typical.

bottom A specimen in the Founders Memorial Garden at the UGA.

left An old specimen on the UGA campus.   *right* A screening in Athens, Ga.

Ilex × *attenuata* 'Fosteri' FOSTER'S HOLLY

Foster's holly is an extremely attractive holly with smaller very dark green leaves, good fruit production, and a handsome upright conical to oval form. The form is quite useful in tight spaces between buildings and in small courtyards or patios or as an accent plant for semiformal compositions. It is beautiful left natural in form but can also be sheared into hedges and topiaries for more formal landscapes, where its dark green foliage and fine texture provide an excellent background for flowering shrubs and perennials. It has the ability to produce fruit without requiring a male holly nearby for fertilization.

ZONES & ORIGIN 6a–9b, a hybrid between native hollies *Ilex cassine* and *I. opaca*.

SIZE & GROWTH RATE 20'–30' tall, 8'–15' wide, medium slow growing.

TEXTURE & FORM Fine texture with a dense symmetrical conical form.

FOLIAGE Dark green alternate simple leaves are 1"–2" long, oblanceolate to obovate in shape, with spines predominantly on the upper half and tip of the leaf.

FLOWERS Inconspicuous white mid-spring flowers.

FRUIT Attractive red berries 3/16"–1/4" diameter color up in mid- to late autumn and remain into early spring. While the fruit is not as numerous or showy as that on Savannah holly, it still provides an added bonus to the formal appearance.

LIGHT & SOIL Full sun to light shade with a moist but well-drained acidic soil. They tolerate light to moderate salt spray and become drought tolerant after establishment.

MAINTENANCE Young plants need to be pruned to develop a strong central leader.

INSTALLATION Container plants in 5- to 25-gallon sizes, as well as field-grown plants 6'–8' tall, are readily available. Space 8'–10' on center for screens.

PESTS & DISEASES Ambrosia beetles, spittlebugs, scale, and leaf miners occur primarily on stressed plants. Deer don't bother them.

NOTES & CULTIVARS
Very popular in the nursery industry, Foster hollies provide the narrowest and most formal option of the three *Ilex* × *attenuata* cultivars. Some nurseries also provide multitrunked versions. 'Sunny Foster' has yellow new foliage.

top Typical deep green shiny foliage and abundant fruit.

bottom If necessary, lower limbs can be removed.

A backdrop to the entrance to Reinhardt University.

Some screening from the street in Watkinsville, Ga. Note how elegant it looks when it is allowed to branch fully to the ground.

Ilex × *attenuata* 'Savannah'   SAVANNAH HOLLY

'Savannah' is very popular across the lower and coastal South and is distinct from the other *Ilex* × *attenuata* crosses due to its bright light green foliage and extremely heavy red fruit production. Its fruit is far heavier and showier than either East Palatka or Foster holly. It has an attractive pyramidal to oval form that can be used for loose screens. It serves as an interesting single or multitrunk tree and can serve as an accent plant in compositions to take advantage of its fairly formal appearance.

Medium to olive-green leaves and always profuse berry production.

ZONES & ORIGIN 6b–9b, a hybrid between native hollies *Ilex cassine* and *I. opaca*.

SIZE & GROWTH RATE 30'–45' tall, 15'–20' wide, medium fast growing.

TEXTURE & FORM Medium texture with a pyramidal to oval form.

FOLIAGE Light green alternate simple leaves are 2"–4" long, elliptic to ovate in shape, with an irregular number (5 to 13) of short spines on the margins and tip.

FLOWERS Inconspicuous white flowers in midspring.

FRUIT Round berries ¼"–⅜" turn deep red in mid- to late autumn and remain through winter. Birds consume the fruit in early to midspring.

LIGHT & SOIL Full sun to light shade with a moist but well-drained slightly acidic soil is ideal. It tolerates moderate salt spray and drought after establishment.

MAINTENANCE While it tolerates severe pruning, to do so will sacrifice the quantity of fruit for that year. Pruning is best done in late winter or early spring before new growth begins. Light annual pruning may be required to maintain a formal appearance. Heavy fruit set can cause branches to droop and even break some years, particularly under winter snow or ice.

INSTALLATION Container and field-grown plants are readily available. Space 10'–15' on center for screens and groupings.

PESTS & DISEASES Ambrosia beetles, spittlebugs, scale, and leaf miners occur primarily on stressed plants. Deer will nibble young growth but rarely cause severe damage to mature plants.

NOTES & CULTIVARS
Probably the most popular of the *Ilex* × *attenuata* cultivars in the nursery industry.

left This plant works well limbed up as a tree form.   *middle* A nice fit in Savannah, Ga.   *right* The more yellow-green color is obvious from a distance.

left Used as a screen.

top right Mature form.

bottom right Limbed up as trees.

Ilex × 'Nellie R. Stevens' NELLIE R. STEVENS HOLLY

This holly has for decades been a top seller, with its extremely deep green foliage and pyramidal form. It forms dense screens of the deepest green imaginable, almost too dark in some contexts, but can prove to be an effective backdrop for other flowering shrubs. Nellie also serves as an effective specimen or accent plant, but be careful of using it around smaller structures, because it grows much larger than many people anticipate. Its popularity has caused it to be overused, so why not choose one of our wonderful native hollies instead to benefit native pollinators?

Incredibly dark green and plastic-like shiny leaves, along with decent berry production.

ZONES & ORIGIN 6b–9b, selected from a hybrid between *Ilex aquifolium* and *I. cornuta*.

SIZE & GROWTH RATE 25'–40' tall, 10'–20' wide, medium fast growing.

TEXTURE & FORM Medium texture with a pyramidal shape in youth, becoming oval with age.

FOLIAGE Lustrous dark blue-green alternate simple leaves are 2"–4" long, mostly elliptic in shape, with five to nine spines on the margins and prominent depressed veins on the upper surface.

FLOWERS Inconspicuous white flowers in midspring.

FRUIT Berries ¼" diameter turn deep red in late autumn and remain into winter. The fruits do not seem to persist as well into winter on Nellie as they do on other species and hybrids.

LIGHT & SOIL Ideally, full sun to light shade and moist but well-drained soil. Plants tolerate moderate shade and drought after establishment but don't tolerate higher pH levels or poorly drained soils.

MAINTENANCE Minor pruning may be required to maintain desired form. Pruning should take place in late winter or early spring before new growth. Avoid pruning in fall.

INSTALLATION Plants are available in a variety of container sizes, as well as field-grown trees up to 12' in height. Space 10'–12' on center for screens or 20' on center to maintain as trees.

PESTS & DISEASES No serious pests, and deer don't bother them.

NOTES & CULTIVARS
The seed was collected by avid gardener Nellie Stevens in 1900 when she visited the United States Botanical Garden in Washington, D.C.

Juniperus virginiana EASTERN RED CEDAR

The beauty and adaptability of this wonderful native are almost unparalleled. One can travel across the eastern United States and see an amazing diversity of forms and foliage colors within the native population, from forms that are pyramidal to rounded and colors that vary from warm yellow green to darker green and even bluish green. The picturesque beauty is perhaps best revealed by old specimens standing stalwart in fields and pastures. At maturity, the canopy flattens, and the tree takes on a gnarled look that is beautiful in its own way. It has long been used for both screens and specimens. Red cedars line the drive of Andrew Jackson's home, the Hermitage, near Nashville, Tennessee. Many wonderful cultivars are readily available for use, providing a range of forms, sizes, and colors. An often overlooked attribute is the wonderful smell of cedars during spring. This is a plant most worthy of use.

clockwise from top

Scaly foliage and attractive frosty berries on female plants.

Columnar juveniles in East Tennessee.

A grove at Berry College in Rome, Ga.

An ancient specimen at Middleton Place Plantation in Charleston, S.C.

A wispy coastal form in Beaufort, S.C.

ZONES & ORIGIN   3b–9b. Native from eastern Texas to southern Ontario.

SIZE & GROWTH RATE   30'–50' tall, 15'–25' wide, medium fast growing.

TEXTURE & FORM   Fine texture with a broadly pyramidal to columnar form in youth, becoming irregular oval with age.

FOLIAGE   Medium green to blue-green scalelike needles, with color varying by tree and season.

FLOWERS   A dioecious plant, with neither sex showy.

FRUIT   Fleshy berry-like oval cones ¼" long are purplish blue and glaucous on female trees. Heavily fruited trees acquire a beautiful frosted appearance and are popular with birds.

LIGHT & SOIL   Full sun with a well-drained soil. It tolerates drought, moderate salt spray, and slightly alkaline soils.

MAINTENANCE   Carefree plants.

INSTALLATION   Container and field-grown trees 6'–8' tall are available. Space 10'–15' apart for screens.

PESTS & DISEASES   No serious problems. Deer don't touch them.

NOTES & CULTIVARS

The heartwood is used to line closets and chests.

'Brodie' reaches 20' tall with a columnar form.

'Burkii' has blue-green foliage that may go off-color in winter.

'Silver Spreader' and 'Grey Owl' are dwarf forms reaching 3' by 6' with silvery foliage.

The southern coastal form *Juniperus virginiana silicicola* has a more tufted and windswept appearance.

Magnolia grandiflora SOUTHERN MAGNOLIA

Few plants conjure up images of the South as powerfully as southern magnolias. The unforgettable fragrance of the flowers hangs heavy in the hot steamy summer air. Magnolia possesses the magical trio of attributes: evergreen foliage, large showy flowers, and fragrance. Its commanding presence can be seen flanking historic buildings across the South. Older cultivars can frame large garden spaces, while newer cultivars provide smaller size options and interesting leaf character for contemporary landscapes. Native understory trees in their Coastal Plain forest habitats can be surprising to see, with thin canopies and vertically stretched forms, versus their robust appearance in full sun.

The large dark green leaves provide the perfect foil for the showy fragrant white flowers.

ZONES & ORIGIN 6b–10a. Native to the southeastern Coastal Plain.

SIZE & GROWTH RATE 60'–80' tall, 30'–60' wide, medium growing.

TEXTURE & FORM Coarse texture with a pyramidal form in youth to rounded with age.

FOLIAGE Glossy dark green simple leaves 5"–10" long are elliptic shaped and alternately arranged, with light to dense brown pubescence beneath.

FLOWERS Lemony sweet wonderfully fragrant creamy-white flowers 8"–12" in diameter appear in late spring to early summer, with some flowering into early autumn. Trees may take up to 20 years from seedling to flower.

FRUIT A cone-like aggregate of follicles 3"–5" long splits open to expose bright red seeds in early fall.

LIGHT & SOIL Full sun with a slightly moist to moist but well-drained soil is ideal. They tolerate moderate shade, moderate salt spray, and drought after establishment.

MAINTENANCE Fallen leaves take a long time to decompose and can be messy. Never remove bottom limbs, as these provide a perfect "curtain," hiding the leaf litter.

INSTALLATION Large field-grown and container trees are readily available. Provide plenty of room for growth. Southern magnolias are surface rooted, which makes growing ground covers and turf underneath them nearly impossible—yet another reason not to remove lower branches.

PESTS & DISEASES No serious issues. Deer don't bother them.

NOTES & CULTIVARS
'Alta' reaches 25' tall.
'Bracken's Brown Beauty' is the most cold-hardy cultivar, reaching 40'.
'Claudia Wannamaker' reaches 60'.
'Little Gem' reaches 35'.

top left Living walls in the Founders Memorial Garden at UGA.

bottom left A 'Little Gem' espalier in Atlanta, Ga., designed by Land Plus Associates.

right Bookends with architecture at UGA—a common yet commanding visual.

Magnolia virginiana SWEETBAY MAGNOLIA

Many designers have sung the praises of sweetbay magnolia, using it frequently in private and public landscapes. To be sure, sweetbay possesses that magic combination of (mostly) evergreen foliage, spring flowers, and fragrance. It also possesses other subtler and desirable characteristics, such as an open density that keeps it from being too visually heavy, making it a great complement to architecture, particularly around restaurant terraces, pools, and patios. Dappled in its appearance and casting a light shade, its leaves are a bright silvery white on their undersides, which provides interest upon close inspection and a dazzling reflectivity when lit up at night. Commonly found as multitrunked trees, they also make wonderful specimen plants. Perhaps the only caution with sweetbay is to avoid the tendency to underestimate its eventual size.

Medium green foliage (silvery undersides) with late spring fragrant white flowers.

ZONES & ORIGIN 5b–10a. Native to the southeastern Coastal Plain.

SIZE & GROWTH RATE 30'–60' tall, 15'–30' wide, with a medium fast growth rate.

TEXTURE & FORM Medium coarse texture with an upright oval form.

FOLIAGE Light green elliptic leaves 3"–5" long, alternately arranged, with smooth margins and fragrant when crushed. Undersides of leaves are silvery white. Semievergreen to deciduous in zones 5–7.

FLOWERS Creamy-white flowers 2"–3" in late spring (May in Athens) are not particularly showy but have a particularly sweet lemony fragrance.

FRUIT A slender cone-like aggregate of follicles to 3" long is not ornamental.

LIGHT & SOIL Full sun to light shade with a moist to moist but well-drained fairly acidic soil is ideal. While commonly found in shady wet areas throughout the southeastern Coastal Plain, it adapts well to drier soils and tolerates moderate shade.

MAINTENANCE A surprisingly clean tree, especially compared to southern magnolia.

INSTALLATION Large container and field-grown plants up to about 12' in height are readily available and often grown as multitrunked plants. Space 12'–15' on center for groves or masses.

PESTS & DISEASES No serious issues. Deer nibble young growth.

NOTES & CULTIVARS 'Green Shadow' and 'Jim Wilson' provide improved cold-hardiness and leaf retention in northern locations.

left An ancient specimen in Columbus, Ga.

top right With sensitive fern and Japanese iris in a rain garden in Boston, Mass., designed by Andropogon Associates.

bottom right Works well as a corner accent.

Creating the gateway to the Arch entrance to the historic North Campus at UGA.

Persea palustris SWAMP BAY

Swamp bay is an evergreen tree native to the southeastern Coastal Plain, where it occurs as a forest understory tree in moist to wet locations. It is useful as a loose evergreen screen similar to *Prunus caroliniana*. Unfortunately, all bay species appear susceptible to laurel wilt, a fungal disease rapidly spread by the accidental introduction of the Asian ambrosia beetle. *Persea* populations have been decimated in only a decade, and other related laurel family species such as sassafras may be the next target. As of this writing, two beautiful specimens of swamp bay remain on the UGA campus, flanking the iconic Arch entrance to the historic North Campus, perhaps located there due to an ancient Egyptian temple inscription, "My divine heart searches for the sake of the future . . . that which it had not known forever because of the command which the hidden persea tree, lord of my years, communicates."

Foliage.

ZONES & ORIGIN 7b–10b. Native to the swamp edges of the southeastern Coastal Plain.

SIZE & GROWTH RATE 30'–50' tall and wide with a medium growth rate.

TEXTURE & FORM Medium coarse texture with an upright oval form in youth, rounded with age.

FOLIAGE Light green simple leaves are alternately arranged, 2½"–6" long, elliptic in shape, with entire margins and acute tips. Young twigs and undersides of leaves are densely pubescent, with a spicy odor when crushed. Colonists used the leaves for seasoning in cooking.

FLOWERS Insignificant creamy-white late spring flowers.

FRUIT Small rounded drupes mature to blue black in autumn.

LIGHT & SOIL Full sun to light shade with moist to moist but well-drained acidic soil is ideal. It tolerates moderate shade and drought with establishment.

MAINTENANCE No serious issues.

INSTALLATION Rare in nurseries, with only small container plants usually available. Space 12'–15' on center for groves or masses.

PESTS & DISEASES Laurel wilt may wipe out the entire population unless resistant forms are found.

NOTES & CULTIVARS
Redbay, *Persea borbonia*, is similar but has darker-green leaves lacking pubescence beneath and glabrous twigs. It occurs on better-drained sites.

Pinus bungeana LACEBARK PINE

Lacebark pine is an extremely rare tree in cultivation and is usually found only in botanical or collectors' gardens and on university campuses. Native to well-drained ridges and mountains of China, it was valued as a specimen tree in temples and imperial gardens due to its attractive bark, and enthusiasts value it for bonsai. Commonly low-branched, with ascending branches providing a multitrunked appearance, it may be selectively pruned to highlight its sycamore-like bark. Trees perform best in cooler locations and are reported to be susceptible to pinewood nematodes. Use with caution, and consider limiting its use to entry ways and courtyards in large planters with sterilized soil mixes.

Short dark green needles.

ZONES & ORIGIN 5a–8a. Native to central and northern China.

SIZE & GROWTH RATE 20'–40' tall, 10'–25' wide, and slow growing.

TEXTURE & FORM Medium fine texture and narrowly conical to oval form.

FOLIAGE Somewhat stiff needles 3"–4" long occur in bundles of threes. Bark is a smooth light gray, with older trees revealing a highly attractive and irregular mosaic of silvery-white and green inner bark reminiscent of sycamore.

FLOWERS Insignificant flowers.

FRUIT Insignificant brown cones 1½"–3" long are rare in cultivation.

LIGHT & SOIL Full sun to light shade with well-drained soils. It tolerates slightly alkaline soils and droughts with maturity.

MAINTENANCE Selective pruning of lower limbs will help reveal the bark.

INSTALLATION Trees are difficult to locate in nurseries due to their extremely slow growth rate. When found, they are quite expensive. Small container plants can sometimes be obtained, and a few nurseries provide field-grown plants up to 20' tall. Ensure attractive bark when selecting trees in nurseries.

PESTS & DISEASES Although long-lived in its native habitat, its performance is questionable in North America due to exposure to insects and pathogens for which it has no natural defense. Its branching habit also makes it susceptible to damage from snow and ice loads.

NOTES & CULTIVARS Although some cultivars are listed, you may have a better chance of winning the lottery than locating one.

left A specimen in a Baltimore, Md., garden by Oehme, van Sweden (OvS) with *Petasites japonicus*, or butterbur, underneath—not a combination that would work just anywhere. *right* Conical form.

Pinus echinata SHORTLEAF PINE

Shortleaf pine is the most widespread of the southern yellow pines. It occurs on well-drained uplands from eastern Texas and Oklahoma to Florida and northward through West Virginia. The sculptural and stately appearance of old specimens with their long, straight trunks is impressive and provides a filtered light shade through a somewhat open canopy that is ideal for azaleas and camellias and other light shade–loving plants. Only existing mature trees are utilized in landscape compositions due to difficulty in transplanting and a slow growth rate when young.

ZONES & ORIGIN 6a–9a. Native to upland soils from eastern Texas to southern New York.

SIZE & GROWTH RATE 80'–100' tall, 40'–60' wide, fast growing.

TEXTURE & FORM Medium texture with an oval to pyramidal canopy.

FOLIAGE Bright green needles 1½"–3" long occur in bundles of twos, rarely threes. Reddish-brown scaly bark on young trees gives way to distinctive flattened plates on mature trees. Dead limbs are quickly dropped as they are shaded out by upper branches.

FLOWERS Insignificant yellow pollen cones occur in early spring (late March to mid-April in Athens).

FRUIT Insignificant gray-brown egg-shaped cones 1½"–2½" long with short stalks and short blunt prickles remain on the tree for several years. The seeds provide food for squirrels and chipmunks.

LIGHT & SOIL Full sun with a moist but well-drained to well-drained acidic soil and very drought tolerant. Young trees tolerate some shade.

MAINTENANCE Mature trees drop needles in early to midautumn and dead cones and branches year-round. Watering during extended drought helps prevent destructive insects.

INSTALLATION Due to difficulty in transplanting, trees are only available as bareroot seedlings in bulk from forestry production nurseries. Plant from late fall through winter.

PESTS & DISEASES During extended droughts, southern pine beetle and pine engraver beetle can destroy hundreds of trees in one season. Deer rub young trees.

NOTES & CULTIVARS
No cultivars available. Shortleaf and loblolly are the pine species most commonly found in southern Piedmont forests.

left A poetic presence in the background of this Columbus, Ga., garden.

middle Often tall and lanky where there is more competition.

right Form in Watkinsville, Ga.

Pinus elliottii SLASH PINE

Slash pine is the fastest-growing southern yellow pine and is the most commonly planted pine for timber production in the Southeast. Slash pine plantations occupy much of the lands once inhabited by longleaf pine. Its fast growth, ease of transplanting, and ability to tolerate moist soils make it popular for temporary screens and buffers on new landscape developments. Older trees provide a rugged appearance and a good canopy for understory plants that prefer light shade.

ZONES & ORIGIN 7b–10b. Native to the southeastern Coastal Plain.

SIZE & GROWTH RATE 80'–100' tall, 40'–60' wide, and fast growing.

TEXTURE & FORM Medium coarse texture and broadly oval canopy.

FOLIAGE Dark lustrous green needles 7½"–10" long occur in bundles of two, occasionally three, in tufts on the ends of branches. Mature gray bark has shallow furrows and scaly ridges that reveal an orange-brown inner bark.

FLOWERS Insignificant purple pollen cones occur in late winter and early spring (late February to late March in Athens).

FRUIT Glossy reddish-brown narrowly conical and slightly curved cones 4"–5" long occur on short stalks beneath the branches. Cones have short prickles that are not as painful to touch as those on loblolly pine. Seeds provide food for squirrels, chipmunks, and turkeys.

LIGHT & SOIL Full sun with a moist but well-drained acidic soil is ideal. Slash pine tolerates moist but not wet soils and is the least drought tolerant of the southern yellow pines.

MAINTENANCE Trees clean themselves of dead branches throughout the year. They are more prone to storm damage than other native pines. Slash pines don't reseed in the upper Piedmont.

INSTALLATION Small container trees are widely available. For temporary screens and buffers, stake trees 10'–15' apart and thin to 25' apart in five years.

PESTS & DISEASES Young trees are highly susceptible to fusiform rust. Engraver beetles attack older trees. Trees are susceptible to storm damage. Deer nibble young trees.

NOTES & CULTIVARS Researchers are crossing slash pine with shortleaf to improve cold-hardiness and resistance to fusiform rust.

A lustrous summer appearance at UGA.

Pinus palustris LONGLEAF PINE

Longleaf pine is distinct among the southern pines for its long lifespan, coarse texture, and gnarled, somewhat ghoulish demeanor. Longleaf heartwood is resistant to decay and termites, making it a favored tree for colonial construction, while turpentine and tar for waterproofing ships are derived from its sap. "Tarheels" was the name given to those who labored to produce the tar. The distinctive parklike appearance of longleaf pine / wiregrass communities is a result of periodic natural fires that killed other trees, but longleaf was capable of surviving. With the suppression of fire and heavy logging from the eighteenth to the early twentieth century, less than 6 percent of longleaf pine communities still exist. Surviving stands are often replaced with faster-growing slash pine or converted to pasture.

Long shiny three-sided needles reflect the sunlight.

ZONES & ORIGIN 7a–10b. Native to the southeastern Coastal Plain and lower Piedmont.

SIZE & GROWTH RATE 60'–100' tall, 30'–60' wide, and medium slow growing.

TEXTURE & FORM Coarse texture and oval canopy.

FOLIAGE Bright green needles 9"–20" long occur in bundles of three clustered on the ends of the branches with silvery-white terminal buds. Mature bark is gray brown and scaly, revealing a reddish-brown inner bark.

FLOWERS Insignificant purple pollen cones release yellow pollen in early spring (mid-March to early April in Athens).

FRUIT Large dull brown cones 7"–10" long mature in autumn and are often used in holiday decorations. The seeds are eaten by small mammals. Pure stands of longleaf are preferred habitat for quail.

LIGHT & SOIL Full sun with a moist but well-drained to well-drained acidic soil. Longleaf tolerates fire, drought, and salt spray.

MAINTENANCE Large cones, dead branches, and fallen needles can be a nuisance in highly maintained landscapes.

INSTALLATION Space small container plants 30' apart. They produce little top growth for several years while the root system becomes established.

PESTS & DISEASES Few serious problems. Rabbits eat young seedlings.

NOTES & CULTIVARS
Mature trees provide nesting habitat for the red cockaded woodpecker. *Pinus* × *sondereggeri* is a naturally occurring cross between longleaf pine and loblolly pine.

left Lush yet coarse in appearance.

middle and right Juveniles at UGA create a coarse silhouette.

left More ancient trees with sculptural form at Longwood. *middle* A specimen at Longwood Gardens. *right* A juvenile with a feathery form.

Pinus strobus EASTERN WHITE PINE

White pine occurs from the mountains of northeastern Georgia to southern Canada and is the most shade tolerant of the native pines. Preferring cooler climates, it is usually limited to cool moist streambanks in the southern Appalachians, where it provides shade for stream habitats. Its shade tolerance and low-branching habit make it useful for buffers, sheared hedges, and windbreaks. While strongly pyramidal in youth, like many evergreen trees, older specimens become flat topped and almost windswept, ghostly and hauntingly beautiful.

ZONES & ORIGIN 3a–8a. Native from north Georgia to Canada.

SIZE & GROWTH RATE 60'–80' tall, 40'–60' wide, and fast growing.

TEXTURE & FORM Fine texture and conical to oval form.

FOLIAGE Silvery blue-green needles 3"–5" long occur in bundles of five, with distinctive white lines along their length. Young bark is smooth light gray, eventually becoming dark gray, with shallow furrows and ridges. Yearly growth occurs in whorls, making it easy to determine the tree's age and growth rate.

FLOWERS Insignificant midspring flowers (mid-April in Athens).

FRUIT Cylindrical-shaped cones are 3½"–6" long and ¾"–1" wide.

LIGHT & SOIL Full sun to moderate shade and moist but well-drained acidic soil. It prefers consistent moisture during summer droughts and suffers from alkaline soils, road deicing salts, and high ground-level ozone levels.

MAINTENANCE It is difficult to grow other plants beneath its dense shade.

INSTALLATION Field-grown trees are available and easily transplanted. For sheared hedges, plant 10'–12' apart.

PESTS & DISEASES Rabbits and deer eat young seedlings.

NOTES & CULTIVARS
'Blue Shag', 'Minuta', and 'Nana' grow slowly to 3' with rounded forms.
'Fastigiata' reaches 50' with a 10'–15' spread.
'Pendula' and 'Angel Falls' reach 10'–15' tall with rounded forms and pendulous branches.
Spruce pine, *Pinus glabra*, is native to the Southeast from zones 8b to 10a, reaching 40'–60' with a medium growth rate, oval to broadly oval form, and fine texture. It tolerates light to moderate shade and moist to slightly wet soils.

Fresh new-season cones in midsummer.

left A mature form at UGA.

middle High canopy and low density of foliage providing filtered light for dogwoods.

right Fast-growing juvenile form.

Pinus taeda LOBLOLLY PINE

Loblolly pine is native to the southeastern Coastal Plain and Piedmont and is one of the southern yellow pine group species used for timber production. It is sometimes called "old field pine," since it invades old abandoned farmland, where it grows faster than shortleaf pine on soils with adequate moisture. For designs, loblolly is sometimes planted to provide a quick tall temporary buffer or screen until more shade-tolerant shrubs reach the desired size. Mature trees provide light shade that is ideal for azaleas and camellias.

Needles usually in threes.

ZONES & ORIGIN 6b–9b. Native from eastern Texas to Delaware.

SIZE & GROWTH RATE 80'–120' tall, 40'–70' wide, and fast growing.

TEXTURE & FORM Medium coarse texture. A pyramidal form in youth becomes broadly oval with age.

FOLIAGE Needles 5"–8" long occur primarily in clusters of three, rarely two. Young bark is reddish brown and scaly, while mature bark is gray brown, with deep vertical ridges and furrows.

FLOWERS Insignificant yellow pollen cones occur in early spring (mid-March to mid-April in Athens).

FRUIT Conical-shaped reddish-brown cones 4"–6" long have sharp prickles on the individual scales that are extremely painful to handle. The cones are sessile, lacking a stalk that separates them from the branch.

LIGHT & SOIL Full sun and a moist slightly acidic soil are ideal. It tolerates light shade when young and moderate drought.

MAINTENANCE Trees can be messy over refined lawn areas, with needles dropping in early autumn and dead cones and limbs falling year-round, so consider using them to provide light shade over bed plantings. Seedlings are common in sunny beds.

INSTALLATION Small container-grown trees are often difficult to locate. For quick buffers, plant 10'–15' apart, and be prepared to thin in five to seven years.

PESTS & DISEASES Trees are susceptible to southern pine beetle and borers during extended droughts. Deer will rub upon young trees.

NOTES & CULTIVARS
Loblolly and shortleaf pines are the predominant species in the upper Piedmont, often occurring together. Loblolly becomes prevalent on moister soils, while shortleaf dominates on drier uplands.

Pinus thunbergii JAPANESE BLACK PINE

Japanese black pine is native to coastal areas of southern Japan and South Korea, becoming a large tree in its native habitat but rarely exceeding 40' in the United States. It can provide a focal point in the garden due to its short stature, crooked trunk, and horizontal branches, which lend a picturesque windswept appearance. Trees are highly valued in Japanese gardens, where the trees' natural form is accentuated by pruning and wiring selective branches, cleaning the foliage of dead needles, and clipping live needles to provide the desired appearance. Bonsai enthusiasts usually employ similar techniques. Its low-branching habit and slow growth rate also make it suitable for screens and buffer plantings.

ZONES & ORIGIN 6a–8b. Native to Asia.

SIZE & GROWTH RATE 20'–40' tall, 15'–25' wide, medium slow growing.

TEXTURE & FORM Medium coarse texture and oval to broadly oval form.

FOLIAGE Stiff dark green twisted needles 3"–5" long occur in tufts on the ends of branches in bundles of two. Hairy silvery-white terminal buds are prominent against the dark needles in winter and early spring. A dark gray scaly bark becomes ridged and furrowed with age.

FLOWERS Insignificant flowers.

FRUIT Insignificant brown cones 2"–3" long remain for several years.

LIGHT & SOIL It performs best in full sun with moist but well-drained acidic soil, but it tolerates light shade, drought, slightly alkaline soils, and salt spray.

MAINTENANCE Ensure good drainage.

INSTALLATION Container and field-grown trees are available. A few nurseries provide trees that are 15'–20' tall. For screens, space 15'–20' apart.

PESTS & DISEASES Trees tend to be short-lived in the Southeast, particularly in coastal locations, where it is highly susceptible to pinewood nematodes and pine wilt disease. Perhaps the best way to utilize this tree is in container plantings with sterilized soil mixes to minimize exposure to soil-borne pathogens.

NOTES & CULTIVARS
'Majestic Beauty' reaches 30'–40' with dark green needles.
'Ogon' reaches 12' with bright yellow-green needles.
'Thunderhead' is slow growing, with a dense rounded form to 10'.

top Needles in twos.

bottom Bonsai-like pruning in a rooftop garden in Vancouver, B.C.

left A pruned form in the Japanese garden at the Bloedel Reserve.

right A sculptural form in Vancouver, B.C.

Pinus virginiana VIRGINIA PINE

Virginia pine thrives on drought and neglect. It occurs from lower elevations of the mountains to the Coastal Plain on extremely thin rocky or sandy soils and can survive conditions where other pines fail to thrive. A low-branching habit makes it popular for Christmas tree nurseries and allows it to be used for buffers and even sheared hedges. However, mature trees are probably the least attractive of the native pines due to crooked trunks, hundreds of old cones, and numerous dead limbs. The crooked trunk and knots from the limbs render it unsuitable for lumber operations.

ZONES & ORIGIN 5b–8b. Native from Mississippi to Pennsylvania.

SIZE & GROWTH RATE 40'–60' tall, 20'–40' wide, and fast growing on good soils.

TEXTURE & FORM Medium texture. A pyramidal form in youth becomes broadly oval with a flattened top at maturity.

FOLIAGE Yellow-green twisted needles 1½"–2½" long occur in bundles of two, rarely three, along the length of the branches. Young bark has a reddish-orange tint. Mature trunks develop a scaly gray bark with a hint of red orange between the scales.

FLOWERS Insignificant yellow pollen cones occur in early spring (late March to early April in Athens).

FRUIT Small reddish-brown cones turn gray and remain for several years on the tree, creating an unsightly appearance.

LIGHT & SOIL Provide full sun. It performs best on moist but well-drained soils but is very tolerant of drought and highly acidic to slightly alkaline soils.

MAINTENANCE Mature trees are very messy. They don't clean themselves well of dead branches and cones. Avoid using other plants beneath them, and be content with leaving the accumulated litter beneath them.

INSTALLATION Virginia pine is available in containers and as field-grown plants 6'–8' tall. For screens, space 12'–15' apart in full sun and well-drained soils.

PESTS & DISEASES Virginia pine is susceptible to the usual native pine culprits like beetles and borers. It is also very shallow rooted and more susceptible to uprooting by heavy winds than are other pines.

NOTES & CULTIVARS
None available.

top left Twisted needles.

bottom left Always a heavy producer of small cones.

right It retains a shrub-like appearance for much of its life.

left A loose billowy tree.
top right A clipped hedge in Beaufort, S.C.
bottom right A loose screening at Hills and Dales in Lagrange, Ga.

Prunus caroliniana CAROLINA CHERRY LAUREL

Cherry laurel is an important native evergreen tree that occurs primarily on the southeastern Coastal Plain as an understory tree but has naturalized on the Piedmont as well. It is a tough and adaptable plant that tolerates all but the darkest shade, as well as soils ranging from dry to slightly moist. In the South it has long been used for loose screens or even sheared hedges in more formal applications. The fruit is a favorite of birds, and seedlings are a nuisance in highly maintained landscapes. However, the tree's ease of use and ability to tolerate dry shade under mature trees make this a very useful tree for planting design, in addition to the wildlife value of the seeds.

ZONES & ORIGIN   7a–10b. Native to the southeastern Coastal Plain.

SIZE & GROWTH RATE   20'–30' tall, 15'–25' wide, and fast growing.

TEXTURE & FORM   Medium texture and broadly oval to rounded form.

FOLIAGE   Lustrous dark green alternate simple leaves 2"–4" long are oblong to oblong-lanceolate shaped, with entire margins on mature plants, but often serrate on young trees. Leaves often have a reddish petiole and smell slightly like maraschino cherries when crushed. Foliage is poisonous to livestock.

FLOWERS   Lightly fragrant tiny white flowers are borne on racemes 2"–3" long in early spring (late March to early April in Athens).

FRUIT   Lustrous dark black drupes ripen in October and remain into winter. Birds devour them in early spring about the same time as new flowers emerge.

LIGHT & SOIL   Full sun to light shade with a moist but well-drained acidic soil is ideal. It tolerates moderate shade, drought, and salt spray.

MAINTENANCE   Seedlings spread by birds arise in ground covers, shrub beds, and hedges.

INSTALLATION   Small container plants are readily available. Space 6'–8' apart for hedges or 12'–15' on center for groves or masses. Makes a nice multistemmed evergreen specimen tree. Easily transplanted.

PESTS & DISEASES   No major issues. Deer don't bother them.

NOTES & CULTIVARS
'Bright 'N-Tight' and 'Compacta' stay somewhat smaller in size with denser foliage.

Profuse spring flowers.

Sabal palmetto CABBAGE OR SABAL PALM

Sabal palms herald one's arrival to the lower Coastal Plain of the Southeast, where they occur as understory trees as part of the pine / bay / myrtle / yaupon / live oak maritime forest mix. The visual energy of a palm is arresting, and its tendency to become telephone pole–like makes them somewhat challenging to use well in designs. However, carefully placed palms make wonderful complements and help soften architecture. They combine well with lower-growing shrubs and ornamental trees, making a multilayered composition of plants possible. Consider installing them at staggered heights to help draw the eye through the composition.

ZONES & ORIGIN 8a–11a. Native to the southeastern Coastal Plain.

SIZE & GROWTH RATE 40'–60' tall, 10'–20' wide, slow growing.

TEXTURE & FORM Coarse texture with an upright single prominent gray trunk.

FOLIAGE Olive-green fan-shaped leaves occur on long spiny-edged petioles. Leaves generally fold and twist in three directions. The fronds, 3'–6' wide, are deeply dissected into numerous leaflets, some stiff, others drooping with age. Old brown fronds hang on the tree for years if not pruned.

FLOWERS Creamy-greenish-white somewhat showy flowers occur on arching stalks 4'–5' long in summer.

FRUIT Berry-like drupes mature to black in autumn and are eaten by birds on the tree and small mammals when the drupes drop to the ground.

LIGHT & SOIL Full sun to moderate shade with well-drained soil. They tolerate acidic to slightly alkaline soil and are very tolerant of drought and salt spray.

MAINTENANCE Remove dead leaves and leaf bases for tidier landscapes. Fallen fruit can be messy in pedestrian areas.

INSTALLATION Trees transplant easily even when 20'–30' tall. After planting, remove leaves or tie them up to reduce sun and wind desiccation, and stake the palm for the first year until the roots become established.

PESTS & DISEASES No major issues, and deer don't bother them.

NOTES & CULTIVARS
- Withstands hurricane damage. Good for urban environments, especially street plantings. It is the state tree of Florida and South Carolina.
- The seed-produced cultivar 'Lisa' has a more compact appearance with more upright and less divided leaves.

top left A young tree at the State Botanical Gardens of Georgia.

top right Street trees in the I'on neighborhood in Mt. Pleasant, S.C.

middle At the marsh edge in Wormsloe Plantation, Isle of Hope, Ga.

bottom Flowers.

Trachycarpus fortunei WINDMILL PALM

Windmill palms are one of the most cold-tolerant palms known, surviving into zone 7b with protection. Slow growing and of tough constitution, they tolerate a wide range of conditions, from sun to moderate shade to wind and salt spray, and they only need well-drained soils. While certainly tropical, their fronds are not as large as many palms, making them less obviously tropical in appearance and therefore a little easier to sneak into temperate landscapes as a special accent. They look fabulous in containers and will stay small enough to remain in the container for several years before needing to be bumped up or transplanted into the garden, where they should be used as an accent or perhaps in groves.

ZONES & ORIGIN 7b–10a. Native to southeastern Asia.

SIZE & GROWTH RATE 15'–35' tall, 6'–10' wide, slow growing.

TEXTURE & FORM Coarse texture with an upright form and rounded crown.

FOLIAGE Palmate leaves 1½'–2' long and up to 3' wide are held on flattened stems with toothed edges. Leaves are dissected into 40 to 50 pleated segments 2"–3" wide. Some leaves have stiff segments, while others droop. The trunk is covered with brownish-gray fibers.

FLOWERS A dioecious plant with fragrant yellow flowers that appear on a large inflorescence among the foliage and occur unpredictably spring through fall.

FRUIT Bluish-black fruit on female palms are popular with birds.

LIGHT & SOIL Light to moderate shade and well-drained soil are ideal. The trees tolerate full sun, drought, and salt spray.

MAINTENANCE Periodic removal of old leaves produces a tidier appearance.

INSTALLATION It is easy to transplant container or field-grown plants. After planting, remove leaves or tie them up to reduce sun and wind desiccation, and stake the palm for the first year until the roots become established.

PESTS & DISEASES No major issues.

NOTES & CULTIVARS
Old specimens can appear top-heavy and unstable as old leaf scars on the lower portions of the trunk shed, making the trunk appear as if a beaver whittled away some of the trunk near the ground.

top Lush foliage.

middle Someone's trophy in Athens, Ga.

left A container of "thrillers" in this garden by Bill Smith and Associates.

right Elegant foliar habit with dangling fringe-like leaf tips.

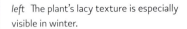

Tsuga canadensis CANADIAN HEMLOCK

The rich and protected cove forests of the Appalachian Mountains are robed in the splendor and grace of Canadian hemlock from southern Canada to northern Georgia and Alabama. A winter hike alongside singing streams in the lower elevations of the mountains reveals the presence of hemlock and its love of moist well-drained coves and valleys, where it provides important shade for stream habitats. There is perhaps no more refined evergreen for its conical form, soft texture, fine foliage, and slightly upswept branch tips. It has long been used as a specimen accent, as a screening plant whether loose or sheared, or as evergreen understory to take advantage of its shade tolerance.

ZONES & ORIGIN 3b–8a. Native from northern Alabama to Canada.

SIZE & GROWTH RATE 40'–70' tall, 25'–35' wide, medium slow growing.

TEXTURE & FORM Fine texture with a pyramidal form.

FOLIAGE Dark green linear needles ½" long with two whitish bands beneath occur in two flattened ranks along stems.

FLOWERS Insignificant.

FRUIT Insignificant short brown cones.

LIGHT & SOIL Light to full shade with moist but well-drained slightly acidic soils. Provide supplemental water during drought for several years after planting.

MAINTENANCE Trees are most graceful when branched fully to the ground, but they tolerate pruning for size control or even shearing for hedging.

INSTALLATION Small field-grown trees transplant well. Space 6'–10' apart for hedges; otherwise, plan for eventual mature spread.

PESTS & DISEASES Woolly adelgid aphids have devastated native Appalachian hemlocks, making their use in designs questionable. Entire forests have succumbed, leaving the trunks still standing in testament to what once was. Let us hope that research under way to develop resistant stock is successful. Deer and small mammals browse the foliage.

NOTES & CULTIVARS
- 'Sargentii' or 'Pendula' grow 10'–15' tall and 20'–25' wide with a pendulous habit.
- Carolina hemlock, *Tsuga caroliniana*, is native from southwest Virginia to north Georgia but only available from specialty native plant nurseries.
- Western hemlock, *Tsuga heterophylla*, is similar in appearance but doesn't do well outside its native habitat.

Delicate lacy needles held in two ranks, with small dainty seed cones.

left The plant's lacy texture is especially visible in winter.

top right 'Pendula'.

bottom right This plant is often hedged.

LARGE EVERGREEN SHRUBS

As the category name implies, these plants are generally not well suited for small spaces. Many of them tend to grow fairly quickly and as a result can be difficult to maintain if forced into locations unsuited for their ultimate size.

As a result, one of the most common uses of these shrubs is to place them toward the rear of borders and allow them to serve as background for other flowering plants. In these locations, they can also often serve as screens or, essentially, walls that form spaces in the garden or hide any undesirable views that may lie beyond the designed space. Those with showy or highly fragrant flowers can function in this capacity, as well as provide their own seasonal interest in the garden.

Often overlooked is the fact that a number of these shrubs can be limbed up into attractive small trees. Doing so may provide the best opportunity to utilize these plants in smaller spaces, such as in courtyards or near patios. In these situations, the ultimate size of these plants lends a comforting scale to the space while still allowing them to demonstrate their own particular attributes.

Southern indica azaleas in the Founders Memorial Garden.

BOTANICAL NAME	SUNLIGHT	SOILS	TEXTURE	ATTRACTIVE FLOWERS	ORNAMENTAL ATTRIBUTES	NATIVE TO SOUTHEAST
Abelia × grandiflora	Full sun to light shade	Well drained	Medium fine	Fragrant white summer flowers	Reddish-purple winter foliage	No, Asia
Agarista populifolia	Light shade	Moist to moist but well drained	Medium	Fragrant creamy-white midspring	Upright arching branches	Yes
Agave americana	Full sun	Well drained to dry	Coarse	Only flowers once in its life	Exotic, arid character	No, Mexico
Callistemon citrinus	Full sun to light shade	Well drained	Fine	Showy bright red	Repeat flowering during season	No, Australia
Camellia japonica	Light shade	Moist but well drained, acidic	Medium coarse	Showy red, pink, or white	Late fall to spring flowering	No, Asia
Camellia sasanqua	Light shade	Moist but well drained, acidic	Medium	Showy red, pink, or white	Early to late fall flowering	No, Asia
Chamaecyparis obtusa 'Gracilis'	Full sun to light shade	Moist but well drained, acidic	Medium fine	No	Unique foliage Upright form	No, Asia
Cotoneaster lacteus	Full sun to light shade	Moist but well drained	Medium	Creamy-white late spring	Red fall and late winter fruit	No, Asia
Eriobotrya japonica	Full sun to light shade	Well drained	Coarse	Fragrant creamy white late fall	Edible orange late spring fruit	No, Asia
Feijoa sellowiana	Full sun to light shade	Well drained	Medium	Creamy white with red centers	Edible flowers and fruit	No, South America
Ilex vomitoria	Full sun to light shade	Moist to well drained	Fine	No	Showy red fruit on female plants	Yes
Ilex vomitoria 'Folsom's Weeping'	Full sun to light shade	Moist to well drained	Fine	No	Showy red fruit, salt tolerance	Yes
Illicium floridanum	Light to moderate shade	Moist to moist but well drained	Medium	Somewhat showy maroon	Unusual star-shaped fruit	Yes
Illicium parviflorum	Full sun to moderate shade	Wet to moist but well drained	Medium coarse	No	Light green foliage	Yes
Kalmia latifolia	Light shade	Moist but well drained, acidic	Medium	Showy pinkish white late spring	Available pink and red cultivars	Yes
Ligustrum japonicum	Full sun to moderate shade	Well drained	Medium	Creamy white late spring	Purple-black winter fruit	No, Asia
Loropetalum chinense	Full sun to moderate shade	Moist but well drained, acidic	Medium fine	White midspring	Lightly fragrant flowers	No, Asia
Loropetalum chinense rubrum	Full sun to light shade	Moist but well drained, acidic	Medium fine	Pink to red early spring	Maroon to burgundy foliage	No, Asia
Magnolia figo	Light shade	Moist but well drained acidic	Medium	Creamy yellow midspring	Fruity flower fragrance	No, Asia
Morella cerifera	Full sun to light shade	Moist to well drained	Medium fine	No	Fruit are wildlife food source	Yes
Nerium oleander	Full sun to light shade	Well drained	Medium fine	Showy reds, pinks, and white	Flowers attract hummingbirds	No, Mediterranean
Osmanthus americanus	Light to moderate shade	Moist to moist but well drained	Medium	Not showy lightly fragrant	Open canopy and black fruit	Yes
Osmanthus fragrans	Full sun to moderate shade	Moist but well drained	Medium	Fragrant creamy white	Repeat flowering fall and spring	No, Asia
Osmanthus heterophyllus	Full sun to light shade	Moist but well drained acidic	Medium fine	Lightly fragrant late fall white	Upright oval form	No, Asia
Osmanthus × fortunei	Full sun to light shade	Well drained	Medium	Fragrant white midautumn	Dense dark green canopy	No, a man-made cross
Photinia × fraseri	Full sun to light shade	Well drained	Medium coarse	White in midspring	Coppery-red new foliage	No, a man-made cross

BOTANICAL NAME	SUNLIGHT	SOILS	TEXTURE	ATTRACTIVE FLOWERS	ORNAMENTAL ATTRIBUTES	NATIVE TO SOUTHEAST
Pittosporum tobira	Full sun to full shade	Moist but well drained acidic	Medium	Fragrant creamy white midspring	Suited for bonsai and small tree	No, Asia
Podocarpus macrophyllus	Full sun to moderate shade	Well drained	Fine	No	Upright form, salt tolerant	No, Asia
Prunus laurocerasus	Light to moderate shade	Well drained	Coarse	White in early to midspring	Tolerant of salt spray	No, Europe
Pyracantha spp.	Full sun to light shade	Well drained	Fine	White in mid- to late spring	Showy orange to red fall fruit	No, Europe and Asia
Rhododendron catawbiense	Light shade	Moist but well drained acidic	Coarse	Lavender mid- to late spring	Mixes well with ferns and hostas	Yes
Rhododendron × indicum	Light shade	Moist but well drained acidic	Medium	Showy early spring	Various colors available	No, Asia
Rhododendron maximum	Moderate shade	Moist but well drained acidic	Coarse	White in early summer	Mixes well with ferns and hostas	Yes
Rhododendron minus	Light to moderate shade	Moist but well drained acidic	Medium	White mid- to late spring	Loose, open canopy	Yes
Ternstroemia gymnanthera	Light to moderate shade	Moist but well drained acidic	Medium	Slightly showy white late spring	Coppery-red new growth	No, Asia
Thuja occidentalis 'Degroot's Spire'	Full sun to light shade	Moist to well drained	Fine	No	Formal, columnar form	No, Northern North America
Viburnum awabuki	Full sun to moderate shade	Moist but well drained	Coarse	Slightly showy white midspring	Upright form	No, Asia
Viburnum odoratissimum	Full sun to moderate shade	Moist but well drained	Coarse	White early spring	Lightly fragrant flowers	No, Asia
Viburnum rhytidophyllum	Light to moderate shade	Moist but well drained	Coarse	Creamy white early spring	Lightly fragrant flowers	No, Asia
Viburnum suspensum	Full sun to moderate shade	Moist but well drained	Medium coarse	Pinkish-white early spring	Fragrant flowers, salt tolerance	No, Asia
Viburnum × pragense	Full sun to light shade	Well drained	Medium	Showy white midspring	Lightly fragrant flowers	No, man-made cross
Yucca aloifolia	Full sun to light shade	Well drained to dry	Coarse	White in summer	Salt spray and drought tolerant	Yes

top left In bloom in Athens.
bottom left As a hedge.
right Abelia × 'Edward Goucher'.

Foliage and flowers.

Abelia × grandiflora GLOSSY ABELIA

Glossy abelia is a versatile and dependable semievergreen shrub that has been popular for over a century. Its drought tolerance, summer-long flowers, lack of serious pest problems, and colorful fall and winter foliage make it a requirement for many designers. Its fine texture and arching cascading branches soften hard edges at steps or retaining walls. It can also serve for background plantings or screens or even in semiformal clipped hedges. Too often, homeowners don't realize its ultimate size and end up shearing it into an unsightly appearance.

ZONES & ORIGIN 6a–9b. A cross between two Asian species.

SIZE & GROWTH RATE 8'–10' tall and wide, fast growing.

TEXTURE & FORM Medium fine texture and upright arching broadly oval form.

FOLIAGE Dark glossy green opposite leaves ¾"–1¾" long emerge coppery red, with dentate margins and acuminate tips. Foliage turns reddish purple in late autumn, with some leaves remaining through winter.

FLOWERS Funnel-shaped lightly fragrant white flowers occur in panicles on the ends of stems from late spring to autumn, attracting insects and butterflies. In Athens a heavy flush of flowers occurs in early May, with flowers on new growth into mid-November.

FRUIT Insignificant fruit, but coppery-pink sepals remain after flower petals have fallen.

LIGHT & SOIL Full sun to light shade with a well-drained soil is ideal. It tolerates moderate shade, drought, and a near-neutral pH.

MAINTENANCE To control size and maintain a natural form, remove the tallest stems at the ground each spring. For hedges, abelia requires frequent shearing. Shape the base broader than the top to maintain foliage to the ground.

INSTALLATION Space plants 6' on center. Provide supplemental water until well established.

PESTS & DISEASES No serious issues. Deer rarely browse them.

NOTES & CULTIVARS

Abelia × 'Edward Goucher' reaches 6'–8' with lavender-pink flowers that aren't as prominent as those of glossy abelia and a medium fast growth rate. It can be identified by its flower color and its dull lumpy-looking leaves.

'Raspberry Profusion' is similar to 'Edward Goucher' but with glossier foliage, heavier flowering, and prominent pink sepals.

Agarista populifolia FLORIDA LEUCOTHOE

Florida leucothoe is a somewhat rare shrub found on moist acidic soils along streams and edges of wetlands of the Southeast. Also known as pipestem leucothoe due to its hollow stems, it is becoming more popular due to its fairly fast growth, attractive midspring flowers, and lack of pest problems. An upright arching branching habit lends itself to use as an informal hedge or screen. Take advantage of its informal habit for woodland edge and streamside plantings with oakleaf hydrangea, bigleaf magnolia, and native rhododendrons. Just remember how large it ultimately grows.

top Flowers.
bottom Foliage.

ZONES & ORIGIN 6b–9b. Native to the southeastern Coastal Plain.

SIZE & GROWTH RATE 8'–12' tall, 6'–12' wide, medium fast growing.

TEXTURE & FORM Medium texture with upright arching branches and broadly oval form.

FOLIAGE Simple lustrous green alternate leaves 2"–4" long are ovate shaped with finely serrate margins and acuminate tips. New leaves emerge coppery red. Young yellow-green stems are hollow, with a zigzag growth habit.

FLOWERS Creamy-white lightly fragrant bell-shaped flowers in drooping axillary racemes occur in midspring (mid- to late April in Athens).

FRUIT Insignificant capsules remain through winter, making identification easy.

LIGHT & SOIL Light shade and a slightly moist acidic soil are ideal. It grows in full sun to moderate shade with moist but well-drained soils and tolerates short droughts. It is not as particular about its culture and lacks the leaf spot diseases associated with *Leucothoe* genus members.

MAINTENANCE To control size, prune branches to lower nodes or to the ground in late spring after flowering. Maintain the soil pH in the range of 5.0–5.5. Mulch twice per year, and provide supplemental water during extended droughts.

INSTALLATION Container plants can be planted year-round on 6'–8' centers in a loose soil mix amended with organic material. Provide supplemental water for the first summer.

PESTS & DISEASES No serious problems. Deer don't bother them.

NOTES & CULTIVARS
'Leprechaun' grows 3'–4' in height and spread with a fine texture and could be used for border plantings.

left Form. *right* As a screen.

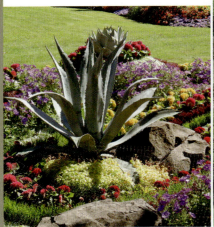

top left At Queen Elizabeth Park.
top right At a residence in Columbus, Ga.
middle and bottom At Chanticleer Garden.

Agave americana CENTURY PLANT

Century plants are extremely difficult plants to utilize in compositions due to their extremely coarse texture. Their bold striking form and gray-green rosette of foliage are reminiscent of arid desert landscapes. With that in mind, the century plant could be used to invoke an exotic playful composition with other drought-tolerant plants such as junipers, yuccas, rosemary, verbenas, and purple heart plant to provide year-round interest and color. Due to its sharp leaf tips, avoid using it near walkways or around small children.

ZONES & ORIGIN 8a–11a. Native to arid parts of Mexico.

SIZE & GROWTH RATE 6'–8' tall and wide, slow growing.

TEXTURE & FORM Extremely coarse texture and rounded form.

FOLIAGE Thick fleshy gray-green lanceolate-shaped leaves 3'–6' long occur in a rosette, with hooked spines along their margins and a stout sharp spine at their tips.

FLOWERS Century plant requires from 10 to 50 years to flower, dying afterward. It is not known what stimulates the plant to flower. A panicle 12' tall with yellow-white individual flowers emerges from the center of the plant over several months.

FRUIT Insignificant capsules remain for several months.

LIGHT & SOIL Full sun with well-drained soil is ideal. It tolerates light shade, drought, alkaline soils, and salt spray.

MAINTENANCE Provide good drainage. Supplemental water in summer in sandy soils improves the growth rate.

INSTALLATION Young sucker plants known as pups emerge around the parent plant when flowering starts. Transplant these pups to containers for planting year-round in zone 9 southward or spring to early autumn in zone 8.

PESTS & DISEASES No serious problems. Deer don't touch them.

NOTES & CULTIVARS
New Mexico hardy century plant, *Agave parryi neomexicana*, grows 2' by 4' in zone 7a.
'Silver Surfer' reaches 5' by 9' with silvery-blue-green foliage to 7b.
Agave weberi 'Arizona Star' grows 4' by 7' with cream-colored margins to zone 8b.
Weber Blue agave, *Agave tequilana azul*, is hardy to 9b and is the agave used in tequila production.

Callistemon citrinus BOTTLEBRUSH

Bottlebrushes are extremely popular plants in Florida and California, but their lack of cold-hardiness has limited their use through much of the Southeast. Valued for their highly attractive red flowers, which attract hummingbirds and insects, they bloom repeatedly throughout the season and thrive in sunny well-drained locations. In warmer climates where they reach 15' in size, they are often utilized as small multitrunked trees around pools or hot tubs to lend a tropical appearance. They can also be utilized for backgrounds of borders or for vertical accents in smaller, more intimate compositions. If you're in an area where bottlebrushes survive the winter, you won't be disappointed in them, either up close or from a distance.

ZONES & ORIGIN 8b–11a. Native to Australia.

SIZE & GROWTH RATE 8'–12' tall and wide, fast growing.

TEXTURE & FORM Fine texture and broadly oval form.

FOLIAGE Narrowly lanceolate simple leaves 1½"–3½" long appear spirally arranged around the stems. The upper third of the leaf has an extremely finely serrate margin and an acute tip ending with a short bristle. Crushed leaves smell like citrus.

FLOWERS Showy scarlet-red flowers occur in columnar-shaped spikes 3"–5" long near the end of the branches on new growth and are extremely attractive to hummingbirds. In Athens, flowering may begin in early spring, with subsequent rounds of flowers in summer and early autumn.

FRUIT Insignificant capsules remain into winter.

LIGHT & SOIL Full sun with a moist but well-drained soil is ideal. It tolerates light shade, salt spray, and drought.

MAINTENANCE To stimulate new growth and flowering, prune old flower heads and provide supplemental water during droughts.

INSTALLATION Plant small container-grown plants 6'–8' apart during spring and early summer. Avoid late season planting, since the roots may not have the opportunity to become established before severe freezes. Make sure the plant has not become root-bound in the container.

PESTS & DISEASES No serious problems. Deer don't touch them.

NOTES & CULTIVARS
'Woodlanders Hardy' and 'Clemson Hardy' reach 6'–10' and are promoted as hardy to zone 8a.

clockwise from top
Foliage and flowers.
Form in Savannah.
A hedge in Savannah.
A young plant in Athens.

At Hills and Dales.

Camellia japonica CAMELLIA

Camellias are the state flower of Alabama and are staples of large southern gardens, but they offer more than just lining formal walkways. Their ability to tolerate some shade and their low-branching habit allow them to be used along woodland paths and edges, as screens, or as backgrounds for other plants. Take advantage of their upright form for accent plants in compositions, or even limb them up into small trees. A continuous show of color is possible from autumn to spring if the appropriate cultivars are selected.

ZONES & ORIGIN 7a–9b. Native to Asia.

SIZE & GROWTH RATE 10'–20' tall, 8'–15' wide, medium slow growing.

TEXTURE & FORM Medium coarse texture and oval to broadly oval form.

FOLIAGE Simple lustrous green alternate leaves 2"–4½" long are elliptic to ovate shaped, with serrate margins and acuminate tips.

FLOWERS Showy flowers up to 5" wide with single or multiple petals in reds, pinks, and whites occur over several weeks from late autumn to spring. Early season cultivars bloom from November through December, midseason cultivars bloom in January and February, and late season cultivars bloom from early March to mid-April in Athens. Some cultivars provide variegated flowers.

FRUIT Insignificant oval capsules.

LIGHT & SOIL Light shade with a moist but well-drained acidic soil is ideal. Camellias tolerate full sun to moderate shade, but flowering is reduced in shade.

MAINTENANCE Provide several inches of organic mulch in late spring and late fall. Prune as necessary to shape the plant in spring. Ensure water every seven to ten days for the first few years and during extended droughts.

INSTALLATION Container-grown plants are readily available in sizes from 1 to 7 gallons. For best results, plant in mid- to late autumn or early spring at 8'–12' on center.

PESTS & DISEASES Aphids and scale are common under less than ideal cultural conditions. Petal blight and leaf gall are two common fungal diseases that can be prevented with proper hygiene. Deer nibble young foliage.

NOTES & CULTIVARS
These common cultivars are organized by flower color and include japonica-like hybrids.

Reds
'Adolph Audusson' has large bright red semidouble midseason blooms.
'Bob Hope' has dark red semidouble to peony-type midseason blooms.
'C. M. Hovey' has crimson-red formal double mid- to late season blooms.
'Christmas Beauty' has bright red semidouble early to midseason flowers with dark green foliage.
'Daikagura' has rosy-red peony-type early to midseason blooms.
'Glen 40' is a slow grower with deep red semidouble to rose-form mid- to late season flowers.
'Governor Mouton' has semidouble to loose peony-type and often variegated mid- to late season blooms.
'Kramer's Supreme' is heavy flowering, with large bright red peony-type midseason flowers.
'Mathotiana' has large crimson-red formal double mid- to late season blooms.
'Mathotiana Supreme' has large semidouble to peony-type mid- to late season blooms.
'Miss Charleston' has large semidouble to peony-type and often variegated mid- to late season blooms.
'Mrs. Charles Cobb' has semidouble to peony-type mid- to late season blooms.
'Professor Sargent' is a deep red anemone-form early to midseason plant.
'Spring's Promise' has salmon-red single mid- to late season flowers.
'Tom Knudson' has velvety-red rose-form to formal double mid- to late season blooms.

Pinks
'Bernice Boddy' has semidouble light pink midseason flowers.
'Coral Delight' has semidouble dark pink midseason flowers.
'Debutante' has early to midseason light pink peony-type flowers.
'Kumasaka' has late season dark rosy-pink double to peony-type blooms.
'Pearl Maxwell' has mid- to late season light pink formal double flowers.
'Pink Perfection' has small pink formal double early to late season flowers.
'R. L. Wheeler' has large semidouble to anemone-type early to midseason flowers.
'Rose Dawn' has dark green foliage and deep pink rose-type to formal double midseason flowers.

Whites
'Alba Plena' has formal double mid- to late season blooms.
'Finlandia' has early to midseason semidouble flowers.

top In Beaufort, S.C.
bottom A camellia walk in Athens.

'Frost Queen' has mid- to late season semidouble flowers.
'Nuccio's Gem' has midseason pure white formal double blooms.
'Silver Waves' has large semidouble early to midseason flowers with wavy petals.

Variegated
'Betty Shefield' has midseason white with pink and red blotches semidouble to peony-type flowers.
'Daikagura Variegated' has early to midseason red peony-type flowers with white blotches.

In Savannah.

Camellia sasanqua SASANQUA CAMELLIA

Just as the crape myrtles, summer annuals, and perennials start to fade, sasanqua camellias emerge from their slumber to brighten the autumn landscape. Less pretentious than the japonicas, sasanquas are sometimes overlooked when one considers camellias for the garden. Though a little less cold-hardy than japonicas, sasanquas' fall flowers are less likely to be damaged by freezing temperatures, and their smaller lighter flowers allow them to be used as both accents and espaliers. As an added bonus, their dark green foliage provides an excellent background for other plants while serving to enclose garden spaces.

Early season and late season sasanquas in the Founders Memorial Garden.

ZONES & ORIGIN 7a–9b. Native to Japan.

SIZE & GROWTH RATE 4'–15' tall, 5'–12' wide, medium growing.

TEXTURE & FORM Medium texture and oval to broadly oval form.

FOLIAGE Simple dark lustrous green alternate leaves 1¼"–2½" long are elliptic to ovate shaped with crenate-serrate margins, acute to abruptly acuminate tips, and pubescent young stems.

FLOWERS Showy flowers up to 3" wide with single or multiple petals in reds, pinks, whites, and variegated colors occur over a month or more in autumn. Early season cultivars bloom from late September through October, midseason cultivars bloom in October and November, and late season cultivars bloom from mid-November to mid-December in Athens. Flowers shatter as they mature, scattering individual petals.

FRUIT Insignificant oval capsules.

LIGHT & SOIL Light shade with a moist but well-drained acidic soil is ideal. They tolerate full sun to moderate shade and moderate drought with maturity. Flowering is reduced with increased shade.

MAINTENANCE Prune late winter to early spring to shape or control the size. Pruning too late prevents flower bud formation. Maintain 2"–3" of organic mulch and an acidic soil pH, and provide supplemental water during summer droughts.

INSTALLATION Plant container-grown plants in early spring or autumn at 6'–10' on center.

PESTS & DISEASES Similar problems to those of *Camellia japonica*.

NOTES & CULTIVARS Listed are those most available, including some sasanqua-like hybrids.

'Apple Blossom' has fragrant single white mid- to late season flowers with pink edges.

At the Ram Giberson residence.

'Bonanza' has early to late season rosy-red peony-type flowers.

'Cleopatra' has dark pink semidouble midseason flowers.

'Jean May' has early to midseason light pink peony to formal double flowers.

'Kanjiro' has early to midseason single pink flowers.

'Mine-no-yuki' is an early season heavy bloomer with white peony-type flowers and small dark green foliage.

'Pink Snow' has pink rose-form double early to midseason flowers.

'Setsugekka' has large white single flowers with wavy petal margins in early to midseason.

'Shishigashira' has a broad spreading form with rosy-pink peony-type mid- to late season flowers.

'Showa-no-Sakae' has a broad spreading form with light pink peony-type early to midseason flowers.

'Snow Flurry' has mid- to late season white peony-type flowers.

'Star Above Star' has midseason light pink semidouble flowers.

'Stephanie Golden' has early to midseason bright pink semidouble blooms.

'Winter's Charm' has mid- to late season pink peony-type flowers.

'Winter's Snowman' has mid- to late season large white semidouble to anemone-type flowers.

'Winter's Star' has midseason single pink flowers.

'Yuletide' has mid- to late season single bright red flowers with prominent yellow stamens.

A sasanqua espalier in the Founders Memorial Garden.

Chamaecyparis obtusa 'Gracilis'
SLENDER HINOKI FALSECYPRESS

Hinoki falsecypresses are native to the mountains of Japan and prefer cool humid climates similar to those of the Pacific Northwest. They are limited in how far south they survive and thrive in the hot southeastern states. 'Gracilis' is the most common cultivar and is popular for its conical form, which lends itself to use as an accent or even specimen plant in designs. Its clean appearance and slow growth make it a favorite for conifer gardens and rock gardens with junipers, podocarpus, and arborvitae. An attractive branching habit makes it a natural for bonsai collections as well. It could also serve for low-maintenance informal hedges and for background plantings for flowering plants.

top Winter foliage.
middle At an Atlanta residence.
bottom left At Chanticleer.
bottom right At Stanley Park.

ZONES & ORIGIN 5a–8b. Native to Japan.

SIZE & GROWTH RATE 8'–12' tall, 4'–8' wide, slow growing.

TEXTURE & FORM Fine texture and upright oval to conical form.

FOLIAGE Dark green scalelike foliage is arranged in flattened sprays with pendulous tips and whitish markings on the undersides. Foliage may turn a bronze purple in winter. Inner branches often turn brown and remain for several years.

FLOWERS Insignificant.

FRUIT Insignificant small spherical cones.

LIGHT & SOIL Provide full sun to light shade with a moist but well-drained acidic to neutral pH soil.

MAINTENANCE Prune in early spring before growth begins to control size and form. Their appearance can suffer under repeated drought stresses, so provide supplemental water during summer droughts.

INSTALLATION Container plants are readily available. Plant at least 8' apart for full branching over time. Avoid planting them where they are exposed to high winds.

PESTS & DISEASES Bagworms occasionally appear but rarely cause severe problems. Deer will browse them and can cause severe foliage loss.

NOTES & CULTIVARS
'Crippsii' reaches 12' with yellow-green foliage and is hardy to zone 4b.
'Filicoides' reaches 12'–15' with very attractive and fine-textured fernlike foliage.
'Nana' reaches 2'–3' with a rounded form.
'Nana Gracilis' is extremely slow growing, eventually reaching 6' tall and 4' wide.
'Nana Lutea' reaches 8' with golden foliage.

Cotoneaster lacteus PARNEY COTONEASTER

Parney cotoneaster is a loose semievergreen shrub that is more popular on the West Coast than in the Southeast. Upright arching branches develop a loose informal habit that blends more easily into many designs than do shrubs with stiffer habits. Showy late fall and winter fruit and white spring flowers provide added attractions virtually year-round. Consider placing it on top of a slope or retaining wall and allow the branches to arch over to soften harsh edges. It also functions as a trained espalier, providing similar attributes to pyracantha but without the painful spines and unpleasant flower odor.

ZONES & ORIGIN   6a–8b. Native to China.

SIZE & GROWTH RATE   8'–12' tall, 6'–10' wide, medium growing.

TEXTURE & FORM   Medium texture and broadly oval to mounded form.

FOLIAGE   Simple dull green alternate leaves 1"–3" long are elliptic shaped, with entire margins and rounded to acute tips. Upper surfaces of the leaves have prominent depressed veins, while the undersides are covered with a fine soft white pubescence. Tardily deciduous, it often retains some green leaves into mid-January in Athens.

FLOWERS   Somewhat showy creamy-white flowers on rounded corymbs 2" wide occur in midspring (late April to early May in Athens).

FRUIT   Small pomes mature to orange red in autumn and remain into spring. They don't seem to be favored by wildlife.

LIGHT & SOIL   Full sun to light shade with a moist but well-drained soil. Mature plants tolerate drought and slightly alkaline soils.

MAINTENANCE   Pruning anytime of the year will sacrifice either flowers or fruit. Pruning before midsummer avoids removing next year's flower buds. Water only during droughts as the plant matures.

INSTALLATION   For informal hedges, space container-grown plants 6'–8' apart during the dormant season.

PESTS & DISEASES   A member of the rose family, it has fewer problems than many rose-family members, especially under good cultural conditions. That said, aphids, lace bugs, and spider mites, as well as fire blight and various fungal diseases, occasionally find it. Deer don't usually cause damage.

NOTES & CULTIVARS   None available.

top left At a Birmingham residence.
top right In a border planting on the UGA campus.
middle Fall fruit.
bottom Foliage and midspring flowers.

top and middle Late spring fruit in the Founders Memorial Garden and in the State Botanical Garden of Georgia.

bottom Foliage and late autumn flowers.

Eriobotrya japonica LOQUAT · JAPANESE PLUM

Loquats are coarse-textured shrubs with a low-branching habit and dense canopy, making them effective for screens and background plantings. With an upright habit, they can also be limbed up into accent trees in compositions. Their dark green foliage is outstanding in front of dark red brick or natural stone walls. Loquats are good plants for courtyards, where their flower fragrance fills the space but they are somewhat protected from cold winter temperatures and winds. They even function as small specimen trees and can be used for interior plantings in high-light areas.

ZONES & ORIGIN 8a–11a. Native to Asia.

SIZE & GROWTH RATE 15'–20' tall, 10'–15' wide, medium growing.

TEXTURE & FORM Coarse texture and broadly oval form.

FOLIAGE Simple lustrous dark green alternate leaves 5"–10" long are elliptic to narrowly obovate shaped, with depressed veins, coarsely serrate margins, and acuminate tips, densely pubescent beneath and on young twigs. Mature bark is smooth gray.

FLOWERS Sweetly fragrant creamy-white flowers occur in terminal panicles 4"–6" long in late autumn (mid-November to mid-December in Athens). While the flowers are not terribly showy, their fragrance is outstanding on warm autumn afternoons.

FRUIT Oval pomes 1" long with a citrus taste mature to orange yellow in late spring and are edible but often killed by freezes in zone 8. Like those of peaches, the pits are poisonous.

LIGHT & SOIL Provide full sun to light shade with well-drained soil. It tolerates drought, slightly alkaline soils, and moderate salt spray.

MAINTENANCE Mature fruit can cause messes on pavements and attract insects. Seedlings occur beneath mature fruiting loquats. The thin bark is easily damaged by maintenance equipment.

INSTALLATION Container-grown plants are available from Florida and south Texas nurseries. Plant in well-drained soil, and space 10'–15' on center.

PESTS & DISEASES Fire blight can affect fast-growing plants. Deer don't touch them.

NOTES & CULTIVARS
Several cultivars have been selected for their fruit, but little work has been done on improving cold-hardiness. Cultivars are predominantly found in California nurseries.
'Champagne' is noted for its heavy fruiting.

Feijoa sellowiana PINEAPPLE GUAVA

Pineapple guava is not well known but should be considered when situations call for tough evergreens that tolerate adverse conditions. Few plants exceed its performance in sunny well-drained locations. It develops a loose sprawling form, but annual pruning helps maintain a denser habit. Unusual-looking late spring flowers attract hummingbirds and are best appreciated up close. For a more refined appearance, consider training it as an espalier, or limb it up into a small tree.

Foliage and late spring flowers in bloom at UGA.

ZONES & ORIGIN 8a–10b. Native to South America.

SIZE & GROWTH RATE 12'–15' tall and wide, medium growing.

TEXTURE & FORM Medium texture with a sprawling, mounded form.

FOLIAGE Simple opposite leaves 1½"–3½" long are elliptic shaped, with entire margins and blunt or acute tips. The silvery undersides of the leaves are covered in a soft dense pubescence.

FLOWERS Flowers occur along the stems of new growth in late spring (May in Athens), with sporadic flowers into early summer. Flowers 1½" in diameter have four petals that are maroon on the inside and white on the margins and undersides, with crimson stamens in the center. They are eaten in salads. While attractive up close, the flowers aren't prominent from a distance.

FRUIT Oval edible green berries 1½"–2½" long, with a gritty texture and minty pineapple taste, mature in early autumn. Fruiting requires minimal winter chilling hours and multiple plants.

LIGHT & SOIL Full sun to light shade with well-drained soil is ideal. It tolerates a near-neutral pH, drought, and salt spray.

MAINTENANCE Prune in late winter or early summer after flowering. Feijoa has a low nutritional requirement and a shallow fibrous root system, so avoid excessive fertilization and cultivation around the plant.

INSTALLATION Plants are available in small containers only from specialty nurseries in the Southeast. Plant from mid-spring to midautumn on 8'–10' centers.

PESTS & DISEASES No serious problems. Deer rarely browse them.

NOTES & CULTIVARS Feijoa is popular in New Zealand, where it is grown for its fruit and for windbreaks. Self-fruiting cultivars are available from California nurseries.

left Forming an arch in Charleston, S.C.
top right Foliage and late spring flowers in bloom at UGA.
bottom right Winter in the State Botanical Garden of Georgia.

Ilex vomitoria YAUPON HOLLY

Yaupon holly is a tough versatile large shrub or small tree of the southeastern Coastal Plain that has been naturalized in the Piedmont. Thriving in a variety of soils and solar exposures, it develops into a multitrunked shrub that often forms dense thickets. A dioecious species, females in sunny locations produce attractive glossy red fruit that remains through the winter. While performing well for informal or sheared hedges, it is perhaps most impressive when limbed up into a multitrunked small tree. A tea brewed from the foliage was reportedly consumed in large quantities in Native American rituals to cleanse the spirit.

top Foliage and winter fruit.
middle A yellow-fruited cultivar.
bottom left With a dwarf yaupon hedge.
bottom right Form.

ZONES & ORIGIN 7a–10a. Native to the southeastern Coastal Plain.

SIZE & GROWTH RATE 12'–20' tall and wide, medium growing.

TEXTURE & FORM Fine texture with an oval form in shade, rounded in full sun.

FOLIAGE Simple alternate leaves are ½"–1½" long and broadly elliptic shaped, with crenate margins and blunt tips. Containing caffeine, young leaves can be used to brew a delightful tea. Young twigs are light gray, and bark is a smooth gray.

FLOWERS Insignificant white early spring flowers.

FRUIT Small berry-like drupes cluster about the stems on female plants, turning glossy red in late autumn and remaining through winter. While eaten by birds in early spring, they don't seem to be a favored food.

LIGHT & SOIL Full sun to light shade with a moist but well-drained acidic soil is ideal. It tolerates moderate shade, slightly alkaline soils, drought, and salt spray.

MAINTENANCE Protect the bark from lawn maintenance equipment. Pruning or shearing to maintain hedges will impact the following year's flowers and fruit. Yaupons invade Piedmont landscapes and woodlands.

INSTALLATION Container-grown plants transplant well year-round. Space 6'–8' apart for hedges or 15' for trees.

PESTS & DISEASES No problems. Deer ignore it.

NOTES & CULTIVARS
Nurseries predominantly grow female cultivars. The most common female cultivars are 'Pride of Houston', 'Kathy Ann Batson', and 'Hightower', with an oval to pyramidal form.
'Will Fleming' is a male with a columnar form.

Ilex vomitoria 'Folsom's Weeping'
WEEPING YAUPON HOLLY

Weeping yaupon has a very different form from yaupon holly. With its pendulous branching, weeping yaupon tends to take on an upright oval to columnar habit, making it highly suited for tucking into narrow spaces near buildings or between buildings and nearby pavements. As a result of its form and tough nature, it is a favored shrub for urban courtyards and plazas, but it can also be used effectively as an accent plant in larger compositions to take advantage of its pendulous branching habit. 'Folsom's Weeping' is a female plant, so there is never any question that it will provide attractive fall and winter fruit. Just remember that plants in the shade of nearby buildings will not fruit as heavily as those in sunnier locations.

ZONES & ORIGIN 7a–10a. Native to the southeastern Coastal Plain.

SIZE & GROWTH RATE 10'–20' tall, 5'–10' wide, medium growing.

TEXTURE & FORM Fine texture with a columnar to upright oval form.

FOLIAGE Simple alternate leaves ½"–1½" long are broadly elliptic, with crenate margins and blunt tips. Twigs and bark are a smooth light gray. Stems tend to arch over after several years, providing a weeping effect.

FLOWERS Insignificant white spring flowers.

FRUIT Showy glossy red berry-like drupes make a show from late fall to early spring.

LIGHT & SOIL Full sun to light shade with moist but well-drained acidic soils is best. It tolerates moist to dry and slightly alkaline soils, salt spray, and moderate shade, with reduced fruiting.

MAINTENANCE Seedlings can be problems in shrub and ground cover beds.

INSTALLATION Container plants can be installed year-round. Plants intended for moist sites may need to be acclimated.

PESTS & DISEASES No serious problems. Deer rarely touch them.

NOTES & CULTIVARS
'Pendula' is a catchall cultivar name for any yaupon with a pendulous branching habit. Most nurseries that list 'Pendula' carry female plants, but some male plants have a pendulous habit as well, so select plants that exhibit some fruit to ensure you have a female.

top left In downtown Athens.
top right At an Athens residence.
middle On the UGA campus.
bottom Foliage and fruit.

Illicium floridanum STARBUSH

Starbush is a native shrub that is suited for buffers in shaded woodland gardens. Preferring moist soils but tolerating moist but well-drained sites, it is a dependable but somewhat rare plant. While the spring flowers are not terribly showy, they do provide an added bonus, and the star-shaped fruit is interesting up close. Starbush looks good combined with ferns around shaded water features and/or with irises and spiderworts in sunnier locations.

top Foliage and winter buds.
bottom Flowering in Athens.

ZONES & ORIGIN 6a–10b. Native to moist woodlands of the southeastern Coastal Plain.

SIZE & GROWTH RATE 8'–12' tall, 6'–10' wide, medium growing.

TEXTURE & FORM Medium texture and oval form.

FOLIAGE Dark lustrous green simple leaves 2½"–5½" long are elliptic shaped, with entire margins and short acuminate tips, and they tend to cluster near the ends of the twigs. Crushed leaves have an odor that hints of anise and reportedly repels insects, but they are toxic to cattle and humans if ingested.

FLOWERS Flowers are approximately 1" in diameter and have a faint fishy odor and multiple crimson- to maroon-colored strap-shaped petals. They occur in early spring (early to mid-April in Athens).

FRUIT Yellow-green capsules join at their base in a wheel arrangement ¾" in diameter. While not showy, the star-like shape is unusual and interesting viewed up close.

LIGHT & SOIL Starbush performs best in light shade and loose moist acidic soils. Plants in moderate shade have sparser canopies and fewer flowers.

MAINTENANCE Provide supplemental water during droughts and several inches of organic mulch to keep roots cool and moist.

INSTALLATION Although somewhat rare in nurseries, 3- to 7-gallon container plants can be installed year-round. Provide supplemental water during the first summer and during moderate periods of drought thereafter. Space 6'–8' for massing.

PESTS & DISEASES Few issues under good cultural conditions. Deer don't like them.

NOTES & CULTIVARS
'Alba' has white petals.
'Pink Frost' has variegated foliage with white margins that turn pink in late fall and winter.
Illicium henryi has similar foliage to starbush but produces smaller watermelon-pink flowers.

left In the Founders Memorial Garden.
right At the Atlanta Botanical Garden.

Illicium parviflorum ANISE TREE

Anise tree is native to a small area of the Southeast on moist sandy soils often near bodies of water. Producing multiple stems from root suckers, it forms a sprawling habit. A fairly coarse texture and light green foliage provide contrast with many other plants. An ability to grow in either sun or shade and from wet to well-drained soils makes it ideal for background plantings, buffers, and screens in larger landscapes. Its low-maintenance requirement has caused it to rapidly gain popularity in the nursery industry.

top Foliage and flowers.
bottom Fruit.

ZONES & ORIGIN 7a–10a. Native from central Florida to southern Georgia.

SIZE & GROWTH RATE 8'–15' tall, 6'–15' wide, medium growing.

TEXTURE & FORM Medium coarse texture and broadly oval to rounded form.

FOLIAGE Simple light green alternate leaves 2"–6" long are elliptic in shape, with entire margins and bluntly acute to rounded tips. Young leaves arise at a 45-degree angle to the stems and have a pungent licorice odor when crushed.

FLOWERS Insignificant tiny white flowers in late spring to early summer.

FRUIT Insignificant light green star-shaped collection of capsules ½" in diameter.

LIGHT & SOIL Performance is best in light to moderate shade and loose moist acidic soils, but anise performs well in full sun and moist but well-drained soils. It tolerates wet soils and short summer droughts.

MAINTENANCE Provide several inches of mulch to keep roots moist in summer. Selectively prune to maintain a desired size and density. Never shear.

INSTALLATION Readily available container-grown plants can be installed year-round on 6'–10' centers. Provide supplemental water during extended summer droughts.

PESTS & DISEASES No significant problems. Deer don't like them.

NOTES & CULTIVARS

Although related to the Chinese star anise, *Illicium verum*, which is used for spice, anise tree's foliage is poisonous and should not be ingested.

Japanese star anise, *Illicium anisatum*, has darker-colored leaves that are held more perpendicular to the stems and flowers in early spring. It produces only a few stems and is thus a better selection for pruning into a small tree.

Used as a screen in Athens and in Baton Rouge.

left Planted with hemlock along a mountain stream.

top right Planted with catawba rhododendron.

bottom right 'Sarah' at Callaway Gardens.

Kalmia latifolia MOUNTAIN LAUREL

Few shrubs rival mountain laurel in mid- to late spring. Its clusters of pinkish-white flowers last several weeks in late spring. Mountain laurel forms dense thickets along mountain streams and sandy streambanks of the Coastal Plain. Use it for naturalizing along woodland edges and paths combined with native stone, rhododendrons, and ferns.

ZONES & ORIGIN 5a–8b. Native from Louisiana to Maine.

SIZE & GROWTH RATE 8'–15' tall, 6'–12' wide, slow growing.

TEXTURE & FORM Medium texture and broadly oval form.

FOLIAGE Simple lustrous green alternate leaves 2"–4½" long are mostly elliptic shaped, with entire margins and acuminate tips. Ingested foliage is poisonous to humans and cattle.

FLOWERS Pink flower buds open to reveal pinkish-white five-sided cup-shaped flowers with 10 red stamens in midspring (late April to mid-May in Athens). The extremely showy flowers are not fragrant.

FRUIT Insignificant capsules.

LIGHT & SOIL Light shade with a loose and moist but well-drained acidic soil is ideal. Avoid midday summer sun, and provide regular moisture during summer.

MAINTENANCE Maintain soil pH below 5.5. Prune in late spring to allow time for next year's flower buds to form, and maintain several inches of mulch all year.

INSTALLATION Mountain laurel is tricky to establish in disturbed landscapes. Container-grown plants perform best when planted in early autumn in organic soils. Ensure good surface drainage, and water every week or so for the first few summers.

PESTS & DISEASES Deer usually don't bother it. Several fungal diseases cause discolored foliage.

NOTES & CULTIVARS

'Carol' reaches 6' with dark pink buds and light pink flowers.

'Elf' reaches 3' with pink buds and white flowers.

'Firecracker' reaches 3' with red buds and pinkish-white flowers.

'Heart of Fire' reaches 8' with pinkish-red buds and light pink flowers.

'Minuet' reaches 3' with white flowers that have a dark red band inside.

'Olympic Fire' reaches 6' with dark red buds and pinkish-white flowers.

'Pristine' reaches 4' with pure white flowers.

'Sarah' reaches 4' with pinkish-red buds and pink flowers.

'Tiddlywinks' reaches 3' with pink buds and flowers.

Foliage and flowers.

top left A sheared hedge in Vancouver.

bottom left A tree form at a residence in I'on in Mt. Pleasant, S.C..

right A sheared tree form at a residence in Columbus, Ga.

Ligustrum japonicum WAXLEAF LIGUSTRUM

Waxleaf ligustrum is a favorite plant for screens and buffers or as a background plant in compositions. Its dense canopy and ability to tolerate severe pruning, sun to shade, and salt spray have made it popular in a variety of applications. It performs well when limbed up into a small tree near entries and patios and is often treated as a topiary plant in formal gardens. Although occasionally reported as invasive, it does not appear to be in the Piedmont and may be confused with the tree ligustrum, *Ligustrum lucidum*.

ZONES & ORIGIN 7b–10a. Native to Japan.

SIZE & GROWTH RATE 10'–15' tall, 10'–20' wide, medium fast growing.

TEXTURE & FORM Medium texture and broadly oval form.

FOLIAGE Simple dark lustrous green opposite leaves 2"–4" long are elliptic shaped, with entire margins and acute tips. Young gray stems have prominent raised lenticels. Mature bark is a smooth gray.

FLOWERS Showy creamy-white flowers with an unpleasant odor arise from terminal panicles 4"–6" long in midspring (late April to mid-May in Athens).

FRUIT Small oval drupes mature to purple black in late autumn and are highly attractive to birds in late winter.

LIGHT & SOIL Full sun to light shade with a well-drained soil is ideal. It tolerates moderate shade, slightly alkaline soils, moderate salt spray, and drought with establishment.

MAINTENANCE Protect the thin bark from maintenance equipment. If flowers aren't a priority, pruning can be done from early spring to early autumn.

INSTALLATION Sizes up to 30 gallons are readily available. Plant year-round in zones 9 and 10, midspring to midautumn in zones 7 and 8, and space 10'–12' on center.

PESTS & DISEASES Whiteflies and scale occur with poor drainage and excessive shade. Deer don't seem to be a problem.

NOTES & CULTIVARS
'Howard' produces bright yellow new foliage that turns green in summer.
'Recurvifolium' produces wavy green leaves with curled tips and reaches 6'–8'.
'Rotundifolium' produces curly rounded leaves and an upright form to 4'.
'Variegatum' and 'Jack Frost' provide creamy-white leaf margins.

Foliage.

Loropetalum chinense CHINESE WITCH HAZEL

Chinese witch hazel is an extremely versatile shrub that can fit a number of niches in the landscape. Its adaptability to diverse cultural conditions allows it to be used for borders, background plantings, and screens, and it can even be used as a specimen tree in full sun to moderate shade locations. It can be trained as an espalier and could be woven through unattractive fencing for tennis courts and athletic fields or just to soften the appearance of security fencing. Older plants are highly attractive as small multitrunked trees to highlight their exfoliating bark.

Foliage and flowers.

ZONES & ORIGIN 7a–10a. Native to Asia.

SIZE & GROWTH RATE 15'–25' tall and wide, medium fast growing.

TEXTURE & FORM Medium fine in texture with a broadly oval form.

FOLIAGE Simple alternate leaves ¾"–2¼" long are ovate shaped, with rounded to acute tips and asymmetrical bases. Leaves have a sandpapery feel above and tiny hairs along the margins. Young stems are densely pubescent, while older trunks have a somewhat attractive exfoliating bark.

FLOWERS Lightly fragrant and somewhat showy flowers with creamy-white strap-shaped petals occur for several weeks in early spring (late March to mid-April in Athens).

FRUIT Fruit is an insignificant capsule.

LIGHT & SOIL Performs well in full sun to moderate shade with a moist but well-drained acidic soil and is drought tolerant when well established.

MAINTENANCE Prune in mid- to late spring after flowering is completed to maintain desired size and shape. If flowers aren't a priority, it can be sheared into a semiformal hedge. Wear gloves and long sleeves while pruning loropetalums to avoid a skin rash.

INSTALLATION Container-grown plants are readily available and can be installed year-round. Space 6'–10' on center for massing.

PESTS & DISEASES No significant problems. Deer don't care for the pubescent stems and foliage.

NOTES & CULTIVARS
'Carolina Moonlight' reaches 6' in height and spread with a medium growth rate.
'Emerald Snow' provides a dense rounded form to 4' in size.
'Snow Panda' reaches 10' with an oval form.

top left A sheared hedge with Japanese cryptomeria.
bottom left A form on the UGA campus.
right An informal hedge.

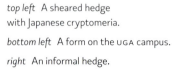

Loropetalum chinense rubrum
REDLEAF CHINESE WITCH HAZEL

About every 10 years, a new plant is introduced and becomes so popular and overplanted that it becomes tacky. Variegated euonymus, redtip photinia, Bradford pear, several ornamental grasses, and now redleaf Chinese witch hazel cultivars assumed that role with their introduction in the 1990s. To be honest, they have a place in the landscape, just not every place. They obviously provide color contrast in compositions. The larger cultivars can be attractive small trees when they mature. Smaller cultivars can serve as semiformal borders or hedges. A low-growing ground cover cultivar provides potential for rock gardens and container plantings. Just be careful and remember that more is not always better.

Foliage and flowers.

ZONES & ORIGIN   7a–10a. Native to Asia.

SIZE & GROWTH RATE   15'–25' tall and wide, medium fast growing.

TEXTURE & FORM   Medium fine texture and broadly oval form.

FOLIAGE   Foliage is similar to *Loropetalum chinense*, but with a reddish-purple to burgundy tint, particularly in spring and early summer. Foliage color declines in shade, turning dark green. Some cultivars are better at retaining their foliage color throughout the year.

FLOWERS   Strap-shaped flower petals are dark pink to red, depending on the cultivar. Some cultivars begin blooming several weeks before the species (often early to mid-March in Athens).

FRUIT   Insignificant capsules.

LIGHT & SOIL   Full sun to light shade with a moist but well-drained acidic soil. The foliage turns green in some shade.

MAINTENANCE   The best foliage color is achieved on new active growth. Supplemental water during summer droughts helps maintain new growth. Prune after flowering in spring. Wear gloves and long sleeves while pruning to avoid a skin rash.

INSTALLATION   Readily available container plants can be installed year-round on 8'–10' centers.

PESTS & DISEASES   No problems.

NOTES & CULTIVARS
'Ever Red' reaches 8' with bright red flowers and burgundy year-round foliage.
'Plum Delight' and 'Purple Majesty' reach 10'–15' with pink flowers and purple foliage.
'Purple Pixie' has a low-mounding habit, reaching 2' tall and 4' wide.
'Zhuzhou Fuchsia' reaches 20' with an oval form, dark maroon foliage, and pink flowers.

left A tree form in Savannah.

top right At Young Harris United Methodist Church in Athens.

bottom right An informal hedge in Athens.

top left Form on the UGA campus.

top right With rosemary and *Loropetalum chinense*.

middle Flowers and foliage.

bottom Foliage and flower buds.

Magnolia figo BANANA SHRUB

Banana shrub is primarily noted for its fragrant but nonshowy spring flowers. While tough and versatile, it is not as popular as shrubs that display showy flowers or foliage. Its dense canopy enables it to be used for screens and background plantings, while its somewhat slow growth rate enables it to be used for informal hedges or borders. Like camellias, it can be used to line informal pathways. Mature shrubs can be pruned into attractive multitrunked small trees. Use it near patios and courtyards to take full advantage of its fragrance, since it is not as powerful as that of tea olive, pittosporum, or gardenia.

ZONES & ORIGIN 7b–11a. Native to China.

SIZE & GROWTH RATE 10'–20' tall and wide, medium slow growing.

TEXTURE & FORM Medium texture and broadly oval form.

FOLIAGE Simple lustrous dark green alternate leaves 2"–3½" long are elliptic shaped, with entire margins and acuminate tips. Pubescent brown conical buds ½" long occur in the leaf axils. Young twigs have a dense brown pubescence.

FLOWERS Small cup-shaped creamy-yellow flowers with purple at the base and margins of the petals occur along the stems for an extended period in midspring (mid-April to mid-May in Athens). Though not very showy, they have a pleasant banana fragrance.

FRUIT Insignificant aggregate of follicles.

LIGHT & SOIL Light shade with a moist but well-drained slightly acidic soil is ideal. Err on the side of well drained. Plants tolerate full sun to moderate shade and become fairly drought tolerant with maturity.

MAINTENANCE Prune to control size and shape in late spring after flowering has finished. Provide supplemental water for the first few summers during droughts.

INSTALLATION Plants are somewhat rare in nurseries but can be located in containers up to 7 gallons. Plant slightly above the surrounding soil in a loose soil mix at 6'–8' apart for low borders and hedges or 10'–15' for backgrounds and screens.

PESTS & DISEASES No serious problems. Deer rarely bother them.

NOTES & CULTIVARS
No cultivars are commonly available.

Morella cerifera SOUTHERN WAX MYRTLE

Wax myrtle is a tough native that adapts to a variety of sites. Popular for screening unsightly objects or views due to its very fast growth, it can also be maintained as an informal hedge. In addition, wax myrtle performs well as a multitrunked small tree for courtyards and patios. Its ability to tolerate both moist and dry soils makes it a good choice for wetland restorations and stormwater retention areas, where its dense canopy serves as cover for wildlife. Many publications list it as *Myrica cerifera*.

ZONES & ORIGIN 7b–11a. Native to the southeastern Coastal Plain.

SIZE & GROWTH RATE 12'–20' tall, 10'–15' wide, fast growing.

TEXTURE & FORM Medium fine texture and rounded form.

FOLIAGE Simple light green alternate leaves 1½"–4" long are oblanceolate shaped, with acute tips, a few serrations near the tips, and a slightly spicy odor when crushed. Young yellow-green stems are hairy. Mature bark is smooth gray.

FLOWERS A dioecious plant, with neither sex showy.

FRUIT Small round drupes occur in clusters along the stems of female plants. While not showy, the fruit turns bluish purple with a waxy coating in autumn and provides food for several migratory bird species. Colonists boiled the fruit to extract wax for candles.

LIGHT & SOIL Wax myrtle prefers full sun and moist soils. It tolerates light shade, wet to well-drained soils, drought, and salt spray.

MAINTENANCE While short-lived in nature, wax myrtle can thrive for 30 years or more in garden settings. For screening, frequent pruning is necessary to maintain density to the ground. To maintain tree forms, remove root suckers. Protect the trunks from lawn equipment.

INSTALLATION Containers and field-grown plants are readily available. Due to wax myrtle's fast growth, smaller container plants are recommended and should be spaced 8'–10' apart for massing.

PESTS & DISEASES Branches are easily damaged by snow and ice. Deer leave them alone.

NOTES & CULTIVARS
'Fairfax', with light green foliage, and 'Don's Dwarf', with darker foliage, reach 6' in size.
'Georgia Gem' grows 2' tall and 4' wide.

above and top left Flowers and fruit in the Founders Memorial Garden.

middle left A tree form on the UGA campus.

bottom left As a sheared hedge

Nerium oleander OLEANDER

Oleander is a highly popular flowering shrub in warmer areas of the Southeast due to its extended summer flowering and tough drought-resistant nature. In zones 9 and 10, oleander is often utilized for highway median and interchange plantings and is popular for informal hedges, screens, and background plantings or even as small multitrunked trees. Dwarf cultivars can be used for low borders. In cooler climates, oleander is employed for colorful container plantings on patios and decks and in courtyards.

top Foliage and flowers.
bottom A container plant at the National Arboretum.

left With rosemary and *Antigonon leptopus* on Hilton Head Island.
right Planted in a border.

ZONES & ORIGIN 8a–11a. Native to the Mediterranean region.

SIZE & GROWTH RATE 10'–20' tall, 6'–10' wide, fast growing.

TEXTURE & FORM Medium fine texture with an oval form.

FOLIAGE Simple leathery dark green opposite leaves 3"–6" long are linear to lanceolate shaped, with entire margins and acuminate tips, and often appear whorled at the ends of the stems. Foliage is frequently injured by hard freezes in zone 8.

FLOWERS Showy terminal flowers in singles and doubles in red, white, yellow, and pink occur in clusters on new growth in late spring (mid-May to early June in Athens), with some flowering throughout the summer. The flowers attract hummingbirds, and a few cultivars are lightly fragrant.

FRUIT Nonshowy green cylindrical capsules should be removed to encourage new growth.

LIGHT & SOIL Full sun to light shade with well-drained soils. It tolerates drought, salt spray, and alkaline soils.

MAINTENANCE Prune in early spring. Avoid fall pruning to prevent winter injury to new growth.

INSTALLATION Container-grown plants are readily available in sizes up to 7 gallons and should be planted in early spring to early summer in zone 8 on 6'–10' centers.

PESTS & DISEASES Aphids and mealybugs are issues on plants in damp soils. Deer don't touch them.

NOTES & CULTIVARS
Foliage is used for several chemotherapy drugs but is toxic if consumed.

The following cultivars are promoted as hardy to zone 8a:

'Calypso' has single red flowers to 18'.
'Hardy Pink' and 'Hardy Red' reach 10'.
'Matilda Ferrier' reaches 10' with double yellow flowers.
'Sister Agnes' has white flowers to 12'.

Osmanthus americanus DEVILWOOD

Devilwood is native to the maritime forest and portions of the southeastern Coastal Plain, but it is never abundant in nature. It acquired its name from early colonists who found its dense hard wood extremely difficult to cut. In its native environment, devilwood forms a low-branched, somewhat open-canopied shrub and is often associated with live oak, swamp bay, wax myrtle, and yaupon holly. Devilwood is rarely used in designs due to the difficulty of locating it from growers and the fact that, to be perfectly honest, several more widely available species offer better attributes for consideration. It is best suited for naturalizing along woodland edges and shaded paths.

ZONES & ORIGIN 6b–9b. Native to the southeastern Coastal Plain.

SIZE & GROWTH RATE 15'–25' tall and wide, medium slow growing.

TEXTURE & FORM Medium texture with an oval form in shade, broadly oval in sun.

FOLIAGE Simple lustrous dark green opposite leaves 2½"–5" long are narrowly elliptic to obovate shaped, with entire margins and acuminate tips. A smooth gray bark develops warty lenticels with maturity.

FLOWERS Creamy-white flowers in axillary cymes occur in early spring (mid-March to early April in Athens). The tiny flowers are not showy and only slightly fragrant. Next year's flower buds form in late summer and are visible throughout fall and winter.

FRUIT Devilwood is a dioecious species. With males nearby, female plants produce small oval drupes that mature to bluish purple in midautumn and remain until eaten by songbirds in midspring.

LIGHT & SOIL Light to moderate shade with a moist to moist but well-drained acidic soil is ideal. Devilwood tolerates full sun to full shade, well-drained soils, and salt spray.

MAINTENANCE Provide supplemental water for the first few summers after planting and during severe droughts.

INSTALLATION Devilwood is rare in nurseries. A few specialty growers provide it in small containers. For screens, plant 6'–10' on center in a loose organic soil mix.

PESTS & DISEASES No serious problems, although borers sometimes occur. Deer don't seem to like them.

NOTES & CULTIVARS None reported.

top to bottom

Foliage and early spring flowers.

Summer foliage and fruit.

A tree form on the UGA campus.

LARGE EVERGREEN SHRUBS

Osmanthus fragrans TEA OLIVE

Anyone who has ever experienced fragrant tea olive in bloom has probably imagined growing it in their own garden. The flowers aren't especially showy, but their fragrance can be enjoyed from far away on warm autumn evenings. With an upright form and dense canopy, tea olive can be used for accent plants, massed for informal buffers or backgrounds, or limbed up into small trees. Make sure to plant it upwind to appreciate the full fragrance.

ZONES & ORIGIN 8a–10a. Native to Asia.

SIZE & GROWTH RATE 15'–20' tall, 8'–15' wide, medium slow growing.

TEXTURE & FORM Medium texture and oval to broadly oval form.

FOLIAGE Simple leathery green opposite leaves 1½"–3¼" long are elliptic shaped, with acuminate tips. Finely serrate leaf margins on young plants become entire on mature foliage. New foliage is coppery colored. Gray-green twigs have prominent lenticels.

FLOWERS Clusters of extremely fragrant tiny creamy-white flowers occur in cycles from early to late autumn and early to midspring. Fall flowering seems to be initiated by changes in temperature and humidity. In Athens, the first flush usually occurs in mid- to late September and continues into November. Spring flowering is not as abundant or as fragrant. Petal extracts are used in perfumes and cosmetics and to flavor teas.

FRUIT Plants rarely fruit in the Southeast.

LIGHT & SOIL Full sun to moderate shade with moist but well-drained soil. While tea olive is drought tolerant, protection from early morning winter sun may help prevent foliage burn in cooler zones.

MAINTENANCE Prune in midspring to allow time for growth and flower bud formation.

INSTALLATION Container-grown plants are commonly available in sizes up to 7 gallons. Plant in well-drained soil on 8'–12' centers from early spring to midautumn in zones 7b–8b.

PESTS & DISEASES No serious problems. Deer don't eat them.

NOTES & CULTIVARS
'Fodingzhu' produces larger flower clusters but is less cold-hardy.
Osmanthus fragrans aurantius produces fragrant orange flowers in autumn. *O. fragrans thunbergii* produces yellow flowers. Both varieties are hardy to zone 7b.

top left Planted as a sheared hedge at Hills and Dales.
top right A young accent plant.
middle Foliage and flowers.
bottom Form in Athens.

Osmanthus heterophyllus HOLLY OSMANTHUS

Holly osmanthus is an extremely tough shrub with a dense canopy and spiny leaf margins that causes many designers to consider it as only being suitable for barrier plantings. But that overlooks the potential of holly osmanthus in compositions. Utilize its upright oval form for accents in shrub and perennial borders, or train it as an espalier in narrow spaces. Its dark green foliage is suited for backgrounds for other flowering plants in narrow borders.

ZONES & ORIGIN 6b–9b. Native to Asia.

SIZE & GROWTH RATE 12'–20' tall, 8'–15' wide, medium slow growing.

TEXTURE & FORM Medium fine texture and upright oval to oval form.

FOLIAGE Simple lustrous dark green opposite leaves 1"–2½" long are elliptic shaped, with spiny margins and acuminate tips. Foliage on mature plants has mostly entire margins.

FLOWERS Lightly fragrant nonshowy white flowers occur in late autumn (mid- to late November in Athens). Their fragrance is nowhere near as powerful as that of *Osmanthus* × *fortunei* or *O. fragrans*, and they are the last to flower in the autumn.

FRUIT Insignificant small oval drupes ripen to bluish black on female plants when both sexes are present.

LIGHT & SOIL Full sun with moist but well-drained slightly acidic soils is ideal. It tolerates light to moderate shade and is very drought tolerant after establishment.

MAINTENANCE Prune from late winter to midspring to allow time for flower bud formation on new growth over the summer. Provide supplemental water over the first summer during prolonged drought.

INSTALLATION Container-grown plants in sizes up to 7 gallons are widely available and can be planted year-round on 6'–8' centers for massing.

PESTS & DISEASES No serious problems. Deer don't touch them.

NOTES & CULTIVARS
'Goshiki' has light green foliage with creamy-white margins and a pinkish-red tint on new foliage.
'Gulftide' maintains its very spiny leaf margins and is hardy to zone 6a.
'Rotundifolius' is hardy to zone 7a, with rounded leaves, entire margins, and an oval form.
'Sasaba' has an extremely fine texture, with narrowly lanceolate leaves.

top to bottom

Foliage.

'Gulftide'.

'Goshiki' at Hills and Dales.

A tree form in Columbus.

Osmanthus × fortunei   FORTUNE'S OSMANTHUS

For many people, the first thing that comes to mind about Fortune's osmanthus is its powerfully sweet midautumn flowers. For locations too cool for tea olive, it provides the closest alternative for flower fragrance. The dark green foliage and dense canopy make a good buffer or screen and provide an outstanding year-round background for other flowering shrubs and perennials. And when autumn comes, the fragrance can be appreciated from well over 30' away. Mature plants make attractive small trees near patios or decks.

above Foliage.

top right A tree form in Athens.

middle right A sheared hedge.

bottom right In the Founders Memorial Garden.

ZONES & ORIGIN   7a–9b. A cross between *Osmanthus heterophyllus* and *O. fragrans*.

SIZE & GROWTH RATE   15'–25' tall, 10'–20' wide, medium slow growing.

TEXTURE & FORM   Medium texture and broadly oval form.

FOLIAGE   Simple lustrous dark green opposite leaves 2"–4" long are elliptic shaped, with acuminate tips. Leaves on young plants have 8–12 pairs of spines on the margins, while mature plants eventually develop entire margins.

FLOWERS   Highly fragrant tiny white flowers appear in cymes along the stems for about two weeks in midautumn (usually mid- to late October in Athens).

FRUIT   A dioecious plant that rarely fruits, since male plants are usually propagated.

LIGHT & SOIL   Plants perform well in full sun to moderate shade and slightly acidic well-drained soil. They are very drought tolerant.

MAINTENANCE   Prune in late winter to early spring to avoid removing new flower buds. Pruning can be a painful experience because of the spiny-margined foliage. Their dense canopy makes it very difficult to grow other plants beneath them.

INSTALLATION   Container-grown plants can be installed year-round at 8'–12' centers for massing. Provide supplemental water for the first summer during droughts.

PESTS & DISEASES   No serious problems. Deer don't touch them.

NOTES & CULTIVARS
Fortune's osmanthus has been available for many years but is not as popular with nurseries today as are tea olive and holly leaf osmanthus. Only a couple of cultivars, 'San Jose' and 'Fruitlandii', appear. Both are difficult to locate and slightly less cold-hardy while providing little significant ornamental difference.

Photinia × *fraseri* FRASER'S

Fraser's photinia has traditionally been promoted for its dense canopy and showy red new foliage. It can function as an accent plant to take advantage of its foliage color and upright habit but is more often used for tall screens and hedges. It can certainly improve the appearance of a chain-link security fence. Many people shear it several times per year to promote new foliage. Due to its fast growth and ultimate size, it is not a plant for small spaces. Overgrown plants can be pruned into small multitrunked trees. Extreme care should be taken with using it in the Southeast due to a debilitating leaf spot fungus.

ZONES & ORIGIN 6b–8b in the Southeast. A cross between two Asian species.

SIZE & GROWTH RATE 15'–25' tall, 10'–20' wide, fast growing.

TEXTURE & FORM Medium coarse texture and broadly oval form.

FOLIAGE Simple alternate leaves 3"–5" long are elliptic to oblong shaped, with serrate margins and acuminate tips. New growth throughout the season is coppery red before fading to a dark lustrous green.

FLOWERS Showy creamy-white flowers with a strong odor of well-aged roadkill occur in terminal panicles 3"–4" long in early spring (early to mid-April in Athens).

FRUIT Somewhat showy small berry-like pomes turn red from fall through winter.

LIGHT & SOIL Provide full sun to light shade with well-drained soil. It tolerates drought after establishment.

MAINTENANCE Pruning to encourage new growth can occur until late summer with the added benefit of reducing the volume and odor of next year's flowers.

INSTALLATION Container plants, mostly from West Coast nurseries, are available. Plant on 8'–10' centers virtually year-round in zones 7 and 8.

PESTS & DISEASES Plants are highly susceptible to leaf spot disease and thus are recommended for cooler drier climates. Frequent spraying with fungicides may be required to control severe outbreaks in warm damp springs. Deer will browse them.

NOTES & CULTIVARS
'Birmingham' is the original cross and the most common cultivar.

top New growth in Vancouver, B.C.
middle Foliage.
bottom Early spring flowers.

Pittosporum tobira PITTOSPORUM

Pittosporums are versatile shrubs that are highly popular in coastal areas of the Southeast. They develop a dense compact canopy that provides an outstanding background for smaller flowering plants or for screens or informal hedges in designs. Their ability to grow in full sun to full shade while maintaining their dense canopy only adds to their versatility. Their fragrant midspring flowers are particularly nice in close intimate spaces. An attractive branching habit makes them popular for bonsai specimens and for interior plants in cooler climates. Limbed-up mature plants make attractive multitrunked small trees.

top Foliage and flowers.
bottom 'Variegata' foliage.

ZONES & ORIGIN 8a–11a. Native to Asia.

SIZE & GROWTH RATE 10'–20' tall, 10'–25' wide, medium slow growing.

TEXTURE & FORM Medium texture and rounded to mounded form.

FOLIAGE Simple leathery dark green alternate leaves 1½"–3½" long are obovate shaped, with entire margins and blunt or rounded tips, and they cluster into a whorled appearance near the ends of stems.

FLOWERS Sweetly fragrant and somewhat showy creamy-white flowers in terminal clusters 1½" in diameter fade to yellow with age in midspring (mid- to late April in Athens).

FRUIT Fruits are nonshowy small green capsules that split open in early autumn to reveal tiny red seeds.

LIGHT & SOIL Light shade with a moist but well-drained slightly acidic soil is ideal. They tolerate full sun to full shade, moderate drought, salt spray, and slightly alkaline soils.

MAINTENANCE Prune after flowering in late spring to avoid removing next year's flower buds.

INSTALLATION Container plants are readily available in sizes up to 7 gallons and should be spaced 6'–10' apart in early spring or early to midautumn in zone 8.

PESTS & DISEASES While disease problems are few, deer cause serious damage.

NOTES & CULTIVARS
'Mojo' and 'Crème de Mint' are both dwarf forms reaching 2'–3' in size. 'Mojo' has yellow leaf margins, while 'Crème de Mint' has creamy-white margins.
'Variegata' reaches 6'–10' with gray-green foliage that has creamy-white margins.
'Wheeler's Dwarf' reaches 4' but is considered cold-hardy only to zone 8b.

left Form in Columbus, Ga.
right Planted with live oak and southern indica azaleas in Savannah.

Podocarpus macrophyllus PODOCARPUS

Podocarpus is a fine-textured large shrub or small tree that is quite flexible in how and where it is used. It is most frequently utilized as a sheared hedge 6'–8' tall to take advantage of its upright form and somewhat slow growth rate. Adaptable to sun or shade, it also performs well as an accent plant near doorways or garden entries. With light pruning, it serves as a specimen plant around patios or courtyards. Left unpruned, it reaches the size of a small tree over many years and could be trained as a low-maintenance espalier to cover blank walls. Podocarpus are often used for interior plantings in colder climates due to their lower light requirements.

ZONES & ORIGIN 8a–10b. Native to Asia.

SIZE & GROWTH RATE 25'–40' tall, 15'–30' wide, slow growing.

TEXTURE & FORM Fine texture and upright oval form.

FOLIAGE Dark lustrous green lanceolate-shaped alternate leaves 2"–4½" long are spirally arranged, with acute tips and prominent midribs. Mature plants have a light gray shredding bark.

FLOWERS A dioecious plant, with neither sex significant.

FRUIT Female plants produce insignificant berry-like dark purple cones that are mildly toxic if ingested.

LIGHT & SOIL Full sun to moderate shade with a well-drained soil. It tolerates near-neutral pH, drought after establishment, and moderate salt spray but cannot tolerate poorly drained soils.

MAINTENANCE Lightly prune in early spring to maintain a desired size and form. Sheared hedges typically require only one trim per year, but shearing should begin at an early age to establish desired density.

INSTALLATION Container plants in sizes from 3 to 7 gallons are available from Gulf Coast nurseries. Space 6'–8' apart in early spring for sheared hedges or 10'–12' apart for larger informal screens.

PESTS & DISEASES No serious issues. Deer don't like them.

NOTES & CULTIVARS
'Pringle's Dwarf' reaches 5' with a very slow growth rate, and could serve for border plantings.
Podocarpus macrophyllus maki reaches 10'–12' with a denser habit and smaller leaves. It is cold-hardy only to zone 8b.

top Foliage.
bottom A tree form at Louisiana State University.

left A privacy hedge in Charleston.   *right* A sheared formal privacy hedge.

Prunus laurocerasus ENGLISH LAUREL

English laurel is far more popular in the Pacific Northwest, where it is often used for tall hedges and screens. A tolerance of substantial shade allows it to maintain its branches low to the ground. Its modest growth rate allows it to be maintained at lower sizes than it could ultimately grow. It lacks appreciable attributes up close, so take advantage of its coarse texture and dense canopy and plant it in the rear of border plantings or in locations of dry shade where other plants struggle. It was reportedly used for hedges in colonial Williamsburg.

Foliage in Seattle.

ZONES & ORIGIN 6b–8b. Native to southeastern Europe.

SIZE & GROWTH RATE 15'–20' tall, 20'–25' wide, medium growing.

TEXTURE & FORM Coarse texture and rounded to spreading form.

FOLIAGE Simple stiff leathery lustrous green oblong alternate leaves 2½"–6" long have serrate margins and abruptly acuminate tips.

FLOWERS Somewhat showy white flowers with a slight grapelike fragrance are held on ascending racemes 2"–5" long along the stems in early spring (early to mid-April in Athens).

FRUIT Small rounded drupes turn purple and black in late summer and fall but are somewhat obscured by new foliage growth.

LIGHT & SOIL Light shade with well-drained soil is ideal. It tolerates full sun to moderate shade, moderate drought, salt spray, and a near-neutral pH but is very sensitive to wet soils.

MAINTENANCE Prune from midspring to early summer to control size. Never shear them, since cut leaves have an unsightly appearance. Older plants can be limbed up into small trees.

INSTALLATION English laurel is not nearly as common as its smaller cultivars. With searching, container plants from 3 to 7 gallons and a few field-grown plants can be found. Plant above surrounding grades in well-drained soils at 8'–12' apart for larger screens and buffers.

PESTS & DISEASES No serious problems in well-drained soils. Deer don't like them.

NOTES & CULTIVARS
'Magnoliifolia' produces large dark green foliage but is very difficult to locate.
See "Medium Evergreen Shrubs" for information on more popular smaller cultivars.

top left Foliage in Seattle.
bottom left Form in Vancouver, B.C.
right A form at Hills and Dales.

Pyracantha spp. FIRETHORN

Pyracanthas are dense drought-tolerant shrubs known for their showy late spring flowers and fall and winter fruit. With a stiff branching habit, they appear like small explosions in the landscape. They are often trained as an espalier on fences or walls to highlight their winter fruits but can also serve for informal hedges and barrier plantings or even to soften retaining walls and fences. Newer hybrid cultivars offer improved disease resistance in the southeastern climate.

Foliage and flowers

ZONES & ORIGIN 6a–9a. Native to Europe and Asia.

SIZE & GROWTH RATE 10'–15' tall and wide, medium fast growing.

TEXTURE & FORM Fine texture and broadly oval form.

FOLIAGE Simple alternate leaves 1"–2½" long are elliptic to oblanceolate in shape, with finely serrate margins and acute to truncate tips, depending on the cultivar. Stems have sharp stout spines at the nodes.

FLOWERS Showy tiny white flowers with an unpleasant roadkill odor are held in rounded corymbs 1"–2" long in midspring (late April to early May in Athens).

FRUIT Showy pomes ⅜" in diameter turn orange red to deep red in autumn and remain into spring before birds devour them.

LIGHT & SOIL Full sun with a well-drained slightly acidic soil is ideal. Firethorns tolerate light shade, drought, and near-neutral soils.

MAINTENANCE Prune after flowering, recognizing that you are sacrificing some fall fruit.

INSTALLATION Container plants can be installed from late winter to midautumn at 8'–12' spacing.

PESTS & DISEASES Aphids, scale, lace bugs, scab, and fire blight are potential problems. Choose disease-resistant cultivars. Deer don't like them.

NOTES & CULTIVARS
'Apache' reaches 4'–6' with red fruit and resistance to scab and fire blight.
'Lalandei' is hardy to 5b, reaching 15' with orange-red fruit.
'Lowboy' reaches 2'–4' and has a spreading form, but it is susceptible to scab.
'Mohave' reaches 12'–15' with orange-red fruit and resistance to scab and fire blight.
'Red Cushion' reaches 4' with a mounded form for ground covers and borders.
'Red Elf' is hardy to 7b and reaches 2' with a mounded to spreading form.

left Late fall and winter fruit on the UGA campus.

top right Espalier in Charleston.

bottom right In Savannah.

Foliage and flowers at Chanticleer, at Bethesda Terrace in Central Park in New York City, and in Chattanooga.

Rhododendron catawbiense CATAWBA RHODODENDRON

Catawba rhododendrons are slow-growing long-lived shrubs forming dense, nearly impenetrable thickets in their native habitats. They are often hybridized by growers to take advantage of their cold-hardiness and large showy flowers. Consider them for woodland trails and informal gardens, where they combine well with native stone, ferns, hostas, and stained wood. Just remember that they are more sensitive than many other shrubs to cultural conditions.

ZONES & ORIGIN 4b–8a. Native to the southern Appalachian Mountains.

SIZE & GROWTH RATE 6'–12' tall and wide, slow growing.

TEXTURE & FORM Coarse texture and broadly oval to rounded form.

FOLIAGE Simple leathery olive-green alternate leaves 2½"–6" long are elliptic to oblong shaped, with entire margins and acute tips. Foliage is toxic.

FLOWERS Extremely showy rosy-pink to purple funnel-shaped flowers occur in rounded terminal clusters in midspring (late April to mid-May in Athens).

FRUIT Insignificant capsules.

LIGHT & SOIL Light shade with a loose and moist but well-drained acidic soil is ideal. Though not drought resistant, they tolerate moderate shade, with reduced flowering.

MAINTENANCE Mulch and provide supplemental water during summer droughts. Avoid disturbance around established plants.

INSTALLATION Container plants from 2 to 7 gallons are readily available. Reject root-bound plants. Plant above the surrounding soil level in a rich organic soil at 6' on center.

PESTS & DISEASES Droughts and damp soils make them more susceptible to lace bugs, scale, borers, and twig blight. Deer nibble but don't like them.

NOTES & CULTIVARS
According to the American Rhododendron Society, these are selected hybrids with Catawba rhododendron as one parent.

'Album Elegans' reaches 8' with a round form and white flowers with a mauve blush.
'Catawbiense Album' reaches 6' with dark green leaves, pink buds, and white flowers.
'English Roseum' grows 6'–8' with an upright form and rosy-pink flowers.
'Nova Zembla' grows 5'–7' with an upright form and red flowers.
'Purpureum Elegans' reaches 5' with a rounded form and light purple flowers.
'Roseum Elegans' reaches 6'–8' with a rounded form and lavender flowers.

Rhododendron × *indicum* SOUTHERN INDICA AZALEA

Like camellias, azaleas are staples of traditional southern gardens. Southern indicas are the favored azaleas for zones 8 and 9 due to their large showy spring flowers, faster growth rate, and somewhat more forgiving nature compared to other evergreen azaleas. Available in a variety of colors, these azaleas show their stuff in early to midspring as the camellias are ending and native dogwoods are peaking. In the rear of borders, they serve as backgrounds for other plants when not in bloom or as evergreen foundations for large deciduous shrubs like spiraea, viburnum, hydrangea, and beauty bush.

'Formosa' flower and foliage.

ZONES & ORIGIN 7b–9b. Native to Asia.

SIZE & GROWTH RATE 6'–10' tall and wide, medium growing.

TEXTURE & FORM Medium texture and broadly oval to rounded form.

FOLIAGE Simple alternate leaves 1½"–3" long are elliptic to slightly obovate shaped, with entire margins and acuminate tips. Young leaves are densely pubescent.

FLOWERS Large showy clusters of funnel-shaped flowers in shades of red, pink, purple, and white occur in early spring (early to mid-April in Athens).

FRUIT Insignificant capsules.

LIGHT & SOIL Light shade with a moist but well-drained acidic soil is ideal. They grow in full sun to moderate shade and are slightly drought tolerant with age.

MAINTENANCE Maintain several inches of mulch and provide supplemental water during extended summer drought. Prune after spring flowering to avoid sacrificing next year's flower buds.

INSTALLATION Ensure that container plants are not root-bound. Plant 6' on center in autumn or early spring in loose acidic soil mixtures.

PESTS & DISEASES Lace bugs, aphids, and spider mites are major pests of stressed plants. Deer nibble young plants but rarely damage mature ones.

NOTES & CULTIVARS
'Fielder's White' provides frilly white flowers.
'Formosa' has rosy-purple flowers.
'G. G. Gerbing' provides white flowers with chartreuse throats and light green foliage.
'George L. Tabor' has light pink flowers with rosy-purple throats and light green foliage.
'Judge Solomon' has salmon-pink flowers with crimson throats.
'President Clay' has bright red midseason flowers.
'Pride of Mobile' has dark pink flowers.

top 'G. G. Gerbing' at Middleton Place Plantation.

middle 'George L. Tabor' (pink) and 'G. G. Gerbing' (white).

bottom 'George L. Tabor' and flowering dogwood.

Rhododendron maximum ROSEBAY RHODODENDRON

Rosebay rhododendron is the coarsest of the native rhododendrons and the last to bloom. Pink buds open to reveal white flowers in early summer (early to mid-June in Athens). Though rare in nurseries, they are common along cool streambanks at lower elevations of the Appalachians. Combine them with native ferns and stone for naturalizing along woodland edges. Older plants make attractive multitrunked small trees.

ZONES & ORIGIN 3b–8a. Native to the Appalachians from Georgia to Maine.

SIZE & GROWTH RATE 10'–15' tall and wide, slow growing.

TEXTURE & FORM Coarse texture with a mounded form.

FOLIAGE Leathery green simple leaves with a dense brown pubescence beneath are up to 8" long, narrowly elliptic in shape, with entire margins and acute tips. The leaves curl under drought and cold temperatures. Ovate flower buds are over 1" in size.

LIGHT & SOIL Provide light to moderate shade and loose, cool, and moist but well-drained acidic soil.

MAINTENANCE Provide supplemental water during summer droughts and maintain several inches of organic mulch. Prune after flowering in early summer. Deer don't touch them.

NOTES & CULTIVARS Remove fruit capsules to stimulate new growth. Ingested foliage is toxic.

top Foliage.

bottom Early summer flowers in north Georgia.

Rhododendron minus PIEDMONT RHODODENDRON

Piedmont rhododendron is the least prominent and well known of the native rhododendrons. Unlike rosebay and catawba, it has a loose open canopy with only 6–8 flowers per cluster. Its pinkish-white early to mid-May flowers are somewhat obscured by new growth. If you can find them, take advantage of their loose open form for the rear of borders and woodland edges. Piedmont rhododendron is one of the parents of the P.J.M. group of hybrid azaleas.

ZONES & ORIGIN 5b–8a. Native to the upper Piedmont and mountains of the Southeast.

SIZE & GROWTH RATE 6'–8' tall and wide, medium slow growing.

TEXTURE & FORM Medium texture and broadly oval form.

FOLIAGE Simple medium green elliptic leaves 2"–3¾" long have entire margins and acuminate tips. Foliage turns bronze in winter sun.

LIGHT & SOIL Provide light shade with moist but well-drained acidic soil.

MAINTENANCE Provide supplemental water during summer droughts and maintain several inches of organic mulch. Prune after flowering in late spring. Deer don't touch them.

NOTES & CULTIVARS Though rare in nurseries, they are easily propagated from cuttings. Leaf spot fungus is common but not serious.

top Late spring flowers.

bottom Mixed with azaleas.

left An informal hedge in Columbus.
top right A sheared privacy hedge.
bottom right At the Founders Memorial Garden.

Ternstroemia gymnanthera CLEYERA

Many people are familiar with cleyera, but they may not be aware of its full potential. It is often severely pruned or sheared to maintain it as a hedge, screen, or border plant to take advantage of its dark green foliage. But left to its own, cleyera develops an upright habit that allows its use in narrow spaces, with a minimal amount of pruning required. Plus, allowing it to grow provides opportunities to appreciate its fragrant late spring flowers, since annual pruning often removes many of its flower buds.

ZONES & ORIGIN 7a–10a. Native to Asia.

SIZE & GROWTH RATE 10'–15' tall, 6'–8' wide, medium growing.

TEXTURE & FORM Medium texture and upright oval to oval form.

FOLIAGE Simple lustrous dark green alternate leaves 1¾"–3" long are elliptic to oblanceolate shape, with entire margins, red petioles, and acute tips, and they appear whorled near the ends of twigs. New growth is coppery red. Winter foliage develops a reddish tint in sun.

FLOWERS Small but very fragrant white flowers are held along the stems in late spring (late May in Athens). The flowers are somewhat obscured by the new spring growth, since they occur on the previous year's growth lower on the stems.

FRUIT Insignificant small rounded berries mature in late summer and fall.

LIGHT & SOIL Light to moderate shade with a moist but well-drained acidic soil is ideal. Cleyera tolerates full sun with adequate moisture and is somewhat drought tolerant after establishment.

MAINTENANCE Prune in late spring after flowering to maintain desired size.

INSTALLATION Container plants are readily available in sizes up to 7 gallons. Space 6' on center for massing and provide supplemental water during summers for several years until well established.

PESTS & DISEASES Leaf spot fungus can occur in shade with overhead watering but is usually not serious. Deer nibble young plants but don't significantly damage mature ones.

NOTES & CULTIVARS
'Bronze Beauty' develops coppery-red new foliage.
'Clemson' develops purple-red new growth.
'LeAnn' has coppery-red new growth and improved leaf spot resistance.

Foliage.

Thuja occidentalis 'Degroot's Spire'
DEGROOT'S SPIRE ARBORVITAE

American arborvitae is 30'–50' tall with a pyramidal form that is native across northern portions of the United States and Canada. Degroot's spire is considered a dwarf cultivar, and it was selected because it develops a highly formal columnar form that functions like a sentinel in the landscape. It can be massed and sheared to form a tall formal hedge to serve as a garden wall. More often it is utilized as an accent plant in shrub borders or foundation compositions. Plant two or more to provide a gateway or sense of entry between rooms of the garden. It's not fond of summer heat, so use it with caution in the Southeast.

ZONES & ORIGIN 3b–8a. Native to the northern United States and Canada.

SIZE & GROWTH RATE 10'–15' tall, 3'–4' wide, medium slow growing.

TEXTURE & FORM Fine texture and columnar form.

FOLIAGE Fernlike sprays of medium green scale-type foliage are held along flattened branches that are oriented parallel to the ground.

FLOWERS Insignificant.

FRUIT Insignificant.

LIGHT & SOIL Full sun to light shade with a slightly moist and slightly acidic soil is ideal. It tolerates light salt spray, moist but well-drained soils, slightly alkaline soil, and short droughts after establishment.

MAINTENANCE Provide supplemental water during summer droughts. Prune in early spring before new growth begins, and mulch in spring to help the roots stay cool and moist during summer.

INSTALLATION Plants are widely available in a variety of sizes both in containers and as field-grown specimens. Plant in early to midautumn or early spring at 3' apart for massing.

PESTS & DISEASES Deer are the biggest problems. Avoid arborvitae if deer are in your neighborhood. Bagworms and spider mites are common but usually not serious under good cultural conditions. Twig blight can occur with overhead watering.

NOTES & CULTIVARS
'Brandon' and 'Smargd' reach 12'–20' with narrowly conical forms.
'Hetz Wintergreen' reaches 20'–30' tall.
'Holmstrup' reaches 10' with vertical foliage sprays.

top and middle Foliage at the Giberson residence.
bottom left Accents at a Signal Mountain, Tenn., residence.
bottom right At an Athens residence.

Viburnum awabuki CHINDO VIBURNUM

Unlike other viburnums, Chindo viburnum is valued more for its foliage than for its flowers or fruit. A relatively recent introduction by the nursery industry, it is gaining popularity as a cold-hardy alternative to sweet viburnum, *Viburnum odoratissimum*. With a tolerance for sun or shade, a dense canopy, and a low-branching habit, it can be used for background plantings, buffers, and tall screens. Take advantage of its somewhat formal upright habit as an accent plant in compositions where its coarse texture will almost always provide contrast with surrounding plants. Mature plants perform well as small trees for courtyards and patios.

ZONES & ORIGIN 7b–9b. Native to Asia.

SIZE & GROWTH RATE 12'–20' tall, 10'–15' wide, medium growing.

TEXTURE & FORM Coarse texture and oval to broadly pyramidal form.

FOLIAGE Simple dark glossy green opposite leaves 3"–7" long are narrowly elliptic in shape, with crenate margins and acute tips. A few red dying leaves are usually present.

FLOWERS Somewhat showy creamy-white flowers on terminal panicles occur in mid- to late spring (late April to late May in Athens). The flower heads are somewhat obscured by new growth. Plants take several years before flowering.

FRUIT Red drupes appear in midsummer, but many Chindos don't fruit, because they require cross-pollination from nearby genetically different plants.

LIGHT & SOIL Chindo viburnum grows in full sun to moderate shade, with moist but well-drained slightly acidic soil. Early morning shade in zones 7b and 8a helps prevent burned foliage from excessive transpiration while the ground is frozen in winter. Established plants are fairly drought resistant.

MAINTENANCE Several inches of mulch help prevent burned winter foliage in northern zones.

INSTALLATION Plants are primarily available from Florida nurseries. Plant from early to midautumn or in spring at 12'–15' apart.

PESTS & DISEASES Downy mildew and leaf spot fungus can defoliate plants during cool damp springs. Avoid overhead watering, and remove and destroy all dead leaves on the ground below diseased plants.

NOTES & CULTIVARS
A variegated foliage cultivar is reported but is rarely available.

top left On the UGA campus.
top right Form in flower.
middle Foliage.
bottom Flower buds.

Viburnum odoratissimum SWEET VIBURNUM

Sweet viburnum is a popular large shrub that grows in warmer climates. With its fast growth, dense canopy, and adaptability to sun or shade, it is frequently used for background plantings, large buffers, and even sound barriers. It can even be sheared into formal hedges. Older plants make attractive small trees for courtyards or patios, where their fragrant early spring flowers are particularly appreciated. Use with caution in the northern portions of zone 8b due to risks from freeze damage to the foliage.

Foliage.

ZONES & ORIGIN 8b–10b. Native to Asia.

SIZE & GROWTH RATE 15'–25' tall, 10'–15' wide, fast growing.

TEXTURE & FORM Coarse texture with an oval to broadly pyramidal form.

FOLIAGE Simple bright green leathery opposite leaves 3"–6" long are broadly elliptic shaped, with mostly entire margins and acute tips. Crushed leaves have an unpleasant odor.

FLOWERS Somewhat showy white flowers on pyramidal panicles in early spring have a light sweet odor.

FRUIT Insignificant drupes mature to black, but fruiting may not occur without cross-pollination from other viburnums.

LIGHT & SOIL Light shade with a moist but well-drained slightly acidic soil is ideal. Sweet viburnum tolerates full sun to moderate shade, light salt spray, and moderate drought with age.

MAINTENANCE Prune in spring after flowering. Avoid late summer and fall pruning in zones 8b and 9a to reduce risk of freeze damage to new growth. Selectively thin the dense canopy of plants being used as small trees.

INSTALLATION Container plants in a variety of sizes are readily available from many Gulf Coast nurseries. Avoid late fall and winter planting in borderline cold-hardy areas. Space 10'–12' apart for massing.

PESTS & DISEASES Scale, aphids, and whiteflies can cause problems on plants growing under less than ideal conditions. Deer nibble small plants but don't damage mature ones.

NOTES & CULTIVARS
'Emerald Lustre' with coppery-pink new growth is difficult to locate.
Viburnum bracteatum 'Emerald Luster' is a deciduous shrub reaching 8' with a rounded form, medium texture, and zone 5b hardiness.

At residences in Beaufort, S.C.

Viburnum rhytidophyllum LEATHERLEAF VIBURNUM

Leatherleaf viburnum is rarely among the first plants designers consider when they contemplate large evergreen shrubs for their designs. Yet few plants tolerate sun, shade, or drought with as few problems or maintenance issues. Take advantage of its dark green foliage for a background for other flowering shrubs in the rear of borders. In the Southeast, they are attractive in woodland gardens or the north side of buildings under light shade combined with natural stone walls and pavements.

ZONES & ORIGIN 5b–8a. Native to China.

SIZE & GROWTH RATE 10'–15' tall and wide, medium growing.

TEXTURE & FORM Coarse texture and broadly oval form.

FOLIAGE Simple lustrous leathery dark green opposite leaves 2½"–8" long are lanceolate shaped, with entire margins, acute tips, and prominent depressed veins. The leaves tend to droop in cold weather, and their lower sides, petioles, and young twigs are covered in a dense pubescence.

FLOWERS Lightly fragrant, creamy-white flowers occur on flattened cymes in early spring (early to mid-April in Athens). Next year's brown flower buds become evident in late summer.

FRUIT Though the fruit are fairly showy, they are rarely seen, since the flowers require cross-pollination with other genetically different viburnums to set fruit. Genetically similar clones don't suffice.

LIGHT & SOIL Light to moderate shade with moist but well-drained slightly acidic soil is ideal. It tolerates full sun to full shade, drought, and slightly alkaline soils.

MAINTENANCE Prune immediately after flowering in spring to avoid removing next year's flower buds.

INSTALLATION Specialty nurseries grow them in small containers. Plant 8'–10' apart year-round.

PESTS & DISEASES No serious problems. Deer don't like them.

NOTES & CULTIVARS
Nurseries usually grow one of these cultivars rather than the species.

'Cree' is a medium slow grower reaching 8'–10'.
'Roseum' produces pink flower buds that open to creamy white.

Viburnum × *rhytidophylloides* is a cross between leatherleaf viburnum and *V. lantana*. The most popular cultivar, 'Alleghany', has a similar appearance to leatherleaf viburnum but broader ovate-shaped leaves and is hardy from zones 4a to 8a.

top left Viburnum × rhytidophylloides in bloom.

top right In Vancouver, B.C.

middle Spring flowers.

bottom Late summer foliage and flower buds.

top left and right Foliage and flowers in Savannah.
bottom Foliage.

Viburnum suspensum SANDANQUA VIBURNUM

Sandanqua viburnum is a popular shrub in warmer portions of the Southeast. With its dense rounded canopy and fragrant early spring flowers, it is widely used for borders, screens, and background plantings. It is easily maintained as a lower plant, and as a result, many people maintain it as a 4'–8' semiformal hedge. However, excessive pruning greatly reduces the abundance of flowers and accompanying fragrance. It looks good in combination with dark brick or natural stone walls and when combined with finer-textured shrubs like spiraea and jasminum.

ZONES & ORIGIN 8b–10b. Native to Asia.

SIZE & GROWTH RATE 8'–12' tall and wide, medium fast growing.

TEXTURE & FORM Medium coarse texture and broadly oval to rounded form.

FOLIAGE Simple leathery dark green opposite leaves 2"–4½" long are ovate to elliptic in shape, with serrate margins and acute tips. Young stems have a rough sandpapery feel. Severely freeze-damaged plants emit a strong foul odor.

FLOWERS Somewhat showy and pleasantly fragrant pinkish-white tubular-shaped flowers appear on small panicles that tend to droop below the branches in very early spring.

FRUIT Attractive red drupes form in spring after flowering before turning black in early summer.

LIGHT & SOIL Best performance is in light shade with a moist but well-drained soil. It tolerates full sun to moderate shade and drought and is highly tolerant of salt spray.

MAINTENANCE Prune to desired size and shape in spring after flowering is completed.

INSTALLATION Container-grown plants are readily available from many Florida growers and can be planted year-round except in zone 8b, where they should be planted no later than midautumn. Space plants 4'–6' on center for lower borders or 6'–8' apart for higher screens.

PESTS & DISEASES Few serious problems with good cultural conditions. Deer don't bother them.

NOTES & CULTIVARS
Laurustinus viburnum, *Viburnum tinus*, is similar to Sandanqua but larger in size, with larger and showier lightly fragrant early spring flowers and bluish-purple fruit. The most popular cultivar, 'Spring Bouquet', reaches 6' with a rounded form to zone 7b.

top left and right Flowers in bloom on the UGA campus.

bottom Late summer foliage and flower buds.

Viburnum × *pragense* PRAGUE VIBURNUM

Many people don't care for the coarse texture of many evergreen viburnums but are looking for something that provides their toughness and dependability. The Prague viburnum may be just what they are searching for. Providing fast growth, attractive spring flowers, and the ability to thrive under less than ideal conditions, it may be just the ticket for people who need an attractive tall screen or buffer. Unlike many other large shrubs, it is easily manageable and provides dependable flowers each year. Like the leatherleaf viburnum, Prague viburnum looks good combined with natural stone or stained woods and could be used as an accent in a shrub border. Just make sure to allow it enough room to spread.

ZONES & ORIGIN 5b–8b. A man-made cross between *Viburnum rhytidophyllum* and *V. utile*.

SIZE & GROWTH RATE 10'–12' tall and wide, fast growing.

TEXTURE & FORM Medium texture with a broadly oval form.

FOLIAGE Simple lustrous dark green opposite leaves 2"–4½" long have entire margins and acute tips. The narrowly ovate leaves have prominent depressed veins above, with dense pubescence beneath and on the petioles and young stems.

FLOWERS Pink flower buds give way to lightly fragrant white flowers in rounded terminal cymes in early spring (late March to mid-April in Athens). Tan flower buds become evident in autumn.

FRUIT Rarely sets fruit, requiring cross-pollination with other viburnum species.

LIGHT & SOIL Best performance is with full sun to light shade and moist but well-drained soils. It is very drought tolerant and tolerates full shade, but with reduced flowering.

MAINTENANCE Prune branches back to a node after flowering in spring to maintain desired size and form.

INSTALLATION Container-grown plants are readily available and can be planted year-round. Space 8'–10' on center.

PESTS & DISEASES No serious problems. Deer browse them but usually don't cause serious problems.

NOTES & CULTIVARS None available.

top left At the State Botanical Garden of Georgia.

top right At Middleton Place Plantation.

middle and bottom In Athens.

Yucca aloifolia SPANISH DAGGER

Few plants are more difficult to effectively utilize in compositions than yuccas. Spanish dagger, the largest of the native yuccas, will immediately catch everyone's attention. Since it is readily visible from a distance, keep it away from walks and pathways. In rock gardens, provide it with a base of other sun-loving and drought-tolerant plants such as junipers, lantanas, and verbenas. Since it tolerates moderate shade and neglect, take advantage of its stout multiple trunks for interior courtyards that are not accessible to the public, such as for zoo exhibits.

ZONES & ORIGIN 7a–11a. Native to coastal dunes and marshes of the southeastern United States.

SIZE & GROWTH RATE 6'–10' tall, 3'–4' wide, slow growing.

TEXTURE & FORM Coarse texture and upright oval form.

FOLIAGE Lustrous bright green lanceolate leaves 18"–24" long and ¾"–1¼" wide are spirally arranged, with finely serrate margins and sharply pointed tips. The margins can cause paper cuts, while the tips are quite painful and dangerous around children.

FLOWERS Showy white flowers on terminal panicles arise 1'–2' above the foliage, usually in early summer, but are unpredictable and can occur anytime between late May and October in Athens.

FRUIT Fruit are unsightly oval capsules 2"–3" long.

LIGHT & SOIL Plants prefer full sun and well-drained soils but tolerate alkaline soils, drought, salt spray, and up to moderate shade.

MAINTENANCE Wear gloves and thick clothes when working around this yucca. Remove the flower stalk after flowering.

INSTALLATION Container-grown plants can be planted year-round on 3'–5' centers.

PESTS & DISEASES No problems under good cultural conditions. Deer don't touch them.

NOTES & CULTIVARS
'Marginata' has cream-colored variegated foliage.
Yucca treculeana is native to southwestern Texas and Mexico. Hardy to zone 7a, it reaches 10'–12' with a stout trunk and leaves up to 4' long that are broader and coarser in texture than *Y. aloifolia*. The flower panicle reaches about 2' above the foliage, and it can flower more than once each year.

LARGE DECIDUOUS SHRUBS

Doublefile viburnums in Chattanooga.

Due to their size, the shrubs in this group require a good deal of space to utilize them in a design, thus mostly limiting their effectiveness to large properties and gardens. In those situations, they are generally reserved for use toward the rear of border plantings or woodland edges, where their showy flowers or brilliant fall foliage allows them to be appreciated from a distance. In many instances, these shrubs can be somewhat unattractive up close, providing further reason to place them away from the viewer.

Many of these large shrubs were once highly popular and heavily used in landscapes. Many are considered as old-garden plants that our grandparents and great-grandparents may have used on their own properties in the early to mid-1900s. Today, several of them are not as popular as they once were. There are likely several reasons why they have declined in popularity over the decades.

As we have evolved from a largely agrarian society to a more urban one, our properties have decreased in size. Further, as the progression from large-lot suburban homes to smaller lots of only a quarter acre or less becomes more prevalent, there is less available space to fill with ornamental plants. If your front or rear yard is only 10'–20' deep, you often don't have enough space to use one of these large shrubs while still providing space for circulation and outdoor living.

Also, during the latter part of the twentieth century, air-conditioning systems became much more common for homes in the Southeast. As a result, fewer folks spend their spring and summer evenings outside enjoying and maintaining their yards. This is particularly true as our population has aged. As a result, smaller and more manageable plants that don't require as much maintenance have exploded in popularity. At the same time, our recent addiction to electronic gadgetry for entertainment and communication appears to have further reduced some people's interest in spending time outdoors working in their yards. How important can pruning a mock orange or viburnum be if it causes you to miss a celebrity's latest Tweet?

Finally, many of these shrubs tend to be one-trick ponies. Their mostly nondescript appearance when not in bloom, fruiting, or exhibiting their fall foliage probably tends to reduce their allure to the general public.

So if you have the space to layer plants in borders, are willing to provide the necessary pruning and care, and are looking for a shrub that will make an impression in a season, these large shrubs may do the trick for you. They certainly have a lot to offer. Just ask your grandparents.

BOTANICAL NAME	SUNLIGHT	SOILS	TEXTURE	NOTABLE ATTRIBUTES	FALL FOLIAGE	NATIVE TO SOUTHEAST
Aesculus parviflora	Light to moderate shade	Moist but well drained	Coarse	Early summer white flowers	Attractive yellow fall foliage	Yes
Buddleja davidii	Full sun to light shade	Moist but well drained	Medium coarse	Summer flowers attract butterflies	None	No, Asia
Cephalanthus occidentalis	Full sun to light shade	Moist to wet	Medium	Fragrant white summer flowers	None	Yes
Chimonanthus praecox	Full sun to moderate shade	Moist but well drained	Medium coarse	Fragrant yellow winter flowers	Fair yellow late autumn	No, Asia
Deutzia scabra	Full sun to light shade	Well drained	Medium coarse	White late spring flowers	None	No, Asia
Euonymus alatus	Full sun to light shade	Well drained	Medium	Drought and pH tolerant	Outstanding deep red	No, Asia
Exochorda racemosa	Full sun to light shade	Well drained	Medium	White early spring flowers	None	No, Asia
Ficus carica	Full sun to moderate shade	Well drained	Coarse	Edible fruit	None	No, western Asia and north Africa
Hamamelis virginiana	Light shade	Moist but well drained acidic	Medium coarse	Fragrant late fall yellow flowers	Good yellow	Yes
Hamamelis × intermedia	Full sun to moderate shade	Moist but well drained acidic	Medium coarse	Mid- to late winter flowers	Good yellow	No, man-made cross
Hibiscus syriacus	Full sun to light shade	Well drained	Medium coarse	Colorful early summer flowers	None	No, Asia
Hydrangea paniculata	Full sun to light shade	Moist but well drained acidic	Coarse	White midsummer flowers	None	No, Asia
Hydrangea quercifolia	Light to moderate shade	Moist but well drained	Coarse	White late spring flowers	Outstanding red fall foliage late	Yes
Ilex decidua	Full sun to moderate shade	Moist but well drained	Medium fine	Showy fall and winter fruit	Fair to good yellow	Yes
Ilex verticillata	Full sun to moderate shade	Moist but well drained to wet	Medium	Showy fall and winter fruit	Poor yellow green	Yes
Kolkwitzia amabilis	Full sun to light shade	Well drained	Medium	Attractive midspring flowers	Fair red orange	No, Asia
Lonicera fragrantissima	Full sun to light shade	Moist but well drained	Medium	Fragrant white winter flowers	None	No, Asia
Philadelphus coronarius	Full sun to light shade	Well drained	Medium	Fragrant late spring flowers	Poor yellow green	No, Europe and Asia
Punica granatum	Full sun to light shade	Well drained	Medium	Edible fruit and showy flowers	Poor yellow	No, Europe and Asia
Rosa banksiae 'Lutea'	Full sun to light shade	Moist but well drained	Medium fine	Showy midspring flowers	None	No, Asia
Rosa laevigata	Full sun to light shade	Moist but well drained	Medium	Fragrant midspring flowers	None	No, Asia
Sambucus nigra canadensis	Full sun to light shade	Moist to moist but well drained	Medium coarse	Early summer flowers and fruit	None	Yes
Viburnum macrocephalum 'Sterile'	Full sun to light shade	Moist but well drained	Coarse	Showy white spring flowers	None	No, Asia
Viburnum plicatum tomentosum	Full sun to light shade	Moist but well drained	Medium coarse	Showy white spring flowers	Good red to crimson	No, Asia
Viburnum × burkwoodii	Full sun to light shade	Moist but well drained	Medium	Fragrant white spring flowers	None	No, Asia
Vitex agnus-castus	Full sun	Well drained	Medium fine	Purple early summer flowers	None	No, Persia
Weigela florida	Full sun to light shade	Well drained	Medium	Showy spring flowers	None	No, Asia

Aesculus parviflora BOTTLEBRUSH BUCKEYE

Few plants provide as many attractive attributes as the bottlebrush buckeye. Its coarse texture, attractive early summer flowers, and yellow fall foliage are all reasons to highlight this plant in woodland garden compositions. It combines well with other informal native plants such as mountain laurel, rhododendron, itea, and deciduous azaleas. Its only real drawback might be its slow growth, requiring several years to achieve a fullness deserving of respect. Keep in mind that the fruit is poisonous when chewed, so keep it away from young children who might enjoy grazing the garden between meals.

ZONES & ORIGIN 5a–9a. Native to shaded streambanks of southwest Georgia and central Alabama.

SIZE & GROWTH RATE 8'–12' tall, 8'–15' wide, slow growing.

TEXTURE & FORM Coarse texture and rounded to mounded form.

FOLIAGE Palmately compound opposite leaves have five obovate leaflets with acuminate tips and crenate-serrulate margins. Fall foliage is an attractive bright yellow in early to midautumn.

FLOWERS Showy white flowers in panicles 8"–15" long appear above the top of the foliage in early to mid-June in Athens, with a few flowers into early July.

FRUIT Light brown pear-shaped capsules appear in midsummer and remain into late autumn. They are not particularly attractive, and the seeds are toxic if eaten.

LIGHT & SOIL Light shade and moist but well-drained acidic soil are ideal. Plants are not very drought resistant, preferring consistent moisture availability throughout the summer. They perform well in full sun to moderate shade, but flowering is limited under moderate shade.

MAINTENANCE With age, it produces a spreading habit, with new plants forming from root suckers that can be separated from the parent plant to provide new plants or allowed to remain to facilitate the spread of the plant.

INSTALLATION Amend clay soil with organic material to keep it loose to facilitate the spread of the roots. Specialty nurseries carry container plants. Space plants 6'–8' apart, and provide supplemental water during summer droughts.

PESTS & DISEASES No serious diseases. Deer don't touch them.

NOTES & CULTIVARS None listed.

May foliage and flower panicles.

top June flowers in the Founders Memorial Garden.

middle In bloom at the Taylor-Grady residence in Athens.

bottom Fall color in Athens.

Buddleja davidii BUTTERFLY BUSH

Butterfly bush is often treated like a herbaceous perennial in many landscapes. It is frequently pruned back to about 24" each spring to promote new stems with showy flower panicles. Butterfly bush performs best when used toward the rear of border plantings to allow its branches to arch over and exhibit its showy flowers but hide its woody stems. It is semievergreen in zone 9, treated as an annual in zone 4, and invasive in the Pacific Northwest.

ZONES & ORIGIN 5a–9b. Native to China.

SIZE & GROWTH RATE 8'–12' tall, 6'–8' wide, fast growing.

TEXTURE & FORM Medium coarse texture and broadly oval form.

FOLIAGE Simple opposite leaves are narrowly ovate to lanceolate shaped, 2½"–6" long, with serrate margins and acuminate tips. Leaf color varies by cultivar. No fall color.

FLOWERS Tiny individual flowers with four petals and orange centers occur on slender panicles 4"–10" long throughout the summer on new growth and attract butterflies and hummingbirds. Flowers are lightly to moderately fragrant, depending upon the cultivar. In Athens, flowering begins in mid-May, peaking in early June.

FRUIT Insignificant capsules provide another reason to prune.

LIGHT & SOIL It needs full sun and a moist but well-drained soil. Flowering is greatly reduced in shade. While it is drought tolerant, it requires adequate moisture to produce new growth and flowers throughout the summer.

MAINTENANCE Periodic pruning and supplemental summer water promote new growth and flowering.

INSTALLATION Container plants are readily available. Plant year-round in zones 6–9. Space larger cultivars 8'–12' apart, 4'–6' for smaller cultivars.

PESTS & DISEASES No serious problems. Deer don't touch them.

NOTES & CULTIVARS
The following cultivars are grouped by color:

Purples: 'Black Knight', 'Dartmoor', 'Potter's Purple', 'Violet Eyes', 'Wine'
Blues and lavenders: 'Bonnie', 'Guinevere', 'Lavender Eyes', 'Lochinch'
Reds: 'Attraction', 'Summer Beauty', 'Royal Red'
Pink: 'Pink Delight'
Whites: 'White Bouquet', 'White Profusion'
Yellow: 'Honeycomb'

These cultivars grow 4'–6'. The name provides an indication of color: 'Adonis Blue', 'Lavender Eyes', 'Miss Ruby', 'Nanho Blue', 'Peacock', 'Petite Snow'.

top Foliage and flower panicles.
bottom Early summer flowers.

top Early summer flowers in a border planting.
bottom With crocosmia in Vancouver, B.C.

Cephalanthus occidentalis BUTTONBUSH

Buttonbush is a native wetland shrub found on the edges of swamps and other damp soils across much of the United States. Considered a pioneer species in those locations, it is somewhat brittle-wooded and tends to be short-lived due to shading by taller but slower-growing trees. While an excellent choice for wetland or stream restorations, it is a difficult plant to effectively utilize in most gardens. In designed landscapes, severe pruning each year keeps it dense and flowering heavily.

top left At the J. C. Raulson Arboretum in Raleigh, N.C.

top right Early summer flowers and foliage.

bottom Midsummer flowers and fruit.

ZONES & ORIGIN 4a–10b. Native to the eastern United States to southern Canada.

SIZE & GROWTH RATE 12'–15' in height and spread, fast growing.

TEXTURE & FORM Medium texture with a loose and irregular rounded form.

FOLIAGE Simple leaves are mostly opposite but occasionally whorled. The lustrous green leaves, 2"–5½" long, are elliptic to ovate in shape, with entire margins and acute tips. Leaves usually drop in midautumn without developing any color.

FLOWERS Lightly fragrant tiny white flowers occur in 1" rounded heads in terminal panicles of three to nine in early to midsummer. Mid- to late June is the peak in Athens, with sporadic flowers into early September. The flowers are popular with honeybees and other insects.

FRUIT Flowerheads turn into rounded reddish-brown nutlets in mid- to late summer and remain into the winter. Waterfowl are known to eat the seeds.

LIGHT & SOIL Full sun to light shade and moist to wet soils. It doesn't tolerate drought well, and flowering is reduced in light shade.

MAINTENANCE Since buttonbush flowers on new growth, selective pruning to keep it lower and denser in habit can occur from midsummer through early spring.

INSTALLATION Buttonbush is available in small containers from specialty growers. Plant from midautumn to midspring in a consistently moist soil. Space plants 3'–5' apart for wetland restorations or 8'–12' apart for borders. Young stem cuttings can root when placed in moist locations.

PESTS & DISEASES No serious diseases. Deer browse the foliage.

NOTES & CULTIVARS
'Sputnik' produces light pink flower heads that fade to white.

Chimonanthus praecox WINTERSWEET

Wintersweet is a difficult plant to utilize in designs. For much of the year it is somewhat unsightly in appearance. Only in the winter does it provide a reason for its use when its fragrant yellow flowers are highlighted against a bright blue winter sky. Therein lies the dilemma. To take advantage of its fragrance, you want it fairly close. Yet for the rest of the year, it is better suited to obscurity in the background. However, placing it too far away denies viewers the full benefit of its fragrance.

ZONES & ORIGIN 6b–9b. Native to China.

SIZE & GROWTH RATE 10'–15' tall and wide, medium slow growing.

TEXTURE & FORM Medium coarse texture with a flat-topped broadly oval form.

FOLIAGE Simple ovate-lanceolate opposite leaves are 2"–7" long, with entire margins and acuminate tips. The dark green leaves have a rough sandpaper-like feel to the upper surface. They develop a fair yellow late fall color and often hold some leaves into midwinter.

FLOWERS Fragrant single yellow flowers with purple centers occur along the stems for an extended period in winter. On warm winter days, the fragrance fills a courtyard. Flowering is never very showy, since buds don't all open at once. In Athens, flowering occurs from late December to late February, peaking in late January. Freezing temperatures don't seem to adversely affect the flowers.

FRUIT Unattractive pear-shaped capsules 2" long turn brown in summer and remain into winter.

LIGHT & SOIL Full sun and moist but well-drained soils are ideal. It tolerates up to moderate shade and drought after establishment.

MAINTENANCE To control size, prune in early spring after flowering is completed. Removing the fruit will help the appearance.

INSTALLATION Although wintersweet easily germinates from seed, its slow growth to marketable sizes discourages growers. As a result, relatively few nurseries grow it, and those that do only offer it in small containers. Plant in early spring after flowering or in mid- to late autumn.

PESTS & DISEASES No serious problems.

NOTES & CULTIVARS
Several cultivars are listed in the literature but aren't available.

top Foliage.
middle Early winter flowers.
bottom Fall color in the Founders Memorial Garden.

Deutzia scabra FUZZY DEUTZIA

Fuzzy deutzia is an old-garden plant that has fallen out of favor in recent years. Its arching branches provide an outstanding display of white flowers for a couple of weeks in late spring but are mostly nondescript the rest of the year. As with pearlbush, wintersweet, and beauty bush, use fuzzy deutzia in the rear of border plantings to display its spring flowers and allow it to disappear afterward.

ZONES & ORIGIN 5a–8a. Native to Japan.

SIZE & GROWTH RATE 8'–12' tall, 6'–10' wide, medium growing.

TEXTURE & FORM Medium coarse texture with fountain-like branching habit and broadly oval form.

FOLIAGE Simple opposite dull green leaves 2"–3" long are ovate in shape, with serrate margins, acuminate tips, and a sandpapery surface. They lack any fall color. Showy terminal panicles of white flowers arise in late spring (mid-May in Athens).

LIGHT & SOIL Full sun to light shade with a well-drained soil.

MAINTENANCE No serious disease problems. Prune older stems annually after flowering to control size and preserve the fountain-like form. Do not shear.

NOTES & CULTIVARS
'Pride of Rochester' provides pink flowers. *Deutzia* × *magnifica* reaches 10' with double white flowers. Both are rare in today's nurseries.

top and bottom Foliage and late spring flowers with catawba rhododendrons.

Euonymus alatus
WINGED EUONYMUS · BURNING BUSH

The brilliant red fall foliage of burning bush against a blue autumn sky or in front of a dark green background catches everyone's attention. The showy foliage lasts for several weeks in mid- to late autumn. An ability to tolerate adverse urban conditions also contributes to its popularity. But like many deciduous shrubs, a little of this one goes a long way. Try tucking a few into a shrub border to add autumn interest rather than using it as a clipped hedge, where it offers little interest throughout the year.

Fall foliage and fruit.

ZONES & ORIGIN 4b–8b. Native to Asia.

SIZE & GROWTH RATE 12'–16' tall, 10'–15' wide, medium growing.

TEXTURE & FORM Medium texture with a rounded flat-topped form.

FOLIAGE Simple opposite leaves are elliptic to obovate shaped, ¾"–2½" long, with serrate margins and acuminate tips. Fall foliage is an outstanding scarlet to crimson in sunny locations in mid- to late autumn. Young stems are green, with second-year growth developing prominent brown corky wings for several years.

FLOWERS Insignificant tiny yellow-green midspring flowers.

FRUIT Small red capsules open in autumn to reveal orange-red seeds but are usually obscured by the brilliant red fall foliage.

LIGHT & SOIL Full sun to moderate shade and well-drained soils. It tolerates drought and near-neutral to slightly alkaline soils.

MAINTENANCE Burning bush is invasive in northeastern states but is currently not considered a problem throughout the Southeast. It adapts well to annual pruning to maintain the desired size.

INSTALLATION Burning bush is readily available and can be planted year-round. For massing, plant 8'–10' apart, or 5'–7' for the smaller cultivars. Ensure good drainage.

PESTS & DISEASES Scale is a problem in damp locations. Deer don't like them.

NOTES & CULTIVARS
'Compactus' and 'Chicago Fire' reach 6'–10' tall, with slower growth rates, making them better selections for most homeowners and more common in nurseries. 'Little Moses' and 'Rudy Haag' reach 4'–6'.
Strawberry bush, *Euonymus americanus*, is native to well-drained eastern and midwestern woodlands.

top Fall color in north Georgia.

bottom Fall color on the UGA campus.

Flower buds and flowers in the Founders Memorial Garden and in a north Georgia pecan orchard.

Exochorda racemosa PEARLBUSH

Pearlbush is a little-known shrub whose flowers provide an early springtime show. It is a pest-free plant that tolerates drought and neglect, and its white early spring flowers appear just as the native dogwoods and Kurume azaleas begin to bloom. Unfortunately, it doesn't offer much else to recommend it when it is not in bloom, so careful siting is essential. Consider providing a foundation for it with evergreen azaleas, Otto Luyken laurels, or a spreading camellia. Upright camellias, osmanthus, or cleyera could provide a suitable backdrop to highlight pearlbush's flowers.

ZONES & ORIGIN 4b–8b. Native to China.

SIZE & GROWTH RATE 10'–15' tall and wide, medium growing.

TEXTURE & FORM Medium texture with upright arching branches and a broadly oval form.

FOLIAGE Simple alternate leaves are 1½"–2½" long, with a blue-green tint in spring and early summer. The elliptic to slightly obovate leaves emerge with the flowers in early spring, with entire margins, rounded or blunt tips, and an occasional short bristle. They produce no significant fall color. Light brown twigs produce a bitter odor when scratched.

FLOWERS Pearl-like white buds open to reveal showy white flowers with five petals in short racemes along the branches for about 10 days just before and with the new foliage in early spring (late March to early April in Athens).

FRUIT Insignificant capsules.

LIGHT & SOIL Full sun to light shade and moist but well-drained soils are ideal. Pearlbush tolerates drought and a near-neutral soil pH.

MAINTENANCE To maintain the desired size, prune by late spring to allow the plant time to form next year's flower buds. To maintain an upright arching habit, prune older limbs back to the ground. Pearlbush doesn't look well when sheared.

INSTALLATION Pearlbush is rare in southeastern nurseries. Where found, it is usually grown in containers and can be planted virtually year-round. For grouping or masses, plant at 6'–10' centers in well-drained soil.

PESTS & DISEASES No serious problems, but deer heavily browse the foliage.

NOTES & CULTIVARS
Exochorda × *macrantha* 'The Bride' reaches 4' with a rounded form.

Flower buds and flowers.

Ficus carica FIG

Most figs are planted for their edible fruit. However, their coarse texture and tropical appearance can be assets in a design. An ability to grow in moderate shade allows them to be used in courtyards and other shaded locations where their exotic appearance can be featured. Their drought tolerance also allows them to be used in raised planters or planted in movable containers in colder locations.

Foliage.

ZONES & ORIGIN 7a–10b. Native to Asia and northern Africa.

SIZE & GROWTH RATE 8'–12' in zones 7 and 8, but 20' farther south. Medium growing.

TEXTURE & FORM Coarse in texture with a broadly oval to rounded form.

FOLIAGE Simple alternately arranged lustrous dark green leaves 4½"–9" long have an ovate shape and three prominent lobes and are covered with short stiff hairs. Yellow fall foliage is undependable. Bark is a smooth light gray.

FLOWERS Insignificant flowers.

FRUIT Edible pear-shaped fruit 2"–3" long turns reddish purple when mature. Figs taste like a mixture of strawberry and raspberry but don't last long after maturing. Plants in warmer climates often produce two crops, one in spring from the previous year's wood and another in early autumn on new growth. The spring crop is usually considered inferior to the fall crop.

LIGHT & SOIL Full sun to moderate shade and moist but well-drained soil. Plant in full sun for fruit production.

MAINTENANCE Ripened fruits ferment quickly after falling, attracting numerous insects and producing an unpleasant odor. Mulch regularly to keep the roots cool and moist in summer and warm in winter. Prune in early spring to control size, and protect the skin when pruning. Broken stems and branches exude a sticky milky-white sap that can irritate the skin, especially upon exposure to sunlight.

INSTALLATION Late winter to early spring is the best time to transplant container-grown figs.

PESTS & DISEASES No serious problems. Deer don't like them.

NOTES & CULTIVARS
'Brown Turkey' produces large reddish-brown fruit. 'Celeste' produces small but very sweet fruit with a brown skin.

top left Behind a Knock Out Rose and a ginger lily in Athens.
bottom left Behind a 'Silver Spreader' juniper in Athens.
right At the T. R. R. Cobb House in Athens.

Hamamelis virginiana WITCH HAZEL

Witch hazel is a widely dispersed small native tree found along small streambanks and on lower slopes but occasionally on drier sites as well. Usually multitrunked, witch hazel is noted for its yellow fall foliage and lightly fragrant late fall flowers. Use it for naturalizing woodland edges or in shaded border plantings. A lotion derived from the twigs and bark relieves pain and itching from insect bites, burns, and small cuts. The forked twigs were used by water diviners to locate underground water sources.

ZONES & ORIGIN 4a–9a. Native from Texas to southern Canada.

SIZE & GROWTH RATE 15'–25' tall and wide, slow growing.

TEXTURE & FORM Medium coarse texture and broadly oval form.

FOLIAGE Simple alternately arranged dark green broadly oval to obovate leaves have crenate margins, short acute to rounded tips, and prominent depressed veins. Late autumn yellow fall color is good. Smooth light gray young twigs have a zigzag growth habit. Older trunks are gray, with warty growths.

FLOWERS Lightly fragrant flowers with yellow strap-shaped petals occur for several weeks in mid- to late autumn but are somewhat obscured by the yellow fall foliage. In Athens, flowering is usually throughout November. Fragrance depends upon the genetics of each plant, so select plants while in bloom.

FRUIT Insignificant mustard-colored capsules are helpful in identification, since they remain throughout the year.

LIGHT & SOIL Light shade with moist but well-drained slightly acidic soils is ideal. It tolerates full sun to moderate shade but not extended droughts.

MAINTENANCE Prune in early spring to shape or control the size to allow time for the fall flower buds to develop.

INSTALLATION Specialty nurseries may grow container plants or small field-grown plants. Plant in winter and amend the soil to improve the texture in heavy clay soils.

PESTS & DISEASES Leaf galls are common but not serious. Deer seldom browse them.

NOTES & CULTIVARS
'Harvest Moon' flowers after the foliage has dropped.
Vernal witch hazel, *Hamamelis vernalis*, occurs on well-drained streambanks of the southern plains. Hardy from zones 5b to 8b, it reaches 6'–15' with fragrant yellow-red winter flowers and yellow fall foliage.

top Foliage.

bottom Late autumn flowers.

Flowering in the Founders Memorial Garden.

Flowering in north Georgia.

Hamamelis × *intermedia* HYBRID WITCH HAZEL

Hybrid witch hazels are selections of man-made crosses with similar features to the native witch hazel, but they bloom in mid- to late winter. As a group, they tend to be better adapted to cooler climates than those found in the Southeast and are very popular in Europe. Often treated as large shrubs in compositions, they can also be limbed up to form multitrunked small trees.

Flowers.

ZONES & ORIGIN 5a–8a. Cross from two Asian species.

SIZE & GROWTH RATE 10'–20' tall and wide, slow growing.

TEXTURE & FORM Medium coarse texture and a broadly oval form with ascending branches.

FOLIAGE Simple broadly oval to obovate dark green alternate leaves have depressed veins, crenate margins, and short acute to rounded tips. Fall color is mostly bright yellow to orange red, depending upon the cultivar.

LIGHT & SOIL Full sun to moderate shade with a moist to moist but well-drained acidic soil.

MAINTENANCE Prune in spring after flowering to avoid removing next year's flower buds.

NOTES & CULTIVARS
'Arnold's Promise' is the most popular cultivar, with fragrant yellow flowers with red centers in late winter.
'Diane' has coppery-red flowers.
'Jelena' has coppery-colored flowers.
'Sunburst' has bright yellow midwinter flowers.

Hibiscus syriacus ROSE OF SHARON · HIBISCUS

Hibiscus has experienced a resurgence of popularity in recent years as larger flowers and varied colors have been introduced. Its ability to tolerate drought and continue to flower over much of the summer has proven to be a valued asset in areas with outdoor water restrictions. Like many large deciduous shrubs, it is somewhat unsightly in winter and benefits by having an evergreen foundation in front of it and a dark background behind it.

ZONES & ORIGIN 5b–9a. Native to Asia.

SIZE & GROWTH RATE 8'–12' tall, 5'–10' wide, medium growing.

TEXTURE & FORM Medium coarse texture and oval to broadly oval form.

FOLIAGE Simple ovate alternate leaves are 1½"–3" long, with three lobes and coarsely rounded toothed margins. Twigs and branches are light gray. Fall foliage is poor.

FLOWERS Showy nonfragrant flowers in a variety of colors occur from early summer into early autumn, peaking in early to midsummer (June in Athens). Individual flowers with single or double petals are 2"–4" wide in whites, pinks, reds, blues, and purples but last only one day.

FRUIT Unattractive capsules remain year-round. The ascending branches often bend due to the weight of the flowers and capsules.

LIGHT & SOIL Full sun with moist but well-drained soils is ideal. They tolerate light shade, drought, moderate salt spray, and slightly alkaline soil pH.

MAINTENANCE Older cultivars were notorious for producing numerous seedlings. Newer cultivars released by the National Arboretum are sterile. Prune from late autumn to late winter.

INSTALLATION Container plants can be planted year-round at 6'–10' spacing.

PESTS & DISEASES Whiteflies, aphids, and a leaf spot fungus that causes early defoliation are common.

NOTES & CULTIVARS
'Aphrodite' has single dark pink flowers with red eyes.
'Ardens' has large double dark pink flowers.
'Blue Satin' has large single blue flowers with maroon centers.
'Blush Satin' has light pink flowers with red eyes.
'Diana' has large single white flowers.
'Lavender Chiffon' has double lavender-pink flowers.
'Red Heart' has single white flowers with red eyes.
'White Chiffon' has large single white flowers.

top Early summer flowers and foliage in Vancouver, B.C.

bottom A sidewalk composition with herbaceous perennials.

Early summer flowers at Stanley Park (*left*) and in downtown Vancouver, B.C. (*right*).

Hydrangea paniculata PANICLE HYDRANGEA

Panicle hydrangeas are large shrubs with floppy branches bending to the ground. 'Grandiflora', with large and mostly sterile flower heads, is the largest and most common cultivar. With their coarse texture and extremely showy flowers, they catch the eye in compositions but can be unsightly in fall and winter. Available smaller cultivars may be easier to incorporate in border plantings.

Foliage and panicles.

ZONES & ORIGIN 3a–8b. Native to Asia.

SIZE & GROWTH RATE 10'–12' tall, 8'–12' wide, fast growing.

TEXTURE & FORM Coarse texture and broadly oval to rounded form.

FOLIAGE Simple elliptic to ovate opposite leaves are 2¾"–5" long, with finely serrate margins and acuminate tips. Leaves at the ends of the stems appear whorled. Fall color is poor.

FLOWERS Showy terminal panicles 10"–15" long occur in mid- to late summer (early July to mid-August in Athens). Sterile flowers are creamy white and cover the panicles. The nonfragrant flowers last for several weeks before fading to pink and then tan; they remain into winter.

FRUIT Fruit are small insignificant capsules. Old flower panicles remain through the winter and become unattractive.

LIGHT & SOIL Provide full sun to light shade with a moist but well-drained slightly acidic soil. It tolerates moderate drought.

MAINTENANCE Since they bloom on new seasonal growth, they can be pruned from late winter to midspring. Remove old flower heads in autumn to provide a tidier appearance.

INSTALLATION Container plants can be planted virtually year-round in warmer climates. Space 8' apart.

PESTS & DISEASES Deer browse new foliage and cause problems for small young plants. Brittle limbs are easily broken under snow or ice loads, particularly if the old flower heads remain.

NOTES & CULTIVARS
'Chantilly Lace' reaches 6'–8' with early summer flowers fading to light pink.
'Limelight' reaches 6'–10' with white flowers fading to rosy pink.
'Little Lamb' reaches 6'–8' with smaller midsummer flowers.
'Quick Fire' reaches 8' with early summer flowers fading to deep pink.
'Tardiva' reaches 12' with pyramidal panicles of late summer flowers.

top left At the Edmonds residence in Athens.
bottom left On the UGA campus.
right Summer flowers at the Doherty residence in Athens.

Hydrangea quercifolia OAKLEAF HYDRANGEA

Oakleaf hydrangea is a tough versatile shrub with many attractive attributes. Its showy late spring flowers catch the eye from quite a distance away, while its deep red to reddish-purple foliage in late fall and early winter provides interest at those times of year as well. A coarse texture provides design contrast opportunities throughout the year. Its adaptability to a range of soil and light conditions allows its use in situations from enclosed spaces, woodland plantings, or borders to masses in more open areas.

Fall foliage.

ZONES & ORIGIN 5b–9b. Native to established wooded slopes of the southeastern United States.

SIZE & GROWTH RATE 6'–10' tall and wide, medium growing.

TEXTURE & FORM Coarse texture with a broadly oval to mounded form.

FOLIAGE Simple opposite leaves 4"–8" long have three to eight coarsely serrate lobes. The undersides of the leaves and young stems are densely pubescent, while older stems exhibit a cinnamon-brown exfoliating bark. Fall foliage is an outstanding deep red to purple in November and early December.

FLOWERS Large showy terminal panicles of white flowers arise in late April, peaking in mid-May in Athens, before turning pink in June and fading to tan. Old flower heads remain into winter and are often used in dried flower arrangements.

FRUIT Nondescript capsules.

LIGHT & SOIL Light shade with a loose, moist, but well-drained soil is ideal. Plants in too much shade will not bloom heavily and are less likely to develop colorful fall foliage. Plants in full sun may develop burned leaf tips during dry summers. Established plants tolerate moderate droughts.

MAINTENANCE Prune in early summer. Never shear this plant. Maintain an organic mulch to keep the roots cool.

INSTALLATION Amend heavy clay or sandy soils with organic material. Space 6'–8' on center.

PESTS & DISEASES No serious problems with well-drained soils. Deer nibble young stems, leaves, and flower buds.

NOTES & CULTIVARS
'Alice' and 'Snowqueen' reach 10'–12' in height.
'Pee Wee' grows 3'–5' tall.
'Snowflake' reaches 6'–8' with large panicles of double flowers.

left Along a stream at a Columbus, Ga., residence.

top right In the Founders Memorial Garden.

bottom right Late spring flowers.

Ilex decidua POSSUMHAW

Possumhaw is a deciduous holly of the Southeast usually found along small streambanks and bottomlands but occasionally along upland forest edges and fencerows. A multitrunked large shrub or small tree, it is best known for its showy red fruit, held along the branches from autumn into late winter, but can also provide some fairly showy yellow fall foliage in sunny locations. Possumhaw performs well in masses along woodland edges, within evergreen border plantings, or even as a specimen tree near entrances.

Foliage and fruit at the Birmingham Botanical Garden.

top At the Birmingham Botanical Garden.

middle Along a fencerow in Oconee County.

bottom At the University of the South.

ZONES & ORIGIN 5b–9b. Native to bottomlands from Arkansas to Virginia.

SIZE & GROWTH RATE 10'–20' tall, 12'–15' wide, slow growing.

TEXTURE & FORM Medium fine texture and broadly oval form.

FOLIAGE Simple lustrous dark green alternate leaves are 1½"–3" long, mostly obovate or occasionally elliptic shaped, with crenate margins. Fall color is bright yellow. Light gray twigs have numerous short spurs, while mature bark is light gray and slightly warty.

FLOWERS Mostly inconspicuous tiny white flowers with four petals occur in clusters along the branches in midspring (late April in Athens).

FRUIT Bright orange-red berry-like drupes are clustered on short stalks along the branches of female plants from midautumn into late winter. American holly, *Ilex opaca*, reportedly pollinates the possumhaw.

LIGHT & SOIL Light shade and a moist but well-drained acidic soil are ideal. It performs well in full sun to moderate shade and tolerates near-neutral pH soils and slightly wet winter soils.

MAINTENANCE Possumhaw may not be a good choice for locations heavily populated by deer due to its slow growth. Young plants could be destroyed after deer take a few mouthfuls.

INSTALLATION Possumhaw is rarely available in anything other than small containers. Plant in late winter to early spring on 10'–12' centers for massing.

PESTS & DISEASES Few serious problems, but deer browse young foliage.

NOTES & CULTIVARS
- 'Council Fire' has a shrubby form and orange-red fruit and reaches about 15' tall.
- 'Warren's Red' reaches 25' with vase-shaped branching and heavy fruiting.

Ilex verticillata WINTERBERRY

Winterberry is a native shrub of low woods, streambanks, and swamp edges throughout the eastern United States. Best known for its showy fall and winter fruit and ability to tolerate moist to wet soils, it is nondescript for much of the year until autumn, when the fruit on female plants turns bright red. Use it in borders with a small evergreen foundation and a larger evergreen background. Cut stems are popular for floral arrangements because the fruit remains on the stems for several weeks.

Midautumn foliage and fruit.

ZONES & ORIGIN 4a–9a. Native from northern Florida to southern Canada.

SIZE & GROWTH RATE 8'–12' tall, 6'–10' wide, medium slow growing.

TEXTURE & FORM Medium in leaf, fine in winter, with an oval form in youth becoming rounded with maturity.

FOLIAGE Simple alternate leaves 2"–4" long with prominent depressed veins are elliptic or occasionally obovate shaped, with serrate margins and acute tips. Yellow-green fall color is poor, with the leaves falling early.

FLOWERS Inconspicuous white flowers along the branches occur in late spring (late May in Athens).

FRUIT Bright red berry-like fruits are clustered along the branches on female plants, maturing in early autumn and remaining into late winter until eaten by birds. Male plants should be nearby for pollination.

LIGHT & SOIL Light shade with a moist but well-drained acidic soil is ideal. Winterberry tolerates full sun to moderate shade, moist to wet soils, and light salt spray.

MAINTENANCE Maintain the soil pH below 5.8. Prune in late winter.

INSTALLATION Winterberry is most often found in 3- or 5-gallon containers. Plant from late winter through midspring on 6'–10' spacing in a loose soil to facilitate the spread of the root suckers.

PESTS & DISEASES Plants become chlorotic under near-neutral or alkaline soil pH. Few pest problems are reported, and deer don't seem to like them.

NOTES & CULTIVARS
'Red Sprite' is a slow-growing female reaching 3'–4' in size.
'Southern Gentleman' and 'Jim Dandy' are male cultivars for pollination.
'Winter Red' is promoted for its heavy fruiting.

top Form at Longwood Gardens.
middle Winter fruit.
bottom 'Red Sprite' at Atlanta's Fourth Ward Park.

LARGE DECIDUOUS SHRUBS

top left Midspring foliage and flowers.
top right At Swarthmore College.
middle At Chanticleer Garden.
bottom In the Founders Memorial Garden.

Kolkwitzia amabilis BEAUTY BUSH

Beauty bush is a somewhat rare shrub in southeastern landscapes. Fast growing and tolerant of adverse conditions, it is worthy of greater consideration in border compositions. Beauty bush provides highly attractive flowers in midspring and upright arching branches that provide a fountain-like effect in compositions. It benefits from regular pruning to maintain a dense upright arching canopy, becoming sprawling with an unkempt appearance without such attention. Combine it with evergreen azaleas or Japanese plum yew as a base and surround it with something like camellias, rhododendrons, or evergreen viburnums for contrast in texture and form.

ZONES & ORIGIN 5b–8a. Native to China.

SIZE & GROWTH RATE 8'–12' tall, 6'–8' wide, fast growing.

TEXTURE & FORM Medium fine texture in leaf in the spring, medium and broadly oval form in the winter.

FOLIAGE Simple opposite leaves are 1½"–3" long, ovate shaped, with very finely serrate margins and acuminate tips, softly pubescent above and on the veins beneath. Fall color is only a fair red orange. Young reddish-brown twigs turn tan colored, while older branches near the ground have an exfoliating bark.

FLOWERS Tiny bell-shaped white flowers with a flush of pink are held in clusters 2" wide along the stems for about two weeks in midspring (early to mid-April in Athens). The flowers are not fragrant but are quite attractive in bloom and somewhat resemble those of the glossy abelia.

FRUIT Insignificant bristly capsules remain into winter.

LIGHT & SOIL Provide full sun to light shade and moist but well-drained soil. Beauty bush tolerates moderate drought and near-neutral pH soils.

MAINTENANCE Prune older branches near the ground to control the overall height of the shrub. Younger branches can be pruned back to a main node after flowering in late spring.

INSTALLATION Most beauty bushes are grown in midwestern nurseries in small containers. They can be planted virtually year-round on 6'–8' centers. Provide supplemental water during extended droughts.

PESTS & DISEASES No problems in well-drained soils. Deer rarely cause serious damage.

NOTES & CULTIVARS 'Pink Cloud' provides pink flowers.

Lonicera fragrantissima WINTER HONEYSUCKLE

Winter honeysuckle is known primarily for its highly fragrant late winter flowers. It is semievergreen in zones 7a southward, depending upon the severity of the winter. It is fast growing, with upright arching branches, and its flowers are not showy and would be overlooked if not for their lemony aroma, which fills winter gardens to announce that spring is coming soon. The fragrance can be appreciated from quite a distance, so winter honeysuckle could be tucked into a courtyard corner or toward the rear of a shrub border and still be appreciated. Cut stems in water will fill a room with fragrance.

ZONES & ORIGIN 5a–9a. Native to China.

SIZE & GROWTH RATE 8'–10' tall, 6'–12' wide, fast growing.

TEXTURE & FORM Medium texture with upright arching branches and a broadly oval form.

FOLIAGE Simple blue-green opposite leaves are 1"–2½" long, with a broadly elliptic to ovate shape, entire margins, acute tips, and no fall color. Young stems are reddish purple, eventually turning brown.

FLOWERS Tiny white paired flowers occur along the branches in late winter. While not showy, they open over several weeks and have a sweet lemony fragrance. In Athens, flowering may begin in mid-January and continue into early March. Flowering is usually a briefer time period in cooler climates.

FRUIT Tiny bright red early summer berries are mostly hidden by the foliage.

LIGHT & SOIL Full sun to light shade and a moist but well-drained soil. It tolerates summer droughts and near-neutral pH soils but not consistently damp soils.

MAINTENANCE Selectively prune in early spring after flowering to maintain the desired overall size. Prune back to lower branch nodes or to the ground to maintain the upright arching character. Avoid shearing.

INSTALLATION Container-grown plants can be installed year-round in the Southeast. Provide well-drained locations and water every 10 to 14 days during the first summer. Space 6'–8' on center.

PESTS & DISEASES No serious problems. Deer browse them but seldom cause serious damage.

NOTES & CULTIVARS No cultivars available.

top Summer foliage.
bottom Late winter flowers.

left Late spring in the Founders Memorial Garden. *right* New spring foliage.

left Midspring blooms at the Founders Memorial Garden.

top and bottom right At the Fernandez residence in Athens.

Philadelphus coronarius SWEET MOCK ORANGE

Sweet mock orange is an old-garden plant valued for its late spring blooms and overall toughness. It showcases its attributes between the rush of spring blooming plants and the onset of summer perennials when few other plants are in bloom. It has fallen out of favor in recent years as new large evergreen options such as *Loropetalum chinense* and smaller fragrant deciduous shrubs such as edgeworthia have become increasingly popular. Allow it to arch over the rear of evergreen border plantings.

Foliage and flowers.

ZONES & ORIGIN 4b–9a. Native to Asia.

SIZE & GROWTH RATE 8'–12' tall, 6'–10' wide, medium fast growing.

TEXTURE & FORM Medium texture with an upright arching broadly oval form.

FOLIAGE Simple ovate to elliptic opposite leaves 2"–6" long have acuminate tips and serrate margins. Fall color is poor. Young stems are cinnamon brown. Older stems develop exfoliating bark near the ground.

FLOWERS Fragrant white four-petaled flowers 1"–1½" wide with 20–30 prominent yellow stamens occur in 5–7 racemes in late spring (late April to mid-May in Athens). The degree of fragrance varies, so select plants while blooming.

FRUIT Unattractive capsules remain into winter.

LIGHT & SOIL Full sun to light shade and a moist but well-drained slightly acidic soil are ideal. It tolerates drought, moderate shade, near-neutral pH soils, and light salt spray.

MAINTENANCE Prune in early summer back to lower branch nodes or to the ground to maintain the upright arching character. Avoid shearing.

INSTALLATION Container plants can be installed year-round on 8'–10' spacing. Mulch in late autumn to keep the roots warm.

PESTS & DISEASES Few problems in well-drained soils. Deer ignore them.

NOTES & CULTIVARS

Hybrids with other *Philadelphus* species provide a number of cultivars. Most are fragrant, but again, select while in bloom to judge the degree of fragrance. *Philadelphus inodorus* is a rare native of the eastern United States, growing from zones 5b to 8b, with flowers that appear identical to sweet mock orange. Two slight differences are flowers occurring in 1–3 racemes with 40–60 stamens.

Punica granatum POMEGRANATE

An Old World plant valued for its fruit and prominent flowers, pomegranate has played a prominent role in Middle Eastern cultures and was often planted near French and Italian villas. Use it judiciously toward the rear of sunny shrub borders. Prune it into a small tree or espalier it on a fence to utilize its fruit.

Foliage and flower close up.

ZONES & ORIGIN 7b–10b. Native to the Mediterranean region.

SIZE & GROWTH RATE 8'–15' tall, 6'–12' wide, medium growing.

TEXTURE & FORM Medium fine texture and broadly oval form.

FOLIAGE Simple narrowly elliptic opposite leaves 1"–2½" long have entire margins and rounded tips. Showy orange-red flowers resembling carnations occur in late spring and early summer, with sporadic flowers into September. Leathery berries 2"–3" in diameter mature in late summer. The juicy seeds are valued for their antioxidant properties and made into jellies, juices, and grenadine.

LIGHT & SOIL Full sun to light shade with a moist but well-drained soil. It tolerates slightly alkaline soil and drought.

MAINTENANCE Prune in early spring. Leaf spot diseases are common but usually not serious. Space container plants 6'–8' apart.

NOTES & CULTIVARS Specialty growers provide numerous cultivars selected for their flowers and fruit.

left and below Fruit at a Columbus, Ga., residence.

Rosa banksiae 'Lutea' LADY BANKS' ROSE

Lady Banks' rose puts on a show of midspring yellow flowers that is second to none. For several weeks, it is covered by small creamy-yellow blossoms. With its fairly fine texture and tardily deciduous foliage, it is not a shrub that necessarily needs to be hidden when not in bloom. However, it is not a plant for small spaces. It forms a dense sprawling mass 20' or greater in size that can swallow nearby plants or structures. While often trained as a vine, it doesn't have any mechanisms to actually climb but rather uses nearby structures or adjacent plants to sprawl up and over, providing a vine-like appearance. Train it on a fence or attach it to a wall as an espalier, but remember that periodic pruning is necessary to maintain the desired shape and size.

ZONES & ORIGIN 7b–11a. Native to China.

SIZE & GROWTH RATE 12'–25' tall, 10'–20' wide, fast growing.

TEXTURE & FORM Medium fine texture and broadly oval to rounded form.

FOLIAGE Pinnately compound alternate leaves have five leaflets. Narrowly elliptic to lanceolate leaflets 1"–2½" long have serrate margins and acute tips. It is tardily deciduous, with no fall foliage color. Stems lack thorns and eventually develop a cinnamon-brown exfoliating bark.

FLOWERS Nonfragrant double yellow flowers that are 1" wide occur in clusters along the branches in midspring (April in Athens).

FRUIT Insignificant rounded hips ¼" long turn yellow green in summer.

LIGHT & SOIL Full sun to light shade with a moist but well-drained soil. It tolerates some salt spray and drought after establishment.

MAINTENANCE Prune after flowering and before early summer to avoid removing next year's flower buds.

INSTALLATION Avoid late fall to midwinter planting in zones 7 and 8 to allow the roots to become established before a hard freeze. Space multiple plants at least 10' apart.

PESTS & DISEASES Surprisingly few problems with good cultural conditions. Young plants should be protected from deer.

NOTES & CULTIVARS
'Alba Plena' has double white flowers.

Midspring flowers in the Founders Memorial Garden.

From top right to bottom In the Founders Memorial Garden, on an arbor in Athens, and at a residence in Athens.

Rosa laevigata CHEROKEE ROSE

Similar to Lady Banks' rose, Cherokee rose is a fast-growing sprawling rose that swallows nearby shrubs and small trees. Imported from China, it was used in the 1700s for hedges to enclose gardens and livestock. Naturalizing across the Southeast, it was misidentified as a native by French botanist André Michaux in 1803. The state flower of Georgia and valued for its large fragrant white spring flowers, it is often trained as an espalier on an arbor, fence, trellis, or wall. It also provides an excellent screen, buffer, or background plant due to its dense branching habit and semievergreen to evergreen nature.

top left In the Founders Memorial Garden.
bottom left Behind Sherwood abelias on the UGA campus.
right Flowers on a Charleston fence.

ZONES & ORIGIN 7b–9b. Native to China.

SIZE & GROWTH RATE 10'–12' tall, 10'–15' wide, fast growing.

TEXTURE & FORM Medium texture with a broadly oval to rounded form.

FOLIAGE Alternately arranged lustrous dark green trifoliate leaves have three, rarely five, leaflets. Ovate leaflets are 1½"–3½" long, with serrate margins and acute tips. Undersides of the rachis and leaflet have prickles, while the stems have prominent hooked thorns. Tardily deciduous or semievergreen with no fall color in zone 8, but evergreen in zone 9.

FLOWERS Showy white flowers appear for several weeks in midspring (late March to mid-April in Athens). The lightly fragrant 3" flowers have five petals and prominent yellow anthers.

FRUIT Prominent rose hips covered with painful prickles are green in summer before turning orange red in autumn and remaining into winter.

LIGHT & SOIL Provide full sun to light shade and a moist but well-drained slightly acidic soil. It tolerates light salt spray.

MAINTENANCE With its fast growth, it requires pruning several times per year, a painful endeavor due to its numerous hooked thorns.

INSTALLATION Container plants can be planted year-round. Space 10'–12' apart for screens and barrier plantings.

PESTS & DISEASES Plants are particularly prone to powdery mildew and witches'-broom and are susceptible to leaf spot diseases and aphids. Deer rarely browse young foliage.

NOTES & CULTIVARS
Cherokee rose is somewhat invasive in zones 8b and 9.

Foliage and midspring flowers.

Sambucus nigra canadensis ELDERBERRY

Elderberry is a fast-growing pioneer species of moist open sites across most of the United States. Similar to sumac, elderberry is short-lived in nature but can be longer-lived in maintained landscapes. It is noted for its summer fruit, which is popular with birds, and its showy white late spring and early summer flowers, which are favored by pollinators. It is a shrub that is more attractive from a distance than up close. Place it in the rear of open borders, and take advantage of its fast growth for streambank and wetland restorations with buttonbush, clethra, and juncus.

top Foliage and late spring flowers.
bottom 'Black Lace' foliage.

ZONES & ORIGIN 3b–10b. Native across eastern North America.

SIZE & GROWTH RATE 10'–12' tall, 10'–20' wide, fast growing.

TEXTURE & FORM Medium coarse texture and rounded form.

FOLIAGE Opposite pinnately compound leaves have five to nine, usually seven, leaflets, which are 2"–5" long and narrowly elliptic or occasionally ovate shaped, with serrate margins and acuminate tips. Fall color is poor. Dark gray stems have prominent lenticels.

FLOWERS Showy creamy-white flowers in 4"–8" flattened terminal cymes occur in late spring and early summer (mid-May to mid-June in Athens).

FRUIT Small black rounded drupes mature in late summer but are eaten by birds before they fully ripen. The bitter raw fruit is high in vitamin C and cooked for pies and jellies or fermented for wine.

LIGHT & SOIL Full sun to light shade with a moist acidic soil. It tolerates a near-neutral pH and moist but well-drained soils.

MAINTENANCE Brittle branches are easily damaged under snow and ice loads. A fibrous root system tends to sprout new plants. Prune older taller canes in late winter to early spring to maintain a manageable size.

INSTALLATION While rare in nurseries, small container plants can be planted during the dormant season with 10' spacing.

PESTS & DISEASES Few serious problems, but deer heavily browse them.

NOTES & CULTIVARS
Several cultivars are listed but rarely available.
European black elderberry, *Sambucus nigra*, has dark foliage, with several common cultivars, including 'Black Beauty' and 'Black Lace'.

left Flowering on the UGA campus.
right 'Black Lace' with weigela in Boston.

Viburnum macrocephalum 'Sterile'
CHINESE SNOWBALL VIBURNUM

Probably no other large shrub provides the eye-opening early spring flower display of the Chinese snowball viburnum. Large rounded flower heads with numerous small bright white individual flowers literally cover the shrub like snowballs. Unfortunately, this viburnum doesn't offer much else to recommend its use after flowering. It has no showy fruit or fall color, so its only other attribute is a coarse texture that provides contrast with surrounding plants. Since it looks better from a distance, consider contrasting snowball viburnum's texture in the rear of borders by surrounding it with Florida leucothoe or abelia and perhaps a foreground of boxwood or Schip laurel. Combine it with some red- or purple-flowered southern indica azalea cultivars that bloom at the same time.

ZONES & ORIGIN   6a–8b. Native to China.

SIZE & GROWTH RATE   10'–15' tall, 10'–12' wide, medium fast growing.

TEXTURE & FORM   Coarse texture and dense broadly oval form.

FOLIAGE   Dark green simple opposite leaves 2"–4" long are elliptic but occasionally ovate shaped, with finely dentate or occasionally crenate margins, acute tips, and depressed veins. Young stems are thick and gray brown in color. No fall color.

FLOWERS   Sterile white flowers in rounded cymes 4"–8" in diameter appear in midspring (late March to mid-April in Athens), with a few flowers in mid-autumn. The flowers cover the cymes and are quite showy, even from a long distance.

FRUIT   No fruit, but old flower heads turn tannish brown and remain into summer.

LIGHT & SOIL   Full sun to light shade with a moist but well-drained slightly acidic soil.

MAINTENANCE   Prune heavily every few years after flowering to maintain its density. Provide supplemental water during extended droughts.

INSTALLATION   Container plants are readily available and can be planted virtually year-round. Space 10'–12' apart for massing.

PESTS & DISEASES   No serious disease issues, but deer occasionally browse the foliage.

NOTES & CULTIVARS
Viburnum opulus 'Roseum', the European snowball viburnum, is similar in size and appearance but blooms several weeks later and is hardy from zones 3b to 8a.

left Midspring flowers with Japanese kerria in Watkinsville.
top right In Chattanooga.
middle At Chanticleer.
bottom With azaleas in Athens.

Viburnum plicatum tomentosum
DOUBLEFILE VIBURNUM

Doublefile viburnum offers several seasons of interest for the garden that allow it to be showcased throughout a composition. A distinctly layered horizontal branching habit accentuates showy white spring flower heads held in double rows above the branches as the foliage emerges in spring. Attractive red fruit in summer is a magnet for birds, while deep red fall foliage completes the season. Its refined appearance allows doublefile viburnum to be used for accents near entrances or to soften steps or other grade changes. Use it beside water features with native stone and ferns.

Foliage and early spring flowers.

Foliage and early spring flowers in Boothbay, Maine, and in Stockbridge, Mass., and with azaleas in Chattanooga.

ZONES & ORIGIN 5b–8a. Native to Asia.

SIZE & GROWTH RATE 8'–10' tall and wide, medium fast growing.

TEXTURE & FORM Medium coarse texture, pyramidal form in youth becomes broadly oval with age.

FOLIAGE Simple ovate-shaped opposite leaves 2"–6" long have dentate-serrate margins, acuminate tips, and prominent depressed veins. Fall color is a good deep red to reddish purple. Horizontal branching lends a layered appearance.

FLOWERS Double rows of flattened cymes 3"–5" in diameter are held above the stems in early spring (late March to early April in Athens). The lacecap cymes contain bright white sterile flowers surrounding nonshowy fertile flowers.

FRUIT Attractive oval drupes turn red and finally black in early fall and are eaten by birds before fully maturing.

LIGHT & SOIL Full sun to light shade with a moist but well-drained soil is ideal. It tolerates moderate shade, but flowering is reduced, and it is susceptible to droughts.

MAINTENANCE Provide supplemental water during extended summer droughts. Prune after flowering in spring to control size.

INSTALLATION Container-grown doublefiles are readily available and can be planted from early spring to late autumn. Space 8'–10' apart for massing.

PESTS & DISEASES No serious problems, but deer browse new foliage.

NOTES & CULTIVARS
'Pink Beauty' reaches 8' with an upright habit and pink flowers.
'Mariesii' and 'Shasta' reach 10'–12' with large flower heads and excellent fall foliage.
Japanese snowball viburnum, *Viburnum plicatum*, has rounded cymes 3" in diameter with sterile flowers and blooms several weeks later.

Viburnum × *burkwoodii* BURKWOOD VIBURNUM

Burkwood viburnum is noted for its showy fragrant early spring flowers. It tends to be more refined in appearance than other large deciduous shrubs. As a result, it doesn't need to be tucked into the rear of borders but can be used closer to the observer to take advantage of its fragrance. Use it near entrances, in patios and enclosed courtyards, or even as a semiformal hedge or screen.

ZONES & ORIGIN 5b–8a. A cross between two Asian species.

SIZE & GROWTH RATE 6'–10' tall, 4'–8' wide, medium growing.

TEXTURE & FORM Medium texture and oval to broadly oval form.

FOLIAGE Simple lustrous dark green opposite leaves 2"–4" long are ovate to occasionally elliptic, with minutely serrate margins and acute or short acuminate tips. It often holds a few leaves into midwinter in zones 7 and 8.

FLOWERS Rounded cymes 2"–3" in diameter with small white individual flowers occur in early spring (late March to early April in Athens). Flowers are pink in bud before opening, with an outstanding sweet fragrance for 10 days.

FRUIT Plants usually provide only a few insignificant oval drupes at best and require other viburnums nearby for cross-pollination.

LIGHT & SOIL Full sun to light shade with a moist but well-drained slightly acidic soil. Light shade may be better in zones 7 and 8. Flowering is reduced in moderate shade.

MAINTENANCE Prune after flowering, and maintain a 2" mulch to keep the roots cool in summer.

INSTALLATION Container-grown plants are common and transplant well in early spring on 6'–8' spacing. Provide supplemental water for the first summer.

PESTS & DISEASES No serious disease issues. Deer occasionally browse the foliage.

NOTES & CULTIVARS

'Conoy' develops a rounded to spreading form to 6' tall and 8' wide, with a medium fine texture and evergreen foliage that turns maroon in winter. The leaves and flower heads are about half the size of Burkwood viburnum but lack fragrance. Hardy to zone 6a.

'Mohawk' is similar in size, with red flower buds and fragrant white flowers.

Foliage and early spring flowers.

top Foliage and early spring flowers at an Athens residence.

middle 'Conoy' foliage and flowers.

bottom 'Conoy' in the Founders Memorial Garden.

Vitex agnus-castus CHASTETREE

Chastetree is a large shrub or small multitrunked tree primarily known for its showy early summer flowers and drought tolerance. Pruning after flowering promotes new growth and additional flowering into midautumn. Chastetree is not particularly attractive up close, especially in winter, but its flowers are readily visible from a distance. Consider placing it in the rear of borders so that its flowers can be appreciated and its warts partially obscured.

Compound leaves and early summer flowers.

ZONES & ORIGIN 7a–10b. Native to the Mediterranean region.

SIZE & GROWTH RATE 12'–20' tall and wide, fast growing.

TEXTURE & FORM Medium fine texture in leaf, but medium in winter with a rounded form with maturity.

FOLIAGE Opposite palmately-compound leaves have five to seven leaflets. The dark green leaflets are 2"–5" long and lanceolate in shape, with mostly entire margins and acute tips. No fall color.

FLOWERS Showy panicles of lavender-purple flowers 8"–12" long occur in early summer (late May to mid-June in Athens), with sporadic flowers into early autumn on new growth. The flowers are highly attractive to insects but are not fragrant.

FRUIT Nonshowy berry-like drupes remain into winter if not removed. Extracts from the fruit were used by monks to decrease sexual desire, although there is no clinical evidence to support this. However, extracts have proven to be useful in treating PMS in clinical trials.

LIGHT & SOIL Provide full sun and a well-drained soil. Chastetree tolerates drought, salt spray, and slightly alkaline soils.

MAINTENANCE Pruning old flower heads and providing supplemental water stimulate new flowers throughout the summer. Older trunks should be removed at ground level to maintain a lower plant. It reportedly produces numerous seedlings in zone 9.

INSTALLATION Chastetree is available in containers and field-grown trees and can be successfully transplanted virtually year-round. Provide well-drained soils and space 15'–20' apart for massing.

PESTS & DISEASES No serious problems. Deer hate them.

NOTES & CULTIVARS
'Abbeville Blue' provides deep blue flowers.
'Alba' and 'Silver Spires' are white-flowered cultivars.
'Lavender Lady' provides light bluish-purple flowers.
'Shoal Creek' has violet-blue flowers.

top left At an Athens area office.
bottom left At the T. R. R. Cobb House.
right At the Giberson residence.

With hostas and with blue stars at Chanticleer.

Weigela florida WEIGELA

Weigela is an old-garden favorite that has experienced a resurgence of interest in recent years. It was once considered only for its spring flowers, but recently released cultivars provide new flower and foliage color options, as well as an expanded selection of sizes from which to choose. Larger cultivars are still best viewed from a distance in the back of border plantings, but smaller cultivars can be used for border plantings or even as informal ground covers. The dense spreading form of some of the dwarf cultivars could be used to soften grade changes around steps.

ZONES & ORIGIN 5a–8b. Native to Asia.

SIZE & GROWTH RATE 6'–10' tall, 8'–12' wide, medium fast growing.

TEXTURE & FORM Medium texture and rounded to spreading form.

FOLIAGE Simple opposite leaves 2"–4" long are elliptic or occasionally obovate shaped, with serrate margins and acuminate tips. Fall color is usually poor, with some crimson-colored foliage in cooler climates.

FLOWERS Trumpet-shaped light pink flowers occur in clusters along the stems in midspring (late April to early May in Athens).

FRUIT Insignificant.

LIGHT & SOIL Weigela prefers full sun and moist but well-drained soils, but it tolerates light shade, moderate drought, and slightly alkaline soils.

MAINTENANCE Prune in late spring after flowering to size and shape.

INSTALLATION Container-grown plants can be planted year-round. Provide supplemental water for the first year, and space 4'–10' on center, depending upon the cultivar.

PESTS & DISEASES No serious problems. Deer browse them but seldom cause serious damage.

NOTES & CULTIVARS
'Fine Wine' reaches 2'–4' with burgundy foliage and dark pink flowers.
'French Lace' reaches 6' with red flowers.
'Java Red' reaches 6' with dark reddish-green foliage and dark pink flowers.
'Midnight Wine' reaches 2' with burgundy foliage and pink flowers.
'Minuet' reaches 3' with dark green foliage and pinkish-red flowers.
'Pink Poppet' reaches 3' with a mounded form and pink flowers.
'Red Prince' reaches 6' with red flowers that attract hummingbirds.
'White Knight' reaches 6' with pinkish-white flowers.
'Wine and Roses' reaches 6' with burgundy foliage and rose-pink flowers.

top Foliage and midspring flowers in Boston.

bottom 'White Knight'.

MEDIUM EVERGREEN SHRUBS

Medium sized evergreen shrubs serve a variety of uses in garden design. They are substantial enough to help delineate space in compositions or to provide an evergreen base foundation for larger deciduous shrubs. They can also provide a green backdrop for smaller deciduous shrubs or herbaceous plants in the composition.

top Buxus sempervirens at the T. R. R. Cobb House in Athens.
bottom Buxus sempervirens at Hills and Dales.

BOTANICAL NAME	SUNLIGHT	SOILS	TEXTURE	ORNAMENTAL FLOWERS	ORNAMENTAL ATTRIBUTES	NATIVE TO SOUTHEAST
Aucuba japonica	Moderate shade	Moist but well drained	Coarse	No	Variegated foliage cultivars	No, Asia
Berberis julianae	Full sun to light shade	Well drained	Fine	Yellow in midspring	Winter foliage color and fruit	No, Asia
Buxus microphylla japonica	Light to moderate shade	Moist but well drained	Fine	No	Dense, rounded form	No, Asia
Buxus sempervirens	Light to moderate shade	Moist but well drained	Fine	No	Dense, broadly oval form	No, Europe and Asia
Camellia sinensis	Full sun to moderate shade	Moist but well drained acidic	Medium	White in midautumn	Source of green and black teas	No, Asia
Cephalotaxus harringtonia	Light to moderate shade	Moist but well drained	Fine	No	Dense, mounded to columnar form	No, Asia
Chamaecyparis pisifera 'Filifera Aurea'	Full sun to light shade	Moist but well drained	Fine	No	Fine texture, weeping habit	No, Asia
Cycas revoluta	Full sun to moderate shade	Well drained	Coarse	No	Exotic-looking form and foliage	No, Asia
Fatsia japonica	Moderate to heavy shade	Moist but well drained, salt tolerant	Coarse	White in late autumn	Exotic, tropical-looking foliage	No, Asia
Gardenia jasminoides 'August Beauty'	Full sun to light shade	Moist but well drained acidic	Medium	White in early summer	Fragrant flowers	No, Asia
Ilex crenata	Full sun to light shade	Moist but well drained fairly acidic	Fine	No	Dense canopy in variety of sizes	No, Asia
Ilex glabra	Full sun to moderate shade	Moist to moist but well drained acidic	Medium fine	No	Salt tolerant	Yes
Ilex vomitoria 'Nana'	Full sun to moderate shade	Moist to well drained acidic to alkaline	Fine	No	Salt tolerant	Yes
Juniperus × pfitzeriana 'Wilhelm Pfitzer'	Full sun to very light shade	Well drained, drought tolerant	Fine	No	Dense windswept canopy	No, Asia
Leucothoe fontanesiana	Light to heavy shade	Moist but well drained acidic	Medium	White in mid to late spring	Relaxed informal character	Yes
Mahonia aquifolium	Light to heavy shade	Moist but well drained, fairly acidic	Medium coarse	Yellow in early spring	Red-purple winter foliage in sun	No, Pacific Northwest
Pieris japonica	Light to moderate shade	Moist but well drained, fairly acidic	Medium	White in midspring	Clean appearance Red new foliage	No, Asia
Prunus laurocerasus 'Otto Luyken'	Full sun to moderate shade	Moist but well drained, fairly acidic	Medium	White in midspring	Broadly spreading form	No, Europe
Rhapidophyllum hystrix	Full sun to full shade	Moist to moist but well drained	Coarse	No	Exotic, tropical-looking foliage	Yes
Rhaphiolepis umbellata	Full sun to light shade	Moist but well drained, fairly acidic	Medium	White in midspring	Dense form, black fruit	No, Asia
Rhododendron × obtusum	Light shade	Moist but well drained acidic	Medium fine	Various colors in midspring	Inexpensive spring color	No, Asia
Yucca gloriosa	Full sun to light shade	Well drained, salt tolerant	Coarse	White but timing varies	Coarse, exotic foliage and form	Yes

Aucuba japonica JAPANESE AUCUBA

Japanese aucuba is a shade-loving evergreen that is a staple of many shade gardens of the Southeast. Its coarse texture provides a contrast with other shade-loving plants such as ferns and azaleas, and it combines well with native stone and natural woods. The most popular cultivar, 'Variegata', can tastefully brighten dark corners of the garden, so consider using it in shaded courtyards and patios. Its dense canopy also allows it to serve as a background for other plantings.

ZONES & ORIGIN 6b–10a. Native to Japan.

SIZE & GROWTH RATE 5'–8' tall, 4'–6' wide, slow growing.

TEXTURE & FORM Coarse texture and oval to broadly oval form.

FOLIAGE Simple oppositely arranged leaves are 4"–8" long, with coarsely serrate margins. The elliptical- to lanceolate-shaped leaves have a lustrous surface and leathery texture and are often clustered near the ends of the stems.

FLOWERS Aucuba is dioecious, with neither sex producing very showy flowers.

FRUIT With a male pollinator nearby, female plants produce clusters of berry-like red fruit in late autumn and into winter that are somewhat obscured by the foliage.

LIGHT & SOIL Moderate to full shade with a loose and moist but well-drained and somewhat acidic soil is ideal.

MAINTENANCE Prune stems back to lower nodes in late spring or early summer to size and shape. Never shear aucuba, or you'll be left with ragged browning leaves. Provide supplemental water during severe droughts. Maintain mulch year-round.

INSTALLATION Container plants are readily available. Space on 4'–6' centers for massing.

PESTS & DISEASES Excessive sunlight causes the foliage to become burned. Temperatures just below 0°F turn foliage to brown mush. Deer rarely cause problems.

NOTES & CULTIVARS
Gold dust plant, 'Variegata', is a female plant with yellow-flecked foliage. It is one of the few variegated plants that combines well with other plants without calling attention to itself.
'Picturata' has a large yellow center to its leaves.
Aucuba japonica borealis 'Honshu' is a dwarf female cultivar with smaller and narrower green leaves.

top left Gold dust plant in the Founders Memorial Garden.
top right Gold dust plant in Portland, Ore.
middle 'Variegata' foliage and fruit.
bottom Foliage and fruit.

left Flowers, foliage, and thorns.

right Flowers in bloom on the UGA campus.

Berberis julianae WINTERGREEN BARBERRY

Wintergreen barberry is a well-known plant for all the wrong reasons. It is commonly used for barrier plantings and sheared into tall hedges, and the perception that most people have of it is forbidding and dangerous due to its prominent spines. However, it does well in mixed shrub borders to take advantage of its lightly fragrant early spring yellow flowers and fall foliage color. Avoid using around children.

ZONES & ORIGIN 6a–9b. Native to China.

SIZE & GROWTH RATE 6'–8' tall, 4'–6' wide, medium growing.

TEXTURE & FORM Medium fine texture and oval form.

FOLIAGE Narrowly elliptical simple leaves have sharp spiny teeth along their margins and cluster near stem nodes along with prominent thorns. Autumn foliage may turn wine red in zones 6 and 7.

LIGHT & SOIL Full sun to light shade with well-drained soils.

MAINTENANCE Older dead stems in the center of the plant will need removal occasionally. If you insist upon shearing it into a hedge, provide a trapezoidal form with a broader base so that sunlight can reach the lower portions of the plant.

NOTES & CULTIVARS
For massing, space 3'–4' apart. Deer don't touch them.

Buxus microphylla japonica LITTLELEAF BOXWOOD

Littleleaf boxwood is a commonly used plant for formal gardens of the Southeast. For borders, hedges, and parterre gardens, its slow growth rate and tolerance to shearing have made it a favored choice for many years. Several commonly available cultivars provide the opportunity to select plants to fit the mature size that the designer desires. Just keep in mind that boxwoods can be somewhat particular about soil pH, soil moisture, and light requirements.

ZONES & ORIGIN 5b–10a. Native to Asia.

SIZE & GROWTH RATE 5'–6' tall and wide, slow growing.

TEXTURE & FORM Fine texture and dense broadly oval to rounded form.

FOLIAGE Simple glossy green opposite leaves arranged along the green four-sided stems are 3/8"–3/4" long, oval to obovate shaped, with entire margins and occasionally emarginate tips. Some cultivars develop bronze or orange winter foliage.

FLOWERS Insignificant midspring flowers.

FRUIT Insignificant.

LIGHT & SOIL Light to moderate shade with a loose and moist but well-drained near-neutral pH soil.

MAINTENANCE Boxwoods are sensitive to soil moisture levels and soil pH. Water deeply each week during the summer, and maintain 2" of an organic mulch to protect the shallow root system. Check the pH annually, and provide lime as necessary to maintain a near-neutral pH.

INSTALLATION Container-grown plants can be planted throughout the year on 2'–4' centers for borders. Amend the soil mix with organic material, and plant slightly higher than the plant was grown in the container.

PESTS & DISEASES Boxwood blight is becoming a big problem, with infected plants rapidly dying. Volutella blight looks similar but can be treated. It is questionable whether boxwoods should be considered for new plantings or replacements due to these diseases. Deer generally leave them alone.

NOTES & CULTIVARS
'Faulkner' reaches 4' tall.
'Green Beauty' reaches 4'–5' with bronze winter foliage.
'Kingsville Dwarf' reaches 2' with extremely fine texture.
'Winter Gem' and 'Wintergreen' are cultivars of *Buxus sinica insularis*. They reach 4' with dense rounded forms, and maintain their color over winter.

top Littleleaf boxwood border in Vancouver, B.C.
bottom A formal sheared hedge.

left A sheared border in San Francisco.
right A border in Savannah.

Buxus sempervirens BOXWOOD

The common boxwood has been part of American gardens since colonial times. It functions in a variety of applications, from formal plantings to specimen plants around structures, in perennial borders, as backgrounds or screens, and even sheared into garden ornaments. A range of available cultivars provides a variety of forms from columnar to rounded and sizes from 3' to over 20' in height.

Foliage.

ZONES & ORIGIN 5b–9a. Native to the Mediterranean region.

SIZE & GROWTH RATE 6'–12' tall, 4'–10' wide, slow growing.

TEXTURE & FORM Fine texture with a billowy broadly oval form.

FOLIAGE Simple dark green opposite leaves are ½"–1" long, ovate shaped, with entire margins and blunt or emarginate tips and a slightly foul odor when crushed.

FLOWERS Insignificant.

FRUIT Insignificant.

LIGHT & SOIL Although boxwood can tolerate full sun under ideal cultural conditions, for most applications, light to moderate shade is preferred. A loose, moist, but well-drained soil with a near-neutral pH is essential for good performance.

MAINTENANCE Its shallow root system requires deep watering weekly during summer droughts and a 2" layer of mulch throughout the year. Check the soil pH annually, and maintain within a range of 6.5–7.5. Fertilize and prune in late winter before new growth begins.

INSTALLATION Container plants can be installed throughout the year. Amend the soil with organic material. For borders, space 4'–6' depending upon the cultivar selected.

PESTS & DISEASES Boxwood has far more problems than many people realize. Provide optimum soil conditions to avoid many of the pests. Snow and ice, as well as intoxicated humans who lose their footing, can severely damage plants. Boxwood blight kills, and volutella blight disfigures. At least deer are not usually a problem.

NOTES & CULTIVARS
'Green Gem' and 'Green Velvet' are crosses between *Buxus sempervirens* and *B. sinica insularis* that reach 4'–6' with dense rounded forms.
'Graham Blandy' reaches 10' with a narrow columnar form.
'Pyramidalis' reaches 8'–10' with a narrow conical form and dark green foliage.

Form at the Founders Memorial Garden, at the T. R. R. Cobb House, and at Hills and Dales.

Chamaecyparis pisifera 'Filifera Aurea'
THREADLEAF FALSECYPRESS

Threadleaf falsecypress is used solely for its foliage effect. It develops a lacy canopy with yellow-green threadlike foliage and a weeping pendulous habit. It is a favored plant for conifer gardens and rock gardens due to its fine texture, color, and form. Use it to brighten winter landscapes by contrasting it with the darker foliage and coarser texture of rhododendrons and camellias. It can reach 8' or more in size but is fairly easy to maintain at lower sizes by annual pruning of the upper branches and is often maintained at 3'–4' in size.

'Golden Charm'.

ZONES & ORIGIN 5a–8b. Native to Japan.

SIZE & GROWTH RATE 6'–8' tall and wide, medium slow growing.

TEXTURE & FORM Fine texture with pendulous branches and mounded form.

FOLIAGE Yellow-green awl-shaped needles are finely appressed, providing a threadlike appearance. The tips of the branches droop, providing a pendulous habit.

FLOWERS Insignificant.

FRUIT Insignificant.

LIGHT & SOIL Full sun to light shade with a moist but well-drained slightly acidic soil is ideal. It becomes moderately drought tolerant with age.

MAINTENANCE Provide supplemental water during droughts for the first summer. Prune from late winter to midsummer to maintain the desired size and form.

INSTALLATION Small container-grown plants are commonly available and can be installed year-round on 4'–6' centers.

PESTS & DISEASES No serious problems. Deer don't like them.

NOTES & CULTIVARS
'Golden Charm' reaches 5'–6' in size, while 'Golden Mop' grows 3'–4' in size. Both have yellow-green foliage with rounded forms and perform best in light shade.
'Sungold' reaches 5'–6' tall and up to 8' wide, with yellow new foliage.
Chamaecyparis obtusa 'Lemon Twist' grows to 4' in size with a rounded form and yellow-green foliage on twisted branches.
Threadleaf arborvitae, *Thuja occidentalis* 'Filiformis' is hardy from zones 3b to 7b and reaches 7'–8' tall and 3'–4' wide with an oval form and threadlike foliage but is susceptible to deer browsing.

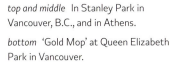

top and middle In Stanley Park in Vancouver, B.C., and in Athens.

bottom 'Gold Mop' at Queen Elizabeth Park in Vancouver.

Cycas revoluta SAGO PALM · CYCAD

Fossil records show that sago palms have been around for hundreds of millions of years. Classified as conifers rather than palms, they are valued for their attractive foliage, which resembles the combination of a bird's nest and a giant fern. They combine well with other shade-loving drought-resistant plants such as liriopes, hellebores, tea olives, cast iron plants, and camellias. Often used as specimen plants, they perform well in raised planters and in protected courtyards and are valued as interior plants in cooler regions.

Sago palm in Savannah.

ZONES & ORIGIN 8b–10b. Native to Japan.

SIZE & GROWTH RATE 4'–8' tall and wide, extremely slow growing.

TEXTURE & FORM Coarse texture and mounded form.

FOLIAGE Whorled pinnately compound lanceolate leaves are 2'–5' long, with numerous dark lustrous green needle-like leaflets with sharply pointed tips.

FLOWERS Sago is dioecious, with neither sex being showy. Flowers occur in the top of the crown and may not occur until twenty years or more of age. Yellow male flowers are conical in shape, while females are a flattened rounded form.

FRUIT Female plants with males nearby produce orange seeds that are interesting but not very showy.

LIGHT & SOIL Light shade and a well-drained soil are ideal. They tolerate full sun to full shade and become very drought tolerant.

MAINTENANCE Avoid overfertilization, and allow the soil to dry between watering. Remove dead foliage from the lower part of the plant each year. With age, sago develops new plants around its base that can be removed and planted elsewhere or allowed to remain to form a larger mass.

INSTALLATION While expensive due to its slow growth, it is easily transplanted throughout the year. Ensure good surface drainage away from the plant, and space 4' apart for massing.

PESTS & DISEASES Sago was long considered to be problem-free. However, an introduced scale species in Florida is proving deadly, so closely inspect new plants before purchasing. Temperatures in the low to midteens will damage the foliage. Deer don't touch them.

NOTES & CULTIVARS None widely available.

Top left Female (left) and male (right)

Bottom left and right Common under live oaks in Savannah

Fatsia japonica   FATSIA · JAPANESE FATSIA

For detail plantings in heavily shaded locations, few shrubs perform better than fatsia. It is an outstanding choice for shady corners of courtyards or patios where you want a coarse-textured tropical-looking shrub that can be appreciated up close. A fairly slow grower, fatsia can be easily maintained in the 5'–6' range as a dense shrub with foliage to the ground. Consider combining it with hostas and aspidistras beside a water feature or with native stone and ferns. It makes an outstanding house plant in colder climates.

ZONES & ORIGIN   7b–10b. Native to Japan.

SIZE & GROWTH RATE   6'–10' tall and wide, medium slow growing.

TEXTURE & FORM   Coarse texture with a broadly oval form.

FOLIAGE   Simple palmately lobed leaves are alternately arranged but tend to cluster near the ends of the stems. Individual leaves are a lustrous dark green color, 6"–12" long, with 5 to 11 lobes and coarsely serrate margins.

FLOWERS   Somewhat showy white flowers are held on rounded panicles 12"–18" above the foliage in late autumn. In Athens, flowering typically occurs from mid-November to early December.

FRUIT   Somewhat showy black berry-like drupes appear in winter and early spring. Birds eat the mature fruit, but it isn't reported to be invasive.

LIGHT & SOIL   Fatsia tolerates salt spray and grows well in moderate to heavy shade and a moist but well-drained slightly acidic soil. Avoid midday sun everywhere and early morning sun in zones 7b and 8a, since the warming sun on cold winter days may cause foliage burn.

MAINTENANCE   Maintaining mulch year-round helps prevent foliage burn during periods of drought and when the ground is frozen in winter. Plants that are not pruned become very leggy over time.

INSTALLATION   Plant in protected locations in zones 8a and 7b in mid- to late spring to allow time to establish its root system before winter.

PESTS & DISEASES   Aphids and scale are frequent pests, and deer may cause problems on younger plants.

NOTES & CULTIVARS
'Variegata' has creamy-white margins on the leaves.

top In a Land Plus Associates design in Atlanta.

middle Foliage and immature fruit.

bottom Late autumn flowers at the Founders Memorial Garden.

top left 'August Beauty' at UGA.
top right 'Shooting Star' in Athens.
middle 'August Beauty' foliage and flowers.
bottom 'Shooting Star'.

Gardenia jasminoides 'August Beauty'
AUGUST BEAUTY GARDENIA

In many gardens of the warmer zones of the Southeast, gardenias are as prevalent as magnolias, camellias, and azaleas. They are an old-garden plant, and the sweet scent of their early summer flowers serves to entice all who are fortunate enough to be located where gardenias survive the winters. For cooler areas, they are popular as interior plants in conservatories or as container plants that can be placed outside in spring. They combine well with virtually everything and can even be sheared into hedges. Just be sure to place them near a path, sitting area, or window where their fragrance can be fully appreciated.

ZONES & ORIGIN 8a–10b. Native to China.

SIZE & GROWTH RATE 6'–8' tall, 4'–6' wide, medium growing.

TEXTURE & FORM Medium texture with an oval form.

FOLIAGE Elliptic to obovate lustrous green simple leaves 2"–5" long are mostly opposite, with entire margins, acute tips, and prominently depressed veins on their upper side. Leaves are clustered near the ends of stems in a whorled appearance.

FLOWERS Attractive and highly fragrant white flowers with double petals are produced from late spring to midsummer. In Athens, flowering begins in late May and extends through June. A few flowers occur through September on new growth.

FRUIT Insignificant capsules.

LIGHT & SOIL Full sun to light shade with a moist but well-drained moderately acidic soil is ideal. It is drought tolerant. Plants in moderate shade become leggy, with fewer flowers.

MAINTENANCE Prune in early summer to size and shape after flowering has peaked.

INSTALLATION Gardenias can be planted virtually year-round. For massing, plant on 3'–5' centers, depending upon the cultivar selected. Ensure good surface drainage away from the gardenia.

PESTS & DISEASES Aphids, scale, and whiteflies are regular guests on gardenias but can be controlled with dormant oils or systemic insecticides. Deer don't like them.

NOTES & CULTIVARS
'Daisy' and 'Kleim's Hardy' reach 3' with single flowers and are hardy to zone 7b.
'Shooting Star' reaches 6' with single flowers to zone 7b.

Ilex crenata JAPANESE HOLLY

Japanese hollies have long been used for borders and background plantings in southern landscapes. Their fine texture, dense canopy, and relatively slow growth rate provide an alternative to boxwoods for formal parterres, hedges, or even tall ground covers where boxwoods may not be well suited. The species is seldom seen in cultivation, but numerous cultivars are widely available, offering a variety of mature sizes to fit any design niche.

ZONES & ORIGIN 5b–8b. Native to Asia.

SIZE & GROWTH RATE 3'–10' tall and wide, depending upon the cultivar, medium slow growing.

TEXTURE & FORM Fine texture and mounded to columnar form, depending upon the cultivar.

FOLIAGE Simple alternately arranged leaves are dark green in color, ½"–1¼" long, oval to occasionally obovate in shape, with acute tips and crenate margins. Young stems are green in color, and some cultivars have convex leaves.

FLOWERS A dioecious species, with neither sex producing significant flowers.

FRUIT Small insignificant black berries on female plants.

LIGHT & SOIL Provide full sun to light shade with a moist but well-drained acidic soil. They become moderately drought resistant with age but suffer under excessively damp soils.

MAINTENANCE Although they tolerate shearing to maintain the desired size and form, be sure to select an appropriate cultivar to reduce the required maintenance.

INSTALLATION Plant with the top of the root ball higher than the surrounding soil and ensure good surface drainage. For massing, plant on 2'–3' centers for smaller cultivars and 3'–5' centers for larger cultivars.

PESTS & DISEASES Provide good drainage! Japanese hollies are very sensitive to poorly drained soils, which contribute to numerous other problems. Deer usually aren't a problem.

NOTES & CULTIVARS
'Chesapeake' reaches 7' with a 4'–5' spread and an upright oval form.
'Compacta' reaches 6' in height and spread, with dark green leaves and a rounded form.
'Convexa' reaches 8' tall and 10' wide, with convex-shaped glossy green leaves.
'Sky Pencil' grows to 8' tall and 2'–3' wide with a columnar form.

top 'Compacta' foliage.
middle 'Convexa' with bergenia.
bottom left 'Sky Pencil'.
bottom right A 'Convexa' hedge in Boston.

Ilex glabra INKBERRY GALLBERRY

Inkberry is a native evergreen shrub that adapted to periodic fires in the longleaf pine forests of the Southeast. Following a fire, it regrows numerous sprouts from its root system, particularly in loose moist soil locations. As a landscape plant, it has gained popularity in recent years as a substitute for boxwoods and Japanese hollies due to its ease of propagation, salt tolerance, and noninvasive properties. Its drawbacks are a somewhat slow growth rate and an inability to maintain foliage low to the ground as it matures, which may not present problems when it is utilized for background plantings.

Foliage and fruit.

ZONES & ORIGIN 5a–10a. Native to moist locations of the southeastern Coastal Plain.

SIZE & GROWTH RATE 6'–8' tall, 5'–7' wide, medium slow growing.

TEXTURE & FORM Medium fine texture with a broadly oval form.

FOLIAGE Simple alternately arranged leaves are a lustrous green color, ¾"–2" long, elliptic to oblanceolate in shape, with a few teeth on the upper third of the margins.

FLOWERS A dioecious species, with neither sex producing showy flowers.

FRUIT Female plants produce small black berry-like drupes in autumn that remain through winter but are mostly obscured by the foliage. In its native habitat, the fruit is eaten by quails and turkeys.

LIGHT & SOIL Full sun to light shade with a moist acidic soil is ideal. It tolerates salt spray and moderate shade but becomes more open in shade. It prefers consistent moisture throughout the summer.

MAINTENANCE To maintain the desired size and form, prune stems back to a lower node. To maintain a dense canopy to the ground, prune the entire plant down to 12" above the ground every five years.

INSTALLATION Container-grown plants are readily available. Space 3'–5' apart.

PESTS & DISEASES No serious problems with adequate summer moisture. Deer rarely cause significant damage.

NOTES & CULTIVARS
'Compacta' is a female plant growing 4'–6' tall.
'Nordic' reaches 5' and is hardy to zone 4b.
'Shamrock' reaches 4'–6' with a dense canopy and dark green leaves.

left With dwarf yaupon holly at an Athens residence.

right A hedge on the UGA campus.

Ilex vomitoria 'Nana' DWARF YAUPON HOLLY

Landscape architects sometimes overuse a favorite plant because they can count on it to survive tough situations. Thus is the fate of the dwarf yaupon holly. Forming a dense mounded outline, dwarf yaupon holly has been used as a substitute for boxwood for sheared formal plantings due to its ability to tolerate soil conditions such as moist or acidic soils that would spell doom for boxwoods. It can also serve as an evergreen foundation for larger deciduous shrubs or as a background for smaller flowering shrubs or perennial border plantings.

ZONES & ORIGIN 7a–10b. Native to the southeastern Coastal Plain.

SIZE & GROWTH RATE 5'–7' tall and wide, medium slow growing.

TEXTURE & FORM Fine texture with a mounded form.

FOLIAGE Simple alternate leaves ½"–1½" long are ovate to elliptic in shape, with crenate margins. New foliage emerges with a purple-bronze color, with some cultivars providing deep purple winter foliage.

FLOWERS Insignificant.

FRUIT None.

LIGHT & SOIL Full sun is ideal, but it tolerates up to moderate shade with anywhere from moist to well-drained soils. Dwarf yaupons are very tolerant of drought and salt spray and are not particular about pH.

MAINTENANCE Allow plants to grow together as a mass rather than shearing them into individual globes. Mature plants are very slow to recover their form if heavily damaged, leaving large voids for many years. Consider cutting them back to near the ground after traumatic damage.

INSTALLATION Plant on 4' centers for massing anytime of the year.

PESTS & DISEASES No significant pest problems. Deer will nibble on young plantings but rarely cause severe damage to mature plants.

NOTES & CULTIVARS
'Schillings' and 'Stokes Dwarf' produce purplish winter foliage, particularly in sunny locations, and mature in the 3'–5' range.
'Bordeaux' produces purplish new growth and winter foliage.

top left A parterre at the State Botanical Garden of Georgia.

top right A parterre at Belfair Plantation.

middle At the Affolter and Pringle residence in Athens.

bottom An example on the UGA campus.

Layered branching of a Pfitzer juniper in Athens.

Juniperus × *pfitzeriana* 'Wilhelm Pfitzer'
PFITZER JUNIPER

Pfitzer juniper, listed in most nursery catalogs as *Juniperus chinensis* 'Pfitzeriana', has been utilized for many years to provide a dense evergreen screen or background for other plants. It can also be used to provide a foundation for a large flowering deciduous shrub such as beauty bush, weigelia, and butterfly bush. Older Pfitzers assume an attractive windswept coastal appearance resembling a large bonsai. Just make sure to provide enough space for its ultimate size.

'Pfitzeriana Glauca' in Chattanooga.

ZONES & ORIGIN 4a–9a. A cross between two species from China.

SIZE & GROWTH RATE 6'–8' tall, 8'–16' wide, medium fast growing.

TEXTURE & FORM Fine texture with a spreading form.

FOLIAGE Foliage is dull green with predominantly scalelike needles. With time, the branches provide a layered appearance, with the ends of the twigs drooping.

FLOWERS Junipers are dioecious, with neither sex showy.

FRUIT None.

LIGHT & SOIL Provide full sun to light shade with well-drained soils. It is quite tolerant of drought and alkaline soils.

MAINTENANCE With age, the lower foliage is shaded out, providing a windswept appearance that exposes the lower trunk and branches. Many people find this look attractive. For continuous foliage to the ground, prune back new growth in the upper canopy annually to keep the lower branches exposed to full sun.

INSTALLATION Container-grown plants up to 5 gallons are readily available and easily transplanted year-round. Space plants 6'–10' on center.

PESTS & DISEASES Bagworms and spider mites are common problems, but deer are not.

NOTES & CULTIVARS

'Aurea Improved' and 'Old Gold' grow 3'–5' tall and 6'–8' wide, with yellow-green foliage.

'Pfitzeriana Aurea' has yellow-green new foliage.

'Pfitzeriana Glauca' has silvery-blue-green foliage.

Juniperus chinensis 'Angelica Blue' is slightly smaller, with striking blue-green foliage.

'Hetzii Glauca' grows 5'–7' tall and 8'–12' wide, with silvery-blue-green foliage.

'Torulosa', the Hollywood juniper, reaches 10'–15' tall with an oval form.

Leucothoe fontanesiana
DROOPING LEUCOTHOE · FETTERBUSH

Drooping leucothoe is a native evergreen shrub of cool mountain slopes and streambanks. Fairly attractive mid- to late spring white flowers on 2"–3" drooping racemes beneath the stems have a slightly unpleasant odor. Consider it for woodland gardens and water features with ferns and native stone.

ZONES & ORIGIN 5a–7b. Native to the southern Appalachian Mountains.

SIZE & GROWTH RATE 4'–6' tall and wide, slow growing.

TEXTURE & FORM Medium texture and arching broadly oval form.

FOLIAGE Simple leaves are 2"–5" long, ovate-lanceolate shaped, with finely toothed margins and acuminate tips, and emerge coppery red.

LIGHT & SOIL Provide light to moderate shade with a loose, moist, but well-drained acidic soil containing plenty of organic material. Droughts can be deadly.

MAINTENANCE Without ideal cultural conditions, leucothoe is susceptible to leaf fungal diseases and is often short-lived in zones 7 and 8 planting designs.

INSTALLATION Rare in nurseries. Space small container plants 4' apart for massing.

NOTES & CULTIVARS
Swamp leucothoe, *Leucothoe racemosa*, is a deciduous shrub native to moist sites in the lower Piedmont and Coastal Plain with showy white late spring flowers on curving racemes and red fall foliage.

Foliage and spring flowers along a north Georgia stream.

Mahonia aquifolium OREGON GRAPEHOLLY

Oregon grapeholly provides a loose and somewhat rambling character with colorful late fall and winter foliage. It is the state flower of Oregon, where it is widespread in dry shady woodlands. It combines well with other shade-loving plants such as fatsias, pachysandras, hellebores, and ferns in informal garden compositions. Take advantage of its shade tolerance for woodland paths. It is known for its ability to sprout new stems and spread from its root system but is easily kept in bounds.

top Winter foliage and flower buds.
middle Summer fruit and foliage.
bottom left In bloom.
bottom right Form.

ZONES & ORIGIN 5b–9a. Native to shady woods of the Pacific Northwest.

SIZE & GROWTH RATE 4'–6' tall and wide, medium slow growing.

TEXTURE & FORM Medium coarse texture with a loose and rambling rounded form.

FOLIAGE Alternately arranged odd pinnately compound leaves tend to cluster near the ends of the stems. Individual leaves have seven, rarely five or nine, sessile lustrous green leaflets that are ovate in shape, with 13 to 21 spiny teeth on the margins. New foliage emerges coppery red, while mature foliage turns reddish purple in late fall in sunny locations.

FLOWERS Bright yellow flowers occur on short racemes on the ends of the stems for an extended time in early to midspring (typically early March to early April in Athens). The flowers are very lightly fragrant, but not significantly so.

FRUIT Small grapelike berries turn purple in late summer and often remain into winter.

LIGHT & SOIL Light to moderate shade with loose, moist, but well-drained slightly acidic soils is ideal. It tolerates heavy shade.

MAINTENANCE Foliage on plants in excessive sun may become desiccated and turn brown during winter freezes. To maintain a denser canopy, remove a few older stems near the soil every other year.

INSTALLATION For massing, plant 4'–5' on center, or 3' for the dwarf cultivars.

PESTS & DISEASES No significant problems. Deer don't bother them.

NOTES & CULTIVARS
'Compacta' grows 3'–4' in height and spread.
'Orange Flame' reaches 3' with rusty-pink to orange new foliage that turns to green with maturity.

Pieris japonica PIERIS · JAPANESE ANDROMEDA

Pieris is an attractive shade-loving plant whose attributes are best appreciated up close. Its lightly fragrant white flowers resemble those of the native sourwood tree. A clean neat shrub with attractive coppery-red new spring foliage and an attractive branching habit make it popular for bonsai. It is frequently used as a specimen plant in detailed designs. Use it along shaded woodland trails with rhododendrons, mountain laurels, and native wildflowers and ferns.

ZONES & ORIGIN 5b–8b. Native to Asia.

SIZE & GROWTH RATE 6'–10' tall, 4'–8' wide, slow growing.

TEXTURE & FORM Medium fine texture with an oval form.

FOLIAGE New foliage emerges coppery red in color. Simple alternately arranged leaves 1"–3" long tend to cluster near the ends of the stems, where they appear opposite or whorled. Leaves are oblanceolate to narrowly oblong in shape and frequently have serrate margins on the upper half of the leaf.

FLOWERS Very lightly fragrant bell-shaped creamy-white flowers occur on pendulous panicles at the ends of the stems in early spring (late March to early April in Athens). New flower buds form in summer and are visible through winter, aiding in identification.

FRUIT Small capsules are not showy, remain on the panicles through the winter, and aid in identification.

LIGHT & SOIL Light to moderate shade with a moist but well-drained acidic soil is ideal. Protect it from afternoon summer sun, and provide supplemental water during summer droughts.

MAINTENANCE Maintain 2"–3" of organic mulch. Selectively prune to control size immediately after flowering in midspring. Summer pruning removes next year's flower buds.

INSTALLATION Add organic material to the soil mix and ensure good surface and internal drainage. Space 4'–6' apart for larger cultivars or 3' for smaller cultivars.

PESTS & DISEASES Deer don't bother them, but lace bugs can require attention.

NOTES & CULTIVARS
'Compacta' and 'Debutante' are smaller and denser in habit, reaching 4'–6'.
'Mountain Fire' produces bright red new foliage.
'Valley Rose' has light pink flowers, while 'Valley Valentine' produces deep red flowers.
'Variegata' produces foliage with creamy-white margins.

top At Portland State University and at the Portland Japanese Garden.
middle Spring flowers.
bottom Summer foliage and fruit.

Prunus laurocerasus 'Otto Luyken'

OTTO LUYKEN LAUREL

Otto Luyken, Schip, and Zabel laurels are popular landscape plants with a spreading habit. They are easy to combine with other plants yet provide a comfortable contrast to those plants. All are outstanding choices for informal hedges and borders, to provide backgrounds for smaller plants, or as foundations for taller shrubs. Their lightly fragrant and somewhat showy white spring flowers provide an added bonus. Though they are tough plants once established, all of these laurels are sensitive to poorly drained soils.

ZONES & ORIGIN 5b–8b. Native to Europe.

SIZE & GROWTH RATE 4'–6' tall, 4'–8' wide, medium slow growing.

TEXTURE & FORM Medium texture with a broadly oval form.

FOLIAGE Simple alternately arranged leaves are a lustrous dark green in color, 2"–4" long, and narrowly elliptical in shape, with mostly entire margins and acute tips. Leaves on the Otto Luyken are held upright at an angle of 45° to the stems.

FLOWERS Somewhat showy lightly fragrant white flowers occur on upright racemes along the stems in early spring (late March to early April in Athens), with some flowering in autumn as well.

FRUIT Purple to black berry-like drupes in late summer.

LIGHT & SOIL Light shade and moist but well-drained soils are ideal. These laurels tolerate full sun to moderate shade and become fairly drought resistant with establishment, but they cannot tolerate damp soils.

MAINTENANCE Easily maintained at smaller sizes by selective pruning in late spring and early summer.

INSTALLATION Container plants are readily available. Space 4'–5' apart.

PESTS & DISEASES No serious problems. Deer are not a problem.

NOTES & CULTIVARS
- Schip laurel, 'Schipkaensis', reaches 8' tall and 12' wide, with a branching habit and form that are more horizontal than Otto Luyken. The leaves are lighter green, slightly longer and broader than 'Otto Luyken', and tend to have serrate margins on their upper half.
- Zabel laurel, 'Zabeliana', is an older cultivar reaching 6' tall and 10' wide, with a spreading form similar to Schip. Its leaves are similar to 'Schipkaensis' but with entire margins.

Zabel laurel.

left 'Otto Luyken' at Swarthmore College.
top right 'Otto Luyken'.
bottom right Zabel laurels with hostas.

Rhapidophyllum hystrix NEEDLE PALM

Needle palm, sometimes called porcupine palm, is so named for the extremely sharp needle-like spines arising from its short trunk. While its use should be curtailed where children might fall into the palm while playing, it nevertheless offers a number of attributes of interest to the designer. Its attractive and exotic-looking foliage, ability to tolerate a range of environmental conditions, and rugged nature provide ample reasons to consider its use. The fact that it is a native palm and is hardy throughout the Southeast adds to its appeal. Consider it for shaded courtyards or container plantings where it can be appreciated up close or as a natural buffer viewed from afar.

The needles on a needle palm.

ZONES & ORIGIN 6b–10b. Native to moist woodlands of the southeastern Coastal Plain.

SIZE & GROWTH RATE 6'–10' tall and wide, very slow growing.

TEXTURE & FORM Coarse texture with a rounded form.

FOLIAGE Dark glossy green deeply divided fan-shaped leaves are 3'–5' long and arise from the crown on three-angled petioles. The crown eventually reaches 3'–4' tall and is covered by narrow needle-like black spines 6"–12" long.

FLOWERS The flowers are held down near the crown of the palm and hidden by the foliage. It is reported to be dioecious in nature.

FRUIT Insignificant drupes near the crown are obscured by the foliage.

LIGHT & SOIL Light to moderate shade with a loose and consistently moist soil is ideal. It tolerates full sun to full shade and moist but well-drained soils as well.

MAINTENANCE Mulch several times per year and remove older dying leaves as needed to maintain a clean appearance. New plants emerge around the crown with time and can be transplanted to other locations.

INSTALLATION Needle palm is considered a threatened species in Florida, so purchase nursery-grown container plants. For masses, plant on 4' centers virtually anytime of the year.

PESTS & DISEASES No significant problems. Deer don't bother them.

NOTES & CULTIVARS
No cultivars reported.

A needle palm at the State Botanical Garden of Georgia and with fatsia in the Founders Memorial Garden.

Rhaphiolepis umbellata INDIAN HAWTHORN

Indian hawthorn is a versatile shrub possessing a number of attributes for designers. Its dense canopy and mounded form are suited for informal borders and low hedges or to provide a foundation for deciduous shrubs. Attractive midspring flowers, fall and winter fruit, and salt tolerance provide additional reasons to consider its use. Cultivars are available that only reach 3' in height. However, it is susceptible to leaf spot disease, so be sure to select cultivars with improved resistance.

ZONES & ORIGIN 8a–10a. Native to China.

SIZE & GROWTH RATE 4'–6' tall and wide, medium growing.

TEXTURE & FORM Medium texture and mounded form.

FOLIAGE Simple alternate leaves 1½"–3½" long tend to cluster near the ends of the stems. Leathery dark green individual leaves are ovate to obovate shaped, with acute tips and serrate margins on their upper half, and they emerge with a coppery tint.

FLOWERS Attractive white flowers occur on short panicles at the ends of the stems of the previous year's growth in midspring (April in Athens).

FRUIT Small berry-like pomes turn black in autumn and remain into winter but are somewhat obscured by the current season's growth.

LIGHT & SOIL Full sun to light shade with a moist but well-drained acidic soil is ideal. It tolerates moderate salt spray but not poorly drained soils.

MAINTENANCE To control size, selectively prune back to lower stem nodes after flowering is completed. Avoid overhead irrigation, provide early morning sunlight to dry the foliage, and select resistant cultivars to minimize leaf spot diseases.

INSTALLATION Ensure good surface drainage away from the plants, and space 3'–4' apart.

PESTS & DISEASES Deer may cause severe damage.

NOTES & CULTIVARS
'Eleanor Tabor' produces pink flowers and improved resistance to leaf spot diseases.
'Georgia Petite' produces dark green leaves, light pink flowers, a low mounding form, and improved leaf spot resistance.
'Jack Evans' produces pink flowers.
'Minor' has smaller dark green leaves and a broadly oval form.
'Snow White' provides a low spreading form and good disease resistance with white flowers.

top Flowers and foliage.
middle With spiderworts in bloom.
bottom In bloom beneath Japanese maples on the UGA campus.

As a border in a Land Plus Associates project in Atlanta.

Rhododendron × *obtusum* KURUME AZALEAS

Few people consider spring to have arrived until the colorful flowers of the Kurume azaleas emerge. With attractive flowers in white, pink, salmon, and red, Kurumes are selections from crosses between several species of rhododendrons. Mass them with native dogwoods and spiraeas to provide spring color for several weeks. They can also be used for borders, sheared hedges, informal woodland plantings, and even bonsai. They can be temperamental about their placement, planting, and care.

ZONES & ORIGIN   6b–9b. Native to Japan.

SIZE & GROWTH RATE   3'–6' tall and wide, medium growing.

TEXTURE & FORM   Medium fine texture and broadly oval form.

FOLIAGE   Simple alternate leaves ¾"–1½" long are oval to obovate shaped, with blunt tips. Some cultivars produce reddish-purple winter foliage.

FLOWERS   Attractive funnel-shaped flowers in pink, red, and white occur in clusters in early spring (late March to mid-April in Athens). Some cultivars produce hose-in-hose flowers.

FRUIT   Insignificant capsules.

LIGHT & SOIL   Light shade with a loose, moist, but well-drained acidic soil is ideal. Avoid midday to midafternoon summer sun.

MAINTENANCE   Maintain 2"–3" of organic mulch year-round and a soil pH around 5.5 to avoid iron chlorosis. Provide supplemental water during droughts.

INSTALLATION   Plants frequently arrive root-bound from nurseries. Slice the root ball vertically at least twice, spread the roots out in the planting hole, and plant higher than the surrounding grade on 3'–4' centers.

PESTS & DISEASES   Lace bugs are a common problem, ultimately weaken-

top to bottom

Assorted Kurume azaleas.

'Coral Bells'.

'Snow'.

ing the plant if not controlled. Deer will browse them.

NOTES & CULTIVARS

'Appleblossom' reaches 6'–10' with pinkish-white early flowers.

'Christmas Cheer' is low growing, with red hose-in-hose flowers.

'Coral Bells' has pink hose-in-hose early season flowers.

'Delaware Valley White' has large white midseason flowers and better cold-hardiness.

'Hershey's Red' produces large bright red hose-in-hose early season flowers.

'Hino Crimson' has crimson midseason flowers and bronze fall foliage.

'Hinode-giri' has single pinkish-red midseason flowers and a rounded form.

'Mother's Day' produces bright red hose-in-hose midseason flowers.

'Pink Pearl' is upright, with midseason hose-in-hose salmon-pink flowers.

'Sherwood Red' produces orange-red early season flowers.

'Snow' has white hose-in-hose early season flowers; spent flowers persist.

Encore Series azaleas are similar to Kurumes, with additional early autumn flowering. Cultivars are available in single and hose-in-hose flowers in white, pink, red, and purple, with some cultivars providing variegated flowers. Provide full sun to light shade and adequate moisture in sunny locations.

top to bottom

'Hino Crimson' azaleas with a fescue lawn and dogwoods in Athens.

'Hinode-giri' and 'Delaware Valley White' azaleas.

'Coral Bells' and 'Snow' with flowering dogwoods.

Yucca gloriosa MOUNDLILY YUCCA · SPANISH DAGGER

Moundlily yucca has broad gray-green foliage with stiff needle-like tips that are painful to the touch. It reaches about 6' tall before falling over onto the ground and sprouting new plants along its stem. Yuccas can be difficult to combine with many plants due to their bold striking form, which hints of arid southwestern landscapes. Take advantage of their drought tolerance and preference for full sun by combining them with junipers, purple heart plants, rosemarys, lantanas, or ornamental grasses in perennial borders.

ZONES & ORIGIN   7a–10b. Native to southeastern dunes and brackish marshes.

SIZE & GROWTH RATE   4'–6' tall, 3'–5' wide, slow growing.

TEXTURE & FORM   Coarse texture and oval form.

FOLIAGE   Thick gray-green leaves are 15"–30" long, 1½"–2½" wide, with entire margins and spiny tips. Dead leaves remain along the trunk and appear unsightly.

FLOWERS   Showy creamy-white flowers emerge from crimson buds on panicles 4' tall. Flowering occurs from late May through late September and with the timing varying on the same plant from one year to the next.

FRUIT   Green capsules are neither showy nor attractive.

LIGHT & SOIL   Full sun to light shade with well-drained soils. They tolerate drought, salt spray, and higher pH levels.

MAINTENANCE   Tough fibrous dead leaves remain and become unsightly. To improve the plant's appearance, remove the dead foliage from the stem each year, as well as old flower structures. New plants arise from older stems that have fallen over.

INSTALLATION   Plant 3'–5' on center.

NOTES & CULTIVARS

Yucca recurvifolia is native to the Southeast and hardy from zones 7a to 10a. Reaching 5'–6' in height and 3' in width, it has blue-green leaves, with the older leaves curving downward. Although providing a softer appearance than *Yucca gloriosa*, it also has needle-like tips to its foliage, so avoid using it near small children. Its showy creamy-white flowers arise in early autumn in Athens.

top left Yucca recurvifolia in Athens.

top right and middle Moundlily or Spanish dagger on the UGA campus.

bottom Flowering.

MEDIUM DECIDUOUS SHRUBS

Hydrangea arborescens at Chanticleer.

Medium sized deciduous shrubs are primarily used to provide seasonal interest in garden designs. In some cases, that interest may extend to more than one season of the year. Since they are not evergreen, they are rarely used to help form and define spaces in the design. Instead, they augment the spaces that are created through the use of evergreen shrubs such as camellias and hollies or spaces created by structures such as walls and fences. Due to their lack of foliage from late autumn to midspring, consider using them in groupings of no more than three to five plants rather than in larger masses.

Fortunately, many of these shrubs reveal their attractive character at a considerable distance from the viewer. In fact, they may not provide any greater appeal up close than they do from a distance. So give them ample room to grow and show off their attributes, but don't feel like they necessarily need to be placed beside a doorway or walk to be enjoyed.

BOTANICAL NAME	SUNLIGHT	SOILS	TEXTURE	ORNAMENTAL FLOWERS	ORNAMENTAL ATTRIBUTES	NATIVE TO SOUTHEAST
Berberis thunbergii	Full sun to light shade	Well drained	Medium fine	Insignificant	Red to purple fall foliage	No, Japan
Callicarpa americana	Full sun to light shade	Moist but well drained to well drained	Coarse	Insignificant	Showy purple fruit attract birds	Yes
Calycanthus floridus	Full sun to moderate shade	Moist but well drained	Medium	Maroon in mid- to late spring	Some yellow fall foliage	Yes
Chaenomeles speciosa	Full sun to light shade	Well drained	Medium	White, pink, red in early spring	Edible fruit but not showy	No, Asia
Clethra alnifolia	Full sun to moderate shade	Moist to moist but well drained	Medium	White in midsummer	Attractive yellow fall foliage	Yes
Edgeworthia chrysantha	Light to full shade	Moist but well drained	Coarse	Fragrant yellow in early spring	Prominent buds in fall and winter	No, Asia
Forsythia × intermedia	Full sun to light shade	Well drained	Medium	Yellow in early spring	Some yellow to purple fall color	No, cross of two Asian species
Fothergilla × intermedia 'Mount Airy'	Light shade	Moist but well drained acidic	Medium	White in midspring	Outstanding red fall foliage	No, cross from two U.S. species
Hydrangea arborescens	Light shade	Moist to moist but well drained	Coarse	White in early summer	Cultivars provide showy flowers	Yes
Hydrangea macrophylla	Light shade	Moist but well drained	Coarse	Blue to pink in early summer	Some blooms to late summer	No, Asia
Itea virginica	Full sun to light shade	Moist to moist but well drained	Medium fine	White in late spring	Outstanding red fall foliage late	Yes
Jasminum floridum	Full sun to light shade	Well drained	Medium fine	Yellow in mid- to late spring	Semievergreen and green stems	No
Kerria japonica	Full sun to moderate shade	Well drained	Medium fine	Yellow in mid- to late spring	Some flowers into summer	No, Asia
Rhododendron canescens	Light shade	Moist but well drained	Medium	Fragrant light pink midspring	Attractive branching habit	Yes
Rhododendron prunifolium	Light shade	Moist but well drained	Medium	Red in mid- to late summer	Attracts hummingbirds	Yes
Rosa 'Radrazz'	Full sun to light shade	Well drained	Medium	Red from spring to late autumn	Heavy flowering in cycles	No, man-made hybrid group
Spiraea cantoniensis	Full sun to light shade	Well drained	Medium	White in midspring	Slight yellow fall foliage color	No, Asia
Spiraea prunifolia 'Plena'	Full sun to light shade	Well drained	Medium fine	White in early spring	Slight yellow fall foliage color	No, Asia
Spiraea thunbergii	Full sun to light shade	Well drained	Fine	White in late winter	Slight yellow fall foliage color	No, Asia
Spiraea × vanhouttei	Full sun to light shade	Well drained	Medium fine	White in midspring	Some orange to red fall color	No

Foliage at Queen Elizabeth Park in Vancouver, B.C., at Mt. Auburn Cemetery, Cambridge, Mass., and in Stanley Park in Vancouver, B.C.

Berberis thunbergii JAPANESE BARBERRY

Japanese barberry is rarely used in the landscape. However, several of its cultivars are popular due to their colorful foliage. The fine texture, colorful foliage, and toughness of this plant make it worthy of consideration for use in shrub borders, informal hedges, or even sheared formal plantings. All forms of barberry have prominent spines along the stems, which, unfortunately, often restrict their usage to barrier plantings. While it is not a problem in zone 8, the plant is reportedly invasive in the mid-Atlantic states and New England.

ZONES & ORIGIN   4a–9b. Native to Japan.

SIZE & GROWTH RATE   4'–6' tall, 3'–5' wide, medium growing.

TEXTURE & FORM   Medium fine texture and rounded form.

FOLIAGE   Simple obovate-shaped alternate leaves ½"–1½" long are often clustered at the nodes of the stems and turn an attractive reddish purple in fall.

FLOWERS   Small yellow flowers are obscured by the foliage in mid-April.

FRUIT   Small berries turn bright red in fall and often remain through winter.

LIGHT & SOIL   Full sun to light shade with well-drained soil. Cultivars with colored foliage will revert to green under light shade. Barberry is drought and pH tolerant but can't tolerate wet soils.

MAINTENANCE   Lower stems will lose their foliage and become leggy in appearance over time. To maintain a dense outline, prune barberry at any time of the year.

INSTALLATION   Ensure good drainage by amending heavy clay soils and planting high. For massing, plant 3'–4' on center.

PESTS & DISEASES   No serious problems with good drainage. Deer don't bother them.

NOTES & CULTIVARS
'Aurea' and 'Bonanza Gold' develop bright yellow foliage.

The variety *atropurpurea* has reddish-purple foliage and serves as a parent for the following cultivars:

'Atropurpurea Nana' or 'Crimson Pygmy' grows 2'–3' in height and spread.
'Concorde' grows 2'–3' with dark purple foliage.
'Rose Glow' reaches 5'–6' with mottled foliage that matures to deep purple.

Berberis × *mentorensis* is a cross between Japanese barberry and wintergreen barberry, *Berberis julianae*, that reaches 7' tall and is semievergreen, with orange to deep red fall foliage.

Foliage.

Callicarpa americana AMERICAN BEAUTYBERRY

A pioneer species of well-drained woodland edges of the Coastal Plain and lower Piedmont, beautyberry is nondescript for much of the year. Only when its fruit matures in early autumn do many people recognize its presence. Large masses can be boring, so a key to utilizing beautyberry in designs is to surround it with plants that provide interest at other times of the year but allow it to shine in early autumn. Consider adding some yellow-colored flowers, such as goldenrods and sunflowers, nearby to complement beautyberry's attractive fall fruit.

Early summer foliage and flowers.

ZONES & ORIGIN 6a–10b. Native from Texas to Virginia.

SIZE & GROWTH RATE 5'–8' tall and wide, medium fast growing.

TEXTURE & FORM Coarse texture and sprawling broadly oval form.

FOLIAGE Simple light green elliptic opposite leaves 4"–7" long have crenate margins and acuminate tips. Their upper sides have a sandpapery feel, while the lower sides, petioles, and young stems are densely pubescent. While leaves develop some yellow fall color, they're usually gone by midautumn.

FLOWERS Tiny light pink flowers are not showy but cluster around the stems in early to midsummer (late May to early July in Athens).

FRUIT The small berry-like drupes clustered around the stems turn purple violet in color in late August and early September and are extremely popular with birds, which usually devour them by late October.

LIGHT & SOIL Full sun to very light shade and moist but well-drained soil are ideal. They are quite drought tolerant.

MAINTENANCE Prune in late winter to encourage greater density for greater flowering and fruit. Without pruning, beautyberry declines in vigor and production after several years.

INSTALLATION Specialty growers carry small container plants that can be planted 4'–6' apart year-round. Young seedlings are easily transplanted successfully.

PESTS & DISEASES None reported. Deer gobble the fruit but don't care for the foliage.

NOTES & CULTIVARS
Callicarpa americana lactea produces white fruit.
Callicarpa dichotoma grows 4'–6' tall, with a denser rounded form, a more refined appearance, and fruit held above the foliage rather than clustered around the stems.

Early autumn fruit in north Georgia.

Calycanthus floridus CAROLINA SWEETSHRUB

Sweetshrub is an old-garden plant used at colonial Williamsburg. While nondescript for much of the year, it stands out in spring when blooming and with its golden-yellow foliage in autumn. While not particularly interesting in large masses, individual plants can be used in mixed shrub and perennial borders. To take advantage of its flower fragrance, locate it near a walkway or lightly shaded woodland path.

ZONES & ORIGIN 4b–10a. Native to moist shaded slopes of the southeastern United States.

SIZE & GROWTH RATE 6'–8' tall, 5'–8' wide, medium growing.

TEXTURE & FORM Medium texture and broadly oval form.

FOLIAGE Simple elliptic opposite leaves 2"–6" long have a rough sandpapery feel to the upper surface, soft pubescence beneath, and a spicy odor when crushed. Plants develop a good yellow fall color.

FLOWERS Somewhat showy maroon flowers with strap-shaped petals begin in Athens in early April, peak in mid- to late April, and continue sporadically into mid-May. Flowers smell like fermented apples, with the degree of fragrance varying greatly with the individual genetics of each plant. Most plants are only lightly fragrant.

FRUIT Nonshowy pear-shaped capsules containing approximately 30 dark brown seeds mature in late summer and remain on the plant through winter.

LIGHT & SOIL Light shade is best, but the plant grows in full sun to moderate shade with moist but well-drained acidic soil and tolerates moderate drought after establishment.

MAINTENANCE Mature plants produce suckers from the roots. Leave them alone to produce a small thicket, or remove them and transplant the young plants.

INSTALLATION For masses, plant no closer than 4' on center. Provide supplemental water during the first summer while becoming established.

PESTS & DISEASES No issues. Deer browse the foliage.

NOTES & CULTIVARS
'Athens' produces creamy-white flowers with a stronger fragrance.
'Michael Lindsey' produces dark green foliage, a denser form, and fragrant flowers.
Calycanthus × *raulstonii* cultivars are crosses between *C. floridus* and *C. chinensis*. 'Hartlage Wine' reaches 10'–12' with crimson flowers larger than those of sweetshrub.

top left 'Hartlage Wine' at Berkshire Botanical Garden.

top right and bottom Foliage and spring flowers in north Georgia woods.

middle 'Hartlage Wine'.

Chaenomeles speciosa FLOWERING QUINCE

Flowering quince makes a show in late winter and early spring, when its vivid flowers come to life, reminding us that spring is coming. However, from a design standpoint, quince appears better from a distance than up close. Its flowers are impressive from afar, but it loses much of its attraction after flowering. Quince produces a better floral display in cooler climates, where the flowers open over a shorter period of time, but its extended flowering in warmer climates means its flowering overlaps with a wider array of other plants. Use it in mixed borders with camellias, forsythias, edgeworthias, and Loebner or star magnolias.

top Foliage with kidney-shaped stipules.
middle A white-flowered cultivar.
bottom left A scarlet-flowered cultivar.
bottom right Behind Schip laurels on the UGA campus.

ZONES & ORIGIN 5a–8b. Native to Asia.

SIZE & GROWTH RATE 5'–8' tall, 4'–6' wide, medium slow growing.

TEXTURE & FORM Medium texture in leaf, medium fine in winter, and broadly oval form.

FOLIAGE Simple ovate or oblong alternate leaves 1"–3" long have sharply serrate margins. Kidney-shaped stipules at the leaf base frequently disappear by early summer. Twigs produce sharp thorns.

FLOWERS Showy single and double flowers in red, pink, white, and peach usually begin in late January in Athens. Peak flowering is mid-February to mid-March, with some flowers into early April. In cooler climates, flowering may last only two to three weeks, providing a more intensive display than in the Southeast.

FRUIT A hard and nonshowy small green pome sometimes used for jellies develops in early summer and remains into fall.

LIGHT & SOIL Full sun to light shade and well-drained soils.

MAINTENANCE Prune after flowering in midspring to avoid removing next year's flower buds.

INSTALLATION Container plants are readily available. Space 4' apart and ensure good surface drainage.

PESTS & DISEASES Leaf fungal diseases frequently defoliate plants by midsummer, particularly in warm humid climates. Aphids and scale are also common. Deer don't bother them.

NOTES & CULTIVARS
'Cameo' has peach-colored double flowers.
'Double Take' has deep red double flowers.
'Texas Scarlet' has deep red flowers and mounded form.
'White Trail' produces white flowers.
Chaenomeles × superba cultivars typically grow only 3'–4' tall.

top Pink spires on the UGA campus.
bottom Foliage and summer flowers

Clethra alnifolia SUMMERSWEET CLETHRA

Summersweet clethra is an attractive shrub with a neat demeanor and several ornamental attributes. The lightly fragrant midsummer flowers, while not as showy as those of a crape myrtle, are still eye-catchers, and the yellow fall foliage adds interest to the autumn garden. Combine these features with a durable plant that tolerates a wide range of cultural conditions with few problems, and you have a plant that is worth consideration. Take advantage of its fragrance and attractive branching habit by keeping it close to where people congregate. Native to low moist sites of the Coastal Plain, clethra is also tough enough to be used in stormwater retention areas that are both wet and dry during the year.

ZONES & ORIGIN 4b–9a. Native to the Coastal Plain from Texas to Maine.

SIZE & GROWTH RATE 5'–8' tall, 4'–6' wide, medium growing.

TEXTURE & FORM Medium texture and oval form.

FOLIAGE Simple elliptic to obovate-shaped alternate leaves 1½"–3½" long have sharply serrate margins, acute tips, and prominent depressed veins. Fall foliage turns bright yellow in sunny locations.

FLOWERS Lightly fragrant white flowers occur on upright terminal racemes 2"–5" long in midsummer (mid-July to early August in Athens).

FRUIT Insignificant capsules remain into winter and are helpful in identification.

LIGHT & SOIL Full sun to light shade and a moist to moist but well-drained fairly acidic soil are ideal. It tolerates moderate shade, wet soils, and moderate salt spray.

MAINTENANCE Clethra flowers on new growth, so it can be pruned in late winter and early spring to control the size. Provide supplemental water during extreme summer droughts.

INSTALLATION Container plants are readily available and easily transplanted year-round. Space 4'–5' apart.

PESTS & DISEASES No disease problems. It suffers under prolonged droughts on well-drained sites, so be prepared to water deeply at 10- to 14-day intervals. Deer browse it.

NOTES & CULTIVARS
'Hummingbird' is a dwarf cultivar that only reaches 4' with dark green foliage. 'Pink Spires' has light pink flowers. 'Ruby Spice' has deep pink flowers.

Edgeworthia chrysantha PAPERBUSH

Oriental civilizations made fine papers from the crushed stems of paperbush, which is how the common name was derived. Still a somewhat rare plant in the Southeast, paperbush offers attributes that make it worthy of greater use. A very clean nontemperamental plant that tolerates shade, a good reason in itself, but the prolonged fragrant showy late winter and early spring flowers are what attract most of the attention to this plant. With its attractive sympodial branching, prominent winter buds, and fragrance, make sure to plant it close enough to a patio or walkway to be fully appreciated.

top Late winter flowers.
bottom Foliage at the Giberson residence.

ZONES & ORIGIN 6b–8b. Native to China.

SIZE & GROWTH RATE 4'–7' in height and spread, medium slow growing.

TEXTURE & FORM Medium coarse texture and broadly oval to rounded form.

FOLIAGE Softly pubescent blue-green leaves are 3"–8" long, narrowly elliptic in shape. Although technically alternately arranged, leaves are clustered at the ends of the stems, providing a whorled appearance. Fall foliage is a pale yellow.

FLOWERS Tiny yellow trumpet-shaped flowers are produced in heads of 30 or more for several weeks in late winter. In Athens, flowering begins in mid-February and continues to mid-March. Flowers are sweetly fragrant. Prominent flower buds appear on the ends of the stems by mid-autumn and are prominent over winter.

FRUIT Insignificant drupes may not be produced on plants in the Southeast.

LIGHT & SOIL Light to moderate shade with a loose, moist, but well-drained soil is ideal. Paperbush tolerates full shade, but flowering is reduced with increasing shade.

MAINTENANCE Paperbush often produces shoots from the base of the plant that can be removed to reveal more of the trunk and stems.

INSTALLATION Container plants are becoming more frequently available. Amend the soil with organic material to keep it loose, mulch periodically to keep the roots cool, and space plants 4'–6' on center.

PESTS & DISEASES No serious problems have been reported. Deer don't appear to like them.

NOTES & CULTIVARS
'Akebono', 'Red Dragon', and 'Rubra' produce reddish-orange flowers.

left At Swarthmore College.
right In a Land Plus Associates design in Atlanta.

Forsythia × *intermedia* FORSYTHIA · GOLDEN BELLS

Forsythia is a tough and dependable old-garden plant whose blooms are the first sign of spring in many gardens. Forsythia looks like a small explosion of bright yellow in the late winter landscape. Take advantage of its upright arching habit by mixing it in shrub borders. Since the flowers can be appreciated from a distance, give it a foundation and place toward the rear of shrub borders with a dark green or even purple-foliaged background such as loropetalum, camellia, or osmanthus.

left Late winter flowers in Oconee County.

top right Purple late fall foliage.

bottom right In bloom at the T. R. R. Cobb House.

ZONES & ORIGIN 5a–9a. A cross between two Asian species.

SIZE & GROWTH RATE 6'–8' tall and wide, fast growing.

TEXTURE & FORM Medium texture with upright arching branches and broadly oval form.

FOLIAGE Simple elliptic opposite leaves 1"–4" long have serrate margins and acute tips. Late fall foliage turns dark purple in sunny locations.

FLOWERS Bright yellow nonfragrant bell-shaped flowers emerge in late winter (late February to early March in Athens). Flowering continues for almost a month in zone 8a but is condensed to about two weeks in northern locations.

FRUIT Insignificant capsules.

LIGHT & SOIL Full sun and well-drained soils are ideal. It tolerates drought and up to moderate shade with reduced flowering.

MAINTENANCE Avoid shearing, since this eliminates forsythia's natural form. Instead, selectively remove some of the older and taller stems near ground level after flowering in spring to avoid removing next year's flower buds. Stems that arch to the ground can take root.

INSTALLATION Container plants are readily available and can be planted year-round in zones 7 and 8 on 6' centers.

PESTS & DISEASES None serious. Deer nibble them but don't seem to care for them.

NOTES & CULTIVARS

'Bronxensis' and 'Citrus Swizzle' are cultivars of *Forsythia viridissima*. Both are dwarf plants, topping out between 2' and 3' in height, with 'Citrus Swizzle' producing yellow-green variegated foliage.

'Golden Peep' only grows 3' tall.

'Lynwood' or 'Lynwood Gold' is the most popular forsythia cultivar.

'Spring Glory' is a more dependable bloomer for zones 7 and 8.

Fothergilla × *intermedia* 'Mount Airy'
MOUNT AIRY FOTHERGILLA

Mount Airy fothergilla is the result of a cross between *Fothergilla gardenii*, a native of the southeastern Coastal Plain, and *F. major*, native to the Appalachian Mountains. Attractive early spring flowers, outstanding late fall foliage, and a clean appearance throughout the year are all reasons to use it in compositions. Its relatively small size and slow growth rate reduce the need to prune it in most gardens. And, unlike many deciduous shrubs, it is as attractive up close as it is from a distance, so don't be afraid to place it near walks, decks, or patios.

top Foliage.
bottom Flowers close up.

ZONES & ORIGIN 4b–8b. Cross from two native species.

SIZE & GROWTH RATE 4'–7' tall, 3'–5' wide, slow growing.

TEXTURE & FORM Medium texture and oval to broadly oval form.

FOLIAGE Simple alternate leaves 1½"–3½" long are elliptic shaped, with dentate margins and prominent depressed veins. Blue green in color in spring and early summer, the leaves develop a brilliant orange-red late autumn color.

FLOWERS Lightly fragrant white flowers occur on conically shaped terminal spikes 1½" long in early spring. In Athens, flowering typically occurs for about 10 days in late March and early April just as the leaves begin to emerge.

FRUIT Insignificant capsules.

LIGHT & SOIL Light shade and moist but well-drained acidic soils are ideal. It tolerates full sun to moderate shade, although flowering and fall color are reduced with shade, and it often loses its foliage under summer drought stress.

MAINTENANCE Mulch plants to keep the roots cool and help conserve soil moisture during summers. Provide supplemental water during prolonged summer droughts. Prune after flowering ends in early spring.

INSTALLATION Space container plants 3'–4' apart.

PESTS & DISEASES No serious disease problems. Deer browse them.

NOTES & CULTIVARS
Fothergilla major is somewhat rare on cool and well-drained lower to midelevation slopes of the Appalachians, where it reaches 12' tall. *F. gardenii* reaches 3' on the edges of moist woods and water bodies of the Coastal Plain.

left Flowers in bloom.
right Fall color.

Hydrangea arborescens SMOOTH HYDRANGEA

Smooth hydrangea is a widespread native shrub that forms dense thickets on shaded slopes of the Appalachian Mountains. It produces flattened flower heads with mostly fertile flowers and few showy sterile flowers in late spring to early summer.

ZONES & ORIGIN 4a–8a. Native to shaded moist slopes of the eastern United States.

SIZE & GROWTH RATE 3'–5' tall and wide, medium growing.

TEXTURE & FORM Coarse texture and mounded form.

FOLIAGE Dark green broadly ovate to cordate leaves 3"–6" long have serrate margins and acuminate tips. Fall foliage is poor.

LIGHT & SOIL Light to moderate shade with consistently moist but well-drained soil.

MAINTENANCE Lightly prune in late winter to encourage stouter stems to support the large flower heads. Provide supplemental water during summer droughts. Deer devour them.

NOTES & CULTIVARS
'Annabelle' and 'Incrediball' are popular commercial cultivars with showy rounded mopheads 6"–12" in diameter of sterile white flowers in late May to mid-June. They combine well with hostas, ferns, camellias, and other plants that prefer light shade. Their heavy flower heads tend to droop over unless properly pruned to encourage stout stems.

'Haas Halo' produces a lacecap-type flower head.

top 'Annabelle' in a private garden by SWH Associates, Knoxville, Tenn.

bottom 'Haas Halo'.

Hydrangea macrophylla
GARDEN OR FRENCH HYDRANGEA

Garden hydrangeas have come back into prominence in the past decade due to the development of numerous cultivars that offer both a choice of flower color and a choice of sizes. Some newer cultivars will even rebloom throughout the summer. Their showy flowers and coarse texture invite their massed use in lightly shaded shrub borders, in courtyards, and beside patios. Mix in some rudbeckias or Shasta daisies for complementary colors.

top Lacecap flowerhead and foliage.
bottom A blue mophead.

ZONES & ORIGIN 5b–9a. Native to Asia.

SIZE & GROWTH RATE 5'–8' tall and wide, medium fast growing.

TEXTURE & FORM Coarse texture and broadly oval to mounded form.

FOLIAGE Simple lustrous opposite leaves 4"–8" long are ovate shaped, with coarsely serrate margins and acuminate tips but no autumn color.

FLOWERS Large rounded (mophead) or flat-topped (lacecap) terminal corymbs with pink to blue petals occur in late spring to early summer (typically late May to late June in Athens). Flower color is influenced by pH and the availability of aluminum ions in the soil. A pH of 5.5 or lower produces blue flowers, 5.5–6.5 produces bluish-purple petals, and 6.5 or greater produces pink flowers. Flowers have no fragrance.

FRUIT Insignificant capsules.

LIGHT & SOIL Light to moderate shade is best with a loose, moist, but well-drained soil. Plants in full shade don't bloom heavily. They tolerate some salt spray.

MAINTENANCE Plants are not drought resistant and need cool roots and consistent summer moisture, so mulch in spring and fall and water weekly during dry summers. Prune immediately after flowering is finished in early summer.

INSTALLATION Container plants are abundant. Space plants 4'–6' apart.

PESTS & DISEASES Deer love them, and slugs cause problems in moist soils.

NOTES & CULTIVARS
Mophead cultivars include the following:

'All Summer Beauty' reaches 5'.
'Dooley' reaches 5' with cold-hardy buds.
'Nikko Blue' reaches 6'.
'Paris Rapa' reaches 3' with pinkish-red blooms.
'Penny Mac' is a rebloomer that reaches 6'.

Lacecap cultivars include the following:

'Blue Wave' reaches 6'.
'Twist and Shout' is a rebloomer that reaches 5'.
'Variegata' reaches 6' with creamy-white-margined foliage.

left Hydrangea heaven.
right Blue lacecaps.

Itea virginica VIRGINIA SWEETSPIRE

Virginia sweetspire is a tough native shrub of streambanks, swamps, and low moist areas of the southeastern Coastal Plain. Attractive late spring flowers and outstanding fall foliage provide opportunities to utilize it in designs. Its fine texture and arching form provide a contrast to other shrubs in compositions. Combine it with other moisture-loving plants such as inkberry, clethra, equisetum, Siberian iris, and sweetbay magnolia near streams or water features and allow it to arch over the water.

Foliage and flowers.

ZONES & ORIGIN 5b–10a. Native from eastern Texas to New Jersey.

SIZE & GROWTH RATE 4'–6' tall and wide, medium growing.

TEXTURE & FORM Medium fine texture with arching branches and mounded form.

FOLIAGE Simple elliptic alternate leaves 1½"–5" long have finely serrate margins and acuminate tips. The leaves turn yellow orange to deep red in autumn. Summer and early autumn droughts may cause early defoliation.

FLOWERS Terminal racemes of lightly fragrant white flowers appear in mid-spring (late April to mid-May in Athens).

FRUIT Insignificant capsules remain into winter, making identification easy.

LIGHT & SOIL Full sun to light shade with slightly acidic and consistently moist soils is ideal. It tolerates moderate shade but becomes more upright and open, with fewer flowers and less fall foliage color.

MAINTENANCE Virginia sweetspire naturally spreads by underground root suckers, so either allow it room to spread or be prepared to remove the new stems on a yearly basis. To maintain its height, prune older stems immediately after flowering. Provide supplemental water for young plants for several years and for more established plants during severe summer droughts.

INSTALLATION Container plants are readily available. Plant 4' on center in a loose soil mixture.

PESTS & DISEASES Leaf spot fungus can cause early defoliation. Deer seem to enjoy it too.

NOTES & CULTIVARS 'Henry's Garnet' has become the standard available cultivar, with longer flower racemes, a deep red to maroon fall foliage, and cold-hardiness to zone 5a. 'Little Henry' and 'Merlot' reach 3'–4' in height and spread, with reddish-purple fall foliage.

Itea with foamflower at Shoemaker Green at the University of Pennsylvania and in a swale with equisetum in Chattanooga.

Jasminum floridum FLORIDA JASMINE

With its arching spreading branching habit, fine texture, and green stems, Florida jasmine is preferred more for its form and habit than for its yellow late spring and early summer flowers. Take advantage of its natural form by planting it above retaining walls or in raised planters to allow it to billow over and soften the edges. Because of its ability to root where the stems reach the ground, it is sometimes used on steep embankments to creep down the slope like a large ground cover.

Foliage.

ZONES & ORIGIN 7b–10b. Native to China.

SIZE & GROWTH RATE 3'–5' tall and wide, medium growing.

TEXTURE & FORM Fine texture with arching stems and a mounded form.

FOLIAGE Compound leaves with three, rarely five leaflets are alternately arranged on green angular stems. Individual leaflets are glossy green, ¾"–1½" long, with finely serrate margins and sharply acute tips. Terminal leaflets are about twice the size of the others. Florida jasmine is semievergreen in zones 7b and 8a.

FLOWERS Lightly fragrant yellow star-shaped flowers emerge in early April in Athens and continue sporadically into June. The flowers arise after the new spring growth, so they are somewhat obscured by the foliage. Since it flowers for an extended period, it never produces a strong show.

FRUIT Insignificant.

LIGHT & SOIL Florida jasmine prefers full sun to light shade and well-drained soils.

MAINTENANCE Arching stems have the ability to root where they touch the ground, so either provide it room to spread or be prepared to severely prune it to maintain a desirable size. After becoming established, it appears to be fairly drought resistant.

INSTALLATION Plants can be difficult to locate. Space 4' on center.

PESTS & DISEASES No significant problems. Deer will nibble but not destroy them.

NOTES & CULTIVARS
Primrose jasmine, *Jasminum mesnyi*, has yellow semidouble midspring flowers. Hardy to zone 8a, it reaches 8' tall and 15' wide. It is often planted on large embankments, where its branches can arch over to cover the slope. It requires pruning to maintain density.

left Jasminum mesnyi at Samford University, Birmingham, Ala.

right In bloom with some spiderworts.

Kerria japonica JAPANESE KERRIA

Japanese kerria is one of those plants that people either love or hate—there's not much middle ground. For the unimpressed, it's a dense pile of twigs that looks like a bird's nest for much of the year. Aficionados recognize its unusual habit, tough nature, and showy yellow flowers, which provide an alternative to azaleas and a complement for spiraeas for spring color. Kerria is an old-garden plant that has enjoyed some resurgence in its popularity in recent years. Consider using it in mixed shrub borders or in masses with an evergreen ground cover or low evergreen shrub such as dwarf gardenia to provide it with a base.

ZONES & ORIGIN   5a–9b. Native to Japan.

SIZE & GROWTH RATE   4'–6' tall, 5'–8' wide, medium fast growing.

TEXTURE & FORM   Medium fine texture in foliage, very fine in winter, with a mounded form.

FOLIAGE   Simple ovate-shaped alternate leaves 1½"–3½" long have doubly serrate margins and long acuminate tips on green zigzag stems. Foliage remains green until late fall, with the green stems quite noticeable in winter.

FLOWERS   Bright yellow nonfragrant flowers arise along the stems in early to midspring (late March with a peak in mid-April in Athens). Light flowering continues into early summer.

FRUIT   Insignificant.

LIGHT & SOIL   Full sun to light shade with a loose well-drained soil is ideal. It tolerates moderate shade and higher soil pH levels and becomes quite drought tolerant with age.

MAINTENANCE   Kerria produces numerous stems from the roots; stems may need to be removed yearly to keep it in bounds. With maturity, it can be severely pruned after flowering to keep it dense and manageable in size.

INSTALLATION   Container plants can be found with some searching. Space plants on 5' centers.

PESTS & DISEASES   With good drainage, very few problems should be expected. Deer rarely damage them.

NOTES & CULTIVARS
'Honshu' produces large single-petaled flowers.
'Picta' produces variegated foliage with creamy-white margins.
'Pleniflora', a double-flowered cultivar, is quite common and very popular.
'Shannon' is a vigorous grower with single flowers.

top left   With Chinese snowball viburnum in Watkinsville, Ga.

top right and middle   At the University of Illinois.

bottom   Foliage

Rhododendron canescens PIEDMONT AZALEA

Why is a native deciduous shrub with such lovely and fragrant spring flowers, an attractive branching habit, and a clean and neat personality not in greater demand? For woodland gardens, especially near footpaths, few plants can compare to the piedmont azalea. It's a plant worthy of consideration for patios, courtyards, and anywhere you might want to place a specimen plant. Combine it with ferns, hostas, and native stone. Mature plants are attractive when limbed up into small trees, especially with night lighting.

top Early spring flowers and foliage.
middle 'Admiral Semmes' azalea at Don Shaw's residence in Athens.
bottom left Rhododendron canescens on Signal Mountain, Tenn.
bottom right Florida flame azalea in the Founders Memorial Garden.

ZONES & ORIGIN 6a–9b. Native to shaded slopes of the southeastern United States.

SIZE & GROWTH RATE 5'–8' tall, 4'–6' wide, slow growing. Plants in nature may reach 12'.

TEXTURE & FORM Medium texture and oval form.

FOLIAGE Simple elliptic to oblanceolate alternate leaves 1½"–4" long are pubescent with entire margins and acute tips and clustered near the ends of the stems without fall color.

FLOWERS Fragrant tubular-shaped pinkish-white flowers appear in rounded clusters of ten or more with the new leaves in early spring (late March to mid-April in Athens). Flower color and fragrance vary with individual plants.

FRUIT Insignificant capsules.

LIGHT & SOIL Piedmont azaleas prefer light shade and a moist but well-drained acidic soil. They tolerate full sun to moderate shade, but plants in full sun are prone to foliage burn in summer, while those in shade have reduced flowering.

MAINTENANCE Maintain 2"–3" of organic mulch. Prune immediately after flowering in midspring, and provide supplemental water during summer droughts.

INSTALLATION Piedmont azaleas are rare in nurseries. Specialty nurseries provide container plants. Space 4'–5' apart.

PESTS & DISEASES Watch for lace bugs and spider mites. Deer eat young stems and foliage.

NOTES & CULTIVARS
'Varnadoes Pink' and 'Camilla's Blush' provide pink flowers.
Florida flame azalea, *Rhododendron austrinum*, blooms at the same time, with yellow-orange flowers.
'Admiral Semmes' is a deciduous hybrid with *Rhododendron austrinum* as one of the parents. Flowering shortly after piedmont azalea, it reaches 8' with an upright form and lightly fragrant bright yellow flowers.

Rhododendron prunifolium PLUMLEAF AZALEA

A rare native plant, plumleaf azalea deserves much greater use. Its midsummer flowers provide color to woodland plantings and shrub borders at a time when few other shrubs are in bloom. Provide this native shrub with some afternoon shade, and locate it where you can appreciate the brilliant red flowers and the hummingbirds that they attract. Like piedmont azalea, its attractive branching habit is suited for consideration as a specimen plant near patios and entryways or in courtyards. Combine plumleaf azaleas in borders with ferns, hostas, hydrangeas, fothergillas, and other plants that prefer light to moderate shade.

ZONES & ORIGIN 5b–9b. Native to wooded slopes near streams in southern Georgia and Alabama.

SIZE & GROWTH RATE 6'–10' tall and wide, slow growing.

TEXTURE & FORM Medium texture and broadly oval form.

FOLIAGE Simple elliptic to slightly obovate alternate leaves 1¾"–3½" long with minutely hairy margins and acuminate tips are clustered near the ends of the stems. They provide no significant fall color. Plumleaf azalea may be differentiated from piedmont azalea by its slightly glabrous leaves and prominent depressed veins.

FLOWERS Orange-red to deep red non-fragrant flowers occur in clusters of eight or more in midsummer and are popular with hummingbirds. Flower color and time seem to vary by individual genetics. In Athens, flowering may occur from late June to mid-August.

FRUIT Insignificant capsules.

LIGHT & SOIL Light shade with a moist but well-drained acidic soil is ideal. They tolerate moderate shade with reduced flowering.

MAINTENANCE Maintain mulch throughout the year, and provide supplemental water during prolonged summer droughts. Pruning at any time of the year destroys flower buds, since the following year's buds are already set when it blooms in summer.

INSTALLATION Plants are difficult to find in nurseries, even from specialty growers. Before planting, loosen the root ball and spread the roots into the soil to facilitate their spread. Space 4'–6' on center.

PESTS & DISEASES Lace bugs and spider mites occur with drought stress. Deer eat young stems and foliage.

top left Flowering in the woods.

top right Flowering at the State Botanical Garden of Georgia.

middle Foliage with depressed veins and flower buds.

bottom Foliage and flowers.

Rosa 'Radrazz' RED KNOCK OUT ROSE

Traditional roses have been relegated to the domain of highly dedicated gardeners due to their high maintenance requirements. The recent introduction of Knock Out Roses has enabled even casual gardeners to enjoy extended floral displays with no greater maintenance efforts than those required for most hydrangeas or spiraeas. Knock Outs are eye-catching in masses, while individual plants are equally effective in mixed borders or containers.

Red Knock Outs in planters on the UGA campus.

top to bottom
Red Knock Outs in Chattanooga.
Drift Series Roses in Chattanooga.
Pink Knock Outs with daylilies in Athens.

ZONES & ORIGIN 5a–10b. A man-made cross.

SIZE & GROWTH RATE 4'–5' tall and wide, fast growing.

TEXTURE & FORM Medium texture and broadly oval form.

FOLIAGE Pinnately compound lustrous green leaves have five ovate leaflets 1¼"–3" long with serrate margins, acuminate tips, a few bristles beneath the rachis, and a short prickle at the node.

FLOWERS Very lightly fragrant pinkish-red flowers occur in clusters of three to five from spring to late autumn (late March into November in Athens). Heaviest flowering occurs in cycles of four to six weeks during the season.

FRUIT Insignificant.

LIGHT & SOIL Full sun with a moist but well-drained soil is ideal. They tolerate light shade and some drought. Consistent summer moisture helps promote new growth and flowers.

MAINTENANCE Prune heavily every other year in early spring. Light pruning in season stimulates new flowers. Avoid overhead watering.

INSTALLATION Container plants are readily available for early spring to midautumn planting. Space 4' apart for massing.

PESTS & DISEASES Rosa rosette disease, a deadly virus spread by mites, is a serious problem for Knock Out and other cultivated roses. At the first sign of distorted new growth, prune back heavily and destroy the cuttings. Deer devour them.

NOTES & CULTIVARS
'Radcon' has single pink flowers.
'Radcor' has single pink petals with yellow centers.
'Radral' has orange-red double flowers.
'Radsunny' has double yellow flowers that fade to white.
'Radtko' has double red flowers.
'Radtkopink' has double pink flowers.
'Radyod' has light pink double flowers.
Drift Rose series have low mounded forms suitable for ground covers or borders, with white, pink, and red-flowered cultivars and some light fragrance.

Spiraea cantoniensis REEVES SPIRAEA

Reeves spiraea is a common component of spring landscapes in the Southeast. Its brilliant white flowers provide an outstanding complement to the purples, reds, and pinks of evergreen or deciduous azaleas, which bloom at the same time. A mounded form with soft gracefully arching branches invites its use in raised planters and retaining walls, where it can soften hard edges, or upon slopes, where it appears to cascade down the hill. A tough nature and easy maintenance make this a mainstay of shrub borders.

ZONES & ORIGIN 6a–9a. Native to China.

SIZE & GROWTH RATE 4'–6' tall and wide, medium fast growing.

TEXTURE & FORM Medium texture in leaf, medium fine in winter, and mounded form.

FOLIAGE Simple bluish-green alternate leaves ¾"–2½" long occur on upright arching branches. Oblanceolate in shape, with doubly serrate margins, they provide no significant fall color.

FLOWERS Showy white nonfragrant flowers are held in rounded clusters along the stems in early spring. In Athens, flowering time ranges from late March to late April, with the best show in early to mid-April. Reeves spiraea makes quite a show in bloom.

FRUIT Insignificant follicle.

LIGHT & SOIL Full sun and a well-drained soil are ideal, but it grows and even flowers well in up to moderate shade. It tolerates near-neutral pH levels and is very drought tolerant after establishment.

MAINTENANCE Reeves is a very low maintenance plant. To control its size while keeping its natural form, prune back older stems to the ground in late spring after flowering. Supplemental water is rarely needed.

INSTALLATION Container-grown plants are readily available and can be planted virtually year-round on 4'–5' centers.

PESTS & DISEASES No serious problems are reported. All of the spiraeas are very tough and tolerant plants. Deer should not present much of a problem with any spiraea.

NOTES & CULTIVARS
The double-flowered Reeves, 'Lanceata', is probably more popular and available than the species. From a distance it appears identical to the species. Only upon close inspection are the double petals evident.

top right and left Double Reeves at Longwood Gardens.

middle Double Reeves spiraea.

bottom Reeves spiraea flowers.

top left and right Form at the Georgia Center and in the Founders Memorial Garden.

middle and bottom Flowers in the Founders Memorial Garden.

Spiraea prunifolia 'Plena' BRIDALWREATH SPIRAEA

Few deciduous shrubs provide a show of flowers in the early spring to compare with bridalwreath spiraea. Flowering several weeks before the dogwoods, azaleas, and other more familiar spiraeas begin, the bridalwreath complements other early spring flowering plants such as quince, edgeworthia, forsythia, and saucer magnolia. Since their flower display can be appreciated from a distance, take advantage of their upright form by using them as accents toward the rear of shrub borders, and provide them an evergreen base of Indian hawthorn, Kurume azalea, 'Vintage Jade' distylium, or even Parson's juniper. Use in moderation, since bridalwreath spiraeas can look nondescript at other times of the year.

ZONES & ORIGIN 5a–8b. Native to Asia.

SIZE & GROWTH RATE 5'–7' tall, 3'–5' wide, medium fast growing.

TEXTURE & FORM Fine texture with upright arching stems and upright oval form.

FOLIAGE Simple glossy dark green ovate to elliptic alternate leaves ¾"–1½" long have finely serrate margins and blunt tips. Their yellow fall color is insignificant.

FLOWERS Showy white nonfragrant flowers with double petals are held in clusters along the stems in early spring (from early to late March in Athens). The rounded flowers are approximately ¼" in diameter with green centers and make quite a show before the foliage emerges.

FRUIT Insignificant.

LIGHT & SOIL It prefers full sun but tolerates up to moderate shade with reduced flowering and well-drained soil. It is drought tolerant and doesn't appear sensitive to pH.

MAINTENANCE To maintain the plant's size while keeping its natural form, prune back older stems to the ground in spring after flowering. Otherwise, it has very few demands or problems.

INSTALLATION Container plants can be found with some searching. They can be planted virtually year-round. For massing, space 3'–4' apart.

PESTS & DISEASES No serious problems are reported. Deer will nibble on the foliage and young stems but seldom do severe damage to mature plants.

NOTES & CULTIVARS
The species with single flowers is extremely rare.

Spiraea thunbergii BABY'S BREATH SPIRAEA

Baby's breath spiraea is a tough and dependable old-garden plant that often provides the first hint of the coming spring. This late winter to early spring bloomer doesn't perform as well in the South as it does in cooler climates. In zones 7 and 8, the flower display occurs over a month or more and rarely achieves enough vitality to merit its consideration. From a design standpoint, its greatest attribute may be its extremely fine texture and billowy habit, which stand out in contrast to other shrubs. Flowering cut stems are effective in flower arrangements.

ZONES & ORIGIN 4b–8b. Native to Asia.

SIZE & GROWTH RATE 5'–7' tall, 4'–6' wide, medium growing.

TEXTURE & FORM Very fine texture and dense billowy rounded form.

FOLIAGE Simple light green alternate leaves ¾"–1¾" long are linear to linear-lanceolate in shape, with finely serrate margins and acute tips, and occur on thin wiry zigzag stems. Its late autumn orange-yellow fall color is usually insignificant.

FLOWERS Tiny white nonfragrant flowers occur along the stems in late winter and very early spring. In Athens, flowering sometimes begins in late January, typically peaking in late February and early March, with flowers extending into late March. The flowers are more effective in cooler locations, where the flowering time is condensed into two to three weeks.

FRUIT Insignificant.

LIGHT & SOIL Provide full sun to light shade with well-drained soil. They are quite drought tolerant.

MAINTENANCE After establishment, plants may need to be pruned annually to thin out older nonproductive stems and encourage a denser habit. Remove older stems down to the ground, never shear. Prune after flowering is completed in spring.

INSTALLATION Container plants are readily available and can be planted year-round on 5' centers.

PESTS & DISEASES No serious problems have been reported. Deer will nibble on the foliage and young stems, but this plant is not their favorite.

NOTES & CULTIVARS
'Fujino Pink' produces pink flower buds. 'Mount Fuji' produces variegated foliage. 'Ogon' produces bright yellow spring foliage that turns green during the season.

top Flowers close up.
middle Foliage.
bottom left Summer foliage color.
bottom right In bloom.

Foliage.

top right and middle Midspring flowers on Signal Mountain, Tenn.

bottom Behind a wall in Chattanooga.

Spiraea × vanhouttei VANHOUTTE SPIRAEA

Vanhoutte spiraea has been a popular and dependable garden plant for decades throughout most of the United States. Its highly attractive midspring flowers complement azaleas, which are in bloom at the same time. Its blue-green foliage, upright arching form, relatively fine texture, and overall tolerance to a range of cultural situations provide opportunities to use it in a variety of situations. From massing to background plantings or in mixed shrub borders, this spiraea performs admirably. Place it behind some southern indica azaleas, spreading camellias, or 'Duke Gardens' plum yews to take advantage of its upright arching branching. Just make sure to provide it with enough space.

ZONES & ORIGIN 3b–8b. A cross between two Asian spiraeas.

SIZE & GROWTH RATE 6'–9' tall, 5'–8' wide, medium fast growing.

TEXTURE & FORM Medium fine texture with upright arching branches and broadly oval form.

FOLIAGE Simple bluish-green alternate leaves ½"–1¾" long are elliptic to ovate shaped with coarse doubly serrate or occasionally lobed margins. In sunny locations, it develops a fair orange to deep red fall color late in the season but is not always consistent.

FLOWERS Showy white nonfragrant flowers occur in clusters 1" in diameter along the stems in early spring. In Athens, flowering typically begins in early April, peaking in mid-April, with some flowers extending to late in the month.

FRUIT Insignificant follicles.

LIGHT & SOIL Provide full sun to light shade and well-drained soil. It tolerates up to moderate shade and moderately acidic to slightly alkaline soil and is quite drought tolerant.

MAINTENANCE To maintain it at a smaller height while keeping its natural form, prune back older stems to the ground in late spring after flowering. Shearing will destroy its form.

INSTALLATION Container plants are readily available and can be planted year-round on 4'–6' centers.

PESTS & DISEASES No serious problems are reported. Deer will nibble on the foliage but are unlikely to severely damage mature plants.

NOTES & CULTIVARS
'Renaissance' is slightly smaller in size.

SMALL SHRUBS

While they may be small in stature, these plants nevertheless have important roles to play in design compositions, providing the very foundation or beginning of most designs. Whether they are used as a ground cover, as a border or edging for larger plants, or even as an accent, their role is to provide a solid footing for all of the other plants in the composition to display their attributes. A few of these plants even provide the added benefit of showy flowers, fragrance, or fruit in addition to their foliage.

Small deciduous shrubs are often most effectively used in groupings of three to five plants in larger compositions. However, occasionally a single plant is all that is necessary to attract attention in a large shrub and perennial border. Due to their small size, make sure to place them at or near the front of the composition. Otherwise, their ornamental attributes will be lost behind larger shrubs or perennials.

Since most of these small deciduous shrubs only draw attention to themselves during one season of the year, make sure to surround them with other plants that will provide interest when they are not in bloom.

One thing you must keep in mind when using these small plants. More so than with any other category of plant

Dwarf English boxwoods in the Founders Memorial Garden.

in this book, it is critical when using small plants such as these to combine them with other plants that share similar cultural requirements. Their small stature generally translates into shallower, less extensive root systems. As a result, their ability to compensate for less than ideal conditions is greatly reduced in comparison with larger plants. So whether you are using them with herbaceous perennials, larger shrubs, or even trees, make sure to give them the chance to survive and thrive. The very foundation of your design depends upon it.

BOTANICAL NAME	SUNLIGHT	SOILS	TEXTURE	ORNAMENTAL FLOWERS	ORNAMENTAL ATTRIBUTES	NATIVE TO SOUTHEAST
EVERGREEN SPECIES						
Abelia × grandiflora 'Sherwoodii'	Full sun to light shade	Well drained	Fine	White from May into November	Dense mass, lightly fragrant flowers	No, man-made cross from Asia
Ardisia japonica	Moderate to heavy shade	Moist but well drained acidic	Medium coarse	No	Groundcovers, detail design	No, Asia
Buxus sempervirens 'Suffruticosa'	Light to moderate shade	Moist but well drained near neutral pH	Fine	No	Formal garden border plantings	No, southern Europe, North Africa
Daphne odora	Light to moderate shade	Moist but well drained	Medium fine	Late winter pink, white, and red	Lightly fragrant flowers	No, China
Distylium × 'Vintage Jade'	Light shade	Moist but well drained acidic	Medium fine	No	Spreading form, tough plant	No, man-made cross from Asia
Gardenia jasminoides 'Radicans'	Full sun to light shade	Moist but well drained	Medium fine	White in late spring	Lightly fragrant flowers	No, China
Ilex cornuta 'Carissa'	Full sun to light shade	Well drained acidic	Medium	No	Dense mounded form	No, Asia
Ilex crenata 'Helleri'	Full sun to light shade	Well drained acidic to neutral	Fine	No	Dense mounded form	No, Asia
Juniperus chinensis 'Parsonii'	Full sun	Well drained to dry	Fine	No	Dense, flat-topped habit	No, Asia
Juniperus conferta	Full sun	Well drained to dry	Fine	No	Fast-growing trailing form	No, Asia
Juniperus horizontalis 'Wiltonii'	Full sun	Well drained to dry	Fine	No	Low, trailing habit	No, Canada and New England
Juniperus procumbens	Full sun	Well drained to dry	Fine	No	Dense, spreading form	No, Asia
Leucothoe axillaris	Light to moderate shade	Moist to moist but well drained	Medium fine	White in mid- to late spring	Loose spreading habit	Yes
Mahonia eurybracteata 'Soft Caress'	Moderate shade	Moist but well drained	Fine	Bright yellow midautumn	Fall flowers winter foliage	No, Asia
Mahonia fortunei	Moderate shade	Moist but well drained	Medium fine	Yellow summer	Informal appearance	No, Asia
Rhododendron × eriocarpum	Light to moderate shade	Moist but well drained acidic	Fine	Multiple colors in late spring	Mounded form late spring color	No, Asia
Rosmarinus officinalis	Full sun	Well drained	Fine	Blue, late fall to early spring	Fragrant foliage Culinary favorite	No, North Africa, southern Europe
Ruscus aculeatus	Moderate to full shade	Well drained	Fine	No	Leaflike stems are an oddity	No, North Africa, southern Europe
Sarcococca confusa	Moderate shade	Moist but well drained	Medium fine	Creamy white late winter	Lightly fragrant winter flowers	No, Asia
Thuja occidentalis 'Danica'	Full sun to light shade	Moist but well drained	Fine	No	Dense, rounded form	No but North American native
Yucca filamentosa	Full sun to light shade	Moist but well drained to dry	Coarse	Creamy white in late spring	Exotic-looking native shrub	Yes

BOTANICAL NAME	SUNLIGHT	SOILS	TEXTURE	ORNAMENTAL FLOWERS	ORNAMENTAL ATTRIBUTES	NATIVE TO SOUTHEAST
DECIDUOUS SPECIES						
Deutzia gracilis	Full sun to light shade	Moist but well drained	Medium fine	White mid- to late spring	Mounding form	No, Asia
Jasminum nudiflorum	Full sun to light shade	Moist but well drained	Medium fine	Yellow mid winter	Green stems, spreading form	No, Asia
Punica granatum nana	Full sun to light shade	Well drained	Medium fine	Orange red early summer	Small edible fruit	No, Europe and Asia
Rhus aromatica	Full sun to light shade	Well drained	Medium	No	Orange to deep red fall foliage	Yes
Spiraea japonica 'Anthony Waterer'	Full sun to light shade	Moist but well drained	Fine	Dark pink late spring	Red new foliage and fall foliage	No, cross from Asian species

Abelia × *grandiflora* 'Sherwoodii' SHERWOOD ABELIA

A dwarf version of glossy abelia, Sherwood abelia forms a dense rounded mass with intertwining branches like a large bird's nest in the landscape. Its flowering is not as heavy or prominent as glossy abelia's, and it is more likely to go fully deciduous in cold winters. Consider it for a medium to large ground cover that will require occasional shearing to maintain a refined appearance or for border plantings to provide a foundation for larger shrubs. It has a tendency to produce branches that revert to its larger parent (known as "sports"), so occasional pruning is required to remove those odd branches and maintain its low dense form.

Foliage and flowers.

top to bottom

An informal border in Athens.

'Rose Creek' with sweetbay magnolia and cleyera.

'Rose Creek'.

ZONES & ORIGIN 6a–9b. A selection of a cross between two Asian species.

SIZE & GROWTH RATE 3'–5' tall, 4'–5' wide, medium growing.

TEXTURE & FORM Fine texture and mounded form.

FOLIAGE Simple glossy green opposite leaves ⅝"–1" long are ovate in shape, with serrate margins and acuminate tips. Emerging leaves are copper colored, with reddish-purple late autumn foliage.

FLOWERS Faintly fragrant white funnel-shaped flowers occur in panicles on new growth from late spring through autumn. In Athens, flowering begins in May, with sporadic flowers into November.

FRUIT Insignificant.

LIGHT & SOIL Full sun to light shade and well-drained soil. It is very drought tolerant.

MAINTENANCE Remove sport branches as they arise during the growing season.

INSTALLATION Small container-grown plants are readily available. Space 4' apart.

PESTS & DISEASES No serious issues. Deer don't like them, but occasional browsing causes problems for small plants like this.

NOTES & CULTIVARS

'Confetti' grows 3' tall with a 4'–5' spread with green foliage and white leaf margins; leaves tinge bright pink in full sun.

'Flat Creek' grows 3'–4' with a 6'–8' spread without the sport branches of 'Sherwoodii'.

'Kaleidescope' grows 2'–3' with a 3'–4' spread and leaves of green, gold, and red.

'Little Richard' is similar to 'Sherwoodii' in size but provides heavier flowering.

'Mardi Gras' is similar to 'Rose Creek' but slightly smaller, with creamy-white leaf margins.

'Radiance' grows 3' tall and 4'–5' wide, foliage green with creamy white margins fading to somewhat silver.

'Rose Creek' grows 4'–5' tall, with flowering in early June and prominent pink sepals that remain into autumn. Leaves are 1"–1½" long, with upright branching and less density than 'Sherwoodii'.

Ground cover at the Ram Giberson residence.

Ardisia japonica JAPANESE ARDISIA

Japanese ardisia is sometimes used as a ground cover for small areas in shaded locations. It combines well with natural stone and stained woods in detail designs and rock gardens and could be used as a substitute for pachysandra. Tiny pinkish-white flowers are mostly hidden on drooping clusters beneath the foliage in summer and produce a few pea-sized red berries in autumn that are not showy nor easily seen.

ZONES & ORIGIN 8a–10b. Native to Japan.

SIZE & GROWTH RATE 4"–8" tall, 2"–4" wide, slow growing.

TEXTURE & FORM Medium coarse texture. Individual plants have an oval form.

FOLIAGE Simple dark lustrous green alternate leaves 1¼"–3" long are elliptic shaped, with serrate margins and acuminate tips, and appear whorled at the ends of the stems.

LIGHT & SOIL Moderate to full shade with moist but well-drained acidic soil. Mature plantings are somewhat drought resistant.

MAINTENANCE Provide a loose soil mix to facilitate the spread of the plants. Space 12" apart and maintain a mulch on new plantings. Avoid foot traffic on the plants. Deer don't bother them.

NOTES & CULTIVARS
'Hakuokan' has foliage with creamy-white margins and reaches 12" tall.

Foliage and fruit.

Buxus sempervirens 'Suffruticosa'
DWARF ENGLISH BOXWOOD

Dwarf English boxwood's dense form is valued for border plantings in formal gardens, where it is often maintained at 6"–18" tall. Dwarf boxwoods require proper and frequent pruning at an early age in order to obtain their desired form and density and as a result can be expensive for their size. They are also particular about their cultural conditions. For sites with acidic clay soils or poor drainage, dwarf yaupon holly may provide a better alternative for formal borders.

Foliage.

ZONES & ORIGIN 5b–8b. Native to southern Europe and northern Africa.

SIZE & GROWTH RATE 4'–5' tall and wide, slow growing.

TEXTURE & FORM Fine texture with a broadly oval to rounded form.

FOLIAGE Simple dark green opposite leaves ½"–⅝" long are elliptic to ovate shaped, with entire margins and rounded or blunt tips.

FLOWERS Insignificant slightly malodorous early spring flowers.

FRUIT Insignificant.

LIGHT & SOIL Light to moderate shade with moist but well-drained, near-neutral pH soil is ideal. It tolerates full sun but neither wet soils nor drought.

MAINTENANCE Provide a deep watering weekly during summer and mulch throughout the year. Check the soil pH annually and add lime as necessary to maintain within a range of 6.5–7.5. Fertilize and prune or shear in late winter before new growth begins.

INSTALLATION Small container-grown plants are readily available and can be planted year-round in zones 7 and 8. Provide a loose soil mix with a well-drained subsoil, and space 6"–12" apart for low borders or 2'–3' for borders 3' or taller in size.

PESTS & DISEASES These aren't low-maintenance plants. Root rot fungus from poorly drained soil causes a gradual decline in vigor and may not be noticeable until too late. Boxwood blight defoliates the plant. Spider mites occur during periods of drought. Fortunately, deer don't touch them.

NOTES & CULTIVARS
Buxus × 'Glencoe' and *Buxus* × 'Green Gem' grow 3'–4' with rounded forms. *Buxus sinica insularis* 'Wee Willie' grows 2' with a rounded form to zone 5a.

left A parterre at the Founders Memorial Garden.

top right As a parterre by SWH in Knoxville, Tenn.

bottom right A sheared hedge at Bloedel Reserve.

Daphne odora WINTER DAPHNE

Winter daphne is ideally suited for detailed designs where viewers will be in close proximity. Its lightly fragrant flowers aren't impressive from more than about 10' away, so it needs to be placed where it can be appreciated. At doorway entrances; along edges of patios, walkways, or woodland paths; or in shaded rock gardens are good locations for daphne. It combines well with shade-loving plants such as ferns, ophiopogons, pachysandras, and hostas. A somewhat temperamental nature regarding its cultural requirements and an expensive price due to its slow growth are reasons to use it judiciously.

ZONES & ORIGIN 7a–9b. Native to China.

SIZE & GROWTH RATE 2'–4' tall and wide, slow growing.

TEXTURE & FORM Medium fine texture and rounded form.

FOLIAGE Simple lustrous green alternate leaves 1¼"–3" long are elliptic shaped, with entire margins and acute tips, and often appear whorled near the stem tips.

FLOWERS Somewhat showy lightly fragrant pinkish-white flowers occur on terminal stem clusters for several weeks in late winter and early spring (mid-February to mid-March in Athens). Flower buds swell and become prominent for several weeks before opening.

FRUIT Insignificant.

LIGHT & SOIL Light to moderate shade with a moist but well-drained slightly acidic to near-neutral soil is ideal. Daphne doesn't tolerate damp soils or extended drought and suffers in full sun.

MAINTENANCE Provide a deep watering weekly during summer and mulch throughout the year. Pruning should be done in early spring after flowering is completed.

INSTALLATION Container plants are available. Modify clay or sandy soils with organic matter and plant high to ensure good surface drainage. Space 2'–3' apart.

PESTS & DISEASES Root rot from excessively damp soils and leaf fungal diseases appear to be the biggest culprits. A few deer nibbles can wreak havoc on small plants like daphne.

NOTES & CULTIVARS
'Alba' produces white flowers and dark green leaves.
'Aureomarginata' and 'Rogbret' have yellow-margined leaves.
Daphne × *burkwoodii* 'Carol Mackie' is hardy from zones 4a to 8a, with creamy-white leaf margins, a mounded form, and lightly fragrant late spring flowers.

top left 'Carol Mackie'.
top right 'Aureomarginata'.
middle Foliage and flower buds.
bottom 'Aureomarginata' in bloom.

Distylium × 'Vintage Jade' VINTAGE JADE DISTYLIUM

A very new introduction, this series of evergreen shrubs seems poised to take off in the nursery industry. For informal borders that require little pruning or special maintenance, they can't be beat. Use them to provide a foundation for a larger shrub that tends to get a little leggy, like inkberry, gardenia, or pieris. Or take advantage of their spreading habit to front more upright perennials, like coneflowers, ornamental garlics, and crocosmias. Maybe even mix them with some native stone and ferns along shaded pathways. They seem to lend themselves to informal designs, but however you use them, you are likely to be pleased with their performance.

Foliage.

top to bottom

Form in Athens.

With hostas and garden hydrangeas.

With hostas and liriope.

ZONES & ORIGIN 7a–9b. A man-made cross of two Asian species.

SIZE & GROWTH RATE 2'–3' tall, 4'–6' wide, medium growing.

TEXTURE & FORM Medium fine texture and a dense spreading to mounded form.

FOLIAGE Simple lustrous green alternate leaves 1½"–2¼" long are elliptic shaped, with entire margins and acute tips.

FLOWERS Slightly showy late winter maroon flowers won't be noticeable from a distance. In Athens, flowering is late February and early March.

FRUIT Insignificant.

LIGHT & SOIL Light shade and moist but well-drained slightly acidic soil are ideal. They are surprisingly tough and perform well in full sun to moderate shade, as well as slightly moist to well-drained soils.

MAINTENANCE Prune in early spring after flowering if needed to shape or control size. Provide supplemental water for the first year and during severe droughts.

INSTALLATION Container plants are readily available. Plant year-round, ensure good surface drainage, and space plants 3' apart.

PESTS & DISEASES No problems have been reported, and deer don't seem to bother them.

NOTES & CULTIVARS

'Blue Cascade' reaches 4' with darker-blue-green foliage and a spreading form.

'Coppertone' is similar in size to 'Vintage Jade' but has coppery-red new growth that matures to a darker blue green.

'Emerald Heights' reaches 6' with a mounded to rounded outline.

'Linebacker' reaches 10' with coppery-red new foliage and a broadly oval form.

Gardenia jasminoides 'Radicans' DWARF GARDENIA

For low informal borders, few plants exceed the appeal of dwarf gardenia. A somewhat slow growth rate allows it to be easily maintained at a desired size to take advantage of its fairly showy and lightly fragrant early summer flowers. But don't limit its use to borders. It can also serve as an informal ground cover for small areas. Its spreading habit serves to soften edges of low retaining walls or the exposed edges of steps. Take advantage of its drought tolerance for sunny rock gardens too. In zones 9 and 10, it can be used for container plantings on patios or decks to take advantage of its fragrance.

Foliage.

ZONES & ORIGIN 8a–10b. Native to China.

SIZE & GROWTH RATE 12"–24" tall, 2'–4' wide, medium slow growing.

TEXTURE & FORM Medium fine texture and mounded form.

FOLIAGE Simple narrowly elliptic to lanceolate bright green opposite leaves 1"–2" long have entire margins and acuminate tips.

FLOWERS Fairly showy lightly fragrant white double-petaled flowers occur in late spring and early summer. In Athens, flowering usually begins in late May, peaking in early to mid-June, with sporadic flowers into September.

FRUIT Insignificant.

LIGHT & SOIL Full sun to light shade with moist but well-drained acidic soil is ideal. Flowering is reduced in moderate shade. They tolerate drought but not damp soils or higher pH levels.

MAINTENANCE Gardenias flower on new growth, so they can be pruned in early spring without losing any potential flowers. Provide 2" of organic mulch in spring and late autumn.

INSTALLATION Small container plants are readily available and easily transplanted from spring to midautumn. Plant high to ensure good surface drainage, and space 3' apart.

PESTS & DISEASES The biggest problems are usually associated with poor soil drainage or excessively high soil pH. Deer don't like them.

NOTES & CULTIVARS
'Frostproof' reaches 3'–4' with double flowers and a more upright habit.
'Kleim's Hardy' grows 2'–3' with single flowers, and is hardy to zone 7b.
'White Gem' has single flowers with a rounded form.

top Form in Athens.
middle and bottom Late spring flowers with lantana in Athens.

top An informal hedge at Gibbs Gardens.

bottom Foliage.

Ilex cornuta 'Carissa' CARISSA HOLLY

Carissa holly is the only member of the Chinese holly group that we can recommend for use in the landscape. A male plant, it doesn't have the invasive potential of other Chinese hollies. It is noted for its dense impenetrable canopy and used for small informal hedges, borders, and edging. For xeric landscapes, it could be combined with yuccas, palms, and junipers for compositions that require low water.

ZONES & ORIGIN 6b–9b. Native to China.

SIZE & GROWTH RATE 3'–4' tall, 4'–5' wide, slow growing.

TEXTURE & FORM Medium texture and dense mounded form.

FOLIAGE Simple medium green leaves are alternately arranged, 1½"–3" long, ovate to elliptical shaped, with entire margins, depressed veins, and a single spine on the tip.

LIGHT & SOIL Full sun to moderate shade with a well-drained soil. It reportedly tolerates salt spray.

MAINTENANCE Due to their slow growth rate, carissas take a long time to recover from severe damage to their branches. Some branches may revert to the rotunda holly. Remove those branches to prevent fruit development and maintain a consistent canopy. Deer don't bother them.

NOTES & CULTIVARS
Space 3'–4' for massing.

Ilex crenata 'Helleri'   HELLERI HOLLY

Helleri holly is used as an alternative to dwarf boxwood in the Southeast for borders and parterre gardens due to its tolerance of acidic soils and lower water requirement. It is an old but still popular cultivar with a mounding form that requires little pruning to maintain the desired size and form. In addition to its use in formal applications, it can provide a foundation for deciduous shrubs such as forsythia and spiraea and herbaceous perennials like rudbeckia and crocosmia or be combined in sunny rock gardens with dwarf conifers.

ZONES & ORIGIN   5b–8b. Native to Asia.

SIZE & GROWTH RATE   2'–4' tall, 3'–5' wide, medium slow growing.

TEXTURE & FORM   Fine texture and mounded form.

FOLIAGE   Simple lustrous dark green alternate leaves ½" long are elliptic shaped, with crenate margins and acute tips. Young yellow-green stems help differentiate them from dwarf yaupon holly's gray stems.

FLOWERS   Insignificant.

FRUIT   Insignificant fruit.

LIGHT & SOIL   Full sun to light shade with moist but well-drained acidic soil is ideal. With maturity, it tolerates some drought but is extremely sensitive to damp soils.

MAINTENANCE   Due to their slow growth, Helleri hollies rarely need pruning or shearing. Maintain several inches of mulch to keep the roots cool in summer.

INSTALLATION   Container plants are readily available and can be planted year-round at 3' apart. Amend clay soils with organic material. Mound the soil and place it slightly higher than the surrounding soil to ensure good surface drainage.

PESTS & DISEASES   Plants are very sensitive to damp soil, which contributes to numerous other problems. Black root rot disease causes a slow ugly death. Spider mites are common in hot dry summers. Deer nibble them but usually don't cause severe problems.

NOTES & CULTIVARS
'Bennett's Compact' reaches 4' with a rounded form.
'Drops of Gold' reaches 4' with a mounded form and hideous yellow foliage.
'Hoogendorn' reaches 2'–3' tall and 3'–5' wide.
'Soft Touch' reaches 2'–3' tall and wide with a rounded form and flexible branches.

top to bottom

Foliage.

Form in the Portland Japanese Garden.

Form.

'Soft Touch' border at the University of Washington.

Juniperus chinensis 'Parsonii' PARSON'S JUNIPER

Parson's juniper is often used for border plantings to take advantage of its upright spreading branching habit. Although it can be utilized for ground covers, its branches remain angled upright instead of spreading along the ground, which prevents it from easily trailing down a slope or over retaining walls and steps. Use it to provide a foundation for larger shrubs or herbaceous perennials behind it. Due to its cold-hardiness, it could be used for container plantings or trained as a bonsai to highlight its upright branching.

Foliage.

ZONES & ORIGIN   5a–10a. Native to Asia.

SIZE & GROWTH RATE   2'–3' tall, 4'–8' wide, medium fast growing.

TEXTURE & FORM   Fine texture with a flattened spreading to mounded form.

FOLIAGE   Grayish-green foliage primarily consists of scalelike needles with a few stems of sharply pointed awl-shaped foliage. The branches ascend upward between 30° and 45° above horizontal.

FLOWERS   Insignificant flowers.

FRUIT   A female plant, its insignificant blue berry-like cones are helpful in identification.

LIGHT & SOIL   Full sun to light shade with well-drained soil. It tolerates drought, slightly alkaline soils, and moderate salt spray.

MAINTENANCE   Avoid watering except during extreme drought. Plants can be lightly pruned from late winter to late summer.

INSTALLATION   Container-grown plants are readily available and can be planted year-round. Amend and mound clay soils to ensure good surface and internal drainage. Space plants 4' on center.

PESTS & DISEASES   Parson's juniper can be somewhat short-lived due to excessive soil moisture causing fungal root diseases. Deer don't touch them.

NOTES & CULTIVARS

Parson's juniper was previously listed as *Juniperus davurica* 'Expansa', *J. davurica* 'Parsonii', and *J. squamata expansa* 'Parsonii'.

Juniperus chinensis 'Sea Green' reaches 4'–5' with a feathery appearance and light green ascending branches.

Juniperus virginiana 'Grey Owl' reaches 3' tall and 6' wide, with gray-green foliage and ascending branches that are pendulous on their ends. Hardy to zone 3b, it produces numerous blue berry-like cones.

Juniperus virginiana 'Silver Spreader' reaches 3' tall and 4'–8' wide, with silvery-green foliage and ascending branches.

top and bottom left   Informal ground covers in Athens.

right   Foliage at Belfair Plantation near Hilton Head, S.C.

Juniperus conferta SHORE JUNIPER

For low maintenance ground covers in well-drained sunny locations, few choices fit the bill like shore juniper. What could be better than a ground cover that tolerates drought, salt, alkaline soils, and deer and doesn't require any supplemental water or pruning? In fact, it's too easy. Too often, shore juniper is specified for every parking lot island, street embankment, or roadway median to the point of monotony. Like everything else, use it in moderation. A little goes a long way. Consider it for rock gardens or to soften retaining walls or edges of steps to take advantage of its branches, which turn upward and lend a sweeping appearance.

ZONES & ORIGIN 5b–8b. Native to Japan.

SIZE & GROWTH RATE 12"–18" tall, 4'–8' wide, medium fast growing.

TEXTURE & FORM Fine texture and spreading form.

FOLIAGE Blue-green awl-like needles, approximately ½" long, occur in clusters along the stems, providing a whorled appearance. The needles have a silvery band, and the entire foliage develops a yellow-green tint in winter.

FLOWERS A dioecious plant, with neither sex producing significant flowers.

FRUIT Blue pea-sized berry-like cones on female plants are insignificant.

LIGHT & SOIL Full sun with well-drained soils is ideal. It is highly tolerant of drought, salt spray, and slightly alkaline soil pH but only tolerates light shade.

MAINTENANCE Normally, little maintenance is required. Watch for yellow jacket and wasp nests should you decide to prune it in summer. Mulches and preemergent herbicides help control invasive grasses and other plants until junipers grow together.

INSTALLATION Container plants are readily available. Plant in well-drained sunny locations on 4' centers or on 3' centers for the smaller cultivars.

PESTS & DISEASES Spider mites and bagworms can occur. With good cultural conditions, serious problems are rare. Deer don't even look at them.

NOTES & CULTIVARS
'Blue Lagoon' grows 8" tall, forming a dense mat, with plum-colored winter foliage.
'Blue Pacific', the most common cultivar, reaches 12" tall with a more refined appearance than the species and silvery-blue-green foliage that doesn't discolor in winter.

Covering a retaining wall in winter.

left 'Blue Pacific' in Athens.
top right 'Blue Pacific' covering a retaining wall above Indian hawthorns.
bottom right 'Blue Pacific' with 'Sea Green' juniper.

Juniperus horizontalis 'Wiltonii' BLUE RUG JUNIPER

Too often, people are tempted to use blue rug and other creeping junipers to cover large open areas. While they generally perform well in those situations, they can be quite boring and have maintenance issues until they become well established. Instead of planting them in large massive areas, consider using them to soften tops of retaining walls, or utilize their spreading habit to hide the edges of exposed steps. Combine them in rock gardens with other sun-loving and drought-resistant plants like rosemary, lantana, salvia, yucca, or other conifers. Just be sure to use them in moderation.

At the University of Illinois.

top to bottom
Covering a retaining wall in Athens.
At Longwood Gardens.
'Plumosa Compacta' winter foliage color.

ZONES & ORIGIN 3a–9a. Native from New England to Nova Scotia.

SIZE & GROWTH RATE 2"–4" tall, 4'–6' wide, medium fast growing.

TEXTURE & FORM Fine texture and prostrate trailing form.

FOLIAGE Scalelike silvery-blue-green needles are predominant, with a few sharply pointed needles. The foliage takes on a light purple tint over winter.

FLOWERS Insignificant.

FRUIT Insignificant.

LIGHT & SOIL Full sun and well-drained soil are best. It tolerates drought, moderate salt spray, and alkaline soils but only light shade.

MAINTENANCE The biggest problem involves invading weeds until the junipers have grown together. Common Bermuda grass thrives in those open sunny locations, but other grasses and even tree seedlings invade as well. Providing a landscape fabric over the soil at the time of planting is a good start, but preemergent herbicides may still be required.

INSTALLATION Container plants are readily available and should be planted 3'–4' on center.

PESTS & DISEASES Generally, no serious problems in well-drained soils. Twig blight and spider mites can occur. Deer don't touch them.

NOTES & CULTIVARS
'Bar Harbor' reaches 12" tall, with awl-shaped foliage that turns purple in winter.
'Blue Chip' grows 8"–12" tall but is better adapted to cooler climates.
'Hughes' grows to 12" tall, with just a hint of purple in winter.
'Plumosa', the Andorra juniper, grows about 2' tall, with purplish winter foliage.
'Plumosa Compacta', dwarf Andorra juniper, is similar to Andorra but only grows 12"–18" tall.

Juniperus procumbens JAPANESE GARDEN JUNIPER

From a design aspect, Japanese garden juniper shares many similar attributes with Parson's juniper. Similar in size, it differs by being a little slower growing and by having the ability for its branches to spread along the ground or trail over retaining walls. The primary difference in identification deals with the needles: Parson's juniper has primarily scalelike foliage, while Japanese garden juniper foliage consists of sharp awl-shaped needles. Like Parson's juniper, it can be used for borders and edging, but it is equally capable of softening the tops of retaining walls and the edges of steps, and it makes a good large container plant. Use it with native stone in rock gardens, and combine it with other drought-tolerant species like yuccas, palms, and chastetrees.

Foliage.

ZONES & ORIGIN 4b–9a. Native to Asia.

SIZE & GROWTH RATE 18"–30" tall, 6'–10' wide, medium growing.

TEXTURE & FORM Fine texture and spreading form.

FOLIAGE Sharply pointed blue-green awl-shaped needles can be painful to touch. Stiff spreading branches form a dense mass.

FLOWERS A dioecious species; neither sex provides significant flowers.

FRUIT Insignificant silvery-blue berry-like cones are produced on female plants.

LIGHT & SOIL Full sun with well-drained soil is ideal. It tolerates drought and alkaline soils but only light shade.

MAINTENANCE Prune from late winter to late summer to control size if necessary. Pruning and removing debris and tree leaves can be difficult and painful without adequate protection. Provide supplemental water only during cases of severe drought.

INSTALLATION Container-grown plants are widely available. Plant 4' apart in well-drained soils year-round in zones 7–9.

PESTS & DISEASES No serious problems, provided the soil is well drained. Deer don't eat them.

NOTES & CULTIVARS
Dwarf Japanese garden juniper, 'Nana', grows approximately 1' tall, with a more refined appearance and slower growth rate that may suit many homeowners better. It develops a mounded form until it completely grows together, when it becomes more flattened in appearance.
'Greenmound' is similar to 'Nana' in habit but only reaches 6"–10" tall, with a bright green foliage color.

top to bottom

'Nana' at the Vince Dooley residence in Athens.

'Nana' in Gainesville, Ga.

'Nana' at Gibbs Gardens near Atlanta.

Winter foliage and form in Mobile, Ala.

Leucothoe axillaris
COASTAL LEUCOTHOE · DOGHOBBLE

Coastal leucothoe is a native evergreen shrub with an arching branching habit that prefers consistently moist soils. Attractive white mid- to late spring flowers occur on short drooping racemes below the stems. Use it for informal borders for larger shrubs or perennials, or combine it with native stone and ferns beside streams or water features.

ZONES & ORIGIN 5b–9b. Native to wetland edges of the southeastern Coastal Plain.

SIZE & GROWTH RATE 2'–4' tall, 4'–6' wide, slow growing.

TEXTURE & FORM Medium fine texture with a loose mounded form.

FOLIAGE Leaves emerge coppery red before becoming a lustrous dark green along zigzag stems. Simple alternate lustrous dark green leaves 2"–4" long are ovate to elliptic in shape, with finely serrate margins and acuminate tips. They turn reddish purple in winter.

LIGHT & SOIL Light shade is ideal, but it tolerates full sun to moderate shade with a loose and moist but not wet acidic soil.

MAINTENANCE Several leaf fungal diseases can be disfiguring or even fatal, but deer don't seem to bother them.

INSTALLATION Space 3' apart for massing in a loose soil mix.

NOTES & CULTIVARS
No cultivars listed.

Mahonia eurybracteata 'Soft Caress'
'SOFT CARESS' MAHONIA

'Soft Caress' mahonia is poised to become very popular in the landscape industry. If you haven't seen it before, you will soon. Its extremely fine texture lends an almost fern- or bamboo-like appearance to this shrub. With its mounded form, attractive yellow autumn flowers, and a much friendlier disposition than other mahonias, it provides a number of opportunities to use it in designs. Consider it for informal border plantings and for detailed designs around entryways, patios, or courtyards. Take advantage of its fine texture by combining it in the landscape or in container plantings with coarser-textured plants like hellebore, Adam's needle yucca, aspidistra, and ardisia or even some coarser evergreen ferns like autumn or tassel fern.

ZONES & ORIGIN   7a–9b. Native to Asia.

SIZE & GROWTH RATE   3'–4' tall, 2'–3' wide, medium growing.

TEXTURE & FORM   Fine texture and broadly oval to mounded form.

FOLIAGE   Dark green pinnately compound leaves are 10"–14" long, with 15–19 lanceolate-shaped leaflets. The leaflets are 3"–5" long and have finely toothed margins and acuminate tips. New foliage is coppery colored, while winter foliage develops a purple tint.

FLOWERS   Attractive and very lightly fragrant bright yellow flowers are held on terminal racemes for several weeks in mid- to late autumn (November in Athens).

FRUIT   Reportedly produces small silvery-blue berry-like fruit over winter into early spring, but we haven't seen it do so.

LIGHT & SOIL   Moderate shade with a moist but well-drained soil is ideal. It tolerates light shade but suffers under full sun and becomes fairly drought tolerant after establishment.

MAINTENANCE   If necessary, prune in late winter to midspring to avoid removing the coming autumn's flower buds.

INSTALLATION   Container plants are readily available. Make sure to slice and spread the roots of any root-bound plants before spacing 3' apart in loose well-drained soil from early spring to midautumn.

PESTS & DISEASES   None reported. We suspect deer don't like them.

NOTES & CULTIVARS
None reported.

top and middle Foliage and late autumn flowers with a gold dust plant in Athens.

bottom left In the Founders Memorial Garden.

bottom right At an Athens residence.

Mahonia fortunei Chinese Mahonia

Chinese mahonia is a plant best utilized in detailed designs. Its foliage resembles that of holly fern, and it has similar cultural requirements. Combine it with other shade-loving plants like hellebores, ferns, hostas, aspidistras, and fatsias to provide a tropical feel in courtyards or patios, along shaded woodland paths, or even in shaded rock gardens. Massed plants can provide an informal foundation for taller deciduous shrubs like edgeworthias and hydrangeas. Just make sure to provide it with midday to early afternoon shade to prevent foliage burn.

Foliage.

ZONES & ORIGIN 8a–9b. Native to China.

SIZE & GROWTH RATE 3'–5' tall and wide, slow growing.

TEXTURE & FORM Medium fine texture and rounded form.

FOLIAGE Pinnately compound alternate leaves have five to nine but mostly seven leaflets. The dark green lanceolate leaflets are 2½"–5" long and have spiny margins and acuminate tips. New foliage emerges with a hint of purple. Both the leaf petiole and rachis are triangular in shape.

FLOWERS Tiny yellow flowers are held on terminal racemes 2"–3" long in late summer (late July to late August in Athens). While interesting up close, the flowers are not noticeable beyond 30'.

FRUIT Insignificant dark purple fruit are rarely produced.

LIGHT & SOIL Moderate shade with a moist but well-drained slightly acidic soil is ideal. It tolerates light to heavy shade but not damp soils.

MAINTENANCE Plants in zone 8a are susceptible to winter foliage damage, particularly if located in too much sun. Provide several inches of mulch in mid- to late autumn. Chinese mahonia is easily pruned to maintain a smaller size. Early to midspring pruning doesn't disturb the current year's flowers.

INSTALLATION Although not as readily available as other mahonias, container-grown plants can be found. Young plants are thin and awkward looking for several years until they have the opportunity to fill out. Plant 3' on center.

PESTS & DISEASES Leaf spot disease rarely causes serious problems. Deer don't like them.

NOTES & CULTIVARS
No cultivars are listed.

Late summer flowers in a courtyard at the Georgia Center and at Callaway Gardens.

Rhododendron × *eriocarpum* Satsuki Azaleas

Satsuki azaleas are highly valued in bonsai collections due to their slow growth, attractive branching, and longevity. They provide showy late spring flowers and dense mounded forms. In Japanese gardens, they are appreciated more for their form and are often sheared to mimic rounded stones at the expense of their flowers. They are now considered crosses with *Rhododendron indicum* as one of their parents. Use them for borders and informal ground covers, or combine them with ferns in shaded rock gardens.

ZONES & ORIGIN 7a–9b. A cross between two Japanese species.

SIZE & GROWTH RATE 1'–2' tall, 2'–4' wide, slow growing.

TEXTURE & FORM Fine texture and mounded form.

FOLIAGE Simple lightly pubescent alternate leaves ½"–1⅜" long are elliptic to obovate shaped, with entire margins and acute tips. Winter foliage on some cultivars has a purple tint.

FLOWERS Large funnel-shaped flowers in reds, pinks, and whites arise for several weeks in late spring (early to late May in Athens).

FRUIT Insignificant.

LIGHT & SOIL Light shade and loose moist but well-drained acidic soil is ideal. They tolerate full sun, moderate shade, and short droughts.

MAINTENANCE Provide supplemental water during the first two summers, then every other week under summer droughts. Maintain mulch throughout the year.

INSTALLATION Container plants are readily available and should be spaced 3' apart. Loosen the roots before planting.

PESTS & DISEASES With fewer problems than other evergreen azaleas, their biggest issues are soil drainage, pH, and tightly bound root balls. Deer nibble the ends of stems.

NOTES & CULTIVARS
'Gunbi' and 'Gunrei' have white flowers with red stripes or flecks and frilled petals.
'Higasa' has dark pink flowers with white margins and reddish-purple throats.
'Johga' has mostly white flowers with dark red throats.
'Pink Gumpo' has light pink frilled petals and darker-pink throats.
'Red Gumpo' has salmon-red flowers.
'Shugetsu' has white flowers with purple borders.
'Wakaebisu' has salmon-pink hose-in-hose flowers.
'White Gumpo' has white flowers with dark pink throats.
Robin Hill Hybrids are similar in size, with late spring flowers.

Foliage.

left Beginning to bloom.
top right 'Wakaebisu' in bloom.
bottom right Robin Hill Hybrid 'Hilda Niblett'.

Rosmarinus officinalis ROSEMARY

Many people are familiar with the culinary and medicinal applications of rosemary but rarely consider it for garden compositions. While often used for container plantings near doorways or patios or for incorporating into herb or kitchen gardens, rosemary can also provide an informal border or foundation for larger shrubs. Use it for rock gardens, or take advantage of its fine texture to mix it into perennial borders with other low-water-requiring plants. With a little patience, it can even be trained as an espalier or topiary. The trailing cultivars are useful as informal ground covers and to soften retaining walls and steps.

top left An informal hedge on Hilton Head Island.

top right 'Prostratus' with agaves at the Los Angeles County Natural History Museum.

middle 'Prostratus'.

bottom Foliage and flowers.

ZONES & ORIGIN 7b–10b. Native to the Mediterranean area.

SIZE & GROWTH RATE 3'–5' tall and wide, medium growing.

TEXTURE & FORM Fine texture and broadly oval to rounded form.

FOLIAGE Simple grayish-green linear opposite leaves ¾"–1½" long are sessile, with entire margins that roll underneath and acute tips. Leaves have a somewhat sticky feel and are extremely fragrant when brushed against.

FLOWERS Slightly showy tiny lavender-blue flowers occur from autumn to spring.

FRUIT Insignificant.

LIGHT & SOIL Full sun to very light shade with well-drained soil and a neutral pH are ideal. It tolerates salt spray, drought, and alkaline soils.

MAINTENANCE Excessive soil moisture is the primary reason for its decline, so avoid supplemental watering. Prune to shape from early spring to early autumn.

INSTALLATION Small container plants are readily available and can be planted year-round. Ensure good surface drainage, and space 3'–4' apart. For container plantings, amend commercial potting soil mixtures with perlite and shredded pine bark to ensure good drainage.

PESTS & DISEASES No problems under ideal cultural conditions. Rosemary makes a good deer repellent.

NOTES & CULTIVARS

'Arp' has ascending branches and an oval form and is hardy to zone 6b.

'Blue Spire' grows 6'–8' tall with an upright habit.

'Huntington Carpet' and 'Prostratus' grow 1'–2' tall with spreading forms but are only hardy to zone 8a.

'Tuscan Blue' grows 4'–6' with a broadly oval form.

Ruscus aculeatus BUTCHER'S BROOM

Butcher's broom's name came from its foliage being bound together to clean butchers' blocks. Its slow growth tends to limit its use to detail plantings near entrances and courtyards. Its ability to tolerate dry shady locations is a rare attribute among landscape plants, so it could provide informal borders under mature trees or on north sides of buildings. Its dried foliage is popular for use in floral arrangements. Compounds derived from the rhizomes have been used to treat cardiovascular disease and edema. Young stems can be cooked and eaten like asparagus.

ZONES & ORIGIN 6b–9b. Native to the Mediterranean area.

SIZE & GROWTH RATE 2'–4' tall, 2'–3' wide, slow growing.

TEXTURE & FORM Fine texture and oval form.

FOLIAGE What most people would think are leaves are actually, according to botanists, stems called cladodes. These stiff leathery leaflike stems are alternately arranged, 1"–1½" long, ovate in shape, with entire margins and acuminate tips that end in a stiff bristle that is painful to touch.

FLOWERS Butcher's broom is dioecious, with neither sex being showy. Flowers held on top of the cladodes appear like tiny insects.

FRUIT Round pea-sized berries occur on top of the cladodes of female plants, turning bright red in autumn and remaining into winter, but they must be viewed up close to be appreciated.

LIGHT & SOIL Provide moderate shade with a moist but well-drained soil. It tolerates heavy shade, drought, and salt spray.

MAINTENANCE Maintain a loose soil mixture to allow below-ground rhizomes to spread.

INSTALLATION While this plant is rare, specialty growers provide small container plants that can be planted 30" apart in loose well-drained soils.

PESTS & DISEASES No issues. Deer don't touch them.

NOTES & CULTIVARS
'Wheeler's Variety' is a female with the ability to produce fruit without a male plant.
Danae racemosa, 'Poet's Laurel', is similar in appearance, but its fruit are held in clusters of three to five beneath the branches. Tolerating heavy shade and dry soils, it reaches 2'–3' tall and wide with a slow growth rate.

top Foliage.
bottom Fruit.

left In the Founders Memorial Garden.
right Poet's laurel at the Birmingham Botanical Garden.

Sarcococca confusa SWEETBOX · CHRISTMAS BOX

Sweetbox is one of the few plants that tolerates dry shade. It is better appreciated up close than from a distance, so use it near building entrances, patios, and courtyards. It could serve as a substitute for boxwood in shaded borders or in sunnier locations to provide a foundation for taller shrubs like gardenia and inkberry. While few people are familiar with sweetbox, its lightly fragrant late winter flowers provide a reason to find a place for it in the garden.

ZONES & ORIGIN 7a–9a. Native to Asia.

SIZE & GROWTH RATE 3'–5' tall and wide, medium slow growing.

TEXTURE & FORM Medium fine texture and oval form that becomes rounded at maturity.

FOLIAGE Simple lustrous dark green alternate leaves 1"–2½" long are lanceolate shaped, with entire margins and acuminate tips that end with a short bristle.

FLOWERS Somewhat showy small fragrant flowers with white threadlike petals occur along the stems in late winter (mid-February to early March in Athens). Their fragrance can be appreciated from about 20' away.

FRUIT Slightly showy berries are held along the stems before ripening to purple black in autumn and remaining into early spring.

LIGHT & SOIL Moderate shade with a loose and moist but well-drained soil is ideal. It tolerates light to full shade, drought, and slightly alkaline soils.

MAINTENANCE Prune in early spring to control size and form. It can be sheared without disfigurement.

INSTALLATION Sweetbox is more popular in cooler regions like the Pacific Northwest. Specialty nurseries carry it in gallon containers. It slowly spreads by root suckers, so plant in loose well-drained soil at 2'–3' on center in spring, and provide water every seven to ten days for the first summer.

PESTS & DISEASES Sweetbox is slightly susceptible to boxwood blight, a fungal disease that kills stems and foliage. Deer don't like them.

NOTES & CULTIVARS
No cultivars listed.
Sarcococca hookeriana humilis, 'Himalayan Sweetbox', reaches 12"–18" tall. Hardy to zone 6b, it spreads slowly by stolons, forming a dense ground cover with lightly fragrant late winter flowers.

top to bottom

Sweetbox foliage and winter flowers.

At the United Parcel Service Waterfall Garden Park in Seattle.

Himalayan sweetbox at Chanticleer.

At the Giberson residence.

left With Annabelle hydrangea in Athens.
top and bottom right Foliage and form at Queen Elizabeth Park.

Thuja occidentalis 'Danica'   DANICA ARBORVITAE

This dwarf arborvitae is valued for its dense canopy, formal appearance, and slow growth rate. Commonly used in dwarf conifer collections and rock gardens, it could also be utilized as an accent in traditional foundation compositions or massed to provide informal borders that require little pruning in sunny parterre gardens. Take advantage of its extreme cold-hardiness for use in raised planter compositions by combining it with trailing plants like confederate jasmine, bigleaf periwinkle, and pachysandra.

ZONES & ORIGIN 3b–8a. Native across northern portions of North America.

SIZE & GROWTH RATE 2'–3' tall and wide, slow growing.

TEXTURE & FORM Fine texture and rounded form.

FOLIAGE Bright green scalelike foliage is held along flattened branches. On most *Thuja occidentalis* cultivars, the branches are held horizontally, but they tend to be more vertically oriented on many of the dwarf cultivars.

FLOWERS Insignificant.

FRUIT Insignificant.

LIGHT & SOIL It prefers full sun to light shade with a moist but well-drained soil. It tolerates alkaline soils but suffers under the heat and dry summers of the Southeast.

MAINTENANCE Maintain several inches of mulch, and provide supplemental water during summer droughts.

INSTALLATION Most nurseries carry these dwarf cultivars in small containers. Best results are achieved by planting in late winter to early spring in sunny well-drained locations at 2'–3' apart. Ensure new plants receive sufficient water every seven to ten days for the first few summers.

PESTS & DISEASES Bagworms and spider mites are common but usually not severe. Don't even consider using it if deer are present.

NOTES & CULTIVARS
'Golden Globe' grows 3'–4' with bright yellow-green foliage.
'Hetz Midget' grows 2'–4' tall and 3'–5' wide with a mounded form.
'Little Gem' grows 2'–3' tall and 3'–5' wide.
'Little Giant' grows 2'–3' in size.
Thuja orientalis 'Aurea Nana', Berckman's Golden Arborvitae, is hardy from zone 6a to 10a and grows 4'–6' tall, 3'–4' wide, with bright yellow-green foliage and a dense broadly pyramidal form.

In a container with creeping jenny and blue spruce sedum.

Foliage and in bloom at the Founders Memorial Garden.

Yucca filamentosa ADAM'S NEEDLE YUCCA

The smallest of the native yuccas, Adam's needle yucca still carries a bold striking form that is bound to catch the eye. A native of sandy soils and dry open woodlands of the Southeast, it has naturalized throughout the mid-Atlantic states and is surprisingly cold-hardy. Though it is commonly used in rock gardens, consider grouping several together in sunny perennial borders to take advantage of their showy late spring flowers. Combine them with other sun-loving and drought-resistant perennials such as butterfly weed, purple heart plant, daylily, and crocosmia or with shrubs like butterfly bush and hibiscus.

ZONES & ORIGIN 5a–10a. Native to the southeastern United States from eastern Texas to Virginia.

SIZE & GROWTH RATE 2'–3' tall and wide, slow growing.

TEXTURE & FORM Coarse texture and mounded form.

FOLIAGE Lanceolate-shaped blue-green leaves 24"–32" long have threadlike filaments along their margins and sharply pointed tips. Young foliage is held upright at a 45- to 60-degree angle. Older foliage bends about midleaf, with the oldest leaves angling toward the ground.

FLOWERS Extremely showy bell-shaped creamy-white flowers are held on panicles that arise 4'–5' above the top of the foliage for several weeks in late spring (mid-May to early June in Athens).

FRUIT Fruit are unattractive oblong capsules.

LIGHT & SOIL Full sun to light shade with a moist but well-drained soil is ideal. It tolerates drought, moderate salt spray, and a neutral to slightly alkaline soil pH.

MAINTENANCE Remove unsightly flower stalks after flowering to stimulate vegetative growth. Removing old dead foliage, while difficult, improves the appearance.

INSTALLATION Container-grown plants are readily available. Plant in sunny locations in well-drained soils at 3' on center.

PESTS & DISEASES No serious problems. Deer don't touch them.

NOTES & CULTIVARS
The leaves are somewhat flexible and will give when pressed from the tip without causing much pain. Nevertheless, use with caution around walkways and small children.
'Bright Edge' has green foliage with yellow margins.
'Color Guard' and 'Golden Sword' have bright yellow foliage with green on the margins.

left At Longwood Gardens.
right 'Sword' in Athens.

In a border with a buckeye.

Deutzia gracilis SLENDER DEUTZIA

Deutzias are old-garden plants that are more common in cooler climates. Known for their dense mounded canopy and white late spring flowers and valued for their drought and pest resistance, deutzias are commonly used for pockets of color near the front of border plantings or in rock gardens to take advantage of their mounded habit. They could also serve to soften a retaining wall or the edges of steps.

ZONES & ORIGIN   4b–8a. Native to Japan.

SIZE & GROWTH RATE   2'–4' tall and wide, medium slow growing.

TEXTURE & FORM   Medium fine texture and mounded form.

FOLIAGE   Simple narrowly ovate to lanceolate opposite leaves 1½"–3" long have serrate margins and acuminate tips. Fall color is poor.

LIGHT & SOIL   Full sun to light shade with a moist but well-drained soil is ideal. It tolerates drought and slightly alkaline soils.

MAINTENANCE   Prune after flowering is completed every few years to maintain a dense canopy, or else they become open and scraggly in appearance.

NOTES & CULTIVARS
Small container plants are somewhat available and can be planted year-round in zones 7 and 8 on 3' centers. 'Nikko' is the most popular cultivar, developing some burgundy fall color.

Form in flower.

Jasminum nudiflorum Winter Jasmine

Few plants brighten up the dreary midwinter like winter jasmine. Its bright yellow blooms are a welcome hint of the distant spring to come. It blooms about the same time as the fragrant winter honeysuckle, and many people mistakenly believe it is winter jasmine's flowers that they smell, since the honeysuckle flowers are obscured from a distance. A tough resilient plant with a spreading habit, winter jasmine is often grown in containers or used to soften the hardscape edges of retaining walls and exposed steps. As a ground cover or border planting, it requires regular pruning to maintain its density. With support, it can also serve as a vine for fences.

Midwinter flowers.

ZONES & ORIGIN 6b–10a. Native to China.

SIZE & GROWTH RATE 2'–4' tall, 6'–8' wide, medium fast growing.

TEXTURE & FORM Medium fine texture and spreading form.

FOLIAGE Dark green trifoliate leaves are oppositely arranged with ovate to elliptic finely serrate leaflets ⅝"–1¾" long. Leaves remain green into late autumn without color. Square-shaped young green twigs have the ability to root where they meet the ground.

FLOWERS Swelling crimson flower buds open into extremely showy bright yellow flowers for four to six weeks in midwinter (late January to early March in Athens). During mild winters, flowering may begin in late December. Cut stems are easily forced indoors to brighten a room.

FRUIT Insignificant.

LIGHT & SOIL Full sun with a moist but well-drained soil is ideal. It tolerates light to moderate shade and is drought resistant after establishment.

MAINTENANCE Established plants require heavy pruning every two to three years after blooming in early spring to maintain dense centers. Without pruning, the foliage will grow at the edge of the plants, leaving a bare area in the center.

INSTALLATION Container plants are readily available. Plant year-round in zones 7 and 8 on 4' centers, and provide good surface drainage.

PESTS & DISEASES No problems. Deer don't like them.

NOTES & CULTIVARS
'Mystique' has foliage with creamy-white margins but is extremely difficult to find.

top left An informal ground cover in Columbus, Ga.

bottom left At a Birmingham residence.

right On the UGA campus.

With Chindo viburnum and Chinese silvergrass.

Punica granatum nana Dwarf Pomegranate

Dwarf pomegranates provide spots of color in landscape borders to help bridge the gap between spring and summer flowering plants. Since they are borderline cold-hardy, be careful in their use. Consider them for interior plants, and move them outside in midspring.

ZONES & ORIGIN 8a–10b. Native to Asia and southeastern Europe.

SIZE & GROWTH RATE 3'–4' tall, 2'–3' wide, medium slow growing.

TEXTURE & FORM Medium fine texture and oval form.

FOLIAGE Simple linear to oblanceolate opposite leaves ½"–1" long have entire margins and rounded tips. New foliage is coppery tinted. Attractive orange-red flowers occur on new growth in early summer, with sporadic flowers into early autumn, with ¾" rounded orange to reddish-purple fruit.

LIGHT & SOIL Provide full sun and moist but well-drained soil. It tolerates light shade, drought, and slightly alkaline soils.

MAINTENANCE Small container plants are available and should be spaced 2'–3' apart. Prune in early spring if necessary to shape. Light pruning and supplemental water in early summer stimulate new growth and flowering.

NOTES & CULTIVARS
'Chico' produces double orange flowers. 'Orange Blossom' has orange flowers and grows 2'–3' in size.

As an informal border in Italy.

Rhus aromatica FRAGRANT SUMAC

Fragrant sumac is a rarely encountered native shrub that occurs throughout much of the United States in dry open woods and fields. Closely resembling poison oak and poison ivy, it is differentiated from both by its sessile leaflets, red fruit, and lack of aerial rootlets. Spreading by underground stems that provide a sprawling habit, it is most noted for its colorful fall foliage. Use it for informal ground covers in xeric landscapes, particularly on embankments or roadsides where maintenance will be minimal.

ZONES & ORIGIN 3a–9a. Native to eastern North America.

SIZE & GROWTH RATE 3'–6' tall, 4'–8' wide, medium growing.

TEXTURE & FORM Medium texture with an irregular mounding form.

FOLIAGE Alternately arranged trifoliate leaves are thick and densely hairy when young. Ovate to obovate-shaped leaflets are 1"–3" long and have crenate to lobed margins. Crushed foliage and stems have a pleasant citrus odor. Fall foliage is an outstanding orange to deep red.

FLOWERS Fragrant sumac is dioecious, with neither sex being particularly showy. Yellow flowers appear in early spring with emerging leaves. Terminal male catkins are visible from late summer through winter.

FRUIT Drooping clusters of hairy berry-like drupes on female plants turn red in summer and remain into winter.

LIGHT & SOIL Full sun with well-drained soil is ideal. It tolerates light shade, drought, and alkaline soils.

MAINTENANCE Fragrant sumac thrives in drier situations, so avoid overwatering, which leads to foliage fungal diseases. It benefits from heavy pruning or mowing every few years to maintain its density. When combining it with other plants, use some type of edge restraint to keep it in bounds.

INSTALLATION Container plants from specialty nurseries can be planted year-round in zones 7 and 8 at 4' on center, or 3' apart for 'Gro Low'.

PESTS & DISEASES Leaf spot and powdery mildew often occur during cool damp springs and early summers. Deer don't like them.

NOTES & CULTIVARS
'Gro Low' is more widely grown than the species, reaching 2'–3' tall and 6'–8' wide, with orange-red fall foliage.

top to bottom
Foliage.
As a ground cover.
Planted in a border at Cornell University.

At Swarthmore College.

Spiraea japonica 'Anthony Waterer'
ANTHONY WATERER SPIRAEA

Anthony Waterer spiraea provides interest throughout much of the year. From its emerging red foliage to its showy late spring flowers and reddish-purple fall foliage, it offers much to appreciate. Add a disease-free and drought-resistant disposition, and you have a plant that provides a number of benefits in landscape compositions. Work it into border plantings to complement yellow-flowered late spring bloomers like daylily, rudbeckia, and achillea. Also take advantage of its cold-hardiness for use in containers on patios or decks with a trailing rosemary, juniper, or pachysandra.

ZONES & ORIGIN 3b–8b. A cross between two Asian species.

SIZE & GROWTH RATE 3'–4' tall and wide, fast growing.

TEXTURE & FORM Fine texture and rounded to mounded form.

FOLIAGE Simple narrowly ovate to lanceolate alternate leaves 1"–2½" long have serrate or occasionally doubly serrate margins and acuminate tips. Reddish-purple new foliage fades to blue green in summer. Late autumn color is a fairly good reddish purple.

FLOWERS Showy dark pink flowers occur on 2"–4" rounded terminal corymbs in late spring. In Athens, flowering usually begins in late April and peaks in early to mid-May, with sporadic flowering into midautumn.

FRUIT Insignificant dried fruit remain into late winter.

LIGHT & SOIL Full sun with moist but well-drained soil is ideal. It tolerates moderate shade and drought.

MAINTENANCE Blooming on new growth, it can be pruned in late winter and still flower in late spring. Promoting summer growth stimulates flowering into autumn.

INSTALLATION Container plants are readily available. Space 4' apart year-round in zones 7 and 8.

PESTS & DISEASES No serious problems with well-drained soil. Deer will nibble them, although spiraeas aren't their favorite.

NOTES & CULTIVARS
Spiraea japonica cultivars produce sports with stems displaying different-colored foliage and dark pink to white flowers.
'Crispa' and 'Dolchica' have foliage with deeply cut margins.
'Goldflame' has red new foliage that turns yellow and finally green in summer.
'Goldmound's' foliage remains greenish yellow during summer before turning orange red in fall.
'Limemound's' yellow-green new foliage matures to bright green.

top left In the Founders Memorial Garden.

top right and middle In full bloom in Chattanooga.

bottom Foliage and midspring flowers.

ORNAMENTAL GRASSES

Grasses contribute to many of North America's iconic landscapes, from flat coastal marshes, to rolling Piedmont meadows and farmland, to the tallgrass prairie. Grasses evoke a sense of the temporal as they sway in the wind and catch the sunlight. Their movement in the landscape creates a dynamic sense of life and energy that is attractive and engaging. Grasses for landscape purposes continue to gain in popularity, as their loose and energetic aesthetic appeals to many wanting to depart from tight and formal landscapes of clipped evergreens.

Grasses fit in many landscape contexts. In terms of scale, grasses relate well to the pedestrian and are therefore good choices for adding interest to a small space such as a residential yard or as part of a perennial or shrub border or container planting. Grasses are equally good when used in grand sweeping masses in larger landscapes such as corporate campuses, collegiate landscapes, and roadsides.

This section includes grasslike plants that are not technically grasses, such as sedges, sweet flag, and juncus, but that have a very grasslike effect visually in the landscape. Grasses have flat leaves, whereas sedges have triangular leaves and flower stems, and juncus have leaves that are cylindrical and feel rolled to the touch. Grass flowers are called inflorescences, and there are many types, from the showy plumelike panicles of pampas grass to subtler panicles, spikes, or racemes. Some of these flowers, such as those of juncus, are of little ornamental consequence. Grasses may form clumps or spread by underground root structures called rhizomes. Growth habit is important, as spreading types may be desirable for ground cover or even lawn use, depending on context and maintenance. Clumping types may make better accent plants but can also be used as ground covers if spaced correctly.

Grasses can contribute greatly to the winter landscape whether they are de-

Calamagrostis, among many perennials and shrubs in the always exemplary Tennis Court Garden at Chanticleer, June 2009.

ciduous or evergreen. Many of the deciduous grasses covered in this section provide dramatic fall and winter form in the landscape, as well as foliage colors of gold and tan that provide dramatic combinations with evergreens, snow, and blue winter skies. Fortunately, this winter aesthetic is increasingly appreciated, and for this reason maintenance personnel should refrain from trimming grasses until late winter, just before the new foliage emerges. Uncut winter foliage also provides much-needed habitat and is a food source for birds and small mammals, providing, to paraphrase Doug Tallamy, a last refuge for fauna increasingly displaced by human development.

Grasses are also an important functional component to stormwater treatment and biofiltration. Many species tolerate or prefer moist to wet environments and develop thick networks of roots and foliage, holding soils in place and filtering out particulates and pollution that would otherwise move downstream. Contemporary stormwater designs such as green streets and open stormwater management systems often utilize grasses, rushes, and sedges to help handle stormwater in a way that mimics natural wetlands while creating places for people to engage with the natural world. Fourth Ward Park in Atlanta, Georgia, provides an excellent example. Altogether, the plants in this section provide many opportunities for provocative planting design in conditions of sun or shade, wet or dry.

Meadows

The design and installation of a meadow is a beautiful art and science and must be considered carefully based on the geographic region, climate, soils, and aesthetic goals. Meadow design in the United States typically favors grasses as the dominate ground cover layer, with only a few herbaceous perennial species added for some seasonal color. This approach works well in many rural and more natural settings or for habitat restoration and land reclamation. An opposite approach can be found in contemporary urban projects such as the High Line in Manhattan or the Lurie Garden in downtown Chicago, where public visibility is so high that herbaceous perennials dominate the species list and grasses serve as filler, often comprising only 20 percent of the seed or plug mix. Dr. James Hitchmough, University of Sheffield in the United Kingdom, has pioneered this approach with success in such projects as the 2012 London Olympic Park. These highly designed meadow-like creations incorporate annuals and bulbs along with grasses and perennials as part of the continual show of bloom and dormant-season interest. For an authoritative exploration, we point you to the book *Sowing Beauty: Designing Flowering Meadows from Seed*, by James Hitchmough, along with the excellent book *Planting in a Post-wild World: Designing Plant Communities for Resilient Landscapes*, by Thomas Rainer.

Many of the grasses featured in this section can be found as part of today's designed meadows along with perennials. They are often seeded in the fall or installed as plugs in combination with seeding where budget allows.

Calamagrostis × acutiflora 'Karl Foerster' at the University of Washington.

BOTANICAL NAME	FOLIAGE TYPE	SUNLIGHT	SOILS	SALT TOLERANCE	TEXTURE	NATIVE TO SOUTHEAST
EVERGREEN VARIETIES						
Acorus calamus	Evergreen	Full sun to moderate shade	Evenly moist to water's edge	No	Fine	No
Acorus gramineus	Evergreen	Full sun to moderate shade	Moist well drained to wet	No	Fine	No
Carex spp.	Evergreen or deciduous	Varies by species	Varies by species	No	Fine	Yes
Cortaderia selloana	Semievergreen	Full sun to light shade	Moist well drained to dry	No	Medium	No
Festuca glauca	Evergreen	Full sun to light shade	Moist well drained to dry	No	Fine	No
Juncus spp.	Evergreen	Morning sun to moderate shade	Moist well drained to wet, water's edge	No	Fine	Yes
Sisyrinchium angustifolium	Semievergreen	Full sun to light shade	Moist to moist well drained	No	Fine	Yes
DECIDUOUS VARIETIES						
Andropogon virginicus	Deciduous	Full sun to moderate shade	Moist well drained to dry	No	Fine	Yes
Calamagrostis × acutiflora 'Karl Foerster'	Deciduous	Full sun to light shade	Moist well drained to dry	No	Fine	No
Chasmanthium latifolium	Deciduous	Full sun to moderate shade	Poorly drained to well drained & dry	No	Medium fine	Yes
Eragrostis spectabilis	Deciduous	Full sun	Moist well drained to dry	Light	Fine	Yes
Leymus arenarius 'Blue Dune'	Deciduous	Full sun to light shade	Moist well drained to dry	Yes	Fine	No
Muhlenbergia capillaris	Deciduous	Full sun to light shade	Poorly drained, moist well drained	No	Fine	Yes
Nassella tenuissima	Deciduous	Full sun to light shade	Moist well drained to dry	No	Fine	Yes
Panicum virgatum	Deciduous	Full sun to light shade	Poorly drained, moist well drained to dry	Yes	Medium fine	Yes
Pennisetum alopecuriodes	Deciduous	Full sun to light shade	Moist but well drained to dry	No	Fine	No
Schizachyrium scoparium	Deciduous	Full sun to light shade	Moist well drained to dry	No	Fine	Yes
Sorghastrum nutans	Deciduous	Full sun to light shade	Poorly drained, moist well drained to dry	No	Fine	Yes
Sporobolus heterolepis	Deciduous	Full sun to light shade	Moist well drained to dry	No	Fine	Yes
Tripsacum dactyloides	Deciduous	Full sun to light shade	Poorly drained to moist well drained	Low	Medium	Yes
Typha angustifolia	Deciduous	Full sun to moderate shade	Wet and water's edge	No	Medium	Yes

Acorus calamus 'Variegatus' at Chanticleer Garden.

Acorus calamus SWEET FLAG

Sweet flag is not technically a grass. However, the linear foliage and soft fine texture give the appearance of a grass in the landscape. It has several wonderful attributes, including its medium size, fine texture, evergreen foliage, and ability to tolerate wet soils and water edges, as well as full sun to partial shade. The species is a bright solid green, while the cultivar 'Variegatus' offers bold cream-colored variegated foliage. Sweet flag is an obligate wetland plant, so the designer must site it correctly and avoid confusion with the popular Asian species, *Acorus gramineus*, which will tolerate slightly drier conditions. Sweet flag reaches 2'–4' in height, and its textural effects at the water's edge are quite striking.

ZONES & ORIGIN 4–8. Native to Europe.

SIZE & GROWTH RATE 2'–4' tall, 18"–24" wide, with a medium growth rate.

TEXTURE & FORM Fine texture and upright oval form.

FOLIAGE Evergreen fan-shaped tufts of narrow leathery sword-shaped leaves are 2'–4' long and ½"–¾" wide. When bruised, the foliage releases a sweet cinnamon-like scent.

FLOWERS Tiny yellow flowers occur along a nonshowy yellowy-green spadix that is held down within the foliage.

FRUIT Not significant.

LIGHT & SOIL Provide full sun to light shade and moist to wet soils such as those found at the edge of a pond or stream. It can grow in standing water.

MAINTENANCE Little maintenance required once a thick mass is established.

INSTALLATION Plant plugs or small container plants on 12"–2' centers depending on desired thickness slightly below the soil in moist locations or standing water. If used in containers in water features, make sure the container is below the water level.

PESTS & DISEASES None major.

NOTES & CULTIVARS
Sweet flag spreads by underground rhizomes. Some type of edge restraint may be needed to prevent it from spreading beyond the desired niche.
'Variegatus' or 'Argentostriatus' has bold creamy-white striped foliage.

Acorus gramineus JAPANESE SWEET FLAG

Though Japanese sweet flag is not technically a grass, its linear foliage and soft fine texture give it the appearance of a grass in the landscape. Its small size, fine texture, evergreen foliage, and ability to tolerate slightly moist to wet soils in full sun to light shade provide many opportunities to utilize Japanese sweet flag in designs. Several design-worthy cultivars offer various shades of green, cream, and golden-yellow variegated foliage that offer exciting choices for planting design. The species has a bright solid green foliage that is evergreen in zone 9 but semievergreen to deciduous in cooler locations.

ZONES & ORIGIN 6–9. Native to Asia.

SIZE & GROWTH RATE 6"–15" height and spread with a medium growth rate.

TEXTURE & FORM Fine texture with a mounded form.

FOLIAGE Narrow fan-shaped tufts of leathery iris-like leaves are 4"–12" long and about ¼" wide.

FLOWERS Flowers occur on a nonshowy yellowy-green spadix that most people never see.

FRUIT Not significant.

LIGHT & SOIL Ideally, light shade with a moist to wet soil. It tolerates full sun to moderate shade but does not like to dry out.

MAINTENANCE While not native, Japanese sweet flag does not appear to be invasive in the Southeast. Little maintenance is required once a thick mass is established. As with all mass ground cover plantings, hand weeding is necessary for the first few years.

INSTALLATION Plant plugs or small containers on 8"–18" centers depending on cultivar, desired thickness, and budget.

PESTS & DISEASES Very pest and disease free.

NOTES & CULTIVARS
'Golden Edge' has golden variegation to 12" tall.
'Golden Pheasant' leaves mature to a solid golden green to 12" tall.
'Masamune' has creamy variegation to 8".
'Minimus' is dark green and only 3" tall.
'Minimus Aureus' has bright gold variegation and is only 3" tall.
'Ogon' has chartreuse-and-cream variegated foliage to 10" tall.
'Pusillus Nanus' is solid green and only 4" tall.
'Variegatus' has white variegation to 12" tall.

top to bottom

Acorus gramineus 'Nana', Gainesville Medical Center, by the Fockele Garden Co.

Happy at the water's edge in the garden of the Giberson residence, Athens, Ga.

At Gibbs Garden outside Atlanta.

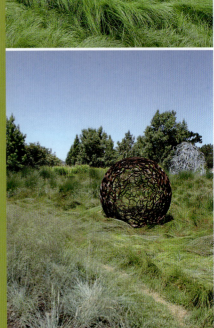

top left Carex oshimensis 'Everillo' with giant alliums at Chanticleer Garden, Wayne, Pa.

top right A designed wetland near Olympic Park, Vancouver, B.C.

middle C. stricta on the Shoemaker Green, University of Pennsylvania, by Andropogon Associates.

bottom Various species in Sonoma, Calif.

Carex spp. SEDGE

To lump all the *Carex* species into one category is a terrible injustice; however, doing so may inspire your love affair with them. Thousands of species occur in North America, Europe, Asia, and New Zealand, often in shady and moist or wet places, but some also occur in dry sunny or dry shady sites. We tell our students there's a *Carex* for every situation. Several of the species below make effective ground covers and even lawn alternatives for difficult shady and wet soil locations. Others make fine accents in containers, courtyards, or perennial borders. Nearly all have a very fine texture and a low mounding and clumping form. This account focuses mostly on native species; however, there are many attractive species from other continents. Installation is best from plugs or small containers at a close spacing for massing.

Carex appalachica, Appalachian sedge, is native to woodlands of the eastern United States and hardy from zones 3 to 8. It is 12" tall and wide with a clumping habit, and it tolerates light to moderate shade and well-drained to dry soils. Because it is a great accent or walkway border plant, it combines well with other woodland plants.

Carex flaccosperma, blue wood sedge, is native to southeastern woodlands from zones 6b to 8b. It is 6"–10" tall and wide with a clumping habit. With glaucous blue-green foliage, it prefers light to moderate shade in well-drained to moist soils.

Carex muskingumensis, palm sedge, is native to woodlands and moist creek banks of the Ohio River Valley and Great Lakes states from zones 5 to 8. It is 12"–24" high and wide and slowly spreading and requires moist soils in full sun to moderate shade. A nice massing plant or accent with several great cultivars such as 'Oehme', with yellow leaf edges, and 'Ice Fountains', with green-and-white variegated foliage.

Carex oshimensis is a Japanese species with several commonly available cultivars, such as 'Everillo', with yellow foliage, and 'Evergold', with creamy-white variegated leaves. All prefer moist to wet soils and light to moderate shade but will tolerate short dry periods.

Carex pennsylvanica, Pennsylvania sedge, is native to woodlands from northern Georgia to Minnesota and New Hampshire in zones 4 to 8. It is 8"–10" high and wide but spreading and tolerates light to moderate shade and well-drained to dry soils. It makes a good ground cover for dry shade and is a shady lawn alternative.

Carex stricta, tussock sedge, is native to stream and bog edges from zones 5 to 8. It is 24"–36" tall and wide with a clumping habit. Growing in full sun to light shade, it prefers consistently moist to wet soils and is useful in wetland restoration, rain gardens, and drainage swales.

Cortaderia selloana Pampas Grass

Pampas grass is native to the Pampas or plains region of Argentina. It has long been cultivated in the United States as an ornamental with its impressive size and flowering. Indeed, it makes such a statement in the landscape that it is difficult to use in combination with other plants, since it always steals the show. Large swaths planted along highways in the coastal South or perhaps specimen plantings as a focal point may work. Pampas is a tough-as-nails grass with razor-sharp leaf blade edges. It is mostly evergreen and can provide a considerable screen or buffer. While not known as invasive in the Southeast, it has become quite problematic in southern California.

ZONES & ORIGIN 7a–10. Native to Argentina.

SIZE & GROWTH RATE 8'–12' tall and wide with a fast growth rate.

TEXTURE & FORM Medium coarse texture and upright arching fountain-like form.

FOLIAGE Long slender arching leaves are ½" wide, 6'–8' long, and light green in color with razor-sharp scabrous margins. Foliage remains evergreen in zones 9 and 10 but turns tan in winter in zone 7.

FLOWERS Impressive large fluffy white plumes are held above the foliage in late summer.

FRUIT Large plumes turn brown and remain through winter and often into the second growing season if not removed.

LIGHT & SOIL Full sun to light shade with well-drained soils. It tolerates drought and is very tolerant of salt spray.

MAINTENANCE Pampas grass becomes very unkempt by late winter or early spring and should be cut back unless it is planted in a very naturalistic location. This is a daunting task, so wear long sleeves and gloves.

INSTALLATION Plant 8'–10' on center for mass plantings from containers.

PESTS & DISEASES None major.

NOTES & CULTIVARS
'Albolineata' reaches 6'–8' tall with leaves with white stripes.
'Andes Silver' and 'Patagonia' are hardy to zone 6.
'Aureolineata' reaches 6'–8' with gold striped leaves.
'Bertini' and 'Pumila' grow to 6'.
'Pink Feather' and 'Rendatleri' have plumes with a pink blush.

top Dramatic summer flower spikes, always an attention hog.

bottom left A border planting in Birmingham, Ala.

bottom right A front yard in Athens, Ga., with windmill palm.

Festuca glauca BLUE FESCUE

The ornamental blue fescue grass is a clump-forming cool season grass native to southern France. It prefers dry well-drained soils and full sunlight. The extremely fine texture, small size, and evergreen silvery-blue foliage make it irresistible to garden designers and plant enthusiasts. Be warned that clumps can develop center die-out in the summer heat of zones 7 and 8 and will need to be dug and reset in the fall. For this reason, blue fescue may best be used in hotter zones as an accent plant or in containers but not in large quantities, and avoid sweeping masses where complete coverage and long-term durability will be difficult to achieve.

ZONES & ORIGIN 4–8. Native to southern France.

SIZE & GROWTH RATE 8"–12" tall and wide with a medium growth rate.

TEXTURE & FORM Fine texture with a mounded form.

FOLIAGE Evergreen silvery-blue narrow rolled leaves to 12" long occur in tight clumps.

FLOWERS Light and airy panicles are held above foliage to 18" tall in late spring or early summer. Panicles become lax and unkempt by fall and may need to be trimmed in manicured landscapes.

FRUIT They produce tiny delicate seeds that are not ornamental.

LIGHT & SOIL Full sun with well-drained or even dry soils. Good drainage is essential.

MAINTENANCE Center die-out is a problem in hot humid climates. Dig and divide at least every other year.

INSTALLATION Plant on 8"–12" centers for masses. Blue fescue is an excellent container plant.

PESTS & DISEASES None major with good drainage.

NOTES & CULTIVARS
'Boulder Blue' has intense blue foliage to 16" in flower.
'Elijah Blue' is a time-tested cultivar with silvery-blue foliage to 16" in flower.

top to bottom

With sedum, liriope, and nasella in Vancouver, B.C.

A successful planting in the Southeast.

A border at Longwood Gardens, with senecio, Mugo pine, yucca, clematis, and white petunias.

Juncus spp. RUSH

The rushes comprise a large genus of many species native to the eastern United States and abroad. Rushes are not technically grasses, but their thin cylindrical upright foliage provides a grassy effect that is most often seen in grand sweeps at the water's edge or in poorly drained locations, although some also tolerate periodic drought. Most species are evergreen or semievergreen. This combination of wet soil tolerance and evergreen character makes rushes an irresistible choice in design for waterside plantings, bioswales, detention ponds, and wetland reclamation projects. Research shows that rushes can serve as a water-filtering and water-cleaning agent. This account provides a short listing of the best available species and cultivars for southeastern landscapes. The number of species grown will undoubtedly increase in the coming years as more environmentally responsible stormwater management systems become standard.

ZONES & ORIGIN 3–10. Many species native to North America and worldwide.

SIZE & GROWTH RATE 12"–36" tall and wide with mostly medium growth rates.

TEXTURE & FORM Fine texture with a spiky mounded form.

FOLIAGE Cylindrical hollow upright stems are mostly evergreen.

FLOWERS Flowering is not showy but occurs as small brownish clusters of three near the tops of stems.

FRUIT Small rusty-brown seeds form in a sideways-leaning spray from the stem.

LIGHT & SOIL Full sun to light shade. All tolerate moist to wet soils, with some species also tolerating drier conditions.

INSTALLATION Space approximately 2' apart for massing from plugs or containers.

PESTS & DISEASES None major.

NOTES & CULTIVARS

Juncus coriaceus, leathery rush, is native to the Southeast and hardy from zones 5 to 9. It is 1'–2' tall and prefers moist to wet soils and full sun.

Juncus effusus, common rush, is native across North America and Japan in zones 4–10. It requires moist to wet soils and sun to light shade, and it grows 2'–4' tall with dark green foliage. 'Spiralis' provides interesting corkscrew foliage for detail plantings and containers.

Juncus inflexus, hard rush, is from Europe but has naturalized in the eastern United States with blue or gray-green foliage. It is 2'–4' tall and tolerates dry conditions quite well. 'Afro' is 12" tall with twisted stems. 'Lovesick Blues' is a weeping clump form to 14" tall with bluish-green foliage.

Juncus patens 'Carmen's Gray', California gray rush, is native to the West Coast and hardy from zones 5 to 9. It is 1'–2' tall with bluish-gray foliage and grows in full sun to light shade, but it tolerates drought once established.

Juncus roemerianus, black needle rush, is native to coastal marshes from Maryland to Florida and Texas. Hardy from zones 4 to 10, it reaches 3'–5' tall and requires wet soils and sun. Salt tolerant, it is useful in shoreline stabilization.

top to bottom

Summer flowers occur on one-sided cymes in a rich warm brown color.

On the banks of the New River in Carroll County, Va.

Sweeps on the waterfront park in Vancouver, B.C., by PWL Partnership, also in Vancouver.

A smart planting in Fourth Ward Park, Atlanta, by HDR in Atlanta.

359

ORNAMENTAL GRASSES · EVERGREEN GRASSES

Sisyrinchium angustifolium BLUE-EYED GRASS

The grasslike effect of *Sisyrinchium* hides its real identity as a member of the Iris family. This low-growing native is found in open woods and makes a lovely low ground cover. It provides an exciting alternative to plants such as mondo grass and liriope. The pale blue flowers in spring are profuse and quite lovely. It prospers in even moisture and needs to be planted in good soils where conditions will not become too dry. In zones 7 and 8 some afternoon shade is advantageous. Use it in lightly shaded rock gardens and along paths or the front of the border as the last and lowest layer of the composition.

top to bottom

A perfect container accent at Mt. Cuba Center.

The blue spring flowers of 'Lucerne'.

'Lucerne' in the garden of Shannon Currey with daylily foliage behind.

ZONES & ORIGIN 4–9. Native from Florida and Texas to Canada.

SIZE & GROWTH RATE 8"–12" tall and 6"–12" wide with a medium growth rate.

TEXTURE & FORM Fine texture with a clumping habit and mounded form.

FOLIAGE Medium green narrow and pointed leaf blades to 12" long are arranged in small flat fans like all irises and form tight clumps.

FLOWERS Delicate sky-blue to white flowers with yellow centers ¼" wide are held just above the foliage and occur in April and May in Athens.

FRUIT They produce tiny delicate insignificant seeds.

LIGHT & SOIL Provide full sun to light shade with moist to moist but well-drained soil. Morning sun with afternoon shade is best in the Southeast.

MAINTENANCE Occasional division and resetting are necessary to maintain full masses. Hand weeding will be necessary in sunnier locations.

INSTALLATION Plant on 8"–12" centers for quick masses with plugs or containers.

PESTS & DISEASES None major.

NOTES & CULTIVARS
'Lucerne' has larger ¾" flowers and is reported to self-seed less.

Andropogon virginicus BROOM SEDGE

Broom sedge is native across most of North America and extends south to Mexico and into South America. It occurs in dry well-drained soils in full sunlight. It often grows where nothing else could survive in the poorest of soils and on hot exposed sites. It is a frequent pioneer species on recently disturbed land and is therefore useful in land restoration as part of a native seed blend. The fall and winter character is striking and memorable as the clumps stand erect and turn a delightful warm orangey-amber color—beautiful against the clear blue winter sky, evergreens, or snow. Several other important related species are available and listed below.

ZONES & ORIGIN 3–10. Native to the Southeast and across North America.

SIZE & GROWTH RATE 2'–3' moderate growth.

TEXTURE & FORM Fine texture with a stiff upright form.

FOLIAGE Clump forming, with stems and leaves bright green, hairy, and sticky to the touch in summer, finally turning rich shades of orange and amber for winter.

FLOWERS Insignificant late summer flowers with touches of red and purple atop green stems.

FRUIT Seed covered with fuzzy white hairs that glow in winter sunlight. Very attractive across a meadow in winter.

LIGHT & SOIL Full sun to light shade. Tolerates poor dry soils of sand or clay but fails in soils that are too rich in organic matter or are too moist—a plant that thrives on neglect.

MAINTENANCE Carefree once established. As with all grasses, the winter effect is destroyed if the grass is cut too early. In the Southeast, trim back or burn grasses in late February or early March before new spring growth begins.

INSTALLATION Space plugs 12"–24" on center. Very light or zero mulch may be best to avoid excessive soil moisture. Seeding is a common method, and care must be taken to control weeds during establishment through mowing at 8" height or short periods of grazing.

PESTS & DISEASES None major.

NOTES & CULTIVARS

Andropogon gerardii 'Big Bluestem' reaches 5'–8' in height. It was once the dominant grass of the tallgrass prairie and is useful in native seed mixes for land restoration. It needs full sun and dry conditions. It provides great winter color. Southern ecotypes need development.

Andropogon var. *glaucus* has a distinct and attractive silvery-blue color in summer.

Andropogon glomeratus differs significantly from other species in its tolerance of wet soil conditions. Occurs along the Coastal Plain and Piedmont from Massachusetts to Florida. It grows 2'–3' tall, with extremely showy and bushy flower heads that command attention with their winter color.

Andropogon gyrans is native to eastern North America and differs from *A. virginicus* in its showy inflorescences and sheaths clustered atop the stems. This upside-down paintbrush effect is quite showy in winter with the typical copper-orange color. Grows 2'–3' tall in zones 5–9.

Andropogon ternarius 'Splitbeard Bluestem' is tough as nails. It grows to 2' tall. The inflorescences are "split" in two and fuzzy white in the dormant season. Provides amber winter foliage color.

top to bottom

Andropogon virginicus inflorescens.

A. glomeratus.

A. virginicus at Bellingrath Plantation near Mobile, Ala.

A. virginicus in the fall with smooth sumac, Oconee County, Ga.

Calamagrostis × *acutiflora* 'Karl Foerster'
'KARL FOERSTER' FEATHER-REED GRASS

The genus *Calamagrostis* is quite large, with species occurring around the world and often in cooler climates. However, the cultivar 'Karl Foerster', a selection from an interspecific hybrid between European and Asian species, has been utilized with great success in the eastern United States as far south as zone 8. It is prized for its strictly upright habit and tall narrow seed heads, which sway in the slightest breeze. It makes a wonderful vertical accent in small numbers or large sweeping masses. Though not native, this hybrid does not produce viable seed and will not invade local ecosystems.

ZONES & ORIGIN 4–8. Native to Europe and Asia.

SIZE & GROWTH RATE 4'–6' tall in flower, medium growth.

TEXTURE & FORM Fine texture with a stiff upright form.

FOLIAGE Clump forming, with deep green foliage emerging very early in spring and turning tan in winter. Holds its tight vertical form in the winter landscape.

FLOWERS Showy and linear terminal inflorescences form by late May.

FRUIT Upright inflorescences hold well through winter and are ornamental.

LIGHT & SOIL Full sun to light shade. Prefers moist but well-drained to moist soils.

MAINTENANCE Cut back in late winter before new foliage emerges.

INSTALLATION Space 2' on center for mass plantings, plugs, or containers.

PESTS & DISEASES None major.

NOTES & CULTIVARS
'Karl Foerster' is the mainstream form, selected for its impressive flowers and seed structures.

top to bottom

Attractive inflorescens.

With catmint, sedums, and little bluestems in Portland, Ore.

Chasmanthium latifolium INLAND SEA OATS

Inland sea oats is native to the Coastal Plain, inland floodplains, riverbanks, and low woods from New Jersey to Florida and west to Kansas. This grass tolerates a wide range of conditions, from soils that are periodically wet and poorly drained to drier upland soil conditions, and it grows quite well in light shade, where many grasses flop. This adaptability and its manageable size have made it quite popular for landscape design and land restoration. The summer and winter foliage character is handsome. Foliage emerges early in spring, with bright green summer color. Showy and pendant terminal panicles are held above the foliage from midsummer through fall. They turn shades of bronze and salmon before yielding to a handsome light golden winter color.

ZONES & ORIGIN 5–9. Native to the eastern United States.

SIZE & GROWTH RATE 2'–4' fast growing.

TEXTURE & FORM Fine texture and upright, slightly arching form.

FOLIAGE Clump forming with attractive lanceolate foliage that is bright green in summer and turns golden in winter.

FLOWERS Showy terminal panicles of spikelets and seed are somewhat pendulous and elegant. Green in summer, then turning golden and bronze in fall and winter, they resemble something from the Art Deco period.

FRUIT Angular seeds dangle from terminal panicles well through winter and are quite attractive.

LIGHT & SOIL Full sun to light shade. Prefers moist or even poorly drained soils but also tolerates more upland sites and will survive drought.

MAINTENANCE May reseed in moist environments. Cut back in late February before new foliage.

INSTALLATION Space mass plantings, plugs, containers, and seeds 18"–2' apart on center.

PESTS & DISEASES None major.

NOTES & CULTIVARS Freely self-seeds and can become aggressive in some contexts.

top to bottom

Summer seed heads.

Lush summer foliage.

October in Georgia, a mass planting under river birches.

Eragrostis spectabilis PURPLE LOVE GRASS

Purple love grass is a native grass to the eastern United States and occurs over a large range in sunny open environments such as meadows, roadsides, and woodland edges. It prefers full sun and will prosper in well-drained soils, but it also does quite well in hot, dry, and poor sites. Flowering occurs in early to midsummer in the Southeast and creates a soft purple haze hanging over the low-growing foliage. In fall the leaves turn an attractive orangey-golden color. Winter presence is admittedly iffy, and overall this is a grass that leans toward the wilder side, aesthetically making it perhaps more suitable for meadow mixes and more naturalistic-looking planting designs.

A cloudy pink haze of midsummer flowers, Rougemont, N.C.

ZONES & ORIGIN 5–9. Native to eastern North America.

SIZE & GROWTH RATE 1'–2' slow growing.

TEXTURE & FORM Fine texture with a low mounding form.

FOLIAGE Spreads slowly by rhizomes forming a dense mat of green foliage.

FLOWERS Delicate airy flower panicles of soft purple float just above the foliage in midsummer. Attractive in flower, but only for a few weeks.

FRUIT Seed panicles turn a tan color and blow around like tumbleweeds by late summer.

LIGHT & SOIL Full sun. Tolerates well-drained soils of clay or sand and drought. Salt spray tolerant.

MAINTENANCE It is slowly rhizomatous, so utilize it where spreading will not be a problem or can be maintained. Cut back in late winter.

INSTALLATION Space 12"–18" on center for mass plantings, plugs, containers, or seeds.

PESTS & DISEASES None major.

NOTES & CULTIVARS

Large masses were planted on campus at UGA and then removed two years later. We suspect that their appearance was too weedy for the green meatball aristocracy.

Eragrostis curvula 'Weeping Lovegrass' is from South Africa and invasive. Often used for erosion control.

Eragrostis elliottii 'Wind Dancer' has an upright form to 30" tall and a delicate and perhaps more visual presence throughout the year than *E. spectabilis*.

Massing just past peak color in July in Athens, Ga.

left Color contrast with *Carex*, *Hosta*, and more at Swarthmore College.

right Grand Park, Los Angeles, Calif.

Leymus arenarius 'Blue Dune'   BLUE DUNE GRASS

Blue Dune grass is native to coastal areas of northern and western Europe; however, it is quite tolerant of heat and humidity. It is salt and drought tolerant and provides an excellent low-spreading ground cover of silvery-blue fine-textured foliage, an attractive foil for other plantings as a low ground cover mass. It is a cool-season grower and spreads by rhizomes, forming a dense cover and maintaining its silver-blue color through the heat of summer. Leymus may be evergreen in zones 9 and 10. In cooler zones the winter color is an attractive bright tan.

ZONES & ORIGIN   4–10. Native to northern Europe.

SIZE & GROWTH RATE   3' tall in flower and fast growing.

TEXTURE & FORM   Fine texture with a spreading, spiky appearance.

FOLIAGE   Spreads by rhizomes forming a dense mat of silvery-blue glaucous foliage.

FLOWERS   Flower spikes 3'–4' tall are held above the foliage in late spring. While this plant is attractive in flower, it is used primarily for the unique foliage color.

FRUIT   Wheat-like seed heads mature in midsummer to a dull beige color for late summer through early winter.

LIGHT & SOIL   Full sun to light shade. Tolerates well-drained soils of clay or sand. Salt spray tolerant.

MAINTENANCE   It is strongly rhizomatous, so use it where spreading will not be a problem or can be maintained.

INSTALLATION   Space 12"–18" on center for mass plantings, plugs, and containers.

PESTS & DISEASES   None major.

NOTES & CULTIVARS   Deer and rabbit resistant and highly salt spray tolerant. Leaves used for making mats and ropes.

Massing in Rabun Gap, Ga., with 'Forest Pansy' redbud, butterfly bush, and gold spirea by Fockele Garden Co., based in Gainesville, Ga.

top left October flowering at the gates of UGA.

top right Summer in the Botanical Garden at the University of Tennessee, Knoxville.

bottom right Winter foliage.

bottom Airy inflorescences appear as pink fog in the fall.

Muhlenbergia capillaris PINK MUHLY GRASS

Pink muhly grass is native to the Southeast, occurring from Massachusetts to Florida and Texas and into Mexico on the Coastal Plain. It grows in lower-elevation meadows and woodland edges in relatively dry soils or in wet and boggy low-lying areas. In summer, the foliage is a wispy fine-textured clump of dark green followed by a fall display of pink flower panicles. These create a pink fog hovering above mass plantings; they are dreamy and memorable when lit by the autumn sun. In winter the foliage and flower heads turn a distinct tan and should not be trimmed back until late winter, if at all. The only potential drawback to this grass is its tendency to begin spring growth late in the season, causing one to wonder if it is still alive. This is remedied in planting design by placing muhly with other plants to distract the eye during muhly's extended slumber.

ZONES & ORIGIN 6–10. Native to the southeastern Coastal Plain.

SIZE & GROWTH RATE 3' tall and wide with a medium growth rate.

TEXTURE & FORM Fine texture and mounded form.

FOLIAGE Thin leaves 2' long with a clumping habit are deep dark green in summer, turning a rich straw tan in winter. New growth is late to emerge in spring.

FLOWERS Evocative clouds of pink panicles float above the foliage in September through early November in the Southeast. In mild winters, flowering may extend well into late December.

FRUIT Panicles turn an attractive tan for the winter landscape with small oval seeds.

LIGHT & SOIL Provide full sun to light shade. It tolerates a range of soils from clay to sand and constantly moist to well drained.

MAINTENANCE In tidier landscapes, a late winter haircut may be desired. Pest and disease free.

INSTALLATION Space 2' on center for mass plantings, plugs, and containers.

PESTS & DISEASES None major.

NOTES & CULTIVARS
'White Cloud' is an exquisite white-flowered cultivar.

Nassella tenuissima   MEXICAN FEATHER GRASS

Mexican feather grass is native to Texas and New Mexico and south to Mexico and Argentina and occurs in very sunny dry locations. It is incredibly drought tolerant as it blooms in spring and goes dormant in the heat of the summer. The dormancy period is attractive, with an irresistible fine wispy character to the thin leaves, which provide soft movement in the breeze. Its small size makes Mexican feather grass a great front layer in design or an accent plant in creating a soft foil for other plants in a herbaceous border.

ZONES & ORIGIN   7–10. Native to Texas, New Mexico, Mexico, and Argentina.

SIZE & GROWTH RATE   1'–2' tall with a medium growth.

TEXTURE & FORM   Fine texture with an upright fountain-like form.

FOLIAGE   Thin leaf blades in clumps are dark green in late winter and early spring before turning golden tan with summer dormancy. Foliage remains attractive all year.

FLOWERS   Fluffy terminal inflorescences occur in spring as creamy white and then turning tan with summer dormancy, providing lovely light and wind effects through early fall.

FRUIT   Delicate inflorescences are somewhat insignificant in that they blend into the dormant tan-colored foliage in winter.

LIGHT & SOIL   Full sun to light shade. Well-drained to dry soils are essential.

MAINTENANCE   Extremely low maintenance, with perhaps only an occasional trim needed in winter before new foliage emerges.

INSTALLATION   Space 12"–18" on center for mass plantings and containers.

PESTS & DISEASES   None major.

NOTES & CULTIVARS   The rather xeric appearance and tan color of the summer dormant foliage can be awkward in some contexts while everything else is green.

top to bottom

Late spring inflorescence.

Popping out of creeping phlox at Duke Gardens, Durham, N.C.

Summer dormancy on a rooftop in Seattle.

Panicum virgatum SWITCHGRASS · PANIC GRASS

The development of switchgrass and its many cultivars in recent years has provided an exciting and versatile native grass for diverse landscapes. Why invasive species of *Miscanthus* continue to be planted when so many great *Panicum* species are available is a mystery. Switchgrass is native across a large range from Canada to the West Indies and as far west as Montana and Arizona. It occurs in moist coastal environments and is mildly salt tolerant, and it grows in more upland prairie or open woodland sites. This versatile grass makes a strong upright statement in the landscape, with bright shades of green or blue green in summer and shades of rich gold and tan in winter. Size, form, and seasonal color vary greatly with cultivar. Some of the best cultivars are listed below.

ZONES & ORIGIN 4–10. Native throughout the eastern and midwestern states and southern Canada.

SIZE & GROWTH RATE 3'–9' in bloom depending on cultivar, fast growing.

TEXTURE & FORM Fine texture and upright oval form.

FOLIAGE Primarily a clump-forming grass with stiff upright or lax and arching leaf blades in colors ranging from deep green to blue green to burgundy red depending upon the cultivar. Fall colors range in golds and even red. Winter form and foliage colors range from golds to tan.

FLOWERS Light and airy terminal panicles float above the foliage in early summer in white, cream, and pink.

FRUIT Panicles turn tan and hold through winter, offering pleasing light effects in the winter sunlight.

LIGHT & SOIL Provide full sun to light shade. It tolerates a wide range of soils, from sandy, dry, and well drained to heavy clay and soggy soil, and is salt tolerant.

MAINTENANCE Trim back to 12" in late winter to preserve winter form and visual interest.

INSTALLATION Space 3'–6' on center depending on cultivar for mass plantings with plugs or containers. Species will seed effectively.

PESTS & DISEASES None major.

NOTES & CULTIVARS
'Cape Breeze' is only 30" tall, holding green color late into fall, golden winter color.
'Cloud Nine' grows to 8' with a slightly blue-green fine-textured inflorescences, golden in fall.
'Dallas Blues' has an arching form. It is blue green to 6' and its flowers change from pink to red purple, light amber in winter. It is very drought tolerant.
'Heavy Metal' has a very upright form. It is bluish gray to 5' and has pink-tinted flowers, with red and gold color in autumn and tan color in winter. Drought tolerant.
'Northwind' has a stiff upright form to 6' in flower. Its blue-green leaves turn golden in fall. Very drought tolerant.
'Shenandoah' has an upright form to 4'. It is green in summer, turning red and wine by July, with strong wine fall color and an attractive tan color in winter.

top to bottom

'Heavy Metal' summer foliage.

'Heavy Metal' massed at the State Botanical Garden of Georgia.

'Shenandoah' in Rabun Gap, Ga., with perennials, by the Fockele Garden Co.

'Shenandoah' in winter with dwarf winterberry holly, Fourth Ward Park, Atlanta, by HDR.

Pennisetum alopecuriodes FOUNTAIN GRASS

Fountain grass has long been utilized as an ornamental grass and is valued for its gracefully arching fountain-like form, fine texture, attractive flowering, low height in the landscape, and respectable winter presence. There are many good cultivars available that can be used as specimen accents in detail plantings or in large sweeping masses as a ground cover. Fountain grass tolerates the hot wet summers of the South well but is also fairly drought tolerant. It is invasive in the southwestern United States. Confusion often exists between the purple fountain grasses, which are borderline cold-hardy in zones 8, and this species, which will grow much farther north.

In Costa Mesa, Calif., where it is invasive.

ZONES & ORIGIN 6–9. Native to Japan and southeastern Asia.

SIZE & GROWTH RATE 1'–5' depending on the cultivar, and fast growing.

TEXTURE & FORM Fine texture with an upright arching form.

FOLIAGE Clump-forming and gracefully arching leaf blades are rich green in summer and light tan in winter, providing a good winter presence.

FLOWERS Distinctive fuzzy terminal panicles (like fuzzy caterpillars) 1" wide and 4"–6" long are held above the foliage from June through fall depending on the cultivar. Colors vary from white to cream or pink purple.

FRUIT The fuzzy panicles often last well through winter and offer a beautiful winter presence.

LIGHT & SOIL Full sun to light shade. Tolerates a variety of soils, but good drainage is essential, especially in winter.

MAINTENANCE Long-lived and drought tolerant once established. Cut back where necessary in late winter before new foliage emerges.

INSTALLATION Space containers 18"–3' apart depending on the cultivar for masses.

PESTS & DISEASES None major.

NOTES & CULTIVARS
'Cassian' grows to 3' tall, with cream flowers in August and gold with red-tinted fall color.
'Caudatum' grows to 3' tall, with nearly white flowers in August.
'Hameln' is 2'–3' tall in flower, light green to white flowers, and amber fall color.
'Little Bunny' is under 18" tall in flower; otherwise, it is similar to 'Hameln'.
'Moudry' grows 2'–3' tall, with distinctive dark purple to almost black-gray flowers in September. This color can be off-putting in the wrong context.

top to bottom

The soft fluffy inflorescences from midsummer on invite one to touch.

'Moudry'.

In a design by Robert Murase near Portland, Oreg.

top left Early autumn amber color.

top right Clumps show subtle blue and pink tints compared with other greens. All photos courtesy of Hoffman Nursery.

bottom Inflorescences beautifully catch the winter sunlight.

Schizachyrium scoparium LITTLE BLUESTEM

Little bluestem is a refined-looking, fine-textured, clumping native grass with a tough constitution. It can be found across all North America in open, sunny, and well-drained sites. Its smaller size and attractive, often blue-tinged foliage are easy to use in masses, as part of meadow mixes, or as part of a perennial border. It wants to be planted on hot dry sites and prefers to be neglected. Soils that are too rich and applications of thick mulch can cause decline. In fall the foliage turns a rich combination of rusty orange and purple, finally resting into a warm amber color for the winter. It is widely available and useful in so many applications, from seeds to plugs to containers.

ZONES & ORIGIN 3–9. Native from southern Florida and Arizona to southern Canada.

SIZE & GROWTH RATE 2'–4' tall, 2'–3' wide, and slow growing.

TEXTURE & FORM Fine texture with a stiff upright oval form.

FOLIAGE Narrow upright clumps of green foliage with cultivars selected for blue foliage. Russet red to amber fall and winter foliage.

FLOWERS Blooms in August and September atop green stems with fuzzy white inflorescences ¼" long that last through winter and glow in winter sunlight.

FRUIT Insignificant seed.

LIGHT & SOIL Full sun to light shade. Well-drained to dry soil is essential.

MAINTENANCE Trim back in late winter or burn where possible.

INSTALLATION Space containers or plugs 12"–18" on center for mass plantings.

PESTS & DISEASES None major.

NOTES & CULTIVARS
'The Blues' provide superb blue-tinted foliage.
'Standing Ovation' has bluish foliage and slightly thicker leaf blades with an upright form.

Sorghastrum nutans INDIAN GRASS

Indian grass is a common native occurring in a wide variety of habitats, including prairie, savannah, well-drained slopes, and open woods from Canada to Florida and west to Arizona and Mexico. It is one of the dominant warm-season grasses along with panic grass and big and little bluestem. Indian grass is primarily clump forming or slowly rhizomatous and provides upright green or blue-green summer foliage topped with slender chestnut-brown seed heads in mid- to late summer. It is useful planted in large sweeps from plugs or from seeds and works well as part of a native seed mix for land restoration projects. Several handsome blue-green-leaved cultivars have been selected mostly from western provenance. Southeastern selections are needed.

top Flowers.

bottom 'Indian Steel' at Hoffman Nursery.

ZONES & ORIGIN 3–10. Native throughout eastern North America into Canada.

SIZE & GROWTH RATE 3'–5' tall, 2'–3' wide, and medium fast growing.

TEXTURE & FORM Fine texture with an upright oval form.

FOLIAGE Slender upright clumps of green to blue-green foliage turn amber colored in fall and hold their winter form well.

FLOWERS Slender flower and seed heads held well above the foliage in mid- to late summer.

FRUIT Slender seed heads turn from green to chestnut brown in fall and winter and do not typically remain upright all winter.

LIGHT & SOIL Provide full sun to light shade. It tolerates a variety of soils, from dry slopes to seasonally moist floodplains.

MAINTENANCE Trim back in late winter where needed before new spring growth.

INSTALLATION Space containers or plugs 18"–3' on center for mass plantings. It can also be seeded effectively.

PESTS & DISEASES None major.

NOTES & CULTIVARS

'Indian Steel' has bluish-green foliage 3'–4' tall with an upright form and attractive fall foliage.

'Sioux Blue' has glaucous gray-blue foliage and very attractive golden-brown winter foliage.

left 'Indian Steel' with sedum and fountain grass at Hoffman Nursery.

right A floodplain meadow of Indian grass along the New River, Carroll County, Va., with *Juglans cinerea*, white walnut, forming much of the overstory.

Sporobolus heterolepis PRAIRIE DROPSEED

Prairie dropseed naturally occurs on North American prairies from Quebec south to Colorado and Texas; however, it has also proven to be quite happy planted in the hot humid Southeast. It is long-lived and drought tolerant and is highly desirable in planting design for its small size, usefulness as a ground cover, and delicate and refined fine texture. The softness of a mass of prairie dropseed is pleasing to the eye and peaceful to the soul. The flowering is also delicate, with fine-textured seed heads floating above the foliage and glinting in the sunlight in late summer to early fall. Fall color is exquisite as warm orange copper, fading to light amber for winter.

ZONES & ORIGIN 3–8. Native to the midwestern North American prairies.

SIZE & GROWTH RATE 2'–3' tall and wide. Slow growing.

TEXTURE & FORM Fine texture with an arching habit and mounded form.

FOLIAGE Threadlike shiny dark green foliage in weeping clumps in summer turns orange copper in fall and fades to soft amber in winter.

FLOWERS Delicate creamy-white seed heads held above the foliage in late summer to early fall are noticeably fragrant.

FRUIT Delicate inflorescences turn tan for winter and offer minimal ornament.

LIGHT & SOIL Provide full sun to light shade. It tolerates sandy or clay soils but must have good drainage and is drought tolerant.

MAINTENANCE Trim back old foliage in late winter before new spring growth.

INSTALLATION Space plugs or containers 18"–2' on center for mass plantings.

PESTS & DISEASES None major.

NOTES & CULTIVARS
Prefers poor soils and is easily outcompeted by other faster- and taller-growing grasses on rich moist sites.

top to bottom

A soft bed for sculpture at Chanticleer.

Summer texture at Chanticleer Garden.

With false blue indigo at Chanticleer Garden.

Tripsacum dactyloides EASTERN GAMAGRASS

Eastern gamagrass, also often referred to as fakahatchee grass, is native to the Southeast and beyond, occurring in wet drainage swales and in moist soils from Massachusetts to Florida and west to Texas and Kansas and Iowa. It is a commonly used landscape plant in the Gulf Coast South and can be used in more well drained soils in addition to moist areas. It forms a large bold medium-textured upright clump to as much as 10' in flower. It is useful in creating informal vegetative screens and buffers, as well as bioswale plantings and land restoration, and is tolerant of salt spray.

ZONES & ORIGIN 5–10. Native from Florida and Texas to Iowa.

SIZE & GROWTH RATE 3'–10' tall, 4'–6' wide, and fast growing.

TEXTURE & FORM Medium texture and upright oval form.

FOLIAGE Leaf blades are 1" wide with sharp edges. They are a shiny medium green in summer and occur in very upright clumps. The foliage is evergreen in zones 9 and 10 but deciduous elsewhere.

FLOWERS Thin terminal spikes occur in mid- to late summer. Flower structures are dark red tinged with pink seeds hanging sideways off the stem, reaching high above the foliage to 10'.

FRUIT Seed may remain above foliage into winter and is somewhat ornamental.

LIGHT & SOIL Full sun to light shade. It tolerates regular well-drained soils of clay or sand or moist soils in drainage swales. Salt spray tolerant.

MAINTENANCE Trim back in late winter before new spring foliage emerges.

INSTALLATION Space 4'–5' on center for mass plantings from plugs or containers.

PESTS & DISEASES None major.

NOTES & CULTIVARS
Florida gamagrass, *Tripsacum floridanum*, is a lower-growing form to 30" tall and is hardy to at least zone 8a.

top to bottom

Solid mass planting at the State Botanical Garden of Georgia.

Linear inflorescences erupt out of the lush foliage.

Typha angustifolia NARROW-LEAVED CATTAIL

Narrow-leaved cattail is native to moist areas across North America, South America, and Eurasia. It is an obligate wetland plant (it must be in water or wet soils at all times) and is usually found in moist drainage swales and along pond and river edges. It provides a bold upright linear texture that is quite beautiful at the water's edge. In summer the distinctive tails are produced above the foliage as spikes of dark cinnamon brown. These will often hold well into winter and provide visual interest. Cattails spread by rhizomes or seed and are quite aggressive; they may outcompete other more desirable species. The plant has been used worldwide for food and for making baskets. A similar species, *Typha latifolia*, is also very common and is listed below.

top to bottom

October at Fort Mountain State Park, Ga., with the black gums turning red.

Granville Island, Vancouver, B.C.

ZONES & ORIGIN 3–10. Native throughout North America.

SIZE & GROWTH RATE 4'–6' tall, 3'–5' wide, and fast growing.

TEXTURE & FORM Medium texture with a stiff upright habit and oval form.

FOLIAGE Strap-like linear foliage of medium green to 4'–5' long.

FLOWERS Prominent terminal spike-like inflorescences 4"–6" long have a short space separating the male and female segments.

FRUIT Inflorescences are warm cinnamon brown, turning nearly black in fall and winter.

LIGHT & SOIL Full sun to light shade with moist to wet soil is essential.

MAINTENANCE Spreads aggressively and can overwhelm moist-soil plantings. Utilize it where large masses will be acceptable.

INSTALLATION Space 2'–4' on center for initial establishment from bare-root seedlings or plugs.

PESTS & DISEASES None major.

NOTES & CULTIVARS

Typha latifolia is a visually similar species, although it is taller growing to as much as 10'. Flower spikes lack the separation between male and female segments. Native and hardy in zones 3–10.

PERENNIALS, BULBS, AND GROUND COVERS

To plant and tend a perennial garden is to become intimate with the incredibly diverse growth habits and personalities of plants. The number of combinations and possibilities in a temperate garden is an almost endless source of wonder and delight. While perennials are popular in America, the average landscape is sadly typically missing this more detailed element. In garden design it is generally understood that the bones of the garden are the trees, shrubs, and architectural features such as fences, walls, and buildings. This is indeed true, but to have a landscape of only bones is to miss the depth and complexity that perennials have to offer. Perennials are human scale, and they put the flesh on a garden's bones. They are the smile and the kiss of color and texture and the breath that elevates a simple landscape to that of a garden—a place where one can get lost in the wonder and beauty of the natural world as it has been lovingly tended and shaped by human hands.

Perennial gardens can be rich and complex, as in the incredible perennial beds at Chanticleer estate in Wayne, Pennsylvania, or the famous border at the J. C. Raulston Arboretum in Raleigh, North Carolina. However, they can also be very low maintenance additions to simpler landscapes of shrubs and grasses when used in masses. Altogether, their versatility creates endless opportunities for landscapes that capture the imagination and invite human and animal interaction. Many perennials are extremely attractive to pollinators, and this activity adds a significant layer of interest and ecological function. Take a risk and lose some turf to make way for perennial plantings, and watch the ecology of your piece of the earth become far more engaging.

We have designed this section to capture a wide range of plants, including traditionally defined perennials, as well as bulbs and ground covers. The idea is that scale in the human-dominated landscape is almost always of utmost importance. Once the correct scale has been chosen, more detailed decisions can be made regarding color, texture, and seasonal change. The 0'–8' range in the landscape can encompass an amazing variety of plants, from bulbs and perennials to grasses and shrubs. All of these should be considered when doing a planting design in order to create landscapes that appeal to the human senses—making livable and beautiful places for people that are also of greater benefit to the overall environment.

Perennials, grasses, and bulbs are woven into an exquisite tapestry by the talented horticulturalists at Chanticleer Garden in Wayne, Pa.

EVERGREEN PERENNIALS

BOTANICAL NAME	SUNLIGHT	SOILS	SALT	TEXTURE	DROUGHT	SEASONAL ATTRIBUTES	NATIVE TO SE
UNDER 12" TALL (GENERALLY)							
Dianthus spp.	Full sun to light shade	Dry to moist well drained	Yes	Fine	Yes	Spring flowers	No
Iberis sempervirens	Full sun to moderate shade	Dry to moist well drained	Yes	Fine	Yes	Spring flowers	No
Liriope muscari	Light to heavy shade	Moist well drained to dry	Moderate	Medium	Yes	Late summer flowers	No
Mazus reptans	Full sun to moderate shade	Moist well drained	No	Fine	No	Spring flowers	No
Ophiopogon japonicus	Light to moderate shade	Moist well drained to dry	Yes	Fine	Yes	—	No
Pachysandra terminalis	Light to moderate shade	Moist well drained	No	Medium fine	No	Spring flowers	No
Phlox subulata	Full sun to light shade	Dry to moist well drained	No	Fine	Yes	Spring flowers	Yes
Rubus calycinoides	Full sun to light shade	Moist well drained	No	Medium	No	Winter foliage color	No
Sedum sarmentosum	Full sun to light shade	Dry to moist well drained	No	Fine	Yes	Spring flowers	No
Vinca major	Light to moderate shade	Dry to moist well drained	No	Medium	Yes	Spring flowers	No
Vinca minor	Light to moderate shade	Dry to moist well drained	No	Fine	Yes	Spring flowers	No
12" – 36" TALL							
Aspidistra elatior	Moderate shade	Dry to moist well drained	No	Coarse	Yes	—	No
Equisetum hyemale	Full sun to moderate shade	Moist well drained to wet or submerged	No	Fine	No	—	Yes
Helleborus orientalis	Light to moderate shade	Dry to moist well drained	No	Coarse	Yes	Winter and spring flowers	No
Heuchera spp.	Light to moderate shade	Moist well drained	No	Medium coarse	No	Foliage colors	No

DECIDUOUS PERENNIALS

BOTANICAL NAME	SUNLIGHT	SOILS	SALT	TEXTURE	DROUGHT	SEASONAL ATTRIBUTES	NATIVE TO SE
UNDER 12" TALL							
Ajuga reptans	Light to moderate shade	Moist well drained	No	Medium	No	Spring flowers, foliage color	No
Conoclinium coelestinum	Full sun to moderate shade	Moist well drained	No	Medium	Yes	Fall flowers	Yes
Crocus spp.	Full sun to light shade	Dry to moist well drained	No	Fine	Yes	Spring flowers	No
Epimedium spp.	Light to moderate shade	Dry to moist well drained	No	Medium	Yes	Spring flowers, foliage nearly evergreen	No
Glandularia canadensis	Full sun to light shade	Dry to moist well drained	Mildly	Fine	Yes	Flowers spring and summer	Yes
Hosta spp.	Light to moderate shade	Moist well drained	Mildly	Coarse	Yes	Foliage color and texture, summer flowers	No
Iris cristata	Light to moderate shade	Dry to moist well drained	No	Medium	Yes	Spring flowers	Yes

BOTANICAL NAME	SUNLIGHT	SOILS	SALT	TEXTURE	DROUGHT	SEASONAL ATTRIBUTES	NATIVE TO SE
Iris tectorum	Light to moderate shade	Dry to moist well drained	No	Medium	Yes	Spring flowers, foliage interest	No
Leucojum vernum	Full sun to light shade	Dry to moist well drained	No	Fine	Yes	Spring flowers	No
Lycoris radiata	Full sun to light shade	Dry to moist well drained	No	Fine	Yes	Late summer flowers	No
Lysimachia nummularia 'Aurea'	Light to moderate shade	Moist well drained	Yes	Fine	No	Foliage color	No
Narcissus spp.	Full sun to light shade	Dry to moist well drained	Mildly	Medium	Yes	Spring flowers	No
Packera aurea	Light to moderate shade	Dry to moist well drained	No	Medium	Yes	Spring flowers, foliage interest	Yes
Phlox divaricata	Light to moderate shade	Dry to moist well drained	Yes	Fine	Yes	Spring flowers	Yes
Stachys byzantina	Full sun to light shade	Dry to moist well drained	No	Coarse	Yes	Foliage interest, late spring flowers	No
Tiarella cordifolia	Light to moderate shade	Moist well drained	Low	Medium	No	Spring flowers, foliage interest	Yes
Tradescantia pallida 'Purpurea'	Full sun to moderate shade	Moist well drained	Yes	Medium	Yes	Foliage interest, flowers all season	No
Trillium spp.	Light to moderate shade	Moist well drained	No	Medium	No	Spring flowers, foliage interest	Yes

12" – 36" TALL

BOTANICAL NAME	SUNLIGHT	SOILS	SALT	TEXTURE	DROUGHT	SEASONAL ATTRIBUTES	NATIVE TO SE
Achillea spp.	Full sun to light shade	Dry to moist well drained	Yes	Fine	Yes	Spring and summer flowers, foliage	No
Agastache spp.	Full sun to light shade	Dry to moist well drained	No	Medium	Yes	Summer flowers, scented foliage	Yes
Allium spp.	Full sun to light shade	Dry to moist well drained	No	Medium	Yes	Spring flowers, seed heads	No
Amsonia hubrichtii	Full sun to light shade	Dry to moist well drained	No	Fine	Yes	Spring flowers, foliage texture	Midwest native
Amsonia tabernaemontana	Light to moderate shade	Moist well drained	No	Fine	Yes	Spring flowers	Yes
Aquilegia canadensis	Light to moderate shade	Moist well drained	No	Medium	Yes	Spring flowers	Yes
Asclepias tuberosa	Full sun to light shade	Dry to moist well drained	Yes (*A. tuberosa*)	Medium	Many species	Summer flowers	Yes
Aster spp.	Full sun to light shade	Dry to moist well drained	No	Fine	Yes	Fall flowers	Yes
Astilbe spp.	Light to moderate shade	Moist well drained	No	Fine	No	Summer flowers, foliage interest	No
Farfugium japonicum	Light to moderate shade	Moist well drained	No	Coarse	No	Foliage interest, spring flowers	No
Hemerocallis spp.	Full sun to light shade	Dry to moist well drained	Yes	Medium	Yes	Summer flowers	No
Hosta spp.	Light to moderate shade	Moist well drained	Mildly	Coarse	No	Foliage interest, summer flowers	No
Hylotelephium 'Autumn Joy'	Full sun to light shade	Dry to moist well drained	No	Medium	Yes	Fall flowers, foliage interest, seed heads	No
Hypericum spp.	Full sun to light shade	Dry to moist well drained	No	Medium	Somewhat	Summer and fall flowers	Yes
Iris ensata	Full sun to light shade	Moist well drained to moist	No	Medium	No	Summer flowers, foliage interest	No
Iris × germanica	Full sun to light shade	Dry to moist well drained	No	Medium	Yes	Spring flowers, foliage interest	No

BOTANICAL NAME	SUNLIGHT	SOILS	SALT	TEXTURE	DROUGHT	SEASONAL ATTRIBUTES	NATIVE TO SE
Iris sibirica	Full sun to light shade	Moist well drained to moist	No	Fine	Yes	Spring flowers, foliage interest	No
Lantana camara	Full sun to light shade	Dry to moist well drained	Yes	Medium	Yes	Summer and fall flowers	Central America
Leucanthemum × superbum	Full sun to light shade	Moist well drained	No	Medium	No	Summer flowers, foliage interest	No
Liatris spicata	Full sun to light shade	Moist well drained to moist	No	Fine	Yes	Summer flowers	Yes
Lilium spp.	Full sun to light shade	Moist well drained	Yes, *Crinum* spp.	Medium	Yes	Summer and fall flowers, fragrance	Some species
Lobelia cardinalis	Full sun to light shade	Moist well drained to moist	No	Medium	No	Summer flowers	Yes
Monarda didyma	Full sun to light shade	Moist well drained to moist	No	Medium	No	Summer flowers	Yes
Paeonia spp.	Full sun to light shade	Dry to moist well drained	No	Coarse	Yes	Spring flowers, fragrance	No
Penstemon spp.	Full sun to light shade	Dry to moist well drained	No	Medium	Yes	Spring and summer flowers	Some species
Rudbeckia fulgida	Full sun to light shade	Moist well drained to moist	No	Medium	Yes	Summer and fall flowers, seed heads	Yes
Salvia greggii	Full sun to light shade	Dry to moist well drained	No	Fine	Yes	Summer and fall flowers	Texas and Mexico
Salvia sclarea 'Turkistanica'	Full sun to light shade	Dry to moist well drained	No	Coarse	Yes	Spring flowers, foliage interest	No
Salvia 'Cherry Queen'	Full sun to light shade	Dry to moist well drained	No	Fine	Yes	Summer and fall flowers	No
Salvia 'Mystic Spires'	Full sun to light shade	Dry to moist well drained	No	Fine	Yes	Summer and fall flowers	No
Salvia 'Blue Queen'	Full sun to light shade	Dry to moist well drained	No	Fine	Yes	Summer and fall flowers	No
Salvia 'East Friesland'	Full sun to light shade	Dry to moist well drained	No	Fine	Yes	Summer and fall flowers	No
Stokesia laevis	Full sun to light shade	Dry to moist well drained	No	Medium	Yes	Summer flowers	Yes
Solidago spp.	Full sun to light shade	Dry, moist well drained to moist	Yes	Fine	Most forms	Summer and fall flowers	Yes
Tradescantia virginiana	Full sun to moderate shade	Moist well drained to moist	No	Medium	No	Spring flowers	Yes
Tulbaghea violacea	Full sun to light shade	Dry to moist well drained	Yes	Fine	Yes	Summer and fall flowers	No
Verbena rigida	Full sun to light shade	Dry to moist well drained	No	Fine	Yes	Summer and fall flowers	No

36"–60" TALL

BOTANICAL NAME	SUNLIGHT	SOILS	SALT	TEXTURE	DROUGHT	SEASONAL ATTRIBUTES	NATIVE TO SE
Acanthus spinosus	Light to moderate shade	Dry to moist well drained	No	Coarse	Yes	Winter foliage, spring flowers	No
Achillea spp.	Full sun to light shade	Dry to moist well drained	Yes	Fine	Yes	Spring and summer flowers	No
Agapanthus spp.	Full sun to light shade	Dry to moist well drained	Yes	Medium	Yes	Summer and fall flowers	No
Anemone × hybrida	Light to moderate shade	Moist well drained	No	Medium	No	Fall flowers	No
Aster spp.	Full sun to light shade	Dry to moist well drained	No	Medium	Yes	Fall flowers	Yes

BOTANICAL NAME	SUNLIGHT	SOILS	SALT	TEXTURE	DROUGHT	SEASONAL ATTRIBUTES	NATIVE TO SE
Baptisia australis	Full sun to light shade	Dry to moist well drained	No	Medium	Yes	Spring flowers	Yes
Canna × generalis	Full sun to light shade	Moist well drained to submerged	Mildly	Coarse	No	Summer flowers, foliage interest	No
Colocasia esculenta	Full sun to moderate shade	Moist well drained to submerged	No	Coarse	No	Foliage interest	No
Crocosmia × hybrida	Full sun to light shade	Dry to moist well drained	No	Medium	Yes	Summer flowers	No
Echinacea purpurea	Full sun to light shade	Dry to moist well drained	Mildly	Medium	Yes	Summer and fall flowers	Yes
Gaura lindheimeri	Full sun to light shade	Dry to moist well drained	No	Fine	Yes	Summer and fall flowers	Yes
Hedychium coronarium	Full sun to moderate shade	Moist well drained to wet	Yes	Coarse	No	Fall flowers, fragrance	No
Iris × louisiana	Full sun to light shade	Moist well drained to submerged	No	Medium	No	Late spring flowers, foliage interest	Yes
Iris pseudacorus	Full sun to light shade	Moist well drained to submerged	No	Medium	Yes	Spring flowers, foliage interest	No
Lantana camara	Full sun to light shade	Dry to moist well drained	Yes	Medium	Yes	Summer and fall flowers	Mexico
Lilium spp.	Full sun to light shade	Dry to moist well drained	No	Medium	Yes	Summer and fall flowers, fragrance	Some
Perovskia atriplicifolia	Full sun to light shade	Dry to moist well drained	No	Fine	Yes	Summer flowers, foliage interest	No
Phlox paniculata	Full sun to light shade	Moist well drained	No	Medium	No	Summer flowers	Yes
Ruellia brittoniana	Full sun to light shade	Moist well drained to moist	Mildly	Medium	No	Summer and fall flowers	No
Salvia guaranitica	Full sun to light shade	Dry to moist well drained	No	Medium	Yes	Summer and fall flowers	No
Salvia leucantha	Full sun to light shade	Dry to moist well drained	No	Medium	Yes	Fall flowers	Mexico
Salvia 'Indigo Spires'	Full sun to light shade	Dry to moist well drained	No	Medium	Yes	Summer and fall flowers	No
Solidago spp.	Full sun to light shade	Dry to moist well drained	Yes	Fine	Most forms	Fall flowers	Yes
Verbena bonariensis	Full sun to light shade	Dry to moist well drained	No	Fine	Yes	Summer and fall flowers	No

OVER 5' TALL

BOTANICAL NAME	SUNLIGHT	SOILS	SALT	TEXTURE	DROUGHT	SEASONAL ATTRIBUTES	NATIVE TO SE
Alpinia zerumbet	Light to moderate shade	Moist well drained to moist	Yes	Coarse	Yes	Foliage interest, fall flowers	No
Brugmansia spp.	Full sun to light shade	Dry to moist well drained	Mildly	Coarse	Yes	Summer and fall flowers, fragrance	No
Canna × generalis	Full sun to light shade	Moist well drained to submerged	Mildly	Coarse	No	Foliage interest, flowers	No
Eutrochium maculatum	Full sun to light shade	Dry to moist well drained	No	Coarse	Yes	Late summer and fall flowers	Yes
Helianthus spp.	Full sun to light shade	Dry to moist	No	Medium	Yes	Fall flowers	Yes
Hibiscus spp.	Full sun to light shade	Moist well drained to moist	Mildly	Coarse	No	Summer and fall flowers	Some species
Musa spp.	Full sun to light shade	Moist well drained to moist	No	Coarse	No	Tropical summer foliage	No
Salvia madrensis	Full sun to light shade	Dry to moist well drained	No	Coarse	Yes	Fall flowers	No
Vernonia noveboracensis	Full sun to light shade	Moist well drained to moist	Mildly	Medium	Yes	Late summer flowers	Yes

top left In the Founders Memorial Garden at UGA.

bottom left Cast iron plant and holly fern at Bellingrath Gardens near Mobile, Ala.

right In containers in Beaufort, S.C.

Aspidistra elatior CAST IRON PLANT

The cast iron plant earned its name from its ability to tolerate extremely low light conditions and drought. It was also known as parlor plant in the Victorian era, as it can be grown in dark corners of interior rooms. In the landscape it makes a wonderful coarse-textured tall and dark evergreen ground cover under deciduous or evergreen shrubs and trees, coping with the competition for water and nutrients quite well. It is commonly seen under the canopy of live oaks in New Orleans and other cities and towns in the Deep South. In the northern extent of its range, it benefits from a protected location such as a courtyard or a place that is sheltered from winter winds.

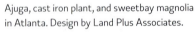

Ajuga, cast iron plant, and sweetbay magnolia in Atlanta. Design by Land Plus Associates.

ZONES & ORIGIN 7–10. Native to China.

SIZE & GROWTH RATE 18"–30" tall and slow growing.

TEXTURE & FORM Coarse texture and grows in an upright clump.

FOLIAGE Radial and arching clumps of oblong and elliptic very dark green leaves to 30" long and 5" wide gradually narrow into a petiole to 15" long. The leaves have acute tapering tips and parallel veins with grooved stalks.

FLOWERS & SEEDS Rarely seen single flowers 1" wide that are brown with purple markings are born in late winter and appear at the soil surface, obscured by foliage and leaf debris.

LIGHT & SOIL Light to moderate shade. They will survive full sun, but the foliage burns and looks horrific. They prefer moist well-drained soil but tolerate poor dry soil and drought once established.

MAINTENANCE This is a carefree plant, although it benefits from selective removal of tired leaves once a year.

INSTALLATION Space 12" on center for mass plantings. It grows very slowly by creeping rhizomes, so the extra cost of closely spaced plants is worth the investment.

PESTS & DISEASES No major issues with good drainage. Deer don't bother them.

NOTES & CULTIVARS 'Milky Way' grows to 24", with slimmer leaves with speckled creamy-white variegation. Other variegated cultivars exist and make interesting specimen plants.

Dianthus spp. PINKS

The genus *Dianthus* includes many annual and perennial species from various parts of Europe. This account is centered on the species and hybrids that are true evergreen perennials and typically have a very low spreading habit with fine-textured silvery-colored foliage, such as *Dianthus gratianopolitanus* and cultivars. These plants make a wonderful drought-tolerant low evergreen ground cover with an impressive floral display in late April and May. Most are also quite fragrant. They are useful as the lowest layer in a planting composition and in an herbal knot garden, and they also work well in cracks and crevices and detail areas. Some division and resetting may be necessary every few years if a large solid ground cover mass is desired.

A double cultivar.

ZONES & ORIGIN 3–8. Native to the British Isles and Europe.

SIZE & GROWTH RATE 6"–12" tall with a medium growth rate.

TEXTURE & FORM Fine texture in a low spreading mass.

FOLIAGE Opposite narrow lanceolate gray or silvery-green foliage ¼" wide to 2" long with entire margins. Foliage is attractive without flowers.

FLOWERS & SEEDS Single or double flowers are born solitary or in pairs from late March through May. They are held above the foliage on thin stems to 12" tall in white, pinks, deep red, and bicolors depending on the cultivar. Most are fragrant. The flowers will reseed themselves. Flowering may be prolonged into summer by removal of spent flowers.

LIGHT & SOIL Full sun to light shade. Prefers moist well-drained soil but tolerates poor dry soil and drought once established. Prefers neutral to alkaline soils but appears to perform well in slightly acidic soils as well. Salt spray tolerant.

MAINTENANCE This is a carefree plant. Reset plants every few years to maintain solid mass plantings.

INSTALLATION Space 12"–18" on center for mass plantings. They spread slowly.

PESTS & DISEASES None major.

NOTES & CULTIVARS
'Bath's Pink' has light pink flowers and gray-green foliage.
'Firewitch' has deep magenta-pink flowers and gray-green foliage.
'Greystone' has white flowers and gray-green foliage.
'Mountain Mist' has pink flowers and gray-green foliage.
'Splendens' has deep red flowers and gray-green foliage.

top to bottom

Dianthus gratianopolitanus on a June visit to New York City.

Ground cover massing in Athens. The foliage is attractive even after flowering ends.

Dianthus is low enough to provide the final layer in the planting scheme.

Equisetum hyemale
HORSETAIL RUSH · SCOURING RUSH

Horsetail rush is a native perennial occurring in moist to wet environments in full sun to light shade across the eastern United States. The foliage may remind one of a horse tail, but it is also called scouring rush because the foliage has a high silica content and was used to scour and polish. It is only fully evergreen in zones 9 and 10, semievergreen above zone 9. The linear quality of the plant is eye-catching and distinctive and lends itself to use in containers and planters, along walls, or next to and in water. The designer must beware of its tendency to spread aggressively by underground stems, particularly in moist environments. A significant soil barrier is necessary to keep the plant in bounds, but the stunning visual effects are often well worth the extra effort.

ZONES & ORIGIN 4–9. Native to the eastern United States.

SIZE & GROWTH RATE 3'–5' tall and fast growing.

TEXTURE & FORM Stiff upright form with a fine texture.

FOLIAGE Stiff upright stems, cylindrical, hollow, jointed, to 5' tall. Dark green in color, with dark bands at stem joints.

FLOWERS & SEEDS Reproductive spores produced in a terminal sporophyll. Insignificant.

LIGHT & SOIL Full sun to light shade. Prefers shallow water, wet, or moist well-drained soil but will tolerate periodic dryness once established.

MAINTENANCE A soil barrier that is 12" deep or deeper is a must; otherwise, the plant spreads rapidly.

INSTALLATION Space containers or cuttings/divisions 12"–24" on center.

PESTS & DISEASES None.

NOTES & CULTIVARS
Equisetum arvense, field horsetail, grows to 9" tall with a grasslike texture.

top Reproductive spores on stem tips in late spring.

midddle *Equisetum arvense*.

bottom left Horsetail's aggressive spreading is kept in check by a container.

bottom right Horsetail makes an architectural statement in this Knoxville residence by SWH Associates.

Helleborus orientalis LENTEN ROSE

Hellebore species are native to Europe and Asia and occur as part of the woodland understory. *Helleborus orientalis* has long been used in cultivation; however, today's nursery plants are often hybrids, listed as *H. × hybridus*, as growers pursue distinct flower coloration and, recently, flowers that hold their heads upright rather than in a nodding posture. Hellebores make wonderful plants for design as they are tough, low, and evergreen, they like shade, and they bloom during the season of Lent, from early March through the end of May, in colors ranging from white to green and various shades of pink, purple, and even black. For an interesting read on historic medicinal use, look up the veterinary medicinal practice of "settering" using the roots of *H. viridis*. All parts of hellebores are toxic to humans and animals if ingested.

ZONES & ORIGIN 3–8. Native to Europe and Asia.

SIZE & GROWTH RATE 12"–18" tall; slow growing.

TEXTURE & FORM Mounding clumps; coarse texture.

FOLIAGE Palmately compound dark green and leathery leaves with coarsely toothed margins grow to 12" across.

FLOWERS & SEEDS Attractive cup-shaped and nodding flowers 1"–2" across bloom from early March through May in white, pinks, purples, green, and black, sometimes speckled. Flowers fade to green and produce seed in three to ten segmented follicles. Reseeds readily.

LIGHT & SOIL Light to moderate shade. Prefers woodland with organic rich and moist but well-drained soil.

MAINTENANCE Reseeds readily, and clumps slowly increase and may be divided.

INSTALLATION Space containers or clump divisions 12"–24" on center.

PESTS & DISEASES None.

NOTES & CULTIVARS
Consult specialty growers for an endless list of named hybrids. New hybrids with outward-facing flowers appear to be slower growing and are reported to be sterile.

top left Hellebore ground cover under a dogwood.

top right Typical *orientalis* mixture of pinks and whites in the Founders Memorial Garden.

midddle Palmate foliage.

bottom Nodding flowers.

Heuchera spp.   CORAL BELLS · ALUM ROOT

Coral bells are grown for their exciting foliage colors, low habit, evergreen leaves, and medium to coarse texture. They need filtered shade and a rich and moist well-drained soil to perform well in the South. At least five species of coral bells are native to various parts of the United States, with two occurring in the Southeast. These are *Heuchera americana* and *H. villosa*. A trip to the garden center today will yield dozens of hybrid choices, many of which may not perform well in all regions. The best ones for heat will have significant genes of either *H. villosa* or *H. americana*. Below is a short list of hybrids that tolerate the heat and humidity well.

Caramel-colored *Heuchera* with yarrow, yucca, and lamb's ear.

left Coral bells and hardy geranium at Chanticleer.

right A tapestry with hostas and creeping jenny forms the last layer at Chanticleer.

ZONES & ORIGIN 4–9. Native to North America.

SIZE & GROWTH RATE 12"–24" tall; medium growing.

TEXTURE & FORM Mounding clumps; medium to coarse texture.

FOLIAGE Rounded, lobed, and often coarsely toothed leaves 4"–6" long on long petioles form a mounded clump of evergreen foliage. Brightly colored cultivars may fade in summer heat.

FLOWERS & SEED Many hybrids do flower quite attractively, with light airy panicles held above the foliage in May and June. Flower colors range from white, pink, red, and purple depending on hybrid and can offer an interesting complement to the foliage color. Insignificant seed.

LIGHT & SOIL Light to moderate shade. Prefers woodland and organic rich, moist, but well-drained soil.

MAINTENANCE May need to be divided and reset every few years. Supplemental water is necessary in hot dry weather.

INSTALLATION Space container-grown plants 12"–24" on center for mass effect.

PESTS & DISEASES None major.

NOTES & CULTIVARS These vigorous cultivars are adapted to hotter regions:

H. americana is a native species that is purple tinted and grows to 18".

H. villosa is also a native species and has green foliage to 18".

'Amethyst Mist' has a purple tint.

'Brownies' is light brown.

'Can Can' has silver venation.

'Caramel' has a peachy color.

'Crimson Curls' is ruffled bronze above and burgundy below.

'Ebony and Ivory' is a ruffled bronze.

'Eco-Improved' is silver with green veins.

'Frosted Violet' has pink/purple colors.

'Green Spice' is green with silver veins.

'Lime Ricky' is chartreuse.

'Obsidian' is black.

'Palace Purple Improved' is purple.

'Regina' is dark bronze.

'Ruby Veil' is red bronze.

'Shenandoah Mountain' is silvery purple.

left Early spring flowering. Candytuft is great at a bed or wall edge.

right A tight ground cover habit allows candytuft to mix well with other perennials.

Iberis sempervirens CANDYTUFT

Candytuft was once a well-known garden plant and is often seen around old homes and gardens. It is a tough-as-nails plant and offers a fine-textured, low-spreading, evergreen ground cover or border plant and attractive white (sometimes pink) spring flowers—what could be better? It tolerates drought well once it is established and is extremely long-lived. It should be used more in contemporary landscapes. Dwarf cultivars offer an even shorter evergreen ground cover option. Fall reblooming cultivars also exist; however, just like in the movies, the sequel is less impressive.

ZONES & ORIGIN 3–8. Native to southern Europe.

SIZE & GROWTH RATE 10"–18" tall with 3' spread, medium growing.

TEXTURE & FORM Fine texture with mounding and spreading clumps.

FOLIAGE Thin lanceolate acuminate leaves are dark green and 1½" long. Leaves are entire, with one to two angles on their margins.

FLOWERS & SEED 1½" umbel-shaped inflorescences lengthen with age. They are white but will sometimes tinge pink. March and April in Athens.

LIGHT & SOIL Full sun to moderate shade. It prefers moist well-drained soil; however, it is tolerant of poor dry soils once it is established. Salt spray tolerant.

MAINTENANCE This is a carefree plant. It will root where its stems touch the ground and can be transplanted to new areas. Cut back after flowering to increase density and reduce legginess.

INSTALLATION Space container-grown plants or divisions 12"–24" on center for a mass effect.

PESTS & DISEASES None major.

NOTES & CULTIVARS
'Autumn Snow' grows 8"–10" tall with large flowers and repeats in the fall.
'Compacta' grows 4"–6" tall with tight foliage.
'Little Gem' grows 5"–8" tall.
'Snowflake' grows 8"–10" tall with inflorescences that are 3" wide.

Candytuft flowers and foliage.

top left Ground cover massing on the UGA campus with hostas, distylium 'Vintage Jade', and hydrangeas.

top right It is commonly used as a bed edge and called "border grass," though spreading can be a problem.

midddle The variegated clumping type in July flower.

bottom Lily turf with July and August flower spikes.

Liriope muscari LIRIOPE, LILY TURF

Liriope is often the go-to ground cover plant for landscape architects either for massing as the lowest layer in a plant composition or as a border plant. Many refer to liriope as border grass. It is easy to understand why, as the plant stays low, is fully evergreen, seems to grow anywhere, and offers showy blue to purple flower spikes in July and August. *Liriope muscari* is known for its more clumping habit than *L. spicata*, but it will still spread by rhizomes and can be somewhat aggressive. This can be a blessing or a curse depending on where the plant is used. *L. spicata* is differentiated by slimmer foliage and typically nonshowy flower spikes that are mostly obscured by and held below the foliage. This form is very aggressive and forms an almost impenetrable mat. Interesting and showy cultivars of *L. muscari* are abundantly available and worthy of consideration.

ZONES & ORIGIN 5–10. Native to China, Taiwan, and Japan.

SIZE & GROWTH RATE 8"–18" tall, creeping, with a medium growth rate.

TEXTURE & FORM Medium fine texture with a creeping mat.

FOLIAGE Thin grasslike leaves grow up to 18" long and ¼"–¾" wide on showier cultivars. Many variegated foliage forms have white or yellow stripes.

FLOWERS & SEED Flower spikes form in July and August. They are held well above the foliage, with blue to purple or white bell-shaped flowers, followed by black pea-sized fruits held into early winter.

LIGHT & SOIL It can be planted in full sun but looks best in light to moderate shade. Prefers moist well-drained soil; however, it is tolerant of poor dry soils and drought once established. Moderate salt spray tolerance.

MAINTENANCE Carefree plant, although it can spread too much over time. Plan to hand weed tree and other seedlings out of large mass ground cover plantings.

INSTALLATION Space container-grown plants or divisions 6"–12" on center for mass effect.

PESTS & DISEASES None.

NOTES & CULTIVARS
- 'Big Blue' grows to 18" tall and has deep green-blue foliage.
- 'Emerald Goddess' is an attractive form that grows to 2' tall but is less cold-hardy.
- 'Gold Band' has yellow leaf edges and grows to 18" tall.
- 'Variegata' has white leaf edges and grows to 15" tall.
- *L. spicata*, aggressive and less showy, grows to 15" tall. It is sometimes preferred as a bullet-proof nonturf ground cover for commercial parking lot islands—the plant equivalent of concrete.

Mazus reptans MAZUS

Mazus provides an excellent and extremely low creeping ground cover for detail areas such as gaps between stepping stones or other garden nooks and crannies. It is best used as a detail plant and not in large ground cover areas, where it may lack the vigor to effectively keep out weeds and young tree seedlings. Native to the Himalayas, it is easy to grow in full sun to light shade, provided there is at least average soil moisture to wet soils. Attractive flowers smother the foliage in periwinkle blue or white in May and June in Athens.

Spring flowering.

ZONES & ORIGIN 5–9. Native to the Himalayas.

SIZE & GROWTH RATE 2"–3" tall, 1'–2' wide, fast growing.

TEXTURE & FORM Fine texture, spreading ground cover.

FOLIAGE Simple leaves ½"–1" wide are densely packed, forming a solid mat. Leaves hold well into fall or remain green for winter in zones 8 and 9.

FLOWERS Two-lipped flowers in pale purple or white with yellow and white markings almost smother the foliage in peak bloom in May and June in zone 8.

FRUIT Insignificant.

LIGHT & SOIL Full sun to light shade and rich moist well-drained to wet soils. More shade and moisture are necessary in zones 8 and 9.

MAINTENANCE New plantings for ground cover will need hand weeding until cover is established.

INSTALLATION Typically container grown. Install on 12" centers between stepping stones or tuck into planted steps or cracks in a stone wall. Plants root at nodes, but mazus is not aggressive.

PESTS & DISEASES None major. Slugs may feed on foliage.

NOTES & CULTIVARS
'Albus' is a white-flowered cultivar readily available from the nursery industry.

top Mazus softens the edges and fills up the gaps by this stream in the Gainesville Botanical Garden, Ga.

bottom Mazus provides the perfect low filler between stepping-stones here in the State Botanical Garden of Georgia.

Ophiopogon japonicus MONDO · MONKEY GRASS

Mondo or monkey grass is a staple ground cover for landscape design. It is hard to beat, with its low height, slow-spreading and thick uniform nature, fine texture, and evergreen foliage. It offers a neat deep green foil for other plants in the landscape. The use of plants like mondo grass reduces the need to mulch and helps keep out weeds over the long term. The shorter cultivar 'Nana' reaches only 3" or so in height and is spectacular around stepping stones or other detail design areas. The popular black mondo is *Ophiopogon planiscapus* 'Nigrescens' and offers a unique color contrast.

Every sliver of green matters in a Charleston, S.C., alley.

ZONES & ORIGIN   6–9. Native to Japan and Korea.

SIZE & GROWTH RATE   8" tall, slowly creeping, medium growing.

TEXTURE & FORM   Forms a creeping mat with a fine texture.

FOLIAGE   Thin grasslike leaves are 15" long and ¼" wide.

FLOWERS & SEED   The flowers are mostly obscured by the foliage. Short racemes of lilac flowers bloom in summer and are followed by metallic-blue berries.

LIGHT & SOIL   Tolerates full sun, but it looks best in light to moderate shade. Prefers moist well-drained soil; however, it is tolerant of poor dry soils and drought once established. Moderate salt spray tolerance.

MAINTENANCE   Carefree plant.

INSTALLATION   Space container-grown plants or divisions 6"–12" on center for mass effect.

PESTS & DISEASES   None.

NOTES & CULTIVARS
'Nana' grows 3"–4" tall.
'Nippon' grows 3"–4" tall and has white flowers.
Ophiopogon planiscapus 'Nigrescens', black mondo, grows to 6" tall and prefers partial sun.

below left *Ophiopogon planiscapus* 'Nigrescens' at Bloedel Reserve, Bainbridge Island, Wash.

right top A soft floor plane at Birmingham Botanical Garden.

right bottom 'Nana' used to fill cracks at Land Plus Associates in Atlanta.

Pachysandra terminalis

PACHYSANDRA · JAPANESE SPURGE

Pachysandra is a sumptuous and refined evergreen ground cover. Give it light to moderate shade and moist well-drained soil, and it can provide an elegant foil for other plantings. It fills in nicely but without being overbearing and preventing other bulbs, shrubs, and perennials from growing in the same bed—in other words, it plays well with others.

ZONES & ORIGIN 4–9. Native to Japan.

SIZE & GROWTH RATE 6"–9" tall, creeping; medium growing.

TEXTURE & FORM A creeping mat with a medium texture.

FOLIAGE Alternate leaves are clustered in a whorled pattern and are 2"–4" long, oval-shaped, toothed toward the apex, shiny medium green.

FLOWERS & SEED Fairly insignificant flowers. The terminal raceme emerges in late spring with creamy-white flowers.

LIGHT & SOIL Light to moderate shade, although it tolerates some morning sun. It prefers moist well-drained soil that is slightly acidic to neutral pH.

MAINTENANCE Carefree plant.

INSTALLATION Space container-grown plants or divisions 6"–12" on center for a mass effect.

PESTS & DISEASES It may contract various fungal diseases in excessively moist conditions. Apply fungicide to treat.

NOTES & CULTIVARS
'Green Carpet' grows to only 8" tall and is dark green.
'Green Sheen' has very shiny dark green foliage.
'Variegata' has white variegation.
Pachysandra procumbens 'Alleghany Spurge' is a native deciduous species. Its leaves are larger, to 6" across, and are somewhat flatter, mottled, and matte. This plant makes an attractive woodland garden ground cover.

top left The sumptuous final layer in this Knoxville garden by SWH Associates.

top right A shady courtyard in Atlanta by Land Plus Associates.

midddle Looking good filling moist nooks and crannies.

bottom The lovely native *Pachysandra procumbens* 'Alleghany Spurge' at Mt. Cuba Center.

Phlox subulata MOSS PINK · CREEPING PHLOX

Most folks are usually surprised to learn that creeping phlox is native to rocky ledges, slopes, and woodlands of the eastern United States. This adequately explains why creeping phlox can be seen virtually everywhere in the spring on slopes and forgotten places in the landscape suddenly exploding into flower. Creeping phlox is tough and durable, drought tolerant, and long-lived. It spreads to create a continuous mat. The only drawback is the somewhat tired and bedraggled appearance of the foliage when the plant is not in flower, so use it where it isn't the center focus during the off-season.

ZONES & ORIGIN 2–8. Native to eastern North America.

SIZE & GROWTH RATE 2"–6" tall, creeping to 24", medium growing.

TEXTURE & FORM Forms a fine-textured creeping mat.

FOLIAGE Stiff narrow leaves to ½" long.

FLOWERS & SEED The foliage is smothered in small star-shaped flowers from mid-March through April in Athens. Available in blue, purple, lavender, pink, red, white, and bicolors. Seeds are insignificant.

LIGHT & SOIL Full sun to light shade. Tolerant of most soils provided drainage is good.

MAINTENANCE Carefree plant.

INSTALLATION Space container-grown plants or divisions 12"–24" on center for mass effect.

PESTS & DISEASES None.

NOTES & CULTIVARS
Too many to list, but here are a few.
'Apple Blossom' is pale pink with a darker eye.
'Candy Stripe' is white striped with pink.
'Crackerjack' is crimson red.
'Drummond Pink' is magenta pink.
'Emerald Cushion Blue' is blue and vigorous.
'Red Wing' is rose red.
'Snowflake' is pure white.

Showy five-petaled flowers.

top to bottom

With azaleas in early April in Athens.

These look great spilling over a wall.

At Glen-Ella Springs Inn in north Georgia.

Rubus calycinoides CREEPING RASPBERRY

This Asian species of raspberry makes an interesting low evergreen ground cover for small areas or for use spilling out of containers. While it does flower and fruit, it does so sparingly and is really best used for its interesting crinkled and hairy foliage. Though a raspberry, it has few if any spines. In zones 7 and 8 it prefers morning sun or light shade and a well-drained location.

ZONES & ORIGIN 6–8. Native to Taiwan.

SIZE & GROWTH RATE 6"–12" tall, creeping to sometimes more than 36", medium growing.

TEXTURE & FORM Low ground cover; medium texture.

FOLIAGE Small 1"–2" dull olive-green leaves, rounded and wavy or crinkled with deeply pressed veins and a dense covering of hairs on leaves and stems. Occasional spines.

FLOWERS & SEED Rarely flowers or fruits much in the Southeast, but it bears creamy-white single flowers that are ½" across in midsummer, followed by golden-yellow raspberries.

LIGHT & SOIL Morning sun or light shade. Needs a well-drained soil, and it is drought tolerant once established.

MAINTENANCE Stems root wherever they touch the ground, so edge restraints may be necessary.

INSTALLATION Space container-grown plants or divisions 12"–18" on center for mass effect.

PESTS & DISEASES None.

NOTES & CULTIVARS 'Emerald Carpet' selected for deep green foliage color, vigor, and spread to a 5" diameter. Winter foliage coloration is a raspberry reddish green.

top Intermingled with acorus, junipers, and stone in the garden of Ram and Tom Giberson, Athens, Ga.

bottom Spilling over a wall in Seattle, Wash.

top Leathery texture and unique leaf shape invite a closer look.

bottom Occasional fruit spotted here in Bainbridge, Wash.

Sedum sarmentosum

SEDUM · GOLD MOSS · STONECROP

Many species of stonecrop are native to Europe, northern Africa, and Asia. As a succulent plant they are generally very sun and drought tolerant and only require good drainage. They are incredibly easy plants to grow and make great low ground covers around stepping stones (although they are not tolerant of foot traffic), filler for cracks between steps and walls, or spillers over the top of a short garden wall, out of a container, or as part of an intricate menagerie of small plants in garden areas where this attention to detail can be appreciated.

ZONES & ORIGIN 3–8. Native to Europe and northern Africa.

SIZE & GROWTH RATE 2"–6" tall, creeping to 24"; fast growing.

TEXTURE & FORM Forms a fine-textured creeping mat.

FOLIAGE Small and narrow elliptic light green leaves 1" by ¼" are arranged in whorls of three. Stems are round and fleshy. Many species exhibit foliage that is a mix of rosy, burgundy, and bronze or is bluish.

FLOWERS & SEED Attractive yellow-flowering corymbs are held above the foliage in April and May in Athens. Insignificant seeds.

LIGHT & SOIL Full sun to light shade. Tolerant of most soils provided drainage is good.

MAINTENANCE Carefree plant. Stem pieces will root wherever they touch the ground. After a few years without careful cleanup, sedum could be everywhere.

INSTALLATION Space container-grown plants or divisions 12"–18" on center for mass effect. Better used in smaller areas.

PESTS & DISEASES None.

NOTES & CULTIVARS
Sedum acre has thick, somewhat rounded green foliage.
S. rupestre 'Angelina' has golden foliage with radial leaves.
S. rupestre 'Blue Spruce' has blue-gray foliage with radial leaves.
S. spurium has rounded green leaves with scalloped edges.

Great for nooks, crannies, and bed edges—seen here at Callaway Gardens.

top to bottom

Perhaps no better plant for cracks and crevices.

Yellow flowers in late spring.

Sedum rupestre 'Angelina' planted atop a wall at Chanticleer Garden in Wayne, Pa.

left Ground cover massing blooming in early March in the Founders Memorial Garden at UGA.

right Cheerful early spring flowers.

Vinca major BIGLEAF PERIWINKLE · VINCA

Bigleaf periwinkle is a common ground cover in the mid-Atlantic states and the Southeast where it has escaped cultivation and can be seen around old homesites and in woodlands near urban areas. It prefers light to moderate shade and can tolerate dry shade quite well, making it useful as a ground cover and one that will not smother bulbs and other low-growing shrubs. It is quite attractive in early spring when it is covered in periwinkle-blue flowers.

ZONES & ORIGIN (6b) 7–9. Native to Europe.

SIZE & GROWTH RATE 12"–18" tall, creeping to 36"+; fast growing.

TEXTURE & FORM Low ground cover; medium texture.

FOLIAGE Small opposite dull green leaves 1"–2", elliptic to almost cordate, entire and hairy margins. Variegated forms available.

FLOWERS & SEED Showy 1" or larger five-petaled flowers in periwinkle blue occur in profusion in March in north Georgia, then very sparingly throughout the growing season. White or purple forms available.

LIGHT & SOIL Morning sun or light to moderate shade. Tolerant of most soils provided drainage is good. Drought tolerant once established.

MAINTENANCE Stem pieces will root wherever they touch the ground, so edge restraints may be necessary.

INSTALLATION Space container-grown plants or divisions 12"–18" on center for mass effect.

PESTS & DISEASES No major issue, but aphids can infect drought-stressed plants in full sun. Deer don't touch them.

NOTES & CULTIVARS
Cultivars are available with variegated foliage and darker or lighter flower color. They are commonly used as the spiller from containers and hanging baskets.

Vinca minor COMMON PERIWINKLE

Vinca minor is a common ground cover in the eastern United States where it has escaped cultivation and can be seen around old homesites and covering large areas of forest floor. Luckily, it does not climb trees like English ivy, and while it does spread, it never becomes thick enough to smother out other woodland plants. This ability to play well with others makes it a useful ground cover for woodland gardens. It prefers light to moderate shade and can tolerate dry shade quite well once it is established. It is quite attractive in early spring, when it is covered in periwinkle-blue flowers set against the deep blue-green foliage.

Early spring flowers in periwinkle blue.

ZONES & ORIGIN 4–9. Native to Europe.

SIZE & GROWTH RATE 4"–6" tall, creeping to more than 36"; fast growing.

TEXTURE & FORM Low ground cover with a fine texture.

FOLIAGE Small narrow glossy deep blue-green leaves are opposite and elliptic to lanceolate and have smooth margins. Variegated forms are available.

FLOWERS & SEED Showy 1" five-petaled flowers in periwinkle blue occur in profusion in March in north Georgia, then very sparingly throughout the growing season. Glorious with spring bulbs.

LIGHT & SOIL Morning sun or light to moderate shade. Tolerant of most soils provided drainage is good. Drought tolerant once established.

MAINTENANCE Stem pieces will root wherever they touch the ground, so edge restraints may be necessary.

INSTALLATION Space container-grown plants or divisions 12"–18" on center for mass effect.

PESTS & DISEASES None major. Deer don't bother it.

NOTES & CULTIVARS
Cultivars are available with variegated foliage and darker or lighter flower color. Commonly used as the spiller from containers and hanging baskets.

left Under a sweetbay magnolia and next to autumn fern. *right* In Vancouver, B.C., with hydrangeas.

Acanthus spinosus BEAR'S BREECHES

Acanthus is native to the Mediterranean region and has long been cultivated. It was the inspiration for the leaves at the top of Greek Corinthian columns. Many species exist; however, the species *mollis* and *spinosus* are most common in the Southeast. While both are grown, *spinosus* and its cultivars have been shown to be more cold-hardy and more tolerant of summer heat and humidity, and they produce early summer flowers with greater consistency. *Acanthus* provides a bold tropical-looking clump of foliage for the shrub or perennial border.

ZONES & ORIGIN 6–10. Native to southern Europe.

SIZE & GROWTH RATE 36"–48" tall and wide; medium growth rate.

TEXTURE & FORM Coarse texture with a mounding form.

FOLIAGE Large 10" lanceolate leaves, deeply divided, have spiny margins, although the spines are actually soft to the touch. Foliage emerges in late winter and may remain all winter in zones 9 and 10.

FLOWERS & SEED Impressive spikes rise above the foliage to 5' in May. They are covered in small white flowers surrounded by showy reddish-purple bracts. Seeds are produced; however, flower spikes do not remain upright for long after flowering, so they are not ornamental.

LIGHT & SOIL Full sun to moderate shade. Tolerant of most soils, provided drainage is good.

MAINTENANCE This is a carefree plant. It spreads slowly by its roots, and small root pieces will produce new plants if divided.

INSTALLATION Space container-grown plants or divisions 24"–36" on center for mass effect. Excellent used singly as a specimen.

PESTS & DISEASES None.

NOTES & CULTIVARS
Acanthus mollis is very common in the South. Its leaves are less divided than those of *Acanthus spinosus*, which is only hardy in zones 7–9, with less flowering and reduced summer heat tolerance. Still, this is a lovely and enduring plant. It needs at least afternoon shade. 'Summer Beauty' is a hybrid with great vigor that grows to 4'–5' tall.

top left A forest floor covered outside Rome, Italy, in early June.

top right June flowers in North Carolina.

midddle Early June flowers in the Founders Memorial Garden at UGA.

bottom Late July flowering in Seattle, Wash.

Achillea spp. YARROW

Yarrows are native to Europe and the Caucasus Mountains between Europe and Asia. In North America, the white-flowering form has naturalized and can be seen along roadsides in early summer. It is a plant with many historic medicinal uses. For design purposes, many color and height variations are available through hybridization of multiple species. Some of the better hybrids for zones 8 and 9 are listed below. Yarrows like full sun and good drainage and are tough and easy plants for perennial borders.

Early August flowers in Vancouver, B.C.

ZONES & ORIGIN 3–9. Native to Europe.

SIZE & GROWTH RATE 24"–48" tall, 24" wide; fast growing.

TEXTURE & FORM Fine texture with an upright clump.

FOLIAGE Soft, feathery, and finely divided alternate leaves are usually gray green or even silvery, and they often have a spicy or pungent smell.

FLOWERS & SEED Distinctly flat corymbs are composed of inner flat yellow flowers surrounded by outer ray flowers in white, yellows, pinks, or reds, depending on the hybrid. Blooms in May and June, sometimes later, in Athens. Seed heads tend to flop before winter and should be cut back in fall.

LIGHT & SOIL Full sun to light shade. Tolerant of most soils, provided drainage is good. Salt spray tolerant.

MAINTENANCE Carefree plant. Spreads by rhizomes, but most hybrids are not too aggressive.

INSTALLATION Space container-grown plants 18"–24" on center for massing.

PESTS & DISEASES None.

NOTES & CULTIVARS
'Appleblossom' grows to 3' with peach or pink flowers.
'Cerise Queen' has cerise-red flowers and grows to 18".
'Coronation Gold' is a fabulous old hybrid that is a rich gold and grows to 3'–4' tall.
'Oertel's Rose' has rosy-pink-and-white flowers and grows to 18".
'Orange Queen' has orange-gold flowers and grows to 30".
'Paprika' has red-and-yellow flowers and grows to 30".

left Huntington Gardens, Pasadena, Calif., in June.

right top With phlox, geum hybrids, orange crocosmia, daylily, and more in July in Vancouver, B.C.

right bottom 'Coronation Gold' in July at Lewis and Clark College, Portland, Ore.

Agapanthus spp. LILY OF THE NILE

The deep blues and violets of *Agapanthus* in full bloom are exquisite and leave a lasting impression. In late summer, *Agapanthus* makes an impressive show of rounded flower clusters, often in vivid shades of blue or purple but also in white. The combination of dark green strap-like foliage in arching clumps with the abundant flowers rising above creates a rich tropical effect in the garden. A few of the hybrids may be overwintered in zone 7 or even farther north if they are protected, but the plant really flourishes in zone 8 and southward. It's a sad reality for most folks north of zone 7, but they can grow the giant *Allium* species. Nobody can have it all.

The white-flowered form 'Albus'.

ZONES & ORIGIN (7) 8–11. Native to South Africa.

SIZE & GROWTH RATE 24"–60" tall and 24"–36" wide; medium growing.

TEXTURE & FORM Medium texture; grows in an arching clump.

FOLIAGE Thick strap-like foliage to 2' in arching clumps; handsome and evergreen in zone 9 and south.

FLOWERS & SEED Incredible rounded flower heads rise above foliage 2'–5' depending on the hybrid, in late summer. Flowers bloom in various shades of light to dark blue, lilac, violet, purple, and white. Choose a hybrid based on the desired color and height. Insignificant seed.

LIGHT & SOIL Full sun to light shade. Prefers a rich and moist but well-drained soil. Salt spray tolerant.

MAINTENANCE Likes moisture. Spreads slowly by rhizomes.

INSTALLATION Space container-grown plants or divisions 18"–36" on center for massing.

PESTS & DISEASES None.

NOTES & CULTIVARS
'Albus' has white flowers and grows to 3'.
'Bressingham Blue' has deep blue flowers and grows to 3'.
'Ellaine' has large blue flower heads and grows to 5'.
'Ellamae' has violet flowers and grows to 3'.
'Loch Hope' has deep violet flowers and grows to 5'.

left top With Chinese silvergrass on the coast of Georgia.

left bottom In the Bainbridge Island, Wash., garden of the great plantsman Dan Hinkley.

right With dwarf nandina on Hilton Head Island, S.C.

top left 'Blue Fortune' with tall verbena and Muhly grass in Sonoma, Calif.

top right 'Blue Fortune' (*right*) and 'Blue Boa' (*left*) with herbs and a waxleaf ligustrum hedge in Sonoma, Calif.

midddle 'Golden Jubilee'.

bottom With echinacea and other perennials in Vancouver, B.C.

Agastache spp. HYSSOP

Agastache is one of those perennials that has risen to stardom in recent years, with many new cultivars and hybrids on the market. The designer in humid climates should be very careful, as many forms with parent plants from the arid Southwest simply do not tolerate year-round humidity and winter moisture. However, the species *foeniculum* and related hybrids have shown themselves to tolerate the South well, and these make wonderful additions to the perennial border, as they attract pollinators, love the heat, and tolerate drought. The list below provides some tried-and-true cultivars for use even in the humid Southeast.

ZONES & ORIGIN 7–9. *Agastache foeniculum* is hardy in the northern United States and Canada; hybrids have multiple origins, from the United States, China, and Japan.

SIZE & GROWTH RATE 18"–36" tall, 18" wide; fast growing.

TEXTURE & FORM Medium fine texture; grows in an upright clump.

FOLIAGE Alternate leaves have simple toothed margins. They are often gray green and usually licorice scented. There is considerable variation among hybrids; see the notes below.

FLOWERS & SEED Terminal spikes of tubular flowers occur from midsummer until fall in blue, purple, lavender, pinks, and white. Hybrids from the Southwest offer tantalizing oranges and yellows but tend not to perform well in the humid South without extremely well-drained rocky soil and full sun conditions.

LIGHT & SOIL Full sun. Must have well-drained soil, and it prefers neutral to slightly alkaline pH.

MAINTENANCE Provide an open, dry, and sunny location. Cut back in fall or early winter.

INSTALLATION Space container-grown plants or divisions 18"–24" on center for massing.

PESTS & DISEASES None major.

NOTES & CULTIVARS
Agastache foeniculum has the following cultivars:

'Alba' has white flowers.
'Black Adder' has rosy-violet flowers.
'Blue Fortune' is vigorous to 3' and its flowers are lavender blue.
'Golden Jubilee' has bright chartreuse-yellow foliage with light blue flowers.
'Licorice Blue' has lavender flowers.
'Licorice White' has white flowers.

Ajuga reptans AJUGA · BUGLE WEED

Ajuga is a low-growing, semievergreen, mat-forming, and slowly spreading perennial with attractive blue to purple spring flower spikes. However, it is primarily grown for its glossy attractive foliage. The foliage of many cultivars displays various shades of pink, white, burgundy, and nearly chocolate brown. The options for design use have grown significantly in recent years with some wonderful new cultivars that really do perform well in zones 8 and 9—no hype!

ZONES & ORIGIN 3–9. Native to Europe.

SIZE & GROWTH RATE 4"–12" tall, 18" wide; fast growing.

TEXTURE & FORM Medium texture; grows in a prostrate spreading clump.

FOLIAGE Simple oblong to obovate glossy and pubescent green, purple, or bronze leaves 3"–4" long have entire to slightly toothed margins. Stoloniferous.

FLOWERS & SEED Terminal spikes rise 4"–8" above the foliage and have whorls of blue tubular flowers (late March to late April in Athens).

LIGHT & SOIL Light to moderate shade best. Needs moist well-drained soil.

MAINTENANCE Divide and reset clumps if die-back leaves holes in mass plantings.

INSTALLATION Space container-grown plants or divisions 6"–12" on center for massing.

PESTS & DISEASES Fungal diseases can attack thick foliage. It is possible to treat the plant with fungicide, but it is best to prevent these diseases with correct siting.

NOTES & CULTIVARS
'Atropurpurea' is bronzy purple and vigorous.
'Bronze Beauty' is bronze.
'Burgundy Glow' has white, pink, rose, and green variegation and large leaves.
'Catlin's Giant' has tall flowers and bronze foliage, vigorous.
'Chocolate Chip' has slim leaves and bronzy foliage and is handsome.
'Silver Beauty' has gray-green foliage edged in white.

Early April flowers in Athens, Ga.

top left Wonderful at the edge of a shaded path.

top right with creeping jenny and Korean rock fern.

bottom This plant is a great filler for nooks and crannies.

Allium spp. ORNAMENTAL ONION

These bulbous perennials are a designer's best friend, as they provide instant visual drama when in flower—total eye candy. Luckily, the hybrids are also quite easy to grow, multiplying over the years and providing plants to share with friends. *Allium* species should be grown in combination with other low perennials or ground covers that will serve as a foil for the dramatic floral display. The slim foliage of the *Allium* typically dies just before or after flowering, creating the need for other plants. This is really where the excitement lies—creating exciting plant combinations out of which the *Allium* varieties can erupt! Spent flower heads remain for several weeks, providing interest even after the color fades. Most of the showy *Allium* cultivars perform best in cooler and drier climates and sadly will not return in the Southeast. However, the recently introduced cultivar 'Millennium' is a breakthrough and a great performer in zone 8 gardens.

ZONES & ORIGIN 4–8 (9). Native to the Middle East and Asia.

SIZE & GROWTH RATE 2'–4' tall, 6" wide; fast growing.

TEXTURE & FORM Coarse texture; forms an upright clump.

FOLIAGE Strap-like foliage to 12" long. There are usually only 6–8 leaves per bulb, fading before the flower appears or sometimes just after. Not significant.

FLOWERS & SEED Terminal scapes erupt in May or June in Athens with perfect spherical purple flower heads that are 2"–6", depending on the hybrid. Spheres persist for weeks, fading to tan or silver.

LIGHT & SOIL Full sun to light shade. Prefers loose, moist, and well-drained soil.

MAINTENANCE Divide and reset clumps every few years. You should be so lucky.

INSTALLATION Best planted in fall. Space bulbs 6"–24" on center for masses, depending on underplantings. Works well as random drifts.

PESTS & DISEASES None major.

NOTES & CULTIVARS
'Gladiator' grows 3'–4' tall, with light purple flowers.
'Globemaster' is aptly named; it is vigorous to 30" tall and has incredible 4"–6" lavender flower heads.
'Lucy Ball' grows to 4' tall and has dark violet flowers.

top to bottom

'Globemaster' in early June at Longwood Gardens.

'Globemaster' at Chanticleer Garden.

June in Manhattan.

June in Boston Common.

Alpinia zerumbet SHELL GINGER

Shell ginger is a staple of warm-climate gardens, especially in zones 9 and 10, where it lends a tropical appearance to hot humid landscapes and attractive sweetly fragrant flower clusters. Flowering is a unique delight, with pendulous clusters of seashell-shaped and highly fragrant flowers of white, pink, and apricot. In warm zones it is often evergreen; farther north in zones 7 and 8 it is killed to the ground in winter and needs a protected position such as a courtyard or a warm wall. In zones 7 and 8 it still offers an exciting coarse-textured accent for the summer garden that is somewhat more refined than *Canna* species.

ZONES & ORIGIN 7b–10. Native to Asia.

SIZE & GROWTH RATE 8'–10' in zones 9 and 10, to 6' in zones 7 and 8; fast growing.

TEXTURE & FORM Elegant upright leaning clumps; coarse texture.

FOLIAGE Attractive dark green simple alternate lanceolate leaves to 18" long, 4" wide, with smooth margins. Stems tend to lean outward from the center, creating an elegant swagger.

FLOWERS & SEED Flowers only on two-year-old stems with racemes that are 12"–18" long and have shell-shaped white and pink flowers, sweetly fragrant. Does not flower where foliage is killed to the ground.

LIGHT & SOIL Full sun to moderate shade. Moist, organic, rich, and well-drained soil. Salt spray tolerant.

MAINTENANCE Selectively prune out tired foliage after flowering where evergreen. Cut back to the ground after the first killing frost farther north.

INSTALLATION Plant containers or divisions of rhizomes 12"–24" on center for masses. Makes an excellent specimen accent.

PESTS & DISEASES None major.

NOTES & CULTIVARS
Alpinia zerumbet 'Variegata' is a popular yellow striped variegated form that grows to 6' tall. It also flowers on old growth. Not as cold-hardy as the species, surviving maybe only in zone 8. It needs light to moderate shade, where it shimmers.

top to bottom

Shell-like flowers.

Attractive yellow variegation.

At the faculty club on the campus of Louisiana State University.

In a Savannah, Ga., courtyard.

Amsonia hubrichtii
AMSONIA · THREADLEAF BLUESTAR

A visit to the incredible Chanticleer estate, now a public garden in Wayne, Pennsylvania, will leave one forever changed. There, soft billowy plantings of *Amsonia hubrichtii* float with other perennials in a dreamlike tapestry—the visual effect is stunning and lingers in the memory. *A. hubrichtii* offers three seasons of beauty, from delicate blue star-shaped flowers in spring, a soft summer texture that serves as an excellent foil for other plantings, and a warm fall display of golden to amber foliage before it drops its leaves. It looks delicate, but it's a tough native plant that tolerates heat and drought well.

ZONES & ORIGIN 6–9. Native to Arkansas and the mid-South.

SIZE & GROWTH RATE 3' tall and wide; moderate growth.

TEXTURE & FORM A fine texture in upright rounded clumps.

FOLIAGE Attractive medium green simple alternate lanceolate leaves are only ¾" wide and 3" long, with smooth margins. The foliage is the real reason to grow the plant.

FLOWERS & SEED Small star-shaped light blue to almost white flowers appear in terminal panicles in April in Athens. They are somewhat obscured by the foliage.

LIGHT & SOIL Prefers full sun to light shade and moist well-drained soil. Also tolerates poor dry soils and drought.

MAINTENANCE A carefree plant.

INSTALLATION Plant containers or divisions of clumps 24"–36" on center for masses.

PESTS & DISEASES None.

NOTES & CULTIVARS
Amsonia ciliata is a Southeast native that grows to 36" tall. The texture of its foliage is extremely fine. It is typically found on sandy soils in full sun but prefers regular moisture.

left In the texture garden at Swarthmore College in Swarthmore, Pa.

right top At Chanticleer, sweetbay magnolias, hydrangeas, and serviceberry filter the house.

right bottom With peonies at the Coastal Maine Botanical Gardens.

April flowers in Athens popping out of lenten rose foliage.

Amsonia tabernaemontana   AMSONIA · BLUE STAR

Blue star is native to the eastern United States and occurs in sunny meadows and roadsides or forest edges and in full sun or light shade. It flowers through most of April in Athens with attractive, star-shaped light blue flowers. Blue star is an easy perennial with good drought tolerance once established. It is delicate enough for the perennial border and tough enough to use in masses in larger commercial or public landscapes.

ZONES & ORIGIN   3–9. Native to the eastern United States.

SIZE & GROWTH RATE   3' tall and wide; moderate growth.

TEXTURE & FORM   Upright rounded clumps with a medium fine texture.

FOLIAGE   Attractive medium green simple alternate lanceolate leaves 1½" wide and 3" long have smooth margins.

FLOWERS & SEED   Small star-shaped light blue flowers appear in terminal panicles in April in Athens.

LIGHT & SOIL   Full sun to light shade. Prefers moist well-drained soil. Also tolerates poor dry soils and short periods of drought.

MAINTENANCE   A carefree plant. May flop in light shade and need support.

INSTALLATION   Plant containers or divisions of clumps 24"–36" on center for masses.

PESTS & DISEASES   None.

NOTES & CULTIVARS
'Montana' has deeper-blue flowers that occur one or two weeks earlier than the species and has wider leaves. It is a more compact plant.

Anemone × *hybrida*

JAPANESE ANEMONE · HYBRID ANEMONE

Many species of anemones exist and can provide flowers for the entire growing season. Of the many species, the fall-blooming hybrids are among the loveliest and easiest to grow. With well-drained soils and partial shade, these hybrids will provide an incredible show in September and October when many other plants are finished and moving into dormancy. The foliage is also quite handsome and complements other plantings long before the fall flowering. Can be a tad aggressive.

ZONES & ORIGIN 4–8. Hybrid origin.

SIZE & GROWTH RATE 3'–4' tall by 24" wide; moderate growth rate.

TEXTURE & FORM Medium texture with upright clumps.

FOLIAGE Attractive dark green simple alternate 3-or-5-lobed and coarsely toothed leaves that are 3"–5" long and nearly as wide, often hairy. Leaves are clumped more at the base, with fewer along the flowering stems.

FLOWERS & SEED Lovely 2"–4" flower heads are actually sepals surrounding true flowers in the center. They bloom in September and October. Available in white and pinks, double and single.

LIGHT & SOIL Light shade or morning sun and afternoon shade. Prefers moist well-drained soil rich in organic matter.

MAINTENANCE This plant spreads by rhizomes where it is happy and may need periodic thinning and removal from unwanted areas.

INSTALLATION Plant containers or divisions 18"–24" on center for masses.

PESTS & DISEASES None.

NOTES & CULTIVARS
'Elegantissima' grows 3'–4' tall with double rosy sepals; vigorous.
'Honorine Jobert' grows 3'–4' tall with single white 2"–3" sepals.
'September Charm' grows 3' tall with single rose-pink sepals.
'White Giant' grows 4' tall with large double white sepals.

At Great Dixter, Northiam, England, in September.

top to bottom

Delicate but showy fall flowers.

Foliage provides an attractive foil for the flowers.

September flowering in a park in London, England.

Aquilegia canadensis COLUMBINE

Columbine is a wonderful native plant for perennial borders or use in less formal areas where plants may naturalize. At least two species occur in the southeastern United States, *Aquilegia canadensis*, with its fantastic yellow-and-red flowers, and *A. longissima*, with its lovely light yellow flowers. These natives are great without any fussing with hybridization. However, the interspecific hybrids are very popular, with parentage from many areas of the world, including western North America. The hybrids offer a wide array of flower colors. Columbine is an easy plant to grow, preferring morning sun or light to moderate shade and moist well-drained soil. It will reseed gently and float about the garden from season to season, never becoming too aggressive and obnoxious. It is great used with ferns and other woodland plants.

ZONES & ORIGIN 3–8. Native to the eastern United States (hybrids are of at least partial nonnative origin).

SIZE & GROWTH RATE 12"–30" tall and 12" wide; fast growing.

TEXTURE & FORM Upright clumps; fine texture.

FOLIAGE Attractive basal clumps of dark bluish-green leaves in groups of three are reminiscent of clover. Emerges early in spring.

FLOWERS & SEED Flower spikes rise above the foliage in April and May in north Georgia with intricate nodding or upright tubular flower heads that are 1" wide to 3" long, with spurs sweeping out from the back of the flower. Hybrids offer a color range of red, yellow, white, blues, purples, pinks, and bicolors. Reseeds well.

LIGHT & SOIL Light to moderate shade (tolerates morning sun); moist well-drained soil.

MAINTENANCE No major maintenance required.

INSTALLATION Plant 12"–18" on center for containers.

PESTS & DISEASES Leaf miners can disfigure the foliage, but they are rarely serious.

NOTES & CULTIVARS There are too many hybrids to list. Consult a reputable local grower or catalog.

top to bottom

A white-flowered form with *Brunerra macrophylla*, geranium, peony, and bottlebrush buckeye at Longwood Gardens.

With azaleas, *Indigofera kirilowii*, and roses in Athens, Ga.

With *Packera aurea*, golden ragwort, at Chanticleer.

With sensitive fern in Boston, Mass.

Asclepias tuberosa BUTTERFLY WEED

All species of *Asclepias* serve as the host plant for the larval stage of the monarch butterfly. As efforts to protect habitat for the monarch have increased, so have interest and nursery production of these great North American native plants. To watch the life cycle of the monarch occur in one's own garden is to be forever seduced by the beauty of nature. Butterfly weed is one of the more noticeable species with its conspicuous bright orange flowers, which occur in midsummer. As with most natives, it is wonderfully heat, pest, disease, and drought tolerant. Use it in the perennial border or as a low accent in front of shrubs or grasses. Descriptions of other species appear below.

At a Baltimore, Md., residence by Oehme, van Sweden (OvS).

left With lavender in the scree garden at Chanticleer.

right top With lavender, grasses, thyme, and oregano in the scree garden at Chanticleer.

right bottom With spiderwort in Georgia.

ZONES & ORIGIN 3–10. Native to North America.

SIZE & GROWTH RATE 12"–24" tall and 24" wide; medium growing.

TEXTURE & FORM Forms upright clumps; medium texture.

FOLIAGE Dark green lanceolate leaves are smooth above and hairy below, 1"–3" long and 1" wide. Stems are also hairy.

FLOWERS & SEED Flat-topped clusters of orange flowers 4"–6" long occur in midsummer. A large seed pod that is 2"–3" long develops, splitting open in late summer or early fall to reveal black seeds, each having long white hairs for wind dispersion. Foliage is toxic to livestock and humans if eaten fresh.

LIGHT & SOIL Full sun to light shade. Tolerates most soils, provided there is good drainage. Salt spray tolerant.

MAINTENANCE None major required.

INSTALLATION Space containers 12"–24" on center for massing. It is somewhat difficult to transplant, as all *Asclepia* varieties develop a fairly deep tuberous root system.

PESTS & DISEASES Warning: this plant is a food source for monarchs and other insects. Install it in a location where possible defoliation won't be a problem. The butterflies are worth it!

NOTES & CULTIVARS

Asclepias incarnata, swamp milkweed, is native to North America in zones 3–9. It grows 3'–4' tall and 2' wide. It prefers moist bottomland soils but will tolerate drier conditions. Flowers are pink.

A. syriaca, common milkweed, is native to North America in zones 3–7. It grows 3'–4' tall and 24" wide and prefers moist well-drained soils. Flowers form as spherical umbels and are greenish white. The foliage is large and coarse. Warning: this plant is aggressive!

Aster spp. ASTER

For the ease of the reader we have kept asters together here as one account; however, in recent years this former genus has been split into at least five new genera (see below). Spend a little bit of time researching asters, and you will quickly realize that many species and possibly hundreds of cultivars exist. Which ones will work well for warmer zones? This account is focused on three common roadside native species and their progeny of improved cultivars that work quite well in zones 7–9 and colder and provide tough, drought-tolerant, late fall–blooming perennials for the border or for massing with grasses in informal landscapes.

ZONES & ORIGIN 4–8. Native to the eastern United States.

SIZE & GROWTH RATE 1'–4' tall and wide, depending on the species and cultivar; fast growing.

TEXTURE & FORM Upright clumps; medium fine texture.

FOLIAGE Simple alternate lanceolate leaves clasp the stem and are sometimes hairy (*Aster novae-angliae*).

FLOWERS & SEED Ray flowers that are 1"–3" are produced in pairs or large corymbs in white, pinks, reds, salmon, blue, lavender, and purple, often with a yellow center. Fall blooming in September until frost in late October or even November.

LIGHT & SOIL Full sun to light shade. Well-drained soil, though it is tolerant of poor soils and drought.

MAINTENANCE Spreads by rhizomes and may need periodic thinning and resetting to maintain healthy clumps. Tall cultivars need support by staking or a shrub to spill over.

INSTALLATION Plant containers or divisions 18"–24" on center for masses.

PESTS & DISEASES None.

NOTES & CULTIVARS
Ampelaster carolinianus is hardy in zones 6–9. It is called "climbing aster" for its long (to 8' or more) lanky stems, which can be trained like a vine. It has fall-blooming pinkish-purple flowers and is stunning on a fence or spilling over a wall.

Symphyotrichum laeve, smooth aster, grows 2'–3' tall in dry to moist well-drained soils. Often blooms in early summer with a bigger fall show. 'Bluebird' is an excellent cultivar.

S. nova-belgii, New York aster, is available in short forms (under 12"), medium forms (1'–2' tall), and tall forms (3'–4') in almost every color. Refer to local growers' listings.

S. novae-angliae, New England aster, has hairy leaves. Many tall (3'–4') cultivars are available (too many to list), such as 'Barr's Pink', 'Lyon's White', 'Purple Dome', 'Rosa Siegar' (salmon), 'September Ruby', and 'Treasure' (light purple).

top left and right In London in September at Olympic Park, by James Hitchmough. Smooth aster, tall verbena, rudbeckias, and more.

middle A. integrifolius, thickstem aster.

bottom Aster × frikartii 'Monch', Frikart's aster.

Astilbe spp. FALSE SPIREA · FALSE GOAT'S BEARD

Astilbe offers a distinctly fine-textured, feathery, and brightly colored accent for the shade garden. They need a carefully chosen spot that both is shady and has consistent moisture, which can be a challenge in zone 8, but moist ravines and pond or water-feature edges make good locations. Hybrid forms offer a wide color range, including true reds, magenta, pinks, salmon, and white. When not in flower the foliage of *Astilbe* offers a handsome fernlike texture and dark green or bronze color, depending on the hybrid.

ZONES & ORIGIN 4–8. Hybrid origin.

SIZE & GROWTH RATE 1'–3' tall and wide, depending on the hybrid; moderate growing.

TEXTURE & FORM Fine texture in upright clumps.

FOLIAGE Leaves are twice or three times divided into many-toothed leaflets that are shiny dark green or bronze to coppery on some hybrids.

FLOWERS & SEED Impressive plumelike inflorescences rise above the foliage from June to mid-August, depending on the hybrid, in reds, magenta, pinks, salmon, and white. Spent flower heads turn buff and can contribute to the fall or winter garden.

LIGHT & SOIL Light to moderate shade. Prefers rich organic and moist but well-drained soil.

MAINTENANCE Spreads slowly by rhizomes. Cut back in late winter before spring growth.

INSTALLATION Plant containers or divisions 18"–24" on center for masses.

PESTS & DISEASES None.

NOTES & CULTIVARS
Astilbe biternata, native astilbe, occurs in the Southeast in moist shady locations and is 3'–5' tall, with creamy-yellow to white inflorescences.

top to bottom

In the Portland, Ore., Rose Garden with a boxwood hedge.

A white cultivar with Solomon's seal.

At Longwood Gardens, Kennett Square, Pa., with a boxwood parterre and arborvitae hedge.

In Portland, Ore., with maidenhair fern, black mondo grass, rhododendron, and fuchsia.

Baptisia australis FALSE BLUE INDIGO

The tough and durable constitution of our native plants is no better illustrated than by the *Baptisia* species. This perennial has the seductive look of a lupine from out west but is in fact native all over the eastern United States, where it occurs in sunny well-drained locations. As a mostly clump-forming plant (slowly rhizomatous), it produces gray-green foliage topped by showy spikes of pea-like flowers in midspring. It is heat and drought tolerant and very easy to grow as part of a perennial border, but it is substantial enough to find a place with shrubs and is tough enough to work in less-cared-for public or commercial landscapes. Several species are native to the Southeast, and growers now offer a wide range of colors, from white to yellow, blue, and purple. See the excellent trial results from Mt. Cuba Center in Hockessin, Delaware.

ZONES & ORIGIN 3–8. Native to eastern North America.

SIZE & GROWTH RATE 3'–4' tall, with nearly equal spread; medium growing.

TEXTURE & FORM Medium fine texture with a rounded form.

FOLIAGE Waxy-looking blue or gray-green alternate, compound, and trifoliate leaves have smooth margins. Stems look like asparagus when they emerge in spring and may be black or green.

FLOWERS & SEED Lovely 12" or taller flower spikes emerge above the foliage in April in north Georgia. Spikes are lined with 1"–2" pea-like flowers in shades of blue purple. Showy seed pods develop. Other species flower in white and yellow as well.

LIGHT & SOIL Full sun to light shade. Prefers moist well-drained soils to dry, and it is drought tolerant.

MAINTENANCE None.

INSTALLATION Install containers or rhizome divisions 3'–4' on center for massing.

PESTS & DISEASES Voles are reported to love the roots.

NOTES & CULTIVARS
This plant is difficult to divide, as the rhizomes are tough and woody—get the axe!

Baptisia alba, white wild indigo, is native to the Southeast and grows well in zones 5–8 to 3' tall and wide. Its flowers are white.

B. spaerocarpa, yellow wild indigo, is from the midwestern United States. It grows well in zones 5–9 to 4' tall and wide. The flowers are yellow.

B. tinctoria is yellow and grows in zones 5–8.

The hybrid 'Purple Smoke' reaches 4' by 4' with showy flowers for up to a month.

top left Early June at a park in Philadelphia, Pa.

top right *Baptisia* 'Carolina Moonlight' in the garden of Mike and Bonnie Dirr, near Watkinsville, Ga.

midddle A blue-purple cultivar with alliums.

bottom Foliage in late summer.

top left A tree form in Los Angeles, Calif.
top right In San Diego, Calif.
middle In Portland, Ore.
bottom A yellow form at Butchart Gardens, Vancouver Island, B.C.

Brugmansia spp. ANGEL'S TRUMPET

Like most tropicals grown in temperate regions, angel's trumpet is not for the faint of heart, with its bold coarse texture, light green color, and showy dangling trumpet-shaped flowers. In addition to being showstoppers, the flowers emit an incredibly rich musky fragrance, particularly at night, making those evening parties on the patio and in the garden all the richer. Use it as an accent next to a warm wall where someone will walk by it frequently and be able to enjoy the wonderful fragrance and beautiful flowers. Just don't eat it, as all parts of the plant are toxic.

ZONES & ORIGIN 7b–10. Native to South America.

SIZE & GROWTH RATE 6' tall, with a nearly equal spread (to 12' in warmer zones); fast growing.

TEXTURE & FORM Coarse texture with a rounded form.

FOLIAGE Large 12" or greater alternate simple leaves are light green, with entire to coarsely dentate margins, pubescent. Variegated forms available.

FLOWERS & SEED Impressive trumpet-shaped flowers with twisted petals hang 6"–12" long below the foliage in white, pink, salmon, orange, and yellow. Single or double forms are available. Extremely fragrant at night. Insignificant seed.

LIGHT & SOIL Full sun to light shade. Moist but well-drained soil and regular moisture are best. Salt spray tolerant.

MAINTENANCE In zones where it is killed back to the ground, cut it back anytime after the first freeze. In warmer zones and protected locations, it may not be killed at all and can become a handsome small tree in the landscape.

INSTALLATION Typically used singly as a specimen.

PESTS & DISEASES None major.

NOTES & CULTIVARS
'Charles Grimaldi' is salmon pink.
'Cherub' is a rich pink and floriferous.
'Double White' has double petals and yes, it is white.
'Ecuador Pink' is an excellent pink.
'Snowbank' has variegated white-and-green foliage and apricot flowers.
'Yellow' has the classic yellow form.

Canna × *generalis* CANNA

Cannas offer a bold tropical-looking coarse texture and bright colored flowers for the summer and fall garden. Many hybrids exist, offering both subtle and dramatic combinations of foliage and flower colors. The contrast with other perennials in a border, as accents in containers, or even with woody shrubs in larger landscapes can be very exciting. Go ahead, take the leap and use some coarse textures in your planting composition! Most hybrids are of at least partial nonnative origin and like full sun. They tolerate wet soils such as a pond edge or regular moist but well-drained garden soils. Hummingbirds love cannas.

ZONES & ORIGIN 7b–10. Hybrids are native to many parts of the world.

SIZE & GROWTH RATE 3'–8' tall, depending on the hybrid, creating a thick mass in a few years; fast growing.

TEXTURE & FORM Coarse texture; forms upright clumps.

FOLIAGE Large alternate simple leaves are 8"–2' long, with smooth margins. They are light and dark green, purple and bronze; variegated forms are yellow, white, orange, and purple and sometimes shiny (see hybrids).

FLOWERS & SEED Impressive flower heads rise above the foliage from June to frost, 3'–8' tall, depending on the hybrid, in reds, oranges, yellows, pinks, salmon, and creamy white. Interesting (or heart-stopping) in combination with foliage colors. Interesting spiky seed pods until frost.

LIGHT & SOIL Full sun to light shade. They prefer moist but well-drained soil. Some hybrids tolerate wet soils at the water's edge to even being submerged in water a few inches. They are also drought tolerant once established, but their growth and appearance will not be as luxurious. Mildly salt spray tolerant.

MAINTENANCE Cannas melt to the ground with the first hard frost. Clean up the foliage by cutting it off at ground level, and mulch for winter protection. As with most tropicals, spring or summer installation increases winter hardiness.

INSTALLATION Install 12"–24" on center for mass plantings.

PESTS & DISEASES For leaf rollers and Japanese beetles, treat the plant with beneficial bacteria or neem-oil.

NOTES & CULTIVARS
'Apricot Dream' is 3' tall, with gray-green leaves and salmon flowers.
'Australia' is 5' tall, with purple leaves and red flowers.
'Bengal Tiger' is 5' tall, with yellow-and-green striped leaves and orange flowers.
'Brandywine' is 5' tall, with green foliage and red flowers.
'Ermine' is 3' tall, with green foliage and creamy-white flowers.
'Musifolia' is 12' tall! It has green leaves and red flowers, but it is grown for the architectural effect.
'Pink President' is 3' tall, with green foliage and pink flowers.
'Richard Wallace' is 4' tall, with green foliage and yellow flowers.
'Tropicanna' is 5' tall, with green, purple, and orange striped foliage and orange flowers.

top to bottom

'Tropicana'.

'Bengal Tiger' in the Founders Memorial Garden at UGA.

A dark-foliage form with dahlias, *Agapanthus*, and crocosmias.

At Great Dixter with too many plants to list!

Colocasia esculenta ELEPHANT EAR

Elephant ears have long been a popular garden plant for warm climates. They, along with cannas, are often the token tropical flare in an otherwise uninteresting or strange planting composition around a southern homestead. (You've seen that house, haven't you?) However, they can make an exciting contribution to the well-planned border, container, or water's-edge planting with their coarse texture and lush tropical look. A good designer can find the right place for just about every plant. Be careful, however, in wet areas, as this plant can become invasive. It may be better to use it in a contained area.

ZONES & ORIGIN 7–10. Native to tropical Asia and the East Indies.

SIZE & GROWTH RATE 3'–5' tall, forming a colony; fast growing.

TEXTURE & FORM Coarse texture in upright individual clumps.

FOLIAGE Large ovate-cordate simple leaves emerge out of one stem to 2' long, with smooth margins and ruffled edges. Leaves face out or are almost perpendicular to the ground. Green, black, and white variegated forms are available.

FLOWERS & SEED The pale yellow spathe flower emerges below the foliage. The seed pod is insignificant. Grown for the foliage.

LIGHT & SOIL Full sun to light shade. Likes moist to wet soils at the water's edge. Can also be submerged in water a few inches.

MAINTENANCE Foliage melts to the ground with the first hard frost. Clean up the foliage by cutting it off at ground level, and mulch for winter protection. As with most tropicals, spring or summer installation increases winter hardiness. Becomes invasive in wet areas and needs containment.

INSTALLATION Install 18"–24" on center for mass plantings.

PESTS & DISEASES None major.

NOTES & CULTIVARS
'Black Magic' has black and dark green foliage to 5' tall.
'Elena' has chartreuse leaves to 3'.
'Ruffles' is green and grows to 6' tall.

top Black foliage form at Berry College in Rome, Ga.

midddle With creeping jenny, dwarf mondo grass, fatsia, and pachysandra in an Atlanta garden by Land Plus Associates.

bottom left With begonias and sweet flag in an Atlanta garden by Land Plus Associates.

bottom right In the Gainesville, Ga., Botanical Garden.

Conoclinium coelestinum
MIST FLOWER · WILD AGERATUM

Mist flower is an extremely underutilized native perennial occurring in damp roadside swales, woods, and creek bottoms. It offers a low overall height and fall blooming and is the prettiest cobalt blue, which is the perfect complement to other warm autumn colors. It is great for naturalizing with other plants in bioswales or for use as part of a loose informal ground cover, mixing with ferns, hostas, and other woodland plants. It will also perform well in sun, provided there is ample moisture. Its only drawback is that in moist locations it can become aggressive and spread rapidly by rhizomes, so use it where spreading is welcome.

top left At the State Botanical Garden of Georgia.

top right In Atlanta in October.

bottom Flowers.

ZONES & ORIGIN 6–10. Native to the eastern United States.

SIZE & GROWTH RATE 1'–2' tall to 24" wide and spreading; fast growing.

TEXTURE & FORM Upright clumps, medium texture.

FOLIAGE Simple opposite bright green triangular leaves are 2"–3" long, with toothed margins and veins pressed into the leaf surface.

FLOWERS & SEED Showy corymbs display fuzzy-looking light blue to cobalt-blue flowers from August to October. Insignificant seed.

LIGHT & SOIL Full sun (with moisture) to moderate shade. Prefers rich organic and moist well-drained soil.

MAINTENANCE This is a carefree plant unless spreading is deemed a problem. Can be cut back in midsummer to increase density.

INSTALLATION Space 12" on center for mass plantings.

PESTS & DISEASES None major.

NOTES & CULTIVARS 'Album' is a white-flowered form.

Crocosmia × *hybrida*   CROCOSMIA · MONTBRETIA

Looking for hot colors in the landscape? Then crocosmia is your plant, with its color range of red, orange, and yellow and its blazing floral display in early to midsummer. The flowers are quite elegant, with arching stems and nodding tubular flowers, borne above very attractive dark green iris-like clumps of foliage. It makes an attractive accent in the shrub or perennial border and is an easy drought-tolerant plant to grow—a hummingbird favorite.

top to bottom

'Lucifer' at Butchart Gardens, Vancouver Island, B.C.

An orange form in Portland, Ore.

Yellow form in Seattle, Wash.

With hybrid anemone foliage and sedum in Portland, Ore.

ZONES & ORIGIN   6–8. Hybrid origin.

SIZE & GROWTH RATE   3'–4' tall and 2' wide; fast growing.

TEXTURE & FORM   Upright individual clumps with a fine texture.

FOLIAGE   Swordlike foliage arises to 3' in clumps from underground corms. Attractive even without flowers.

FLOWERS & SEED   Nodding tubular flowers borne on zigzagging and arching stems in June in the South. Hybrids offer reds, oranges, and yellows. Insignificant seed.

LIGHT & SOIL   Full sun to light shade. Likes moist but well-drained soil.

MAINTENANCE   Most hybrids need division every few years to maintain heavy flowering.

INSTALLATION   Install corms 3"–4" deep in spring at 4"–6" on center for mass effect. Space container-grown plants 6"–12" on center.

PESTS & DISEASES   None major.

NOTES & CULTIVARS

'Emily McKenzie' is orange with a crimson throat.

'Jenny Bloom' is butter yellow.

'Lucifer', popular and vigorous, is dark red.

'Star of the East' is orange with a cream throat.

'Walburton Yellow' is golden yellow.

Crocus spp. CROCUS

Crocuses are one of the first harbingers of spring with their delicate funnel-shaped flowers, which often appear as early as February in the South, smiling with the promise of warmer weather just around the corner. The sight of crocus flowers popping through the snow brings joy to the winter-weary heart. The popular Dutch hybrids offer exciting colors and dependable bulbs for naturalizing in large masses or tucking into nooks and crannies in detail areas. Fall-blooming species also exist and are quite showy—the common orchid-pink color is such a surprise when everything else is going into fall color.

ZONES & ORIGIN 5–8. Hybrid origin.

SIZE & GROWTH RATE 2"–6" tall; fast growing.

TEXTURE & FORM Forms clumps that are low to the ground; fine-textured foliage that is coarser in flower.

FOLIAGE Extremely thin blades channeled with a white stripe arise from corms. Disappears by midsummer on spring-blooming hybrids.

FLOWERS & SEED Cup- or funnel-shaped flowers 3"–4" long and 3" wide rise above the foliage in late February through March in the South in white, yellows, blues, lavender, purple, and bicolors. Insignificant seed.

LIGHT & SOIL Full sun to light shade. Likes moist but well-drained soil. Drought tolerant.

MAINTENANCE Effective naturalized in lawns, but mowing must be performed high enough to allow foliage to remain and collect energy for the next year.

INSTALLATION Install corms 2"–3" deep in fall at 6" on center for mass effect.

PESTS & DISEASES Squirrels, chipmunks, voles, and so on love to eat the corms.

NOTES & CULTIVARS
Crocus speciosus is a fall-blooming species with lavender flowers and bright orange stigmas. It is from Turkey and is hardy in zones 5–7.

top Fall-flowering species in the State Botanical Garden of Georgia.

middle Spring flowers in the Founders Memorial Garden.

left Late February in Georgia.

right Fall-flowering species in September at Great Dixter.

Echinacea purpurea PURPLE CONEFLOWER

Purple coneflower is native to open meadows of the eastern and central United States. It ranks as a tough and durable native perennial. It is outstanding as part of a perennial garden or a grassy meadow or en masse in just about any planting composition. It is often correctly listed as drought tolerant, but this doesn't mean that it looks its best in dry weather. A little supplemental water goes a long way. As with so many plants today, the release of cultivars is out of control. *Echinacea purpurea* and its purple cultivars 'Magnus' and 'Kim's Knee High' tend to outperform many of the newly released hybrids, but for the collector or adventurous designer, there are now yellows, peaches, oranges, mangos, and reds to choose from. See a partial list of the better hybrids below.

Flowers.

ZONES & ORIGIN 3–8. Native to the eastern and central United States.

SIZE & GROWTH RATE 2'–3' fast growing.

TEXTURE & FORM Upright clump; medium texture.

FOLIAGE Lanceolate dark green leaves are 4"–8" long and covered in stiff white hairs that are rough to the touch. The leaves are clumped around the base, with fewer and smaller clasping leaves along the stems.

FLOWERS & SEED Striking flowers 3"–4" in diameter have a central cone that is deep brown, almost black, surrounded by rose-to-purple-colored petals. Heavy flowering in June in Athens, with sporadic flowers until frost. Old flower heads make a significant contribution to the winter landscape. Cones full of seeds attract goldfinches and other seed-eating birds.

LIGHT & SOIL Full sun is best, although it will tolerate light shade. Prefers moist but well-drained soil to a fairly poor and dry soil. Drought tolerant. Mildly salt spray tolerant.

MAINTENANCE This is a carefree plant. It will reseed, and clumps can also be divided.

INSTALLATION Space 18"–2' on center for mass plantings.

PESTS & DISEASES None major.

NOTES & CULTIVARS
'After Midnight' is 12"–18" tall, with magenta flowers and black stems.
'Harvest Moon' is 2'–4' tall, with golden flowers and cone.

June at J. C. Raulston Arboretum with canna, *Eucomis comosa*, pineapple lily, bee balm, hibiscus, and variegated giant reed grass.

'White Swan' with tall verbena and grasses in Sonoma, Calif.

'Kim's Knee High' is 2' tall and vigorous, with rosy-pink flowers.
'Magnus' is 4' tall, vigorous, and time tested. It has large rosy flowers.
'Pink Double Delight' is 2' tall, with double pink flowers.
'Ruby Giant' is 4' tall, with deep purple flowers.
'Summer Sky' is 2'–4' tall, with reddish flowers.
'Sunrise' is 3'–4' tall, with lemon-yellow flowers with a golden cone.
'Twilight' is 2'–4' tall, with red flowers and cones.
'White Swan' is a time-tested and dependable, with a white flower.

Flowers.

top March flowers in the Lurie Garden, Chicago.

midddle A tidy border at Great Dixter.

bottom left Epimedium × perralchicum 'Frohnleiten' in Gainesville, Ga. Design by the Fockele Garden Co.

bottom right Sumptuous ground cover at Bloedel Reserve, Bainbridge Island, Wash.

Epimedium spp. BARRENWORT

Epimedium species are destined to become a favorite of landscape architects and designers, as they provide a good ground cover option for dry shady areas on a plant with showy spring flowers—and a few forms are even evergreen. Their growth is not overly aggressive, making them very compatible with bulbs and other shade garden plants such as hostas, ferns, and Lenten roses. The evergreen forms offer garden hope to those who are tired of monotonous plantings of Ophiopogon and Liriope.

ZONES & ORIGIN 5–8. Hybrid origin—many forms from Asia.

SIZE & GROWTH RATE 8"–12" tall to 24" wide; slow to moderate growth.

TEXTURE & FORM Mounding clump, medium texture.

FOLIAGE Compound lanceolate dark green leaflets are 3"–6" long in two groups of three, with smooth or serrate margins. Many hybrids exhibit early spring foliage with pink to bronze or burgundy coloration, which later turns green. Evergreen and deciduous forms are available.

FLOWERS & SEED Showy flower panicles are held above foliage in early spring in white, yellows, pinks, reds, burgundy, and purple, as well as many bicolors. Insignificant seed.

LIGHT & SOIL Light to moderate shade. Prefers organic rich, moist, and well-drained soil. Will tolerate drought and tree competition once established.

MAINTENANCE A carefree plant.

INSTALLATION Space 12" on center for mass plantings.

PESTS & DISEASES None major.

NOTES & CULTIVARS
Evergreen: *Epimedium acuminatum* 'Frohnleiten' has yellow flowers.
'Hot Lips' is deep red.
'Pink Champagne' has two-tone pink flowers with attractive purple-and-green foliage.
'Pink Constellation' has pink flowers and dark green foliage.
'Pink Elf' is light pink and bronze.
Deciduous: *Epimedium grandiflorum* has pale pink flowers.
E. × *rubrum* has crimson-and-white flowers.
E. × *youngianum* 'Niveum' has white flowers.
E. × *youngianum* 'Roseum' has rosy flowers.

Eutrochium maculatum JOE PYE WEED

Several species of Joe Pye weed are native to the eastern United States and are quite common in moist meadows from Canada to Georgia. It has long been appreciated in English gardens but only recently seems to be catching on in the United States as a cultivated plant. It is called queen of the meadow, as it stands tall, to 8' or even 12' in midsummer, with impressive 12" mauve to purple panicles held atop stems. Pollinators love the plant, and it is an easy perennial for a large back border where its height is not a problem or for bioswales and meadow plantings. If height is a problem, there are several great shorter cultivars—see below.

ZONES & ORIGIN 4–8. Native to the eastern United States.

SIZE & GROWTH RATE 4'–8' (12') tall, to 3' wide; fast growing.

TEXTURE & FORM Tall upright clumps; coarse texture.

FOLIAGE Three to five whorled leaves, each 8"–12" long, are coarsely serrate. Stems are hollow, with purple mottling.

FLOWERS & SEED Show-stopping 1' panicles occur in midsummer and are mauve to light purple in color. Butterfly magnets.

LIGHT & SOIL Full sun to light shade. Prefers organic rich, moist, and well-drained soil.

MAINTENANCE A carefree plant.

INSTALLATION Space 3'–4' on center for mass plantings.

PESTS & DISEASES None major.

NOTES & CULTIVARS
Euotrochium fistulosum is a Southeast native with hollow stems and a slightly more mauve color. It loves wet to regularly moist soils.
E. purpureum 'Gateway' is shorter than the species but may still reach 6'.
'Little Joe' is 4' tall, with large purple flower heads.
'Phantom' is a hybrid that grows to only 3' with lavender flowers.

top left E. maculatum with tall phlox, canna, lily, and a *Persicaria* hybrid, lady's thumb, at Butchart Garden on Vancouver Island, B.C.

top right A wet meadow in Georgia.

middle Eutrochium fistulosum.

bottom E. fistulosum in the Founders Memorial Garden at UGA.

top In Beaufort, S.C.

midddle *Farfugium stenocephala* 'The Rocket' in Portland, Ore. (This form hates humidity.)

Farfugium japonicum LEOPARD PLANT

Leopard plant, once lumped in the genus *Ligularia*, is an eye-catching clump-forming plant for the shade garden. Its coarse texture and shiny leaves have a similar visual effect as hosta but with a slightly more tropical and lush feel, and leopard plant is only hardy in zones 7b–9. Several cultivars have ruffled leaf margins or golden spots on the dark green leaves, hence the name leopard plant. They make an exciting contribution to shady and moist garden areas as a specimen or in mass plantings and are useful in combination with ferns and other shade lovers.

ZONES & ORIGIN 7b–9. Native to Japan.

SIZE & GROWTH RATE 18"–24" tall and wide; moderate growth rate.

TEXTURE & FORM Mounding clumps; coarse texture.

FOLIAGE Clumps of dark green glossy cordate to rounded leaves are 4"–10' across, depending on the cultivar. Margins are wavy or ruffled. Gold-spotted variegated cultivars are available.

FLOWERS & SEED Daisy-like yellow flowers rise above the foliage to 2' tall from midsummer through fall. The flowers are interesting, although the foliage is the real reason to use the plant. Seeds are produced, but they are not showy.

LIGHT & SOIL Light to moderate shade. Prefers moist and rich organic well-drained soil.

MAINTENANCE Little required other than selective leaf removal to tidy the appearance.

INSTALLATION Space clumps 18"–2' on center for massing or use as a specimen in a small detailed area.

PESTS & DISEASES None major, although foliage may be eaten by insects and rabbits.

NOTES & CULTIVARS
'Aurea-maculata' has yellow leopard spots.
'Crispata' has heavily ruffled gray-green leaves.
'Giganteum' is dark green and 3' by 3'.

left March in Maastricht, the Netherlands, with *Ipheion uniflorum*, spring starflower, in bloom.

below At Wormsloe Plantation near Savannah, Ga.

Gaura lindheimeri GAURA · WHIRLING BUTTERFLIES

This wonderful native perennial has yet to really become mainstream. Perhaps it is slightly too "wild" looking for the average consumer? Its heat and drought tolerance and tendency to bloom the entire growing season make it a highly valuable plant, and it should be used more. Many cultivars have been introduced with white to deep pink flowers and some foliage variegation of pink and white. This plant is versatile and tough enough to be at home in the traditional perennial border or used in sweeping masses together with grasses and shrubs.

ZONES & ORIGIN   5–8. Native to Louisiana and Texas.

SIZE & GROWTH RATE   3' by 3' fast growing.

TEXTURE & FORM   Mounding form with a fine texture.

FOLIAGE   Mostly basal and narrow lanceolate gray-green foliage to 3" long. Some cultivars have burgundy to gold variegated leaves.

FLOWERS & SEED   Prolific flowering from spring until frost with four-petaled white to pink 1" flowers that continue to open up the flower stems. The flowers look like butterflies perched on the thin airy flower stems. May self-seed.

LIGHT & SOIL   Full sun to light shade. Prefers moist well-drained to dry soil. Drought tolerant.

MAINTENANCE   A carefree plant. May need cutting back in midsummer to rejuvenate tall plants that have flopped.

INSTALLATION   Space 3' on center for mass plantings.

PESTS & DISEASES   None major.

NOTES & CULTIVARS
'Passionate Blush' has reddish buds opening deep pink. It is more compact, to 24".
'Pink Cloud' has a vigorous and floriferous pink-flowered form.
'Whirling Butterflies' has white flowers.

top to bottom

Delicate butterfly-like flowers.

Interplanted with grasses in Tongva Park, Santa Monica, Calif., by Field Operations.

With Japanese roof iris at J. C. Raulston Arboretum.

With annual cleome, or spider flower, spiderwort, star juniper, and abelia in Athens, Ga.

Glandularia canadensis CLUMP VERBENA

This spreading verbena became wildly popular with the introduction of the cultivar 'Homestead Purple', and for good reason, as it is a vigorous and floriferous ground cover plant. The designer must be careful not to be swayed by the many forms of verbena on the market. Many of the hybrids are effectively annuals, and even some reported to be perennials are only half hardy. Our advice is to stick with the hybrids that have been trialed and are known to perform well. It should be noted that even top performers like 'Homestead Purple' will fail to overwinter if drainage is poor. All forms seem to explode into flower in late April through early June but then rest during the heat of the summer, often reblooming in fall. If they are cut back in midsummer, then rebloom is encouraged. This plant is great at the front of the border spilling out of other perennials, bulbs, or low shrubs or as the "spiller" from a container.

top to bottom
Flowers.
A white form with annual globe amaranth and southern shield fern.
'Homestead Purple' with creeping jenny in Athens, Ga.

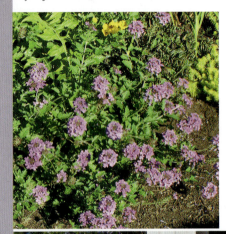

ZONES & ORIGIN 6–10. Native to North America.

SIZE & GROWTH RATE 8"–12" tall and 36" wide; fast growing.

TEXTURE & FORM Low spreading clumps; fine texture.

FOLIAGE Deep green deeply lobed ovate leaves are 1"–3" long and 1" wide. Stems are square and pubescent.

FLOWERS & SEED Terminal rounded 1"–3" clusters of tubular flowers occur heavily in May and early June and then sporadically until frost in lavender, pink, red, purple, and white, depending on the hybrid.

LIGHT & SOIL Full sun to light shade. Needs moist well-drained soil. Mildly salt spray tolerant.

MAINTENANCE Cut back in midsummer to encourage repeat flowering and dense growth. Winter hardiness is reduced by poor drainage.

INSTALLATION Space containers 12"–24" on center for massing.

PESTS & DISEASES Powdery mildew and spider mites.

NOTES & CULTIVARS
These hybrids are noted for good vigor:
'Abbeville' has lavender flowers.
'Fiesta' has a pink-and-purple bicolor.
'Homestead Purple' is a rich purple.
'Silver Anne' is pink.
'Snowflurry' is white.
'Summer Blaze' is red.

Verbena tenuisecta, moss verbena, and related cultivars from South America have finely cut foliage and are floriferous and vigorous, but they are not cold-hardy above zone 8. They are best used as annuals.

Hedychium coronarium BUTTERFLY GINGER

The sweet fragrance of butterfly ginger in bloom, hanging thick in the humid August and September air, is something to look forward to. In late summer and early fall, the white or even pink or peach flowers open in the shape of a butterfly and release their heavy perfume. Besides the wonderful fragrance, the foliage is very attractive and offers an elegant medium coarse texture that isn't overtly tropical like cannas or elephant ears; therefore, the designer can usually sneak these into temperate gardens where clients sometimes reject the use of coarse textures. Butterfly ginger works as part of the perennial border or together with shrubs and foundation plantings, provided there is ample moisture. It should be used where one must pass by it frequently.

ZONES & ORIGIN   7b–10. Native to Asia.

SIZE & GROWTH RATE   4'–6' tall to 4' wide and spreading; fast growing.

TEXTURE & FORM   Upright clumps that lean outward; medium coarse texture.

FOLIAGE   Thick stems arch elegantly outward as they mature, with simple alternate oblong bright green leaves that are 3"–5" wide and 24" long. The edges are often rolled under, with smooth margins. Leaves often have a ladder-like appearance, with nearly equal spacing along the stem.

FLOWERS & SEED   Exquisite five-petaled flowers resembling a butterfly open one or two per day on a large cone-shaped cluster for four to six weeks in late August through early October. They have a heavy sweet scent. White is most common; however, pink, orange, peach, and yellow cultivars are available.

LIGHT & SOIL   Full sun to moderate shade. Prefers organic rich, moist, and well-drained soil. Also performs well in wet soils. Salt spray tolerant.

MAINTENANCE   Clumps may need staking as they lean outward. Likes moisture. Spreads by rhizomes quickly where moisture is abundant and may need partial removal every few years.

INSTALLATION   Space containers or divisions 2'–3' on center for mass plantings.

PESTS & DISEASES   None major.

NOTES & CULTIVARS
'Carnival' is butterscotch yellow.
'Elizabeth' grows to 9' tall and is pinkish red.

top left Ladder-like foliage with sweet flag.

top right and middle With southern shield fern and tall phlox in the Founders Memorial Garden at UGA.

bottom Butterfly-like flowers.

top left *Helianthus angustifolius* flowers in October.

top right *H. angustifolius*—perfect position exploding from behind a fence in Savannah, Ga.

middle *H. divaricatus*.

bottom *H. divaricatus* with Mexican petunia and dwarf banana.

Helianthus spp. SUNFLOWER

Helianthus is a large genus with both annual forms and some truly wonderful but less well known perennial species. The word "explosion" most succinctly describes the visual effect of the perennial species in full bloom in late summer or early fall. All love full sun and moist well-drained soils or even periodically wet soils. They should be a common fixture of bioswales and water filtration systems, provided their tall height is acceptable. In the back of a large perennial border or just erupting from behind shrubs, *Helianthus* is an exciting and durable perennial providing an exquisite fall show and a food source for birds. See individual species descriptions below.

ZONES & ORIGIN (4) 5–9. Native to the eastern United States.

SIZE & GROWTH RATE 4'–8' tall, nearly equal spread; fast growing.

TEXTURE & FORM Upright clumps that lean outward when in flower; medium texture.

FOLIAGE Most species have simple alternate narrow leaves with entire margins to 7" long that are hairy and rough, but this quality is variable. Medium to dark green.

FLOWERS & SEED Ray flowers 2"–3" wide are produced in abundance. They are bright sunny yellow with either a dark brown or purple center, as in *Helianthus angustifolius*, or yellow like the petals in other species. Flower in September and October until frost in the South. Seed heads are visited by many birds.

LIGHT & SOIL Full sun to perhaps light shade. Prefers moist well-drained soil. Also performs well in periodically wet soils.

MAINTENANCE Clumps may need staking if they are in partial shade. Likes moisture. Spreads by roots and seed quickly where moisture is abundant, and may need partial removal every few years.

INSTALLATION Space containers or divisions 4' on center for mass plantings, although one (perhaps three) makes a fine specimen and quite a display.

PESTS & DISEASES None major.

NOTES & CULTIVARS

Helianthus angustifolius, swamp sunflower, is a native species to 8' (10') tall. It has yellow flowers with a dark center and spreads aggressively.

H. mollis, ashy sunflower, is native to the Midwest. It has handsome gray felt-like foliage and grows to only 4'–5' tall, with solid yellow flowers. It is not as aggressive—one of the best!

H. salicifolius, willowleaf sunflower, is native to the Midwest. It has very narrow leaves and grows to 8' tall. The flowers are a solid yellow. It is more drought tolerant than other species.

H. tuberosus, Jerusalem artichoke, is a native that is grown primarily for its edible tubers.

Hemerocallis spp. DAYLILY

To tackle such a popular and long-hybridized plant in such little space is impossible, but let this account lead you to lists by many growers of countless named hybrids that offer easy sun-loving perennials in almost every color imaginable. Some hybrids, such as 'Stella d'Oro', 'Happy Returns', and 'Rosy Returns', offer a shorter height and repeat flowering and have been a landscape favorite—to the point of complete boredom. The larger-flowered and often taller once-blooming hybrids offer some truly exquisite flowers that are worth waiting for each year.

ZONES & ORIGIN 3–9. Hybrid origin—often China and Japan.

SIZE & GROWTH RATE 1'–4' tall, depending on hybrid, with a 24" spread; fast growing.

TEXTURE & FORM Mounding clumps; medium texture.

FOLIAGE Mounding clumps of grasslike narrow foliage arranged in a fan and arching outward. Some hybrids are listed as evergreen; however, most are deciduous.

FLOWERS & SEEDS Beautiful five-petaled flowers that are 3"–7" across are tubular at the base and sometimes fragrant, occurring in a wide color range. They are sometimes bicolored and have single and double forms. Some hybrids repeat flowering, but most flower once in June to early July.

LIGHT & SOIL Full sun to light shade. Prefers moist well-drained soils. Salt spray tolerant.

MAINTENANCE Clumps may need division every three to five years. Foliage can become tired and too messy looking for highly maintained landscapes.

INSTALLATION Space containers or divisions 18"–2' on center for mass plantings. Ground cover types may work at 12" on center.

PESTS & DISEASES None major, although aphids, thrips, and daylily rust can be problems. Deer and rabbit candy!

NOTES & CULTIVARS

It is impossible to list all the cultivars here. Refer to the tested hybrids and award winners listed by the American Hemerocallis Society and the All American Daylily Selection Council.

Hemerocallis fulva is a common naturalized roadside species from China that blooms bright orange.

top left A red cultivar in bloom at Huntington Botanical Gardens, Pasadena, Calif.

top right 'Happy Returns' in Athens, Ga.

middle A tall deep orange form.

bottom A repeat flowering yellow in Athens, Ga.

top left Hibiscus coccineus at the State Botanical Garden of Georgia.

top right A dwarf white hybrid in the Birmingham Botanical Garden.

middle A popular tropical form that is hardy to zone 9b and works well as a container plant farther north.

bottom The hybrid 'Raspberry Rose' in its July glory.

Hibiscus spp. HARDY HIBISCUS · SWAMP MALLOW

Are you looking for traffic-stopping dinner-plate-sized flowers? The collective group of cold-hardy hibiscus species and their hybrids offers large deciduous shrubs that love moist soils to actual submersion in shallow water and full sun and are covered in enormous flowers from June through about August, depending on the cultivar. These plants are outstanding as part of retention ponds or other wet-soiled landscapes, and they are hummingbird magnets. Some also tolerate regular well-drained garden soils. Several Southeast native species have been used to create today's popular hybrids (see below).

ZONES & ORIGIN (5) 6–9, but varies with cultivar. Native to the eastern United States.

SIZE & GROWTH RATE 4'–8' tall and wide, depending on hybrid; fast growing.

TEXTURE & FORM Rounded form and coarse texture.

FOLIAGE Large simple alternate leaves vary from elliptic or cordate with smooth margins and solid green color to palmate or heavily lobed and having coppery to reddish color, depending on the hybrid.

FLOWERS & SEEDS Incredibly showy large single flowers range in size from 4" to some hybrids that have 12" flowers! Most flower in June and July in north Georgia. Brown stems and seed pods add interest to the winter garden.

LIGHT & SOIL Full sun to light shade. Most prefer moist to consistently wet soils or even shallow submersion. Mildly salt spray tolerant.

MAINTENANCE Cut back last year's stems in late winter just before new stems emerge.

INSTALLATION One may be plenty, but if space permits, install 5' or greater on center.

PESTS & DISEASES Japanese beetles can mangle the foliage.

NOTES & CULTIVARS

Hibiscus coccineus, swamp mallow, is native to the Coastal Plain. It grows best in zones 7–9 to 5'–7' tall and wide, with bright scarlet-red flowers in midsummer.

H. moscheutos, common mallow, is native to low-lying areas of the eastern United States. Thrives in zones 5–9 to 3' tall and wide, with white to pink midsummer blooms.

H. mutabilis, Confederate rose, is from China. It grows to 15' tall and wide but is hardy only to zone 7. The double flowers emerge pink and then mature to red, but it does not flower until October.

There are too many hybrids to name, but here are a few.

'Fantasia' grows to 3' by 3', with green leaves and 9" orchid-pink flowers.

'Kopper King' grows to 4' by 4', with coppery foliage and pink-tinged white flowers.

'Lady Baltimore' grows to 6' by 6', with pink flowers with red centers.

'Lord Baltimore' grows to 6' by 6', with red flowers.

'Raspberry Rose' grows to 7' by 7', with raspberry-pink flowers in profusion.

Hosta spp. HOSTA · PLANTAIN LILY

A shade garden without hostas is almost unthinkable. Hostas provide low clumps of luxurious foliage in many shades of green, yellow green, and blue green, as well as variegated forms. They create great interest for the ground plane in shade gardens. While they are grown primarily for their foliage, hostas do flower, with fairly impressive flower stalks held well above the foliage in summer. The number of hybrids available is mind boggling, and many are exquisite. One warning: hostas are deer candy!

A blue form in Stanley Park, Vancouver, B.C.

ZONES & ORIGIN 5–9. Hybrid origin—often China and Japan.

SIZE & GROWTH RATE 1'–4' tall and wide, depending on hybrid; moderate growth rate.

TEXTURE & FORM Mounding clumps; medium to coarse texture.

FOLIAGE Mounding clumps of rounded or ovate to lanceolate foliage with entire margins. The leaves can be ruffled, cupped, or puckered, and they radiate outward from the center. Foliage size and coloration vary greatly from solid or variegated, chartreuse green to almost blue.

FLOWERS & SEEDS Showy tubular florets in white or lavender are sometimes fragrant and are held above the foliage on stems up to 4' tall in June and July. Insignificant seeds.

LIGHT & SOIL Light to moderate shade, and it tolerates morning sun. Prefers rich organic, moist, and well-drained soil. Mildly salt spray tolerant.

MAINTENANCE Lightly mulch it, and then leave it alone.

INSTALLATION Very effective in mass plantings or as specimens. Spacing varies with the size of the hybrids from 12" to 4' on center.

PESTS & DISEASES Unfortunately, several significant threats include deer, slugs, snails, voles, and leaf-eating insects.

NOTES & CULTIVARS
It is impossible to list many cultivars here. Refer to local growers and award winners listed by the American Hosta Growers Association.

'Aureo-Marginata' is green with yellow margins.
'Francee' is green with white variegation. It is somewhat sun tolerant and grows 12" tall and 24" wide.
'Frances Williams' is blue-green and puckered. It grows 2' tall and 3' wide.
'Guacamole' is chartreuse with darker-green edges. It is 18" tall by 3' wide.
'Halcyon' is large, blue, and pleated to 18" tall and 3' wide.
'Sum and Substance' is an impressive chartreuse to 3' tall and 5' wide.

top to bottom

A chartreuse form in the Japanese Garden, Portland, Ore.

At Chanticleer Garden.

'Frances Williams' with 'Annabelle' hydrangea and common periwinkle at a residence in Knoxville, Tenn., by SWH.

Hylotelephium 'Autumn Joy' AUTUMN JOY SEDUM

'Autumn Joy' sedum has reached stardom in American gardens with its use by famous designers in large sweeping masses together with ornamental grasses and other perennials. The combos can be quite effective in creating color and textural drama on the ground for summer, as well as in the fall and winter landscape where dried grasses and flower heads are appreciated as unique and beautiful expressions of the changing seasons. Whether used in mass plantings or in smaller clumps for perennial borders or containers, this sedum performs well and looks good even in hot humid climates. This is not true of many sedums, which may survive in the Southeast but look rather terrible in summer, recovering in cooler drier weather. 'Autumn Joy' is a winner, tolerating full sun and drought and delivering at least three seasons of interest, with attractive foliage in early spring and summer, late summer flowers, and dried flower heads in fall that last until about midwinter.

top left In a rooftop garden in Vancouver, B.C., with Mexican feather grass and Japanese black pine.

top right With lavender and annual rudbeckia, early August in Vancouver, B.C.

middle Flowers.

bottom In September in London.

ZONES & ORIGIN 3–8. Hybrid origin.

SIZE & GROWTH RATE 12"–24" tall and wide; moderate growth rate.

TEXTURE & FORM Upright clumps; medium texture.

FOLIAGE Simple alternate light gray-green leaves are thick and waxy and 2"–3" long, with toothed margins.

FLOWERS & SEEDS Showy corymbs are 4"–6" wide and start out as green, flushing a mauve pink in August and turning a rich bronze red by fall. Dried seed heads are attractive through midwinter.

LIGHT & SOIL Full sun is best, because plants flop in any shade. Prefers dry or moist well-drained soils.

MAINTENANCE None major.

INSTALLATION Space containers 12"–18" on center for massing.

PESTS & DISEASES None major.

NOTES & CULTIVARS Purchase propagated plants only to ensure they are 'Autumn Joy'. Seed-grown plants may bloom earlier and not perform like 'Autumn Joy'.
Hylotelephium spectabile is similar in appearance, although it is perhaps pinker, and is native to Europe and Asia.

Hypericum spp.   ST. JOHN'S WORT

Several species and hybrids of *Hypericum* are commonly available. Perhaps the most common species, *H. calycinum*, is a great ground cover option for zones 5 and 6, but it suffers in the summer heat and humidity below zone 6. Many a landscape architect has specified *H. calycinum* (and others), excited by the thought of a semievergreen ground cover with yellow flowers in summer, only to watch the installation fizzle out in the heat. For southern landscapes in zones 7 and 8, designers should specify *H. buckleyi*, *H. densiflorum*, or *H. frondosum* (all Southeast natives), which have a larger and more shrub-like character, which is disappointing if you're wanting the ground cover effect of *H. calycinum* but realistic for southern growing conditions. Many native species exist and should be made more available.

ZONES & ORIGIN   5–9. *Hypericum calycinum* is native to Europe and Asia; *H. densiflorus*, *H. buckleyi*, *H. frondosum*, and *H. prolificum* are from the southeastern United States.

SIZE & GROWTH RATE   1'–4' tall and wide, depending on the species; moderate growth rate.

TEXTURE & FORM   Mounding clumps; fine to medium texture.

FOLIAGE   Generally blue-green ovate leaves with entire margins that are ½"–4" long, depending on the species. Several species are semievergreen and may develop reddish to bronze winter coloration.

FLOWERS & SEEDS   Showy yellow five-petaled flowers occur in midsummer to fall. *Hypericum frondosum* has a puffy rounded cluster of stamens in the center.

LIGHT & SOIL   Full sun to light shade. All prefer excellent drainage. Southeast native species tolerate drought and poor soils fairly well.

MAINTENANCE   Cut back in late winter to rejuvenate.

INSTALLATION   Very effective in mass plantings or as specimens—spacing varies with the size of the species from 12" to 3' on center.

PESTS & DISEASES   None major if sited correctly and heat-tolerant species are selected for the South.

NOTES & CULTIVARS
Hypericum species for cooler zones 5–6:

Hypericum calycinum is a low ground cover to 12" tall, semievergreen, reddish-bronze winter coloration.

Hypericum 'Hidcote' forms a beautiful 3' by 3' mound where it grows well.

Hypericum species for zones 5–9 (all native):

Hypericum buckleyi does well in zones 5–8 and grows 2' by 2'.

H. densiflorum grows in zones 5–9 to 4' by 4' and has shiny foliage.

H. frondosum 'Sunburst' grows in zones 5–8, forming a 3' by 3' mound with impressive puffball flowers.

H. prolificum grows in zones 3–8 to 4' by 4'.

top to bottom

Hypericum 'Hidcote' flower.

H. calycinum.

Hypericum 'Hidcote' form.

H. calycinum ground cover in Queen Elizabeth Park, Vancouver, B.C.

Flowers.

top to bottom
Flowers.
Summer foliage at Callaway Gardens.
A skillful use in Athens, Ga.

Iris cristata DWARF CRESTED IRIS

Dwarf crested iris is a wonderful and demure native occurring across the eastern United States on shady slopes and in ravines often near lakes and streams. It is, however, a tough and durable plant that tolerates drought well and provides an extremely low ground cover option for small or detail areas in the woodland garden or next to a walkway or other place where small detailed plants can be appreciated. It flowers in April in north Georgia, and native populations can be light blue to pure white, with flowers held just above the foliage.

ZONES & ORIGIN 3–9. Native to the eastern United States.

SIZE & GROWTH RATE 4"–6" tall and spreading; moderate growth rate.

TEXTURE & FORM Low ground cover; fine texture.

FOLIAGE Medium green flat blades are arranged in fans.

FLOWERS & SEEDS It forms showy flowers with three short upright "standard" petals and three longer drooping petals, called "falls." They have a fuzzy crest in golden yellow. Most flowers occur primarily in pale blue and white.

LIGHT & SOIL Light to moderate shade, and it tolerates morning sun. Prefers moist well-drained soil.

MAINTENANCE None.

INSTALLATION Very effective in mass plantings as a small-area ground cover. Space containers or divisions 12" on center. Clumps spread by rhizomes.

PESTS & DISEASES None.

NOTES & CULTIVARS
'Eco Bluebird' has darker blue flowers.
'Tennessee White' has a vigorous white form.
Iris verna var. *verna*, vernal iris, is native to the Coastal Plain and Piedmont (zones 6–10) in dry woods. Appears somewhat like a large version of *I. cristata*, reaching 12" tall. Its dark blue flowers have an orange blotch on the falls. *I. verna* var. *smalliana* occurs in upland mountain locations (zones 4–8).

A blue form in a rain garden by Andropogon and Associates near Philadelphia, Pa., with foamflower, Virginia sweetspire, inkberry holly, fothergilla, and more.

Iris ensata JAPANESE IRIS

The Japanese irises are one of the water-loving types, and they make a fabulous textural statement at the water's edge, not to mention their typically large and showy flowers. They will also tolerate regular moist garden soils but will be shorter and less vigorous. Use these to soften water-body edges or provide textural contrast in perennial and shrub borders.

ZONES & ORIGIN   4–9. Native to eastern Asia and Japan.

SIZE & GROWTH RATE   24"–36" tall and spreading; moderate growth rate.

TEXTURE & FORM   Upright clumps; fine texture.

FOLIAGE   Thin grasslike bright green blades to 1" wide and 30" tall are arranged in very stiff upright fans. Variegated (white) cultivars are available.

FLOWERS & SEEDS   Extremely showy flowers to 10" across occur above foliage for several weeks in late May to early June. The falls are much larger than the standards. Colors range from white to blues, purples, violet, pinks, and burgundy. The noticeable cylindrical seed pod turns from green to brown in fall.

LIGHT & SOIL   Full sun to light shade. It loves standing water and moist soils, although it also tolerates regular moist well-drained soils. The soil must have an acid pH.

MAINTENANCE   Divide every three to five years or so to increase flowering.

INSTALLATION   Space containers or rhizome divisions 24" on center. Plant shallow.

PESTS & DISEASES   None major.

NOTES & CULTIVARS
Consult the American Iris Society for a list of many wonderful cultivars.

'Agripinella' is a violet-and-white bicolor.
'Bellender Blues' is cobalt blue.
'Mt. Fuji' is large and white.

A purple cultivar in Athens, Ga.

top left At Chanticleer Garden.

top right Old-fashioned bicolor in Johnson City, Tenn.

middle April in Athens, Ga., with 'Blushing' Knock Out Rose and spiderwort.

bottom In Manhattan in June.

Iris × *germanica* BEARDED IRIS

Bearded irises have been grown in American gardens since colonial days, and old plantings can be seen around homesteads and on roadsides, as well as in many contemporary gardens. They are a tough, easy, and drought-tolerant perennial for borders or for massing along with low shrubs or ground covers. Several common white, purple, and light blue flowering forms have been passed along between neighbors and friends and are everywhere you look. However, this iris has been heavily hybridized, and cultivars in every color and bicolor imaginable are available from specialty growers. The American Iris Society designates award winners each year, and its lists may be helpful in culling a few good ones from the thousands.

ZONES & ORIGIN 3–8 (10). Hybrid origin, with many parent species native to Europe and Asia.

SIZE & GROWTH RATE 12"–3' tall and spreading; moderate growth rate.

TEXTURE & FORM Upright clumps; medium coarse texture.

FOLIAGE Often gray or blue-green and glaucous flat blades are 1"–2" wide to 24" long and arranged in extremely upright fans. It is somewhat evergreen in zones 9 and 10 and is early to emerge where it is deciduous.

FLOWERS & SEEDS Usually fragrant six-petaled flowers with three upright standards and three cascading falls are large and impressive. The falls have a fuzzy "beard." Flowers rise above the foliage in late March through April in north Georgia.

LIGHT & SOIL Full sun to light shade. Must have excellent drainage and be able to tolerate poor and dry soils. It prefers alkaline pH but will tolerate slightly acidic soils as well.

MAINTENANCE Cut back the foliage in fall to clean plants and reduce the chance of disease, especially in warmer zones.

INSTALLATION Space containers or rhizome divisions 12"–18" on center. Must be planted shallow, with the top of the rhizome even with the soil surface.

PESTS & DISEASES Few problems, if drainage is good. Plants struggle south of zone 8 but are occasionally seen.

NOTES & CULTIVARS

Far too many to attempt to list here. Cultivars are often divided by height, as very dwarf forms under 12" exist all the way to the more common tall hybrids, which may reach more than 3' when they are in flower.

Iris × *louisiana* LOUISIANA IRIS

The Louisiana irises include a collection of hybrids developed from several species native to the swamps and lowlands of southern Louisiana. Though native to the Coastal Plain, they are hardy much farther north and will grow in conditions from standing water to regular but moist garden soils. These and the other water-loving irises provide sumptuous texture and flowering at the water's edge or as part of a perennial and shrub border.

ZONES & ORIGIN   4–9. Native to south Louisiana.

SIZE & GROWTH RATE   36"–54" tall and spreading; fast growing.

TEXTURE & FORM   Upright clumps; fine texture.

FOLIAGE   Thin and often somewhat yellow-green grasslike blades grow to 2" wide and 36" tall arranged in very stiff upright fans. May be evergreen in southern locales.

FLOWERS & SEEDS   Showy 4" flowers occur above the foliage for several weeks in May. The falls are much larger than the standards. Colors range from white to blues and purples, pinks, burgundy, yellow, and rust. The noticeable cylindrical seed pod turns from green to brown in fall.

LIGHT & SOIL   Full sun to light shade. Loves standing water and moist soils, but it also tolerates regular moist well-drained soils.

MAINTENANCE   Divide every few years to increase flowering.

INSTALLATION   Space containers or rhizome divisions 24" on center. Plant shallow.

PESTS & DISEASES   None major.

NOTES & CULTIVARS   There are many wonderful cultivars.

'Black Gamecock' has deep purple to almost black flowers and grows to 5' tall.
'Brushfire Moon' has large butter-yellow flowers and grows to 3'.
'Now and Forever' has large lavender flowers and grows to 3'.
'Red Velvet Elvis' has large burgundy flowers and grows to 3'.

top and middle With spiderwort.

bottom With yellow flag iris in the far container in the Founders Memorial Garden at UGA.

left top In a private courtyard in Augusta, Ga., next to creeping fig.

left bottom Pond edge at Callaway Gardens.

right With Japanese garden juniper and Japanese maple.

Iris pseudacorus YELLOW FLAG IRIS

The sight of the foliage of yellow flag iris (or any water-loving iris) next to water is quite beautiful and lends the perfect vertical contrast to the horizontal plane of the water. Yellow flag has naturalized in many areas of the United States and can be quite aggressive in moist environments. Its growth is much slower and more manageable in regular well-drained garden soils, where it makes a nice contribution to perennial borders or larger shrub borders as a mass. In spring it produces majestic golden-yellow flowers, which hover just above the foliage.

ZONES & ORIGIN 4–10. Native to Europe and western Asia.

SIZE & GROWTH RATE 4'–6' tall and spreading; grows fast in wet soils.

TEXTURE & FORM Upright clumps; medium texture.

FOLIAGE Rich yellow-green flat blades that are 1" wide are arranged in extremely upright fans. Evergreen in zones 9 and 10. It is early to emerge where it is deciduous.

FLOWERS & SEEDS Golden-yellow flowers have three falls that are longer than the three standards. They hover over the foliage for about two weeks in late March to early April in north Georgia. The falls might have a brown blotch and some brown venation. Large seed pods develop.

LIGHT & SOIL Full sun to moderate shade. Tolerates shallow water and wet boggy soils to regular moist well-drained soil.

MAINTENANCE Aggressive where moisture is plentiful. May need a barrier or periodic removal.

INSTALLATION Space containers or rhizome divisions 24" on center.

PESTS & DISEASES None.

NOTES & CULTIVARS
'Variegata' emerges in spring with yellow leaf variegation that fades to green by midsummer.

With royal fern and black willow at Chanticleer Garden.

left In a sunny perennial garden.
right top and bottom On campus at UGA.

Iris sibirica SIBERIAN IRIS

If you've spent any time gardening, then you've probably been given some Siberian or bearded irises. The Siberian form that is common to American gardens has thin grasslike upright foliage and blooms white or deep purple in May. It is an easy plant to grow, performing well in full sun to light shade, and it prospers in a moist location but also tolerates regular garden soils and drought.

ZONES & ORIGIN 3–9. Native to central Europe and Russia.

SIZE & GROWTH RATE 12"–24" tall and spreading; moderate growth rate.

TEXTURE & FORM Upright clumps; fine texture.

FOLIAGE Thin grasslike blades to 1" wide and 18" long are often somewhat yellow green and are arranged in upright fans.

FLOWERS & SEEDS Showy 2" flowers occur above the foliage for two weeks in May. The falls are much larger than the standards. Colors range from white to blues and purples. A noticeable cylindrical seed pod develops, turning from green to brown in fall.

LIGHT & SOIL Full sun to light shade. It loves moist soils, but it will also tolerate regular garden soils and drought, being shorter and less vigorous in the latter.

MAINTENANCE None.

INSTALLATION Space containers or rhizome divisions 12"–18" on center. Plant shallow.

PESTS & DISEASES None major.

NOTES & CULTIVARS
There are many wonderful cultivars.

'Caesar's Brother' has large blue-purple flowers.

'White Swirl' has huge white flowers.

Many cultivars with 'Aurea' catalpa tree, a lime-green dwarf bamboo, with switchgrass behind at Chanticleer Garden.

Iris tectorum JAPANESE ROOF IRIS

Japanese roof iris takes its name from its traditional use in Japan on thatched roofs. As one might guess from this environment, it is a tough species that loves full sun and regular garden soils to fairly dry conditions. Its low height and attractive pleated foliage are basically evergreen, although it flops during winter. It provides a nice texture when used in combination with other low perennials or ground covers, and the white or bluish-purple flowering in April is quite attractive.

ZONES & ORIGIN 4–9. Native to Japan.

SIZE & GROWTH RATE 12"–18" tall and spreading; moderate growth rate.

TEXTURE & FORM Upright clumps; medium texture.

FOLIAGE Flat pleated blades to 2" wide and 18" long are arranged in wide fans that are often somewhat yellow green. Fairly evergreen in zones 7 and 8, although the foliage flops a bit in cold weather.

FLOWERS & SEEDS Showy light blue to light purple lightly fragrant flowers are 4"–6" wide. The three standards lie somewhat flat just above the three falls, which have a whitish crest. It blooms in late April to early May.

LIGHT & SOIL Full sun to light shade. It prefers moist well-drained to fairly dry soils.

MAINTENANCE Cut back the foliage in late winter to make way for new spring leaves.

INSTALLATION Space containers or rhizome divisions 12"–18" on center. Plant shallow.

PESTS & DISEASES None major.

NOTES & CULTIVARS
'Alba' has white flowers with a yellow crest.

top left In the Founders Memorial Garden at UGA.

top right With Kurume azalea in the Atlanta Botanical Garden.

middle In the Gainesville Botanical Garden.

bottom In the Birmingham Botanical Garden with Chinese silvergrass.

Lantana camara LANTANA · HAM AND EGGS

Lantana is a mainstay of gardens in zones 7b–11, particularly the old ham and eggs variety, which can grow to 6' tall by the end of summer and is covered in multicolored flowers of deep orange, yellow, and pink. Hummingbirds and other pollinators love lantana, and breeding in recent years has produced several new cold-hardy forms that are dependable perennials. Purchasing lantana can be confusing, because the annual types far outnumber the perennial forms. Be sure to look for specific cultivars that are known to return each year if a perennial is what you want. The ones listed below are excellent and provide several size and color options.

ZONES & ORIGIN 7b–11. Native to Mexico.

SIZE & GROWTH RATE 1'–5' tall and wide, depending on the cultivar; fast growing.

TEXTURE & FORM Mounding clumps; medium texture.

FOLIAGE Opposite ovate toothy yellow-green leaves are 1"–5" long and are scabrous above and pubescent below. The stems are square. The foliage is aromatic.

FLOWERS & SEEDS Rounded flower clusters to 2" across begin in June and continue until frost. Shiny black seeds may develop, and they are poisonous.

LIGHT & SOIL Full sun to light shade with moist well-drained to dry soil. The plants are drought tolerant once established, and they are salt tolerant.

MAINTENANCE To ensure winter hardiness, wait until new foliage begins to emerge in spring at the base before removing last year's woody stems.

INSTALLATION Space containers 1'–3' on center, depending on the cultivar.

PESTS & DISEASES None major.

NOTES & CULTIVARS
'Chapel Hill Gold' grows 3' by 3' with golden-yellow flowers.
'Chapel Hill Yellow' grows 3' by 3' with sunny-yellow flowers.
'Miss Huff' grows to 4' by 4' with flowers that are orange, yellow, and peachy pink in the center.
'Mozelle' has flowers that are light and dark pink with a cream center, to 3' by 3'.
'New Gold' is a prostrate form that is 12" tall and 24" wide, with golden-yellow flowers.
Lantana montevidensis is a ground cover form to 12" tall and 4' wide, with lavender flowers.

Seed.

top to bottom

'Chapel Hill Yellow' in the author's (Davis) garden.

'Miss Huff' and 'New Gold' at Crane Cottage, Jekyll Island, Ga.

Annual types with purple fountain grass and *Tradescantia pallida* 'Purpurea', purple heart.

Leucanthemum × superbum SHASTA DAISY

Shasta daisies have long been grown in American gardens and provide each generation of schoolchildren an opportunity to play "she loves me / she loves me not." The cultivars available today are hybrids resulting from crosses between several European species. They provide a very classic look for perennial gardens and border plantings with their white flowers and dark green basal foliage. They perform a little better in areas with cool nights, such as zone 6 and north, but they can be grown in warmer zones with the realization that they may have to be replanted or divided and reset every few years to produce vigorous new growth.

With a leopard plant 'The Rocket' and sea holly near Vancouver, B.C.

ZONES & ORIGIN 3–8. Native to Europe.

SIZE & GROWTH RATE 1'–3' tall and wide, depending on the cultivar; fast growing.

TEXTURE & FORM Upright clumps; medium texture.

FOLIAGE Basal clumps of dark green and shiny leaves to 12" long are toothed with a long petiole. The leaves become smaller and sessile up the flower stem.

FLOWERS & SEEDS Showy single or double white daisies have a yellow center and are produced in May and June in north Georgia. Flowering can be prolonged by deadheading. Yellow-flowering cultivars exist.

LIGHT & SOIL Full sun to light shade. Prefers moist well-drained soil.

MAINTENANCE Divide every few years to rejuvenate.

INSTALLATION Space containers 1'–2' on center, depending on the cultivar.

PESTS & DISEASES None major, but foliar fungal diseases can wipe out mature clumps in hot humid climates.

NOTES & CULTIVARS
'Alaska' has 3" flowers on 2'–3' plants.
'Becky' has 3"–4" flowers on 3' plants.
'Ice Star' has double flowers on 2' plants.
'Snowcap' has smaller, 18" plants.
'Snow Lady' has 12" plants and 2" flowers.
'Sunshine' has 4" lemon-yellow flowers on 3' plants.

top to bottom

With Chinese silvergrass and bee balm in Virginia in June.

With yarrow at the always nicely planted Asheville, N.C., rest stop on I-40.

Looking storybook perfect on the Oregon Coast in early August.

Leucojum vernum SPRING SNOWFLAKE

Spring snowflakes are a common heirloom old-garden bulb and can be seen along with narcissus by the thousands around old homesteads and in historic gardens. They are an easy bulb to grow and make a graceful display in early spring when used in large drifts. They look great popping out of other ground covers or informal lawn areas that can wait to be mowed until after the snowflake foliage disappears in late May. They are also useful in smaller pockets and more detailed areas, offering a glimpse of spring when temperatures are still cold and winter seems as if it will never end.

ZONES & ORIGIN 3–9. Native to Europe.

SIZE & GROWTH RATE 12" tall and 6" wide; moderate growth rate.

TEXTURE & FORM Upright clumps; fine texture.

FOLIAGE Clumps of dark green strap-like leaves grow to 12" tall. Foliage begins to emerge in February in north Georgia and disappears by late May, storing energy in the bulb for the next year.

FLOWERS & SEEDS Delicate white bell-shaped flowers nod on 12" hollow stems. Each flower is tipped in light green.

LIGHT & SOIL Full sun to light shade with moist well-drained soil. Drought tolerant.

MAINTENANCE Avoid cutting back foliage until it dies to ensure flowering the next year.

INSTALLATION Plant in the fall, and space bulbs 6"–12" on center for massing, 3"–4" deep.

PESTS & DISEASES None major.

NOTES & CULTIVARS
Plants are slow to recover after division and are reported to tolerate significant soil moisture. Several species are native to Europe.

top left February in Savannah, Ga., with camellia, boxwood, and Satsuki azalea.

top right With hellebores.

middle March in Athens, Ga.

bottom February at Magnolia Plantation.

top left A white form with a variegated sedge in a Portland, Ore., rain garden.

top middle and right *Liatris spicata* with sedum and *Persicaria* hybrid, lady's thumb, in Vancouver, B.C.

bottom In the author's (Davis) garden.

Liatris spicata BLAZING STAR

Blazing star is a striking native perennial that occurs in moist meadows and sunny sites across much of the eastern United States. It is tough and provides a showy display of rich purple flowers in midsummer on a spike that gets 3'–4' tall. It is very attractive to pollinators and will gently reseed itself around the garden. It is a useful companion to grasses in perennial borders and containers and is tough enough to mass and use in public landscapes. Many other species are native to North America and offer diversity in site appropriateness from moist to dry. These can be a useful component of meadow seed mixes. Blazing star is a great choice for gardens, as it typically remains erect even in wetter summers when others get too tall and flop.

ZONES & ORIGIN 3–9. Native to the eastern United States.

SIZE & GROWTH RATE 24"–48" tall, 12"–18" wide; moderate growth rate.

TEXTURE & FORM Upright clumps; fine texture.

FOLIAGE Clumps of thin grasslike dark blue-green leaves to 12" long grow in a mounded clump. Leaves also radiate out from the flower spike and become smaller up the stem.

FLOWERS & SEEDS Showy spikes of reddish-purple flowers open at the top of the spike first and continue downward, blooming over a long period from late June through early August in north Georgia. This is a popular cut flower. It will reseed itself lightly.

LIGHT & SOIL Full sun to light shade in moist but well-drained soil. Fairly drought tolerant.

MAINTENANCE None major.

INSTALLATION Install 12"–18" on center for massing.

PESTS & DISEASES None major.

NOTES & CULTIVARS
'Alba' is a white-flowered form.
'Kobold' is a dwarf cultivar to only 2' tall, with purple flowers.

Lilium spp.   LILY

Few flowers offer such sophistication and elegance as a lily. A lily in bloom is an architectural marvel, and its inclusion in the garden shows great attention to detail. To try and discuss the many species of lilies available to designers in this short account is impossible; however, there are a few that are commonly available and of widespread appeal for use in garden settings. No fine garden should be without a few lilies. In general, they need full sun and rich and moist well-drained soil. They look wonderful popping out of other ground cover plants as part of a perennial border or as an accent in a detail area. Most must be ordered as bulbs and planted in the fall, although some can be found as container-grown plants. Many possess an intoxicating fragrance.

ZONES & ORIGIN   5–8. Multiple origins.

SIZE & GROWTH RATE   2'–6' depending on the species; moderate growth rate.

TEXTURE & FORM   Upright stems; medium texture.

FOLIAGE   Generally upright stems with dark green and glossy narrow lancelike leaves that are 6"–8" long. The leaves are arranged spirally up the stem.

FLOWERS & SEEDS   Star or trumpet-shaped (depending upon the species) five-petaled flowers are as much as 10" across, often nodding and borne in clusters on top of the stems. Bloom time varies with species, from early summer through fall. Various species and cultivars offer many colors, from white, reds, yellows, oranges, pinks, peach, and bicolors. Flowers are sometimes marked with spots or stripes. Many forms are highly fragrant.

LIGHT & SOIL   Full sun to light shade in moist organic and rich well-drained soil.

MAINTENANCE   Taller species often need staking for support.

INSTALLATION   Space bulbs 12"–18" apart in groups or drifts for maximum effect. In general, plant bulbs at a depth three times the bulb diameter.

PESTS & DISEASES   Bulbs may be eaten by moles and voles. Many species are susceptible to lily mosaic virus, so plant resistant species.

NOTES & CULTIVARS

There are many colors available in the Aurelian hybrid group, with large funnel- or trumpet-shaped flowers on impressive 6'–8' stems.

'Casa Blanca' has large fragrant white flowers to 4' tall in midsummer.
'Stargazer' is pink and white with dark flecks, fragrant, midsummer, to 3' tall.
Lilium formosanum, Formosa lily, grows to 6'. Its white trumpet flowers are produced in September. It forms attractive seed heads and self-seeds readily. It is susceptible to mosaic virus.
L. superbum, Turk's cap, is native to the eastern United States in damp woodsy areas. It grows to 5' tall, with small orange-red flowers that nod—lovely.
L. tigrinum, tiger lily, is a common pass-along lily seen around old homesteads. It blooms orange with dark spots in midsummer to 5' tall and vigorous.

top left   A yellow modern hybrid.

top right   Lily displays at the J. C. Raulston Arboretum.

middle   A modern pink hybrid.

bottom   An older form commonly shared as a pass-along plant called tiger lily.

Lobelia cardinalis CARDINAL FLOWER

Cardinal flower is an excellent native occurring across the eastern United States in partially shaded damp meadows and on banks along rivers and streams. It also performs well in regular moist well-drained garden soil with some afternoon shade. Its dark green foliage and intense red flowers are quite showy. Cardinal flower is at home in bioswales and water treatment plantings, as well as in a lightly shaded perennial border. Hummingbirds love it.

ZONES & ORIGIN 2–9. Native to the eastern United States.

SIZE & GROWTH RATE 2'–3' tall and 12" wide; moderate growth rate.

TEXTURE & FORM Upright stems; medium texture.

FOLIAGE Mostly basal leaves are dark green and glossy, 4" long, narrow and toothed.

FLOWERS & SEEDS Tubular flowers of deep cardinal red are produced on terminal spikes in August in north Georgia. Self-seeds. Pink and white cultivars are available.

LIGHT & SOIL Light shade or morning sun with afternoon shade. Prefers moist organic well-drained soil to somewhat damp soil.

MAINTENANCE Little required, although in riparian zones, naturalistic plantings and selective reduction of neighboring plants may help cardinal flower to thrive, as it is not very competitive. Some rebloom will occur if the plant is deadheaded.

INSTALLATION Space containers 12"–18" on center for massing.

PESTS & DISEASES None major.

NOTES & CULTIVARS
'Alba' is a white-flowered form.
'Golden Torch' has golden foliage with red flowers.
'Rosea' has pink flowers.

top to bottom

Flowers.

A shorter form in this dry location in Alabama.

With water lettuce and lotus.

An ornamental planting with annual rudbeckia in Vancouver, B.C.

September in the Founders Memorial Garden at UGA.

Lycoris radiata SURPRISE LILY

Surprise lilies spark great curiosity when their showy flower heads suddenly rocket from the ground in late summer to early fall seemingly from nowhere. The secret of *Lycoris* is that the foliage emerges in the fall, lasts through the winter, and then disappears by the heat of summer. Flowers are not produced until late summer, and by this time most folks have forgotten they existed. The visual effect can be quite stunning, as the flower heads are large and showy. *Lycoris* bulbs are easy to cultivate, simply needing good drainage and sunny conditions. They multiply rapidly and share well with friends and neighbors.

ZONES & ORIGIN 6b–9. Native to China.

SIZE & GROWTH RATE 24" tall and 6" wide; moderate growth rate.

TEXTURE & FORM Upright clumps; fine texture.

FOLIAGE Clumps of thin dark blue-green strap-like leaves to 6" long. Foliage appears after flowering in the fall and lasts until late spring, disappearing by summer.

FLOWERS & SEEDS Delicate yet showy rounded flower heads of tubular azalea-like flowers in deep red are 4"–6" across. Flowers occur in mid-August in north Georgia.

LIGHT & SOIL Full sun to light shade in moist well-drained soil. Drought tolerant.

MAINTENANCE Divide every five years if flowering is reduced from overcrowded bulbs.

INSTALLATION Plant in the fall and space bulbs 6"–12" on center for massing, 3"–4" deep.

PESTS & DISEASES None major.

NOTES & CULTIVARS
Lycoris squamigera, pink surprise lily, with large pink showy flowers, is equally popular as the red form and blooms a little earlier than *L. radiata*. The bulbs are tough as nails, multiply rapidly, and last forever. It is more cold-hardy (zones 4–9).
Other rare species and hybrids exist with flowers of yellow and orange.

Lysimachia nummularia 'Aurea' CREEPING JENNY

Creeping jenny is a wonderful little ground cover for use around stepping stones or next to a pathway, stream, or pond where its low height and bright yellow-green foliage can be appreciated. It makes a wonderful finish to a perennial border as the final and lowest element and works well as a spiller for containers. It prefers moist soils and light shade but will tolerate full sun, provided moisture is adequate. In dry conditions the foliage may disappear, but it will return with cooler temperatures and more moisture. While an effective ground cover, it is not suitable for large areas, as it will not outcompete weeds or other more aggressive plants. Utilize it in smaller areas.

ZONES & ORIGIN 3–9. Native to Europe.

SIZE & GROWTH RATE 3" tall and 24" wide (plus); moderate growth rate.

TEXTURE & FORM Low ground cover; fine texture.

FOLIAGE Small 1" oval to rounded leaves are opposite and bright yellow green.

FLOWERS & SEEDS Single yellow 1" flowers occur in early summer but do not stand out against the bright yellow-green foliage.

LIGHT & SOIL Prefers light shade, but it will tolerate full sun if soils are moist. Moist well-drained soil is best. Salt spray tolerant.

MAINTENANCE Will spread quickly by rooting stems in moist environments, but it is easily removed.

INSTALLATION Install 12"–18" on center for massing.

PESTS & DISEASES None major.

NOTES & CULTIVARS
The species has naturalized in the eastern United States and is a darker green.

top to bottom

Foliage.

In a border with Japanese forest grass, Japanese painted ferns, and hostas at the Swarthmore Arboretum.

With hostas and dwarf mondo.

A shady tapestry in this garden by Land Plus Associates in Atlanta, Ga.

Monarda didyma BEE BALM

Bee balm is a native perennial occurring in moist locations such as streambanks and damp meadows across the eastern United States. It is a fast-growing and easy perennial, providing rich red summer flowers that are attractive to pollinators. Many hybrids have been produced by crossing *Monarda didyma* with *M. fistulosa*, yielding many color options from red to white, pinks, and violet purple. Drawbacks to bee balm include aggressive spreading by underground stems and a tendency to get powdery mildew; however, many of the newer hybrids may be more resistant to powdery mildew, and the tendency to spread is not a negative in all situations. The shallow-rooted plants are easily divided and removed, or in less formal situations large swaths of bee balm make a lovely display. Recent *Monarda* trials at Mt. Cuba Center have shed light on better cultivars for the mid-Atlantic regions and perhaps farther south.

ZONES & ORIGIN 3–7. Native to the eastern United States.

SIZE & GROWTH RATE 2'–3' tall and spreading; fast growing.

TEXTURE & FORM Mounding clumps; medium texture.

FOLIAGE Simple opposite leaves are 4"–6" long, with irregularly toothed margins. They are often hairy and aromatic when bruised. The stems are four angled.

FLOWERS & SEEDS Flowers and showier bracts are clustered at the tops of stems in June and July in north Georgia. Available in red, pinks, violet purple, and white. Insignificant seeds.

LIGHT & SOIL Full sun to light shade, with moist well-drained to damp soils.

MAINTENANCE Aggressive plants may need division and/or removal every few years in highly maintained landscapes. Will rebloom if cut back after flowering.

INSTALLATION Space containers 18"–24" on center for massing.

PESTS & DISEASES Powdery mildew is common, especially in dry soils.

NOTES & CULTIVARS
'Alba' is white.
'Jacob Cline' is deep red.
'Violet Queen' is deep purple. Dwarf forms also exist.

top left *Monarda bradburiana* with amsonia in late May on the High Line in Manhattan.

top right With Shasta daisy, Chinese silvergrass, Asiatic lily, backed by spruce.

middle Hummingbirds can't resist this plant.

bottom Showy flowers in summer.

Musa spp. BANANA

Most species of banana are native to the tropical regions of the globe, from the Caribbean and Central America around to tropical Africa and Asia. The large fruiting types grown for commercial production and the grocery store produce section must be grown in warm climates. However, many interesting and varied species with greater cold-hardiness exist and provide incredibly dramatic tropical foliage for temperate gardens. *Musa basjoo*, Japanese cold hardy banana or fiber banana, is reported to overwinter as far north as zone 5. In early spring, new leaves emerge from the previous year's roots or pseudostems, and by midsummer the foliage can be 15'–20' tall and wide. As with any coarse tropical-looking plant, the designer must be careful to position bananas in a garden context with other coarse-textured plants. A hidden tropical-pool garden can work well with bananas exploding out of a corner. Bananas also work well as part of large and bold herbaceous border.

ZONES & ORIGIN 5–12 for *Musa basjoo*; zone 9 and warmer for most other species. *M. basjoo* is native to Japan.

SIZE & GROWTH RATE 4'–18' tall, 4'–18' wide, depending on species, fast growing.

TEXTURE & FORM Coarse texture, upright oval form with an irregular outline.

FOLIAGE Simple opposite leaves 6"–2' wide and to 8' long clasp to form a trunk-like pseudostem. Leaves are paddle shaped with smooth margins on long petioles. With age, leaves become wavy and crinkled and are easily damaged by heavy winds.

FLOWERS Flowers emerge at the end of long panicles with pale pink to pale purple or cream bracts, depending on the species. True flowers are small and yellow in the center. Panicles become large and heavy and arch over toward the ground.

FRUIT Bananas form in linear bunches on large multibranched panicles, bending toward the ground under the weight of ripening fruit. Size, color, and taste vary greatly with species.

LIGHT & SOIL Full sun to light shade and rich moist to moist but well-drained acidic soils.

MAINTENANCE Bananas are heavy feeders and need constant moisture. With the first freeze, foliage is instantly turned into what looks like brown paper. Cut back but leave as much of the pseudostem upright as possible, as this will provide a jump start on the next season in milder climates.

INSTALLATION Typically container grown. Install as a specimen accent, or if a massive grove is desired, consider spacing new plants 6'–8' on center.

PESTS & DISEASES Aphids, thrips, nematodes, and mosaic virus.

NOTES & CULTIVARS
Ensete ventricosum 'Maurelii', red Abyssinian banana, formerly *Musa ensete*, has new foliage emerging with reddish striping and petioles. Grows to 15' tall. Only hardy in zones 10 and 11. Often used in conservatories and other indoor gardens in colder climates.

top to bottom

M. basjoo, the Japanese banana, in the tropical courtyard at Chanticleer Garden.

A Japanese banana in Victoria, B.C.

Musa spp. popping out of annuals coleus and *Ipomea batatus*, ornamental sweet potato, at the Birmingham Botanical Garden.

Musa siam 'Ruby'.

Narcissus spp. DAFFODIL

Daffodils light up the landscape in mid- to late winter and herald the coming of spring. A field or old homestead ablaze with daffodils in late February to early March is a cure for the winter blues. Today's daffodils are the result of many species crosses to produce bigger and more impressive flowers. Bulb growers offer many exciting choices. The temptation to order a few hundred when the catalogs arrive requires great self-control. Daffodils are excellent when used in mass plantings to create large drifts that pop out of ground covers or lawn areas, provided the lawn can wait to be mowed until the daffodil foliage yellows in late spring.

ZONES & ORIGIN 5 or colder–9. Native to Europe.

SIZE & GROWTH RATE 8"–14" tall and clump forming; moderate growth rate.

TEXTURE & FORM Upright clumps; medium texture.

FOLIAGE Strap-like or cylindrical foliage is 14" tall, depending on the hybrid, and is bright or sometimes gray green.

FLOWERS & SEEDS Flowers are 1"–4" and are composed of a cup (corona) surrounded by petals (perianth). They bloom in late February through mid-March in north Georgia, although some species bloom earlier or later. Colors and bicolors range from white, yellows, oranges, and peachy pink. Highly fragrant. Insignificant seed.

LIGHT & SOIL Full sun to light shade in moist well-drained soils. Drought tolerant. Mildly salt spray tolerant.

MAINTENANCE Do not remove the foliage before it yellows.

INSTALLATION In fall space bulbs 8"–12" on center for massing, 4"–6" deep for most species. Existing clumps may be divided and reset, although flowering may be delayed until the second year.

PESTS & DISEASES None major. They are never bothered by deer or other animals, as they are poisonous.

NOTES & CULTIVARS
Consult bulb growers and the American Daffodil Society for specific information. Here are a few popular hybrids:

'Chromacolor' is white with a pink cup.
'Fortune' is a deep yellow with an orange cup.
'Ice Follies' is a popular solid creamy white.
'King Alfred' is large and a solid yellow.

top left Grand sweeps on the North Campus of UGA.

top right Many species in sweeps at the UGA Botanical Garden.

middle 'Ice Follies'.

bottom Classic yellow 'King Alfred' type.

Packera aurea GOLDEN RAGWORT

This little native plant is easy to grow and makes a delightful contribution to the woodland garden. It has clean dark green foliage that is nearly evergreen, with attractive flower heads and buds that emerge as deep purple and open as a bright sunny yellow in April in north Georgia. It tolerates a fairly wide range of conditions, from full sun (if ample moisture is available) to woodsy locations with moist to fairly dry soils. It spreads gently by underground stolons and also reseeds. Growth in moist environments is fairly fast.

top A wonderful edge plant.

bottom With columbine at Chanticleer Garden.

ZONES & ORIGIN 3–9. Native to the eastern United States.

SIZE & GROWTH RATE 6"–12" tall and wide; moderate growth rate.

TEXTURE & FORM Upright clumps; medium texture.

FOLIAGE Deep-green basal leaves are heart shaped and toothed, forming clumps. Leaves along the flowering stems change to an ovate shape and are finely divided. Foliage is very early to emerge in spring.

FLOWERS & SEEDS Showy flowering stems are 12" tall and emerge a deep purple, with buds opening to reveal 1" sunny-yellow daisy-like flowers, which occur in April in north Georgia.

LIGHT & SOIL Prefers light shade to moderate shade; it tolerates full sun only if abundant moisture is present. It tolerates consistently moist to well-drained and even dry soils in shade.

MAINTENANCE None.

INSTALLATION Space containers 12"–18" on center for massing.

PESTS & DISEASES None.

NOTES & CULTIVARS Formerly listed as *Senecio aureus*.

left Looking tidy in Boston with deutzia and boxwood.

right top Fat buds of anticipation and classic white flower heads.

right bottom Pale pink form in a mixed border at the Coastal Maine Botanical Gardens.

Paeonia spp. PEONY

Few plants engender more loyalty than peonies. These rhizomatous perennials have been used in gardens for centuries, and clumps can be seen around old homesteads—the house long gone, the peonies enduring. A drive through the Pennsylvania Dutch country in late May or early June is awe-inspiring, with literal peony hedges growing everywhere. Many peonies (see cultivars) can also grow well in the Deep South as long-lived and durable plants. Their incredible, huge, and fragrant late spring flowers are showstoppers, and even once the flowers are gone, the foliage is quite attractive. They are substantial enough to be used apart from the perennial border in shrub borders or as specimen accents.

ZONES & ORIGIN 3–8. Native to China and Mongolia.

SIZE & GROWTH RATE 2'–3' tall and wide; slow growing.

TEXTURE & FORM Mounding clumps; medium coarse texture.

FOLIAGE Alternate compound leaves have many ovate leaflets, which are dark green and glossy, almost like an evergreen plant. New foliage emerges in spring as copper to crimson red, turning green as it matures.

FLOWERS & SEEDS Impressive large flower heads are 4"–8" across in single or double forms. Reds, wines, pinks, bicolors, and, most rare, yellow. Many are highly fragrant.

LIGHT & SOIL Full sun to light shade in moist, organic, and well-drained soils.

MAINTENANCE Do not overfertilize, as this may decrease flowering. Do not mulch over the crown. Heavy flowers may need staking.

INSTALLATION Peonies are often grown in containers that can be planted anytime. Roots are available for fall planting. Peony roots like to be near the soil surface, so plant them shallow. Space 24"–36" on center for massing.

PESTS & DISEASES None major, if early season bloomers are selected for the South.

NOTES & CULTIVARS Consult specialty and local growers and the American Peony Society for many wonderful named cultivars. The newer intersectional peonies combine the vigor, strong stems, and open flowers of tree peonies with the flowering, fragrance, and smaller overall size of other herbaceous species such as *Paeonia lactiflora*. 'Bartzella' is an excellent example, with strong and incredible yellow flowers in May and attractive foliage all summer long.

One of the yellow intersectional hybrids at Brooklyn Botanical Garden.

top With geraniums and many other perennials at Chanticleer.

bottom 'Husker Red' in June bloom in Philadelphia.

Penstemon spp. BEARDED TONGUE

Penstemons get gardeners excited with their upright spikes of tubular flowers, much like a foxglove or a snapdragon, but on a truly perennial plant. There are many exciting species and hybrids from around the country, but the best ones for warm humid climates are the species native to the eastern United States and their related cultivars or hybrids. Isn't that usually the case? These include *Penstemon digitalis* and cultivars 'Pink Dawn' and wildly popular 'Husker Red', and *P. smalli*. These are sun-loving, tough, drought-tolerant plants that resent pampering.

ZONES & ORIGIN 4 (*Penstemon digitalis*), otherwise 6–8. Native to the eastern United States.

SIZE & GROWTH RATE 2'–3' tall and 18" wide; moderate growth rate.

TEXTURE & FORM Upright clumps; medium texture.

FOLIAGE Mostly basal dark green leaves are simple, opposite, and oblong-lanceolate, 4"–6" long, becoming smaller and sparser up the stem. 'Husker Red' cultivar has burgundy foliage. 'Dark Towers' foliage is deep wine red with pink flowers.

FLOWERS & SEEDS Tubular flowers are 1"–2" long and held on upright spikes in midsummer. They are called "beard tongue" because of the tuft of yellow hairs just outside the throat. White, pink, and lavender cultivars are available. Insignificant seed.

LIGHT & SOIL Full sun to light shade. Well-drained soils are essential. They tolerate thin, dry, and poor soils.

MAINTENANCE Do not pamper them. They may resent fertilizer and heavy mulch.

INSTALLATION Space containers 12"–18" on center for massing.

PESTS & DISEASES None major.

NOTES & CULTIVARS
Penstemon digitalis 'Pink Dawn' has pink flowers on 2' plants.
'Husker Red' has white flowers and burgundy foliage.
P. smalli, Small's penstemon, has pinkish-lavender flowers on 18"–24" plants. It is tough and drought tolerant.
'Dark Towers' has pink flowers and deep wine foliage that holds color well through the summer.

Perovskia atriplicifolia RUSSIAN SAGE

Russian Sage provides a sumptuous combination of gray-green foliage, a soft fernlike texture, and wispy lavender-blue flowers. These qualities make it float among other plants in the border. It loves dry conditions and tolerates heat and full sun. It is quite attractive in informal perennial borders or in large swaths together with grasses. It has a tendency to flop over by late summer while still in flower, but this habit can be attractive with the right plants in place for it to lean on, or use one of the shorter and more upright cultivars listed below.

ZONES & ORIGIN 5–9. Native to eastern Asia.

SIZE & GROWTH RATE 4'–5' tall and wide; moderate growth rate.

TEXTURE & FORM Upright sprawling clumps; fine texture.

FOLIAGE Simple opposite gray-green leaves to 2½" long and 1" wide, coarsely toothed, appearing fine and feathery. Pungent aroma when bruised.

FLOWERS & SEEDS Small tubular lavender-blue flowers are whorled around the stems from July to frost, creating a soft hazy effect. Insignificant seeds.

LIGHT & SOIL Full sun only. Well-drained soils are essential. Drought tolerant.

MAINTENANCE Do not mulch heavily, as excessive moisture is a problem.

INSTALLATION Space containers 2'–3' on center for massing.

PESTS & DISEASES None major in zones 5–7. Moisture causes fungal disease in zones 8–9.

NOTES & CULTIVARS
'Filigran' has more finely divided foliage. It stands upright and has good color.
'Little Spire' is shorter, to 2', and is not as floppy.

Flower stems can get heavy and lean over other plants.

left With lavender and geraniums in July at Villa La Foce, Montepulciano, Italy.

right With rudbeckia in Bainbridge, Wash.

Phlox divaricata WOODLAND PHLOX

Woodland phlox is native to the eastern United States and occurs in moist woods from Canada all the way to the upper Coastal Plain of southeastern states. A sea of soft periwinkle-blue flowers is often the reward for a hike in the woods of north Georgia in late March through April. This phlox is low growing and carefree and makes a wonderful plant for naturalizing in woodland gardens or for use in more structured perennial beds. It spreads slowly by stolons and more quickly by seed, and it can be planted and forgotten about until the wonderful spring display. It is easy to remove if it reseeds into unwanted areas.

top to bottom

With foamflower and Kurume azalea.

Flowering along the wooded path in the Founders Memorial Garden.

With Virginia creeper and Boston ivy climbing the stone wall.

ZONES & ORIGIN 3–8. Native to the eastern United States.

SIZE & GROWTH RATE 12"–15" tall and wide; moderate growth rate.

TEXTURE & FORM Upright clumps; fine texture.

FOLIAGE Dark green leaves are simple and opposite, 1"–2" long and oblong, becoming smaller and sparser up the stem. May be semievergreen in the Deep South.

FLOWERS & SEEDS Loose panicles of lightly fragrant five-petaled light blue to periwinkle flowers are 1½" wide, held atop the foliage in late March through April in north Georgia. Reseeds readily, although cultivars should be divided or vegetatively propagated.

LIGHT & SOIL Light to moderate shade, but morning sun is acceptable. Moist but well-drained soil is best, but it will tolerate thin rocky soils. Salt spray tolerant.

MAINTENANCE Little care is needed unless reseeding becomes rampant.

INSTALLATION Space containers 12"–18" on center for massing.

PESTS & DISEASES None major.

NOTES & CULTIVARS
'Blue Dreams' is shorter, to 10".

'Fuller's White' grows 8"–12" tall and is extremely heavy flowering and pure white.

'Louisiana' has purple flowers with a magenta eye.

Phlox paniculata GARDEN PHLOX

If only ten perennials could be used in gardens, this phlox would surely make the list, particularly the species itself, which is native to the eastern United States. Finding the true species in the nursery industry may be a challenge, as this phlox has been heavily hybridized in pursuit of ever bigger flowers and intense colors. Look for forms listed as 'Lavender' or 'Old Fashioned Purple', which tend to be close to the original species and exhibit great vigor and visual presence in the landscape. To be fair, some of the new hybrids and colors are also very showy and garden-worthy, but one must be careful to specify a cultivar known for disease resistance and vigor, especially in hot humid climates. Cooler drier climates are more forgiving. See the Mt. Cuba Center phlox trials.

Queen Elizabeth Park, Vancouver, B.C.

ZONES & ORIGIN 4–8. Native to the eastern United States.

SIZE & GROWTH RATE 3'–4' tall and 24" wide; moderate growth rate.

TEXTURE & FORM Upright clumps; fine texture.

FOLIAGE Dark green leaves are simple and opposite, 3"–5" long, oblong and tapering to a point, sparse up the stem. Variegated foliage forms exist, but they suffer badly from disease in the Southeast.

FLOWERS & SEEDS Large showy rounded or conical panicles of lightly fragrant five-petaled flowers are 1" wide. The panicles are held atop the foliage in late May through June and July in north Georgia. Can reseed and often spreads by underground roots.

LIGHT & SOIL Full sun to light shade. Prefers moist well-drained soils.

MAINTENANCE Carefree if sited correctly. Cut it back in fall or late winter.

INSTALLATION Space containers 18"–30" on center for massing.

PESTS & DISEASES Powdery mildew can be a major problem in crowded locations with excessive moisture and poor air circulation. Avoid overhead watering.

NOTES & CULTIVARS
'Bright Eyes' has pale pink flowers with darker eye and is vigorous.
'David' has pure white flowers and is a time-tested vigorous cultivar.
'Jeana' has large deep pink flower heads and blooms from July to September, with excellent mildew resistance.
'Lavender' has beautiful flowers and excellent vigor.
'Orange' has salmon-orange flowers and is vigorous.

top to bottom

A perennial border in Atlanta by Land Plus Associates with Annabelle hydrangea and Joe Pye weed.

Queen Elizabeth Park, Vancouver, B.C.

Butchart Gardens, Victoria, B.C., with hosta, canna, and rudbeckia 'Herbstonne'.

Rudbeckia fulgida

BLACK-EYED SUSAN · YELLOW CONEFLOWER

Black-eyed Susans occupy a seat at the table of the great garden perennials. They make dependable carefree plants for many landscapes, providing handsome foliage, showy golden-yellow summer and early fall flowers, and attractive seed heads for the fall and winter landscape. They are effective in large masses with other perennials or ornamental grasses in commercial and institutional settings, as well as in smaller residential plantings. To some degree their drought tolerance has been overstated. While they will survive drought, plants in good garden soils with regular moisture perform and look best.

With milkweed and hibiscus near Clinton, Tenn.

ZONES & ORIGIN 3–9. Native to the eastern United States.

SIZE & GROWTH RATE 24"–30" tall and 24" wide; moderate growth rate.

TEXTURE & FORM Upright clumps; medium texture.

FOLIAGE Dark green simple alternate leaves are 3"–5" long, oblong and tapering to a point, sparse up the stem. Stems branch well to form large flower clusters.

FLOWERS & SEEDS Ray flowers that are 3" wide have golden-yellow petals and a raised brown to black cone in the center. They occur from July to frost in the Southeast. They provide interesting color and texture effects for the winter garden if they are left standing. Can reseed.

LIGHT & SOIL Full sun to light shade. Moist well-drained soils are best, but they will survive short droughts.

MAINTENANCE Carefree if sited correctly. Cut them back in late winter. Spreads by roots in good soils to form large attractive colonies.

INSTALLATION Space containers 12"–24" on center for massing.

PESTS & DISEASES None major.

NOTES & CULTIVARS
'Goldsturm' is a dependable form that blooms from July until frost. Foliage can be evergreen in the Deep South or in the Pacific Northwest.

left Massing in San Francisco, Calif.

right top With crinum lily, *Crinum* spp. in Portland, Ore.

right bottom A border in Georgia.

Ruellia brittoniana MEXICAN PETUNIA

In zones 7 and 8, Mexican petunia functions as a fast-growing and tall perennial plant, supplying a profusion of purple tubular flowers from midsummer to frost. It is fast-spreading by seed and rhizomes and tolerates heat and humidity, making it an easy plant to grow; however, the winters are cold enough in zone 7 to knock it back and keep it somewhat in check. Farther south in the Gulf Coast region and into south Florida, *Ruellia* has become an invasive plant and should not be used.

ZONES & ORIGIN 7–11. Native to Mexico.

SIZE & GROWTH RATE 36"–60" tall, 36" wide, and spreading; fast growing.

TEXTURE & FORM Upright clumps; fine texture.

FOLIAGE Dark green simple opposite leaves are 3"–6" long, lanceolate, and spaced somewhat evenly up the stem. Stems are angled and greenish purple. Dies back in zones 7 and 8 and is evergreen in zones 9–11.

FLOWERS & SEEDS Tubular light purple flowers are 2" long. They last only one day each. They are borne in clusters and produced from July until frost in north Georgia. The plant reseeds and spreads quickly by rhizomes to form large colonies.

LIGHT & SOIL Full sun to light shade. It will spread rapidly in moist soils and moist but well-drained soils and can tolerate short periods of drought. Salt spray tolerant.

MAINTENANCE Spreads quickly. This plant is listed as invasive in the Gulf Coast South and Florida. In north Georgia its spread is checked by winter dieback.

INSTALLATION Space containers 24"–36" on center for massing.

PESTS & DISEASES None major.

NOTES & CULTIVARS
This plant is also listed as *Ruellia simplex*.
'Alba' is a white-flowered form that is less aggressive.
'Katie's Dwarf' is a dwarf form to 8" with a clumpier habit. It is less cold-hardy (maybe zone 8).
'Purple Showers' may be more floriferous than the species and does not produce seed.

Flowers.

left top A clump in the Trial Gardens at UGA.

left bottom In the UGA Founders Memorial Garden border with southern shield fern and 'Fireworks' goldenrod.

right Underplanted with annual vinca.

top left S. guaranitica's cobalt flowers.

top right Salvia purpurescens in September in London.

bottom 'Hot Lips' flower.

Salvia spp.   SALVIA · SAGE

Oh, the many virtues of perennial salvias! *Salvia* is a large genus comprised of annual and perennial species, many of which are from the Southwest, Mexico, and South America. Thus, not all the salvias currently promoted make great plants for all regions. Careful selection based on climate is essential. There are many that are outstanding and provide a long season of bloom in the most delightful shades of red, pink, blue, and purple, with great drought, pest, and disease tolerance and vigorous growth for sunny perennial borders and massing. The notes section below lists several outstanding species and hybrids.

ZONES & ORIGIN   (6) 7–10. Native many places; see description.

SIZE & GROWTH RATE   18"–60" tall and wide, depending on the cultivar; fast growing.

TEXTURE & FORM   Upright clumps; fine texture.

FOLIAGE   Simple opposite dark to light green leaves are 1"–6" long and ½"–1" wide, spaced somewhat evenly up the stem. Square stems, some forms hairy. Their shape varies from ovate to lanceolate with various species. They are typically aromatic and therefore deer and rabbit proof.

FLOWERS & SEEDS   Typically tubular and two-lipped flowers. The calyx on some forms is a different color, borne along terminal flower spikes. Insignificant seeds.

LIGHT & SOIL   Full sun to very light shade, with dry to moist well-drained soils. Winter drainage is essential.

MAINTENANCE   Little maintenance is required. Spreading forms may need containment.

INSTALLATION   Space containers 18"–36" on center for massing, depending on the species.

PESTS & DISEASES   None major.

NOTES & CULTIVARS
Salvia guaranitica is an aggressive species. Plant in zones 7–10. Native to Brazil. 'Amistad' has an outstanding purple form to 4' but it is less cold-hardy. 'Black and Blue' is 3'–6' tall and 3' wide, with outstanding cobalt-blue flowers with black calyxes. It blooms all summer and increases in intensity in the fall.

top, left to right

S. nemerosa cultivars in June on the High Line in Manhattan.

Salvia 'Mystic Spires' with lighter blue *S. uglinosa* in London.

S. leucantha in October in Athens, Ga.

left middle *Salvia* 'Black and Blue' with *Carex* species in London.

left bottom The wispy character of 'Hot Lips'.

right bottom 'Victoria Blue' with petunias in August, Vancouver, B.C.

'Purple Splendor' is similar to 'Black and Blue' but shorter, with lovely purple flowers.

Salvia greggii forms often resent humidity and winter moisture. Plant in zones 6–10. Native to Texas and Mexico.

'Hot Lips' is 2'–3' tall and wide, with two-tone white-and-red flowers.

'Wild Thing' grows to 2' by 2' with coral-pink flowers.

Salvia madrensis, forsythia sage, grows to 5'–7' tall, with large coarse foliage. It does not bloom until October but rewards with striking butter-yellow flower spikes until frost. An interesting complement to other fall plants. Zones 7b–10.

Salvia sclarea 'Turkistanica', clary sage, is an interesting biennial form best used in zones 4–7. It has striking silvery and coarse-textured foliage, with showy light pink to white flower panicles in May or June that have a musky fragrance. Reseeds freely around the garden. Native to Europe.

'Cherry Queen' is 3' tall and wide. It blooms all summer with cherry-red flowers. Plant in zones (6) 7–10. Nonspreading.

'Indigo Spires' is an outstanding hybrid to 4' tall with nonstop indigo-blue flower spikes. Plant in zones 7b–9. Nonspreading.

'Mystic Spires' grows to 2' tall and also has nonstop indigo-blue flower spikes. Plant in zones 7–9. Nonspreading.

'Blue Queen' is a vigorous hybrid that grows to 18"–24" tall and 18" wide, with violet-blue flower spikes all summer. Plant in zones (4) 5–8a. Nonspreading.

Salvia nemorosa hybrids and cultivars such as 'May Night', 'Caradonna', and 'East Friesland' perform best in the cooler zones of 5–7, though a trip to the big-box garden center might suggest otherwise. Clumping, nonspreading, and great performers.

Solidago spp. GOLDENROD

Goldenrod is a common roadside- and forest-edge native perennial that lights up the landscape with its golden-yellow flowers. Some species begin blooming in late July, and others continue until the first frost. Contrary to popular belief, goldenrod is not the cause of allergies in humans. (The culprit is usually ragweed.) There are many native species that cover dry and moist environments; some are aggressive spreaders, and others are more manageably clumping in habit. Goldenrod has long been appreciated in European gardens, and Americans have caught on in the last couple of decades. Goldenrod cultivars and hybrids can now be purchased from growers or at the garden center. The cultivars tend to be lower in height (with less flopover) and are effective used in clumps as part of a perennial border or in large masses together with grasses and other native shrubs.

top to bottom
Flowers on many species occur in a linear arrangement.
In an urban wild park in downtown Portland, Ore.
A roadside species in October in Oconee County, Ga.
'Fireworks' in September in the Founders Memorial Garden at UGA.

ZONES & ORIGIN 3–9. Native from Canada to northern Florida.

SIZE & GROWTH RATE 12"–48" tall and 24" or more wide; fast growing.

TEXTURE & FORM Upright and spreading clumps; medium texture.

FOLIAGE Lanceolate medium green leaves are 1"–5" long, with margins that are smooth or toothed, alternate to almost whorled along usually hairy stems. The leaves are rough and sandpapery to the touch.

FLOWERS & SEEDS Large showy panicles of golden yellow flowers bloom from midsummer to late fall, depending on the species.

LIGHT & SOIL Full sun to light shade. Tolerates moist well-drained to fairly dry soils. Many species are salt spray tolerant.

MAINTENANCE Spreading forms can be aggressive and overrun other plants.

INSTALLATION Space containers 12"–24" on center for massing.

PESTS & DISEASES Foliar rust can be a problem where summer moisture is abundant and there is poor air circulation.

NOTES & CULTIVARS
Solidago rugosa 'Fireworks' is an excellent native cultivar to 3' tall, with linear flowers that are striking in the landscape in September and October. It is not too aggressive.
S. sempervirens, seaside goldenrod, grows to 5' tall, flowering August to frost. It withstands salt spray, and it does spread.
S. sphacelata 'Golden Fleece' grows to only 18" tall and forms a dense ground cover.

left With *Coreopsis verticillata* 'Moonbeam', moonbeam coreopsis or hybrid tickseed, and switchgrass 'Dewey Blue' at the State Botanical garden of Georgia.

right Clumps accent this border on Granville Island, Vancouver, B.C.

Stachys byzantina LAMB'S EAR

Lamb's ear is a common garden perennial much loved for its woolly soft gray foliage, which begs to be touched. Its low height and unique color and texture make it a nice foil for other taller perennials. It is a great plant for children's or sensory gardens. It is easy to grow in well-drained soils and sun to part shade; however, in zones 7b and warmer the fuzzy foliage can retain too much moisture in the heat and humidity of the summer and quickly melt away from fungal disease. Like most perennials, its attractiveness ebbs and flows throughout the growing season.

ZONES & ORIGIN 4–8. Native to the Caucasus Mountains and the Middle East.

SIZE & GROWTH RATE 12"–24" tall and 24" or more wide; fast growing.

TEXTURE & FORM Low spreading clumps; coarse texture.

FOLIAGE Large lanceolate to elliptic leaves that are 4"–8" long and covered in thick gray to whitish hairs, giving a fuzzy feel and appearance. Can look bedraggled in late summer and fall.

FLOWERS & SEEDS Flower spikes rise above the foliage in late spring with subtle pink flowers mostly obscured by the corolla and foliage. Flowering tends to take energy and attention away from the foliage, and it may be best to remove it.

LIGHT & SOIL Full sun to light shade. Tolerates moist well-drained to fairly dry soils.

MAINTENANCE Remove flowers to promote foliage. In late summer remove diseased foliage to promote new clean growth.

INSTALLATION Space containers 12"–18" on center for massing.

PESTS & DISEASES Fungal diseases attack foliage in hot humid summer weather in zone 7 and south. Siting for good drainage and air circulation helps.

NOTES & CULTIVARS
'Countess Helene von Stein' and 'Big Ears' are excellent cultivars with large showy foliage and reduced flowering. Widely available.

Flower stalks.

Stokesia laevis STOKES' ASTER

Stokes' aster is a native perennial that occurs across the Southeast in sunny well-drained locations. There are few flowers that offer the pure clear blue of Stokes' aster, and for this reason it can be an irresistible choice for perennial borders and containers. Once established it is fairly drought tolerant, but it will look its best in rich moist soils. It forms a heavy clump of foliage at the base that is evergreen and quite attractive, adding interest to the front of the border in winter. Many cultivars have been developed, but the best by far is 'Peachie's Pick'.

ZONES & ORIGIN 5–9. Native to the southeastern United States.

SIZE & GROWTH RATE 12"–24" tall and 18" wide; fast growing.

TEXTURE & FORM Low spreading clumps; coarse texture.

FOLIAGE Large lanceolate leaves 6"–8" long with a white midrib are clumped at the base, becoming smaller and more spread out up the flowering stem. The basal foliage is evergreen.

FLOWERS & SEEDS Ray flowers of a clear cobalt to lavender blue are 4" in diameter, flowering from late May through late June in north Georgia. Makes an excellent cut flower. It will reseed near the mother plant.

LIGHT & SOIL Full sun to light shade. Prefers moist but well-drained soils and is drought tolerant once established.

MAINTENANCE Cut back stems just after flowering for a few repeat blooms, or leave to allow seeding. This is a carefree plant.

INSTALLATION Space containers 12"–18" on center for massing.

PESTS & DISEASES None major.

NOTES & CULTIVARS
'Alba' has white flowers.
'Peachie's Pick' is the best, with large blue flowers and flower stalks that never flop.

top Flowers.

middle and bottom Exquisite midsummer blue flowers with daylilies just past bloom in Oconee County, Ga.

left top Flowers.

left bottom With Virginia sweetspire and Japanese iris in a raingarden in Boston, Mass.

right Massing with sedge, trilliums, and Christmas fern at Chanticleer.

Tiarella cordifolia FOAMFLOWER

Foamflower is native to moist woodland locations in the lower elevations of the Appalachian Mountains and moist ravines of the piedmont regions from Canada south to Georgia and Alabama. It is a delicate little ground cover that must be given rich moist soils in a shady location for good performance; however, when sited correctly it produces a lovely display of green- or bronze-colored foliage and small white flowers that hover just above the foliage in April and May in north Georgia. Where it is happy it is stoloniferous and forms a low ground cover that mixes well with ferns, bulbs, and other shade-loving plants along a woodland path or near a bench or other place that offers the opportunity for close inspection.

ZONES & ORIGIN 3–8. Native to the eastern United States.

SIZE & GROWTH RATE 6"–12" tall and 12" wide; medium growth rate.

TEXTURE & FORM Low spreading clumps; medium texture.

FOLIAGE Rounded leaves with three to five lobes, coarsely toothed, 3"–4" across, green, bronze green, or even gray, depending on the cultivar. Some leaves remain green all winter.

FLOWERS & SEEDS Delicate stalks rise 3"–4" above the foliage in April or May in north Georgia. The buds are pink, opening to reveal white star-shaped flowers.

LIGHT & SOIL Light to moderate shade. Prefers rich moist well-drained soils.

MAINTENANCE None.

INSTALLATION Space containers 12"–18" on center for massing.

PESTS & DISEASES None major.

NOTES & CULTIVARS
'Dark Eye' is vigorous, and its leaves have a burgundy center.
'Pink Bouquet' is vigorous and has pink flowers.
'Spring Symphony' is reported as good for the South.

Tradescantia pallida 'Purpurea' PURPLE HEART PLANT

If you like a little tropical flare and the color purple, this is the plant for you! It has become quite common in warm-climate landscapes in recent years as a reliable perennial. It emerges in midspring and quickly fills out with its fleshy eggplant-colored foliage. It tolerates a wide range of growing conditions; however, the foliage color is most intense under full sun with regular moisture. It is mostly clump forming, but stems will root to form new clumps. The small light pink flowers are an added bonus up close, but the main event is the foliage effect.

ZONES & ORIGIN 7–10. Native to Mexico and Central America.

SIZE & GROWTH RATE 12"–18" tall and 24" or more wide; fast growing.

TEXTURE & FORM Upright and spreading clumps; medium texture.

FOLIAGE Fleshy deep purple and lanceolate leaves clasp the thick stems. Color fades more toward green in shady locations.

FLOWERS & SEEDS Three-petaled light pink flowers that are ½" wide occur atop the stems all summer until fall but are eclipsed by the foliage. Not known to reseed.

LIGHT & SOIL Full sun to moderate shade. Tolerates moist to well-drained soils. Will survive drought, but it looks best with regular moisture. Salt spray tolerant.

MAINTENANCE None.

INSTALLATION Space containers 12"–18" on center for massing.

PESTS & DISEASES None.

NOTES & CULTIVARS
'Tricolor' has hot pink striped variegation in the leaves.

top A courtyard planting in Columbus, Ga., by Bill Smith and Associates with sedum (*Hylotelephium*) and Boston ivy.

middle left Foliage and three-petaled flower.

middle right Unique eggplant foliage color.

bottom A border in the President's Garden at UGA.

left With other natives at Mt. Cuba Center.

right top Popping out of Mondo grass with Indian hawthorn.

right bottom A happy accident? With hosta and creeping jenny.

Tradescantia virginiana SPIDERWORT

Spiderwort is a moisture-loving perennial that can be found in moist ravines near streams or other locations with rich moist soils across much of the eastern United States. Starting in April in north Georgia, its two-foot-tall stems are topped by light purple to blue triangular-shaped flowers, which continue through midsummer. It makes a good filler plant for perennial borders or lightly shaded woodland gardens, mixing well with bulbs and ferns and the like, or it can be useful in bioswales or other locations with periodically inundated soils. It is not a plant to feature by itself, as the foliage tends to yellow and wither after flowering and may need removal.

ZONES & ORIGIN 4–9. Native to the eastern United States.

SIZE & GROWTH RATE 18"–36" tall and 18" wide; medium growth rate.

TEXTURE & FORM Upright clumps; medium texture.

FOLIAGE Strap-like thin medium green leaves to 8" long with a fleshy and glaucous appearance clasp the stems, which are thick and fleshy.

FLOWERS & SEEDS Flower clusters or cymes are held atop stems. One flower opens per day over a two-month period from late April through early June in north Georgia. Seeds are produced abundantly. Multiple cultivars and hybrids exist, offering a color range of blue, purple, white, pink, and red.

LIGHT & SOIL Full sun to light shade. Rich moist well-drained soils.

MAINTENANCE Trim back the foliage after flowering for tidier landscapes. The plant can seed itself and be aggressive in suitable locations.

INSTALLATION Space containers 12"–18" on center for massing.

PESTS & DISEASES None major.

NOTES & CULTIVARS
Many hybrids and cultivars exist based on the flower colors listed above, as well as some with a dwarf habit. 'Sweet Kate' has chartreuse foliage and purple flowers.

With Louisiana iris.

Trillium spp.   Trillium, Wake Robin

To take a walk down a woodland path in early spring and happen upon a drift of trilliums in flower is to experience one of nature's rare treasures. To include them in garden design one must be very careful to provide site conditions mimicking those of the native habitat: shade and rich moist but well-drained soil. Their diminutive size makes them a plant for detail areas, such as near a path or sitting area where they can be appreciated. Both flowers and the mottled foliage are lovely. A few great native species that can be found as nursery-grown plants are listed below.

ZONES & ORIGIN See the species descriptions below for zones. Native to the eastern United States.

SIZE & GROWTH RATE 8"–12" tall and 12" wide; slow growing.

TEXTURE & FORM Upright clumps; medium texture.

FOLIAGE All species produce leaves in a whorled group of three, like a little umbrella atop the stems. Leaves can be green or handsomely mottled with silver, purple, or coppery tones, depending on the species. Foliage emerges in late winter and often disappears by late summer.

FLOWERS & SEEDS Flowers can be sessile, held on top of the foliage, or pedunculate, meaning they nod just below or above the foliage. They occur in late March through April in north Georgia in white, yellow, pink, maroon, purple, and almost brown.

LIGHT & SOIL All species need light to moderate shade and organic rich moist well-drained soil.

MAINTENANCE Site carefully, and mulch lightly with leaf litter.

INSTALLATION Space containers 12" on center for massing.

PESTS & DISEASES None major.

NOTES & CULTIVARS
Trillium cuneatum, toad trillium, grows to 12" tall, with mottled green foliage and maroon sessile flowers. Zones 5–9.
T. erectum, purple trillium, grows to 12" tall, with green foliage and maroon flowers atop the foliage. Zones 4–9.
T. flexipes, bent white trillium, grows to 18" tall, with green leaves and large outward-facing white flowers. Prefers acid and alkaline soils. Zones 4–7.
T. grandiflorum, snow trillium, grows to 12" tall, with green leaves and large showy white flowers fading to light pink. Zones 3–9.
T. luteum, yellow trillium, grows to 12" tall, with green-and-silver-flecked foliage topped by fragrant butter-yellow flowers in mid-April. Tolerates acid or alkaline soils. Zones 4–8.

top *Trillium grandiflorum*.

middle top Yellow species with mottled foliage.

middle bottom and bottom Yellow form with mottled foliage in the woodland gardens at Mt. Cuba Center.

Tulbaghea violacea Society Garlic

For the warmer zones, society garlic makes a steadfast and productive flowering perennial. It is covered the entire growing season with lilac-pink flowers and never exceeds 24" in height. It is very effective in mass plantings and tolerates heat well. It is used in highway medians in Florida and California—ultimate proof of its tough nature. The flowers and foliage do emit a garlicky odor. Deer and rabbits leave it alone. It is effective in containers, in perennial or other flower borders, or in large masses for larger landscapes.

left top At Villa La Foce in Montepulcano, Italy, with lavender on the left.

left bottom With annual summer snapdragons on Hilton Head Island, S.C.

right Also at Villa La Foce in Montepulciano, Italy.

ZONES & ORIGIN 7b–10. Native to South Africa.

SIZE & GROWTH RATE 24" tall and 18" wide; fast growing.

TEXTURE & FORM Upright clumps; fine texture.

FOLIAGE Thin strap-like leaves of grayish light green form grasslike clumps.

FLOWERS & SEEDS Flower stems are held above the foliage nearly the entire growing season, from May to October at least. The spherical flowers of light pinkish purple are 1"–2" in diameter and sweetly fragrant.

LIGHT & SOIL Full sun to light shade. Tolerates most soils, provided drainage is good. Salt spray tolerant.

MAINTENANCE Cut back in winter to rejuvenate the foliage.

INSTALLATION Space containers 12"–18" on center for massing. Mature clumps are easily divided by separating the tuberous roots.

PESTS & DISEASES None major. Deer don't touch them.

NOTES & CULTIVARS
'Variegata' has cream stripes running the length of the leaves.

A variegated form at the Getty Center in Los Angeles, Calif.

Verbena bonariensis

BRAZILIAN VERBENA · TALL VERBENA

Tall verbena is an elegant perennial with a soft veil-like quality and great lines. Some have called it a "see-through" plant because it produces thin wiry stems topped by delicate purple flowers. This quality lends itself to creative use in the landscape when tall verbena is placed in combination with shorter plants that act as filler under the airy verbena. It also serves as an airy complement to other perennials and grasses. It can be massed for greater visual weight, but it's the delicate qualities of the plant that impart an air of sophistication. Although it has a delicate appearance, tall verbena is tough and tolerates drought, heat, and poor soils well. Originally from Brazil, it has naturalized in the Southeast.

ZONES & ORIGIN 6–10. Native to South America.

SIZE & GROWTH RATE 3'–5' tall and 2' wide; fast growing.

TEXTURE & FORM Upright airy clumps; fine texture.

FOLIAGE Thin dark green and leathery leaves to 4" long, serrate at the tips, clasping the square stems in opposite pairs.

FLOWERS & SEEDS Tubular purple ¼" flowers in 1"–3" panicles bloom from May to frost. It is long lasting as a cut flower. May reseed gently around the garden.

LIGHT & SOIL Full sun to light shade. Tolerates most soils, provided drainage is good. Drought tolerant.

MAINTENANCE Cut it back in midsummer if you desire a bushier plant.

INSTALLATION Space containers 18"–24" on center for massing. This is a great plant to intersperse with other perennials.

PESTS & DISEASES Powdery mildew and rust can be problems, although plant vigor does not seem to be impacted by them.

NOTES & CULTIVARS
Verbena rigida, rigid verbena, is like a miniature version of tall verbena. It grows to 24" tall and is hardy in zones 7–10.

top to bottom

Early August in Stanley Park, Vancouver, B.C.

With 'Blue Fortune' hyssop and muhly grass in Sonoma, Calif.

With purple coneflower and Muhly grass in Sonoma, Calif.

At Huntington Gardens in Pasadena, Calif.

Vernonia noveboracensis IRONWEED · TALL IRONWEED

Ironweed announces its presence in July and August with deep purple flower heads at a staggering 8'–10' towering above grasses and other forbs in moist meadows and woodland edges in the eastern United States. The flower color is exquisite and occurs when so many other plants are finished blooming and before most fall-blooming species. The challenge lies in its incredible height, so use it behind shrubs or grasses where space permits, or look for a shorter form, such as the wonderful fine-textured species *Vernonia lettermannii*, which is from Missouri and Arkansas.

ZONES & ORIGIN 5–9. Native to the eastern United States.

SIZE & GROWTH RATE 6'–10' tall and 3' wide; fast growing.

TEXTURE & FORM Upright airy clumps; medium fine texture.

FOLIAGE Lance-shaped alternate dark green leaves grow to 8" long, with rough serrate margins.

FLOWERS & SEEDS Large showy cymes to 6" wide. Fluffy composite flowers of deep magenta to amethyst purple bloom in July and August, fading to a rich rusty color in fall. This is a prolific self-seeder.

LIGHT & SOIL Full sun to light shade. Loves moist soils and tolerates drought. Salt spray tolerant.

MAINTENANCE Cut back in midsummer if you desire a bushier plant.

INSTALLATION Space containers 24"–36" on center for massing. Effective as a specimen in the back of the border or as part of a seeded tall meadow.

PESTS & DISEASES None significant.

NOTES & CULTIVARS
Veronia angustifolia is native to moist meadows in the Southeast and shorter, to 4' tall.

V. lettermannii is an exquisite species that is only 2' tall, with fine-textured foliage similar to *Amsonia hubrichti* and more delicate late summer purple flowers.

top to bottom

Striking in stature and color.

Terminating the sumptuous tall border at Great Dixter, Northiam, England.

Amethyst purple and 8' tall.

TURFGRASSES

St. Augustine grass in a Charleston courtyard.

When selecting a particular turfgrass, the designer must consider several things. First and foremost, what will be the level of maintenance provided for the turf? The finest-textured grasses show the least imperfection in the ground surface or in the turf itself. Weeds and lumpy soils stand out like a black eye with a fine-textured grass. Very fine textured grasses typically require the highest levels of maintenance, meaning frequent mowing, high nutrition, and supplemental water, in order to hide any imperfections and present their best face. If the property owner is not prepared to go to the lengths necessary to properly maintain a fine-textured turfgrass, then a coarser-textured grass may be a better choice for that situation.

An equally important consideration is the level of shade provided by adjacent trees and large shrubs. The vigor of any turfgrass diminishes with any degree of shade, but some can still provide a quality appearance under light or, in a few cases, moderate shade. Since shade trees are an important component of many landscapes in southeastern states, make sure to select a turf that can accommodate the level of shade that is expected. As the trees and large shrubs grow and mature, you may need to convert areas that become too shaded to ground covers or a different type of turfgrass.

Finally, while turfgrass is by far the least expensive ground cover material to initially install, a good designer should be judicious in its use. Too much turf can be quite drab and uninteresting. While it provides a great play surface for children, excessive turf can be quite boring for anyone but a dedicated turfgrass scientist. The turf should be subservient to the other plants in the design. Just as you wouldn't think of furnishing your house with only carpet and no furniture, don't furnish the landscape with only turf and no trees, shrubs, or herbaceous plants. The thoughtful use of turfgrass in a composition provides an opportunity for the designer to contrast the colors, forms, and textures of other types of plants against the turf. Regardless of the type of turfgrass chosen for the design, it will have a much finer texture than will any of the other plants used in the composition. So even a novice designer can appear knowledgeable by thoughtfully combining turf with other types of plants.

Plus, let's face it, any turfgrass is expensive to maintain. It requires a great deal of water and nutrition to survive and thrive in hot dry summers. In light of dwindling water resources, other types of ground covers may be a better choice to serve as the "flooring" material of the design.

BOTANICAL NAME	SEASON	TEXTURE	SHADE TOLERANCE	MAINTENANCE REQUIREMENTS	MOWING HEIGHT	HARDINESS ZONES
Agrostis stolonifera	Cool	Fine	None	High	¼"–1½"	3a–8a
Cynodon dactylon	Warm	Medium fine	Light	Medium high	¾"–1½"	6b–10
Cynodon spp.	Warm	Fine	None	High	¼"–1½"	6b–10
Eremochloa ophiuroides	Warm	Medium	Light	Low	1"–1½"	7b–10
Festuca arundinacea	Cool	Medium	Light	Medium low	2½"–3½"	6a–8a
Lolium perenne	Cool	Medium	Moderate	Medium	½"–1½"	4a–9a
Paspalum vaginatum	Warm	Medium fine	Light	Medium	¼"–1½"	8b–10
Stenotaphrum secundatum	Warm	Coarse	Moderate	Medium	2½"–3½"	7b–10
Zoysia japonica 'Meyer'	Warm	Medium	Light to moderate	Medium	1½"–2"	6b–10
Zoysia × 'Emerald'	Warm	Fine	Light to moderate	Medium high	¾"–1"½	6b–10

Agrostis stolonifera CREEPING BENT GRASS

For cool humid climates, creeping bent grass is considered to provide the best turf for golf greens. A cool-season grass from Europe that spreads by stolons, it forms a fine-textured turf and can be established by either seed or sod. It requires moist but well-drained soils and mowing heights under ½". But even in ideal climates it is not recommended for homeowners due to its high maintenance requirements and susceptibility to numerous fungal diseases. In the Southeast, it has been used to provide a green turf year-round on golf greens without the need for overseeding with ryegrass. However, due to its lack of heat tolerance, it requires frequent syringing with water and the use of fans to keep it cool during the summer months. 'Penncross' and 'Crenshaw' are two of the more widely regarded cultivars that can be seeded. Recommended seeding rates are ½–1 pound per 1,000 square feet in early fall.

Creeping bent grass golf green.

Cynodon dactylon COMMON BERMUDA GRASS

Common Bermuda grass is an aggressive drought-tolerant turf that is suited for lawns and golf course roughs where a highly refined appearance is not required. Although it is able to go dormant during extreme droughts, it appears best in situations where it receives at least 1" of water per week during the summer. It tolerates salt spray.

Common Bermuda grass.

ZONES & ORIGIN 6b–10b. Native to Africa.

TEXTURE Medium fine texture compared with other turfgrasses.

LIGHT & SOIL Provide full sun to very light shade and a moist but well-drained moderately acidic to near-neutral pH soil. It is highly tolerant of salt spray but not poorly drained soils.

INSTALLATION Bermuda grass seeds are quite small, so recommended seeding rates are 1½–2 pounds per 1,000 square feet. The seeds require seven to ten days to germinate, and best results are obtained when hulled seeds are in place as the soil temperatures reach 55°F–60°F, typically early to mid-May in Athens. Seeding after July may not provide adequate time to establish deep roots to survive a cold winter.

GROWTH RATE Fast growing.

MOWING HEIGHT ¾"–1½".

MAINTENANCE For an acceptable-looking turf, common Bermuda grass should be mowed regularly so that no more than a third of the foliage is removed at one time. It should also receive at least ½ pound of nitrogen per 1,000 square feet per month during the growing season.

NOTES & CULTIVARS
The cultivars listed are actually hybrids that may be established by seeding. All are slightly finer in texture than common Bermuda.

'La Prima' provides a dark green color, with quicker germination and establishment.
'Princess 77' produces a dense fine texture with a dark green color; suitable for golf tee areas.
'Sahara' provides improved density and drought tolerance.
'Yukon' provides improved cold-hardiness and fall color retention.

At Beech Haven Baptist Church off Atlanta Highway in Georgia.

Cynodon spp. HYBRID BERMUDA GRASS

Hybrid Bermuda cultivars are mostly a result of crosses between common Bermuda and African Bermuda (*Cynodon transvaalensis*). They produce very dense, fast-growing, and very fine textured turfs that are predominantly suited for athletic fields and golf courses. For most homeowners and commercial applications, hybrid Bermudas require too great a level of maintenance to produce a refined appearance. Their appearance quickly declines with any shade, inadequate nutrition, drought, or irregular mowing intervals.

Hybrid Bermuda grass.

ZONES & ORIGIN 6b–10b. Cross from African species.

TEXTURE Fine.

LIGHT & SOIL Provide full sun and moist but well-drained slightly acidic soil. They tolerate some salt spray and brief droughts but not wet soils.

INSTALLATION Hybrid Bermudas must be installed by vegetative methods such as stolons or sod. Stolons are small pieces of the grass's stems that are spread over bare soil, lightly disked and rolled to establish soil contact, and kept lightly moist for several weeks while they develop a root system. Stolons are used primarily for large areas such as athletic fields and golf courses, and they need to be spread no later than midsummer in order to root deeply before winter. Establishment by sod can occur from midspring to early fall.

GROWTH RATE Fast growing.

MOWING HEIGHT ¼"–1½".

MAINTENANCE Hybrid Bermuda requires high levels of maintenance. For a quality appearance, use reel mowers at intervals of one to five days. Mowing higher than 1½" creates a lumpy appearance. Provide a pound of nitrogen per 1,000 square feet per month during the growing season and 1" of water per week—more on athletic fields. Their fast growth makes them susceptible to several fungal diseases that thrive on tender growth.

NOTES & CULTIVARS
- 'Celebration' and 'TifGrand' provide slightly improved shade tolerance but still perform best in full sun.
- 'Midiron' is slightly coarser than Tifway and performs well at slightly higher mowing heights.
- 'Tifsport' has better cold tolerance and density compared to 'Tifway' but is slower growing.
- 'Tifway' has been popular for many years, producing a very fine texture but requiring a low mowing height to look its best.

In Athens, Ga.

Eremochloa ophiuroides CENTIPEDE GRASS

Centipede grass is a popular turfgrass in the Southeast due to its comparatively low maintenance requirements. Light green in color, centipede grass is called the "poor man's turfgrass" due to its low nutritional requirements and less frequent mowing intervals. A misconception is that centipede grass requires no maintenance. In fact, it declines in vigor over time without adequate maintenance due to drought, inadequate nutrition, and excessive mowing height. While slow growing, it can be established by either seed or vegetative methods.

ZONES & ORIGIN 7b–10b. Native to Southeast Asia.

TEXTURE Medium.

LIGHT & SOIL Full sun with a moist but well-drained acidic soil is best. It tolerates light shade but is sensitive to pH levels higher than 6. It is not as tolerant of salt spray or of extended periods of drought as are the other warm-season grasses.

INSTALLATION Centipede grass can be established by seeding at a rate of ¼–½ pound per 1,000 square feet from early May to mid-July. Plugs at 8" on center or sod may be installed from late April to mid-August. Because of its slow growth rate, installing centipede grass after midsummer is risky, since the roots may not grow deep enough to withstand cold temperatures.

GROWTH RATE Slow.

MOWING HEIGHT 1"–1½".

MAINTENANCE Centipede grass benefits from 1"–1½" of water per week during summer and 1–2 pounds of nitrogen per 1,000 square feet during the growing season at a rate of ½–¾ pounds per application. Ideal times to fertilize are in early May, late June, and early to mid-August. Excessive nitrogen makes it susceptible to fungal disease. Unlike other warm-season grasses, it does not produce rhizomes, only stolons. If it grows too tall between mowings, then excessive amounts of foliage will be removed when it is mowed, allowing the stolons to grow upright rather than horizontally and thus reducing their soil contact.

NOTES & CULTIVARS
'Oaklawn' and 'Tennessee Hardy' have improved cold-hardiness.
'TifBlair' has greater density and improved cold-hardiness and can be established by seed or vegetatively.

Centipede grass.

In an Athens medical park.

Festuca arundinacea TALL FESCUE

Tall fescue is a cool-season, bunch-forming turfgrass best suited for zones 5 and 6. Unlike the warm-season grasses, fescue turfs remain green year-round, even though they may be dormant in the summer heat. With adequate supplemental water during summer, this medium-textured grass can provide an attractive turf year-round at a very low installation cost. Most seed companies provide a combination of cultivars in their seed mixes to create a uniform appearance in full sun to moderately shaded areas. Improved cultivars in recent years have greatly improved heat tolerance. However, most tall fescue yards still benefit from rejuvenation every few years, especially after hot dry summers.

Fescue.

ZONES & ORIGIN 3b–8a. Native to Europe.

TEXTURE Medium to medium fine, depending upon the cultivar.

LIGHT & SOIL Full sun to light shade with a moist but well-drained slightly acidic soil is ideal. Some cultivars tolerate moderate shade.

INSTALLATION Seed at 7 pounds per 1,000 square feet, with a "starter" fertilizer incorporated into the top 4" of the seedbed in early to midfall (mid-September to mid-October in Athens). Seeding can also be done in early spring, mid-March to early April, but spring installation doesn't allow as much time for root establishment before summer's heat and drought. Some nurseries provide fescue sod.

GROWTH RATE Fast.

MOWING HEIGHT 2½"–3½".

MAINTENANCE Ensure 1"–1½" of water per week throughout the year. Rainfall usually provides adequate water from late fall through midspring, but supplemental water is often necessary from May to early November. Provide 3 pounds of nitrogen per 1,000 square feet per year in increments of ¾ pound in early and midautumn, late winter, and midspring. Remove autumn leaves promptly, since fall is its peak growing season.

NOTES & CULTIVARS
Avoid 'Kentucky 31'. Although it has been sold for many years, its coarse texture and poor heat and drought tolerance make newer cultivars better choices.

With azaleas and dogwood in Athens.

Lolium perenne RYEGRASS

Ryegrass is a clump-forming cool-season annual grass from Europe that is used primarily to overseed dormant hybrid Bermuda on golf courses and athletic fields or to provide a quick temporary cover to stabilize soils on construction sites. Germination typically occurs in three to five days under optimum conditions. A fast-growing grass, it tolerates light shade and moist to well-drained soils, and it can be mowed from ½" to 2½" in height. Although ryegrass can be seeded at any time of the year, it performs best when seeded in early to midautumn. Seeding rates are 5–7 pounds per 1,000 square feet to overseed Bermuda, or 3–5 pounds per 1,000 square feet for temporary cover. From zone 6b southward, the summer heat will weaken and kill the ryegrass.

Perennial ryegrass close-up.

Paspalum vaginatum SEASHORE PASPALUM

Seashore paspalum is a warm-season grass that is native to tropical and subtropical coasts and is slightly coarser in texture than hybrid Bermuda. It has quickly gained acceptance as an alternative for hybrid Bermuda for coastal golf course applications due to its extreme salt tolerance, extreme range of pH tolerance, and slightly lower nutritional requirements. Seashore paspalum is a fast-growing fine-textured grass that spreads by rhizomes and stolons and can be established vegetatively or by seed. It performs best with mowing heights from ½" to 1½". It tolerates light shade and well-drained to moist soils and is hardy from zone 8b through zone 11. 'Sealsle I' and 'Sealsle 2000' are two cultivars developed by the University of Georgia. 'Sea Spray' is also a UGA cultivar that can be established by seed.

Sea spray paspalum close-up.

Seashore paspalum golf hole.

Stenotaphrum secundatum ST. AUGUSTINE GRASS

St. Augustine grass is a coarse-textured, fast-growing grass with a blue-green foliage color. It is the most shade tolerant of the warm-season grasses and can hide many imperfections in the turf due to its coarse texture. It is probably the most popular turf for Florida and the Gulf Coast areas of the Southeast, but its lack of cold-hardiness has limited its use in the upper Piedmont and mountains. Its long flattened stolons growing along the ground provide a good method of identification.

St. Augustine grass.

ZONES & ORIGIN 7b–11. Native to Central and South America.

TEXTURE Coarse.

LIGHT & SOIL Full sun to light shade with a moist but well-drained slightly acidic soil is ideal. It survives but doesn't thrive in moderate shade. Although highly tolerant of salt spray, it is not as drought tolerant as Bermuda or zoysia.

INSTALLATION St. Augustine grass is established by vegetative means, primarily sod or plugs. Plugs planted 12" on center in late April or early May will cover in two to three months under optimal conditions. Stolons can root in seven to fourteen days.

GROWTH RATE Fast.

MOWING HEIGHT 2½"–3½" with mowing every five to seven days during the summer.

MAINTENANCE Provide 1"–1½" of water per week and 2–3 pounds of nitrogen per 1,000 square feet during the summer. Apply the fertilizer in increments of ¾ pound every six weeks starting in late spring. Under these conditions, it may require annual thatch removal in late spring or early summer.

St. Augustine grass is susceptible to a viral disease called St. Augustine Decline Virus (SAD), although newer cultivars provide resistance. It is also highly susceptible to chinch bugs when stressed by drought. Preventing drought stress with supplemental irrigation and regular mowing provides the best protection. Finally, many broad-leaf herbicides commonly used on other turfgrasses can damage St. Augustine grass.

NOTES & CULTIVARS
'Delmar' has good shade and cold tolerance.
'Palmetto' produces a denser, finer texture with improved drought tolerance and good shade tolerance.
'Raleigh' has better cold-hardiness but is susceptible to chinch bugs and is less heat tolerant.

At a Baton Rouge residence.

Zoysia japonica 'Meyer' MEYER ZOYSIA

'Meyer' is the oldest cultivar of *Zoysia japonica* and has been an industry standard for many years. It is a tough dependable grass with few insect or disease problems associated with it. Meyer zoysia is an excellent choice of turf for lawns with some shade and where the owner is not interested in an intense level of maintenance yet wants an attractive turf. It forms a very dense turf that feels like a carpet, but due to its slow growth rate, it cannot recover quickly from excessive wear and tear.

Meyer zoysia.

ZONES & ORIGIN 6a–10b, but it is best adapted for 7a–9a. It is native to Asia.

TEXTURE Medium.

LIGHT & SOIL While preferring full sun, it performs well in light shade and does best with a moist but well-drained slightly acidic soil. It is slightly drought resistant and tolerates salt spray.

INSTALLATION Meyer zoysia must be established by vegetative methods, including sprigging, plugs, or sod. Sod should be installed from late April to no later than late August and is expensive due to its slow growth. Plugs planted at 6"–8" on center will require two years to establish a uniform surface under ideal conditions.

GROWTH RATE Slow.

MOWING HEIGHT 1"–2".

MAINTENANCE Meyer zoysia has moderate maintenance requirements, lower than those of fine-textured zoysias, because its coarser texture tends to hide more surface imperfections. It benefits from being fertilized two or three times per growing season and receiving at least 1" of water per week. The stiff leaves of Meyer zoysia quickly dull mower blades.

NOTES & CULTIVARS
'Compadre' and 'Zenith' are similar to 'Meyer' in appearance and can be seeded but are slow to establish from seed. 'Compadre' provides a greater salt tolerance.
'El Toro' and 'Belaire' provide a slightly coarser texture and improved cold tolerance and are slightly faster growing than 'Meyer'.
'Jamur' provides a faster growth rate than 'Meyer'.

On the UGA campus.

Zoysia × 'Emerald' EMERALD ZOYSIA

Emerald zoysia is an expensive turfgrass that tolerates light shade, making it a good choice for many homeowners. Once established, it has few insect or disease issues and will look good with slightly lower levels of maintenance than those required for hybrid Bermudas. However, the least little surface imperfection, such as an uneven soil surface or weeds, will stand out in this fine-textured turf, just as they will in hybrid Bermuda.

Emerald zoysia.

ZONES & ORIGIN 6b–10b. Parent plants are from Asia.

TEXTURE Fine.

LIGHT & SOIL Provide full sun to light shade with a well-drained slightly acidic soil. It is slightly tolerant of drought and highly tolerant of salt spray.

INSTALLATION Emerald zoysia must be established by vegetative methods, including sprigging, plugs, or sod. Sod can be installed from late April to late August in Athens and is very expensive due to its slow growth rate. Plugs planted at 6"–8" on center require two years to establish a uniform surface. Sprigs are the least expensive method but may require two or more years to become fully established, and weed invasion during the interval is a great concern. Sprigs should be planted between early May and no later than early August in order to be rooted prior to winter.

GROWTH RATE Slow.

MOWING HEIGHT ¾"–1½".

MAINTENANCE For an attractive appearance, Emerald zoysia has a fairly high maintenance requirement, but it is not as high as that required by hybrid Bermuda. Fertilize with 1 pound of nitrogen per 1,000 square feet in early May, mid-June, and early August. Providing 1" of water per week is usually adequate. Mowing at higher heights requires mowing no more than once per week. Under higher nutrition levels, it will benefit from dethatching once per year.

NOTES & CULTIVARS
- 'Geo' is a fine-textured zoysia with better shade tolerance than either 'Emerald' or 'Zeon'.
- 'Zeon' is a cultivar of *Zoysia matrella* with better cold tolerance, slightly improved shade tolerance, and a slightly coarser texture compared with 'Emerald'.

In the Founders Memorial Garden.

ANNUALS

Pink and purple petunias with coleus.

se colorful annuals to bring gaiety and life to the garden. Even those designers who prefer the subtlety of seasonal changes in perennial plants benefit from utilizing annuals to provide sparkle and zing to specific locations, such as a patio or deck. Let's face it, even the best-designed gardens have periods during the year when nothing else can provide color.

We've made the effort in this section to cover only what we consider to be the major annuals, those tried-and-true plants that can be expected to produce a show each year. Within these groups of plants, researchers are continually striving to improve such things as heat tolerance and disease resistance. New cultivars, even new series, of many of these plants are introduced each year that perform much better than plants from just a few years before. Any effort to name cultivars of these plants would quickly become outdated.

Annuals are classified as plants that complete their life cycle in one year and decline and die with the changing of the seasons. In fact, the majority of the plants in this section are actually perennials in their native environments, commonly, tropical areas of the world. None of these plants are native to the Southeast. Because they are unable to withstand freezing temperatures or, in some cases, hot summers, they are considered to be annuals in temperate zones. Most of the plants in this section are termed summer or warm-season annuals because they grow and flower from spring to autumn. A few are cool-season annuals because they grow and flower between autumn and the onset of summer.

A common misconception is that these plants provide color with minimal maintenance. In reality, annuals demand very high levels of maintenance in order to perform well. Basically, they must continually produce new growth in order to produce new flower buds. They are heavy feeders, requiring fertilization at regular intervals throughout the season, and they require regular water as well. Even those annuals that are considered drought tolerant do not produce new growth under moisture stress, and without new growth, there are no new flowers. In addition, many of these plants require removal of old flowers or flower stalks in order to encourage new flower production throughout the season. The removal of old flowers, called "deadheading," must be done periodically, or the plants' performance will disappoint.

We've tried to include a little information about disease issues and deer resistance with each plant. While much research has been conducted and published regarding disease problems of these plants, little has been published regarding deer preferences. Most of what we say about deer is based upon our own personal experience and observations.

From a disease and maintenance standpoint, if you had disease issues one year with your annual plantings, you really need to replace the soil mixture before installing new plants the following year. The pathogens in the soil from the previous year are ready to spring to life on new plants. Even if you didn't have any disease issues one year, it is still a good idea to replace the soil mixture each year to facilitate healthy happy annuals.

BOTANICAL NAME	PLANTING TIMES	SUNLIGHT	DEADHEADING	ATTRACTIVE FLOWERS	ATTRACTIVE FOLIAGE	SOILS	SIZE
Angelonia angustifolia	Mid- to late spring	Full sun	Recommended	Blue, purple, pink, white	No	Moist but well drained	12"–24" tall
Antirrhinum majus	Early fall or early spring	Full sun	Recommended	White, red, pink, yellow	No	Moist but well drained	12"–30" tall
Begonia semperflorens-cultorum	Midspring	Full sun to moderate shade	Not necessary	White, pink, and red	Some bronze or variegated	Moist but well drained	8"–16" tall
Caladium bicolor	Mid- to late spring	Light shade	Required	No	Variegated pink, white, and red	Consistently moist	12"–24" tall
Calibrachoa × hybrida	Mid- to late spring	Full sun to light shade	Not necessary	Every color	No	Moist but well drained	4"–8" tall
Catharanthus roseus	Mid- to late spring	Full sun	Not necessary	White, pink, red, and purple	No	Well drained	6"–12" tall
Digitalis purpurea	Early autumn	Moderate to light shade	Not necessary	Purple, pink, and white	No	Consistently moist	24"–60" tall
Gomphrena globosa	Late spring or early summer	Full sun	Recommended occasionally	White, pink, red, and purple	No	Well drained	12"–24" tall
Impatiens hawkeri	Midspring	Light to moderate shade	Not necessary	White, pink, red, and salmon	No	Moist but well drained	12"–24" tall
Ipomoea batatas	Mid- to late spring	Full sun to light shade	Not necessary	No	Lime, black, and purple	Moist but well drained	6"–12" tall
Pelargonium × hortorum	Mid- to late spring	Full sun to light shade	Required	Red, pink, and white	No	Moist but well drained	12"–24" tall
Pennisetum × advena 'Rubrum'	Midspring	Full sun to light shade	Not necessary	Reddish purple	Reddish purple	Well drained	36"–60" tall
Pentas lanceolata	Mid- to late spring	Full sun to light shade	Not necessary	Red, pink, violet, and white	No	Moist but well drained	12"–30" tall
Petunia × hybrida	Early to midspring	Full sun to light shade	Recommended occasionally	All colors and stripes	No	Moist but well drained	6"–30" tall
Plumbago auriculata	Mid- to late spring	Full sun to light shade	Not necessary	Light blue and white	No	Well drained	24"–36" tall
Salvia splendens	Mid- to late spring	Full sun to light shade	Required	Red, white, and purple	No	Well drained	12"–24" tall
Solenostemon scutellarioides	Mid- to late spring	Full sun to light shade	Required	No	Variegated red, purple, and yellow	Moist but well drained	8"–30" tall
Tagetes patula	Midspring or late summer	Full sun	Required	Yellow, orange, and orange red	No	Moist but well drained	6"–18" tall
Tulipa × hybrida	Late autumn to early winter	Full sun to light shade	Not necessary	Yellow, pink, red, white, and purple	No	Well drained	6"–24" tall
Verbena × hybrida	Early to midspring	Full sun	Recommended	Purple, red, pink, and white	No	Well drained	4"–18" tall
Viola × wittrockiana	Midautumn to early spring	Full sun	Not necessary	Every color, even blues	No	Moist but well drained	6"–12" tall
Zinnia angustifolia	Midspring	Full sun	Not necessary	Orange, white, and yellow	No	Moist but well drained	10"–18" tall
Zinnia elegans	Midspring	Full sun	Required	Red, yellow, pink, and white	No	Moist but well drained	12"–30" tall

Angelonia angustifolia SUMMER SNAPDRAGON

Summer snapdragons are relatively low-growing plants with an upright habit that makes them valuable for borders, edging, container plantings, and cut flower arrangements. Their relatively small but abundant flowers come in a variety of colors. They are promoted for their drought resistance and because they do not require deadheading, but in reality, they benefit from not being allowed to become too dry and having their older flowering stems periodically removed.

SIZE & GROWTH RATE 12"–24" tall, 8"–15" wide, fast growing.

TEXTURE & FORM Medium fine texture and oval form.

FOLIAGE Simple dark green sessile leaves are lanceolate shaped.

FLOWERS Upright racemes 4"–8" long in shades of white, pink, purple, and blue, as well as variegated colors, occur from midspring to frost.

LIGHT & SOIL Full sun to very light shade and a loose and moist but well-drained soil. Allow them to dry out slightly between watering.

MAINTENANCE Pinch tips of new stems to promote dense branching and multiple flower stalks. Fertilize every three to four weeks with a balanced fertilizer like 10-10-10, and remove older stems to encourage new growth.

INSTALLATION Incorporate a slow-release fertilizer in the soil mix. Plant 12"–15" apart after nighttime temperatures remain above 45°F.

top With society garlic and roses on Hilton Head Island.

bottom Purple summer snaps with yellow trailing petunias.

Antirrhinum majus SNAPDRAGON

Snapdragons are considered cool-season annuals or short-lived perennials in the Southeast. Known for their showy upright spikes of pastel-colored flowers, they are highly popular for cut flower arrangements. With their upright form, they are popular as focal points in container plantings and for background plantings when combined with lower-growing plants. Snapdragons perform best in early to midspring and decline as hot summer temperatures arrive.

SIZE & GROWTH RATE 12"–30" tall, medium fast growing.

TEXTURE & FORM Medium texture and upright oval to oval form.

FOLIAGE Simple linear to lanceolate alternate leaves.

FLOWERS Flowers are held on terminal racemes ranging from 6" to 24" above the foliage from early to late spring. Colors include white, pink, yellow, red, and purple.

LIGHT & SOIL Provide full sun to light shade, but recognize that the taller varieties may fall over with any shade. Provide a loose and moist but well-drained soil, and don't let them dry out too much.

MAINTENANCE Pinch tips of new plants to encourage multiple stems, and remove older flower stalks.

INSTALLATION Incorporate a slow-release fertilizer into the soil at planting, and plant 8"–12" apart in early fall or early spring.

top Snapdragons.

bottom Orange and yellow snapdragons with yellow flag iris.

Begonia semperflorens-cultorum WAX LEAF BEGONIA

Wax leaf begonias have been around forever but have varied in popularity over the years. For a pure show of flowers, several other warm-season annuals provide better displays. But while begonias' flowers may be somewhat subtle, their ability to grow in full sun to moderate shade and their lower maintenance requirements make them a great option for masses or borders, as well as in containers and hanging baskets. Bronze-leafed varieties' attractive foliage make up for any lack of flower power.

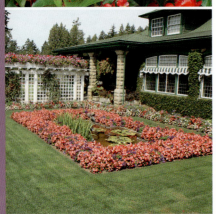

SIZE & GROWTH RATE 8"–16" tall, 12"–24" wide, medium growing.

TEXTURE & FORM Medium coarse texture and rounded to mounded form.

FOLIAGE Simple glossy leaves are ovate to rounded in shape with serrulate margins.

FLOWERS Flowers from spring to frost in colors of white, pink, and red, with some varieties providing double flowers.

LIGHT & SOIL Plant bronze-leafed forms in full sun to light shade. Green-leafed forms prefer light shade. Provide a loose and moist but well-drained soil.

MAINTENANCE Pinch back young stems to promote branching. Provide continuous nutrition with a slow-release fertilizer, and allow the soil to dry slightly between watering.

INSTALLATION Plant 12"–18" apart in a loose soil mix in midspring.

top Wax leaf begonia.
bottom Begonias at Butchart Gardens.

Caladium bicolor FANCY LEAF CALADIUM

Caladiums are grown for their foliage rather than their flowers. They provide a bold and exotic tropical feel to the landscape. They do best in light shade with a continuous source of moisture. White-colored varieties brighten up shady spaces, and all of them enliven border plantings or containers. Purchase multiple colors for use in masses. They benefit by planting in later spring as soil temperatures rise and decline earlier in autumn as nighttime temperatures fall into the low 50s.

SIZE & GROWTH RATE 12"–24" tall and wide, fast growing.

TEXTURE & FORM Coarse texture and broadly oval form.

FOLIAGE Simple hastate or cordate-shaped leaves in variegated colors of white, pink, green, purple, and red.

FLOWERS Insignificant flowers should be removed to encourage more foliage.

LIGHT & SOIL Provide light shade and a loose and moist but well-drained soil.

MAINTENANCE Don't allow caladiums to dry out, and fertilize them every three to four weeks with a higher nitrogen fertilizer.

INSTALLATION Plant tubers 2"–4" deep, 8"–12" apart in a loose soil mix in late spring. Squirrels and chipmunks damage tubers until they sprout, so an alternative is the presprouted container plant.

top Foliage.
bottom Mixed caladiums with variegated shell ginger.

Calibrachoa × *hybrida*
MILLION BELLS · TRAILING PETUNIA

Introduced into nursery production in the early 1990s, trailing petunias are prolific bloomers that produce a spectacular show throughout the summer with very little maintenance. Available in a wide range of colors, they perform best in planters, window boxes, or hanging baskets to take advantage of their trailing habit and preference for well-drained soils. They can also be used as ground covers but are somewhat susceptible to soil-borne fungal and viral diseases.

SIZE & GROWTH RATE 4"–8" tall, 24"–36" wide, medium growing.

TEXTURE & FORM Medium fine texture and dense prostrate trailing form.

FOLIAGE Simple elliptic leaves are covered with fine hairs.

FLOWERS Trumpet-shaped flowers approximately 1" in diameter are attractive to hummingbirds and available in yellow, white, pink, red, purple, and some blues from midspring to frost.

LIGHT & SOIL Provide full sun to very light shade with moist but well-drained acidic soil.

MAINTENANCE Allow them to dry out slightly between watering. No deadheading is required, but fertilizing every three to four weeks stimulates new growth, as it does in other warm-season annuals.

INSTALLATION Pinch young stems of new plants to encourage branching, and plant 18"–24" on center for massing.

Trailing petunias in Athens.

Catharanthus roseus
ANNUAL VINCA · MADAGASCAR PERIWINKLE

Periwinkle is one of the oldest and most dependable of the warm-season annuals for borders, edging, and massing. They perform best in the heat of summer when other annuals go into a stupor. Available in a variety of colors, they require no deadheading and prefer to dry out slightly between watering. Periwinkle is one of the few summer annuals resistant to deer and some salt spray. It is an important medicinal plant: a chemotherapy drug, vincristine, has been developed from it for use in cancer treatments.

SIZE & GROWTH RATE 6"–12" tall, 4"–8" wide, medium growing.

TEXTURE & FORM Medium texture and oval form.

FOLIAGE Simple dark glossy green opposite leaves are elliptic to oblong shaped, with a white midrib and veins.

FLOWERS Five-petaled flowers in whites, pinks, reds, and purples. Many varieties have darker throats.

LIGHT & SOIL Full sun with a loose well-drained soil mix.

MAINTENANCE No deadheading is required, but pinching young plants to encourage branching is recommended. Fertilize every two to three weeks. It can reseed itself in zone 8a.

INSTALLATION Space plants 6"–8" apart in a loose well-drained soil mix.

top Annual vinca.

bottom With yellow coleus and purple fountain grass.

Digitalis purpurea FOXGLOVE

Technically a biennial, foxglove is considered a cool-season annual across much of the Southeast. Planted in early autumn, it develops a rosette of foliage over fall and winter and a stalk of showy spring flowers. Foxglove is frequently used in perennial borders, where its upright form, coarse texture, and flowers contrast with surrounding plants. Resistant to deer, its foliage is poisonous and is the source of the drug digitalis, which is used to regulate heart rate. While foxglove can reseed itself, replanting each year is a more dependable option.

SIZE & GROWTH RATE 2'–5' tall, 1'–2' wide, medium growing.

TEXTURE & FORM Coarse texture and upright oval form.

FOLIAGE Ovate leaves have a hairy crinkled surface.

FLOWERS The flower stalk elongates in early spring and is covered with bell-shaped flowers in purple, pink, apricot, or white in mid- to late spring.

LIGHT & SOIL Light shade with a consistently moist soil is ideal. They tolerate full sun to moderate shade.

MAINTENANCE Flower stalks on plants in moderate shade need support. Don't allow foxglove to dry out, so mulch heavily, and provide water during dry periods.

INSTALLATION Plant 12"–24" apart in early autumn.

top Foxglove in the Founders Memorial Garden.

bottom With Virginia creeper on a fence.

Gomphrena globosa GLOBE AMARANTH

Few warm-season annuals thrive in the heat of summer as globe amaranth do. When the other annuals are catching their breath in the dog days of July and August, globe amaranths just keep on blooming. Somewhat informal in appearance, they are commonly used for masses or border plantings in full sun locations and are popular for cut flowers and dried flower arrangements. Globe amaranth performs best when planted or started from seed in late spring when nighttime temperatures remain in the 50s.

SIZE & GROWTH RATE 12"–24" tall, 6"–15" wide, medium growing.

TEXTURE & FORM Medium texture and oval to broadly oval form.

FOLIAGE Simple opposite elliptic leaves are covered with white hairs.

FLOWERS Rounded flower heads resembling buttons in white, red, pink, or purple occur from early summer to frost.

LIGHT & SOIL Full sun with a loose well-drained soil.

MAINTENANCE Periodic deadheading is recommended but not required. Allow the soil to dry out between watering. They may reseed themselves in zones 7 and 8.

INSTALLATION Often started from seed sown directly in the garden. Young seedlings should be pinched to encourage branching and thinned or spaced 12"–15" apart.

top Purple globe amaranth with white verbenas.

bottom 'Fireworks' amaranth with salvia and sunflowers.

Impatiens hawkeri NEW GUINEA IMPATIENS

For endless summer color, impatiens are hard to beat. Whether used in borders or containers, they demand little more than regular watering and fertilization. Midday shade is ideal, but they will grow in full sun with adequate water. Pinching plants periodically maintains a dense mounded form. In recent years downy mildew has devastated *Impatiens walleriana*, long a garden staple, but New Guinea impatiens are resistant to downy mildew. Until resistant impatiens are developed, stick with New Guinea varieties.

SIZE & GROWTH RATE 12"–24" tall and wide, fast growing.

TEXTURE & FORM Medium texture with a broadly oval to mounded form.

FOLIAGE Simple bronze-colored narrowly ovate to lanceolate-shaped leaves are alternately arranged along succulent green stems.

FLOWERS Single and some double flowers are available in whites, pinks, reds, salmon, and variegated colors. Hornlike stems beneath the petals help differentiate impatiens from *Catharanthus roseus*.

LIGHT & SOIL Light shade is ideal with a loose and moist but well-drained soil.

MAINTENANCE Impatiens quickly wilt when dry, so provide consistent moisture and fertilize every three to four weeks. Deer love impatiens.

INSTALLATION Incorporate a slow-release fertilizer in the soil, and plant on 12" centers.

top New Guinea impatiens.
bottom In a border.

Ipomoea batatas SWEET POTATO VINE

For eye-catching color in the summer landscape, few plants rival the potential of sweet potato vine. Grown for its colorful foliage rather than its flowers, it is commonly used as a ground cover but also does very well in planters and hanging baskets and even on a trellis, provided it receives plenty of sun. Its fast growth, relatively low moisture requirement, superior heat tolerance, deer resistance, and comparatively low maintenance requirements allow gardeners to concentrate their time on other plants.

SIZE & GROWTH RATE 6"–12" tall, 4'–10' wide, fast growing.

TEXTURE & FORM Coarse texture with a trailing form.

FOLIAGE Simple leaves are cordate or palmately lobed, depending on the cultivar. Leaf colors commonly available are dark purple ('Blackie' and 'Ace of Spades'), chartreuse ('Margarita' and 'Sweet Caroline'), and variegated ('Pink Frost' and 'Tricolor').

FLOWERS Insignificant flowers are obscured by the foliage.

LIGHT & SOIL Full sun to light shade with a loose well-drained soil.

MAINTENANCE Provide consistent but not excessive moisture. Burned foliage may indicate that the soil is too dry, as well as too moist. Provide a slow-release fertilizer with a high nitrogen ratio.

INSTALLATION For massing, space plants 30"–36" apart.

top Chartreuse sweet potato vine with fountain grass.
bottom Burgundy sweet potato vine with begonias.

Pelargonium × *hortorum* GERANIUM

Geraniums are popular for containers and window boxes or when massed and interplanted with other summer annuals. They flower best in late spring to early summer and early to midautumn but tend to rest during the dog days of summer. They also tend to have more disease issues, particularly fungal issues, than other summer annuals. Ivy-leafed geraniums, *Pelargonium peltatum*, are medium textured with a more spreading form and smaller flower heads and are recommended for hanging baskets that receive some midday shade.

SIZE & GROWTH RATE 12"–24" tall and wide, medium growing.

TEXTURE & FORM Medium coarse texture and broadly oval to mounded form.

FOLIAGE Simple rounded leaves have crinkled margins. Some varieties have horseshoe-like markings on the leaves and/or variegated foliage.

FLOWERS Flowers in red, pink, white, orange, violet, and salmon are held upright on rounded flower heads. Double-flowered and variegated flower varieties are also available.

LIGHT & SOIL Full sun with a moist but well-drained slightly acidic soil.

MAINTENANCE Remove old flower heads to stimulate new flowering. Avoid overhead watering, and fertilize every three to four weeks with a balanced fertilizer like 10-10-10.

INSTALLATION Plant 12"–18" apart in loose well-drained soils.

top Geraniums.
bottom With mixed annuals.

Pennisetum × *advena* 'Rubrum'
PURPLE FOUNTAIN GRASS

Purple fountain grass is a perennial in zone 9 but is used as an annual in areas farther north. Whether used as a perennial or an annual, purple fountain grass attracts attention with its rich reddish-purple foliage and wine-tinted fuzzy flower heads and its upright arching form in containers or in large sweeps in the landscape. 'Fireworks' has burgundy-red variegated foliage and reaches 3' tall. 'Eaton Canyon' reaches 3' with dark purple foliage. 'Skyrocket' reaches 3' with variegated green foliage.

SIZE & GROWTH RATE 3'–5' tall, 1'–3' wide, fast growing.

TEXTURE & FORM Fine texture and upright arching form.

FOLIAGE Purple and wine-tinted foliage in narrow upright clumps cascades in a fountain-like form.

FLOWERS Prominent bottlebrush-shaped flower heads 12" long begin with a reddish tint before fading to tan from early summer through autumn.

LIGHT & SOIL Full sun to light shade with well-drained soils. Foliage fades to dark green in shade.

MAINTENANCE Although purple fountain grass is considered drought resistant, weekly watering and fertilization every four to six weeks promotes new growth and flower formation.

INSTALLATION Space 12"–18" apart for massing. Purple fountain grass is frequently labeled as *Pennisetum setaceum* 'Rubrum'.

top At Government House, Victoria, B.C.
bottom Purple fountain grass.

Pentas lanceolata PENTAS · STAR FLOWER

Pentas are only recently becoming as available as other summer annuals, but they are proving quite popular, since they tend to require less water and maintenance than many other warm-season annuals. They are suitable for borders and edge plantings, perform well in containers, and might be a good choice for interplanting with geraniums, since the summer heat doesn't deter them. Red-flowering cultivars are promoted for attracting butterflies and hummingbirds.

SIZE & GROWTH RATE 12"–30" tall, 12"–24" wide, medium fast growing.

TEXTURE & FORM Medium texture and broadly oval form.

FOLIAGE Simple ovate to lanceolate-shaped opposite leaves have prominent depressed veins. Some cultivars have variegated leaves.

FLOWERS Tiny star-shaped flowers in reds, pinks, violets, and whites are clustered on oval umbels throughout summer.

LIGHT & SOIL Full sun to light shade with a moist but well-drained and slightly acidic soil.

MAINTENANCE Removing old flower heads and pinching new growth periodically are not required but stimulate new branching and help maintain a dense plant. Apply a balanced fertilizer every four to six weeks, and allow the soil to dry out slightly between watering.

INSTALLATION Space 12"–24" apart. Pinch new plants to encourage branching.

top Star flowers.
bottom Star flowers and annual vinca.

Petunia × hybrida PETUNIA

Petunias are arguably the most popular of the warm-season annuals. An abundance of flowers in a wide range of colors contributes to their popularity. Traditionally, petunias flowered best in the cooler months of midspring to early summer, but breeding efforts have provided greater heat tolerance, so recent variety series such as 'Wave', 'Tidal Wave', 'Surfinia', and 'Supertunia' provide color all summer. Use them as ground covers, in containers, and in hanging baskets.

SIZE & GROWTH RATE 6"–30" tall, 2'–4' wide, fast growing.

TEXTURE & FORM Medium texture and mounded to trailing form.

FOLIAGE Simple ovate-shaped alternate leaves have short sticky hairs.

FLOWERS Funnel-shaped flowers are available in red, pink, purple, yellow, and white. Some cultivars provide striped flowers, double flowers, and flowers with fringed margins to the petals.

LIGHT & SOIL Full sun to light shade with a moist but well-drained soil.

MAINTENANCE Pinching plants periodically helps maintain density, and even the most heat tolerant benefit from a midsummer rejuvenation. Petunias are heavy feeders, so provide a timed-release fertilizer in the soil or fertilize every two to three weeks.

INSTALLATION Space 12"–24" apart with a slow-release fertilizer at planting.

top Pink and purple petunias with coleus.
bottom Pink petunias and elephant ears at Treanor House on the UGA campus.

Plumbago auriculata PLUMBAGO · CAPE LEADWORT

Plumbago is a woody shrub from South Africa that is perennial in the lower parts of zone 8. Farther north, it is treated as a warm-season annual. A fast grower with a sprawling mounded habit and light blue flowers that resemble phlox, it is drought resistant once established. In fact, it tends to bloom more heavily when under some drought stress. Consider it for informal borders, train it on a trellis, or take advantage of its sprawling habit for larger containers. Plumbago attracts butterflies, tolerates some salt spray, and is deer resistant.

SIZE & GROWTH RATE 2'–3' tall, 3'–5' wide, fast growing.

TEXTURE & FORM Medium fine texture and loose sprawling form.

FOLIAGE Simple obovate light green alternate leaves.

FLOWERS Light blue flowers with five petals are held on terminal racemes and continue to flower after light autumn frosts. White- and deep blue-flowered cultivars are also available.

LIGHT & SOIL Full sun to very light shade with a loose, well-drained, and acidic soil.

MAINTENANCE Allow the soil to dry out slightly between watering. Provide a balanced fertilizer every four to six weeks. Prune monthly to keep dense.

INSTALLATION For massing, space 24" apart.

Plumbago at Royal Roads University in Colwood, B.C.

Salvia splendens SALVIA · SCARLET SAGE

Salvia has been a classic option for dependable summer color for decades. It has lost some popularity in recent years to the likes of impatiens and petunias, but it is regaining status due to its ability to tolerate lower water regimens. Its biggest drawback has always been the need to deadhead it to stimulate continued flowers throughout the summer. It is a clump-forming plant, so consider it for borders, masses, and container plantings. Combine red and white cultivars with dark blue plumbagos for a patriotic summer display.

SIZE & GROWTH RATE 12"–24" tall, 6"–12" wide, fast growing.

TEXTURE & FORM Medium texture and oval to pyramidal form.

FOLIAGE Simple ovate leaves are oppositely arranged along square stems.

FLOWERS Tubular-shaped flowers in red, white, salmon, or deep purple occur on upright racemes above the foliage.

LIGHT & SOIL Full sun to light shade with a loose, well-drained, and acidic soil. Allow the soil to dry slightly between watering to discourage slugs and snails.

MAINTENANCE Deadhead every few weeks to promote new flowering racemes. Provide a balanced fertilizer every three to four weeks.

INSTALLATION Space 6"–12" apart, and pinch stems of young plants to encourage branching.

top Salvia.

bottom Red salvia and white annual verbena (Photoshopped).

Solenostemon scutellarioides COLEUS

Traditionally, coleus were grown for their colorful foliage in light to moderately shaded locations. They've long been popular for container plantings, as well as in masses. While they are still grown for their attractive foliage, modern varieties have been developed to grow in full sun. And while older varieties were upright in form, some newer varieties have a trailing habit. So today's designers have far more options in color, habit, size, texture, and sun exposure for these attractive annuals than in years past.

SIZE & GROWTH RATE 8"–30" in size, depending upon the variety, medium fast growing.

TEXTURE & FORM Medium texture and upright oval to mounded form.

FOLIAGE Simple ovate-shaped opposite leaves on square stems have serrate or occasionally lobed margins and are available in colors of red, green, purple, white, and yellow.

FLOWERS Insignificant lavender spikes should be removed throughout the summer.

LIGHT & SOIL Full sun to moderate shade with a loose and moist but well-drained soil. They quickly wilt, so provide consistent moisture.

MAINTENANCE Prune plants, particularly those in some shade, to encourage dense growth, and remove flower spikes. Fertilize every two to three weeks.

INSTALLATION Space 12"–18" apart for massing.

top Coleus.

bottom Red and yellow coleus with purple summer snapdragons, elephant ears, and banana.

Tagetes patula MARIGOLD · FRENCH MARIGOLD

Marigolds have fallen out of favor recently due to the proliferation of other annuals that require less attention. However, their lower water requirements, deer resistance, and fast germination provide reasons to still consider them for summer color. What elementary school child didn't sow a marigold seed in a paper cup to take home for Mother's Day? Use them for borders, window boxes, and container plantings with purple vincas or petunias to complement their warm colors. African marigolds, *Tagetes erecta*, reach 3' with a more upright habit and larger flowers. Crosses between the two species have also been introduced.

SIZE & GROWTH RATE 6"–18" tall, 6"–12" wide, fast growing.

TEXTURE & FORM Fine texture and broadly oval to mounded form.

FOLIAGE Pinnately compound leaves produce a pungent odor when crushed.

FLOWERS Flowers are mostly doubles in colors of yellow, orange, and orange red.

LIGHT & SOIL Full sun with a loose well-drained soil.

MAINTENANCE Deadheading is essential for continuous flowering. Leaf fungal diseases cause midsummer problems and may require replanting for fall color.

INSTALLATION Space 8"–12" apart, and pinch young stems to encourage branching. Incorporate a slow-release fertilizer into the soil mix.

top Orange African and yellow French marigolds.

bottom African marigolds with geraniums, verbena, and Shasta daisies.

Tulipa × *hybrida* TULIP

From zone 6 southward, tulips rarely flower in successive years, so for much of the country, they are treated as cool-season annuals. Tulips look great by themselves in large masses or combined with other early spring flowers such as pansies, daffodils, and snapdragons. They also do well in containers with those same plants or with perennials such as periwinkles, dianthus, and phlox. A word of caution: squirrels and voles eat tulip bulbs, and deer enjoy the flowers.

SIZE & GROWTH RATE 6"–24" tall, 3"–12" wide, depending upon the cultivar.

TEXTURE & FORM Mostly coarse texture with a broadly oval form.

FOLIAGE Silvery-blue-green basal leaves are ovate shaped.

FLOWERS Mostly single flowers in red, pink, white, yellow, purple, and bicolors occur from early to midspring.

LIGHT & SOIL Full sun to light shade in well-drained soils.

MAINTENANCE Remove the bulbs after flowering is completed, and use them for compost.

INSTALLATION In zones 7 and 8, plant refrigerated bulbs about 4" deep and 4"–8" apart in early winter or nonrefrigerated bulbs 6"–8" deep in late autumn.

top Tulips in Chicago.
bottom Tulips at Fuller Gardens in New Hampshire.

Verbena × *hybrida* GARDEN VERBENA

Annual verbenas are a difficult group to define. Depending upon which species are the parents, they may develop either a mounded or a spreading form. Many cultivars require deadheading to continue flower production, and they decline in the summer heat. All provide profuse spring and autumn flowering and benefit from occasional moderate pruning. Verbenas are valued as ground covers or border plantings, do well in containers or hanging baskets, and are somewhat deer resistant.

SIZE & GROWTH RATE 4"–18" tall, 8"–30" wide, fast growing.

TEXTURE & FORM Fine texture and mounded to trailing form.

FOLIAGE Simple opposite leaves on square stems have serrate or dissected margins.

FLOWERS Small individual flowers occur on rounded clusters in red, pink, purple, lavender, white, and bicolors.

LIGHT & SOIL Provide full sun, good air circulation, and well-drained soil.

MAINTENANCE Garden verbenas dislike cool moist soils, so don't pamper them. Allow the soil to dry between watering, and apply a slow-release fertilizer every four to six weeks. Remove old flower heads to encourage consistent flower production, and prune back the entire plant in midsummer.

INSTALLATION Pinch stems of new plants to encourage branching, and space 8"–12" apart.

top Purple verbenas and red petunias.
bottom Annual verbena.

Viola × *wittrockiana* PANSY

Pansies are the backbone of cool-season annual plantings. Available in a huge range of colors and flower sizes, they are often massed by themselves or interplanted with tulips, daffodils, and snapdragons. Pansies are planted in midautumn from zone 6 southward, where they establish their root systems and provide a few flowers in fall and early winter before making their greatest show in early to midspring; they decline in late spring. Farther north, they are planted in early spring.

SIZE & GROWTH RATE 6"–12" tall and wide, medium growing.

TEXTURE & FORM Medium texture and mounded form.

FOLIAGE Simple ovate leaves have crenate to incised margins.

FLOWERS Virtually every color imaginable, many with a "face" of a contrasting color. Violas produce smaller flowers but endure lower winter temperatures. Pansy and viola flowers are edible and used in salads.

LIGHT & SOIL Full sun with a loose and moist but well-drained slightly acidic soil.

MAINTENANCE Water every few days until established and weekly thereafter. Apply a slow-release fertilizer at planting and a liquid fertilizer monthly. Deer devour pansies.

INSTALLATION Pinch stems of young plants to encourage branching. Space 6"–12" apart.

top Pansies at the UGA campus.
bottom At Andrew Low House in Savannah.

Zinnia angustifolia
NARROWLEAF OR MEXICAN ZINNIA

Narrowleaf zinnias provide an abundance of color throughout the spring and summer without the maintenance problems associated with *Zinnia elegans* cultivars. These zinnias like to be kept a little dry and don't require deadheading like their relatives. Outstanding for masses and border plantings, their warm colors combine well with purple-foliaged fountain grass or purple heart plant. Crosses between *Z. angustifolia* and *Z. elegans*, like the Profusion series, combine greater flower color options with improved disease resistance.

SIZE & GROWTH RATE 10"–18" tall and wide, fast growing.

TEXTURE & FORM Medium fine texture, broadly oval to mounded form.

FOLIAGE Simple lanceolate-shaped sessile leaves are oppositely arranged.

FLOWERS Rounded flowers in orange, yellow, and white are mostly singles. Hybrids crossed with *Zinnia elegans* add red and pink options.

LIGHT & SOIL Full sun and a loose well-drained soil.

MAINTENANCE Narrowleaf zinnias have fewer problems than do regular zinnias. They don't require deadheading, bloom all summer with few disease problems, and aren't favored by deer. Allow them to dry between watering, avoid overhead watering, and fertilize every two to three weeks.

INSTALLATION Pinch new plants to encourage branching, and space 12"–15" apart.

top Narrowleaf zinnias.
bottom With red coleus at the T. R. R. Cobb House.

Zinnia elegans ZINNIA

Zinnias make a fantastic show in late spring and early summer in the Southeast. They can be used for borders and cut flowers and massed in full sun in an array of colors, so one wonders why they aren't more heavily used. The reasons are that they require deadheading, are prone to fungal diseases, and tend to decline in the midsummer heat and humidity. Combine them with globe amaranths, and consider replanting them in late summer for fall color.

SIZE & GROWTH RATE 12"–30" tall, 6"–15" wide, fast growing.

TEXTURE & FORM Medium coarse texture and oval to broadly oval form.

FOLIAGE Simple ovate-shaped opposite leaves clasp the hairy stems.

FLOWERS Rounded single and double flowers up to 3" wide are available in white, red, pink, orange, and yellow.

LIGHT & SOIL Full sun with a loose and moist but well-drained slightly acidic soil.

MAINTENANCE Deadheading is required to promote additional flower development. Avoid watering in the evenings and wetting the foliage, and remove old flowers to help prevent fungal diseases. Allow the soil to dry between watering, and fertilize every two to three weeks.

INSTALLATION Space 6"–12" apart, and pinch young stems to encourage branching.

top Zinnias.

bottom With coleus and purple fountain grass.

FERNS

Ferns occupy a unique spot in the environment. Unlike other types of plants, ferns aren't going to enthrall you with their bright colors or catch your eye as you drive down a street. To fully appreciate ferns in a design you have to see them up close and personal. They lend a cool, moist, and lush-tropical feel to the landscape. Their appearance reminds us of the primeval history of our planet, and they are outstanding plants for moist shady environments, where they provide a luxurious level of detail. Just keep in mind that most ferns require a high level of attention to their personal space in order to look their best. All like a loose organic soil mixture and a consistent source of moisture during the summer, and most like moderate to full shade. If you can't ensure those conditions, you may be better off considering something other than a fern for your composition.

Ferns don't produce flowers like other groups of plants. Their reproduction is accomplished by means of spores. The location of the spore cases, called "sori" in fernspeak, is often helpful in identifying the fern. For the majority of the ferns used in southern landscapes, the sori are attached to the underside of the pinnae. In many cases, the sterile and fertile fronds look identical and are separated only by the fact that some hold spore cases and others do not. However, in a few cases, the fertile fronds appear quite different from the sterile fronds. For example, the cinnamon fern, royal fern, and sensitive fern produce fertile fronds that are covered only by bead-like spore cases, giving those fronds a plumelike appearance. The technical term is "dimorphic" for ferns whose sterile and fertile fronds differ in appearance.

A sensitive fern meadow with rhododendrons at Longwood Gardens.

BOTANICAL NAME	SUNLIGHT	SOILS	HARDINESS ZONES	TEXTURE	NATIVE TO SOUTHEAST
EVERGREEEN SPECIES					
Cyrtomium falcatum	Moderate to heavy shade	Moist but well drained	7a–10b	Coarse	No, Asia
Dryopteris erythrosora	Light to moderate shade	Moist but well drained	6a–10b	Medium	No, Asia
Dryopteris marginalis	Light to heavy shade	Moist but well drained	3a–8a	Medium	Yes
Polystichum acrostichoides	Moderate to heavy shade	Moist but well drained	3a–9a	Medium	Yes
Polystichum polyblepharum	Moderate to heavy shade	Moist but well drained to moist	5b–8b	Medium coarse	No, Asia
DECIDUOUS SPECIES					
Adiantum capillus veneris	Moderate to heavy shade	Moist with a neutral or alkaline pH	6b–10a	Fine	Yes
Adiantum pedatum	Moderate to heavy shade	Moist with a slightly acidic to neutral pH	3b–8b	Fine	Yes
Athyrium niponicum pictum	Light to moderate shade	Moist but well drained	4a–8b	Fine	No, Asia
Macrothelypteris torresiana	Light to heavy shade	Wet to moist but well drained	8a–10b	Fine	No, Mariana Islands
Onoclea sensibilis	Moderate to heavy shade	Moist to wet and slightly acidic	3a–9a	Coarse	Yes
Osmunda cinnamomea	Moderate to heavy shade	Moist to wet and acidic	3a–10a	Medium	Yes
Osmunda regalis	Moderate to heavy shade	Moist to wet and slightly acidic	3a–11a	Medium	Yes
Thelypteris kunthii	Full sun to light shade	Moist	7b–11a	Fine	Yes
Woodwardia areolata	Moderate to heavy shade	Moist to wet	5a–9b	Coarse	Yes

Cyrtomium falcatum HOLLY FERN

Holly fern is probably the most popular fern for landscape use in the Southeast and is widely available in the nursery industry. A clump-forming evergreen fern, it is frequently used as a ground cover in densely shaded locations or for border plantings with other shade-loving perennials such as hostas and hellebores. Because it is attractive year-round, you can take advantage of its exotic appearance for interior plantings, in containers on porches and courtyards, or in other intimate shaded locations.

Holly fern in the Founders Memorial Garden.

ZONES & ORIGIN 7a–10b. Native to Southeast Asia.

SIZE & GROWTH RATE 18"–36" tall, 24"–48" wide, and slow growing.

TEXTURE & FORM Coarse texture with a mounded form.

FOLIAGE Dark glossy green fronds resemble artificial plants due to their waxy coating. Pinnate fronds have an arching rachis that is dark brown above, light green beneath, and covered with brown hairlike scales. Pinnae arranged in 12–20 pairs with serrate to coarsely toothed margins are arranged oppositely on the lower half of the rachis but alternately on the upper half. Sori occur along the veins on the underside of the pinnae.

LIGHT & SOIL Moderate to heavy shade with a loose and moist but well-drained acidic soil is ideal. Plants in too much sun easily develop burned foliage if exposed to drying winter winds, while those in moist to wet soils develop root rot. Plants in shade can tolerate some dry periods. It is very tolerant of salt spray, so it makes a good choice for coastal developments.

MAINTENANCE Mulch at least annually in late fall in zones 7 and 8 to keep the roots insulated over the winter. Although this is an evergreen fern, the fronds are frequently damaged by cold winters in those zones and may need to be removed before the new growth appears in the spring.

INSTALLATION Although holly fern can be planted year-round, best results are obtained in late winter or early spring before new fiddleheads emerge. For borders and ground covers, plant 24"–36" on center.

PESTS & DISEASES Florida fern caterpillar defoliates plants in greenhouses and zones 8b southward. Deer don't bother it.

NOTES & CULTIVARS 'Rochfordianum' has coarsely toothed margins.

top to bottom

In front of a Hilton Head residence.

Beneath live oaks at a Marriott resort on Hilton Head Island.

With a southern magnolia espalier in Charleston.

Dryopteris erythrosora AUTUMN FERN

Autumn fern is a clump-forming evergreen fern that has the potential to add spots of color from its new fronds into shaded gardens. Suitable for massing, in border plantings, or in detailed plantings, autumn fern contrasts well with coarse-textured plants such as rhododendrons, fatsias, and hostas. It is particularly attractive when combined with native stone and stained wood. For container plantings, combine it with ajugas, pachysandras, and even shade-loving mosses.

New fronds on autumn fern.

ZONES & ORIGIN 5b–10b. Native to the wooded slopes of Japan, China, and Korea.

SIZE & GROWTH RATE 18"–30" tall and wide with a medium slow growth rate.

TEXTURE & FORM Medium fine texture with a broadly oval form.

FOLIAGE Fronds emerge in midspring with a pink to coppery-red tint and develop a waxy green coating as they mature. Colorful new fronds will continue to emerge throughout the season as long as conditions are suitable for new growth. Bipinnate fronds are triangular in shape, with the pinnae alternately arranged along the rachis. The rachis develops a purplish-brown color as it matures and is covered with short brown hairs. Red spore cases beneath the pinnules turn coppery brown with maturity.

LIGHT & SOIL Moderate shade with a loose and evenly moist but well-drained slightly acidic soil amended with organic matter is ideal. It tolerates light to heavy shade but doesn't like to stay wet.

MAINTENANCE As we do with other ferns, we highly recommend applications of organic mulch in spring and late fall to conserve moisture and moderate soil temperatures. Provide supplemental water during extended summer droughts. Remove old fronds in late winter or early spring and any drought-damaged fronds during the season as needed to maintain a neat appearance.

INSTALLATION For massing, plant 24"–30" on center. Add organic material to the soil mixture when planting, and make certain that there is good surface drainage away from the fern.

PESTS & DISEASES While this fern may go deciduous in zone 6 northward, no serious problems have been reported as long as cultural conditions are suitable. Deer do not seem to be interested in this fern.

NOTES & CULTIVARS
'Brilliance' provides more pronounced foliage color.

left top A border planting in Columbus.
left bottom With pachysandra.
right At an Atlanta residence.

Marginal shield fern.

Dryopteris marginalis MARGINAL SHIELD FERN

Marginal shield fern is a clump-forming evergreen fern native to moist shaded slopes. It is usually found in shallow pockets of soil among rock outcrops and is greatly overlooked as an ornamental fern in the nursery industry. Resembling cinnamon fern, it is a better choice for many situations due to its lower moisture requirements. Use it for detail planting in shaded locations with spring-flowering native plants like the crested iris, foamflower, and trillium and with rhododendrons and other ferns along woodland trails.

ZONES & ORIGIN 3a–8b. Native to cool shaded rocky slopes of eastern North America.

SIZE & GROWTH RATE 18"–36" tall, 12"–24" wide, slow growing.

TEXTURE & FORM Medium texture with upright arching to broadly oval form.

FOLIAGE Dark green bipinnate fronds are lanceolate shaped, with 12–20 pairs of pinnae and sori occurring on the margins of the pinnules. The base of the stipe is covered in light brown hairlike scales.

LIGHT & SOIL Moderate shade with a loose and moist but well-drained acidic soil is ideal. It performs well in light to heavy shade and can dry out some between rainfall events or watering without adverse effects.

Near a north Georgia rock outcrop.

left In a shaded border at Longwood Gardens.

right top In the Founders Memorial Garden.

right bottom With foamflower at Chanticleer.

Polystichum acrostichoides CHRISTMAS FERN

Colonists named the Christmas fern and used it for holiday decorations, since it was one of the few evergreen plants in the woodlands. It is a slow-growing but long-lived clump-forming evergreen fern found on shaded woodland slopes from Florida to Nova Scotia. This is an outstanding plant for use in woodland plantings and shaded rock gardens or near water features. Christmas fern is tough as nails and is one of the easiest ferns to successfully grow for most home gardeners. Consider combining it with rhododendrons, mountain laurels, native wildflowers, and native stone.

Christmas fern.

ZONES & ORIGIN 3a–9a. Native to cool moist slopes from northern Florida to Canada.

SIZE & GROWTH RATE 12"–24" tall, 12"–30" wide, slow growing.

TEXTURE & FORM Medium texture with a broadly oval form.

FOLIAGE Pinnate fronds are dark green and lanceolate in shape. Pinnae have finely bristle-tipped margins with a distinct lobe on the upper edge. Fertile fronds emerge first in the spring and are the tallest fronds, with the sori held on the upper third of the noticeably narrower pinnae. Though the foliage remains green, it flattens to the ground in winter.

LIGHT & SOIL Moderate to heavy shade with a loose and moist but well-drained acidic soil is ideal. Full sun to light shade may cause some singed foliage without adequate moisture. It is surprisingly tolerant of less than ideal conditions and withstands short periods of drought without adverse effects.

MAINTENANCE This fern has probably the lowest maintenance requirements of any of the ferns, but it benefits from the addition of leaf litter or pine straw in late spring to carry it through summer droughts. Water every seven to ten days during droughts. Old fronds may be removed at any time over the winter or early spring with hand clippers to provide a clean appearance.

INSTALLATION Christmas fern can be successfully planted year-round, but planting is best done in late winter before new fiddleheads appear in a loose, well-drained, and moderately acidic soil. Mulch annually with decomposed leaf litter. For massing, plant 18"–24" on center.

PESTS & DISEASES None. White-tailed deer don't even look at it.

Polystichum polyblepharum TASSEL FERN

Tassel fern is an easy-to-grow eye-catching fern for southern gardens with a bold exotic appearance that hints of primeval periods. A clump-forming evergreen fern, its glossy foliage and hairy-looking stems remain attractive throughout the winter and resemble a small sago palm. Use tassel fern in shady rock gardens, along woodland paths, or even as a border planting combined with herbaceous perennials such as foamflower, woodland phlox, and heuchera. Also consider it for container plantings on shaded patios or decks with pachysandra or ajuga. Just make sure to place it close to where people can appreciate it.

left top In a Land Plus Associates design in Atlanta.

left bottom With creeping jenny and ajuga.

right With strawberry begonia, creeping jenny, and hosta.

ZONES & ORIGIN 5b–8b. Native to southern Japan.

SIZE & GROWTH RATE 18"–24" tall and wide, slow growing.

TEXTURE & FORM Medium coarse texture with a mounded form.

FOLIAGE Dark glossy green bipinnate fronds are lanceolate in shape with 20–30 pairs of overlapping pinnae and drooping tips like a tassel. The stipe and rachis of each frond are covered in coarse brown scales that provide a hairy appearance. Unlike those of Christmas fern, tassel fern fronds tend to align themselves parallel to the ground.

LIGHT & SOIL Moderate to heavy shade with a loose and moist but well-drained soil is ideal. It tolerates brief periods of drought but cannot tolerate consistently wet or damp soils.

MAINTENANCE Provide a loose soil mix with added organic material. Mulch in late spring and late fall with decomposed leaf litter or pine straw, and ideally provide at least 1" of water each week during the summer and early fall. While this fern is evergreen, older fronds may appear unkempt, so remove them as they begin to turn yellow or brown to maintain a clean appearance.

INSTALLATION Amend the soil with organic material, and plant the fern a little high to ensure good drainage. Plant 24"–30" on center for massing.

PESTS & DISEASES Slugs and root rot can be problems if the soil is too damp. Deer don't like them.

Korean tassel fern with leopard plant.

top With Boston ivy at the Southern Progress Building, Birmingham, Ala.

bottom Southern maidenhair fern on a wall in Charleston.

Adiantum capillus veneris
SOUTHERN MAIDENHAIR FERN

Southern maidenhair fern is a delicate and fine-textured deciduous fern that spreads slowly by means of rhizomes. In nature, it is often associated with moist locations along limestone outcrops or bluffs such as waterfalls or seeps. The soft pendulous fronds of this fern are ideal for softening low stone retaining walls or tucking into niches in shady rock gardens.

ZONES & ORIGIN 6b–10a. Native to moist limestone soils of the southern United States.

SIZE & GROWTH RATE 8"–12" tall, slow growing.

TEXTURE & FORM Fine texture with an oval form.

FOLIAGE The light green fan-shaped foliage of the southern maidenhair fern resembles that of the ginkgo tree. Bipinnate fronds have alternate fan-shaped pinnules with dichotomous veins and are supported by a dark wiry rachis. Spore cases are held on the underside of the pinnules and are covered slightly by the pinnules' recurved margins.

LIGHT & SOIL Southern maidenhair ferns are somewhat difficult to grow for many people. Moderate to heavy shade is ideal with a loose and consistently moist soil and a neutral to slightly alkaline pH. It tolerates very small pockets of soil as long as there is a consistent moisture source.

Adiantum pedatum NORTHERN MAIDENHAIR FERN

Northern maidenhair is a delicate and fine-textured spreading fern that grows somewhat slowly by creeping rhizomes. It is not quite as picky about its soil requirements as is the southern maidenhair fern, thus making it a better choice for most locations in the Southeast. Native to cool woodland slopes with deep soils, it is ideal for massing or borders, as well as for detailed pockets in rock gardens and along wooded paths.

ZONES & ORIGIN 3b–8a. Native to cool moist woodlands of the eastern United States.

SIZE & GROWTH RATE 10"–18" tall, slow growing.

TEXTURE & FORM Fine texture with a spreading form.

FOLIAGE The spreading fanlike bipinnate fronds are held in a plane parallel to the ground. Each frond's dark and wirelike stipe splits into two parts to form a circular arc. Close inspection of the pinnules reveals a serrate outer margin, while the inner side is entire.

LIGHT & SOIL Moderate to heavy shade is ideal, with a moist but well-drained soil and a slightly acidic to neutral pH. It can tolerate brief periods of drought without adverse consequences.

top Northern maidenhair fern.
bottom With false spirea and crocosmia.

Athyrium niponicum pictum JAPANESE PAINTED FERN

Japanese painted fern is a deciduous clump-forming fern noted for its colorful foliage. The silvery-white foliage and contrasting burgundy-colored rachis of this fern provide the opportunity to add some brightness to heavily shaded parts of the garden. Since this is definitely a plant to enjoy at close range, consider adding a small mass or border planting to courtyards or entry areas, or combine it with other variegated foliage plants or white-flowering plants in a white or moon garden.

Japanese painted fern.

top to bottom
Within a mass of foamflower.
With sweetbox at Chanticleer.
With creeping jenny and annual vinca.

ZONES & ORIGIN 4a–8b. Native to Japan.

SIZE & GROWTH RATE 10"–15" tall, 12"–24" wide, medium growing.

TEXTURE & FORM Fine texture with a mounded form.

FOLIAGE Bipinnate fronds have 12–20 pairs of mostly alternately arranged pinnae. The fronds' rachis and the midrib of the pinnae have a deep red to burgundy color, while individual pinnules have a silvery tint. Coloration is particularly noticeable on new fronds. Sori are located along the veins on the underside of the pinnules.

LIGHT & SOIL Moderate shade is ideal, but it tolerates light to heavy shade. Avoid midday full sun. Provide a loose and moist to moist but well-drained slightly acidic soil.

MAINTENANCE Japanese painted ferns perform best with a consistent source of moisture. Mulch twice per year to keep the roots cool and moist. Remove old fronds in late winter or early spring before new growth emerges.

INSTALLATION For massing, plant 12"–18" on center. Add organic material to the planting mix, and don't be afraid of planting it in a low-lying area that might receive additional water from storm runoff.

PESTS & DISEASES None reported. Although deer reportedly nibble this fern, it is not among their favored plants.

NOTES & CULTIVARS
New fronds on 'Burgundy Lace' exhibit an intense purple color.
'Silver Falls' has brighter silvery-white foliage.

Athyrium filix-femina, lady fern, is a native deciduous fern found in moist locations in light to heavy shade in Georgia and throughout the eastern United States. Reaching 18"–24" and hardy from zones 3a to 8b, it has bright green fronds with a reddish rachis.

Macrothelypteris torresiana MARIANA MAIDEN FERN

Mariana maiden fern is a large, fast-growing, and fine-textured fern that spreads by means of underground rhizomes. An aggressive fern reaching 3'–4' tall, it provides a striking contrast in texture and appearance to surrounding plantings. It could be massed as a tall ground cover, used to provide a foundation for larger shrubs behind it, or simply planted to provide a contrast in border plantings. Although deciduous and easily managed in zone 8a, it is evergreen and has escaped cultivation in zones 9 and 10.

ZONES & ORIGIN 7b–10b. Native to the Mariana Islands of the central Pacific Ocean.

SIZE & GROWTH RATE 36"–54" tall, 12"–24" wide, and fast growing.

TEXTURE & FORM Fine texture, with upright arching fronds and a running habit.

FOLIAGE Bright green fronds are bi- or tripinnately compound with a lacelike appearance. Fronds begin to emerge in mid- to late March and don't go completely deciduous until late December in Athens. New fronds emerge throughout the season as long as growing conditions are suitable. Frond stems are covered in short needle-like hairs. Only about one in ten fronds is fertile.

LIGHT & SOIL Light to moderate shade with a moist to slightly wet soil is ideal, but this fern grows in full sun to heavy shade and in moist but well-drained soils. A loose soil mixture facilitates the spread of the fern's rhizomes.

MAINTENANCE Mariana maiden fern has very few maintenance issues other than the need to restrict its aggressive growth. Some type of edge restraint at least 8" deep is highly recommended to keep it from overwhelming adjacent plantings.

INSTALLATION Bare-root or container plants placed 48" on center in a loose soil mix will grow together in two to three years. Although it can be planted at any time of year, late winter or early spring is preferable.

PESTS & DISEASES No serious problems are reported with this fern. Plants under excessive drought will die back to the ground but reemerge when moisture returns.

Mariana maiden fern in Athens, Ga.

top to bottom

As a shaded ground cover.

Mariana maiden fern in Athens, Ga.

With butterfly bush and ironweed on the UGA campus.

Onoclea sensibilis Sensitive Fern

Sensitive fern is a coarse-textured native fern found in moist shaded areas of the eastern United States that goes deciduous with the first hint of autumn frost. In locations where it is happy, some type of edge restraint may be needed to keep it contained. Use it around water features or drainage downspouts where other plants may not survive the damp soil.

top Sensitive fern with columbine and sweetbay magnolia in Boston.

bottom Fertile fronds of sensitive fern.

ZONES & ORIGIN   3b–9a. Native from Florida and Texas to Canada.

SIZE & GROWTH RATE   12"–18" tall, 6"–12" wide, and medium growing.

TEXTURE & FORM   Coarse texture with a spreading habit.

FOLIAGE   Light green pinnatifid sterile fronds have 8–12 pairs of pinnae arranged along a winged rachis. Lower and middle pinnae have distinct rounded lobes along their margins. The lowest and uppermost pinnae appear alternately arranged, while those in the middle are opposite. Fertile fronds arise 12"–15" tall in mid- to late spring and are covered with bead-like pinnae before turning brown by early summer.

LIGHT & SOIL   Prefers light to full shade and moist slightly acidic soils. Space 24"–36" on center in a loose soil for continuous coverage. Deer don't eat it.

Osmunda cinnamomea CINNAMON FERN

Cinnamon fern is a slow-growing, long-lived, clump-forming, and deciduous fern native to low-damp woods and wetlands from Florida to southern Canada. It is an outstanding plant in woodland plantings and rock gardens and adjacent to water features, provided you can satisfy its thirst for consistent moisture. Mature ferns produce a log-like stem that grows along the ground.

Cinnamon fern's spring fertile fronds.

ZONES & ORIGIN 3b–10a. Native to eastern North America.

SIZE & GROWTH RATE 24"–60" tall and 18"–36" wide with a slow growth rate.

TEXTURE & FORM Medium texture with an oval form.

FOLIAGE Fertile fronds emerge first in early spring, soon turning an orange-brown color that resembles cinnamon sticks as the spores mature. By late spring, the mature fertile fronds wither and die. Bright green sterile fronds are pinnately compound and can remain until late autumn in moist soils. The pinnae are alternately arranged along the rachis with conspicuous tufts of reddish-brown hairs at their base, as well as the lower part of the stipe. Fiddleheads are covered in white hairs as they emerge in early spring.

LIGHT & SOIL Moderate to heavy shade with a moist to wet acidic soil is ideal. Cinnamon fern grows in full sun, provided there is consistent soil moisture, but it doesn't tolerate dry conditions for even short periods. The foliage wilts quickly and will not recover that season.

MAINTENANCE Assure adequate soil moisture for cinnamon fern by planting it in a damp location or providing supplemental water as soon as it shows signs of stress. Old fronds decompose quickly and don't need to be removed from the fern to keep it attractive.

INSTALLATION Plant in late winter or early spring before the new foliage emerges. Provide a moist soil, and loosen existing soil as needed by adding organic material. Since this fern is clump forming, other ferns are better suited for massing than is cinnamon fern. However, it can be planted on 36" centers to provide a mass in two to three years.

PESTS & DISEASES No serious problems are reported with this fern. Deer don't like it.

left At Mt. Auburn Cemetery in Cambridge, Mass.   *right* In Central Park.

Osmunda regalis ROYAL FERN

Royal fern is a slow-growing, clump-forming, and deciduous fern native to low moist sites of the eastern United States and from Central America and the Caribbean into Canada. Mature ferns produce a stump-like crown that may reach as much as 12" above the soil surface and give the fern the appearance of being a shrub. Royal fern provides an exotic tropical look in the landscape and is an excellent plant to use with other moisture-loving plants such as itea and clethra or with hardy perennials like lobelia and equisetum. Consider using it in shady rock gardens, adjacent to water features, or even in low meadow plantings.

ZONES & ORIGIN 3a–11a. Native to eastern North America.

SIZE & GROWTH RATE 24"–48" tall and 30"–48" wide, slow growing.

TEXTURE & FORM Medium texture with a mounded form.

FOLIAGE Bipinnate fronds are bluish green in color, with individual pinnules having blunt or rounded tips that resemble the foliage of the black locust tree. The rachis of the fronds is slightly pink to tan in color. Emerging fiddleheads in the early spring are reportedly edible and prepared like asparagus. Spores are held on the upper third of fertile fronds and dry up in early to midsummer.

LIGHT & SOIL Full sun to heavy shade and moist to slightly wet acidic soils. Plants in sunnier locations need a constant source of moisture.

MAINTENANCE Provide consistent moisture throughout the growing season. Royal fern fronds go dormant if the soil becomes too dry during the season and will not reemerge until the following spring.

INSTALLATION For massing, plant on 36" centers in moist shady locations. Loosen clay soils, and amend them with organic material to improve texture. Maintain an organic mulch around the fern.

PESTS & DISEASES No serious problems are reported with this fern. However, plants under excessive moisture stress will die back to the ground during the growing season. Deer don't like them.

top to bottom

Royal fern.

At a Columbus, Ga., residence.

Royal fern at Chanticleer.

Royal fern at Great Dixter, Northiam, England.

Thelypteris kunthii SOUTHERN SHIELD FERN

Southern shield fern is a fast-growing spreading fern that is native to open damp areas of the Southeast, as well as Central and South America. While deciduous in zones 7b and 8a, it retains its green foliage into early winter and may remain evergreen in zone 8b. It is an outstanding fern for massing or to utilize for border plantings due to its spreading habit, but it may need some type of edge restraint to keep it in bounds. Consider using it in lightly shaded rock gardens or perennial borders or along water features.

ZONES & ORIGIN 7b–11a. Native to open moist locations of the southeastern Coastal Plain.

SIZE & GROWTH RATE 24"–48" tall and 6"–10" wide with a fast growth rate for a fern.

TEXTURE & FORM Fine texture with a spreading habit.

FOLIAGE Bright green pinnate fronds emerge throughout the growing season, provided conditions are suitable for growth. Lanceolate-shaped fronds are 20"–48" long and covered with white hairs along the pinnae and rachis. Fertile and sterile fronds look identical. Over half of the fronds are fertile, with spores on the back of the pinnae.

LIGHT & SOIL Light shade with a moist soil and a near-neutral pH is ideal. It tolerates full sun with adequate moisture and moist but well-drained soils in lightly shaded locations. Unlike most ferns, southern shield languishes in too much shade.

MAINTENANCE Provide consistent moisture throughout the growing season. Plantings in full sun may not be able to outcompete invasive grasses until well established.

INSTALLATION For massing, space 36" on center in a loose moist soil. Provide an edge restraint to control its spread. It is readily available in the nursery industry.

PESTS & DISEASES No serious problems are reported. Extended droughts will cause the fronds to die, but the fern can recover and produce new fronds later in the season with adequate moisture. Deer don't touch it.

NOTES & CULTIVARS
New York fern, *Thelypteris noveboracensis*, is native to low moist woods from eastern Canada to central Alabama and is hardy from zones 4a to 8a.

top left In the Founders Memorial Garden.

top right At the Gary and Joan Bertsch residence in Athens.

middle Southern shield fern.

bottom With spiderwort.

left Netted chain fern.

right Late summer fertile fronds.

Woodwardia areolata NETTED CHAIN FERN

Netted chain fern is similar in appearance and habit to sensitive fern. A deciduous fern native to the eastern United States, it has the ability to spread rapidly by rhizomes in favorable locations. Like sensitive fern, it goes deciduous with the first hint of cold temperatures in autumn. Consider it for shaded wetland plantings, rain gardens, and water features.

ZONES & ORIGIN 5b–9b. Native to moist lowlands from Florida and Texas to Nova Scotia.

SIZE & GROWTH RATE 12"–24" tall and 12" wide, medium growth rate.

TEXTURE & FORM Coarse texture with a spreading habit.

FOLIAGE Sterile pinnate fronds are a glossy light green, with 8–12 pairs of pinnae along a winged rachis. Pinnae are alternately arranged along the entire length of the rachis, with finely serrate margins, versus the lobes of sensitive fern. Fertile fronds arise in mid- to late summer and are much narrower than the sterile fronds.

LIGHT & SOIL Light to full shade with a moist to wet soil.

MAINTENANCE Provide consistent moisture throughout the growing season. Plant 24"–36" apart in a loose soil, and consider some type of edge restraint. Deer don't eat it.

VINES AND CLIMBERS

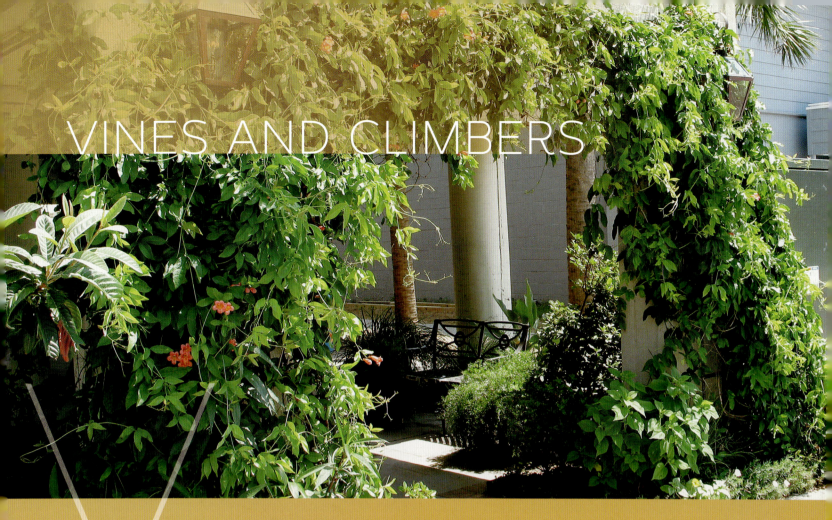

Vines are an extremely versatile medium for planting design. They offer unique solutions to both functional and aesthetic problems in the landscape, as they may be used to climb just about any structure to provide shade, color, or ornament. At times, they can be used to spill over walls and embankments, and some can even serve as ground covers. When you visit a garden and see a vine trained over a doorway or an arbor, you immediately know that you are in someplace special. A carefully tended vine is symbolic of a landscape that is loved and enjoyed. This is not to suggest that all vines are high maintenance and require great effort. For example, using a vine to cover a building facade may involve little maintenance, depending upon the vine. Yet the visual impact may be stunning and memorable, as in the Boston ivy–covered walls of Wrigley Field in Chicago and the Royal Empress Hotel in Victoria, British Columbia, or the thousands of barns and other rustic structures in the Southeast that are often covered in Virginia creeper and a myriad of other vines. These are landscapes that linger in the memory and give character and identity to significant places and landscapes, which is one of the important roles of good planting design and good plant selection.

Good plant selection is critical in choosing the right vine for the right place. Vines climb by two very different mechanisms, twining and clinging. A twining vine twists as it grows, some clockwise and others counterclockwise, and wraps itself around the structure. These types of vines must be planted where they will have a wire, wooden member, or nearby trunk or tree branch to twine on and climb. Clinging vines can attach themselves to surfaces with small suction cup–like discs or by aerial rootlets. These vines are typically able to cling to most any surface and may be more desirable on masonry structures than upon wood, which could be damaged over time. Vines vary in their growth habits, from extremely vigorous and unruly to slow growing and almost too demure. Given the range of growth habits in vines, placement and consideration of the site are paramount to long-term success and decreased long-term maintenance.

As a matter of clarification, climbing roses are not in fact true vines but shrubs. However, climbing roses have been bred and selected for centuries based on their elongated growth habit (long limber canes) and ability to be trained and used like a vine. In planting design, when one is looking for a vine or climber, a climbing rose may be the right choice along with the other true vines; therefore, climbing roses are included here, making this section a full palette of good options.

While we list typical heights for these vines, one should be aware that many will grow as tall as the support provided. Given a tree, building, or other structure large enough to provide support, many of the more aggressive vines can reach heights well beyond those listed.

Native cross vine trained over an entry on Tybee Island, Ga.

BOTANICAL NAME	FOLIAGE	SUNLIGHT	SOILS	CLIMBING METHOD	TEXTURE	NOTABLE ATTRIBUTES	NATIVE TO SE
EVERGREEN SPECIES							
Akebia quinata	Semievergreen	Full sun to moderate shade	Moist well drained to dry	Twining	Fine	Spring flowers	No
Bignonia capreolata	Semievergreen	Full sun to moderate shade	Moist well drained to dry	Clinging	Medium	Showy spring flowers attract hummingbirds	Yes
Clematis armandii	Evergreen	Morning sun to moderate shade	Moist well drained	Twining	Coarse	Spring flowers	No
Cocculus carolinus	Semievergreen	Full sun to moderate shade	Moist well drained to dry	Twining	Medium	Red summer fruit	Yes
Ficus pumila	Evergreen	Full sun to heavy shade	Moist well drained to dry	Clinging	Fine	Dense wall cover	No
Gelsemium sempervirens	Evergreen	Full sun to moderate shade	Moist well drained to dry	Twining	Fine	Spring flowers	Yes
Lonicera sempervirens	Semievergreen	Full sun to light shade	Moist well drained to dry	Twining	Fine	Early spring flowers attract humming-birds	Yes
Smilax smallii	Evergreen	Full sun to heavy shade	Moist well drained to dry	Twining	Fine	Wildlife food, cut foliage for decorations	Yes
Trachelospermum asiaticum	Evergreen	Full sun to heavy shade	Moist well drained to dry	Twining	Fine	Fragrant spring flowers when allowed to climb	No
Trachelospermum jasminoides	Evergreen	Full sun to moderate shade	Moist well drained to dry	Twining	Fine	Late spring fragrant flowers	No
DECIDUOUS SPECIES							
Campsis radicans	Deciduous	Full sun to light shade	Moist well drained to dry	Clinging	Medium	Showy summer flowers attract hummingbirds	Yes
Clematis × jackmanii	Deciduous	Full sun to light shade	Moist well drained	Twining	Medium	Showy flowers	No
Hydrangea anomala petiolaris	Deciduous	Light to heavy shade	Moist well drained	Clinging	Medium	Summer flowers, exfoliating bark	No
Parthenocissus quinquefolia	Deciduous	Morning sun to heavy shade	Moist well drained to dry	Clinging	Coarse	Fall foliage color	Yes
Parthenocissus tricuspidata	Deciduous	Morning sun to heavy shade	Moist well drained to dry	Clinging	Coarse	Fall foliage color	No
Rosa spp.	Deciduous	Full sun to light shade	Moist well drained	Must be trained	Fine	Flowering, fragrance	No
Toxicodendron radicans	Deciduous	Full sun to heavy shade	Moist well drained to dry	Clinging	Coarse	Fall color, wildlife food source	Yes
Wisteria frutescens	Deciduous	Full sun to light shade	Moist well drained	Twining	Medium	Midspring flowers	Yes

Akebia quinata FIVELEAF AKEBIA

Fiveleaf akebia provides a soft texture, interesting foliage, and subtle fragrant flowers that are best appreciated up close. For this reason, the vine may best be used on a vertical structure such as an arbor or over a doorway where one can easily appreciate the flowers, which are small and purple and tend to be somewhat hidden beneath the foliage. The deciduous character of the vine in northern zones makes it useful in places where summer shade and warm winter sun may be desired. In zones 8 and 9 akebia is semievergreen to evergreen. It is a twining vine and needs a trellis, fence, or wire for support. While potentially invasive in the mid-Atlantic states, it doesn't appear to currently be a problem in the Southeast.

ZONES & ORIGIN 4a–9a. Native to China, Korea, and Japan.

SIZE & GROWTH RATE 20'–30' fast growing.

TEXTURE Fine.

FOLIAGE Alternately arranged palmately compound leaves have five elliptic to obovate leaflets 2"–3" long with a dark bluish-green color. They do not provide any significant fall color.

FLOWERS & FRUIT Small lightly fragrant dark reddish-purple flowers 1" wide occur in groups of two to five in March and April in Athens. Sausage-shaped purple pods 2"–4" long ripen in September to October.

LIGHT & SOIL Full sun to moderate shade. It prefers a loose and moist but well-drained soil but tolerates drier sites and drought once established.

MAINTENANCE This is a fairly aggressive vine that will need pruning to keep it in bounds unless it is used on a very large structure.

INSTALLATION One will suffice unless you are attempting to cover a large structure. Space multiple plants 10'–15' on center; complete coverage will occur within three years.

NOTES & CULTIVARS
'Alba' has white flowers.
'Rosea' has light purple flowers.
'Variegata' has white leaf variegation with pink flowers.

top to bottom

Leaves arranged in fives.

Attractive and fragrant pink or purple flowers.

In the Founders Memorial Garden at UGA, continually clipped.

At the State Botanical Garden of Tennessee in Knoxville.

Bignonia capreolata CROSSVINE

Crossvine is found growing in a variety of woodland settings, ranging from dry slopes to moist ravines. It is easy to overlook in nature, as it climbs to the top of deciduous trees with little foliage on the lower portions of the vine. Its presence is often discovered in April and May, when the showy orangy-red tubular flowers are produced and fall to the ground. Crossvine is tough and has great versatility in design, as it has both twining tendrils and clinging discs. Thus, it can be used on any vertical surface, such as the side of a building, or on a trellis or wires. Flowering is profuse and showy in full sun but still significant even in moderate shade.

Flowers on a wild form.

ZONES & ORIGIN 6b–9b. Native from eastern Texas and central Florida to Ohio.

SIZE & GROWTH RATE 40'–60' fast growing.

TEXTURE Medium.

FOLIAGE Opposite compound pinnate leaves have two elliptic leaflets 2"–4" long with entire margins. Three-branched tendrils between the leaves have holdfast discs that allow crossvine to coil around a wire or trellis or adhere to a vertical wood or masonry surface. Foliage is mostly evergreen in the South but may turn reddish purple in winter.

FLOWERS & FRUIT Showy clusters of tubular flowers 2" long are crimson on the outside and red to orange yellow inside. They occur in April and May, with sporadic flowering through the summer. They are attractive to hummingbirds. Insignificant and long slender flat capsules mature by late summer.

LIGHT & SOIL Crossvine grows in full sun to moderate shade and dry to moist, even periodically wet, soils.

MAINTENANCE This is an aggressive vine, producing numerous seedlings that can cover a three-story building or a tall tree. Pruning will be necessary to keep it tidy.

INSTALLATION Space 8' or more on center for fences, pergolas, and walls.

NOTES & CULTIVARS
'Atrosanguinea' has purple-red flowers outside with orange throats.
'Helen Fredel' has flowers that are orange yellow.
'Jekyll' flowers are light orange, with repeat flowering.
'Shalimar Red' flowers are red inside and out, with repeat flowering.
'Tangerine Beauty' has flowers that are reddish orange inside and out.

left At the Atlanta Botanical Garden.

right Summer foliage at a residence in Knoxville, Tenn., by SWH Associates.

left Over a gate in Savannah, Ga.

right top Elegant foliage providing screening in City Park in New Orleans.

right bottom An arbor in Athens, Ga.

Clematis armandii ARMAND CLEMATIS

Armand clematis is an aristocrat of the evergreen vines. Unlike the deciduous clematis species that are grown primarily for their showy flowers, Armand clematis boasts glossy dark green foliage with a slightly drooping appearance, giving it a graceful elegance useful in swagging over a doorway, on an arbor, or along a fence. It also provides small lightly fragrant white flowers in early spring. Maintenance is decreased by using the vine behind a solid wall, where the foliage and flowers can sit on top, and the bare stems below are hidden from view. The older foliage tends to turn brown and remain on the vine under newer growth for some time. This can be unsightly when you are sitting under a pergola and looking up at brown leaves.

ZONES & ORIGIN 7b–10a. Native to China.

SIZE & GROWTH RATE 20'–30' fast growing.

TEXTURE Coarse.

FOLIAGE Pinnately compound leaves with three beautiful dark glossy evergreen lanceolate leaflets, each leaflet 3"–6" long, with entire margins and three noticeable veins. The leaves twine around structures to climb.

FLOWERS & FRUIT Armand clematis sports fragrant white 2"–2½" flowers with four to seven sepals in panicles on old wood in early spring (early to mid-March in Athens).

LIGHT & SOIL Provide either morning sun with afternoon shade or light to moderate shade and moist but well-drained soil. Provide supplemental water during extreme summer droughts.

MAINTENANCE Mulch at least once a year to provide a cool moist environment for the roots, which, like those of all clematis species, like a warm top and a cool root system. If necessary, prune immediately after flowering to avoid losing next year's flowers.

INSTALLATION One Armand clematis can cover a large structure. Provide a wire strung between eyebolts or some other type of structure on which the vine can twine itself.

NOTES & CULTIVARS
'Apple Blossom' has light pink flowers and bronzy new growth.
'Farquhariana' has pink flowers.

Attractive white early spring flowers.

left Late summer fruit.

right Foliage.

Cocculus carolinus CAROLINA SNAILSEED

Carolina snailseed is a semievergreen native vine that occurs in a wide range of environments. Tough as nails, it is usually seen sprawling over shrubs and other vegetation in unmaintained areas. The primary attributes are its colorful red autumn fruit, which is a favorite of birds, and its open habit, which means that it does not become too thick and oppressive, like more aggressive vines. Snailseed could be a good choice for an arbor or fence where the fruit could be appreciated at close range. While rarely found in nurseries, it is easily grown from seeds collected in autumn.

ZONES & ORIGIN 6b–9a. Native across the Southeast.

SIZE & GROWTH RATE 20'–30' fast growing.

TEXTURE Medium coarse.

FOLIAGE Alternate simple bright green leaves are rounded to cordate shaped and occasionally have shallowly lobed margins.

FLOWERS & FRUIT Insignificant clusters of greenish-white flowers occur in spring, followed by berry-like drupes that turn bright red in autumn with snail shell–shaped seeds.

LIGHT & SOIL Full sun to moderate shade with well-drained soil. Flowering and fruit are reduced in shade.

MAINTENANCE Low maintenance, with only occasional trimming needed.

NOTES & CULTIVARS
Space 8' or more apart for fences and trellises.

Ficus pumila CREEPING FIG

Think of walled courtyards and masonry softened by clinging vines in cities like Charleston, Savannah, and New Orleans and in many cities along the West Coast. Creeping fig is often the vine that lends such character to these places. It will cling to wood or masonry, allowing designers and gardeners many creative ways to use it to soften outdoor spaces, such as on the risers of stairs or neatly trimmed into patterns on blank walls. Creeping fig is evergreen in zones 9 and 10 but semievergreen to deciduous in zones 7 and 8, depending on the winter.

ZONES & ORIGIN 7b–10b. Native to China.

SIZE & GROWTH RATE To 40' or more, slow growing initially, but fast with age.

TEXTURE Fine texture on juvenile foliage, medium on mature stems.

FOLIAGE Simple alternate juvenile leaves are set very close to the vine, and all lie in the same plane, making it even more visually effective as a wall covering. Slightly glabrous above, approximately ½" long, and ovate shaped with entire margins. Leaves on mature stems are up to 3" long, lustrous dark green and leathery above, with prominent veins below.

FLOWERS & FRUIT It will only bloom on mature stems held horizontally to the ground. Flowers are insignificant, but light green bell-shaped inedible fruit 2" long droop beneath mature stems.

LIGHT & SOIL Full sun to moderate shade with moist but well-drained soils is ideal, although it tolerates most soils and becomes very drought tolerant once established.

MAINTENANCE As it grows, creeping fig is kept tight against walls by periodic trims, without which it becomes an entirely different-looking plant, with much larger leaves and thick lateral branches extending outward horizontally 3' from the wall. Maintenance becomes difficult on walls where it must be trimmed away from windows, doors, or other architectural features.

INSTALLATION Space 18"–24" apart for faster coverage on walls.

NOTES & CULTIVARS
Cultivars are difficult to locate. Deer don't touch it.

top to bottom

A diamond pattern on a wall in San Diego, Calif.

Over a wall and gate in Savannah, Ga.

So sophisticated on step risers only in Savannah, Ga.

Useful in covering any masonry structure.

Gelsemium sempervirens CAROLINA JESSAMINE

The state flower of South Carolina, Carolina jessamine is a native evergreen vine found along woodland edges and roadsides, particularly on the Coastal Plain of the Southeast, where it clambers over adjacent shrubs and well into the canopies of nearby trees. It is a memorable experience to drive the backroads of the Southeast in late February and early March and find wooded edges and fencerows aglow with the bright sunny-yellow tubular flowers. The combination of attractive flowering and evergreen foliage and the clean nature of this twining vine make it extremely useful for fences, arbors, doorways, and other structures.

top left Trained on the old kitchen house in the Founders Memorial Garden, UGA.

top right Along the fence in front of the Wray Nicholson House at UGA.

middle A sharp-looking gate with redbud in March in Athens, Ga.

bottom Dark green leaves with flower buds in early spring.

ZONES & ORIGIN 7b–10a. Native to the southeastern Piedmont and Coastal Plain.

SIZE & GROWTH RATE 50', medium fast growing.

TEXTURE Medium.

FOLIAGE Simple oppositely arranged dark glossy green lanceolate leaves 1"–3" long with entire margins and short petioles are set close to the stems. All parts of the plant are poisonous, so be careful to keep it away from pasture animals and small children.

FLOWERS & FRUIT Clusters of lightly fragrant bright yellow tubular flowers 1½" long occur in late winter and early spring (late February through March in Athens), with sporadic flowers in mid- to late autumn. Fruit are small insignificant green capsules.

LIGHT & SOIL Carolina jessamine prefers full sun to light shade and moist but well-drained slightly acidic soil. It tolerates moist soils, drought after establishment, and moderate shade with reduced flowering.

MAINTENANCE Carolina jessamine is a very clean vine that must be planted with future growth in mind to avoid the need for constant pruning. Deer don't touch it.

INSTALLATION Carolina jessamine is a twining vine and needs a wire or thin wood member to climb. One vine may cover an arbor or small structure, and spacing depends on the size and length of the structure. A vine placed every 8'–10' will provide complete coverage of a fence or pergola within a few years.

NOTES & CULTIVARS
'Pride of Augusta' or 'Plena' is a double-flowered form that is great for detail plantings where one might notice the double flowers.

Lonicera sempervirens TRUMPET HONEYSUCKLE

Trumpet honeysuckle is a semievergreen vine native to woodlands of the eastern United States, where it twines over small trees and shrubs. Unlike other *Lonicera* species, this one is not aggressive and provides a refined appearance. It possesses the rare quality in vines of being able to provide a softening visual effect without becoming oppressive and overbearing. In spring, it lights up with show-stopping bright cardinal-red flowers, with sporadic flowering into summer and fall. Several cultivars exist, providing a range of colors from scarlet to coral red and pure yellow. It is a twining vine and can be used on fences, lamp posts, and porch columns, trained into small trees, spilled over walls, or anywhere the lines need to be blurred a bit by use of a vine. The flowers attract hummingbirds.

ZONES & ORIGIN 4a–9b. Native from Massachusetts to Florida and Texas.

SIZE & GROWTH RATE 15'–20' slow growing for several years, then becoming fast growing.

TEXTURE Medium.

FOLIAGE Simple opposite bluish-green oval to oblong leaves are 1½"–3" long and have entire margins with short petioles. Upper leaf pairs are sessile and produce terminal flower clusters. Young purple-red stems turn gray with maturity.

FLOWERS & FRUIT Showy terminal clusters of bright red tubular flowers that are 2" long with yellow centers bloom in midspring (early to mid-April in Athens). Showy ¼" orange to red berries are produced in late summer.

LIGHT & SOIL Full sun to moderate shade, with reduced flowering in shade. It is not particular about the soil, provided it is well drained.

MAINTENANCE For use on fences where the objective is to hide most of the fencing, new shoots need to be woven horizontally through the fencing every few weeks. Otherwise, the vine will go to the top of the fence. Very low maintenance, with perhaps only an occasional trim needed.

INSTALLATION Space 8' or more on center for fences and trellises. Needs something on which to twine.

NOTES & CULTIVARS Sadly, not fragrant like the Asian species. Deer eat young shoots.
'Magnifica' provides bright red flowers.
'Sulphurea' has yellow flowers.
'Superba' produces bright scarlet flowers.

top Tubular flowers.
middle A yellow form adorning the lamppost at Chanticleer Garden.

left Hiding the tennis courts.
right Twining the stair rail at the Founders Memorial Garden at UGA.

Smilax smallii JACKSON VINE

Jackson vine is one of the best-kept secrets in the South. In the natural environment, it is found in woods and woodland edges, as well as along fencerows and roadsides, lofting itself into nearby trees or other vegetation. Its identity is unfortunately often obscured and marred by other *Smilax* species, which are known collectively as catbriers for their vicious thorns and unruly growth. Jackson vine is much more refined, as it is nearly thornless with smaller leaves. The upper portions of the vine are loose and pliable, making it very easy to work. On the lovely streets of the Twickenham Historic District in Huntsville, Alabama, it can be found swagged along porch balustrades, around columns, over doorways and windows, or along fences of nearly every house. It has historically been a favorite in the South for holiday and wedding decorations because the foliage lasts a long time indoors. The tubers and new spring growth are edible. Plants require several years to fully reestablish after division; thus, it is seldom offered for sale, but people are usually glad to share.

ZONES & ORIGIN 7b–9b. Native to the southeastern Piedmont and Coastal Plain.

SIZE & GROWTH RATE 25', slow growing initially, becoming vigorous once established.

TEXTURE Fine.

FOLIAGE Simple alternately arranged glossy dark green ovate to lanceolate leaves are 2"–4" long with entire margins and occur on branches off the main stem. It climbs by coiled tendrils, which are present at the base of some leaf nodes. Mature stems develop stout thorns near the ground.

FLOWERS & FRUIT Insignificant yellow-green flowers. Small berries turn red in summer and black by early fall on female plants and are very popular with birds in winter.

LIGHT & SOIL Full sun to full shade with well-drained soils. Very drought tolerant.

MAINTENANCE Needs only a little help getting started around a wire or vertical trellis. New growth is produced from April through summer. Prune older growth in late winter or early spring before new growth emerges.

INSTALLATION One vine will easily extend 25' once mature.

NOTES & CULTIVARS
None available.

top to bottom

In the conservatory at Longwood.

Porch curtains in Savannah, Ga.

Swags in Knoxville, Tenn.

Trachelospermum asiaticum ASIAN JASMINE

Asian jasmine is a twining vine typically used as a ground cover beneath the canopy of live oaks and sabal palms in cities like New Orleans and Charleston. It ranks among the most aggressive of ground cover vines. If an impenetrable mat is desired, this vine will deliver. Use it in situations where the edges can be easily maintained, such as a plaza or other context where hard or mown edges will keep the vine in bounds. In the right spot, it provides a fine-textured sparkling dark evergreen ground cover that outcompetes weeds and unwanted plants. It can also be used to climb fences and trellises with its twining stems.

ZONES & ORIGIN 7b–10b. Native to China.

SIZE & GROWTH RATE 20', fast growing.

TEXTURE Fine.

FOLIAGE Glossy dark green simple leaves are oppositely arranged, 1½" long, ovate to elliptic in shape, with entire margins. Foliage in winter sun develops a reddish tint. Thin wiry light brown stems have milky sap when cut.

FLOWERS & FRUIT As a ground cover, it doesn't bloom. When allowed to climb, it produces fragrant creamy-white star-shaped flowers in late spring and insignificant bean-like capsules.

LIGHT & SOIL Although it tolerates full sun to full shade, as a ground cover it prefers some shade to restrict grasses and other invasives until it becomes established. A loose and moist but well-drained soil is ideal. It tolerates most soils, provided there is good drainage, and it is drought and salt tolerant.

MAINTENANCE To create a dense ground cover, use it where edges can be maintained through trimming or mowing. When planted with other types of vegetation, Asian jasmine dominates, sprawling over adjacent shrubs and small trees without periodic pruning.

INSTALLATION For use as a ground cover, plant 24" on center for coverage within two years. For use as a climbing vine, space 8'–10' apart.

NOTES & CULTIVARS
Several variegated forms are available but may not be as winter-hardy or aggressive.
'Goshiki Kiri' has leaves with pink-and-white variegation.
'Minima' has smaller and more narrow leaves.
'Ogon' has golden leaves.
'Ougon-Nishiki' has orange, red, and yellow leaf variegation.
'Tricolor' has creamy-white leaf margins.

top left Uniform ground cover under river birches at this residence in Augusta, Ga.

top right In the Quad at Louisiana State University.

middle Under live oaks on streets in Savannah, Ga.

bottom Dense foliage.

left May bloom on an arbor in Columbus, Ga.
right top Used as a ground cover.
right bottom Winter color in the sun.

Star-shaped flowers with a heavenly fragrance.

Trachelospermum jasminoides CONFEDERATE JASMINE

Confederate jasmine is a much-loved and well-used vine across the Southeast and other temperate regions. It combines two invaluable traits for the designer: evergreen foliage and highly fragrant spring flowers. It is an easy vine to grow and tolerates a wide range of light and soil conditions, as well as salt spray. As a vigorous twining vine, it can be used on fences, trellises, arbors, and pergolas, above doorways, around lampposts, or over walls. The white flowers are produced in April and May in Athens and provide a heavy sweet fragrance that easily fills a courtyard and wafts a considerable distance. While it never gets as dense as Asian jasmine, it can also serve as a loose ground cover. Some designers mix a few in with an Asian jasmine ground cover to provide fragrance.

ZONES & ORIGIN 7b–10b. Native to China and Japan.

SIZE & GROWTH RATE 20' fast growing.

TEXTURE Medium.

FOLIAGE Simple opposite ovate to elliptic glossy and thick dark green leaves are 2"–4" long with entire margins. Foliage turns reddish in winter sun. Light brown stems are thin and wiry.

FLOWERS & FRUIT Showy and profusely fragrant white ¾"–1" star-shaped flowers with twisted petals hang in axillary clusters for an extended period in late spring (late April through May in Athens). Slender seed pods are hardly noticeable.

LIGHT & SOIL Provide full sun to moderate shade. A loose and moist but well-drained soil is ideal, although it tolerates most soils, provided there is good drainage. Very drought and salt tolerant.

MAINTENANCE Flowers mostly on old wood, so prune after flowering if necessary to keep the vine tidy. It produces a sticky milky sap when pruned that may be a skin irritant.

INSTALLATION One vine easily covers a small arbor. For a pergola or fencing, space 8'–10' on center. As a ground cover, space 24"–36".

NOTES & CULTIVARS
Deer don't bother it.
'Madison' is reportedly more cold-hardy, with pubescent undersides to the leaves.
'Variegatum' has creamy-white leaf variegation.

Campsis radicans TRUMPET CREEPER

Trumpet creeper is native across much of the eastern United States and occurs in a wide range of environments. It tolerates everything but poor drainage and heavy shade. This is an aggressive and unruly vine, but it is strikingly beautiful in bloom with its bright orange tubular flowers, which are produced in abundance throughout the summer and into the fall. Hummingbirds love the flowers. Trumpet creeper is often seen scrambling to the top of utility and fence poles and up the sides of outbuildings. It is primarily a clinging vine, but the new growth will also twine. Several noteworthy cultivars are available with yellow to red flowers that are worthy of use in designs for trellises, fences, and arbors.

left top A yellow cultivar at UGA.
left bottom In the Founders Memorial Garden at UGA.
right An espalier at Longwood Gardens.

ZONES & ORIGIN 4b–9b. Native from central Florida to the Great Lakes states.

SIZE & GROWTH RATE 20'–30' fast growing.

TEXTURE Medium.

FOLIAGE Opposite pinnately compound leaves have 9 to 11 bright green ovate leaflets with coarsely toothed margins. Mature plants develop light gray bark. It climbs primarily by aerial holdfast rootlets.

FLOWERS & FRUIT Showy clusters of 2"–3" orange-red tubular flowers are heaviest in late May and June in Athens, with sporadic flowers into September. While not fragrant, the flowers attract butterflies and hummingbirds. Cylindrical green pods 6"–8" long turn brown in fall and release flat seeds.

LIGHT & SOIL Full sun to light shade is ideal, but it will survive in moderate to full shade with reduced flowering. It tolerates a wide range of soils, from dry to moist, and is salt tolerant.

MAINTENANCE This vine should be used where an aggressive and unruly vine will be acceptable; otherwise, frequent pruning will be necessary to keep it in bounds. Since it blooms on new growth, it can be pruned in late winter without affecting the flowering. Summer pruning may encourage additional flowers.

INSTALLATION Space 12' or more on center for fences, pergolas, and walls.

NOTES & CULTIVARS
'Balboa Sunset' flowers are pure red.
'Flava' has orange-yellow flowers.
'Madame Galen' produces bright orange to scarlet flowers.
'Stromboli' produces blood-red flowers.

Tubular flowers.

Clematis × jackmanii JACKMAN CLEMATIS

This vine is often seen growing over mailboxes. However, it is useful in many situations where a fairly light and manageable vine will add interest, such as spilling over the top of a wall, wrapping a porch column or lamp pole, or growing up the naked canes of a larger shrub or climbing rose. Extremely large showy flowers bloom in profusion from late spring to early summer, with some repeat blooming in autumn. With hundreds of named hybrids available locally and from specialty clematis growers, you can easily outplant your friends. This account lists a few "best of the best" hybrids, but this is merely the tip of the iceberg.

top Showy flowers.

bottom A veritable dollhouse and garden, with clematis climbing the downspout, in Seaside, Ore.

ZONES & ORIGIN 4a–9a. Crosses from Asian species.

SIZE & GROWTH RATE 8'–20' depending on cultivar, medium fast growing.

TEXTURE Medium.

FOLIAGE Opposite compound leaves with three to five coarsely toothed oval to lanceolate leaflets 1"–4" long. Leaf stalks twine like tendrils over fences and railings to climb.

FLOWERS & FRUIT Large showy flat star-shaped flowers with four large dark purple sepals with true flowers held in the center. Sepals on cultivars may be single or bicolored in a range of colors from burgundy and pink to white, blue, and purple, with some lightly fragrant.

LIGHT & SOIL Full morning sun to light shade. Needs moist but well-drained organic-rich soil with mulch to keep roots cool and moist. Warm top and cool bottom is the rule for clematis.

MAINTENANCE This is a manageable vine that does not get out of control. Careful attention to bloom time is necessary for proper pruning. Prune spring bloomers immediately after flowering. Summer bloomers can be pruned from fall or to early spring.

INSTALLATION Space 8' or more for fences and trellises.

NOTES & CULTIVARS
Clematis crispa, swamp leather flower, is native to floodplains of the Southeast, with nodding bell-shaped lavender flowers.

C. glaucophylla, whiteleaf leather flower, is native to the Southeast, with nodding bell-shaped flowers that are deep pink on the outside with yellow inside.

C. × jackmanii 'Alba' has large white flowers.

C. × jackmanii 'Rubra' has large deep red flowers.

top A rustic trellis at Chanticleer Garden.

bottom This mannerly vine easily adorns detail areas.

Hydrangea anomala petiolaris CLIMBING HYDRANGEA

There are several design-worthy climbing hydrangeas; this one possesses some of the greatest ornamental qualities, such as thick woody stems with handsome exfoliating bark, attractive foliage, and white late spring to early summer flowers. In winter, the textural effects of the peeling bark along the woody stems are equally if not more interesting than the summer foliage and flowers. This is a clinging vine that grows slowly. It is best used only on vertical surfaces and not upon overhead arbors, as it becomes too thick, shrub-like, and floppy.

ZONES & ORIGIN 5a–8b. Native to China, Korea, and Japan.

SIZE & GROWTH RATE 40'–60' slow growing when young, medium with maturity.

TEXTURE Medium.

FOLIAGE Simple opposite lustrous dark green leaves 2"–4" long are broadly ovate with acuminate tips, serrate margins, and cordate to rounded bases. They are pale beneath, with tufts of hair along vein axils. Late autumn yellow fall foliage is not always dependable. Young stems are reddish brown, with rootlike holdfasts at the internodes, while mature bark has an attractive exfoliating habit.

FLOWERS & FRUIT Lovely white lightly fragrant corymbs 6"–10" in diameter appear in late May to early June. Subtle inner fertile flowers are surrounded by showy outer sepals like those of other lacecap hydrangeas. Insignificant capsules.

LIGHT & SOIL Like it is for other hydrangeas, light shade is ideal. Grows in full sun to moderate shade, but with reduced flowering with increased shade. It requires an organic-rich, cool, and moist but well-drained soil.

MAINTENANCE Extremely low maintenance, with perhaps only an occasional trim needed.

INSTALLATION Space 8' or more on center for walls.

NOTES & CULTIVARS
Mature plants can be quite heavy, so make sure to provide adequate support. Deer occasionally browse young foliage and stems.
'Miranda' has foliage with light yellow to creamy-white margins.

top left On the house at Chanticleer Garden.

top right Climbing the old gatehouse at the Portland Rose Garden.

middle In flower at the J. C. Raulston Arboretum in Raleigh, N.C.

bottom Foliage and flowers.

A curtain in Rome, Italy. Where else?

Parthenocissus quinquefolia VIRGINIA CREEPER

Virginia creeper is a common native of the eastern United States, occurring across a wide range of environments and beginning as a ground cover until it finds a vertical surface to climb. It is often mistaken for poison ivy but can be differentiated by having five leaflets rather than the three leaflets of poison ivy. Remember: leaves of five, stay alive; leaves of three, leave it be. It is a fast grower, with the ability to cling to any surface, and can often be seen covering the sides of buildings or climbing high into the canopy of a tree with its beautiful scarlet-red fall foliage. The foliage never becomes extremely dense, making it useful as a light wall covering or a loose open ground cover.

top to bottom

Foliage and fruit.

Superb fall color.

Softening a low wall.

ZONES & ORIGIN 3b–10b. Native across eastern North America.

SIZE & GROWTH RATE 50'–80' fast growing.

TEXTURE Coarse.

FOLIAGE Alternate palmately compound leaves with five elliptic leaflets to 6" long are coarsely toothed above the middle, dark green above, but paler beneath. New foliage and stems are reddish, while fall foliage is a beautiful burgundy to red. Stems have branched tendrils with adhesive tips, allowing it to climb, as well as prominent lenticels.

FLOWERS & FRUIT Insignificant greenish midspring flowers. Like other vines, it only flowers when it climbs. Small dark blue round berries are held in clusters and are quite noticeable and attractive in fall with the red foliage. While the fruits are toxic to humans, they are very popular with birds and small mammals.

LIGHT & SOIL Virginia creeper grows in full sun to full shade and well-drained to moist soils. It is extremely tolerant of drought and salt spray.

MAINTENANCE An aggressive vine needing a large surface to cover or woodland to roam. It requires constant pruning if used where space is limited, even though it does not become dense.

INSTALLATION Space perhaps 6' or more on center for wall coverage. As a ground cover, space on 24" centers, and mulch heavily to prevent weeds.

NOTES & CULTIVARS Deer don't bother the foliage.

Parthenocissus tricuspidata BOSTON IVY

Boston ivy is an aggressive clinging vine capable of covering large building facades perhaps as high as 75'. This marvelous effect is memorably displayed on the outfield wall at Wrigley Field in Chicago, on the Royal Empress Hotel in Victoria, British Columbia, and on many other urban buildings and walls around the United States and abroad. It can also be used on smaller residential-scale walls, where it will need to be trimmed to keep it in bounds. The handsome three-lobed dark green leaves turn a magnificent orange to burgundy red in autumn. In winter, the textural effects of the naked vines add interest to otherwise drab surfaces. More buildings should be covered in vines.

ZONES & ORIGIN   4b–8b. Native to China and Japan.

SIZE & GROWTH RATE   30'–50' fast growing.

TEXTURE   Medium coarse.

FOLIAGE   Glossy dark green alternate leaves are broadly ovate to obovate in shape, with three lobes and sharply serrate margins. Some leaves are trifoliate, particularly on younger growth. Fall foliage is a brilliant orange to red. Like Virginia creeper, Boston ivy has branched tendrils with adhesive tips that allow it to climb vertical surfaces.

FLOWERS & FRUIT   Insignificant 3"–5" clusters of greenish-white flowers in spring. Clusters of small but showy bluish-purple berries 2"–6" mature in late summer and fall and are eaten by birds.

LIGHT & SOIL   Full sun to moderate shade, with reduced fruiting in shade, and tolerates dry to slightly moist soils. Plants in zones 7 and 8 may need supplemental summer water to retain foliage into autumn.

MAINTENANCE   High maintenance where space is limited. Care should be taken to avoid allowing Virginia creeper or Boston ivy to climb onto window frames or roof overhangs.

INSTALLATION   Space perhaps 8' or more on center for covering a wall.

NOTES & CULTIVARS
'Lowii' has smaller leaves and is less aggressive, reminiscent of *Ficus pumila*.
'Veitchii' has large shiny leaves.
Parthenocissus henryana is hardy from 6a to 8b and has leaflets with silvery-white veins above. It performs best in light shade.

top to bottom

Three-lobed leaves.

Hotel Sylvia, Vancouver, B.C.

The Royal Empress Hotel, Victoria, B.C.

In Occidental Square in Seattle, Wash.

'Climbing Pinky' in the Trial Garden at UGA.

top White multiflora grown as a large loose shrub on Signal Mountain, Tenn.

bottom Formidable and friendly 'Lady Banks' on the pergola at the Atlanta Botanical Garden.

Rosa spp. CLIMBING ROSES

Is a fine garden complete without a well-placed climbing rose? We think not. Roses ranging from small shrubs to giant ramblers have graced gardens around the world for centuries. *Rosa* is an enormous genus and impossible to cover here, but many great books on roses exist. This account serves as a reminder and a placeholder for today's designer to consider some of the great tried-and-true climbing roses that are still available from the nursery industry and should be used more often. Climbing roses may be petite and manageable or aggressive and capable of devouring small buildings; therefore, great care must be given to placement and selection. As mentioned in the opening paragraphs of this section, roses are technically shrubs, but the "climbers" have been selected for their elongated canes and growth habit for training over doorways, on trellises, over the top of small sheds, and along walls and fences. The roses below are all hardy at least to zone 7. None are native, and all prefer full sun and an organic-rich well-drained soil. Texture is typically medium, with alternate compound leaves and formidable thorns along the canes. Training is typically accomplished by tying the canes with wire or twine to trellises and other structures. The list below is painfully short but a good start for the beginner and a safe bet for the reluctant designer. A visit to the website for the Antique Rose Emporium is a must.

LARGE AGGRESSIVE CLIMBERS
more than 15'

'Cecile Brunner' has light pink and double flowers, repeats, to zone 6.
'Cherokee' has single white flowers, spring only, fragrant, to zone 7 (invasive in the Southeast).
'Lady Banks' has single or double yellow flowers, spring only, to zone 7.
'Madame Alfred Carriere' has double light pink flowers, highly fragrant, repeats, to zone 6.
'Mermaid' has single yellow flowers, repeats, fragrant, attractive foliage, to zone 7.
'Old Blush' has pink and double flowers, repeats, fragrant, to zone 7.

'New Dawn' graces the patio door of this home in Columbus, Ga.

A mystery climber ('Old Blush' maybe?) on the Oregon Coast.

MEDIUM CLIMBERS
10–15'

'American Beauty' has cerise-pink and double flowers, spring only, fragrant, to zone 5.

'Climbing New Dawn' has light pink and double flowers, repeats, fragrant, handsome foliage, to zone 5.

'Crepuscule' has apricot-yellow and double flowers, repeats, fragrant, to zone 7.

'Don Juan' has double red flowers, repeats, fragrant, to zone 6.

'Souvenir de la Malmaison' has light pink to almost white and double flowers, repeats, to zone 6.

SMALL CLIMBERS
less than 10'

'Allister Stella Gray' has pale yellow and double flowers, repeats, fragrant, to zone 7.

'Altissimo' has single red flowers, repeats, fragrant, showy hips, to zone 5.

'Constance Spry' has pink and very double flowers, spring only, to zone 5.

'Iceberg' has double white flowers, repeats, fragrant, to zone 5.

'Zephirine Drouhin' has deep cerise-pink and double flowers, repeats, fragrant, to zone 6.

left to right

Fall color.

Climbing a pine.

Winter stems—very toxic and easily missed.

Leaves of three.

Toxicodendron radicans POISON IVY

Poison ivy is included here for the purposes of identification, because it causes an allergic reaction if touched by most humans. In spite of its adverse effects, poison ivy is quite attractive in fall as it turns brilliant yellowish orange to red. It can be seen across much of the United States as a woodland understory ground cover until it finds a vertical surface and becomes a clinging vine climbing high into the canopies of trees. Birds love the seed—hence its continual emergence in your garden.

ZONES & ORIGIN 3b–10b. Native across eastern North America.

SIZE & GROWTH RATE 60'–80' fast growing.

TEXTURE Coarse.

FLOWERS & FRUIT Trifoliate alternate leaves have coarsely toothed margins and rich orange-red fall color. Stems have rusty-brown aerial rootlets, eventually becoming quite woody, with horizontal branches extending out from the host tree. Mature climbers produce panicles of small creamy-colored berry-like drupes in autumn.

LIGHT & SOIL Grows in full sun to full shade and well-drained to slightly moist soils.

MAINTENANCE Control by selectively spraying individual plants in locations where human contact must be prevented.

NOTES & CULTIVARS
Avoid touching or burning any part of this vine.

Wisteria frutescens AMERICAN WISTERIA

American wisteria is an excellent alternative to the unruly, unkempt, and highly invasive Asian wisterias for use on arbors and trellises. It is a deciduous, fast-growing, and twining vine that is not overwhelming, like the Asian species. Admittedly, the flower effect is not as impressive, but it is still quite nice when the lightly fragrant light purple flower racemes open in late spring, with sporadic flowering continuing throughout summer. The foliage texture is not as coarse as that of the Asian species and is perhaps easier to combine with other plants in the landscape. It occurs on floodplains and moist areas adjacent to waterways from Virginia to Florida and Texas.

ZONES & ORIGIN 5b–9a. Native to the southeastern Coastal Plain.

SIZE & GROWTH RATE 20'–30' fast growing.

TEXTURE Medium.

FOLIAGE Pinnately compound alternate leaves have 9 to 15 leaflets, each bright green above, 1½"–3" long to 1½" wide, glabrous and bright green above, slightly pubescent below, and elliptic ovate or oblong lanceolate in shape.

FLOWERS & FRUIT Showy racemes 4"–6" long of lightly fragrant light purple flowers occur on new growth after the foliage emerges (late April through May in Athens), with sporadic flowering into the summer. Flattened seed pods 4"–5" long turn dark brown in fall.

LIGHT & SOIL Provide full sun to light shade with a moist but well-drained to consistently moist and slightly acidic soil, like its native habitat. Quite drought tolerant after establishment.

MAINTENANCE Very low maintenance, but it still requires an occasional pruning to avoid overwhelming smaller structures.

INSTALLATION Space perhaps 12' or more on center for fences, trellises, and overhead structures.

NOTES & CULTIVARS
'Amethyst Falls' has lavender-blue flowers.
'Magnifica' has lilac flowers with a yellow blotch on the standard.
'Nivea' is a white-flowered cultivar.
American wisteria is a food source for several native butterfly and moth species. Deer should not cause substantial damage to it.

Swags on the fence in the Founders Memorial Garden, UGA.

top Grape cluster–like flowers.
bottom Covering the arbor in the Trial Gardens at UGA.

INTERIOR PLANTS

'Key Largo', Chinese evergreen, and 'Limelight' dracaenas at Longwood Gardens Conservatory.

First, a few thoughts on the interior plants discussed in this section. We selected these particular plants because they are among the most commonly available and sturdiest of interior foliage plants. All are capable of providing an attractive appearance while tolerating neglect and relatively low interior light levels.

Speaking of light levels, all of the plants in this section would be considered shade tolerant in their native habitats. Even those plants that become large trees are able to tolerate a great deal of shade in their natural environments, which is why they serve well as interior plants. Outdoor locations that are in shade all day still have far higher light levels than even the brightest indoor windows can provide.

None of these plants are native to the United States, which is why we've not addressed their origins. Most are native to tropical forests or rainforests of Central and South America or Southeast Asia. Even the most cold-hardy of these plants cannot withstand winters above zone 8b, with the majority being hardy only in zone 10.

The ultimate size of these plants depends upon the size of the container in which they are grown. We have attempted to provide sizes based upon what could reasonably be expected for most interior situations with large containers. Some of the trees listed in this section reach 200' or more in height in nature. But when their root systems are constrained in pots, they rarely reach over 20' in size indoors.

Because they are so far removed from their native environments, interior plants tend to grow slowly, particularly during the winter months, when light and humidity levels are particularly low. As a result, they don't need as much water during the winter. They really don't need any fertilization during winter months and very little fertilization if they remain indoors year-round. Most of the problems interior plants have can be traced to overwatering and excessive fertilization. Speaking of fertilizers, a slow-release formulation with a balanced ratio such as 14-14-14 is always a safe bet for interior foliage plants.

Individual containers are the most common way interior plants are displayed, and they look fine in those situations. Individual containers give you the flexibility to move the plants around to optimize light levels at different times of the year. However, for larger interior planting opportunities like conservatories, hotel lobbies, and shopping malls, the same rules of good composition apply to these plants as the ones that are used for any exterior composition. A good designer must consider the individual light and moisture requirements of each plant. Every attempt must be made to match plants with similar moisture needs and to locate the plants in the composition to accommodate their light requirements.

BOTANICAL NAME	COMMON NAME	TEXTURE	FORM	SOILS	INTERIOR LIGHT REQUIREMENTS
Aglaonema spp.	Chinese evergreen	Medium coarse	Broadly oval to mounded	Well drained	Moderate to low
Araucaria heterophylla	Norfolk Island pine	Fine	Conical to oval	Moist but well drained	High
Asparagus densiflorus 'Sprengeri'	Sprenger's asparagus fern	Fine	Rounded, arching	Moist but well drained	High
Chlorophytum comosum	Airplane plant, spider plant	Fine	Broadly oval to mounded	Well drained	Moderate to low
Dieffenbachia spp.	Dumbcane	Coarse	Upright oval	Moist but well drained	Moderate
Dracaena fragrans	Dracaena	Medium coarse	Upright oval	Well drained	Moderate to low
Dracaena marginata	Red-margined dracaena	Fine	Oval to upright oval	Well drained	Moderate to low
Epipremnum aureum	Devil's ivy, pothos	Medium	Trailing	Moist but well drained	Moderate to low
Ficus benjamina	Weeping fig	Medium fine	Broadly oval	Moist but well drained	High to moderate
Ficus elastica	Rubber plant	Coarse	Oval to upright oval	Moist but well drained	High to low
Pachira aquatica	Money tree	Coarse	Broadly oval	Moist to moist but well drained	High to moderate
Philodendron bipinnatifidum	Split-leaf philodendron, tree philodendron	Coarse	Mounded	Moist but well drained	Moderate to high
Philodendron hederaceum	Heartleaf philodendron	Medium	Trailing	Moist but well drained	Moderate to low
Rhapis excelsa	Lady palm	Medium coarse	Oval	Moist but well drained	Moderate to low
Sansevieria trifasciata	Snake plant, mother-in-law's tongue	Coarse	Upright oval	Well drained	Moderate to low
Schefflera actinophylla	Schefflera, umbrella tree	Coarse	Oval to broadly oval	Moist but well drained	High to moderate
Schefflera arboricola	Dwarf schefflera	Medium	Broadly oval	Moist but well drained	Moderate
Spathiphyllum spp.	Peace lily	Medium coarse	Broadly oval to rounded	Moist	Moderate to low

Aglaonema spp. CHINESE EVERGREEN

Chinese evergreen is a clump-forming plant with variegated foliage that has been a popular interior plant for many years because it tolerates lower light and moisture levels. Combine it in a container with a taller plant such as dracaena or a low-spreading plant such as heartleaf philodendron, or use it for borders in larger compositions. Space it 12"–18" apart for massing. Chinese evergreen sap can cause irritation on the skin and in the mouth if ingested.

SIZE & GROWTH RATE 12"–30" tall and wide, slow growing.

TEXTURE & FORM Medium coarse texture and broadly oval to mounded form.

FOLIAGE Ovate to lanceolate variegated leaves 6"–12" long have silver or creamy-yellow markings.

LIGHT & SOIL Medium to low light and moist but well-drained soil.

MAINTENANCE Allow the soil to dry slightly between watering. Fertilize every other year with a slow-release fertilizer. Maintain between 65°F and 85°F and away from air vents, and remove any flowers and older foliage to maintain appearance.

NOTES & CULTIVARS
'Emerald Bay' has yellow foliage with green margins.
'Emerald Beauty' has green leaves with silver veins.
'Golden Bay' has yellow foliage with green margins.
'Silver Queen' has mostly silver foliage with green veins.

top 'Silver Bay' Chinese evergreen.

bottom 'Gemini' Chinese evergreens with holly leaf fern and dracaenas at Longwood Gardens.

Araucaria heterophylla NORFOLK ISLAND PINE

In their native habitat of Australia, Norfolk Island pines are massive trees, reaching as tall as 200'. As an indoor plant, however, its ultimate size is greatly determined by the container in which it is grown. While it may reach 40' in a conservatory, it rarely grows over 10'–15' in most interior situations. It is often used by itself as a specimen plant, but consider taking advantage of its upright form and fine texture if space is available by combining it with Chinese evergreen, split-leaf philodendron, or dwarf schefflera.

SIZE & GROWTH RATE 4'–12' tall, 3'–8' wide, slow growing.

TEXTURE & FORM Fine texture and conical form.

FOLIAGE Short needle-like leaves are spirally arranged around the stems. The main branches are horizontal, with drooping secondary branches.

LIGHT & SOIL Requires high interior light levels and moist but well-drained soil.

MAINTENANCE Rotate the plant every few weeks to keep it symmetrical, and repot it every two to three years. Keep the soil moist but not wet, and apply a slow-release fertilizer every year. Maintain high humidity levels by avoiding air vents and misting the foliage regularly in winter.

NOTES & CULTIVARS
No cultivars listed.

Norfolk Island pine at Magnolia Plantation and Gardens Conservatory.

Sprenger's asparagus fern.

Asparagus densiflorus 'Sprengeri'
SPRENGER'S ASPARAGUS FERN

Sprenger's asparagus fern is admired for its fine texture and cascading habit. Though hardy to zone 8b, it may be killed to the ground in winters and is invasive in central and southern Florida. It is popular in conservatories as a ground cover, in containers combined with a more upright plant such as schefflera, or in hanging baskets to take advantage of its arching habit. Insignificant white flowers produce attractive but toxic small red berries.

SIZE & GROWTH RATE 2'–3' tall, 2'–4' wide, fast growing.

TEXTURE & FORM Fine texture and mounded form.

FOLIAGE Bright green flattened needle-like branchlets are held on woody spiny stems that can be painful when handled.

LIGHT & SOIL Moderate to high light with moist but well-drained soil.

MAINTENANCE Allow the soil to dry slightly between watering. It performs best with higher humidity levels than found in most homes and benefits from cutting back the stems, applying a slow-release fertilizer, and placing it outdoors during warmer months.

NOTES & CULTIVARS
'Myersii' reaches 30", with plumelike foliage held on upright stems, resembling a bottlebrush.
Fern asparagus, *Asparagus setaceus*, has extremely fine-textured fanlike foliage and a vine-like habit.

Meyer's asparagus fern 'Myersii'.

Chlorophytum comosum
SPIDER PLANT · AIRPLANE PLANT

Spider plants are one of the least expensive and easiest interior plants for most people to grow. They tolerate low to high light levels and slightly dry soils, and they are very forgiving if one forgets to water them for several weeks. Spider plants are often used in hanging baskets to take advantage of their wiry draping stolons with attached new plantlets. Also consider them for borders or as ground covers in larger compositions. While the species has green foliage, variegated cultivars are often more common.

SIZE & GROWTH RATE 10"–15" tall, 24" wide, fast growing.

TEXTURE & FORM Fine texture and broadly oval to mounded form.

FOLIAGE Green grasslike narrowly lanceolate leaves form an arching clump.

LIGHT & SOIL Moderate light is ideal, but they tolerate low to high light with well-drained soils.

MAINTENANCE Water thoroughly every seven to ten days and allow the excess to drain away. Stolons develop when plants become root-bound under moderately high light levels and fertilization every two to three months.

NOTES & CULTIVARS Variegated cultivars require higher light levels.
'Variegatum' has foliage with green midribs and creamy-white margins.
'Vittatum' has creamy-white midribs with green margins.

top Variegated spider plant.
bottom Green spider plant.

Dieffenbachia spp. DUMBCANE

A number of hybrid dumbcane cultivars are available commercially, mostly with variegated foliage. All are coarse textured, produce multiple stems, and are mostly upright in habit. They grow well in moderate to high light levels but survive surprisingly well under low light conditions, although they eventually become thin and leggy in heavy shade. Often used as florist plants, they look good individually or when combined with finer-textured plants. Chewing the foliage leads to numbness and swelling of the mouth and throat.

SIZE & GROWTH RATE 2'–8' tall, 1'–3' wide, medium growing.

TEXTURE & FORM Coarse texture and upright oval form.

FOLIAGE Large lustrous dark green ovate leaves have depressed veins and creamy-white to yellow variegation, depending upon the cultivar.

LIGHT & SOIL Moderate light with moist but well-drained soil.

MAINTENANCE Water when the soil begins to dry out, and maintain air temperatures above 60°F. Clean the large dust-covered leaves monthly indoors. Fertilize yearly if kept indoors or every two to three months in protected outdoor areas.

NOTES & CULTIVARS
'Camille' and 'Marianne' have yellow leaves with green margins.
'Tropic Snow' has dark green leaves with creamy white along the veins.

top 'Camilla' dumbcanes.
bottom 'Camouflage' dumbcanes.

Dracaena fragrans DRACAENA

Dracaenas tolerate low light levels and are drought resistant, making them ideal for people who forget to regularly water or go on two-week vacations. Their upright form makes them ideal for tucking into corners. Variegated cultivars brighten compositions and dark spaces.

Dracaena 'Massangeana'.

SIZE & GROWTH RATE 4'–10' tall, 2'–4' wide, slow growing.

TEXTURE & FORM Medium to medium coarse texture and upright oval form.

FOLIAGE Spirally arranged lanceolate leaves 8"–24" long, with entire margins.

LIGHT & SOIL Moderate light and well-drained soil.

MAINTENANCE Allow the soil to dry slightly between watering. They are sensitive to chlorine and fluoride, so consider using rainwater or distilled water. Plants kept indoors only need fertilization every two to three years. Regular cleaning of dust from leaves keeps them looking their best.

NOTES & CULTIVARS
Dracaena fragrans cultivars include the following:

'Massangeana', corn stalk plant, has leaves with broad yellow bands along the midrib.
'Janet Craig' has lustrous dark green leaves.
'Janet Craig Compacta' reaches 2'–3' tall, with dark green leaves.
Deremensis Group cultivars have variegated leaves with wavy margins.
'Lemon Lime' and 'Lemon Surprise' foliage has dark green centers with chartreuse margins.
'Limelight' has chartreuse-green foliage.
'Warneckii' has green foliage with creamy-white margins.

top Dracaenas 'Lemon Surprise' and 'Ribbon Plant' with 'Janet Craig' behind.
bottom 'Lemon Lime' and 'Limelight' dracaenas at Longwood Gardens Conservatory.

Dracaena marginata RED-MARGINED DRACAENA

Red-margined dracaena is perhaps the most striking of the commonly available dracaenas. Its thin leaves provide a fine texture that appears like a small explosion on top of tall, narrow, and sometimes contorted stems. Consider placing it near an entry wall and lighting it to cast a silhouette on the wall. Like the other dracaenas, it tolerates neglect and low light well but looks best and maintains its foliage color better with moderately high interior light. It is usually sold multitrunked, and the stems can be pruned back to staggered heights to create a layered effect.

SIZE & GROWTH RATE 4'–10' tall, 2'–4' wide, slow growing.

TEXTURE & FORM Fine texture and upright oval form.

FOLIAGE Simple narrowly lanceolate leaves with red margins are spirally arranged, forming a rosette near the top of the thin stems.

LIGHT & SOIL Low to medium high light levels with well-drained soil.

MAINTENANCE Allow the soil to dry between watering, and dust the foliage periodically.

NOTES & CULTIVARS
'Tricolor' has pinkish-red margins with green-and-white stripes.
Lucky bamboo, *Dracaena sanderiana*, is often grown in water in a glass container filled with decorative gravel and is used as a tabletop plant.

top Red-margined dracaena at Magnolia Plantation and Gardens Conservatory.

bottom Red-margined dracaena at the State Botanical Garden of Georgia.

Epipremnum aureum DEVIL'S IVY, POTHOS

Like many vines, devil's ivy has both a juvenile form and an adult form that is only seen when it climbs. Though the juvenile form is most common, pothos can climb by means of aerial roots. It is commonly used in hanging baskets to take advantage of its trailing habit or as a ground cover combined with an upright plant such as dumbcane or schefflera in larger plantings. Space plants 24" apart. The sap reportedly irritates the skin and mouth if ingested. Pothos is invasive in south Florida.

SIZE & GROWTH RATE 4"–8" tall, 2'–10' wide, medium fast growing.

TEXTURE & FORM Medium texture and trailing form.

FOLIAGE Ovate-shaped juvenile foliage is 3"–5" long with entire margins and irregular yellow markings. Mature foliage is 12"–18" long with wavy or lobed margins.

LIGHT & SOIL Moderate light with moist but well-drained soil. Pothos tolerates low light but loses its leaf variegation.

MAINTENANCE Under moderately high light, water every few days, and fertilize every other month. It benefits from pruning the trailing stems to keep the center of the plant full.

NOTES & CULTIVARS
'Jade' has solid green leaves.
'Marble Queen' has silvery-white markings.

top Pothos or devil's ivy.

bottom Trailing pothos with creeping fig at Longwood Gardens.

Ficus benjamina WEEPING FIG

Weeping fig provides an attractive tree that can fill large spaces. Combine it with asparagus fern and split-leaf philodendron. Even use it as a live Christmas tree. Trees are notorious for dropping leaves due to sudden changes in light levels. They're just stressed, so be patient and give them lots of light, and in a few weeks they will look better. Acclimate trees to lower light levels by placing them under outdoor shade for several weeks before bringing them inside.

SIZE & GROWTH RATE 6'–12' tall, 4'–8' wide, medium fast growing.

TEXTURE & FORM Medium fine texture with pendulous branches and broadly oval form.

FOLIAGE Simple elliptic to ovate alternate leaves with entire margins.

LIGHT & SOIL Provide high light and moist but well-drained soils.

top Weeping fig and red-margined dracaena at the State Botanical Garden of Georgia.
bottom Weeping fig behind 'Camouflage' dumbcane at the UGA greenhouses.

MAINTENANCE Under ideal conditions, fertilize every other month. Plants that are looking bare can be heavily pruned to encourage new growth. Scale and aphids are frequent problems, especially on plants that go outside for summer. Treat with a systemic insecticide.

NOTES & CULTIVARS
'Exotica' and 'Monique' have dark green foliage, with 'Monique' being touted for its resistance to leaf drop.
'Starlight', 'Silver Cloud', and 'Variegata' have creamy-white variegated foliage.

Ficus elastica RUBBER PLANT

Most people's experience with the rubber plant is probably disappointing. While often promoted as tolerant of low light and dry soils, rubber plants actually perform much better with moderately bright light, high humidity, and consistently moist but well-drained soils. Use it as a specimen, and consider training it as an espalier on a wall. Take advantage of its coarse texture and upright habit by providing a base of dwarf scheffleras, Chinese evergreens, or heartleaf philodendrons in compositions. Like weeping fig, it drops its foliage under stress.

SIZE & GROWTH RATE 4'–12' tall, 2'–6' wide, medium growing.

TEXTURE & FORM Coarse texture and oval form.

FOLIAGE Leathery and waxy dark green simple leaves 12"–18" long are elliptic shaped.

LIGHT & SOIL Bright light with moist but well-drained soil is preferred. It tolerates moderate to low light and dry soil for short periods.

MAINTENANCE Under optimum conditions, fertilize several times per year. Dust the foliage monthly. Rejuvenate thin plants by pruning and providing ideal growing conditions.

NOTES & CULTIVARS
'Doescheri' has green-and-creamy-white variegated foliage.
'Robusta' provides a denser and more compact habit.
'Rubra' produces deep reddish-purple foliage in bright light.

top Rubber plant at Longwood Gardens.
bottom Rubber plant at Magnolia Plantation and Gardens.

Pachira aquatica Money Tree

A large wetland tree in its native tropical habitat, money tree has been promoted to bring good luck and fortune to the household of its owners. As a result, it has quickly become very popular in the interior plant industry. Most nurseries actually plant several trees in each container and braid their stems together to provide a bonsai-like effect. From a distance, money trees appear similar to scheffleras and could be utilized in a similar manner in compositions, but many people prefer to leave them by themselves to highlight their trunks.

SIZE & GROWTH RATE   2'–10' tall, 4'–6' wide, fast growing.

TEXTURE & FORM   Coarse texture and broadly oval form.

FOLIAGE   Palmately compound leaves with five to seven narrowly elliptic leaflets.

LIGHT & SOIL   Medium to high light with a moist to moist but well-drained soil.

MAINTENANCE   Dust the foliage regularly. Provide a slow-release fertilizer every three months or a liquid fertilizer every month under bright light conditions. Money trees don't like to stay wet, but they don't care to dry out either, so use a loose soil mixture that allows excess water to drain away.

NOTES & CULTIVARS   No cultivars listed.

Money tree at the UGA greenhouses.

Philodendron bipinnatifidum
SPLIT-LEAF PHILODENDRON · TREE PHILODENDRON

Tree philodendron, sometimes listed as *Philodendron selloum*, is a bold, coarse-textured, and broad-spreading plant that will catch your eye wherever it is used. Indoors it is often treated as a specimen or used as a midlevel plant in larger compositions with Chinese evergreens or dwarf scheffleras. Tree philodendron is cold-hardy from zone 8b southward, where it lends a tropical feel to courtyards, fountains, and pools and can reach 12'–15' in size.

SIZE & GROWTH RATE   3'–5' tall, 4'–8' wide, medium growing.

TEXTURE & FORM   Coarse texture and mounded form.

FOLIAGE   Simple leaves 18"–36" long are elliptic shaped, with 15–20 deeply divided lobes. With age, it develops a twisted trunk and aerial roots.

LIGHT & SOIL   Prefers moderate to bright light with moist but well-drained soils. It quickly suffers from drought, as well as from soils that stay too moist. Outdoor plants prefer moderate shade.

MAINTENANCE   Under optimal conditions, provide a slow-release fertilizer every three to four months. Under low light conditions indoors, fertilize annually.

NOTES & CULTIVARS
Philodendron xanadu looks similar to tree philodendron but has smaller foliage and a denser and more compact habit.

top Split-leaf philodendron at Callaway Gardens Conservatory.

bottom Split-leaf philodendron with lady palm behind.

Philodendron hederaceum HEARTLEAF PHILODENDRON

Heartleaf philodendron is one of the most common and versatile interior plants, since it thrives under moderate to low light and moisture levels. Similar to pothos, it can be used as a ground cover or in hanging containers to take advantage of its trailing habit. It also has the ability to climb other plants or structures with its stems. To use it as a ground cover, plant 12"–24" apart, and move the stems periodically to cover open areas. It is sometimes listed in references as *Philodendron scandens* or *P. oxycardium*.

SIZE & GROWTH RATE 4"–8" tall, 2'–10' wide, medium fast growing.

TEXTURE & FORM Medium texture with a trailing form.

FOLIAGE Simple lustrous dark green leaves 3"–6" long are cordate shaped. Leaves on mature foliage are up to 12" in length.

LIGHT & SOIL Low to moderate interior light levels with a moist but well-drained soil.

MAINTENANCE Stems of heartleaf philodendron don't develop secondary branches, so multiple stems are planted in containers. It prefers high humidity levels but can tolerate sporadic watering. If it is under moderate light, apply a slow-release fertilizer every three months. Under low light, fertilize no more than twice per year.

top Heartleaf philodendron.
bottom Trailing heartleaf philodendron at Athens Animal Medical Center.

NOTES & CULTIVARS
No cultivars listed.

Rhapis excelsa LADY PALM

Lady palm is a clump-forming palm valued for its toughness and ability to tolerate low light and low moisture conditions. With its graceful bamboo-like appearance, lady palm lends an Oriental feel to interior compositions and is often used as a bonsai specimen. It is more expensive than many interior plants due to its slower growth, but a 2010 study found lady palm to be among the most effective plants at removing volatile organic compounds from interior spaces.

SIZE & GROWTH RATE 4'–8' tall, 2'–5' wide, slow growing.

TEXTURE & FORM Medium coarse texture and oval form.

FOLIAGE Simple glossy dark green palmate leaves are deeply divided, with six to ten blunt-tipped lobes and stems with brown fibers.

LIGHT & SOIL Moderate light with a moist but well-drained soil is preferred, but it tolerates low light and infrequent watering.

MAINTENANCE Allow the soil to dry slightly between watering. Under low light conditions, fertilize once per year. With brighter light and regular watering, apply a slow-release fertilizer every three months. Remove old foliage as it begins to dull and discolor.

NOTES & CULTIVARS
Variegated cultivars, while rare, are available.

top Lady palm foliage.
bottom Form of three lady palms.

Sansevieria trifasciata
SNAKE PLANT · MOTHER-IN-LAW'S TONGUE

Interior plants don't come much tougher than the snake plant. For people with brown thumbs, this is your plant. Provided the soil is well drained, this plant grows merrily, if slowly, along. One of the few plants that can survive in low light and no water for months at a time, it is ideal for low-maintenance applications. While often used by itself, it is outstanding for border plantings, where its strong upright form provides contrast with everything else in the composition.

SIZE & GROWTH RATE   2'–3' tall, 8"–18" wide, slow growing.

TEXTURE & FORM   Coarse texture and upright oval form.

FOLIAGE   Lustrous leathery dark green lanceolate leaves twist as they arise from underground stems.

LIGHT & SOIL   Moderate light with well-drained soil.

MAINTENANCE   Although this plant tolerates low light and dry soil, best growth is achieved with moderate to bright light and monthly watering. Apply a slow-release fertilizer annually, and clean the foliage regularly.

NOTES & CULTIVARS   Most plants in nurseries have variegated foliage.

'Hahnii', bird's nest, forms a rosette of foliage 8"–12" tall.
'Laurentii' is the most common cultivar, with yellow bands along the leaf margins.
'Moonshine' has silvery-gray banding.

top Snake plant.

bottom Snake plant and peperomia at Longwood Gardens.

Schefflera actinophylla   SCHEFFLERA · UMBRELLA TREE

Scheffleras are coarse-textured multitrunked trees that provide an exotic appearance. While valued for their ease of growth, scheffleras may become too large for many interior situations. They require large containers, at least 15 gallons in size, to accommodate their long-term needs. They perform best with high light levels, but even then they will lose their lower foliage and become leggy over time. Combine them with Chinese evergreen or dumbcane to give them a base in compositions, then add some pothos or heartleaf philodendron for a ground cover. Scheffleras are invasive in south Florida.

SIZE & GROWTH RATE   8'–20' tall, 6'–12' wide, medium fast growing.

TEXTURE & FORM   Coarse texture and oval to broadly oval form.

FOLIAGE   Palmately compound leaves with 7–12 lustrous elliptic leaflets.

LIGHT & SOIL   Medium to high light and moist but well-drained soil.

MAINTENANCE   Wipe the leaves monthly, or take the plant outside on warm days and give it a warm shower. Water when the soil begins to dry, and maintain temperatures above 60°F. When plants become leggy, prune them back about halfway, place them outdoors, and apply a slow-release fertilizer. They drop leaves year-round.

NOTES & CULTIVARS   No cultivars listed.

top Schefflera at UGA greenhouses.

bottom Schefflera at Longwood Gardens Conservatory.

Schefflera arboricola DWARF SCHEFFLERA

Dwarf schefflera is an attractive versatile plant that is fairly forgiving of mistreatment. It tolerates moderate to high light levels and is slightly drought tolerant. It can develop either a dense shrub-like habit or a more upright tree form, depending on the light levels and degree of pruning to which it is subjected. While attractive by itself, in larger compositions dwarf schefflera can be used for borders or midlevel plantings and combined with smaller plants like Chinese evergreen and heartleaf philodendron and larger canopy plants like weeping figs.

SIZE & GROWTH RATE 3'–8' tall, 2'–6' wide, medium growing.

TEXTURE & FORM Medium texture and broadly oval form.

FOLIAGE Palmately compound leaves have seven to nine dark green glossy elliptic to obovate leaflets.

top Dwarf schefflera at Magnolia Plantation and Gardens Conservatory.
bottom Dwarf schefflera and sanseveria at the Washington State Convention Center in Seattle.

LIGHT & SOIL Medium to high light with loose and moist but well-drained soil.

MAINTENANCE Allow the soil to dry slightly between watering. Fertilize every four to six months under moderate to bright light or once per year for lower light locations. Pruning the stems encourages new branches and a dense canopy. Otherwise, they will become leggy.

NOTES & CULTIVARS
'Gold Capella' and 'Jacqueline' have yellow variegated leaflets.
'Trinette' has silver-colored variegated leaflets.

Spathiphyllum spp. PEACE LILY

The clump-forming habit of peace lily makes it an ideal choice for border plantings in interior compositions. In addition to its attractive foliage, the peace lily is one of the few foliage plants that will produce attractive flowers under interior light levels. Their white spathes rise above the foliage and can appear anytime of the year. Plants in the market today are selections of hybrids between several species. In their native habitats, peace lilies grow in moist soil or even standing water.

SIZE & GROWTH RATE 12"–48" tall and wide, fast growing.

TEXTURE & FORM Medium coarse texture and broadly oval to mounded form.

FOLIAGE Simple dark green glossy elliptical leaves 8"–15" long have prominent depressed veins.

top Peace lily and bird of paradise at UGA.
bottom Peace lily with white spathes.

LIGHT & SOIL Moderate light and consistently moist soil are ideal. The plants tolerate low light with diminished flowering but wither quickly when dry.

MAINTENANCE Dust foliage and remove old yellowing foliage regularly. Provide a loose porous soil mixture. Fertilize once per year under low light or twice per year under moderate light with a balanced slow-release fertilizer.

NOTES & CULTIVARS
'Clevelandii' grows to 24".
'Mauna Loa' reaches 36".
'Petite' reaches 12".

INVASIVE EXOTIC PLANTS

Japanese honeysuckle in Athens.

A naturalized plant is one that is not native to a specific ecosystem but is capable of reproducing, growing, and thriving in a new environment. Being capable of naturalizing does not necessarily mean that those plants should not be considered for the landscape. For example, southern magnolia, *Magnolia grandiflora*, yaupon holly, *Ilex vomitoria*, and southern wax myrtle, *Morella cerifera*, are all considered native to the southern Coastal Plain but have now naturalized in the Piedmont region of the Southeast.

On the other hand, invasive exotic plants are species from overseas that have naturalized in new environments to the extent that they have caused environmental harm. Virtually every plant in this section displays one or more features that made it attractive for introduction into the United States. At some point in the past, many were quite popular and frequently used in designed landscapes. Unfortunately, many are still promoted and frequently used. Their ability to reproduce, grow, and thrive in difficult environments is a trait they all share. This ability is attributed to an absence of the animals and diseases that kept them in bounds in their native environments. Unfortunately, as they take over habitats in the Southeast, they crowd out indigenous plants and the animals that depend upon those native plants. Thus as the Chinese privet, *Ligustrum sinense*, invades an open field and inhibits the development of the native butterfly weed, *Ascelpias tuberosa*, we experience a decline in the number of hummingbirds that utilize butterfly weed's flowers, butterflies that feast upon its foliage, and the bird species that feed upon those same butterflies. For this reason, we cannot recommend further use of any of the plants discussed in this section in the southeastern United States.

It is also important to keep in mind that many other nonnative plants besides those noted in this section have the potential to become invasive in other parts of the United States. For example, the butterfly bush, *Buddleja davidii*, is considered invasive in some northern states but doesn't cause problems here in the Southeast. Even some plants indigenous to the Southeast may prove to have invasive potential in other sections of the United States. The native catalpa trees, *Catalpa bignonioides* and *C. speciosa*, are considered invasive in the Pacific Northwest. The native black locust, *Robinia pseudoacacia*, is a pest in New England states. An excellent resource for anyone who is concerned about invasive plants in their particular region is www.invasive.org.

We also cover a few plants in this section that don't currently appear on state invasive lists. As an example, the Chinese elm, *Ulmus parvifolia*, is currently invading moist, open areas of the Georgia Piedmont, yet it does not appear on the Georgia Exotic Pest Plant Council's list of invasive species. Likewise, the Chinese silvergrass, *Miscanthus sinensis*, and the giant reed, *Arundo donax*, are beginning to appear in many well-drained sunny locations in the Southeast. For that reason, we have included those plants in this section.

Finally, there are some plants that may appear on some invasive lists but usually cause no significant economic or environmental harm. Those plants are discussed in other sections of this book. One example is the bugle weed, *Ajuga reptans*. Many people who have planted bugle weed in their landscapes find within a few years that it appears in other areas of the garden, usually because the cultural conditions in its original location became unsuitable for the original plants. The bugle weed is simply taking advantage of its cultural flexibility. If it becomes a problem, it can be easily eradicated.

Ailanthus altissima TREE OF HEAVEN

Tree of heaven is a deciduous tree that has naturalized across virtually the entire United States. It was frequently planted in Williamsburg prior to 1750. Hardy from zones 4b to 8b, it reaches 60'–80' tall and 20'–40' wide, with an extremely fast growth rate. It tolerates full sun to light shade, acidic to alkaline pH levels, and moist to dry soils, and it is even reported to be moderately tolerant of salt spray. Very coarse in texture, with sparse branching, it develops an upright oval form and shades out its lower branches as it matures. Pinnately compound leaves reach up to 3' long with as many as 31 narrowly ovate leaflets, which have a bitter odor when crushed. Female trees produce thousands of samaras. Young seedlings quickly produce deep roots. Mature trees produce young plants from root suckers that inhibit the growth of other species, thus forming thickets.

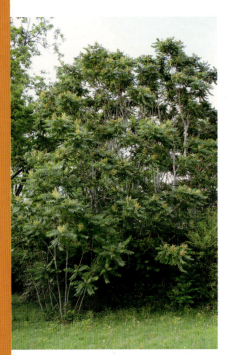

A thicket in Athens.

Spring flowers and foliage.

Albizia julibrissin MIMOSA

What's not to like about a tree with sweetly fragrant showy hot-pink flowers that attract hummingbirds from early to midsummer? Its finely textured bipinnately compound leaves cast a lightly dappled shade and fold up at dusk only to reopen with the morning sun. Cultivars have even been developed that produce deep pink ('Flame') or white ('Alba') flowers or reddish-purple foliage ('Summer Chocolate'). Unfortunately, all produce abundant seed pods that contribute to its invasion of any well-drained sunny location. One only has to drive along a highway during June to observe its spread along the roadside. Hardy from zones 6a to 9a, mimosa is short-lived (about 25 years) but can reach 25'– 35' tall and wide in just four to five years. Intolerant of shade, it forms an umbrella-like canopy by shading out its lower branches. Its extreme drought tolerance, ability to thrive in alkaline soils, and moderate tolerance to salt spray ensure that mimosa will continue its early summer roadside show.

Early summer flowers and foliage.

Form.

Broussonetia papyrifera PAPER MULBERRY

Paper mulberry is a native of China whose wood was used to make cloth and paper. It was planted by early colonists at Williamsburg. A coarse-textured tree with the ability to thrive in virtually any open location, it quickly reaches 25'– 40' tall and 20'– 30' wide with a broadly oval form, and it is hardy from zones 6a to 10a. It tolerates moist to dry sites, alkaline soils, and urban pollution, provided it has adequate sunlight. Mature trees produce ovate- to cordate-shaped leaves with serrate margins. Upper surfaces of the leaves have a sandpapery feel, while the lower surface and young stems are covered with a dense soft pubescence. Leaves on younger plants may have two or three lobes. This is a dioecious species, and female trees produce reddish-orange late summer fruit. It also produces sprouts from its roots and can quickly form a dense impenetrable thicket.

top Various leaf types.
bottom Hairy stems, leaves, and petioles.

Firmiana simplex CHINESE PARASOL TREE

Native to Asia, Chinese parasol tree was valued in designs for its coarse texture, upright oval form, fast growth rate, and exotic appearance. Hardy from zones 7a to 9b, it reaches 30'–50' tall and 10'–20' wide under shade but can be broader in sun. It tolerates full sun to moderately heavy shade and has been utilized for tight spaces adjacent to and between buildings where spatial limitations dictate an upright shade-tolerant plant. Its smooth greenish trunk and umbrella-like canopy are also inviting for use in close intimate spaces. Alternately arranged dark green palmately lobed simple leaves are up to 12" long, with three to five lobes and long petioles. Somewhat showy yellow-orange flowers occur on terminal panicles in late spring. It prefers a moist but well-drained soil but tolerates summer droughts. Its invasive potential appears limited to the immediate surroundings of mature trees where numerous seedlings occur.

top Foliage. *bottom* Smooth green bark.

Ligustrum lucidum TREE LIGUSTRUM

Tree ligustrum typically occurs as a multitrunked evergreen tree or large shrub reaching 30'–50' tall and 15'–25' wide. Hardy from zones 7b to 10b, it poses greater invasive potential from zone 8a southward, where it develops a dense canopy with a coarse texture, oval form, and medium fast growth rate. It prefers full sun but tolerates moderate shade, drought, and salt spray. Ovate-shaped simple leaves are oppositely arranged and 3"–6" long with entire margins. It can be differentiated from wax-leaf ligustrum (*Ligustrum japonicum*) and privet (*L. sinense*) by flowering a month later, in late May to mid-June. The creamy-white flowers have a slightly unpleasant odor and occur on large terminal panicles. Following flowering, it produces numerous berry-like drupes, which turn dark purple in early autumn and often bend the branches due to their weight before migrating birds devour them in late winter.

Foliage and mature fruit.

In bloom in Athens.

left Bipinnately compound leaves.
right Fall color.

Melia azedarach CHINABERRY

Chinaberry provides several ornamental attributes that contributed to its introduction as a street tree in Charleston and Savannah in the early 1800s. In mid- to late spring (late April to early May in Athens), it produces fairly showy lightly fragrant lilac-colored flowers in large terminal panicles. Following flowering, marble-sized berry-like drupes turn yellow in late summer and are popular with birds in late winter. Bipinnately compound leaves produce outstanding bright yellow fall foliage. A fast grower, chinaberry reaches 30'–40' tall and wide, with a medium coarse texture and broadly oval form. It prefers full sun with well-drained soils and tolerates drought, slightly alkaline soils, and salt spray. Hardy from zones 7a to 10b, chinaberry can sprout from its trunk after cutting and reach full size again in four to five years. As a result, it was often cut for firewood around old farmsteads of the Southeast.

Morus spp. MULBERRY

The mulberries, *Morus alba* and *M. rubra*, are being combined under one listing for the purposes of brevity. *M. rubra*, the red mulberry, is a native tree across much of the eastern and midwestern United States. It prefers moist bottomland locations, although it occasionally occurs on upland sites. Rarely available from nurseries, it now appears on some endangered lists in northern states. White mulberry, *M. alba*, is from China and was brought to North America in attempts to establish a silk industry. Although several cultivars of white mulberry are found, particularly a weeping form, 'Pendula', we cannot recommend their use due to their invasive potential. The majority of the trees found in the wild now are either *M. alba* or, more commonly, hybrids of the two species. These hybrids are fast growing, with a medium coarse texture and broadly oval to rounded form, and they reach 40'–50' tall and 30'–50' wide. Simple ovate leaves have serrate margins on older branches but two or three lobes on younger growth. Leaves on younger growth often have a scabrous surface, but the foliage is smooth or even glossy on mature branches. Hardy from zones 5a to 9b, they prefer full sun and tolerate light shade, drought, and alkaline soils. They provide fair yellow fall foliage color in the South that is apparently better than that produced farther north. Flowers are insignificant, but mulberries produce a purple blackberry-like fruit in summer. The sweet edible fruit is consumed by birds in June before fully ripening.

top Foliage. *bottom* Early spring form.

Paulownia tomentosa PAULOWNIA · PRINCESS TREE

Paulownia offers several attributes that made it attractive for designed landscapes. Lightly fragrant trumpet-shaped lavender flowers make a show in midspring before the foliage fully emerges in early to mid-April. Its exotic tropical appearance and coarse texture come from cordate-shaped simple leaves that can reach 12" long. After flowering, it produces woody capsules that remain through much of the year. A native of China, paulownia was introduced into the United States in the mid-1800s. Hardy from zones 6a to 9b, it is a fast grower, reaching 40'–60' tall and 35'–40' wide, with an oval to broadly oval form. It prefers full sun but tolerates light shade, moist to well-drained soils, and near-neutral pH levels, as well as some salt spray. The wood is weak and easily damaged in storms but was used for carving due to its soft and easily worked nature.

Flowers.

Foliage and capsules.

Pyrus calleryana CALLERY PEAR

Although Callery pear isn't grown as an ornamental, several cultivars have been highly promoted in the landscape industry. 'Bradford' was introduced in the 1960s and remains popular today. Subsequent introductions included 'Aristocrat', 'Capital', 'Chanticleer', and 'Redspire'. All were promoted for their fast growth, showy late winter flowers, reddish-purple late fall foliage, and conical to upright oval forms. Unfortunately, these cultivars produce berry-like fruit that is popular with wildlife and whose seeds revert to Callery pears upon germination. Tolerating full sun to moderate shade and well-drained soils, the tree is hardy from zones 5a to 9a, with a medium texture and oval to ovate leaves up to 3" long. Young actively growing branches have sharp, prominent spines. Callery pears reach 30'–40' tall and 20'–35' wide. Their invasive nature is most evident along roadsides and woodland edges in Athens in early to mid-March, when they produce showy white flowers with an odor similar to well-aged roadkill.

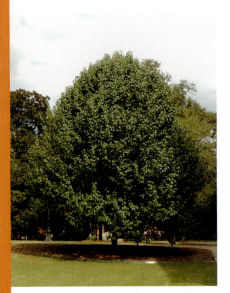

Bradford pear form.

Callery pears in flower.

Triadica sebifera TALLOW TREE · POPCORN TREE

Often identified as *Sapium sebiferum*, Chinese tallow tree is borderline cold-hardy in zones 7b and 8a but is highly invasive across the Southeast from zones 8b to 10b. Reaching 60' tall and 30'– 40' wide, it is a fast grower with a medium fine texture and oval form. Simple leaves are rhombic-ovate in shape and 2"– 5" long, with entire margins and acuminate tips. The foliage develops an outstanding red to reddish-purple late fall foliage that often remains into early winter. Tallow tree produces slightly showy and lightly fragrant flowers in late spring. The fruit is a capsule opening in midautumn to reveal three white waxy seeds. Wax extracted from the seeds has been used in candles, soaps, and lubricants. While the seeds are consumed by birds, the fruit and foliage are poisonous to mammals. It invades wet to well-drained soils in full sun to moderate shade and tolerates salt spray.

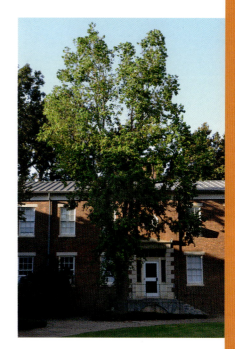

Form.

Foliage.

Ulmus parvifolia CHINESE ELM

It is easy to understand why Chinese elm became popular in the landscape industry. Its tolerance of adverse conditions, ease of transplanting, fast growth, and attractive exfoliating bark all combined to make it one of the most frequently specified trees in recent years. It was promoted as a replacement for American elm due to its resistance to Dutch elm disease, but now we are seeing its darker side. Hardy from zones 5a to 10a, it is listed as invasive from Wisconsin to Florida. Chinese elm develops an upright arching branching habit with a broadly oval form and medium fine texture. It reaches 50'–70' tall and 30'– 50' wide. It prefers full sun with slightly moist soils but tolerates light shade, well-drained soils, and higher pH levels. Simple dark green elliptic leaves are 1"– 2½" long with asymmetrical bases and serrate margins and are held late in fall without significant autumn color. Early autumn samaras are favored by squirrels.

Form in Athens.

Foliage and buds.

left Foliage and fruit.

right Form and habit.

Ardisia crenata CORAL ARDISIA · CORALBERRY

Coral ardisia is an upright evergreen shrub from Japan that forms small mounded thickets over time. Hardy from zones 8b to 10b, it was often used for detailed designs in shaded locations to take advantage of its prominent red fruit. Small white flowers droop beneath the foliage in spring. Pea-sized berries turn bright red in fall and remain into spring. The fruit is not particularly attractive to wildlife, but the seeds appear capable of germinating without being ingested, causing it to be highly invasive in woodlands in Florida and Louisiana. It grows slowly to 2'– 4' tall and 1'– 2' wide, with a medium texture and upright oval form. Simple alternate leaves are a leathery lustrous green, 1½"– 4" long, elliptic in shape, with crenate margins, acuminate tips, and red petioles. Preferring light to moderate shade with a moist but well-drained acidic soil, it tolerates heavy shade and drought.

Hedge.

Elaeagnus pungens THORNY ELAEAGNUS

Often planted as a screen along interstate highway embankments, elaeagnus has proved its ability to survive adverse conditions. Hardy from zones 6b to 10b, it reaches 12'– 18' tall and wide with a mounded form due to arching branches that can root where they meet the ground. Medium in texture, its simple oval leaves are alternate, 1½"– 4¾" long, with entire margins, and they are covered with scales that appear as silvery dots on their upper surface and brown dots beneath. Fast-growing summer shoots produce thorns at their nodes and can grow 10' in a month, providing a wildly unkempt appearance. It produces small white bell-shaped flowers with a perfume-like fragrance along older stems in midautumn. Its oblong orange-red fruit are devoured by birds in early spring. Preferring full sun, it tolerates moderate shade, slightly moist soils, drought, alkaline soils, and salt spray. Autumn olive, *Elaeagnus umbellata*, is a deciduous shrub hardy from zones 3a to 8b that is equally invasive, reaching 10'– 20' tall, with fragrant midspring flowers and red fall fruit.

Foliage and fall flowers.

Ilex cornuta Chinese Holly

While Chinese holly is rarely used in designed landscapes anymore, its many cultivars are still quite popular. Viable seeds from these cultivars revert back to the parent plant, causing an abundance of Chinese hollies in woods around the Southeast. Hardy from zones 7a to 9b, it is an evergreen shrub reaching 12'– 20' tall and 8'– 12' wide, with a moderate growth rate. Dark green glossy leaves are up to 4" long, with five to seven prominent spines and a plastic-like feel. Medium in texture with an oval to broadly oval form, it prefers full sun but tolerates moderate shade on well-drained sites and is very drought tolerant. A dioecious species, it produces somewhat fragrant nonshowy flowers on both sexes in midspring. Female plants produce red berries in late fall that remain on the plant into winter before they are eaten by birds.

Form in Athens.

Foliage and spring flower buds.

Ilex cornuta 'Burfordii' BURFORD HOLLY

Burford holly was once the most popular cultivar of Chinese holly because it is a heavily fruited female plant with less objectionable foliage than the species. Its dark green obovate leaves usually have only one spine at their tip. Burford holly often grows larger than Chinese holly, reaching 20'– 30' tall and 15'– 25' in spread, with a medium fast growth rate. It develops a broadly oval form. Similar to the Chinese holly, it is hardy from zones 7a to 9b and prefers full sun and well-drained soils, becoming quite drought tolerant. It has been often used as a tall screening plant, with its branches remaining low to the ground in open locations, but it could also be limbed up into a small evergreen tree.

Form in Athens.

Foliage and fruit.

Ilex cornuta 'Dwarf Burford' DWARF BURFORD HOLLY

Dwarf Burford holly is probably more popular than Burford holly at this time. Growing 12'–15' tall and 8'–12' wide, it is only about half the size of a mature Burford holly but is not a dwarf compared to other shrubs. Its smaller size and medium growth rate make it easier to maintain than Burford in most situations. Medium fine in texture with an oval to broadly oval form, dwarf Burford develops a dense canopy suitable for screens, buffers, and background plantings. It has glossy dark green leaves that are 1"–2½" long and oval to elliptic in shape, with prominent depressed veins and one spine at their tip. It produces small red fruit clustered about the stems in autumn that are only about half the size of those on the Burford and are far less prominent in appearance.

left In a design.
right Foliage and fruit.

Ilex cornuta 'Rotunda' ROTUNDA HOLLY

A former professor called rotunda holly a "service station plant" due to its ability to tolerate extremely difficult conditions, as well as the fact that no one would ever want to bother it. Since service stations are largely things of the past, perhaps a more relevant term would be a "drive-through fast food restaurant plant." Medium in texture and slowly growing 4'–6' tall and 6'–8' wide, with a densely rounded form, it tolerates full sun to light shade, drought, and higher pH levels with foliage that closely resembles the Chinese holly. While not noted for heavy fruiting, it nevertheless provides some fruit, usually hidden somewhat within the foliage. The seeds revert to the Chinese holly when spread by birds. Hardy from zones 7a to 9b, it was widely used for border or barrier plantings in the past.

Form.

Foliage.

left Foliage.   *right* A sheared hedge in Chattanooga.

Ligustrum sinense   PRIVET, CHINESE PRIVET

Hardy from zones 6a to 10b, privet is a semievergreen large shrub or small tree that reaches 15'– 20' in height and spread. Once a very popular plant for clipped hedges, it is now listed as a severe threat in every state from Virginia and Kentucky to Florida and Texas. Medium fine in texture, with simple opposite leaves that are 1"– 2½" long and oval in shape, with entire margins and acute tips, privet develops a broadly oval to rounded form. Showy terminal panicles of white flowers with a malodorous scent occur in late spring, with small dark purple to black fruit in late autumn through winter. Privet is fast growing and tolerates full sun to full shade, moist to very well drained soils, and salt spray. The University of Georgia proudly promotes it by prominently displaying it as the sideline hedge of Sanford Stadium.

Lonicera maackii   AMUR HONEYSUCKLE

Amur honeysuckle is nearly as great a problem as Chinese privet in the Southeast. Reaching 15'– 18' in height and spread, it is a fast-growing deciduous shrub hardy from zones 4b to 8b. Medium in texture with upright arching branches and a broadly oval form, it tolerates full sun to full shade and is quite drought tolerant. Fairly showy white flowers occur along the stems in midspring (mid- to late April in Athens). Glossy red berries that are very popular with birds occur in October. Oppositely arranged simple leaves are 2"– 4" long and oval to elliptic in shape, with acuminate tips and mostly entire margins. It gets a poor yellow fall color and holds some leaves into early winter. Like many other invasives, amur honeysuckle begins growing before native plants break dormancy and is in full leaf by mid-March in zones 7b and 8a.

Foliage and midspring flowers.

Autumn fruit.

In Charleston.

Mahonia bealei LEATHERLEAF MAHONIA

It is heart-wrenching for any designer to include leatherleaf mahonia in an invasives category. Slowly growing 6'–8' tall and 4'–6' wide, it was often used as a specimen plant in courtyards or near entrances where it could be appreciated up close for its coarse texture, upright layered branching habit, and ability to handle moderate to heavy shade. Leatherleaf mahonia produces yellow lightly fragrant late winter flowers and prominent late spring blue berries. It can be identified by its odd pinnately compound leaves with 9–13 broadly ovate leaflets, which have a plastic-like feel, and 5–9 prominent teeth along their margins. It prefers a moist but well-drained soil but becomes drought tolerant with age and is hardy from zones 6b to 9a. While not as big a pest as privet or elaeagnus, it nevertheless has naturalized in well-drained shaded locations of the Southeast.

Foliage and late spring fruit.

left Winter foliage and fruit in shade.
right Winter foliage and fruit in sun.

Nandina domestica NANDINA · HEAVENLY BAMBOO

Like leatherleaf mahonia, nandina has a number of attributes that make it difficult to exclude it from the design palette. Medium fine texture, attractive white late spring flowers, and showy red late fall and winter fruit and foliage always provided reasons to consider its use. Its ability to grow in full sun to full shade, drought tolerance, and moderate salt spray tolerance allowed it to be used virtually anywhere. Hardy from zones 6b to 9a, with a medium growth rate, it reaches 6'–8' tall and 4'–7' wide. In addition to spreading from seed, it has the ability to sprout new plants from its roots, even small root segments that remain after the original plant has been pulled from the ground. There are reports that its fruit is poisonous to cedar waxwings. Currently, the only nonfruiting or sterile cultivars that can be recommended are 'Firepower', which reaches 3'–5' tall, and 'Filamentosa', which has finely dissected foliage and extremely fine texture and reaches 3' tall.

Photinia serratifolia CHINESE PHOTINIA

While not as aggressive as other plants in this section, Chinese photinia nevertheless has the ability to seed itself into open woods and old fields from zones 7b to 9a. A large evergreen shrub or small tree that reaches 20'–30' tall and 10'–20' wide, it has a coarse texture, broadly oval form, and medium fast growth rate. Growing in full sun to full shade and well-drained soils, it develops a dense canopy with branching low to the ground. Simple opposite leaves 4"–8" long have a leathery texture and oblong shape with coarsely serrate margins. New spring growth emerges coppery bronze. Showy white flowers on terminal panicles in early spring smell like day-old roadkill on hot summer days. Berry-like fruit turn a deep red color from midautumn to spring. Unlike other photinias, Chinese photinia doesn't have severe problems with fungal leaf spot infections.

Foliage.

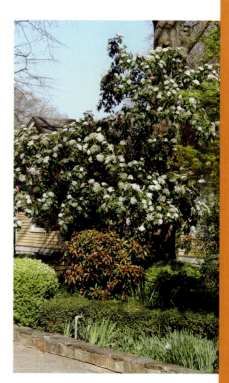

Early spring flowers.

left Late summer flowers.

right Foliage and late summer flowers.

Clematis terniflora SWEET AUTUMN CLEMATIS

Sweet autumn clematis is an aggressive and fast-growing semievergreen to deciduous vine. While not considered as great a problem as Japanese honeysuckle, privet, or kudzu, it nevertheless invades unmaintained areas such as roadsides and alleys. It climbs by twining its compound leaves over adjacent shrubs and is usually limited in size to the height of the plant it is climbing. With a medium texture and hardy from zones 4b to 9a, it tolerates full sun to moderate shade and slightly moist to well-drained soils. Often confused with the native virgin's bower, *Clematis virginiana*, it can be differentiated from the native clematis by having compound leaves with usually five cordate-shaped leaflets with entire margins and by the sweet fragrance of its late summer / early fall white flowers. *C. virginiana* produces compound leaves with three leaflets with serrate margins, and its white flowers lack fragrance.

Euonymus fortunei WINTERCREEPER

Wintercreeper is a difficult plant to describe to someone who is unfamiliar with it. As a ground cover, its branches tend to send shoots upward, requiring shearing at least annually to prevent it from transforming into a shrub. It can also climb vertical surfaces by means of aerial rootlets. With a medium fast growth rate, wintercreeper is hardy from zones 5b to 9a. It grows in full sun to full shade and well-drained soils, and it tolerates drought, higher pH soils, and salt spray. Medium to fine in texture, depending upon the cultivar, its form varies from prostrate as a ground cover to mounded as a shrub. Simple opposite leaves are 1"–3" long, elliptic to ovate shaped, with serrate margins and a waxy coating that helps shed herbicides. It won't flower until it begins to climb or is allowed to develop into a shrub. The flowers aren't showy but produce orange-colored seeds in late fall.

Juvenile foliage.

Mature foliage and fruit.

left Foliage.
right Climbing native deciduous trees.

Hedera helix ENGLISH IVY

English Ivy has been a popular evergreen ground cover for hundreds of years. Like many other vines, it has both a juvenile and an adult form. It is only when it climbs a vertical surface that it evolves into its adult form and develops horizontal branches with creamy-white flowers and black berries that are eaten by wildlife. In its juvenile form as a ground cover, it has simple alternately arranged dark green leaves with usually three to five lobes and is not invasive. As it climbs by means of aerial rootlets, its foliage becomes ovate in shape and lacks lobes. Dozens of cultivars produce foliage that ranges from medium fine to coarse in texture, with some providing variegated foliage. It grows slowly at first but becomes much faster within a few years of planting. It tolerates full sun to full shade, drought, and salt spray. While hardy from zones 5b to 10b, it is susceptible to severe fungal problems in high humidity areas.

Hedera helix subsp. *canariensis* ALGERIAN IVY

Algerian ivy, formerly listed as a separate species, *Hedera canariensis*, and sometimes listed as *H. algeriensis*, is now considered a subspecies of English ivy. It shares virtually all of the traits of English ivy except for having larger leaves with red petioles and a coarse texture, and it is only hardy from zones 8a to 10b. Considered very tolerant of salt spray, it has been primarily used as a substitute for English ivy in zone 8b southward in the southeastern United States due to being less susceptible to fungal diseases in high humidity. Similar to English ivy, if it is maintained in its juvenile form as a ground cover, it is not invasive. Only when it climbs a vertical surface and begins to flower and produce fruit does it become invasive.

Foliage.

With crape myrtles in Savannah.

Lonicera japonica JAPANESE HONEYSUCKLE

Who hasn't enjoyed the fragrance of Japanese honeysuckle on warm late spring evenings? Or spent a childhood afternoon tasting sweet drops of nectar from its flowers? How could such a delightful plant become such a pest? It starts as a fast-growing, medium-textured ground cover vine but becomes a twining climber when encountering a shrub or small tree and can girdle young trees. Hardy from zones 5a to 10b, it is evergreen in zones 9 and 10, semievergreen in zones 7 and 8, and deciduous in zones 5 and 6. Simple opposite leaves are ovate shaped with entire margins. Young stems may be reddish purple in sunny locations. Honeysuckle grows from full sun to full shade and is very drought tolerant. Its fragrant white flowers emerge in late April to early May in Athens and bloom heavily into early summer, with sporadic flowers continuing into autumn. Like other vines, it only flowers and fruits when it climbs, never when it is on the ground.

Foliage and late spring flowers.

Swallowing other plants in Athens.

Pueraria montana lobata KUDZU

Kudzu is an extremely fast-growing deciduous vine from Asia that was introduced in 1876 and promoted for forage and erosion control in the 1920s and 1930s. It quickly found the Southeast to its liking and has taken over large tracts of open land in fields and roadsides, swallowing fences, shrubs, and trees in the process. Coarse textured, it has trifoliate leaves with lobed leaflets. Hardy from zones 5b to 10b, kudzu requires full sun and well-drained soils and is very tolerant of drought and acidic or alkaline soils. Its roots have the ability to fix atmospheric nitrogen in the soil for its use. Similar to other invasive vines, kudzu begins as a ground cover but can climb large trees by twining stems. Short racemes of dark pink flowers are produced in mid- to late summer but rarely seen unless stems are draping from a tree.

top Foliage and summer flowers.
bottom The vine that swallowed the South.

Wisteria sinensis CHINESE WISTERIA

Chinese wisteria has been used as both a deciduous shrub and a twining vine for many years. As a shrub, it reaches about 8' tall with a 12' or greater spread. As a climbing vine, its stems twine in a counterclockwise direction and have the ability to climb as tall as the structure or tree it is using for support. It has been popular for arbors and front porches, since it requires no assistance in climbing. Wisteria's invasiveness becomes evident in early spring, when the fragrant lavender flower racemes appear to drip from the canopies of roadside trees. Wisteria produces pinnately compound leaves with 9–13 leaflets. Hardy from zones 5b to 10b, it is a fast grower with a medium texture that grows in full sun to moderate shade and slightly moist to well-drained soils. Lavender flowers appear in early April, with velvety bean pods in summer. A white-flowered variety is also seen occasionally. *Wisteria floribunda*, Japanese wisteria, has similar attributes and is equally invasive. It differs by having 13–19 leaflets, flower racemes opening from the base downward, less fragrance, and stems twining in a clockwise direction. A recent study indicated that the majority of invasive wisteria in the Southeast is actually a hybrid between the two species.

top Devouring trees and shrubs.
bottom Foliage.

Arundo donax GIANT REED

Giant reed is a deciduous grass from India that naturalized in the Mediterranean area before being brought to the United States. It is considered an invasive species across most of the Southeast and in riparian areas of the Southwest and California. Hardy from zones 6a to 10b, it reaches 12'– 20' tall and 8'– 15' wide, with a coarse texture and an irregular upright form. Gray-green leaves are 12"– 24" long, with sharply scabrous margins and clasping auricles at their base, and they appear two-ranked along the stems. Leaves on young growth are often variegated. A fast grower that prefers full sun to light shade and tolerates wet to well-drained soils, it produces large light red panicles of flowers in early autumn. Unlike most invasive plants that reproduce from seeds, giant reed is reportedly unable to produce viable seeds in the United States. Thus its distribution is attributed to the transport of stem fragments.

Autumn foliage and seed heads.

With Chinese silvergrass in Athens.

Miscanthus sinensis CHINESE SILVERGRASS

Chinese silvergrass is a deciduous bunchgrass introduced from China in the late 1800s and was reported to be invasive as early as the 1940s in the Appalachian Mountains. It grows 6'– 10' tall and 5'– 8' wide, with a medium fine texture, an upright arching habit, and attractive late summer to early autumn flower heads. Promoted for low maintenance, drought resistance, and ability to retain its tan foliage upright over winter, it has been used in perennial borders, masses, and even container plantings. Once a staple in the plant palette of Oehme, van Sweden & Associates (OvS), it became quite popular in the 1980s and 1990s as others attempted to imitate the firm's designs. Its many cultivars offered options in size, texture, and foliage color. Here are some of the more popular cultivars:

'Adagio', which reaches 3'– 5' tall with midsummer flowering.
'Gracillimus' grows 5'–8' with a very fine texture and early autumn flowers.
'Strictus' grows 6'–8' with yellow bands across its leaves and late summer flowers.
'Variegatus' grows 6'–8' with late summer flowers and creamy-white bands running the length of its leaves.

Generally listed as hardy from zones 5 to 9, some cultivars can handle zone 4b, while others are limited to zone 6. They all prefer full sun and moist but well-drained soils. A recent study indicated the species can adapt to open woodlands due to its efficiency in converting short periods of sunlight into energy.

top 'Variegatus'. *bottom* Early autumn flower and seed heads.

Phyllostachys aurea GOLDEN BAMBOO

Thank goodness golden bamboo rarely flowers and produces viable seeds. If it did, we would have to hack a trail home every day. Reports indicate that it may be as long as two decades between flowering. Unfortunately, golden bamboo spreads prolifically simply due to its rhizomes, which can spread 30' or more from the parent plant before breaking the ground. As a result, it develops dense thickets 15'– 25' tall. It is called golden bamboo because its stems turn yellow green in full sun and fishpole bamboo due to its use for cane fishing poles. Hardy from zones 7a to 10b, it is mostly evergreen but may be killed to the ground when temperatures drop to near 0°F. It prefers full sun and tolerates moderate shade and moist to well-drained soils. Golden bamboo is a fast grower with a medium fine texture and lanceolate leaves that are 3"– 5" long. To control its spread, create an impenetrable barrier of steel edging or concrete at least 12" deep around the bamboo.

top In an alley in Madison, Ga.
bottom Foliage.

References

BOOKS

Ambrose, Jonathan, L. Katherine Kirkman, and Leslie Edwards, eds. 2013. *The Natural Communities of Georgia*. Athens: University of Georgia Press.

Armitage, Allan M. 2001. *Armitage's Manual of Annuals, Biennials, and Half-Hardy Perennials*. Portland, Ore.: Timber Press.

———. 2004. *Armitage's Garden Annuals: A Color Encyclopedia*. Portland, Ore.: Timber Press.

———. 2006. *Armitage's Native Plants for North American Gardens*. Portland, Ore.: Timber Press.

———. 2008. *Herbaceous Perennial Plants: A Treatise on Their Identification, Culture, and Garden Attributes*. 3rd ed. Champaign, Ill.: Stipes Publishing.

Atlanta Regional Commission. 2001. *Georgia Stormwater Management Manual*. Vol. 2, *Technical Handbook*. 1st ed.

Beard, James B. 1973. *Turfgrass: Science and Culture*. Englewood Cliffs, N.J.: Prentice-Hall.

Bitner, Richard. 2011. *Designing with Conifers: The Best Choices for Year-Round Interest in Your Garden*. Portland, Ore.: Timber Press.

Booth, Norman, and James Hiss. 2011. *Residential Landscape Architecture: Design Process for the Private Residence*. Pearson, Inc.

Callaway, Dorothy J. 1994. *The World of Magnolias*. Portland, Ore.: Timber Press.

Christians, Nick. 1998. *Fundamentals of Turfgrass Management*. Chelsea, Mich.: Ann Arbor Press.

Copeland, Linda L., and Allan M. Armitage. 2001. *Legends in the Garden: Who in the World Is Nellie Stevens?* Atlanta, Ga.: Wings Publishers.

Cothran, James R. 2003. *Gardens and Historic Plants of the Antebellum South*. Columbia: University of South Carolina Press.

Cox, Tom, and John Ruter. 2013. *Landscaping with Conifers and Ginkgo for the Southeast*. Gainesville: University Press of Florida.

Darke, Rick. 2007. *The Encyclopedia of Grasses for Livable Landscapes*. Portland, Ore.: Timber Press.

Darke, Rick, and Doug Tallamy. 2014. *The Living Landscape: Designing for Beauty and Biodiversity in the Home Garden*. Portland, Ore.: Timber Press.

Dirr, Michael A. 1997. *Dirr's Hardy Trees and Shrubs: An Illustrated Encyclopedia*. Portland, Ore.: Timber Press.

———. 2007. *Viburnums: Flowering Shrubs for Every Season*. Portland, Ore.: Timber Press.

———. 2009. *Manual of Woody Landscape Plants: Their Identification, Ornamental Characteristics, Culture, Propagation and Uses*. Champaign, Ill.: Stipes Publishing.

———. 2011. *Trees and Shrubs for Warm Climates*. Portland, Ore.: Timber Press.

Duble, Richard L. 1996. *Turfgrasses: Their Management and Use in the Southern Zone*. College Station: Texas A&M University Press.

Edgar, Logan A. 1991. *Camellias: The Complete Guide*. Wiltshire, Eng.: Crowood Press.

Flora of North America Editorial Committee. 2003. *Flora of North America*. Vol. 26, *Magnoliophyta: Liliidae: Liliales and Orchidales*. New York: Oxford University Press.

Foster, F. Gordon. 1984. *Ferns to Know and Grow*. Portland, Ore.: Timber Press.

Galle, Fred C. 1997. *Hollies: The Genus Ilex*. Portland, Ore.: Timber Press.

Gardiner, James M. 2000. *Magnolias: A Gardener's Guide*. Portland, Ore.: Timber Press.

Godfrey, Robert K. 1988. *Trees, Shrubs, and Woody Vines of Northern Florida and Adjacent Georgia and Alabama*. Athens: University of Georgia Press.

Griffith, G. E., J. M. Omernik, J. A. Comstock, S. Lawrence, G. Martin, A. Goddard, V. J. Hulcher, and T. Foster. 2001. *Ecoregions of Alabama and Georgia*. Reston, Va.: United States Geological Survey.

Harlow, William M., and Ellwood S. Harrar. 1968. *Textbook of Dendrology: Covering the Important Forest Trees of the United States and Canada*. 5th ed. New York: McGraw-Hill Book Company.

Head, Bob H. 2006. *Hutchinson's Tree Book: A Reference Guide to Popular Landscape Trees*. Taylors, S.C.: Hutchinson Publishing Corporation.

Hitchmough, James. 2017. *Sowing Beauty: Designing Flowering Meadows from Seed*. Portland, Ore.: Timber Press.

Hoshizaki, Barbara Joe, and Robbin C. Moran. 2001. *Fern Growers Manual*. Portland, Ore.: Timber Press.

Irish, Mary, and Gary Irish. 2000. *Agaves, Yuccas, and Related Plants: A Gardener's Guide*. Portland, Ore.: Timber Press.

Jacobsen, Arthur Lee. 1992. *Purpleleaf Plums*. Portland, Ore.: Timber Press.

Kaplan, Rachel, and Stephen Kaplan. 1989. *The Experience of Nature: A Psychological Perspective*. Cambridge: Cambridge University Press.

Kellert, Stephen R., et al. 1993. *The Biophilia Hypothesis*. Washington, D.C.: Island Press.

Kuitert, Wybe, and Arie Peterse. 1999. *Japanese Flowering Cherries*. Portland, Ore.: Timber Press.

Leszczynski, Nancy. 1998. *Planting the Landscape: A Professional Approach to Garden Design*. New York: John Wiley and Sons.

Marston, Ted, ed. 1993. *Annuals: A Comprehensive Guide for Gardeners*. New York: Hearst Books.

Mickel, John T. 1994. *Ferns for American Gardens*. New York: Macmillan Publishing Company.

Miller, James H., and Karl V. Miller. 2005. *Forest Plants of the Southeast and Their Wildlife Uses*. Athens: University of Georgia Press.

Mohlenbrock, Robert H. 1999. *The Illustrated Flora of Illinois*. Carbondale: Southern Illinois University Press.

Nelson, Gil. 2000. *The Ferns of Florida*. Sarasota, Fla.: Pineapple Press.

———. 2011. *The Trees of Florida: A Reference and Field Guide*. Sarasota, Fla.: Pineapple Press.

Odenwald, Neil G., and James R. Turner. 2006. *Identification, Selection, and Use of Southern Plants for Landscape Design*. 4th ed. Baton Rouge, La.: Claitor's Publishing Division.

Olsen, Suzanne. 2007. *Encyclopedia of Garden Ferns*. Portland, Ore.: Timber Press.

Oudolf, Piet, and Noel Kingsbury. 1999. *Designing with Plants*. Portland, Ore.: Timber Press.

Porcher, Richard D., and Douglas A. Rayner. 2001. *A Guide to the Wildflowers of South Carolina*. Columbia: University of South Carolina Press.

Radford, Albert E., Harry E. Ahles, and C. Ritchie Bell. 1968. *Manual of the Vascular Plants of the Carolinas*. Chapel Hill: University of North Carolina Press.

Rainer, Thomas, and Claudia West. 2015. *Planting in a Post-wild World: Designing Plant Communities for Resilient Landscapes*. Portland, Ore.: Timber Press.

Robinson, Nick. 2011. *The Planting Design Handbook*. Surrey, U.K.: Ashgate Publishing Limited.

Snyder, Lloyd H., Jr., and James G. Bruce. 1986. *Field Guide to the Ferns and Other Pteridophytes of Georgia*. Athens: University of Georgia Press.

Spira, Timothy P. 2011. *Wildflowers & Plant Communities of the Southern Appalachian Mountains & Piedmont*. Chapel Hill: University of North Carolina Press.

Tallamy, Doug. 2012. *Bringing Nature Home: How You Can Sustain Wildlife with Plants*. Portland, Ore.: Timber Press.

Trehane, Jennifer. 2007. *Camellias: The Gardener's Encyclopedia*. Portland, Ore.: Timber Press.

Tryon, Rolla. 1980. *Ferns of Minnesota*. Minneapolis: University of Minnesota Press.

Turgeon, A. J. 1999. *Turfgrass Management*. Upper Saddle River, N.J.: Prentice Hall.

Wilson, Edward O. 1984. *Biophilia*. Cambridge, Mass.: Harvard University Press.

Womack, Wayne M. 2006. *A Philosophy for Planting Design*. Baton Rouge: Darbonne and Bartolett Publishers.

PERIODICALS

Ahmad R., P. S. Liow, D. F. Spencer, and M. Jasieniuk. 2008. "Molecular Evidence for a Single Genetic Clone of Invasive *Arundo donax* in the United States." *Aquatic Botany* 88 (2): 113–20.

Anella, Louis B., and Thomas H. Whitlow. 1999. "Flood Tolerance Rankings of Red and Freeman Maple Cultivars." *Journal of Arboriculture* 25 (1): 31–36.

Beckerman, Janna, James Chatfield, and Erik Draper. 2009. "A 33-Year Evaluation of Resistance and Pathogenicity in the Apple Scab-Crabapples Pathosystem." *HortScience* 44 (3): 599–608.

Coder, Kim. 2010. "Live Oak: Historic Ecologic Structures." Tree Dendrology Series. Warnell School of Forest Resources, University of Georgia.

Darke, Rick. 2006. "Halesia in Cultivation." *Plantsman* 5 (December): 253–57.

———. 2008. "Fothergilla in Cultivation." *Plantsman* 7 (March): 10–17.

Del Tredici, Peter. 2005. "Against All Odds: Growing *Franklinia* in Boston." *Arnoldia* 63 (4): 2–7.

Dosman, Michael. 2010. "Beautybush *Kolkwitzia amabilis*." *Arnoldia* 68 (2): 51–52.

Fraedrich, S. W., T. C. Harrington, R. J. Rabaglia, M. D. Ulyshen, A. E. Mayfield III, J. L. Hanula, J. M. Eickwort, and D. R. Miller. 2008. "A Fungal Symbiont of the Redbay Ambrosia Beetle Causes a Lethal Wilt in Redbay and Other Lauraceae in the Southeastern United States." *Plant Disease* 92 (2): 215–24.

Goodell, Edward. 1982. "Two Promising Fruit Plants for Northern Landscapes." *Arnoldia* 42 (4): 103–33. arnoldia.arboretum.harvard.edu/pdf/articles/1138.pdf.

Griffin, Jason J., and Thomas G. Ranney. 2002. "Photosynthetic Capacity of *Illicium parviflorum* and *I. floridanum* Exposed to High Irradiance." SNA Research Conference Proceedings, 433–36.

Guex, J. J., D. M. E. Enriquez Vega, L. Avril, S. Boussetta, and C. Taieb. 2009. "Assessment of Quality of Life in Mexican Patients Suffering from Chronic Venous Disorder: Impact of Oral Ruscus aculeatus–Hesperidin–Methyl-Chalcone–Ascorbic Acid Treatment." *Phlebology* 24:157–65.

Halverson, Howard F., and Donald G. Potts. 1981. "Water Requirements of Honeylocust in the Urban Environment." United States Department of Agriculture Forest Service Research Paper NE-487.

Harris, J. Roger, Patricia Knight, and Jody Fanelli. 1996. "Fall Transplanting Improves Establishment of Balled and Burlapped Fringe Tree (*Chionanthus virginicus*)." *HortScience* 31 (7): 1143–45.

Hawke, Richard. 2014. "A Comparative Study of Joe Pye Weeds (*Eutrochium* spp.) and Their Relatives." *Plant Evaluation Notes,* no. 37. Chicago Botanic Garden.

Held, David W. 2004. "Relative Susceptibility of Woody Landscape Plants to Japanese Beetle (Coleoptera: Scarabaeidae)." *Journal of Arboriculture* 30 (6): 328–35.

Hill, Steven R. 2007. "Conservation Assessment for Yellowwood." Illinois Natural History Technical Report, USDA Forest Service.

Horton, J. L., R. Fortner, and M. Goklany. 2010. "Photosynthetic Characteristics of the C4 Invasive Exotic Grass *Miscanthus sinensis Andersson Growing along Gradients of Light Intensity in the Southeastern USA." *Castanea* 75:52–66.

Hussein, Amer, and Inna Shugaev. 2012. "Phototoxic Response to *Ficus carica* Leaf and Shoot Saps." *Israel Medical Association Journal* 14 (June): 399–400.

Hygnstrom, Scott E., Peter D. Skelton, Scott J. Josiah, Jason M. Gilsdorf, Dallas R. Virchow, James A. Brandle, Anil K. Jayaprakash, Kent M. Eskridge, and Kurt C. VerCauteren. 2004. "White-Tailed Deer Browsing and Rubbing Preferences for Trees and Shrubs That Produce Nontimber Forest Products." *HortTechnology* 19 (1): 204–11.

Iles, Jeff. 2009. "Crabapples . . . with No Apologies." *Arnoldia* 67 (2): 2–13.

Jacobi, W. R. 1992. "Seasonal Effects on Wound Susceptibility and Canker Expansion in Honeylocusts Inoculated with *Thyronectria austro-americana*." *Journal of Arboriculture* 18 (6): 288–93.

Jacobs, K. A., F. S. Santamour Jr., G. R. Johnson, and M. A. Dirr. 1996. "Differential Resistance to Entomosporium Leafspot Disease and Hydrogen Cyanide Potential in Photinia." *Journal of Environmental Horticulture* 14 (3): 154–57.

Juzwik, Jennifer, David N. Appel, William L. MacDonald, and Susan Burks. 2011. "Challenges and Successes in Managing Oak Wilt Disease in the United States." *Plant Disease* 95 (8): 888–900.

Kaplan, Stephen. 1995. "The Restorative Benefits of Nature: Toward an Integrative Framework." *Journal of Environmental Psychology* 15 (3): 169–82.

Knox, Gary W., and Sandra B. Wilson. 2006. "Evaluating North and South Florida Landscape Performance and Fruiting of Ten Cultivars and a Wild-Type Selection of *Nandina domestica*, a Potentially Invasive Shrub." *Journal of Environmental Horticulture* 24 (3): 137–42. http://irrecenvhort.ifas.ufl. edu/Invasiveplants/publications/J%20 Environ%20Hort%202006%20-%20 Nandina.pdf.

Kwang Jin Kim, Myeong Il Jeong, Dong Woo Lee, Jeong Seob Song, Hyoung Deug Kim, Eun Ha Yoo, Sun Jin Jeong, Seung Won Han, Stanley J.

Kays, Young-Wook Lim, and Ho-Hyun Kim. 2010. "Variation in Formaldehyde Removal Efficiency among Indoor Plant Species." *HortScience* 45 (October): 1489–95.

Li, Y. H., M. T. Windham, R. N. Trigiano, D. C. Fare, J. M. Spiers, and W. E. Copes. 2007. "Evaluation for Resistance to Powdery Mildew in *Cornus* Species and Hybrids Using a Leaf Disk Assay." *Journal of Environmental Horticulture* 25 (3): 131–33.

Li, Yonghao, M. T. Mmbaga, A. S. Windham, M. T. Windham, and R. N. Trigiano. 2009. "Powdery Mildew of Dogwoods: Current Status and Future Prospects." *Plant Disease* 93 (11): 1084–92.

McArdle, Alice Jacot, and Frank S. Santamour Jr. 1987a. "Cultivar Checklist of *Quercus* (Excluding Subg. *Quercus*)." *Journal of Arboriculture* 13 (10): 250–56.

———. 1987b. "Cultivar Checklist of White Oak Species (Excluding *Quercus robur* L.)." *Journal of Arboriculture* 13 (8): 203–8.

Metrustry, Deborah, and Dr. Tomasz Anisko. 2006. "Versatile Vitex." *American Nurseryman* 204 (6): 26–34.

Meyer, P. W., and R. Lewandowski. 1985. "The 'Okame' Cherry." *Arnoldia* 45 (1): 23–24.

Neely, Dan, and E. B. Himelick. 1989. "Susceptibility of Honeylocust Cultivars to Thyronectria Canker." *Journal of Arboriculture* 15 (8): 189–91.

Nicholson, Robert. 1989. "*Parrotia persica*: An Ancient Tree for Modern Landscapes." *Arnoldia* 49 (4): 34–39.

Nowak, David J., and Rowan Rountree. 1990. "History and Range of Norway Maple." *Journal of Arboriculture* 16 (11): 291–96.

Pooler, Margaret. 1999. "Preservation and DNA Fingerprinting of the Historic Tidal Basin Cherries." *Journal of Environmental Horticulture* 17 (4): 189–92.

Price, Julie Guckenberger, Amy N. Wright, Robert S. Boyd, and Kenneth M. Tilt. 2010. "Above-Grade Planting with Organic Matter Improves Post-transplant Growth of Two Native Shrub Species." *HortTechnology* 21 (5): 520–24.

Quinn, L. D., D. J. Allen, and J. R. Stewart. 2010. "Invasiveness Poten-

tial of *Miscanthus sinensis*: Implications for Bioenergy Production in the United States." *GCB Bioenergy* 2:310–20. https://doi.org/10.1111/j.1757-1707.2010.01062.x.

Trusty, J. L., B. G. Lockaby, W. C. Zipperer, and L. R. Goertzen. 2007. "Identity of Naturalized Exotic Wisteria (Fabaceae) in the South-Eastern United States." *Weed Research* 47:479–87.

Whittemore, Alan. 2004. "Sawtooth Oak (*Quercus acutissima*, Fagaceae) in North America." *Sida, Contributions to Botany* 21:447–54. http://www.ars.usda.gov/ research/publications/publications. htm?seq_no_115=143169.

Whittemore, Alan T., and Richard T. Olsen. 2011. "Ulmus americana (Ulmaceae) Is a Polyploid Complex." *American Journal of Botany* 98 (4): 1–7.

Williams, J. David, Donna C. Fare, Charles H. Gilliam, Gary J. Keever, Harry G. Ponder, John T. Owen, and Greg Creech. 1995. "Superior Shade Tree Selections for the Southeastern United States." *Journal of Arboriculture* 21 (3): 118–21.

Windham, M. T., E. T. Graham, W. T. Witte, J. L. Knighten, and R. N. Trigiano. 1998. "*Cornus florida* 'Appalachian Spring': A White Flowering Dogwood Resistant to Dogwood Anthracnose." *HortScience* 33 (7): 1265–67.

Windham, M. T., and W. T. Witte. 1998. "Naturally Occurring Resistance to Powdery Mildew in Seedlings of *Cornus florida*." *Journal of Environmental Horticulture* 16 (3): 173–75.

World Health Organization. 2009. "Fructus Agni Casti." In *WHO Monographs on Selected Medicinal Plants*, 4:9–29.

Wyman, Donald. 1951. "Woody Plants Used in Colonial Williamsburg." *Arnoldia* 11 (11): 75–78.

———. 1965. "Plants for Screening Junkyards, Gravel Pits, and Dumps." *Arnoldia* 25 (8): 45–48.

WEBSITES

"About the Fire Effects Information System (FEIS)." U.S. Forest Service. https://www.fs.fed.us/database/feis/AboutFEIS/about.html.

AggieTurf. http://aggieturf.tamu.edu.

American Camellia Society. http://www.americancamellias.org/display.aspx?catid=3,136,137.

American-Lawns.com. http://www.american-lawns.com/index.html#.

American Rhododendron Society. http://www.rhododendron.org/.

American Standard for Nursery Stock. American Horticulture Association and the American National Standards Institute. *https://cdn.ymaws.com/americanhort.site-ym.com/resource/collection/38ED7535-9C88-45E5-AF44-01C26838ADoC/ANSI_Nursery_Stock_Standards_AmericanHort_2014.pdf* https://cdn.ymaws.com/americanhort.site-ym.com/resource/collection/38ED7535-9C88-45E5-AF44-01C26838ADoC/ANSI_Nursery_Stock_Standards_AmericanHort_2014.pdf.

Antique Rose Emporium website. https://antiqueroseemporium.com/.

Antosh, Gary. 2001. *Success with Your Aglaonemas Indoors.* Miami: GHA. http://www.aroid.org/genera/aglaonema/aglaonema_success/aglaonema_success.pdf.

Arnold, Michael A. 2004. "*Sansevieria trifasciata.*" http://aggie-horticulture.tamu.edu/syllabi/608/Lists/second%20ed/Sansevieriatrifasciata.pdf.

———. 2009. "*Chlorophytum comosum.*" http://aggie-horticulture.tamu.edu/syllabi/308/Lists/Fourth Edition/Chlorophytumcomosum.pdf.

"Bacterial Leaf Scorch—Trees." University of Maryland Extension Home and Garden Information Center. https://extension.umd.edu/hgic/bacterial-leaf-scorch-trees.

"Characteristics of Crape Myrtle Varieties." August 12, 2005. http://www.clemson.edu/extension/horticulture/landscape_ornamentals/crapemyrtle/.

Chen, Jianjun, Dennis B. McConnell, Richard J. Henny, and Kelly C. Everitt. "Cultural Guidelines for Commercial Production of Interiorscape Dieffenbachia." University of Florida IFAS Extension. http://edis.ifas.ufl.edu/ep137.

Classic Viburnum Plant Library. http://www.classicviburnums.com/index.cfm/fuseaction/plants.main/index.htm.

"Common Poisonous Plants and Plant Parts." Earth-Kind Landscaping. Texas A&M Agrilife Extension. https://aggie-horticulture.tamu.edu/earthkind/landscape/poisonous-plants-resources/common-poisonous-plants-and-plant-parts/.

"Complete List of HGIC Fact Sheets & Links." Clemson Cooperative Extension Home & Garden Information Center. http://www.clemson.edu/extension/hgic/complete_list.html#lawns.

Cook, Will. "Trees, Shrubs, and Woody Vines of North Carolina." Carolina Nature. http://www.carolinanature.com/trees/.

Crape Myrtles for Texas Database. https://aggie-horticulture.tamu.edu/databases/crapemyrtle/.

"Deer Resistant Plants." High Country Gardens website. http://www.highcountrygardens.com/plant-finder/deer-resistant-plants?gclid=CJOYypD-t9ECFdU7gQodRooBDA.

"Dieffenbachia." September 16, 2015. Clemson Cooperative Extension Home & Garden Information Center. http://www.clemson.edu/extension/hgic/plants/indoor/foliage/hgic1503.html.

"*Epipremnum aureum* (Linden & André) G. S. Bunting." The Exotic Rainforest. http://www.exoticrainforest.com/Epipremnum aureum pc.html.

Feaster, Felicia. "24 Deer-Resistant Plants." HGTV website. http://www.hgtv.com/outdoors/flowers-and-plants/24-deer-resistant-plants-pictures?c1=GA_DGTL_GardenProblems&c2=Google&c3=Deer-Resistant-3&c4=deer-resistant%2520plants.

"Ferns and Fern Allies." *Minnesota Wildflowers: A Field Guide to the Flora of Minnesota.* http://www.minnesotawildflowers.info/page/ferns-and-fern-allies.

"*Ficus elastica.*" http://www.public.asu.edu/~camartin/plants/Plant%20html%20files/ficuselastica.html.

Ficus Production Guide. http://mrec.ifas.ufl.edu/foliage/folnotes/ficus.htm.

"Find Plants." Lady Bird Johnson Wildflower Center. http://www.wildflower.org/plants/.

"Find Plants." Washington State University Clark County Extension PNW Plants. http://www.pnwplants.wsu.edu/FindPlant.aspx.

"Flower and Gardening Articles." Perry Perennial Pages. University of Vermont. http://pss.uvm.edu/ppp/articleS.htm.

"Flower Growing Guides." Cornell University. http://www.gardening.cornell.edu/homegardening/scenee139.html.

"Forest Health Protection." Northeastern Area State and Private Forestry. U.S. Forest Service. http://www.na.fs.fed.us/fhp/invasive_plants/weeds/.

Gilman, Edward F. "*Philodendron selloum* Selloum." University of Florida IFAS Extension. http://edis.ifas.ufl.edu/fp473.

———. "*Philodendron* × 'Xanadu' 'Xanadu' Philodendron." University of Florida IFAS Extension. http://edis.ifas.ufl.edu/fp474.

Gilman, Edward F., and Dennis G. Watson. "*Ilex* × *attenuata* 'Savannah' Savannah Holly." Forest Service Fact Sheet, November 1993. http://hort.ifas.ufl.edu/database/documents/pdf/tree_fact_sheets/ileattc.pdf.

Gilman, Edward F., Dennis G. Watson, Ryan W. Klein, Andrew K. Koeser, Deborah R. Hilbert, and Drew C. McLean. "*Ficus benjamina*: Weeping *figure.*" University of Florida IFAS Extension. http://edis.ifas.ufl.edu/st251.

———. "*Ficus elastica*: Rubber Tree." University of Florida IFAS Extension. http://edis.ifas.ufl.edu/st252.

Goodness Grows website. http://www.goodnessgrows.com/.

"Grasses, Sedges, Rushes, & Non-flowering Plants in Illinois." http://www.illinoiswildflowers.info/grasses/grass_index.htm#mshield_fern.

Griffin, Georgia, National Turfgrass Evaluation Program. http://www.ntep.org/states/ga1/ga1_tf.htm.

Hardy Fern Foundation Database. 2020. https://hardyferns.org/ferns/.

Hartman, John. "Bacterial Leaf Scorch." University of Kentucky—College of Agriculture, Cooperative Extension Service. ppfs-or-w-12. https://plant pathology.ca.uky.edu/files/ppfs-or-w -12.pdf.

Hensley, David, and Jay Deputy. September 1998. "Nandina (Heavenly Bamboo)." College of Tropical Agriculture and Human Resources, Cooperative Extension Service. https://www.ctahr .hawaii.edu/oc/freepubs/pdf/OF-26 .pdf.

Hill, Steven R. May 7, 2007. Conservation Assessment for Yellowwood. inhs Technical Report. usda Forest Service. http://www.ideals.illinois.edu/bitstream /handle/2142/18118/INHS2007_28.pdf ?sequence=2.

Hortanswers. University of Illinois Extension. http://urbanext.illinois.edu /hortanswers/searchplant.cfm.

"Invasive and Exotic Weeds." Invasive. org. http://www.invasive.org/species /weeds.cfm.

King, Gary J., Christopher P. Lindsey, and Mark E. Zampardo. UI Plants. University of Illinois Champaign. https:// wp.hort.net/.

Louisiana Ecosystems and Plant Identification. http://www.rnr.lsu.edu/plantid/.

Lucas, Steve. "Growing Tropical Philodendron Species." The Exotic Rainforest. http://www.exoticrainforest.com /Grow%20or%20Growing%20Phil odendrons.html.

Mayfield, Albert, Stephen W. Fraedrich, and Paul Merten. October 2019. "Pest Alert." United States Department of Agriculture, Forest Service. https:// www.fs.usda.gov/Internet/FSE _DOCUMENTS/fseprd673152.pdf.

Miller, J. H., E. B. Chambliss, and C. T. Baargeron. "Invasive Plants of the Thirteen Southeastern States." http:// www.invasive.org/south/seweeds.cfm ?sort=20.

Missouri Botanical Garden Plant Finder. http://www.missouribotanicalgarden .org/plantfinder/plantfindersearch.aspx.

Morton, J. 1987. "Feijoa." In Fruits of Warm Climates, by Julia F. Morton, 367–70. Miami, Fla. http://www.hort.purdue .edu/newcrop/morton/feijoa.html.

Mt. Cuba Center website. https://mt cubacenter.org/.

National Gardening Association Plants Database. https://garden.org/plants.

National Invasive Species Information Center (nisic). U.S. Department of Agriculture. http://www.invasive speciesinfo.gov/index.shtml.

"National Turfgrass Evaluation Program." http://www.ntep.org/data/pro4/pro4 _10-10/pro4_10-10.pdf.

Nitzsche, Pete, Pedro Perdomo, and David Drake. "Landscape Plants Rated by Deer Resistance." New Jersey Agricultural Experiment Station. http://njaes .rutgers.edu/deerresistance/default .asp.

North Carolina Cooperative Extension. September 24, 2015. "Deer Resistant Plants: Recommended for Central and Southeastern NC Landscapes." https:// chatham.ces.ncsu.edu/wp-content /uploads/2015/09/Deer-Resistant -Plants-Updated.pdf?fwd=no.

North Carolina Cooperative Extension. "Salt Tolerant Plants: Recommended for Pender County Landscapes." Pender County Cooperative Extension, Urban Horticulture Leaflet 14. https://86cb8127dc14737f5057 -7c0671222953158607ea93d5febd68b4 .ssl.cf1.rackcdn.com/888/assets/v1 /489000/489297/salt-tolerant-plants .pdf.

North Carolina Extension Gardener Plant Toolbox. https://plants.ces.ncsu .edu/.

"Oleander." March 14, 2016. Clemson Cooperative Extension Home & Garden Information Center. http://www .clemson.edu/extension/hgic/plants /landscape/shrubs/hgic1079.html.

"Ornamental Cherry, Plum, Apricot & Almond." July 24, 2019. Clemson Cooperative Extension Home & Garden Information Center. http:// www.clemson.edu/extension/hgic /plants/landscape/trees/hgic1018.html.

"Pecan: Carya illinoinensis (Wangenh.) K. Koch." Plant Guide. U.S. Department of Agriculture Natural Resources Conservation Service. http://plants .usda.gov/plantguide/pdf/cs_cail2.pdf.

Pennisi, Bodie V. Native Plants for Georgia Part I: Trees, Shrubs and Woody Vines. University of Georgia Extension, bulletin 987. http://extension.uga.edu /publications/detail.cfm?number=B987.

———. Native Plants for Georgia Part II: Ferns. University of Georgia Extension, bulletin 987-2. http://extension.uga. edu/publications/detail.cfm?number =B987-2.

———. Native Plants for Georgia Part III: Wildflowers. University of Georgia Extension, bulletin 987-3. http://extension.uga.edu/publications /detail.cfm?number=B987-3.

"Philodendron cordatum Kunth." The Exotic Rainforest. http://www.exotic rainforest.com/Philodendron%20 cordatum%20pc.html.

"Philodendron hederaceum (Jacq.) Schott (1829)." The Exotic Rainforest. http:// www.exoticrainforest.com/Philoden dron%20hederaceum%20pc.html.

"Phyllostachys aurea." Fire Effects Information System (feis)." U.S. Forest Service. http://www.fs.fed.us/database /feis/plants/graminoid/phyaur/all.html.

Plant Delights Nursery Inc. http://www .plantdelights.com/.

PlantFacts. http://plantfacts.osu.edu/.

"Plant Type Poisonous." North Carolina Extension Gardener Plant Toolbox. https://plants.ces.ncsu.edu/plants /category/poisonous-plants/.

"Poisonous Plants." aspca website. https://www.aspca.org/pet-care/animal -poison-control/toxic-and-non-toxic -plants.

Poisonous Plants of the Southeastern United States. Alabama Cooperative Extension System. anr-975. https://ssl.acesag .auburn.edu/pubs/docs/A/ANR-0975 /ANR-0975-archive.pdf.

Rawlins, Karan A., Rachel L. Winston, Charles T. Bargeron, David J. Moorhead, and Rachel Carroll. New Invaders of the Southeast. USDA Forest Service, Forest Health Assessment and Applied Sciences Team, Morgantown, W.Va. fhtet-2017-05. https://bugwoodcloud .org/resource/pdf/FHTET-2017-05 _New%20Invaders_SE.pdf.

Royal Horticultural Society Horticultural Database. http://apps.rhs.org.uk/horti culturaldatabase/.

"Rubber Plant." December 15, 2015. Clemson Cooperative Extension Home & Garden Information Center. http://www.clemson.edu/extension/ hgic/plants/indoor/foliage/hgic1510 .html.

Saia, John A, Joseph W. Seamone, and Susanne E. Zilberfarb. "Introduction to Cold-Hardy Tropicals for Virginia Landscapes." Virginia Cooperative Extension. https://www.pubs.ext.vt.edu/content/dam/pubs_ext_vt_edu/3005/3005-1446/3005-1446_pdf.pdf.

"Silverbells." February 21, 2013. University of Maryland Extension Home & Garden Information Center. https://hgic.clemson.edu/factsheet/silverbells/.

Southeastern Palm Society. http://sepalms.org/.

"Toxic Plants (by Scientific Name)." Safe and Poisonous Garden Plants. University of California. https://ucanr.edu/sites/poisonous_safe_plants/Toxic_Plants_by_Scientific_Name_685/.

The Tree and Its Environment. Vol. 1, *Conifers.* https://www.srs.fs.usda.gov/pubs/misc/ag_654/volume_1/vol1_table_of_contents.htm.

The Tree and Its Environment. Vol. 2, *Hardwoods.* https://www.srs.fs.usda.gov/pubs/misc/ag_654/volume_2/vol2_table_of_contents.htm.

Trees and Shrubs That Tolerate Saline Soils and Salt Spray Drift. April 8, 2015. Virginia Cooperative Extension, publication 430-031. http://pubs.ext.vt.edu/430/430-031/430-031.html.

Trenholm, L. E., J. B. Unruh, and T. W. Shaddox. "St. Augustinegrass for Florida Lawns." University of Florida IFAS Extension. http://edis.ifas.ufl.edu/lh010.

"Turfgrass and Environmental Research Online." USGA. http://usgatero.msu.edu/v03/n13.pdf.

Turfgrass Selection: Zoysia. UT Extension. http://utextension.tennessee.edu/publications/Documents/W159-H.pdf.

The UC Guide to Healthy Lawns. University of California Agriculture and Natural Resources Statewide Integrated Pest Management Program. http://www.ipm.ucdavis.edu/TOOLS/TURF/TURFSPECIES/.

University of Georgia College of Agricultural and Environmental Sciences. *GeorgiaTurf: Species.* "Warm Season Turfgrass." https://turf.caes.uga.edu/turfgrass-species/warm-season-turfgrass.html.

U.S. Department of Agriculture Plant Hardiness Zone Map for the United States. 2012. https://planthardiness.ars.usda.gov/PHZMWeb/.

U.S. Department of Agriculture Plants Database. http://plants.usda.gov/java/.

"Viburnum." October 14, 2014. Clemson Cooperative Extension Home & Garden Information Center. http://www.clemson.edu/extension/hgic/plants/landscape/shrubs/hgic1075.html.

Wade, Gary L., and Michael T. Mengak. February 1, 2016. *Deer-Tolerant Ornamental Plants.* University of Georgia Extension, circular 985. http://extension.uga.edu/publications/detail.cfm?number=C985.

"Weeping Ficus." February 15, 2016. Clemson Cooperative Extension Home & Garden Information Center. http://www.clemson.edu/extension/hgic/plants/indoor/foliage/hgic1514.html.

Woodlanders website. http://www.woodlanders.net/.

Woody Plants Database. Urban Horticulture Institute, Cornell University. http://woodyplants.cals.cornell.edu/home.

Image Credits

The authors thank the following individuals and institutions for the use of their images. All other images are by the authors.

p. 12 (fig. 16): https://www.goodfreephotos.com

p. 22 right: Professor Emeritus Bill Mann

p. 31: Griffith, G. E., J. M. Omernik, J. A. Comstock, S. Lawrence, G. Martin, A. Goddard, V. J. Hulcher, and T. Foster, 2001, *Ecoregions of Alabama and Georgia* (Reston, Va.: U.S. Geological Survey)

p. 34 (fig. 35): USDA

p. 287 middle: Maureen O'Brien

p. 360 middle: Shannon Currey

p. 360 bottom: Shannon Currey

p. 364 top: Hoffman Nursery

p. 370 all: Hoffman Nursery

p. 371 top: Hoffman Nursery

p. 371 middle: Hoffman Nursery

p. 371 bottom left: Hoffman Nursery

p. 385 bottom: Andrew Bailey

p. 393 left: Brady Richards

p. 460 middle: Dr. John Ruter

p. 464 middle top: Andrew Bailey

p. 470: Dr. Clint Waltz

p. 475 middle and bottom: Dr. Clint Waltz

Index of Common Names

abelia, 200, 324
accolade cherry, 157
Adam's needle yucca, 344
African marigolds, 489
agave, 202
ageratum, 413
airplane plant, 532, 535
ajuga, 399
Algerian ivy, 557
Allegheny spurge, 389
alum root, 384
amaranth, 484
American beautyberry, 302
American beech, 65
American elm, 93
American holly, 176
American snowbell, 163
American wisteria, 529
amsonia, 402–403
amur honeysuckle, 553
Andorra juniper, 334
anemone, 404
angel's trumpet, 410
anise tree, 215
annual vinca, 483
Anthony Waterer spiraea, 349
Appalachian sedge, 356
arborvitae, 236, 281, 343
ardisia, 325, 550
Armand clematis, 513
ash, 316, 317
ashy sunflower, 424
Asian jasmine, 519
asparagus fern, 534
aster, 407, 460
astilbe, 408
Atlas cedar, 169
August beauty gardenia, 284
autumn fern, 496
autumn joy sedum, 428
autumn olive, 550
azalea, 233, 295–296, 314–315, 339

baby's breath spiraea, 319
bald cypress, 91
bamboo, 555, 561
banana, 446

banana shrub, 220
barberry, 276, 301
barrenwort, 418
basswood, 117
bearded iris, 432
bearded tongue, 450
bear's breeches, 395
beauty bush, 260
bee balm, 445
beech, 65
begonia, 482
bent white trillium, 464
Berckman's golden arborvitae, 343
Bermuda grass, 471–472
big bluestem, 361
bigleaf magnolia, 107
bigleaf periwinkle, 393
black cherry, 112
black-eyed Susan, 454
blackgum, 108
black locust, 113
black needle rush, 359
black oak, 89
black walnut, 69
black willow, 115
blazing star, 440
blue agave, 202
blue dune grass, 365
blue-eyed grass, 360
blue fescue, 358
blue rug juniper, 334
blue star, 403
bluestem, 361, 370
blue wood sedge, 356
Boston ivy, 525
bottlebrush, 203
bottlebrush buckeye, 245
boxelder, 97
boxwood, 277–278, 326
Brazilian verbena, 466
bridalwreath spiraea, 318
broom sedge, 361
buckeye, 98, 128, 245
bugle weed, 399
Burford holly, 551
Burkwood viburnum, 269
burning bush, 250

butcher's broom, 341
butterfly bush, 246
butterfly ginger, 423
butterfly weed, 406
buttonbush, 247

cabbage palm, 194
California gray rush, 359
Callery pear, 548
camellia, 204–206, 279
Canadian hemlock, 196
candytuft, 385
canna, 411
cape leadwort, 488
cardinal flower, 442
Carissa holly, 330
Carolina hemlock, 196
Carolina jessamine, 516
Carolina silverbell, 141
Carolina snailseed, 514
Carolina sweetshrub, 303
cast iron plant, 380
catalpa, 101
Catawba rhododendron, 232
cedar, 169–171, 181
centipede grass, 473
century plant, 202
chastetree, 270
Cherokee rose, 265
cherry, 112, 152, 155–158
cherrybark oak, 77
cherry laurel, 193
chestnut oak, 81
chinaberry, 547
Chindo viburnum, 237
Chinese elm, 549
Chinese evergreen, 533
Chinese flame tree, 142
Chinese holly, 551
Chinese mahonia, 338
Chinese parasol tree, 546
Chinese photinia, 555
Chinese pistache, 111
Chinese privet, 553
Chinese silvergrass, 560
Chinese snowball viburnum, 267
Chinese star anise, 215

Chinese sumac, 159
Chinese wisteria, 559
Chinese witch hazel, 218
Christmas fern, 498
cinnamon fern, 505
clary sage, 457
clematis, 513, 522, 556
cleyera, 235
climbing aster, 407
climbing hydrangea, 523
climbing roses, 526
clump verbena, 422
coastal leucothoe, 336
coastal plain willow, 115
coleus, 489
columbine, 405
common Bermuda grass, 471
common mallow, 426
common milkweed, 406
common periwinkle, 394
common rush, 359
coneflower, 416, 454
confederate jasmine, 520
confederate rose, 426
coral ardisia, 550
coral bells, 384
coralberry, 550
corkscrew willow, 114
crabapple, 149
crape myrtle, 144–145
creeping bent grass, 470
creeping fig, 515
creeping Jenny, 444
creeping phlox, 390
creeping raspberry, 391
crocosmia, 414
crocus, 415
crossvine, 512
cucumber magnolia, 107
cycad, 282
cypress, 91, 173–174

daffodil, 447
daisy, 438
Danica arborvitae, 343
daphne, 327
Darlington oak, 78
dawn redwood, 72
daylily, 425
DeGroot's spire arborvitae, 236
deodar cedar, 170
deutzia, 249, 345
devil's ivy, 537
devil's walkingstick, 130
devilwood, 223
distylium, 328

doghobble, 336
dogwood, 135, 137
doublefile viburnum, 268
dracaena, 536–537
drooping leucothoe, 289
dumbcane, 535
dwarf Andorra juniper, 334
dwarf Burford holly, 552
dwarf crested iris, 430
dwarf English boxwood, 236
dwarf gardenia, 329
dwarf Japanese garden juniper, 335
dwarf pomegranate, 347
dwarf schefflera, 542
dwarf yaupon holly, 287

eastern gamagrass, 373
eastern redbud, 132
eastern red cedar, 181
eastern white pine, 189
East Palatka holly, 177
Edward Goucher abelia, 200
elderberry, 266
elephant ear, 412
elm, 92–93, 118, 549
emerald zoysia, 478
Emily Bruner holly, 175
Encore Series azaleas, 296
English ivy, 557
English laurel, 230
English oak, 112
European beech, 65
European black elderberry, 266
European hornbeam, 100
European snowball viburnum, 267

false blue indigo, 409
falsecypress, 208, 281
fancy leaf caladium, 482
fatsia, 283
feather-reed grass, 362
fern, 495–508, 534
fescue, 358, 474
fetterbush, 289
fig, 252, 515, 538
firethorn, 231
fiveleaf akebia, 511
Florida flame azalea, 314
Florida gamagrass, 373
Florida jasmine, 312
Florida leucothoe, 201
flowering crabapple, 149
flowering peach, 154
flowering quince, 304
foamflower, 461
Formosa lily, 441

forsythia, 307
forsythia sage, 457
Fortune's osmanthus, 226
Foster's holly, 178
fothergilla, 308
fountain grass, 369, 486
foxglove, 484
fragrant sumac, 348
Franklinia, 140
Fraser magnolia, 107
Fraser's photinia, 227
Freeman maple, 60
French hydrangea, 310
French marigold, 489
fringetree, 133–134
fuzzy deutzia, 249

gallberry, 286
gamagrass, 373
garden hydrangea, 310
gardenia, 284, 329
garden phlox, 453
garden verbena, 490
gaura, 421
geranium, 486
giant reed, 560
ginger, 401, 423
ginkgo, 68
globe amaranth, 484
glossy abelia, 200
golden bamboo, 561
golden bells, 307
golden ragwort, 448
goldenraintree, 143
goldenrod, 458
gold moss, 392
grancy graybeard, 134
green ash, 67

hackberry, 64
ham and eggs, 437
hard rush, 359
hardy hibiscus, 426
hawthorn, 139, 294
heartleaf philodendron, 540
heavenly bamboo, 555
hedge apple, 106
Helleri holly, 331
hemlock, 196
hibiscus, 255, 426
hickory, 61, 63
Higan cherry, 157
Himalayan sweetbox, 342
Hinoki falsecypress, 208
holly, 175–180, 212–213, 285–287, 330–331,
    551–552

holly fern, 495
holly osmanthus, 225
Hollywood juniper, 288
honeylocust, 105
honeysuckle, 261, 517, 553, 558
hophornbeam, 109
hornbeam, 100
horsechestnut, 98, 128
horsetail rush, 382
hosta, 427
hybrid Bermuda grass, 472
hybrid witch hazel, 254
hydrangea, 256–257, 309–310, 523
hyssop, 398

impatiens, 485
Indian grass, 371
Indian hawthorn, 294
indigo, 409
inkberry, 286
inland sea oats, 363
iris, 430–436
ironweed, 467
ironwood, 131
Italian cypress, 174
ivy, 525, 528, 537, 557

Jackman clematis, 522
Jackson vine, 518
Japanese andromeda, 291
Japanese anemone, 404
Japanese ardisia, 325
Japanese aucuba, 275
Japanese barberry, 301
Japanese black pine, 191
Japanese cedar, 181
Japanese fatsia, 283
Japanese garden juniper, 335
Japanese holly, 285
Japanese honeysuckle, 558
Japanese iris, 430
Japanese kerria, 313
Japanese maple, 126–127
Japanese pagoda tree, 162
Japanese painted fern, 502
Japanese plum, 210
Japanese plum yew, 280
Japanese roof iris, 436
Japanese snowball viburnum, 268
Japanese snowbell, 163
Japanese spurge, 389
Japanese star anise, 215
Japanese sweet flag, 355
Japanese wisteria, 559
jasmine, 312, 346, 519–520
jelly palm, 168

Jerusalem artichoke, 424
Joe Pye weed, 419
juniper, 288, 332–335

Kanzan cherry, 155
katsura tree, 102
knockout rose, 316
Korean dogwood, 137
Kousa dogwood, 137
kudzu, 558
Kurume azaleas, 295

lacebark pine, 185
Lady Banks rose, 264
lady fern, 502
lady palm, 540
lamb's ear, 459
lantana, 437
laurel, 193, 216, 230, 292, 341
laurel oak, 78
laurustinus viburnum, 240
leather flower, 522
leatherleaf mahonia, 554
leatherleaf viburnum, 239
leathery rush, 359
lenten rose, 383
leopard plant, 420
leucothoe, 201, 289, 336
Leyland cypress, 173
ligustrum, 217, 546
lily, 397, 441–443
lily of the Nile, 397
lily turf, 386
liriope, 386
little bluestem, 370
littleleaf boxwood, 277
littleleaf linden, 117
live oak, 90
loblolly pine, 190
Loebner magnolia, 147
London planetree, 73
longleaf pine, 188
loquat, 210
Louisiana iris, 433
lusterleaf holly, 175

Madagascar periwinkle, 483
magnolia, 107, 146–148, 182–183
magnolialeaf holly, 175
mahonia, 337–338, 554
maidenhair fern, 501
mallow, 426
maple, 56–60, 124–127
marginal shield fern, 497
Mariana maiden fern, 503
marigold, 489

Mary Nell holly, 175
mazus, 387
Mexican feather grass, 367
Mexican petunia, 455
Mexican zinnia, 491
Meyer zoysia, 477
milkweed, 406
million bells, 483
mimosa, 545
mist flower, 413
mockernut hickory, 63
mock orange, 262
mondo, 388
money tree, 539
monkey grass, 388
montbretia, 414
moss pink, 390
moss verbena, 422
mother-in-laws tongue, 541
moundlily yucca, 297
mountain laurel, 216
Mt. Airy fothergilla, 308
mulberry, 545, 547
musclewood, 131

nandina, 555
narrowleaf zinnia, 491
narrow leaved cattail, 374
needle palm, 293
Nellie R. Stevens holly, 180
netted chain fern, 508
New England aster, 407
New Guinea impatiens, 485
New Mexico hardy century plant, 202
New York aster, 407
New York fern, 507
Nikko maple, 125
Norfolk Island pine, 533
northern catalpa, 101
northern maidenhair fern, 501
northern red oak, 85
Norway maple, 56
Nuttall oak, 88

oak, 74–90, 112
oakleaf hydrangea, 257
Ohio buckeye, 98
Okame cherry, 156
oleander, 222
Oregon grapeholly, 290
oriental persimmon, 104
ornamental onion, 400
Osage orange, 106
osmanthus, 225, 226
Otto Luyken laurel, 292
overcup oak, 79

pachysandra, 389
palm, 168, 194–195, 282, 293, 540
palm sedge, 356
pampas grass, 357
panic grass, 368
panicle hydrangea, 256
pansy, 491
paperbark maple, 125
paperbush, 306
paper mulberry, 545
parney cotoneaster, 209
parrotia, 151
Parson's juniper, 332
paulownia, 548
peace lily, 442
peach, 154
pearlbush, 251
pecan, 62
Pennsylvania sedge, 356
pentas, 487
peony, 449
periwinkle, 393–394, 483
Persian ironwood, 151
persimmon, 104
petunia, 455, 483, 487
Pfitzer juniper, 288
philodendron, 539–540
phlox, 390, 452–453
photinia, 227, 555
Piedmont azalea, 314
Piedmont rhododendron, 234
pieris, 291
pignut hickory, 61
pindo palm, 168
pine, 185–192, 533
pineapple guava, 211
pink muhly grass, 366
pinks, 381
pink surprise lily, 443
pin oak, 83
pittosporum, 228
planetree, 73
plantain lily, 427
plum, 153, 210
plumbago, 488
plumleaf azalea, 315
podocarpus, 229
poet's laurel, 341
poison ivy, 528
pomegranate, 263, 347
pond cypress, 91
popcorn tree, 549
possumhaw, 258
post oak, 87
pothos, 537
Prague viburnum, 241

prairie dropseed, 372
primrose jasmine, 312
princess tree, 548
privet, 553
purple coneflower, 416
purple fountain grass, 486
purple heart plant, 462
purpleleaf plum, 153
purple love grass, 486
purple trillium, 464
pyracantha, 231

quince, 304

ragwort, 448
raspberry, 391
red Abyssinian banana, 446
redbay, 184
red buckeye, 128
redbud, 132
red horsechestnut, 128
redleaf Chinese witch hazel, 219
red maple, 57
red-margined dracaena, 537
red mulberry, 547
red oak, 77, 85
Reeves spiraea, 317
rhododendron, 232, 234
rigid verbena, 466
river birch, 99
rock elm, 92
rose, 264, 265, 316, 383, 526
rosebay rhododendron, 234
rosemary, 340
rose of Sharon, 255
rotunda holly, 552
royal fern, 506
rubber plant, 538
rush, 359, 382
Russian sage, 451
ryegrass, 475

sabal palm, 194
sage, 451, 457, 488
sago palm, 282
salvia, 456, 488
sandanqua viburnum, 240
sasanqua camellia, 206
sassafras, 116
Satsuki azaleas, 339
saucer magnolia, 148
Savannah holly, 179
sawtooth oak, 74
scarlet oak, 76
scarlet sage, 488
schefflera, 541–542

schip laurel, 292
scouring rush, 382
seashore paspalum, 475
seaside goldenrod, 458
sedge, 356, 361
sedum, 392, 428
sensitive fern, 504
serviceberry, 129
shagbark hickory, 61
Shasta daisy, 438
shell ginger, 401
Sherwood abelia, 324
shore juniper, 333
shortleaf pine, 186
Shumard oak, 86
Siberian elm, 118
Siberian iris, 435
silver maple, 58
slash pine, 187
slender deutzia, 345
slippery elm, 93
smoketree, 138
smooth aster, 407
smooth hydrangea, 309
smooth sumac, 160
snake plant, 541
snapdragon, 481
snowbell, 163
snow trillium, 464
society garlic, 465
soft caress mahonia, 337
sourwood, 110
southern catalpa, 101
southern Indica azalea, 233
southern magnolia, 182
southern maidenhair fern, 500
southern red oak, 77
southern shield fern, 507
southern sugar maple, 59
southern wax myrtle, 221
Spanish dagger, 242, 297
spider plant, 535
spiderwort, 463
spiraea, 317–320, 349
splitbeard bluestem, 361
split leaf philodendron, 539
Sprenger's asparagus fern, 534
spring snowflake, 439
spruce pine, 189
spurge, 389
staghorn sumac, 161
starbush, 214
star flower, 487
star magnolia, 146
St. Augustine grass, 476
Stellar series dogwood, 137

St. John's wort, 429
Stokes' aster, 460
stonecrop, 392
sugarberry, 64
sugar hackberry, 64
sugar maple, 59
sumac, 159–161, 481
summer snapdragon, 481
summersweet clethra, 305
sunflower, 424
surprise lily, 443
swamp bay, 184
swamp chestnut oak, 80
swamp laurel oak, 78
swamp leucothoe, 289
swamp mallow, 426
swamp milkweed, 406
swamp sunflower, 424
sweet autumn clematis, 556
sweetbay magnolia, 183
sweetbox, 342
sweet flag, 354–355
sweetgum, 70
sweet mock orange, 262
sweet potato vine, 485
sweetshrub, 303
sweet viburnum, 238
switchgrass, 368
sycamore, 73

Taiwan flowering cherry, 152
tall fescue, 474
tall ironweed, 467
tallow tree, 549
tall verbena, 466
tassel fern, 499
tea camellia, 279
tea olive, 224
thorny elaeagnus, 550
threadleaf arborvitae, 281
threadleaf bluestar, 402
threadleaf falsecypress, 281
tiger lily, 441

toad trillium, 464
trailing petunia, 483
tree ligustrum, 546
tree of heaven, 544
tree philodendron, 539
trident maple, 124
trillium, 464
trumpet creeper, 521
trumpet honeysuckle, 517
tulip, 490
tulip poplar, 71
Turk's cap lily, 441
tussock sedge, 356

umbrella tree, 541
upright English oak, 112
upright European hornbeam, 100

Vanhoutte spiraea, 320
verbena, 422, 466, 490
vernal iris, 430
vernal witch hazel, 253
viburnum, 237–241, 267–269
vinca, 393–394, 483
vintage jade distylium, 328
violas, 491
Virginia creeper, 524
Virginia pine, 192
Virginia sweetspire, 311

wake robin, 464
walnut, 69
Washington hawthorn, 139
water oak, 82
wax leaf begonia, 482
wax leaf ligustrum, 217
wax myrtle, 221
Weber blue agave, 202
weeping fig, 538
weeping love grass, 364
weeping willow, 114
weeping yaupon holly, 213
weigela, 271

western hemlock, 196
whirling butterflies, 421
white ash, 66
white fringetree, 133
white mulberry, 547
white oak, 75
white wild indigo, 409
wild ageratum, 413
willow, 114–115
willowleaf sunflower, 424
willow oak, 84
windmill palm, 195
winged elm, 92
winged euonymus, 250
winged sumac, 159
winterberry, 259
wintercreeper, 556
winter daphne, 327
wintergreen barberry, 276
winter honeysuckle, 261
winter jasmine, 346
winter king hawthorn, 139
wintersweet, 248
wisteria, 529, 559
witch hazel, 218, 219, 253, 254
woodland phlox, 452

yarrow, 396
yaupon holly, 212, 213, 287
yellow buckeye, 98
yellow coneflower, 454
yellow flag iris, 434
yellow poplar, 71
yellow trillium, 464
yellow wild indigo, 409
yellowwood, 103
Yoshino cherry, 158
yucca, 297, 344

Zabel laurel, 292
zelkova, 119
zinnia, 491–492
zoysia, 477–478

Index of Scientific Names

Abelia × 'Edward Goucher', 200
Abelia × *grandiflora*, 40, 51, 198, 200
Abelia × *grandiflora* 'Sherwoodii', 322, 324
Acanthus mollis, 37, 395
Acanthus spinosus, 42, 378, 395
Acer barbatum, 59
Acer buergerianum, 122, 124
Acer × *freemanii*, 39, 54, 60
Acer griseum, 122, 125
Acer maximowiczianum, 125
Acer negundo, 39, 96, 97
Acer palmatum, 122, 126–27
Acer platanoides, 54, 56
Acer rubrum, 39, 54, 57
Acer saccharinum, 39, 54, 58
Acer saccharum, 54, 59
Achillea spp., 38, 377, 378, 396
Acorus calamus, 39, 40, 353, 354
Acorus gramineus, 39, 40, 354, 355
Adiantum capillus veneris, 494, 500
Adiantum pedatum, 494, 501
Aesculus × *carnea*, 128
Aesculus flava, 98
Aesculus glabra, 98
Aesculus hippocastanum, 96, 98, 128
Aesculus parviflora, 244, 245
Aesculus pavia, 41, 122, 128
Agapanthus spp., 378, 397
Agarista populifolia, 39, 198, 201
Agastache foeniculum, 398
Agastache spp., 377, 398
Agave americana, 38, 42, 198, 202
Agave parryi neomexicana, 202
Agave tequilana azul, 201
Agave weberi, 202
Aglaonema spp., 532, 533
Agrostis stolonifera, 470
Ailanthus altissima, 544
Ajuga reptans, 376, 399
Akebia quinata, 510, 511
Albizia julibrissin, 545
Allium spp., 377, 400
Alpinia zerumbet, 379, 401
Amelanchier × *grandiflora*, 41, 122, 129
Ampelaster carolinianus, 407
Amsonia ciliata, 402
Amsonia hubrichtii, 377, 402
Amsonia tabernaemontana, 377, 403

Andropogon gerardii, 361
Andropogon glomeratus, 361
Andropogon gyrans, 361
Andropogon ternarius, 361
Andropogon virginicus, 38, 353, 361
Anemone × *hybrida*, 378, 404
Angelonia angustifolia, 480, 481
Antirrhinum majus, 480, 481
Aquilegia canadensis, 41, 377, 405
Aquilegia longissima, 405
Aralia spinosa, 38, 41, 42, 122, 130
Araucaria heterophylla, 532, 533
Ardisia crenata, 550
Ardisia japonica, 322, 325
Arundo donax, 544, 560
Asclepias incarnata, 406
Asclepias syrica, 406
Asclepias tuberosa, 40, 41, 377, 406
Asparagus densiflorus 'Sprengeri', 532, 534
Asparagus setaceus, 534
Aspidistra elatior, 37, 376, 380
Aster spp., 377, 378, 407
Astilbe biternata, 408
Astilbe spp., 377, 408
Athyrium filix-femina, 502
Athyrium niponicum pictum, 494, 502
Aucuba japonica, 274, 275
Aucuba japonica borealis, 275

Baptisia alba, 409
Baptisia australis, 38, 378, 409
Baptisia spaerocarpa, 409
Baptisia tinctoria, 409
Begonia semperflorens-cultorum, 41, 480, 482
Berberis julianae, 38, 42, 274, 276
Berberis × *mentorensis*, 301
Berberis thunbergii, 38, 42, 300, 301
Betula nigra, 39, 96, 99
Bignonia capreolata, 41, 510, 512
Broussonetia papyrifera, 545
Brugmansia spp., 379, 410
Buddelja davidii, 38, 40, 41, 244, 246, 543
Butia capitate, 38, 166, 168
Buxus × 'Glencoe', 326
Buxus × 'Green Gem', 326
Buxus microphylla japonica, 274, 277
Buxus sempervirens, 274, 278

Buxus sempervirens 'Suffruticosa', 322, 326
Buxus sinica insularis, 277, 326

Caladium bicolor, 480, 482
Calamagrostis × *acutiflora* 'Karl Foerster', 38, 353, 362
Calibrachoa × hybrid, 480, 483
Callicarpa americana, 38, 300, 302
Callicarpa dichotoma, 302
Callistemon citrinus, 38, 198, 203
Calycanthus chinensis, 303
Calycanthus floridus, 300, 303
Calycanthus × *raulstonii*, 303
Camellia japonica, 198, 204
Camellia sasanqua, 198, 206
Camellia sinensis, 274, 279
Campsis radicans, 41, 510, 521
Canna × *generalis*, 39, 41, 379, 411
Carex applachica, 356
Carex flaccosperma, 356
Carex muskingumensis, 39, 356
Carex oshimensis, 356
Carex pensylvanica, 37, 356
Carex spp., 353, 356
Carex stricta, 39, 40, 356
Carpinus betulus 'Fastigiata', 96, 100
Carpinus caroliniana, 37, 39, 40, 122, 131
Carya glabra, 38, 54, 61
Carya illinoinensis, 54, 62
Carya ovata, 61
Carya tomentosa, 38, 54, 63
Catalpa bignonioides, 41, 96, 101, 543
Catalpa speciosa, 41, 101, 543
Catharanthus roseus, 480, 483
Cedrus atlantica, 38, 166, 169
Cedrus deodara, 38, 166, 170
Cedrus libani, 169
Celtis laevigata, 39, 54, 64
Celtis occidentalis, 64
Cephalanthus occidentalis, 39, 40, 244, 247
Cephalotaxus harringtonia, 274, 280
Cercidiphyllum japonicum, 96, 102
Cercis canadensis, 38, 41, 122, 132
Cercis canadensis texensis, 132
Chaenomeles speciosa, 42, 300, 304
Chaenomeles × *superba*, 304
Chamaecyparis nootkatensis, 173
Chamaecyparis obtusa 'Gracilis', 198, 208

Chamaecyparis obtusa 'Lemon Twist', 281
Chamaecyparis pisifera 'Filifera Aurea', 274, 281
Chasmanthium latifolium, 39, 353, 363
Chimonanthus praecox, 244, 248
Chionanthus retusus, 122, 133
Chionanthus virginicus, 39, 41, 122, 134
Chlorophytum comosum, 532, 535
Cladrastis kentuckea, 96, 103
Clematis armandii, 510, 513
Clematis crispa, 522
Clematis glaucophylla, 522
Clematis × jackmanii, 522
Clematis terniflora, 556
Clematis virginiana, 556
Clethra alnifolia, 39, 40, 300, 305
Cocculus carolinus, 510, 514
Colocasia esculenta, 39, 40, 379, 412
Conoclinium coelestinum, 39, 40, 376, 413
Cornus florida, 41, 122, 135
Cornus kousa, 122, 137
Cortaderia selloana, 38, 42, 353, 357
Cotinus coggygria, 122, 138
Cotinus obovatus, 138
Cotoneaster lacteus, 198, 209
Crataegus phaenopyrum, 139
Crataegus spp., 41, 42, 122, 139
Crataegus viridus, 139
Crocosmia × hybrida, 379, 414
Crocus speciosus, 415
Crocus spp., 376, 415
Cryptomeria japonica, 166, 171
Cunninghamia lanceolata, 38, 166, 172
Cupressus macrocarpa, 173
Cupressus sempervirens, 38, 167, 174
× Cuprocyparis leylandii, 166, 173
Cycas revoluta, 38, 174, 282
Cynodon dactylon, 470, 471
Cynodon spp., 470, 472
Cyrtomium falcatum, 37, 494, 495

Danae racemosa, 341
Daphne × burkwoodii, 327
Daphne odora, 322, 327
Deutzia gracilis, 323, 345
Deutzia × magnifica, 249
Deutzia scabra, 244, 249
Dianthus gratianopolitanus, 381
Dianthus spp., 37, 38, 376, 381
Dieffenbachia spp., 532, 535
Digitalis purpurea, 41, 480, 484
Diospyros kaki, 104
Diospyros virginiana, 96, 104
Distylium × 'Vintage Jade', 322, 328
Dracaena fragrans, 532, 536
Dracaena marginata, 532, 537

Dracaena sanderiana, 537
Dryopteris erythrosora, 494, 496
Dryopteris marginalis, 37, 494, 497

Echinacea purpurea, 37, 38, 40, 379, 416
Edgeworthia chrysantha, 300, 306
Elaeagnus pungens, 550
Eleagnus umbellata, 550
Ensete ventricosum, 446
Epimedium acuminatum, 418
Epimedium grandiflorum, 418
Epimedium spp., 376, 418
Epipremnum aureum, 532, 537
Equisetum arvense, 382
Equisetum hyemale, 39, 40, 376, 382
Eragrostis curvula, 364
Eragrostis elliottii, 364
Eragrostis spectabilis, 353, 364
Eremochloa ophiuroides, 470, 473
Eriobotrya japonica, 38, 198, 210
Euonymus alatus, 244, 250
Euonymus americanus, 250
Euonymus fortunei, 556
Eutrochium fistulosum, 39, 40, 419
Eutrochium maculatum, 39, 40, 379, 419
Eutrochium purpureum, 39, 40, 419
Exochorda × macrantha, 251
Exochorda racemosa, 244, 251

Fagus grandifolia, 54, 65
Fagus sylvatica, 65
Farfugium japonicum, 377, 420
Fatsia japonica, 37, 40, 274, 283
Feijoa sellowiana, 198, 211
Festuca arundinacea, 470, 474
Festuca glauca, 353, 358
Ficus benjamina, 532, 538
Ficus carica, 37, 244, 252
Ficus elastica, 532, 538
Ficus pumila, 37, 510, 515
Firmiana simplex, 546
Forsythia × intermedia, 300, 307
Forsythia viridissima, 307
Fothergilla gardenii, 308
Fothergilla × intermedia, 300, 308
Fothergilla major, 308
Franklinia altamaha, 122, 140
Fraxinus americana, 54, 66
Fraxinus pennsylvanica, 39, 54, 67

Gardenia jasminoides 'August Beauty', 274, 284
Gardenia jasminoides 'Radicans', 322, 329
Gaura lindheimeri, 379, 421
Gelsemium sempervirens, 41, 510, 516
Ginkgo biloba, 54, 68

Glandularia canadensis, 37, 38, 376, 422
Gleditsia triacanthos inermis, 39, 96, 105
Gomphrena globosa, 480, 484

Halesia diptera, 141
Halesia tetraptera, 122, 141
Hamamelis × intermedia, 244, 254
Hamamelis vernalis, 253
Hamamelis virginiana, 244, 253
Hedera helix, 557
Hedera helix canariensis, 557
Hedychium coronarium, 39, 379, 423
Helianthus angustifolius, 424
Helianthus mollis, 424
Helianthus salicifolius, 424
Helianthus spp., 39, 40, 379, 424
Helianthus tuberosus, 424
Helleborus × hybridus, 383
Helleborus orientalis, 37, 376, 383
Helleborus viridis, 383
Hemerocallis fulva, 425
Hemerocallis spp., 40, 41, 377, 425
Heuchera americana, 384
Heuchera spp., 376, 384
Heuchera villosa, 384
Hibiscus coccineus, 39, 426
Hibiscus moscheutos, 39, 426
Hibiscus mutabilis, 426
Hibiscus spp., 379, 426
Hibiscus syriacus, 38, 41, 244, 255
Hosta spp., 41, 376, 377, 427
Hydrangea anomala petiolaris, 41, 510, 523
Hydrangea arborescens, 41, 300, 309
Hydrangea macrophylla, 41, 300, 310
Hydrangea paniculata, 244, 256
Hydrangea quercifolia, 244, 257
Hylotelephium 'Autumn Joy', 38, 40, 377, 428
Hylotelephium spectabile, 428
Hypericum buckleyi, 429
Hypericum calycinum, 429
Hypericum densiflorum, 429
Hypericum frondosum, 429
Hypericum prolificum, 429
Hypericum spp., 377, 429

Iberis sempervirens, 37, 38, 376, 385
Ilex aquifolium, 180
Ilex × attenuata 'East Palatka', 167, 177
Ilex × attenuata 'Fosteri', 167, 178
Ilex × attenuata 'Savannah', 167, 179
Ilex cassine, 177, 178, 179
Ilex cornuta, 551
Ilex cornuta 'Burfordii', 551
Ilex cornuta 'Carissa', 322, 330
Ilex cornuta 'Dwarf Burford', 552

Ilex cornuta 'Rotunda', 552
Ilex crenata, 274, 285
Ilex crenata 'Helleri', 322, 331
Ilex decidua, 244, 258
Ilex glabra, 39, 274, 286
Ilex latifolia, 166, 175
Ilex × 'Nellie R. Stevens', 167, 180
Ilex opaca, 38, 167, 176
Ilex pernyi, 175
Ilex verticillata, 39, 40, 244, 259
Ilex vomitoria, 38, 39, 198, 212
Ilex vomitoria 'Folsom's Weeping', 198, 213
Ilex vomitoria 'Nana', 274, 287
Illicium anisatum, 215
Illicium floridanum, 39, 198, 214
Illicium henryi, 214
Illicium parviflorum, 39, 198, 215
Impatiens hawkeri, 41, 480, 485
Impatiens walleriana, 41, 485
Ipomoea batatas, 480, 485
Iris cristata, 376, 430
Iris ensata, 39, 377, 431
Iris × *germanica*, 377, 432
Iris × *louisiana*, 39, 40, 379, 433
Iris pseudacorus, 39, 40, 379, 434
Iris sibirica, 39, 377, 435
Iris tectorum, 377, 436
Iris verna smalliana, 430
Iris verna verna, 430
Itea virginica, 39, 40, 300, 311

Jasminum floridum, 300, 312
Jasminum mesnyi, 312
Jasminum nudiflorum, 323, 346
Juglans nigra, 54, 69
Juncus coriaceus, 359
Juncus effusus, 39, 359
Juncus inflexus, 359
Juncus patens, 359
Juncus roemerianus, 359
Juncus spp., 40, 353, 359
Juniperus chinensis, 288
Juniperus chinensis 'Parsonii', 322, 332
Juniperus conferta, 38, 322, 333
Juniperus davurica 'Expansa', 332
Juniperus davurica 'Parsonii', 332
Juniperus horizontalis, 38
Juniperus horizontalis 'Wiltonii', 322, 334
Juniperus × *pfitzeriana* 'Wilhelm Pfitzer', 274, 288
Juniperus procumbens, 322, 335
Juniperus squamata expansa 'Parsonii', 332
Juniperus virginiana, 38, 167, 181
Juniperus virginiana 'Grey Owl', 181, 332

Juniperus virginiana 'Silver Spreader', 181, 332
Juniperus silicola, 181

Kalmia latifolia, 198, 216
Kerria japonica, 38, 300, 313
Koelreuteria bipinnata, 41, 122, 142
Koelreuteria paniculata, 41, 122, 143
Kolkwitzia amabilis, 244, 260

Lagerstroemia spp., 38, 41, 122, 144
Lantana camara, 38, 40, 378, 379, 437
Lantana montevidensis, 437
Leucanthemum × *superbum*, 378, 438
Leucojum vernum, 377, 439
Leucothoe axillaris, 322, 336
Leucothoe fontanesiana, 274, 289
Leucothoe racemosa, 289
Leymus arenarius 'Blue Dune', 38, 353, 365
Liatris spicata, 41, 378, 440
Ligustrum japonicum, 198, 217, 546
Ligustrum lucidum, 546
Ligustrum sinense, 553
Lilium formosanum, 441
Lilium spp., 378, 379, 441
Lilium superbum, 441
Lilium tigrinum, 441
Liquidambar styraciflua, 39, 54, 70
Liriodendron tulipifera, 39, 54, 71
Liriope muscari, 376, 386
Liriope spicata, 386
Lobelia cardinalis, 39, 40, 41, 378, 442
Lolium perenne, 470, 475
Lonicera fragrantissima, 38, 244, 261
Lonicera japonica, 558
Lonicera maackii, 553
Lonicera sempervirens, 41, 510, 517
Loropetalum chinense, 42, 198, 218
Loropetalum chinense rubrum, 42, 198, 219
Lycoris radiata, 377, 443
Lycoris squamigera, 443
Lysimachia nummularia 'Aurea', 377, 444

Maclura pomifera, 38, 42, 96, 106
Macrothelypteris torresiana, 39, 40, 494, 503
Magnolia acuminata, 107
Magnolia denudata, 148
Magnolia figo, 198, 220
Magnolia fraseri, 107
Magnolia grandiflora, 39, 166, 167, 182
Magnolia lilliflora, 148
Magnolia × *loebneri*, 122, 147
Magnolia macrophylla, 96, 107
Magnolia × *soulangeana*, 122, 148
Magnolia stellata, 122, 146
Magnolia virginiana, 39, 167, 183
Mahonia aquifolium, 274, 290

Mahonia bealei, 554
Mahonia eurybracteata 'Soft Caress', 322, 337
Mahonia fortunei, 322, 338
Malus spp., 41, 122, 149
Mazus reptans, 376, 387
Melia azedarach, 547
Metasquoia glyptostroboides, 39, 54, 72
Miscanthus sinensis, 560
Monarda didyma, 39, 40, 41, 378, 445
Monarda fistulosa, 445
Morella cerifera, 39, 40, 198, 221
Morus alba, 547
Morus rubra, 547
Morus spp., 547
Muhlenbergia capillaris, 38, 353, 366
Musa basjoo, 446
Musa ensete, 446
Musa spp., 379, 446

Nandina domestica, 555
Narcissus spp., 377, 447
Nassella tenuissima, 38, 353, 367
Nerium oleander, 38, 198, 222
Nyssa sylvatica, 39, 41, 96, 108

Onoclea sensibilis, 40, 494, 504
Ophiopogon japonicus, 37, 376, 388
Ophiopogon planiscapus, 388
Osmanthus americanus, 39, 198, 223
Osmanthus × *fortunei*, 198, 226
Osmanthus fragrans, 198, 224
Osmanthus heterophyllus, 198, 225
Osmunda cinnamomea, 39, 40, 494, 505
Osmunda regalis, 39, 40, 494, 506
Ostrya virginiana, 37, 39, 40, 96, 109
Oxydendrum arboreum, 41, 96, 110

Pachira aquatica, 532, 539
Pachysandra procumbens, 389
Pachysandra terminalis, 376, 389
Packera aurea, 38, 377, 448
Paeonia lactiflora, 449
Paeonia spp., 378, 449
Panicum virgatum, 38, 39, 40, 353, 368
Parrotia persica, 38, 122, 151
Parthenocissus henryana, 525
Parthenocissus quinquefolia, 510, 524
Parthenocissus tricuspidata, 510, 525
Paspalum vaginatum, 470, 475
Paulownia tomentosa, 548
Pelargonium × *hortorum*, 480, 486
Pelargonium peltatum, 486
Pennisetum × *advena* 'Rubrum', 480, 486
Pennisetum alopecuriodes, 38, 353, 369
Pennisetum setaceum 'Rubrum', 486

Penstemon digitalis, 450
Penstemon smallii, 450
Penstemon spp., 378, 450
Pentas lanceolata, 40, 480, 487
Perovskia atriplicifolia, 37, 38, 379, 451
Persea borbonia, 39, 184
Persea palustris, 39, 166, 184
Petunia × *hybrida*, 41, 480, 487
Philadelphus coronarius, 244, 262
Philadelphus inodorus, 262
Philodendron bipinnatifidum, 532, 539
Philodendron hederaceum, 532, 540
Philodendron oxycardium, 540
Philodendron scandens, 540
Philodendron selloum, 539
Philodendron xanadu, 539
Phlox divaricata, 377, 452
Phlox paniculata, 40, 41, 379, 453
Phlox subulata, 37, 38, 376, 390
Photinia × *fraseri*, 38, 40, 198, 227
Photinia serratifolia, 555
Phyllostachys aurea, 561
Pieris japonica, 274, 291
Pinus bungeana, 166, 185
Pinus echinata, 167, 186
Pinus elliottii, 167, 187
Pinus glabra, 189
Pinus palustris, 167, 188
Pinus × *sondereggeri*, 188
Pinus strobus, 167, 189
Pinus taeda, 167, 190
Pinus thunbergii, 166, 191
Pinus virginiana, 167, 192
Pistacia chinensis, 39, 96, 111
Pittosporum tobira, 41, 199, 228
Platanus × *acerifolia*, 73
Platanus occidentalis, 39, 54, 73
Plumbago auriculata, 480, 488
Podocarpus macrophyllus, 37, 199, 229
Polystichum acrostichoides, 37, 494, 498
Polystichum polyblepharum, 494, 499
Prunus americana, 153
Prunus avium, 157
Prunus campanulata, 41, 122, 152
Prunus caroliniana, 41, 166, 193
Prunus cerasifera, 123, 153
Prunus × *incam* 'Okame', 41, 123, 156
Prunus incisa, 155
Prunus laurocerasus, 37, 40, 199, 230
Prunus laurocerasus 'Otto Luyken', 274, 292
Prunus persica, 123, 154
Prunus persica nucipersica, 43
Prunus salicina, 153
Prunus serotina, 41, 96, 112
Prunus serrulata, 41, 123, 155

Prunus subhirtella, 42, 123, 157
Prunus × *yedoensis*, 42, 123, 158
Pueraria montana lobata, 558
Punica granatum, 38, 244, 263
Punica granatum nana, 38, 323, 347
Pyracantha spp., 38, 42, 199, 231
Pyrus calleryana, 548

Quercus acutissima, 54, 74
Quercus alba, 54, 75
Quercus borealis, 85
Quercus coccinea, 39, 54, 76
Quercus falcata, 39, 54, 77
Quercus hemisphaerica, 54, 78
Quercus laurifolia, 78
Quercus lyrata, 39, 54, 79
Quercus michauxii, 39, 54, 80
Quercus montana, 39, 55, 81
Quercus nigra, 39, 55, 82
Quercus pagoda, 77
Quercus palustris, 39, 55, 83
Quercus phellos, 55, 84
Quercus robur 'Fastigiata', 96, 112
Quercus rubra, 55, 85
Quercus stellata, 39, 55, 87
Quercus texana, 39, 40, 55, 88
Quercus velutina, 39, 55, 89
Quercus virginiana, 55, 90

Rhaphiolepis umbellata, 40, 274, 294
Rhapidophyllum hystrix, 42, 274, 293
Rhapis excelsa, 532, 540
Rhododendron austrinum, 314
Rhododendron canescens, 40, 41, 300, 314
Rhododendron catawbiense, 40, 199, 232
Rhododendron × *eriocarpum*, 40, 322, 339
Rhododendron × *indicum*, 40, 41, 199, 233
Rhododendron maximum, 199, 234
Rhododendron minus, 199, 234
Rhododendron × *obtusum*, 40, 274, 295
Rhododendron prunifolium, 300, 315
Rhus aromatica, 38, 40, 323, 348
Rhus chinensis, 159
Rhus copallinum, 41, 123, 159
Rhus glabra, 41, 123, 160
Rhus typhina, 41, 123, 161
Robinia pseudoacacia, 39, 41, 42, 96, 113
Rohdea japonica, 37
Rosa banksiae 'Lutea', 244, 264
Rosa laevigata, 244, 265
Rosa 'Radrazz', 40, 300, 316
Rosa spp., 42, 510, 526
Rosmarinus officinalis, 38, 322, 340
Rubus calycinoides, 376, 391
Rudbeckia fulgida, 40, 41, 378, 454

Ruellia brittoniana, 39, 379, 455
Ruellia simplex, 455
Ruscus aculeatus, 37, 322, 341

Sabal palmetto, 39, 167, 194
Salix babylonica, 39, 40, 96, 114
Salix caroliniana, 115
Salix matsudana 'Tortuosa', 114
Salix nigra, 40, 96, 115
Salvia greggii, 378, 457
Salvia guaranitica, 456
Salvia madrensis, 457
Salvia nemorosa, 457
Salvia sclarea, 457
Salvia splendens, 480, 488
Salvia spp., 37, 38, 40, 41, 456
Sambucus nigra, 266
Sambucus nigra canadensis, 39, 40, 41, 244, 266
Sansevieria trifasciata, 532, 541
Sapium sebiferum, 549
Sarcococca confusa, 40, 322, 342
Sarcococca hookeriana humilis, 342
Sassafras albidum, 96, 116
Schefflera actinophylla, 532, 541
Schefflera arboricola, 532, 542
Schizachyrium scoparium, 353, 370
Sedum acre, 37, 38, 392
Sedum rupestre, 392
Sedum sarmentosum, 376, 392
Sedum spurium, 392
Sisyrinchium angustifolium, 353, 360
Smilax smallii, 37, 510, 518
Solenostemon scutellarioides, 41, 480, 489
Solidago rugosa, 458
Solidago sempervirens, 458
Solidago sphacelata, 458
Solidago spp., 40, 378, 379, 458
Sorghastrum nutans, 38, 39, 353, 371
Spathiphyllum spp., 532, 542
Spiraea cantoniensis, 40, 300, 317
Spiraea japonica 'Anthony Waterer', 323, 349
Spiraea prunifolia, 300, 318
Spiraea thunbergii, 300, 319
Spiraea × *vanhouttei*, 41, 300, 320
Sporobolus heterolepis, 38, 353, 372
Stachys byzantina, 377, 459
Stenotaphrum secundatum, 470, 476
Stokesia laevis, 378, 460
Styphnolobium japonicum, 123, 162
Styrax americanus, 163
Styrax japonicus, 42, 123, 163
Symphyotrichum laeve, 407
Symphyotrichum novae-angliae, 407
Symphyotrichum novi-belgii, 407

Tagetes erecta, 489
Tagetes patula, 480, 489
Taxodium ascendens, 91
Taxodium distichum, 40, 55, 91
Ternstroemia gymnanthera, 199, 235
Thelypteris kunthii, 39, 494, 507
Thelypteris noveboracensis, 507
Thuja occidentalis, 41
Thuja occidentalis 'Danica', 322, 343
Thuja occidentalis 'Degroot's Spire', 199, 236
Thuja occidentalis 'Filiformis', 281
Thuja orientalis 'Aurea Nana', 343
Tiarella cordifolia, 377, 461
Tilia americana, 117
Tilia cordata, 96, 117
Toxicodendron radicans, 42, 510, 528
Trachelospermum asiaticum, 37, 510, 519
Trachelospermum jasminoides, 510, 520
Trachycarpus fortunei, 39, 166, 195
Tradescantia pallida, 37, 38, 366, 462
Tradescantia virginiana, 39, 40, 41, 378, 463
Triadica sebifera, 549
Trillium cuneatum, 464
Trillium erectum, 464
Trillium flexipes, 464
Trillium grandiflorum, 464
Trillium luteum, 464
Trillium spp., 377, 464
Tripsacum dactyloides, 39, 353, 373

Tripsacum floridanum, 373
Tsuga canadensis, 167, 196
Tsuga caroliniana, 196
Tsuga heterophylla, 196
Tulbaghea violacea, 378, 465
Tulipa × *hybrida*, 41, 480, 490
Typha angustifolia, 40, 353, 374
Typha latifolia, 374

Ulmus alata, 39, 55, 92
Ulmus americana, 40, 55, 93
Ulmus parvifolia, 549
Ulmus pumila, 96, 118
Ulmus rubra, 93
Ulmus thomasii, 92

Verbena bonariensis, 379, 466
Verbena × *hybrida*, 480, 490
Verbena rigida, 378, 466
Verbena tenuisecta, 422
Vernonia angustifolia, 467
Vernonia lettermannii, 467
Vernonia noveboracensis, 379, 467
Viburnum awabuki, 199, 237
Viburnum × *burkwoodii*, 244, 269
Viburnum macrocephalum 'Sterile', 244, 267
Viburnum odoratissimum, 199, 238
Viburnum opulus 'Roseum', 267
Viburnum plicatum plicatum, 268

Viburnum plicatum tomentosum, 244, 268
Viburnum × *pragense*, 241
Viburnum × *rhytidophylloides*, 239
Viburnum rhytidophyllum, 199, 239, 241
Viburnum suspensum, 199, 240
Viburnum tinus, 240
Viburnum utile, 241
Vinca major, 376, 393
Vinca minor, 376, 394
Viola × *wittrockiana*, 41, 480, 491
Vitex agnus-castus, 38, 41, 244, 270

Weigela florida, 41, 244, 271
Wisteria floribunda, 559
Wisteria frutescens, 510, 529
Wisteria sinensis, 559
Woodwardia areolata, 40, 494, 508

Yucca aloifolia, 38, 42, 199, 242
Yucca filamentosa, 38, 42, 322, 344
Yucca gloriosa, 38, 42, 274, 297
Yucca recurvifolia, 297
Yucca treculeana, 242

Zelkova serrata, 96, 119
Zinnia angustifolia, 480, 491
Zinnia elegans, 480, 492
Zoysia × 'Emerald', 470, 478
Zoysia japonica 'Meyer', 470, 477
Zoysia matrella, 478